PROJECT AIR FORCE

CW00408939

PRECISION and PURPOSE

Airpower in the Libyan Civil War

Edited by **Karl P. Mueller**

Contributors:
Gregory Alegi, Christian F. Anrig,
Christopher S. Chivvis, Robert Egnell,
Christina Goulter, Camille Grand,
Deborah C. Kidwell, Richard O. Mayne,
Bruce R. Nardulli, Robert C. Owen,
Frederic Wehrey, Leila Mahnad,
Stephen M. Worman

Prepared for the United States Air Force

For more information on this publication, visit www.rand.org/t/RR676

Library of Congress Cataloging-in-Publication Data

Mueller, Karl P.
  Precision and purpose : airpower in the Libyan Civil War / Karl P. Mueller [and thirteen others].
    pages cm
  Includes bibliographical references and index.
  ISBN 978-0-8330-8793-5 (pbk. : alk. paper)
  1. Libya—History—Civil War, 2011---Aerial operations. 2. Libya—History--Civil War, 2011---Campaigns. 3. Air power—History—21st century. I. Title.

  DT236.M74 2015
  961.205—dc23

                                                                              2015012120

Published by the RAND Corporation, Santa Monica, Calif.

© Copyright 2015 RAND Corporation

RAND® is a registered trademark.

Cover image: Belgian Air Force F-16 over Ghardabiya Air Base, Libya, on
April 29, 2011; courtesy of the Belgian Air Force, photo by Vador.

Support RAND
Make a tax-deductible charitable contribution at
www.rand.org/giving/contribute

www.rand.org

Preface

From March 19 to October 31, 2011, the United States and a coalition of fellow North Atlantic Treaty Organization (NATO) allies and partner states waged a remarkable air war in Libya. Operation Odyssey Dawn and Operation Unified Protector were designed to protect Libya's civilian populace under a United Nations mandate, and in conjunction with the country's new opposition movement, they led to the defeat and removal of the dictatorial regime of Colonel Muammar Qaddafi. The campaign, in which the coalition suffered no casualties and which cost a relatively inexpensive few billion dollars, is now being proffered as a model for future U.S. and NATO expeditionary operations.

This report, written by a team of U.S. and international experts, examines the origins, planning, execution, and results of the air campaign, with the goal of drawing lessons from it that will help prepare the U.S. Air Force and its allies and partners for future operations in which such a strategy of aerial intervention could be a promising policy option.

The research reported here was sponsored by General Philip M. Breedlove, Vice Chief of Staff of the Air Force, and conducted within the Strategy and Doctrine Program of RAND Project AIR FORCE.

RAND Project AIR FORCE

RAND Project AIR FORCE (PAF), a division of the RAND Corporation, is the U.S. Air Force's federally funded research and development center for studies and analyses. PAF provides the Air Force with independent analyses of policy alternatives affecting the development, employment, combat readiness, and support of current and future air, space, and cyber forces. Research is conducted in four programs: Force Modernization and Employment; Manpower, Personnel, and Training; Resource Management; and Strategy and Doctrine. The reserach reported here was prepared under contrat TA7014-06-C-0001.

Additional information about PAF is available on our website:
http://www.rand.org/paf/

Contents

Figures and Tables

Acknowledgments

In researching and writing this volume, the editor and authors benefited from the generous assistance of scores of people who participated in the events and operations described in these pages, or who have studied them since the end of Operation Unified Protector. Among those who agreed to be interviewed (in some cases on multiple occasions), who read and commented on draft chapters of this report, or who provided information or other invaluable help in many different forms to our research effort were the following: Col. Francesco Saverio Agresti, Richard Anderegg, Gp. Capt. Dean Andrew, Gen. (ret.) Mario Arpino, Wg. Cdr. Steve Austin, Maj. Jacob Barfoed, Col. Mike Barker, Dr. Tom Baughn, Brig. Gen. (ret) Bryan J. Benson, Lt Col. Stephen Bergey, Col. Fredrik Bergman, Gen. s.a. Giuseppe Bernardis, Dr. Sven Biscop, Lt.-Gen. (ret.) Charles Bouchard, Lt Col. Luc Boucher, Sqn. Ldr. Andy Brown, William Butler, Prof. Warren Chin, Lt Col. John Christ, Lt Col. Paddy Clarke, Peter Cole, Col. Miguel Colon, Ten. Col. Sandro Cornacchini, Ten. Col. Stefano Cosci, Col. J. William DeMarco, Col. Mark Desens, Lt Chris Devida, Mike Dugree, Lt Col. Hans Einerth, Maj. Gen. Karl Engelbrektson, Col. Torgny Fälthammar, Gen. d.a. Giovanni Fantuzzi, Capt. Jeff Fischer, Brian Fishpaugh, Gen. b.a. Stefano Fort, Col. Bruno Foussard, Jim Frank, Gen. b.a. Silvano Frigerio, Lt Col. Norm Gagne, Dr. Richard Gimblett, Lt Gen. Frank Gorenc, Dr. Stephen Harris, Brig. Gen. Steen Harboe Hartov, Col. Quintin "Q" Hartt, Air Vice-Marshal Mike Harwood, Serge Van Heertum, Lt Col. Dr. Dag Henriksen, Dr. Joseph Henrotin, Lieut. Ken Ingram, Dr. Peter Viggo Jakobsen, Lt. Gen. Ralph Jodice II, Maj. Mat Joost, Brig. Gen. Derek Joyce, Dr. Ken Kan, Wg. Cdr. Paul Kendall, Col. Eric Kenny, Col. Michael Kometer, Lt Col. Guus de Koster, Lt Col. Kevin D. Kozuch, Maj. Gen. Steven Kwast, Lt Jay Landre, Wayne Larsen, Col. Ken Lindberg, Lt. Col. Brian Linvill, Dr. Erwin van Loo, Col. Andy MacLean, Maj. Bill March, Brig. Gen. Larry Martin, Ian McCandie, Brian McQuinn, Gp. Capt. Neil Meadows, David Merrill, Dr. Karim Mezran, Hon. Marco Minniti, Col. John C. "Chris" Moss, Air Cdre. Paul Mulder, Dr. Riccardo Niccoli, Jean-Christophe Notin, Col. Dr. John Andreas Olsen, Air Cdre. Prof. Dr. Frans P. B. Osinga, Gen. b.a. (ret) Vincenzo Parma, Col. Alain Pelletier, Prof. Magnus Petersson, Lt Col. Tommy Petersson, Col. Keith L. Phillips, Col. Todd Phinney, Lt Col. Jeroen Poesen, Oberst Wolfgang Pusztai, Elizabeth

Quintana, Col. Mike Rafter, Air Cdre. Ralph W. Reefman, Dr. Gustaaf Reerink, Gp. Capt. Rocky Rochelle, Gen. b.a. Alberto Rosso, Brigadier Per Egil Rygg, Col. Mike St-Louis, Maj. Gen. Rowayne A. "Wayne" Schatz Jr., Maj. Gen. Anders Silwer, Dr. John Q. Smith, Gp. Capt. Pete Squires, William Stanley, Lt Col. Bradley Stebbins, Col. Eric Steidl, Air Vice-Marshal Edward Stringer, Gp. Capt. Johnny Stringer, John J. C. Sullivan, Maj. Per Harding Svarre, Elise Svarstad, Brig. Gen. David Thompson, Sqn. Ldr. Mark Tillyard, Wg. Cdr. Mike Toft, Prof. Italo Saverio Trento, Amm. Div. Paolo Treu, Gen. s.a. (ret) Leonardo Tricarico, Col. Mike Tronolone, Brig. Gen. Roy E. Uptegraff III, Amb. Veronika Wand-Danielsson, Air Vice-Marshal Gary Waterfall, Gen. Mark A. Welsh III, Col. Geir Wiik, Lt. Col. Stefan Wilson, Master Seaman Victor Wong, Maj. Gen. Margaret H. Woodward, Dr. Stephen Wright, Col. Ancel B. Yarbrough, and Alexander Zervoudakis.

In spite of its length, this list is inevitably incomplete, and we also thank those whose names we have inadvertently omitted. In addition, a number of other participants in the campaign or the related diplomatic efforts helpfully provided information but preferred not to be identified, and we thank them for their invaluable though anonymous assistance.

While writing the chapters in this volume, we enlisted a team of expert reviewers for the initial drafts, and benefited greatly from the comments and insights provided by Philip A. Sabin, Etienne du Durand, Michael Kometer, Dag Henriksen, and RAND's Adam Grissom, David Shlapak, and Paula Thornhill. A wide range of advice, assistance, and support was provided by Thomas P. Ehrhard and the officers of the USAF Chief of Staff's Strategic Studies Group. Later in the process, Jasen Castillo and Thomas Keaney reviewed the draft monograph in detail and provided a host of invaluable comments.

On the RAND research team itself, in addition to the chapter authors, Stephen Worman compiled the timeline in Appendix A and the sortie rate and munitions use data in the introduction and conclusion chapters. Leila Mahnad performed a host of research and editing roles, and managed the development of the maps, which were prepared by Chuck Stelzner. Together Steve and Leila prepared the order of battle in Appendix B. Jocqueline Johnson assisted tirelessly with preparation of the final report and many behind-the-scenes administrative tasks. Without their contributions, the successful completion of this volume, as you see it, would have been impossible.

Abbreviations

AAA	anti-aircraft artillery
AAR	air-to-air refueling
ACC	Air Combat Command
AEW	Air Expeditionary Wing
AFAD	Air Force and Air Defence
AFAFRICA	U.S. Air Forces Africa
AFCENT	U.S. Air Forces Central Command
AFDD	Air Force Doctrine Directive
AFRICOM	United States Africa Command
AFSPC	Air Force Space Command
AFTC	Air Force Targeting Center
AMC	Air Mobility Command
AMRAAM	Advanced Medium-Range Air-to-Air Missile
ANG	Air National Guard
AOC	Air Operations Center
AOR	area of responsibility
ARC	Air Reserve Components
ATO	air tasking order
ATP	Advanced Targeting Pod
AWACS	Airborne Warning and Control System
AWC	Air Warfare Center
BAF	Belgian Air Force
BICES	Battlefield Information Coordination and Exploitation System
BSA	Bosnian Serb Army
C2	command and control

C. Amm.	Contrammiraglio (Cdre [OF-6], Italian Navy)
CAOC	Combined Air Operations Center
CAS	close air support
CCMD	Combatant Command
CEFCOM	Canadian Expeditionary Force Command
CFAC	Combined Forces Air Component
CFACC	Combined Forces Air Component Commander
CFC	Comando Forze di Combattimento (Combat Command)
CGS	Comando Generale delle Scuole (Training Command)
CJTF	Combined Joint Task Force
CJTF-HOA	Combined Joint Task Force—Horn of Africa
COFA	Comando Operativo delle Forze Aeree (Air Force Operational Command)
COMAFFOR	Commander, Air Force Forces
COMAO	composite air operations
COMLOG	Comando Logistico (Logistics Command)
CONUS	continental United States
CSA	Comando della Squadra Aerea (Air Force Command)
CSAR	combat search and rescue
CSDP	Common Security and Defense Policy
CSMD	Capo di Stato Maggiore della Difesa (Chief of Defense Staff)
DACC	Deployable Air Command Center
DAO	Defense Attaché Office
DASS	Defensive Aids Sub-System
DATF	Deployable Air Task Force
DCA	defensive counterair
DDT	deliberate-dynamic targeting
DEAD	destruction of enemy air defenses
DFAIT	Department of Foreign Affairs and International Trade
DIRMOBFOR	Director of Mobility Forces
DMSB	Dual Mode Seeker Brimstone
DOB	deployment operating base
DoD	Department of Defense

EATC	European Air Transport Command
EAW	Expeditionary Air Wing
ECR	electronic combat reconnaissance
EDA	European Defense Agency
EEAW	European Participating Air Forces' Expeditionary Air Wing
EPAF	European Participating Air Forces
EU	European Union
EW	early warning
FAC	forward air controller
FCO	Foreign and Commonwealth Office
FST	Fire Support Team
FTG	Flying Training Group
GCC	Gulf Cooperation Council
Gen. b.a.	Generale di brigata aerea (Brig. Gen., ITAF)
Gen. c.a.	Generale di corpo d'armata (Lt Gen., Italian Army)
Gen. d.a.	Generale di divisione aerea (Maj. Gen., ITAF)
Gen. s.a.	Generale di squadra aerea (Lt Gen., ITAF)
GWAPS	Gulf War Airpower Survey
HARM	high-speed antiradiation missile
HUMINT	human intelligence
IADS	integrated air defense system
ICC	International Criminal Court
ICI	Istanbul Cooperation Initiative
IOC	initial operational capability
ISAF	International Security Assistance Force
ISR	intelligence, surveillance, and reconnaissance
ISRD	Intelligence, Surveillance, and Reconnaissance Division
ISTAR	intelligence, surveillance, target acquisition, and reconnaissance
ITAF	Italian Air Force
JCOA	joint and coalition operational analysis
JDAM	Joint Direct Attack Munition
JFACC	Joint Force Air Component Commander

JFC	Joint Force Command
JFCC	Joint Force Component Command
JFLCC	Joint Force Land Component Commander
JFMCC	Joint Force Maritime Component Commander
JIPTL	Joint Integrated Prioritized Target List
JSOTF	Joint Special Operations Task Force
JSTARS	Joint Surveillance Target Attack Radar System
JSTO	joint space tasking order
JTAC	Joint Terminal Attack Controller
JTF	Joint Task Force
JTF-OD	Joint Task Force Odyssey Dawn
JTWG	Joint Targeting Working Group
KLA	Kosovo Liberation Army
LIFG	Libyan Islamist Fighting Group
LNO	liaison officer
LRPA	long-range patrol aircraft
MARFORAF	U.S. Marine Corps Forces Africa
MARO	mass atrocity response operations
MC	Military Committee (NATO)
MCC	Maritime Component Commander
MEU	Marine Expeditionary Unit
MFFO	mixed fighter force operations
MoD	Ministry of Defence
MPA	maritime patrol aircraft
MPA	military personnel appropriation
MPRS	Multi-Point Refueling System
MRC	major regional contingency
NAC	North Atlantic Council
NATO	North Atlantic Treaty Organization
NAVAF	U.S. Naval Forces Africa
NCCSC	National Coordination Centre and Support Contingent
NFZ	no-fly zone
NSS	National Security Strategy
NTC	National Transitional Council

ODS	Operation Desert Storm
OIC	Organization of the Islamic Conference
OLRT	Operational Liaison and Reconnaissance Team
OOD	Operation Odyssey Dawn
OPCON	operational control
OPIR	overhead persistent infrared
OSC	Office of Security Cooperation
OUP	Operation Unified Protector
PGM	precision-guided munition
PME	professional military education
PSYOP	psychological operations
PTL	prioritized target list
QEAF	Qatar Emiri Air Force
RAF	Royal Air Force
RASP	recognized air and surface picture
RCAF	Royal Canadian Air Force
RCN	Royal Canadian Navy
RDAF	Royal Danish Air Force
RFF	Request for Forces
RJAF	Royal Jordanian Air Force
RNLAF	Royal Netherlands Air Force
RNoAF	Royal Norwegian Air Force
RPA	remotely piloted aircraft
RTP	responsibility to protect
SACEUR	Supreme Allied Commander, Europe
SAM	surface-to-air missile
SAR	search and rescue
SCAR	strike coordination and reconnaissance
SCAR-C	strike coordination and reconnaissance—coordinator
SDSR	Strategic Defence and Security Review
SEAD	suppression of enemy air defenses
SF	special forces
SIGNIT	signals intelligence
SIS	Secret Intelligence Service

SOCAFRICA	Special Operations Command—Africa
SPINS	special instructions
STRATCOM	United States Strategic Command
TACON	tactical control
TAR	tactical air reconnaissance
TCAS	Traffic Collision Avoidance System
TFCHA	Task Force Charlottetown
TFL	Task Force Libeccio
TFN	Task Forces Naples
TGA	task group air
TRAP	tactical recovery of aircraft and personnel
UAE	United Arab Emirates
UAV	unmanned aerial vehicle
UNSC	United Nations Security Council
UNSCR	United Nations Security Council Resolution
USAF	United States Air Force
USAFE	United States Air Forces in Europe
USARAF	U.S. Army Africa
USTRANSCOM	United States Transportation Command

CHAPTER ONE

Examining the Air Campaign in Libya

Karl P. Mueller

Introduction

Between March and October 2011, a coalition of North Atlantic Treaty Organization (NATO) member states, and several partner nations from outside the Alliance, waged a small but remarkable war against the Libyan regime of Colonel Muammar Qaddafi.[1] Through its intervention, the coalition stemmed and then reversed the tide of Libya's civil war, preventing Qaddafi from crushing the nascent rebel movement seeking to overthrow his dictatorship and going on to enable the opposition forces to prevail against an enemy that many had argued the rebels could not defeat without a foreign army invading Libya. The central element of this military intervention was a relatively small, multinational air campaign with forces operating from NATO bases in Italy, France, Greece, and several other countries, as well as from a handful of aircraft carriers and amphibious ships in the Mediterranean Sea.

At first glance, it seems unsurprising that the United States and some of its most powerful allies should have emerged victorious from a conflict against a small dictatorship facing significant internal unrest. What made this victory remarkable was how it was achieved. Politically, the speed and agility of the intervention in a rapidly developing crisis far surpassed widespread expectations about what was realistically possible. Had the response been slower, there is every reason to suspect Qaddafi might have succeeded in crushing the Libyan opposition. Militarily, the fact that Operations Odyssey Dawn (OOD) and Unified Protector (OUP)[2] cost a few billion dollars and that no coalition personnel were killed or seriously wounded stands in stark contrast to the

---

[1] The distinction between "coalition" and "alliance" is problematic when discussing the Libyan intervention. Until March 31, 2011, the intervention was conducted by a coalition of NATO allies. From March 31 to the end of the intervention on October 31, the intervention was an Alliance operation that included four non-NATO partner states. As a matter of convenience, authors in this volume will often refer to the whole as a coalition, but it is equally fair to call even the non-NATO partners "allies" according to traditional usage of that term.

[2] Odyssey Dawn was the U.S. codename for the initial stages of the Libyan operation; some of the other coalition members used it as well, but others adopted their own names for their national efforts in Libya, including Operation Ellamy (United Kingdom), Operation Harmattan (France), and Operation Mobile (Canada). After command of the operation was transferred to NATO on March 31, 2011, it became Operation Unified Protector.

thousands of lives and many hundreds of billions of dollars expended in the contemporaneous wars in Afghanistan and Iraq.

Yet this story is not well known, especially in the United States, for several reasons. At the time, other events often overshadowed the conflict in the Western news media, including the larger, more fraught wars in Afghanistan and Iraq, and the aftermath of the March 11, 2011 earthquake and tsunami in Japan. The small scale of the operation and the lack of coalition casualties also helped to keep it out of the headlines more than most recent wars involving the United States, as did the general tendency for air wars to have limited visibility. Moreover, some of the participants in the intervention were not especially eager to publicize their actions for a variety of political reasons, and so were content to carry on relatively quietly with the campaign. Since the end of the war against Qaddafi's regime, many of the participating forces have conducted "lessons learned" studies of their operations, most of which remain classified or unreleased, but published analyses of the conflict have been comparatively few and far between.

The purpose of this volume is to help fill this shortfall by studying how the coalition used its airpower in Libya, what happened as a result, and what this experience can teach policymakers and military planners that might be beneficial in future situations in which similar interventions are under consideration or are being undertaken. This last consideration is key, for as Libya comes to be held forth as a precedent for how military force might be used in a future in which the military very much wants to avoid the experience of Iraq or Afghanistan, it is imperative to understand what actually happened in Libya in 2011, and why.

Considering the Libyan Air Campaign in Context

The idea of Western military intervention in Libya conjures ghosts of earlier conflicts there. Students of American naval history may be reminded that Tripoli was the principal objective of the first-ever U.S. expeditionary military operation, against the piratical Barbary States during the first Jefferson administration (1801–1805). Those steeped in airpower history will be struck by the fact that 2011 marked the 100th anniversary of the first use of airplanes in warfare, coincidentally by Italian forces fighting the Ottoman Empire for control of Libya in 1911–1912.[3]

To understand what Operations Odyssey Dawn and Unified Protector mean in the course of the development of airpower, the most important historical context can be found in the series of conflicts during the preceding 20 years in the Persian Gulf, the Balkans, and Afghanistan in which relatively independent air campaigns figured

---

[3]   For more details of this often-mentioned but rarely studied event, see Chapter Eight.

prominently (Table 1.1).[4] Each bears certain similarities to the Libyan air campaign, but also differs from it in important ways.

Before enumerating those differences, however, it is important to be clear about the idea of "relatively independent air campaigns," lest this suggest that airpower acted alone in determining the outcome of any of these wars. In fact, ground forces figured significantly in all of them, although differently in each. What they have in common, however, is that for some or all of the operations, airpower was operating more or less "on its own" in a mode other than close integration with co-national conventional ground forces, as is normally envisioned in joint warfighting doctrine. This is quite different from caricature images of airpower operating, or wishing it could operate, with literal independence from other armed forces. As this volume will show, it is quite correct to refer to an "air campaign" in Libya, yet that campaign's strategy, execution, and results all were profoundly shaped by the interaction between air and indigenous land power.

Iraq and Kuwait: Operation Desert Storm, 1991

In January 1991, a multinational coalition led by the United States began a five-week-long air campaign against Saddam Hussein's Iraq and its armed forces as preparation for a joint offensive to expel Iraqi occupation forces from Kuwait and wreck the Iraqi Army. After the ground offensive began, most of the surviving Iraqi forces collapsed or fled, and a ceasefire began after four days of ground combat. Although Operation Desert Storm (ODS) appears quite different from the much smaller air campaign in Libya, it is relevant because it was, at the time, an essentially unprecedented case of modern airpower being employed in a sustained offensive against an entrenched enemy army while friendly ground forces waited for the bombing to inflict enough attrition to shift the battlefield advantage decisively in their favor, well beyond the familiar use of airpower and artillery to "soften up" an enemy as an immediate prelude to a ground offensive. Desert Storm also marked the operational advent of "tank plinking," in which precision-guided munitions (PGMs) were used systematically to destroy stationary armored fighting vehicles.[5]

---

[4] Another set of cases that seemingly call for comparison with the Libyan air campaign is previous "no-fly zones" (NFZs), particularly those that the United States and its allies maintained over Bosnia and Croatia prior to Operation Deliberate Force, and over most of Iraq after the 1991 Gulf War. In fact, the so-called no-fly zone over Libya was quite different from these earlier NFZs because it involved the outright destruction of the Libyan air force rather than a coercive effort to keep it from flying. For an analysis of the subject, see Karl P. Mueller, *Denying Flight: Strategic Options for Employing No-Fly Zones*, Santa Monica, Calif.: RAND, 2013.

[5] The five-volume *Gulf War Airpower Survey* (GWAPS) is available online; the summary volume was published as Thomas A. Keaney and Eliot A. Cohen, *Revolution in Warfare? Air Power in the Persian Gulf*, Annapolis, Md.: Naval Institute Press, 1995. See also John Andreas Olsen, *Strategic Air Power in Desert Storm*, London: Frank Cass, 2003.

Table 1.1
Selected Air Campaigns, 1991–2011

Operation	Sorties Flown	U.S. Sortie %	Total Munitions Expended[a]	% Precision-Guided Munitions[a]
Desert Storm, 1991[b]	118,700	85	*227,000[c]*	6[c]
Deliberate Force, 1995[d]	3,500	66	1,000	69[e]
Allied Force, 1999[f]	38,000	~39[g]	*23,300[c]*	29[c]
Enduring Freedom, 2001[h]	23,900	86	17,500	57
Odyssey Dawn/Unified Protector, 2011[i]	26,300	27[j]	7,642[k]	100

[a] Bombs and missiles only.

[b] Eliot Cohen and Thomas A. Keaney, eds., *Gulf War Air Power Survey: Volume 5—A Statistical Compendium and Chronology*, Washington, D.C.: Government Printing Office, 1993, pp. 232–233, 553–554.

[c] These values reflect only weapons employed by the United States.

[d] Robert C. Owen, ed., *Deliberate Force: A Case Study in Effective Air Campaigning*, Maxwell AFB, Ala.: Air University Press, 2000, pp. 257, 334.

[e] Excludes anti-radiation missiles.

[f] Benjamin S. Lambeth, *NATO's Air War for Kosovo: A Strategic and Operational Assessment*, Santa Monica, Calif.: RAND Corporation, MR-1365-AF, 2001, pp. 61, 88.

[g] Very approximate.

[h] Benjamin S. Lambeth, *Air Power Against Terror: America's Conduct of Operation Enduring Freedom*, Santa Monica, Calif.: RAND Corporation, MG-166-1-CENTAF, 2006, pp. 248, 251.

[i] NATO, "Operational Media Update: NATO and Libya," online, October 25, 2011.

[j] See Chapter Four.

[k] NATO data, in *International Commission of Inquiry on Libya*, Report of the International Commission of Inquiry on Libya—Advance Unedited Version, New York: United Nations Human Rights Council, A/HRC/19/68, March 2, 2012, p. 206. The 7,642 bombs and missiles included 3,544 laser-guided bombs, 2,844 satellite-guided weapons, and 1,150 direct-fire precision-guided munitions (PGMs).

Bosnia: Operation Deliberate Force, 1995

Operation Deliberate Force was a relatively small, three-week-long NATO air campaign against the Bosnian Serb Army (BSA) in the disputed ex-Yugoslavian province. It had the goal of compelling the Bosnian Serbs to agree to a cessation of hostilities and a redistribution of territory with their Bosnian Croat and mostly Muslim Bosnian government enemies. Once the air campaign was under way, the Croatian Army, which had received considerable unofficial organizational and logistical assistance from American ex-military contractors, launched a major offensive against the Serbs, creating synergistic pressures on the BSA from the ground offensive, the air campaign, and artillery attacks from a small Anglo-French United Nations (U.N.) force deployed around Sarajevo. After they had been driven out of approximately as much territory as NATO was demanding that they cede in a peace settlement, the Serbs agreed to a ceasefire and then to the Dayton Accords peace settlement.[6]

Serbia: Operation Allied Force, 1999

Three and a half years later, NATO went to war against Serbia proper to try to end a Serbian ethnic cleansing campaign in its majority-ethnic Albanian province of Kosovo. Operation Allied Force was an 11-week coercive bombing campaign directed both at Serbian military and paramilitary forces in Kosovo and against military and government-related targets in Serbia. Airpower was largely ineffective against the small units doing the ethnic cleansing, but in early June 1999, Serbian president Slobodan Milosevic acceded to NATO's demands for Kosovar autonomy and *de facto* independence. When the war began, NATO leaders ruled out the possibility of a ground invasion of Serbia, in an obvious parallel to the Libyan case, but as the campaign dragged on, NATO reconsidered and began laying the groundwork for launching such an offensive in the autumn. Toward the end of the war, the irregular Kosovo Liberation Army (KLA) began conducting operations significant enough to draw Serbian forces out into the open where they were more vulnerable to air attack, but by this point, the Serbian capitulation was already in the works.[7]

Afghanistan: Operation Enduring Freedom, 2001

The air campaign with perhaps the most important similarities to the Libyan intervention was the initial months of Operation Enduring Freedom in autumn 2001, following the September 11 al Qaeda terrorist attacks against the United States. Operating at long ranges from land bases and aircraft carriers in the Middle East and Indian Ocean, U.S. airpower—which United States and allied special operations forces assisted in many, but not all, parts of Afghanistan—attacked al Qaeda and Taliban government and army targets, enabling forces of the opposition Northern Alliance to gain the upper hand in its long-running war against the Taliban. As the air attacks took effect, the Taliban were routed with a rapidity that took even U.S. planners by surprise— they had expected to achieve a final defeat of the Taliban only after brigades of conventional U.S. Army forces arrived in Afghanistan. Following the airpower-enabled Northern Alliance victory, surviving Taliban scattered or—along with the remnants of al Qaeda—escaped to northwest Pakistan and began laying the groundwork for a

---

6   Owen, *Operation Deliberate Force.*

7   Daniel L. Byman and Matthew C. Waxman, "Kosovo and the Great Air Power Debate," *International Security*, Vol. 24, No. 4, Spring 2000, pp. 5–38; Barry R. Posen, "The War for Kosovo: Serbia's Political-Military Strategy," *International Security*, Vol. 24, No. 4, Spring 2000, pp. 39–84; Lambeth, *NATO's Air War for Kosovo*; Stephen T. Hosmer, *The Conflict over Kosovo: Why Milosevic Decided to Settle When He Did*, Santa Monica, Calif.: RAND Corporation, MR-1351-AF, 2001.

long-running insurgent struggle against the Afghan government, NATO, and coalition forces in Afghanistan that is ongoing.[8]

Why the Libyan Air Campaign Is Important

It goes without saying that every war is worth studying, and none should be forgotten. Some provide cautionary lessons, others reveal potential insights about the future, and in each, the fallen deserve to be remembered. Wars can be particularly noteworthy due to being large, politically consequential, or catastrophic, but for the United States and its allies, at least, the conflict in Libya was none of these. Yet several features of this case make the Libyan intervention important out of proportion to its small size and low cost, and argue for paying serious attention to it.

First is the extent to which it was a multinational operation. For the United States to fight as part of an alliance or coalition is hardly unprecedented, of course—U.S. forces fought alongside multiple allies and partners not only in the recent wars listed above, but also in the Berlin airlift, Korea, and Vietnam. In some cases, such as the invasion of Grenada, the coalition existed for political reasons but had little military significance; in others, allies and partners contributed significant forces, though the United States always played the largest role in air combat operations. But not since World War II was there a war involving the United States in which non-U.S. airpower constituted as large a share of the total as it did in Libya.

Second, Libya was a relatively extreme example of a strategic approach that can be called "aerial intervention," involving external powers intervening in a conflict primarily or entirely through the use of airpower, while cooperating to a greater or lesser degree with indigenous ground forces. Again, this was not a unique feature of the Libyan operation. Precedents can be found in Afghanistan in 2001, in Bosnia, and arguably even in Vietnam in 1972. But never before was aerial intervention pursued so intentionally as a strategy—introducing outside ground forces into the Libyan civil war was proscribed not only by the desire to avoid another quagmire in the region, but explicitly by the very U.N. resolution that the operations were conducted to enforce. The low cost of the campaign was, in turn, tied to the aerial intervention approach, raising tantalizing questions about whether such campaigns might be conducted successfully elsewhere. Understanding what happened in Libya is not enough to provide a conclusive answer, but it is an essential place to start.

In this context, it is worth reiterating a key point about this campaign. The intervention was heavily air-centric, but its success was not a victory by airpower acting alone, nor was it intended to be. The defeat of Qaddafi's regime ultimately was a victory by both air and land forces, albeit one in which the ground combat forces were indig-

---

[8] Lambeth, *Air Power Against Terror.*

enous to the nation's civil war rather than being provided by external powers (beyond their advice and assistance to the rebels' efforts to build an effective army).

In all of these respects, as well as others, the intervention in Libya could be a harbinger of future conflicts. Understanding whether it should be so regarded, and what lessons one ought to take away from it to inform policy and strategy elsewhere, are the core motivations for undertaking this project.

What This Book Is (and Is Not) About

This volume is an examination of the employment of airpower in the 2011 Libyan civil war, or, more precisely, the multinational air campaign in that conflict between March and October 2011. As the following chapters will demonstrate, this is a topic of considerable complexity, so in spite of its length, this study makes no pretense of being the final word about its subject. Instead, it is an initial survey, intended to introduce the Libyan air campaign to new readers, to broaden the knowledge of those whose experience or study of the campaign has focused on parts of the whole, and to facilitate and perhaps to inspire further research on these subjects by others.

In focusing on the air campaign, a number of aspects of this conflict receive relatively little attention in the pages that follow. This lack of emphasis should not be interpreted to mean they do not matter. First, this is not a history of the entire Libyan civil war. The use of airpower was central to the course of the war, but it was nevertheless only part of a larger story. We do address events on the ground, of course, for it is impossible to understand the air campaign and its results in isolation from the ground war. But an exhaustive account of the Libyan opposition's startling victory over the forces of the Qaddafi regime remains to be written.[9] We also are limited regarding the information we can provide about some elements of the operation, particularly the activities of foreign advisors and liaison officers who assisted the Libyan opposition forces, simply because the nations involved are not yet ready to say much about these efforts in public. As this reticence fades, this aspect of the campaign will be ripe for elaboration.

Second, the maritime dimension of the intervention is only briefly mentioned here, aside from the use of airpower based on ships offshore, although arms embargo enforcement and seaborne delivery of humanitarian relief supplies were missions of critical importance.

Third, we do not analyze in depth the question of the intervention's legality, either under international law or the U.S. War Powers Resolution, beyond describing the role that such concerns did or did not play in national decisions regarding whether and how

---

[9] Readers seeking a broader account of the war will be well served to begin with Christopher S. Chivvis, *Toppling Qaddafi: Libya and the Limits of Liberal Intervention*, Cambridge, UK: Cambridge University Press, 2014.

to intervene in the conflict. Beyond that point these legal issues remain important, but they had little effect on the conduct or results of the air campaign.

Finally, in assessing the results of the conflict, we concern ourselves with the outcome of the external military intervention at the operational and campaign-strategic levels associated with the victory of the opposition forces and the overthrow of the regime, rather than with the longer-term questions of whether intervening in Libya was a grand strategic success for the intervening powers. In part, this is because understanding what airpower was able to accomplish in Libya, and what that might portend for other conflicts, has more to do with the results of the campaign than with whether Libya ultimately turns out to be stable or unstable, benign or oppressive, or friendly or hostile to its Western and Arab benefactors. Even more important, we simply do not yet know what that ultimate outcome will be, for Libya itself or for the region more generally, and many years may elapse before the answers to these questions become clear.

Study Approach and Overview

To provide a broad understanding of the use of airpower in Libya, this study is organized around a series of "national experience" chapters, each of which describes and analyzes the role of the air forces of one or several nations.[10] An expert in his or her particular subject has written each chapter.[11] Despite some variations on this theme, and different approaches taken by each chapter author, the basic mission of the authors was to explain: (1) how the country or countries in question decided to participate in the intervention, and in what way; (2) what the air force(s) in question did during the war, from deployment to basing to operations over Libya; and (3) what lessons the nation or air force took away from the experience, or what insights or lessons the author believes ought to be derived from it.[12] Some of these findings are broadly applicable, others are specific to individual countries, but our focus is on operational and strategic implications, rather than narrower tactical or technical lessons (which tend to be well addressed already in the many official, and still predominantly classified, "lessons learned" studies).

In brief summary, the plan of the book is as follows:

In Chapter Two, Christopher Chivvis provides an overview of the conflict and the intervention, focusing on what might be called the Alliance dimension—the aspects

---

[10] Due to limitations of resources and space, the study does not include chapters focusing on several nations that participated in the operation but that did not fly strike missions over Libya. For information about the Spanish Ejército del Aire's participation in OUP, see "Misión Cumplida en Libia," *Revista Española de Defensa*, November 2011, pp. 6–11.

[11] Biographical information about each of the chapter authors can be found at the end of the volume.

[12] In the chapters that follow, we generally use the term "lesson" in its colloquial sense rather than as a rigorous doctrinal label. This volume neither aspires nor claims to be a "lessons learned" study in the formal sense of that phrase.

of the story that underpin each of the other chapters and tend to transcend national boundaries. He also briefly discusses the decisions of several states, particularly Germany, not to participate in the intervention.

Before examining the experiences of the intervening powers in detail, we turn instead to look at the intervention from the point of view of the Libyan opposition forces, who were the first to go to war against the Qaddafi regime and the ones who brought the conflict to its conclusion. In Chapter Three, Frederic Wehrey tells the Libyan side of the story, based on extensive interviews conducted with Libyan opposition leaders and fighters in 2012, to provide an invaluable complement to the perspectives of those who saw the war from the cockpit or the combined air operations center (CAOC).

Because it involves so much ground to cover, the U.S. airpower experience is split between the next two chapters. In Chapter Four, Robert Owen examines American involvement in the Libyan intervention at the broadest, intercontinental level. He describes the road to intervention as it appeared in Washington, then analyzes the functions that U.S. forces performed in supporting the Libyan air campaign with global capabilities, particularly in providing most of the campaign's vital aerial refueling capacity but also considering space and other support. Chapter Five, by Deborah Kidwell, then zooms in to the theater level to focus on the use of U.S. airpower at the theater or operational level of strike, intelligence, surveillance, and reconnaissance (ISR), and battle management. This chapter also describes the evolution of multinational command and control (C2) for the campaign, including the organization and activities of the CAOCs, because so many of the personnel involved in leading and managing the campaign were American.

In Chapters Six and Seven, Christina Goulter and Camille Grand examine respectively the experiences of the United Kingdom and France, the two other states that led the coalition and played the greatest role in causing the intervention to occur in the first place. Chapter Eight, by Gregory Alegi, describes Italy's role in the campaign, which tends to receive scant attention in popular discussions, but was of central importance because of Italy's frontline location.

The next several chapters look at smaller powers in the coalition. Richard O. Mayne describes the role of the Royal Canadian Air Force (as it was renamed in the midst of the campaign) in Chapter Nine. In Chapter Ten, Christian Anrig compares four NATO members—Belgium, Denmark, the Netherlands, and Norway—that deployed similar F-16 forces for the campaign, and ended up playing a larger role in the operation than many observers had expected. Chapters Eleven and Twelve turn to the non-NATO members of the coalition. Robert Egnell presents Sweden's participation in Operation Unified Protector, the Swedish Air Force's first combat deployment in nearly 50 years. Then Bruce Nardulli recounts the roles of the Arab coalition members, principally Qatar and the United Arab Emirates (UAE), in the air campaign.

The final chapter provides a summing up and assessment of the campaign, and focuses on identifying conclusions and implications of the Libyan intervention that may help prepare the United States and other nations to deal with future contingencies that might or might not resemble the Libyan case. This is followed by two appendixes providing additional reference material: a chronology of important political and military events in the campaign (Appendix A), and an air order of battle organized by contributing nation and a list of bases used in the campaign (Appendix B).

Each of the chapters draws heavily on interviews and conversations with military and government personnel from the European and North American nations that participated in the Libyan intervention. Many of these people, particularly those serving in less senior ranks, are not identified by name in the pages that follow. However, it is impossible to overstate the contributions they made to this volume by sharing their experiences and insights with the authors, and we thank them for the indispensible part they played in telling this story.

CHAPTER TWO

Strategic and Political Overview of the Intervention

Christopher S. Chivvis

Introduction

This chapter provides an overview of the 2011 Libya intervention as a foundation for the "national" chapters that follow. It recounts how the coalition was formed, why the United States and its allies went to war, and the deliberations over NATO's role. It then explains the overall course of the campaign as it developed from March through October 2011, identifying some of the implications for the Atlantic Alliance. Many of the events and issues introduced here are examined in more detail in subsequent chapters that focus on participating nations.

Libya and the Arab Uprisings

The Arab Spring began with the self-immolation of a vegetable vendor in Tunisia on December 17, 2010, which sparked a broader uprising against Tunisia's long-standing dictator Zine al-Abidine Ben Ali. Ben Ali was forced into exile on January 14. A wave of revolt then spread across the region, to Algeria, Jordan, Yemen, and especially Egypt, where President Hosni Mubarak was forced to step down on February 11.

Mubarak's departure gave further impetus to unrest across the Middle East and North Africa, first and foremost in Libya, which Colonel Muammar Qaddafi had ruled for 41 years. Initial protests began in the eastern Libyan city of Benghazi, but within a few days, revolutionary councils were springing up nationwide. Regime authorities were chased from their positions in several cities as rebel movements suddenly found themselves in control of a significant part of Libyan territory.

Much of the rebel-held territory was in Libya's eastern province of Cyrenaica, where Qaddafi's hold had always been tenuous. Benghazi was Libya's second-largest city and the main power center of Cyrenaica, which itself was in many ways disconnected from Tripolitania to the west, the location of both the Libyan capital Tripoli and Qaddafi's hometown of Sirte.[1] Eastern Libya had languished under Qaddafi. It was also the home of long-standing Islamist movements—according to the U.S. Army, the eastern town of Darnah sent more jihadis to fight the United States in Iraq than any other town its size.[2] Although Libya is geographically larger than Iran, only a single corridor running along its 1,100-mile coastline joins its east and west (see Figure 2.1).[3] Much of the fighting in the war would eventually become a back-and-forth struggle along this route.

A few days into the revolt, Qaddafi struck back with brutal force against the rebellion, dispatching Libyan and mercenary troops, and using aircraft to launch raids against civilians.[4] On February 22, he gave a rambling television address referencing the Tiananmen Square massacre, promising to stay in power to the end and threatening to "cleanse Libya house-to-house" if the protests did not cease.[5] Fearing the situation would deteriorate into chaos, the United States and most of its European allies started evacuating their nationals from Libya. Hundreds of thousands of refugees fled to neighboring Tunisia and Egypt.

From the 1980s through the 1990s, and into the early 21st century, Qaddafi had been the *bête noir* of the United States and European governments. In the aftermath of the Iraq invasion, however, he had rehabilitated his relationship with the United States and most of the states on the other side of the Mediterranean. He renounced terrorism and gave up his pursuit of weapons of mass destruction. He literally pitched his tent in Paris, within view of the French president's residence at the Elysée Palace, and signed lucrative energy and defense contracts with Italy, France, and other European countries. Relations with the United States also improved. Libya was removed from the official list of state sponsors of terrorism, diplomatic relations were reestablished, and the two countries exchanged ambassadors in 2009.

These halcyon years for Qaddafi came to a screeching halt when the crisis broke. Leaders from the United States, Britain, France, Germany and elsewhere spoke out against his repression and pushed the regime to negotiate with the protestors. Meanwhile, Qaddafi regime officials outside the country started defecting to the opposition en masse. Among these were several Libyan ambassadors, including the ambassador

---

[1] See Saskia van Genugten, "Libya After Gadhafi," *Survival*, Vol. 53, No. 3, June-July 2011, pp. 61–75; William Lewis, "Libya: Dream vs. Reality," *Mediterranean Quarterly*, Vol. 22, No. 3, Summer 2011, pp. 42–52.

[2] David D. Kirkpatrick, "Libya Democracy Clashes with Fervor for Jihad," *New York Times*, June 23, 2012, p. A1.

[3] Central Intelligence Agency (CIA), *World Factbook*, online.

[4] "Révoltes Arabes: Répression Brutale en Libye, à Bahreïn et au Yémen," *Le Monde*, February 20, 2011, p. 1; Anthony Shadid, "Clashes in Libya Worsen as Army Crushes Dissent," *New York Times*, February 18, 2011, p. A1; "Libya Jails Russia, Ukraine, Belarus 'Mercenaries,'" *Agence France Press*, June 4, 2012.

[5] "Live Blog—Libya Feb 22," *Al Jazeera*, February 22, 2011; Kareen Fahim and David D. Kirkpatrick, "Qaddafi's Grip on the Capital Tightens as Revolt Grows," *New York Times*, February 23, 2011, p. A1; "Libye: Kadhafi prend le risque d'encourager une guerre civile," *Le Monde*, February 22, 2011.

Figure 2.1
Libya

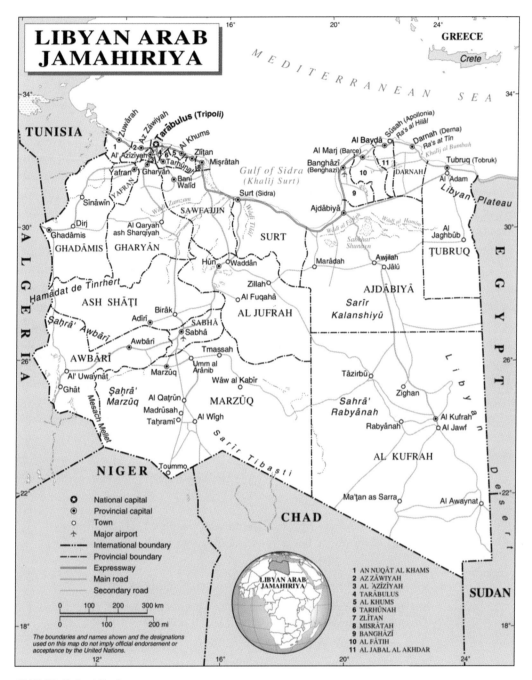

SOURCE: United Nations.
RAND RR676-2.1

to the United States, who defected on February 22. Nearly simultaneously, Qaddafi's representatives at the United Nations also defected and started calling for the establishment of a no-fly zone over their country. On February 26, the U.N. Security Council (UNSC) unanimously passed Resolution 1970, imposing an arms embargo and travel ban on regime officials, freezing the regime's assets, and referring Qaddafi to the International Criminal Court (ICC).[6]

The Debate over Intervention

From the outset of the Libyan crisis, French President Nicolas Sarkozy was the leading voice for military intervention. He deplored Qaddafi's actions and called for his ouster well before most other governments were prepared to do so. He soon gained the support of British Prime Minister David Cameron, who—after initial hesitation—also spoke out clearly against the Libyan regime's repression.

Sarkozy and Cameron had good reasons for stepping out together into the fray. Sarkozy's government had fumbled its initial response to the uprisings in Tunisia, and was eager for an opportunity to show it stood with traditional French liberal values of liberty and human rights—as well as to demonstrate France's continued relevance on the global stage in an election year.[7] Cameron, for his part, was equally eager to demonstrate his leadership on security issues in the wake of domestic criticism of his planned defense cuts that had been announced the previous fall.[8] In addition, both countries saw an opportunity to test the defense cooperation treaties they had signed only a few months earlier.[9]

In the United States, pressure for action also began to develop, mainly in Congress and within policy circles outside the government. While polling by the Pew Research Center showed a solid majority of the U.S. public opposing the use of military force in Libya,[10] interest in the issue was growing.

President Obama had condemned the violence in Libya early on. "The United States," he said,

> strongly supports the universal rights of the Libyan people . . . Like all governments, the Libyan government has a responsibility to refrain from violence, to

---

[6]   United Nations, Security Council Resolution (UNSCR) 1970 (2011), February 26, 2011.

[7]   Natalie Nougayrède, "Recit: Comment la France a-t-elle décidé d'intervenir en Libye?" *Le Monde*, April 19, 2011, p. 12; "On ne s'improvise pas diplomate," *Le Monde*, February 23, 2011, p. 7.

[8]   Interviews with representatives to NATO, Brussels, February 7, 2012.

[9]   "World Cannot Stand Aside from Libya, Says Cameron," *BBC.com*, March 8, 2011; "Cameron: UK Working on 'No-Fly Zone' Plan for Libya," BBC, February 28, 2011; Nicholas Watt and Patrick Wintour, "Libya No-Fly Zone Call by France Fails to Get David Cameron's Backing," *Guardian.co.uk*, February 23, 2011; Sam Coates, "A Lonely War for Cameron . . . But Now He Knows His Comrades in Arms," *The Times*, September 10, 2011.

[10]   "Public Wary of Military Intervention in Libya," Pew Research Center, March 14, 2011.

allow humanitarian assistance to reach those in need, and to respect the rights of its people. It must be held accountable for its failure to meet those responsibilities, and face the cost of continued violations of human rights.[11]

The United States strongly supported UNSCR 1970 and the other actions in late February. By early March, however, international actions had resulted in little change on the ground. As the second week of March opened, the tide was turning sharply against the rebels. As calls for a no-fly zone over Libya intensified, the U.S. administration found itself increasingly on the defensive, under pressure to take military action.

Secretary of Defense Robert Gates was the administration's main spokesperson against these proposals, voicing concern that military action was premature and that proposals for it were naïve. During testimony to Congress on March 2, he pointed out that a no-fly zone would need to begin with strikes against Libya's air defense systems, which could easily be perceived as further U.S. attacks against a Muslim country.[12] The United States could ill afford this, as it was still struggling to disengage and recover from the war in Iraq and deal with the ongoing war in Afghanistan. At a minimum, any action against Libya would therefore require full regional support—and as of early March, this seemed a distant prospect.

Gates also thought the proposals for military action had been made without any serious consideration for postwar planning. Here, the Iraq experience, in which the United States had gone to war without a clear and realistic post-conflict plan,[13] was clearly on his mind. Establishing a no-fly zone in Libya could lead toward regime change, but who was ready to ensure that what came after Qaddafi would be significantly better than Qaddafi's own rule?[14] Moreover, several questions remained not only about the rebels' capabilities, but about their intentions; it was reported that the CIA had deployed operatives to Libya to investigate the rebel movement.[15]

Early in March, a Benghazi-based organization claiming to represent the rebels had emerged called the National Transitional Council (NTC). The NTC quickly became the mouthpiece through which the Libyan opposition movement would communicate its intentions to the world. It also called for international assistance against Qaddafi in the form of a no-fly zone. The precise nature of the NTC and the rebels it

---

[11] The White House, Office of the Press Secretary, "Remarks by the President on Libya," Washington, D.C., February 23, 2011.

[12] Budget Hearing—Department of Defense, Hearing of the Defense Subcommittee of the House Appropriations Committee, March 2, 2011.

[13] Nora Bensahel et al., *After Saddam: Prewar Planning and the Occupation of Iraq*, Santa Monica, Calif.: RAND Corporation, MG-642-A, 2008.

[14] David E. Sanger and Thom Shanker, "Gates Warns of Risks of a No-Flight Zone," *New York Times*, March 3, 2011, p. A12.

[15] Mark Mazzetti and Eric Schmitt, "CIA Agents in Libya Aid Airstrikes and Meet Rebels," *New York Times*, March 31, 2001, p. A1.

represented remained uncertain. Although the NTC was the only organization purporting to represent the rebels, it was clear that the reality of the situation on the ground was a highly fragmented and diverse revolt comprising multiple groups across the country that were united only by their desire to oust Qaddafi. The possibility that al Qaeda was involved was real—the al Qaeda–linked Libyan Islamist Fighting Group (LIFG) was among the groups known to be active in the east.[16]

Furthermore, as several members of the Obama administration noted in public statements during the week of March 7, even if the United States and its allies did agree to impose a no-fly zone over Libya, it would be of only marginal utility. While Qaddafi's use of aircraft against the rebels had made news headlines, his counterattacks primarily were conducted by mechanized and other ground forces. Stopping these forces would require much more assertive action.

However, debate about the options in Libya continued within the administration, and these issues were discussed in a meeting of the President's top national security advisors that took place during the second week of March in order to finalize the U.S. position on Libya before a NATO defense ministerial slated for March 10–11 in Brussels.[17] Despite French and British pressure for action, the principals agreed that the United States would only support a humanitarian role for the Alliance at this time.

When ministers convened in Brussels, NATO had begun so-called "prudent planning"—a form of contingency planning conducted at the discretion of the Supreme Allied Commander, Europe (SACEUR)—and increased aerial surveillance to Libya, tasking Airborne Warning and Control System (AWACS) aircraft to conduct around-the-clock monitoring of the situation.[18] However, NATO Secretary General Anders Fogh Rasmussen insisted the Alliance had "no intention to intervene in Libya."[19]

In fact, no consensus was evident within the Alliance at this point over the use of military force, and the United States remained very hesitant. Germany and the United States appeared reticent about any action, while France was pushing for a no-fly zone, but not under NATO auspices. The consensus that emerged in Brussels was that NATO would increase its naval presence in the region, accelerate the pace of planning for humanitarian relief, and take measures to tighten the arms embargo that had been established under UNSC Resolution (UNSCR) 1970. However, NATO still had no plans for military intervention.[20]

---

[16] "L'opposition libyenne demande l'aide de l'Europe," *LeMonde.fr*, March 10, 2011.

[17] Interview with senior U.S. official, February 6, 2012.

[18] Interview with senior U.S. official, February 6, 2011; interview with member of International Staff, January 30, 2012; Helene Cooper and Mark Landler, "U.S. Imposes Sanctions on Libya in Wake of Crackdown," *New York Times*, February 25, 2011, p. A1.

[19] "NATO Defence Ministers Will Discuss Situation in Libya and Longer Term Prospects in Middle East," Brussels: NATO Press Office, March 7, 2011.

[20] Interview with member of NATO international staff, January 30, 2012.

At the conclusion of the meeting, the British proposed three preconditions for allied military action, and the ministers agreed. These included: (1) demonstrable need, (2) a sound legal basis, and (3) strong regional support.[21] These three conditions would provide the parameters for future discussions within NATO. They implied a U.N. resolution, support from the Arab League or the Gulf Cooperation Council, and a deteriorated situation on the ground. As of March 11, this seemed like a high bar to clear. Events in the next few days, however, would change the situation quickly, and the United States and its allies would shortly be headed for another war in the Middle East.

U.N. Security Council Resolution 1973

The first major development came when the Arab League endorsed the no-fly zone strategy for Libya in a meeting on Saturday, March 12.[22] The Gulf Cooperation Council had endorsed the idea earlier in the week, but the agreement of the Arab League indicated a much broader degree of support than many in Western capitals had anticipated. It was unprecedented that the League should call for military action against one of its own members, though in retrospect not entirely surprising. Many of Qaddafi's fellow Arab leaders despised him, particularly the Saudis for his alleged assassination attempt against the Saudi crown prince in 2004.[23] Arab support for the operation was reinforced when Secretary of State Hillary Clinton met with some Arab leaders on March 14 and was told they were prepared to provide military forces for an intervention—a contribution that would significantly increase the overall legitimacy of such an operation.[24]

A second major change was the rapid advance of Qaddafi's forces. Early in the week of March 7, the regime had regrouped, been reinforced with mercenaries, and was rapidly pushing back the disorganized and ill-equipped rebels. By March 14, Qaddafi's troops were bearing down on the rebel stronghold of Benghazi (see Figure 2.2).

---

[21] Interview with a NATO diplomat, February 7, 2012; U.S. Department of Defense (DoD), Assistant Secretary for Public Affairs, "Media Availability with Secretary Gates at the NATO Defense Ministers Meeting from Brussels, Belgium," March 10, 2011; "NATO Ready to Support International Efforts on Libya," Brussels: NATO Press Office, March 11, 2011.

[22] Richard Leiby and Muhammad Mansour, "Arab League Asks U.N. for No-Fly Zone over Libya," *Washington Post*, March 12, 2011.

[23] Shashank Joshi, "The Complexity of Arab Support," in Adrian Johnson and Saqeb Mueen, eds., *Short War, Long Shadow: The Political and Military Legacies of the 2011 Libya Campaign*, London: Royal United Services Institute (RUSI), Whitehall Report 1–12, 2012, pp. 63–69.

[24] Interview with senior administration official, January 24, 2012. See also Helene Cooper and Steven Lee Myers, "Shift by Clinton Helped Persuade President to Take a Harder Line," *New York Times*, March 19, 2011, p. A1.

Figure 2.2
Approximate Territorial Control in Libya, March 2011

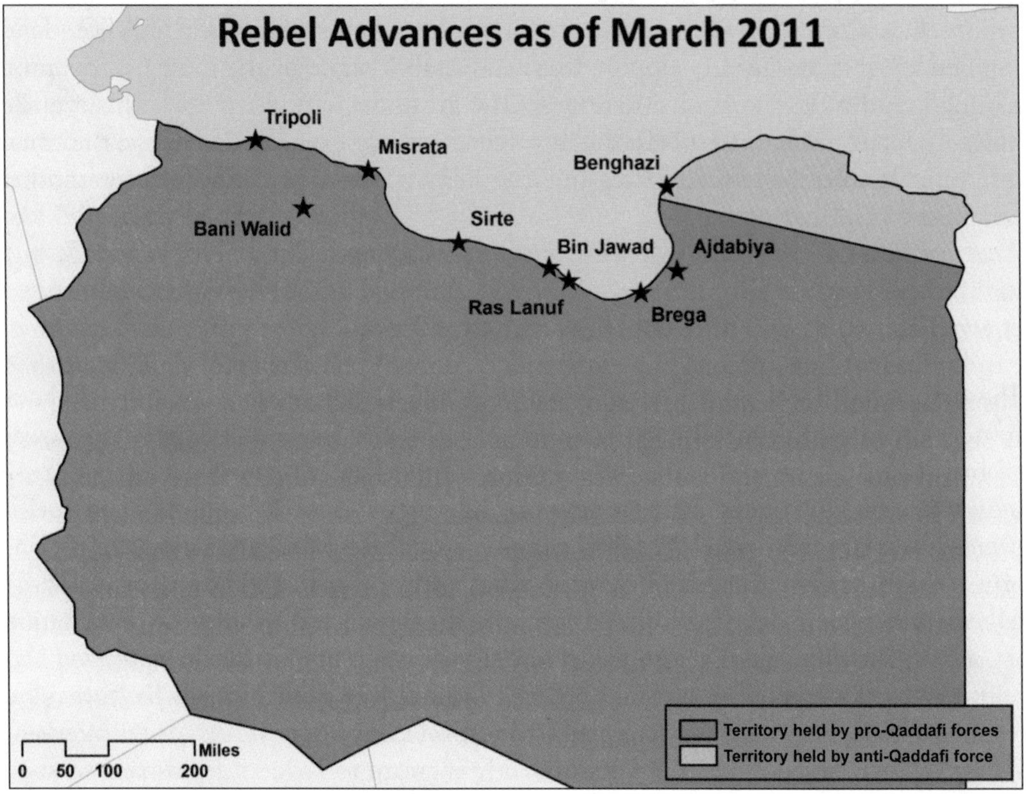

Rebel Advances as of March 2011

Tripoli

Misrata

Benghazi

Bani Walid

Sirte

Bin Jawad   Ajdabiya

Ras Lanuf

Brega

Miles
0   50   100   200

Territory held by pro-Qaddafi forces
Territory held by anti-Qaddafi force

SOURCE: Adapted from NATO, "Evolution of the frontlines in Libya—March–Sept. 2011," online maps, September 22, 2011.
RAND *RR676-2.2*

His public rants gave good reason to fear that when he arrived there, he would slaughter the population indiscriminately.[25]

The pressure for action redoubled. France and Britain increased their public pronouncements in favor of a no-fly zone. But the fact remained that establishing a no-fly zone likely would have little, if any, impact on the situation on the ground. The Arab League vote, in other words, had alleviated one of Secretary Gates's concerns, but it had not changed the strategic argument against a no-fly zone.

On March 15, after hearing Secretary Clinton's report on the willingness of the Gulf states to make military contributions, and with the urgency of the threat to Benghazi increasingly apparent in news and intelligence reporting, President Obama convened a full meeting of his National Security Council to discuss U.S. options. At

---

[25] "Battle for Libya: Key Moments," *Aljazeera.com*, August 23, 2011.

the meeting, he was reportedly frustrated with the choices with which he was presented: On the one hand, his advisors were making it clear that a massacre could very
possibly be in the making in Benghazi. On the other hand, the only military option
they were considering was a no-fly zone, which they themselves agreed would not solve
the problem.[26] He insisted there were better alternatives.

Although Defense Department and other senior officials within the U.S. administration had been reticent about the use of military force, at least two senior officials
had been more openly in favor of some form of military action. The first was Obama's
senior director for multilateral affairs, Samantha Power, author of the Pulitzer Prize–
winning book, *A Problem from Hell*, which chronicled America's failure to intervene in
multiple twentieth century genocides. Although Power's role would later be caricatured
in some reporting, her knowledge of the military possibilities and their application in
past cases enabled her to ensure that more robust military options remained on the
table.[27]

U.S. Ambassador to the United Nations Susan Rice also was more open to the use
of military force than Secretary Gates. Her experience with Rwanda as a White House
official in the first Clinton administration had left her determined that no stone be left
unturned to prevent such atrocities and that all the options should be put before the
president. The week before, she had in fact drafted a stronger, alternative U.N. resolution that was circulating in the event the situation deteriorated—which it now was.[28]
When the President asked for more options, Rice said she believed a tougher U.N.
Security Council resolution going beyond a no-fly zone might be within reach. The
resolution she proposed would call for "all necessary measures" to protect Libya's civilian population from harm—a diplomatic formula for military action.[29]

The President endorsed this option, and the United States introduced the
enhanced text the following day. The draft resolution called for tougher sanctions than
UNSCR 1970, authorized a no-fly zone, and, in a key passage, "all necessary measures" to protect civilians in Libya. The latter reference was the civilian protection mission that became the legal justification for NATO's air campaign. At the insistence of
the Lebanese government, which supported the text, the resolution also ruled out an
"occupying force."[30] France and Britain immediately rallied to support it, while Russia
tabled a much weaker alternative. Germany, meanwhile, expressed its reservations. A
tense debate at Turtle Bay ensued. On March 17, the resolution was put to a vote and

---

[26] Interview with senior White House official, March 29, 2012.

[27] Sheryl Gay Stolberg, "Still Crusading, but Now on the Inside," *New York Times*, March 30, 2011, p. A10. See
also Jacob Heilbrunn, "Samantha and Her Subjects," *The National Interest*, May–June, 2011.

[28] Michael Hastings, "Inside Obama's War Room," *Rolling Stone*, October 27, 2011; Cooper and Myers, "Shift
by Clinton Helped Persuade President to Take a Harder Line."

[29] Hastings, "Inside Obama's War Room."

[30] United Nations Security Council Resolution 1973 (2011).

passed with ten of the Security Council's 15 votes, becoming UNSCR 1973. Brazil, China, Germany, India, and Russia all abstained.

Russian Ambassador Vitaly Churkin said his government had abstained because so many questions remained unanswered, especially with regard to enforcement and the limits of any military action.[31] Reservations notwithstanding, this decision not to block the resolution was a departure from traditional Russian policy. When Russia later reverted to its more traditional position on intervention regarding Syria, it often was portrayed as a result of NATO having stretched the mandate granted in UNSCR 1973, but in reality, Russia's policy on Syria was much closer to its historical norms. Russia had little to lose from an intervention in Libya, and was likely cognizant of appearing reactionary to Europeans by standing in the way of the Arab Spring. For the duration of the Libyan operation, Moscow would complain about NATO's interpretation of UNSCR 1973, arguing—along with China, Brazil, and India—that NATO was stretching the civilian-protection mandate to include regime change. The latter argument ultimately was true, but it would have been difficult for Russia not to recognize this potential when it decided not to veto the use of force in Libya.

Germany's abstention in the UNSCR 1973 vote created one of the most serious rifts in U.S.-German relations since the 2003 Iraq War. It was a clear break with Germany's closest European and American allies, and to make matters worse, it appeared to put Germany on the Russian side against them. The most likely rationale for Germany's abstention, however, is that officials in the German Chancellery failed to recognize the quick turn that policy in the United States had taken. After all, only days before, the U.S. position had been against the use of force. Now the United States was pushing for a much broader mandate—a move that some European diplomats thought was, in fact, a disingenuous tactic aimed at dividing the Security Council. Germany would, as a result, refuse to participate in the military operation. It did not, however, go so far as to block the NATO action—which it might have done—and as the intervention evolved, it increased its financial and diplomatic support.

In a matter of a few days, U.S. policy had taken a major turn. The news media speculated that pressure from Sarkozy and Cameron had played a critical role in the U.S. administration's reversal.[32] Little evidence exists for this, however. While the efforts of the French president and British prime minister kept the issue on the table and held open the door to intervention, and the United States' respect for the role that the allies had played in Afghanistan may on some level have increased its willingness to listen to the allied case for intervention, the United States ultimately did not go to war because its allies asked it to do so. Similarly, while the Arab League vote was an important precondition for action, it was not a determining factor. The two factors

---

[31]   United Nations, "Libya: Full Text, Record of the Debate on Security Council Resolution," March 17, 2011.

[32]   For example, Roger Boyes, "Hesitant Obama Made Up His Mind Thanks to European Resolve," *The Times*, March 18, 2011, p. 7.

that most mattered were the imminent threat Qaddafi's troops posed to the civilian population of Benghazi and the emergence of a workable military option that could help protect those civilians.

Operation Odyssey Dawn

Two days after U.N. Security Council Resolution 1973 passed, a coalition of countries took immediate action to enforce it. On March 19, President Sarkozy hosted a high-level meeting in Paris intended to demonstrate the breadth of the political coalition backing the intervention. Qaddafi had not pulled back his forces. As the meeting in Paris closed, Sarkozy stepped out to announce that two French fighters had struck regime forces outside Benghazi, initiating the intervention.[33]

Within a few hours, the United States fired over a hundred Tomahawk land-attack cruise missiles (TLAMs) at central nodes of Qaddafi's air defense system along the Libyan coast. The Royal Navy also participated in these initial TLAM strikes, though on a much smaller scale.[34] With Libya's air defenses crippled, the coalition proceeded to fly multiple air strikes against other regime targets in Libya, including some B-2 bomber sorties launched from bases in the continental United States. Within 72 hours, the no-fly zone was established (see Figure 2.3). Ultimately, twelve countries would participate in this operation, but the United States flew the vast majority of strike sorties.[35]

The initial operations took place amid some degree of debate about what command and control arrangements should be. As one senior official recounted, "The whole thing ramped up so quickly I don't think anybody saw the speed [with which] the two UNSCRs passed. Everybody was expecting a couple of nations in the Security Council to block it . . . That took everybody by surprise."[36] Only a week before, the expectation in the U.S. Department of Defense (DoD) had been that any operations would be largely humanitarian in nature. U.S. Africa Command (AFRICOM) had been given the lead role, with support from U.S. European Command (EUCOM), U.S. Central Command (CENTCOM), and other combatant commands. The passage of UNSCR 1973, with its civilian-protection mission, however, raised the question of whether EUCOM should be the supported command, given that the operation now had much greater kinetic requirements and that many of the forces necessary would

---

[33] Radio France Internationale (Paris), "French Fighter Jets Fly over Country," March 19, 2011.

[34] Office of the Assistant Secretary of Defense (Public Affairs) (OASD PA), "DOD News Briefing with Vice Admiral Gortney from the Pentagon on Libya Operation Odyssey Dawn," Washington, D.C.: U.S. Department of Defense, March 19, 2011.

[35] OASD (PA), "DOD News Briefing with Vice Adm. Gortney," March 28, 2011.

[36] Interview with senior U.S. official, July 9, 2012.

Figure 2.3
Operation Odyssey Dawn Initial Strikes and No-Fly Zone

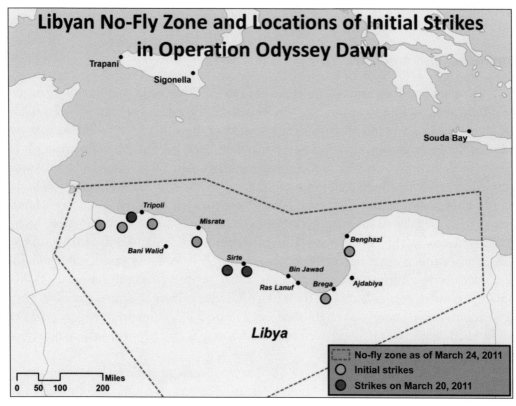

RAND *RR676-2.3*

be generated from or would transit through Europe. In the end, however, AFRICOM retained the lead role, establishing Joint Task Force Odyssey Dawn. Operational command fell to Admiral Samuel J. Locklear III, while AFRICOM's commander, General Carter Ham, had overall strategic command.[37]

While this arrangement answered who would lead U.S. operations, confusion remained about who would be in charge of overall coalition operations. The French had originally sought a joint Franco-British operation, and for the first few days of the campaign the French military continued to insist that the partners' operations were simply concurrent, while AFRICOM claimed that it was the overall lead. Other allies, comfortable with U.S. leadership, already were transferring command of their forces to the U.S. 17th Air Force under AFRICOM, as Denmark did on March 19.[38] Within a

---

[37] Joe Quartararo, Michael Rovenolt, and Randy White, "Libya's Operation Odyssey Dawn," *Prism,* Vol. 3, No. 2, March 2012, pp. 141–156.

[38] "Norway Insists on Acting Under US Command in Libya," *Agence France-Presse,* March 22, 2011.

few days, command relationships between the U.S., British, Italian, and French operations were sorted out, and by March 25, Belgium, Canada, Denmark, the Netherlands,
Norway, Spain, Qatar, and the United Arab Emirates all had joined the operation.

Follow-up strikes in the next few days continued to target Libya's air defenses
while striking regime C2 targets in Tripoli and elsewhere, and addressing the most
immediate regime threats to civilians in Benghazi and Misrata. By midweek, the United
States added A-10 "Warthogs" and AC-130 Spectre gunships to further enhance coalition capabilities against regime forces on the ground.[39] Gradually, however, the newer
members of the coalition were flying more of the sorties, and the United States made a
conscious effort to transition from a lead to a supporting role in military operations. As
Vice Admiral Gortney explained in a March 28 briefing on operations, "U.S. military
participation in this operation is, as we have said all along, changing to one primarily
of support."[40]

Within a week, Odyssey Dawn had succeeded in stopping the advance of regime
forces on Benghazi and allowed the rebels space to move westward, retaking the town
of Ajdabiyah and advancing on the town of Brega. With Benghazi secure, the rebels
had a stronghold and safe haven from which to operate for the rest of the war. There,
they could train their forces and liaise with international actors, significantly strengthening their chances of success against the better-equipped Qaddafi regime. In the west,
only the port city of Misrata was managing to hold off Qaddafi's forces. It was under
brutal siege, and with Qaddafi's forces in flight from Benghazi, the coalition began to
focus on its relief.

These important accomplishments set the stage for the successful NATO operation that followed and the ultimate victory of the rebels over the regime. Much consternation remained, however, over the exact objectives of military operations. President
Obama had clearly called for Qaddafi's departure prior to UNSCR 1973, but that
resolution and the Defense Secretary's warning order (WARNORD) implied that the
objective of military operations was civilian protection.[41] It was not inconceivable in
theory for the military operation to focus on civilian protection and the diplomatic
and political effort to focus on ousting Qaddafi. But in practice, the distinction was
difficult to sustain. In fact, as several commentators pointed out at the time, multiple
outcomes were possible, and the preference of U.S. and allied officials was unclear. It
may be that they themselves were unsure. As one prominent foreign-policy observer
wrote in the *Washington Post*, "The administration has launched the United States into
battle with no clear vision of what a successful and stable outcome looks like."[42]

---

[39] OASD (PA), "DOD News Briefing with Vice Adm. Gortney," March 28, 2011.

[40] OASD (PA), "DOD News Briefing with Vice Adm. Gortney," March 28, 2011.

[41] Multiple interviews. See also, Quartararo, Rovenolt, and White, "Libya's Operation Odyssey Dawn."

[42] Gideon Rose, "Tell Me How This One Ends," *Washington Post*, March 27, 2011, p. B1.

At least three outcomes (not including failure) were imaginable. The first would be a quick collapse of Libyan support for Qaddafi, forcing him from power. Although some leaders—Sarkozy, for example—might have hoped for this outcome, it was soon clear that it would not happen. The second possibility was a partition of Libya between a "free" east and a Qaddafi-ruled west. The third was the rebels' armed overthrow of the regime, as actually occurred. Leaders obviously wanted to avoid stating publicly that regime change was an objective of the military operation for diplomatic reasons, but within allied governments, debate lingered over how the scenario would play out.[43] In general, because the operation had come on so quickly, thinking about end states had received some, but perhaps not enough, attention.

President Obama had declared early on that the American role would be limited, and that after initial operations of roughly a week, the United States would pull back into an overwatch role and provide only those unique assets required to allow its allies to continue the operation.[44] As Odyssey Dawn was under way, therefore, intense discussions occurred in allied capitals about what would follow.

Transition to NATO Command

The United States determined soon after UNSCR 1973 that NATO was its preferred structure for continuing the military action against Qaddafi. Using the Alliance would give the United States significant influence, even after it pulled back its strike aircraft. Moreover, important voices in the U.S. government—including the U.S. ambassador to NATO, Ivo Daalder—believed strongly that NATO was the only organization that could provide the command-and-control facilities required by a broad-based coalition operation of this kind. Of no less importance, NATO's established relationships with the other partners—both from Europe and from the Middle East—would greatly facilitate success in coordinating the efforts of such a broad coalition.[45] Finally, this comparatively low-difficulty intervention against a much-reviled despot could help NATO's reputation, and success might even serve as something of a balm for the wounds the Alliance had suffered in Afghanistan and over Iraq. As one senior U.S. official put it, "There is no such thing as an opportune war, but it was a very opportune time for a war in NATO."[46] NATO Secretary General Rasmussen, a former Danish prime minister, also was eager for an opportunity to get back into the limelight and

---

[43] Interview with senior U.S. official, January 24, 2011.

[44] See Christopher S. Chivvis, *Toppling Qaddafi*, New York: Cambridge University Press, 2013, p. 70.

[45] Interview with senior U.S. official, December 16, 2011.

[46] Interview with senior U.S. official, July 9, 2012.

worked to ensure that all the components of the operation were brought under NATO command.[47]

The British government agreed with the United States' position that NATO was the appropriate organization through which to pursue the operation, as did many of the smaller countries participating in the strikes. Germany indicated a willingness to tolerate a NATO action, provided it was not asked to participate. Even Turkey, which initially had strong objections to the intervention, was willing to go along with NATO, if only because its position within the Alliance afforded it the possibility of greater control over NATO operations.[48]

France, however, disagreed. The French have a long and complicated history with NATO, but under President Sarkozy, France had taken important steps back toward the Alliance, most notably by announcing in 2008 that it would rejoin the NATO integrated military structure following a 42-year absence. But now, the French argued that a coalition of the willing was more suitable than a NATO operation. They hoped this would allow the broad-based political grouping they had gathered in Paris on March 19 to become a guiding political body for military operations, circumventing the Alliance altogether. At the same time, they sought to minimize the influence of countries such as Turkey that were reticent about the operation.[49]

As a result, even as the Franco-British-U.S. coalition struck Qaddafi's forces, French, British and U.S. diplomats were wrangling in Brussels over whether operations would be brought under NATO command. Within a few days, however, French officials agreed to allow the less demanding maritime arms embargo operation to come under NATO command. Shortly thereafter, they also agreed to allow no-fly zone operations to be brought into NATO. Only after a four-way conference call between the French, British, Turks, and Americans, however, was Secretary Clinton able to broker a deal between France and Turkey, and France agreed to allow the entire Libyan operation mission to come under NATO command.[50]

The United States soon began to reduce its role in the strike missions. NATO operations still would rely heavily on a mostly U.S.-provided logistical and ISR backbone, but U.S. strike aircraft would be pulled back and strategic and operational command and control would be transferred from AFRICOM to NATO on March 31.

---

[47] Interview with member of the NATO International Staff, February 6, 2012.

[48] Interview with senior U.S. official, February 6, 2012.

[49] Jean-Pierre Stroobants, "L'alliance atlantique Étale ses divisions à bruxelles sur la gestion de la crise libyenne," *Le Monde*, March 23, 2011; Jean-Pierre Stroobants, "Libye: Batailles diplomatiques en coulisses," *Le Monde*, March 24, 2011, p. 1; Ian Traynor, "Turkey and France Clash over Libya Air Campaign," *The Guardian*, March 24, 2011.

[50] Scott Wilson and Karen DeYoung, "Coalition Nears Agreement on Transition for Operations in Libya," *Washington Post*, March 23, 2011.

The speed with which NATO developed and agreed on its operational plans for what became Operation Unified Protector was unprecedented for the Alliance. NATO developed and agreed upon four operational plans much more quickly after the outbreak of violence than it had in preparing for its interventions in Bosnia and Kosovo. These plans comprised a maritime embargo, a no-fly zone, a civilian-protection mission, and a humanitarian mission. (Of the four, only the humanitarian mission plan would not be activated.[51]) In part, this rapid response was possible because prudent planning already had started in the run-up to the U.N. resolutions, and because NATO could benefit from plans previously developed within AFRICOM and EUCOM. But to say that this pace was an indication of underlying Alliance unity—as some NATO and U.S. officials would later suggest—tends to obscure the fact that operational planning also moved rapidly in part because several countries, notably Germany, absented themselves from the process altogether due to their fundamental disagreement with the entire operation. (See Table 2.1 for a comparison of OOP and OUP command relationship.)

Operation Unified Protector

When OUP began, the preceding coalition operations had prepared the ground for it. Most of the same countries participating in Odyssey Dawn also participated in Unified Protector. The major shift was the reduced operational role of the United States. Bulgaria, Romania, Turkey, and Greece were now added to the coalition as providers of naval assets. Qatar, Sweden, and the United Arab Emirates continued flying alongside

Table 2.1
Comparison of Odyssey Dawn and Unified Protector Command Relationships

	Operation Odyssey Dawn	Operation Unified Protector
Mandate	UNSCR 1970 & 1973	UNSCR 1970 & 1973
Framework	Coalition	NATO Alliance
Authority	National governments	North Atlantic Council
Supported command	AFRICOM	Joint Force Command Naples
Commander	General Carter F. Ham, USA	Admiral Samuel J. Locklear, USN
JTF commander	Admiral Samuel J. Locklear, USN	Lieutenant-General Charles Bouchard, RCAF
JFACC/CFACC	Major General Margaret Woodward, USAF	Lieutenant General Ralph J. Jodice II, USAF
CAOC	617th AOC, Ramstein AB, GER	CFAC, Poggio Renatico, ITA

NOTE: For OOD, only U.S. command arrangements shown.
CFACC=Combined Forces Air Component Commander

---

[51] Interview with senior U.S. official, July 9, 2012.

the coalition's NATO members, and Jordan joined the coalition.[52] At the start of OUP, 14 NATO nations were participating, along with the four non-NATO partners.[53] (See Figure 2.4.) Only six of the NATO states, however, were conducting air-to-ground strike missions.[54]

A combined joint task force (CJTF) was established at Joint Forces Command in Naples, Italy. Admiral Locklear's deputy, Canadian Lieutenant-General Charles Bouchard, took over command. This kept Locklear officially within the chain of command, but freed him to focus on the other ongoing operations with which Joint Force

Figure 2.4
Principal Operating Bases for Operation Unified Protector

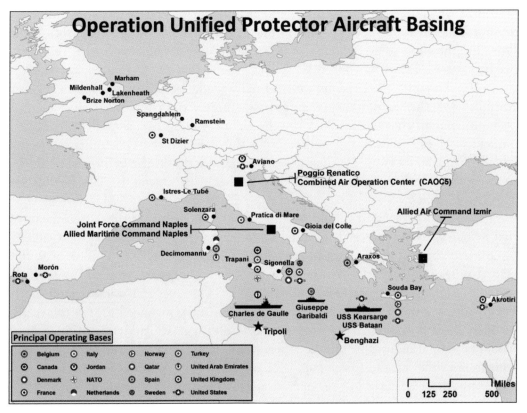

NOTE: Ship icons do not represent actual patrol locations. Aircraft deployed to each base are listed in Appendix B.

RAND RR676-2.4

---

[52] Elizabeth Quintana, "The War from the Air," in Johnson and Mueen, 2012.

[53] Ivo H. Daalder and James G. Stavridis, "NATO's Victory in Libya," *Foreign Affairs*, March/April 2012.

[54] Belgium, Canada, Denmark, France, Norway, and the United Kingdom; Italian aircraft initially flew defense suppression but not strike missions.

Command (JFC) Naples was engaged (including Kosovo, which appeared to be at risk of a flareup), and allowed the United States to step back from the public diplomacy of the operation.[55] Bouchard reported to Admiral James Stavridis, who was dual-hatted as the commander of U.S. European Command and as NATO's Supreme Allied Commander. The North Atlantic Council (NAC) exercised overarching political control of the operation. Control of air operations shifted from the CAOC at Ramstein Air Base (AB), Germany, to the CAOC at Poggio Renatico, Italy, under the command of U.S. Air Force (USAF) Lieutenant General Ralph J. Jodice II.

In the 1999 Kosovo air campaign (Operation Allied Force), allied governments had the opportunity to scrutinize target lists, a practice that led to much criticism from military leadership both during and after the war. (France in 1999 had been one of the countries most adamant about the need for this scrutiny, but it was exactly this problem that the French sought to avoid.) In subsequent years, efforts were made to devolve authority from the NAC to the military commands, and in the case of Unified Protector, the effort to avoid excessive deliberation over targets was further reinforced by the establishment of an internal "striker group" that called most of the shots in the NAC. Although all decisions were formally made "at 28" by all members of the Alliance—whether or not they were participating in the operation—most of these decisions were in effect "precooked" by the eight members that actually were participating in strikes as part of the civilian-protection mission: the United States, France, Britain, Canada, Norway, Denmark, Belgium, and Italy. In the event, the meddling for which political leaders often had been criticized in Operation Allied Force was avoided in Libya.[56]

The NATO operation got off to a difficult start, however. At the outset, the rebels had managed to push several hundred kilometers west from Benghazi as Qaddafi's forces retreated under the shock of coalition airstrikes, but as NATO took over, they started retreating eastward. Within a few days they were nearly pushed from Ajdabiyah, the last town before the rebel stronghold. NATO strikes on Qaddafi's forces at the nearby town of Brega bought them a reprieve, and they managed to halt the regime advance. NATO would carry out repeated airstrikes against Qaddafi's positions, but it would be several months before the rebels would retake any ground. The line of confrontation in the east therefore remained fixed.

After three weeks of NATO operations, little progress was evident. Both NATO and the rebels were suffering from a number of constraints. The rebel forces themselves lacked equipment as well as military experience. This greatly hindered their ability to take advantage of opportunities that NATO strikes provided. Only as they gained capabilities and experience would their ability to take and hold ground increase.

---

[55] Interview with senior U.S. official, July 9, 2012.

[56] Interview with French official, February 7, 2012; interview with UK official, February 7, 2012.

Meanwhile, the Alliance was suffering from shortfalls of tankers and especially ISR. Of the thousands of Alliance member-owned fighter aircraft, fewer than one hundred were participating in the mission. Yet, according to U.S. officials, limited ISR capacity was the principal constraint on operations, especially when it came to targeteers with the skills to support offensive air operations. As OUP began, the United States and other NATO members were forced to surge hundreds of staff from EUCOM and elsewhere to fill gaps in the CAOC in Poggio Renatico.[57]

It is possible that the support staff requirements for the operation were not fully appreciated in some allied capitals when the initial commitments to the operation were made. It took about a week to get the necessary equipment and staff to the CAOC, and another two weeks before all of the kinks were worked out and the allied ISR effort was well integrated. As one senior officer involved in the effort explained, "By the beginning of May, General Jodice had all the necessary tools at his disposal: a good ATO [air tasking order] cycle in place that got all the national targeting packages coordinated, put into NATO, and fed out to the different strike nations."[58]

Another important operational change that took place alongside the transition from coalition to NATO operation was a shift in emphasis from static to dynamic targeting. Most of the targets in the early days of Operation Odyssey Dawn were fixed targets such as surface-to-air missile (SAM) sites, major C2 facilities, and weapon storage bunkers. As these targets were destroyed, the focus of the air campaign increasingly came to rest on dynamic targets identified during the sorties themselves.

Frustrated with the progress on the ground, French and British leaders were already pushing their NATO counterparts for more force contributions by mid-April.[59] In Germany's case, support for the intervention actually grew over time, and eventually would include an offer of post-conflict police trainers as well as significant amounts of financial aid for the new Libyan government. Having abstained from the Security Council vote, however, the Germans would not consider a military contribution.

Poland's absence from the fight was also noteworthy, since the Poles had a sizable force of F-16s, but Warsaw argued that their training was insufficient for the task—an argument that most other nations thought was cover for not wanting to participate. The Polish opt-out was less irksome to U.S. officials than the German abstention, even if it was still regarded as unfortunate. Given Poland's participation in the International Security Assistance Force (ISAF) in Afghanistan, it is possible—though by no means certain—that the United States' decision to step back from strike operations may have lessened the pressure on Poland to contribute to OUP, insofar as it was misinterpreted as a sign of lesser U.S. interest in the overall mission.

---

[57] Multiple interviews.

[58] Interview with senior U.S. official, July 9, 2012.

[59] National Public Radio (NPR), "NATO Allies Question Their Role in Libya," NPR, April 16, 2011.

Some of the other NATO members that did not participate, however, such as the Baltic states, simply lacked capabilities needed to contribute to a modern air war. As a result, U.S. officials would later argue that most of the states that could have participated in the operation did so.[60] The fact was that across Europe, the operation came at a time when the European financial crisis was severely straining defense budgets. Because NATO operates on a costs-lie-where-they-fall basis, any spending on Libya operations would further reduce funds available for the participating militaries, reducing existing training and potentially threatening procurement programs. This—as much as the politics of the operation—clearly played a role in several countries' decisions to stand on the sidelines.

Most military officials also blamed the stalemate on an overall lack of clarity about strategic end states. The U.S. president had called for Qaddafi's ouster prior to UNSCR 1973, as had his British and French counterparts. Yet the U.N. mandate only called for operations to protect civilians. To complicate matters, in a speech at the National Defense University on March 28, President Obama had clearly said regime change was not an objective of the operation.[61] As a result, no small amount of confusion arose about the intervention's actual strategic goals, and this made operational planning more difficult.

The reality, of course, was that the ambiguity in strategic end states was a natural consequence of both the speed with which the operation was undertaken and the breadth of the coalition that had been brought together to support it. After all, the Arab League had called for a no-fly zone, not the civilian protection mission, and had actually wobbled in its support for the operation in the immediate aftermath of UNSCR 1973. A more specific set of objectives—such as calling for Qaddafi's ouster—would have been impossible to get through the U.N. Security Council and likely would have made it much more difficult for some Arab states to support the operation.

A meeting of the NATO foreign ministers in mid-April helped clarify the issue, and eventually, the striker group also decided that Qaddafi's forces were fair game anywhere in Libya as long as attacks against civilians were occurring somewhere because those attacks posed an intrinsic threat to the Libyan populace.[62] NATO thus pursued a two-pronged strategy at the start of its operations, targeting Qaddafi's command and control and lines of supply while also striking directly at forces that were attacking the civilian populace. The focus was accordingly on Qaddafi's forces in Brega, his C2 nodes in and around Tripoli—including the headquarters of Qaddafi's 32nd Brigade, which was responsible for many of the attacks—and the regime forces shelling the port city of Misrata.

---

[60] Interview with senior U.S. official, January 24, 2012; interview with senior U.S. official, February 7, 2012.

[61] The White House, Office of the Press Secretary, "Remarks by the President in Address to the Nation on Libya," Washington, D.C., March 28, 2011.

[62] Interviews with NATO officials, February 7, 2011.

The Relief of Misrata

Misrata was the only city in the western half of Libya that remained under rebel control, and had important symbolic as well as strategic value. By mid-April, however, that control had become extremely tenuous. Rebel fighters were pushed out of the town center from the south and were holding out in the port, which Qaddafi's forces shelled relentlessly. Much of the civilian population had fled the city. Because of the shelling of the port, it was nearly impossible to get humanitarian aid to the civilian population. A major humanitarian crisis was brewing.[63]

Starting in mid-April, NATO focused on striking Qaddafi's forces in and around the city in an effort to relieve the siege. By then, however, Qaddafi's forces had started to adapt to the threat posed by NATO warplanes by making efforts to blend in and disguise themselves as rebels or civilians, imposing even greater difficulties for NATO's already challenged ISR capabilities.

In response, the United States agreed to reintroduce two MQ-1 Predator unmanned aerial vehicles (UAVs) to strike operations in late April (they had been limited to flying ISR missions after the United States withdrew its strike aircraft at the end of Odyssey Dawn). This enhanced NATO's capability to loiter and gather information about regime forces that were hiding in the urban shadows before striking. It also was intended to send a psychological message, helping to succor the rebels in the town and demoralize Qaddafi's troops.[64]

By the second week of May, the rebels had begun to make noticeable progress toward pushing the regime forces out of the town center and into the suburbs. With the port secure, humanitarian shipments began moving back into the town. The line of contact would remain nearby for several months, and some shelling would continue. Nevertheless, the relief of Misrata was, in retrospect, a key turning point in the war. It is possible that without it, anti-regime forces in the east might have sued for peace, dividing the country. With Misrata under rebel control, however, the revolt remained a nationwide uprising.

---

[63] Oana Lungescu, NATO Spokesperson, and Brigadier General Mark van Uhm, Chief of Allied Operations, Allied Command Operations (SHAPE), "Press Briefing on Libya," April 19, 2011; C. J. Chivers, "Taking Airport, Rebels in Libya Loosen Noose," *New York Times*, May 12, p. A1; U.N. Office for the Coordination of Humanitarian Affairs, "Libya: Misrata Is Difficult to Access. Humanitarian Assessment Finds People in Need of Medical Supplies," OCHA Situation Report No. 49, July 16, 2011.

[64] Comments by Secretary Robert Gates, Secretary of Defense and General James Cartwright, vice chairman of the Joint Chiefs of Staff, Washington, D.C., Thursday, April 21, 2011.

Naval Operations

Naval operations played an important role throughout the intervention. The composition of the maritime force coalition differed from that of the striker group in that Bulgaria, Greece, the Netherlands, Romania, Spain, and Turkey also participated, while Denmark and Norway did not.[65] Naval forces played several roles. In Misrata, warships took fire from and fired back at Qaddafi's forces onshore. They also fired illumination rounds for airstrikes and addressed the threat posed by small regime vessels that were seeking to mine and booby-trap Misrata's harbor to stop the flow of aid and other supplies to the city.[66] In June, when regime forces were spotted laying a trap by putting human mannequins and a ton of explosives in an abandoned vessel to lure enemy ships, NATO determined that Qaddafi's naval forces posed enough of a threat to civilians to warrant direct action, and NATO aircraft subsequently destroyed regime vessels in neighboring harbors, eliminating the threat that Qaddafi's navy posed. Sea-basing of fighters, and later attack helicopters, on amphibious vessels and the French aircraft carrier *Charles de Gaulle* brought allied airpower closer to Qaddafi's shores, though the ships had to cycle on and off station for maintenance over the course of the conflict.

Naval operations also were essential to the maintenance of the arms embargo. Although NATO only turned back 11 vessels over the course of the operation, the NATO blockade likely was enough to keep many would-be purveyors of arms to Qaddafi from attempting a breach.[67] Needless to say, the arms embargo was a critical counterpart to efforts to destroy the regime's war-fighting capability. Given the relatively low operational tempo, it is quite possible that Qaddafi would have been able to recoup much of the losses that NATO airstrikes inflicted had the arms embargo not been enforced.

Operations Grind On

Despite the positive momentum that the relief of Misrata had gained, rebel progress was slow over the next three months. A basic divide emerged within the coalition between those countries that, fearing prolonged stalemate, advocated for more forceful measures to bring the conflict to an end and those believing that progress, if slow, was sufficient because they feared the possible consequences or costs of undertaking more

---

[65] Interview with NATO military official, February 10, 2012.

[66] Christian F. Anrig, "Allied Air Power over Libya," *Air and Space Power Journal*, Winter 2011, pp. 89–109.

[67] NATO Media Operations Centre, "Operation UNIFIED PROTECTOR Final Mission Stats," November 2, 2011.

forceful measures. The British and the French were in the first camp, while the United States inclined toward the second.[68]

Both Sarkozy and Cameron felt the pressure of the apparent stalemate. They had been the impetus for the operation in the first place, and had largely operated on the assumption that Qaddafi would be removed from power quickly. The public perceptions of a long-running NATO operation and an apparent stalemate on the ground two months after UNSCR 1973 were bad to begin with, but the two leaders had a greater fear: that stalemate might increase pressure to negotiate a settlement with Qaddafi on unfavorable terms, depriving them of the military and moral victory they both sought. As a result, they pushed for more aggressive action to remove Qaddafi. The British were particularly open in pushing for an expansion of the target list to include more of Qaddafi's military and civilian infrastructure. This was controversial not only because of the impact that it might have on the civilian population, but because corporations in allied countries owned some significant parts of that infrastructure.

In May, France and Britain decided to add attack helicopters to the operation. This came with the risk of both allied and civilian casualties, but like the use of the Predators, it offered the possibility for even more precise strikes and had a certain psychological advantage.[69] By early June, British Apache and French Tigre and Gazelle helicopters based offshore were flying missions in both Brega and Misrata, often in coordination with fixed-wing aircraft.[70]

In June, both France and the UK went a step further, sending trainers, equipment, and supplies to the rebel forces. Although this assistance came in a purely bilateral context, it obviously went beyond the civilian-protection mission and clearly put the French and the British—and, arguably, the whole Alliance—on the side of the rebels. Later reporting would suggest that the numbers of advisors deployed on the ground to assist the rebels was small.[71] Qatar had announced it would send arms to the rebels in April, and eventually deployed special operations forces to train and eventually fight alongside them.[72] Even in small numbers, the marginal impact on rebel tactical and strategic capability of these contributions clearly was significant.

---

[68] Multiple interviews.

[69] Interview with NATO official, February 7, 2012.

[70] "Libya: UK Apache Attack Helicopters Launch First Strikes," *The Telegraph*, June 4, 2011; "Libya: UK Apache Helicopters Used in NATO Attacks," *BBC News*, June 4, 2011; "Des helicopters français participent aux frappes," *France2.fr*, June 4, 2011.

[71] Thomas Harding, "Libya: SAS Leads Hunt for Gaddafi," *The Daily Telegraph*, August 24, 2011; Sam Dagher, Charles Levinson, and Margaret Coker, "Tiny Kingdom's Huge Role in Libya Draws Concern," *Wall Street Journal*, October 17, 2011, p. A1; Ian Black, "Qatar Admits It Sent Troops to Support NTC Fighters," *The Guardian*, October 26, 2011, p. 24.

[72] Dagher, Levinson, and Coker, "Tiny Kingdom's Huge Role in Libya Draws Concern;" Black, "Qatar Admits it Sent Troops to Support NTC Fighters."

For its part, while it generally supported its allies, the United States was concerned that efforts to increase the pressure on Qaddafi might bring unnecessary risks. Actions that could be interpreted as exceeding the U.N. mandate brought criticism from other states—especially Russia and China—and could make it more difficult for some members of the coalition to continue their participation. Increasing the operational tempo and employing attack helicopters also increased the chances that the Alliance would make mistakes. Mistakes, in turn, increased the chances that one or more of the allies would break off from the coalition, scoring a victory for Qaddafi.[73]

Moreover, U.S. officials argued, the progress that was being achieved, even if gradual, was real and eventually would result in Qaddafi's ouster. The number of defections by regime loyalists was steadily rising. By May, Qaddafi's forces already had been weakened to the point at which he could no longer launch a major offensive against the rebels. Meanwhile, the rebels were gaining equipment, organization, and critical know-how that they had lacked at first. Under these conditions, most U.S. officials assessed, patience was the best course of action. The Alliance would eventually grind the regime down, and Qaddafi would either be forced to step down, be overthrown from inside his own coterie, or be defeated outright on the battlefield.

Increasing the Diplomatic Pressure

Military operations in this period were complemented by ongoing diplomatic and political efforts in European and regional capitals. These efforts aimed simultaneously to strengthen the rebels while making Qaddafi's defeat appear to be a foregone conclusion. The main instrument for this was the Libya Contact Group, which grew out of the March 19 Paris meeting and was established at a London meeting ten days later. Largely a French initiative, the Contact Group had a broad and growing membership of more than twenty countries. It met on a monthly basis thereafter, alternating between European and Middle Eastern capitals, with meetings in Doha, Rome, Abu Dhabi, and Istanbul.

In general, the meetings of the Contact Group were designed to demonstrate the political will that backed the military intervention and the Libyan National Transitional Council (NTC). Although the Contact Group never exercised political control over military operations—as the French originally had hoped it would—it did provide an important source of sustained legitimacy for the operation, especially as criticism increased over the course of the summer that NATO was stretching the mandate.

On the most basic level, the meetings provided the opportunity for the rebels to gain the confidence of international actors. The Contact Group was also a forum for discussing means of strengthening the financial situation of the NTC, which needed

---

[73] Interviews with senior U.S. officials, February 7, 2012.

funds not only for military operations, but simply to keep the parts of the country it controlled up and running.[74] A financial mechanism was established in June that facilitated the disbursement of aid, although making the Libyan state assets that had been frozen under UNSCR 1970 available to the NTC would take several months longer—a fact that created much frustration among the rebel leadership. It also irked the White House, where National Security Advisor Tom Donilon reportedly was extremely frustrated with the rebels' inability to access funds that would help their cause on account of the sanctions regime set up against the Qaddafi regime.[75]

The Contact Group also provided a forum for discussions about recognition of the rebels. President Sarkozy had recognized the NTC in early March, but his foreign ministry then attempted to walk back or "interpret" its president's proclamation in subsequent statements. It soon became clear that recognition was a complicated and thorny legal issue.[76] In fact, many forms of recognition are possible, with certain legal criteria coming with each. It was one thing to recognize the NTC as an organization, another to recognize it as the organization that represented the rebels and yet another to recognize it as the government of Libya.[77] By July, however, sufficient confidence existed that the NTC had met the requisite requirements for the United States to recognize the group formally as the government of Libya. Many of the countries that had not yet recognized the NTC soon followed suit (see Table 2.2), expelling any remaining regime diplomats in their capitals and opening the door to further financial aid to the rebels.

Emergence of the Western Front

As part of their efforts to bring the operation to a quicker end, the French reportedly airdropped military equipment to rebels in the Nafusa Mountains west of Tripoli in June.[78] The British also provided the rebels in this area with nonmilitary equipment.[79] A significant uptick in rebel activity in the area followed these insertions. Starting in July, rebel forces began making inroads along the Tunisian border, slowly wresting one small town after another from Qaddafi's grip. In part, these victories were due to the continued defections from Qaddafi's forces. However, they also were due to military

---

[74] Interview with senior U.S. official, January 24, 2012.

[75] Interview with senior White House official, February 13, 2012.

[76] Interviews with U.S. officials, February 13 and February 17, 2012.

[77] Stefan Talmon, "Recognition of the Libyan National Transitional Council," *ASIL Insights*, Vol. 15, No. 16, June 16, 2011.

[78] Philippe Gelie, "La France a parachuté des armes aux rebelles libyens," *Le Figaro*, June 28, 2011.

[79] David Jolly, "Britain Sends Supplies to Libyan Rebels," *New York Times*, June 30, 2011.

Table 2.2
Dates of Recognition of the National Transitional Council

Country	Date
(NTC declares itself the legitimate government of Libya)	March 5
France	March 10
Qatar	March 28
Italy	April 4
Jordan	May 24
Spain	June 8
UAE	June 12
Germany	June 13
Canada	June 14
Denmark	June 22
Turkey	July 3
Poland	July 8
Belgium, Luxembourg, Netherlands	July 13
United States	July 15
United Kingdom	July 27
Egypt	August 22
Norway, Greece	August 23
Russia	September 1
China	September 12
U.N. General Assembly gives Libya's seat to NTC	September 16

SOURCE: NATO, "Evolution of the frontlines in Libya—March–Sept. 2011," online maps, September 22, 2011.

success, presumably aided by the addition of the French weapons and foreign advisors on the ground.[80]

By mid-July, it was clear that a third front, in addition to operations in the east and the territorial perimeter around Misrata, had opened in the war. The introduction of improved communications equipment allowed the rebels to increase not only their tactical effectiveness but also the strategic coordination of their attacks, which previously had been nonexistent. This represented an important strategic advance for the rebels, who now were able to apply strategic pressure on regime forces, and to do so increasingly close to the capital (see Figure 2.5).

Meanwhile, the pressure for a negotiated settlement was growing. Multiple efforts were under way throughout June and July to find a suitable plan for a ceasefire. Qaddafi insisted he wanted a ceasefire, but the rebels responded that his abdication was

---

[80] David D. Kirkpatrick, "Western Libya Earns a Taste of Freedom as Rebels Loosen Qaddafi's Grip," *New York Times*, June 26, 2012, p. A12.

Figure 2.5
Approximate Territorial Control in Libya, June/July 2011

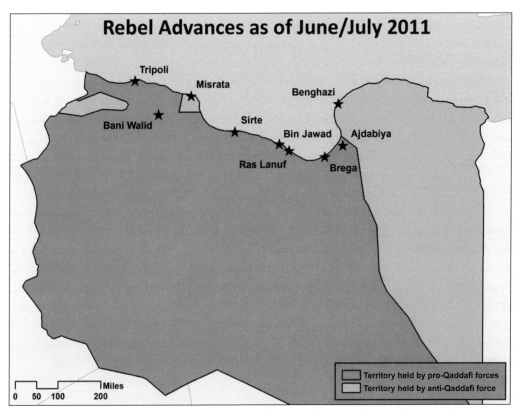

SOURCE: Adapted from NATO, "Evolution of the frontlines in Libya—March–Sept. 2011," online maps, September 22, 2011.
RAND *RR676-2.5*

a prerequisite for any negotiations. The fact that the International Criminal Court had now indicted Qaddafi for crimes against humanity helped legitimize the international intervention, but it further complicated efforts at a negotiated settlement by reducing the number of countries in which Qaddafi might agree to accept exile.[81]

Negotiation efforts by the United Nations, Russia, South Africa, France, and the United States all came to nothing. In mid-July, a U.S. team actually met at the U.S. ambassador's residence in Tunis with members of Qaddafi's inner circle, but that meeting turned into an emotional scene demonstrating only that, despite its difficulties on the ground, the regime had not fully accepted what was happening to it.[82]

---

[81] Interview with senior U.S. official, February 17, 2012.

[82] Interview with senior White House official, February 27, 2012; "U.S. Sends 'Time to Go' Message to Gaddafi," *Al Jazeera*, July 19, 2011.

These negotiations dragged on nevertheless, even as rebel efforts appeared gradually to be gaining momentum in the Nafusa Mountains. In late July, reports broke that rebel military leader Abdel Fatah Younis had been murdered in Benghazi. Although the circumstances of his death remain unclear, it appeared at the time that his death was the result of inter-tribal strife and possibly retribution for repression he carried out in his role as a Qaddafi's interior minister in the 1990s.[83]

The assassination came as a surprise in Washington and disheartened observers at a moment when it seemed that progress on the ground was in sight after months of stalemate.[84] One advantage the rebels possessed was their relative unity. Libya's underlying tribal and ethnic diversity was widely recognized, yet despite the largely organic and dispersed nature of the revolt, the rebels so far had been united in their fight against Qaddafi. Should they fall apart, the rebels' chances of victory could evaporate and the possibility of a Somalia-like scenario in Libya accordingly would grow.

The NTC responded a week later by dissolving its cabinet and forming a new one. By the second week of August, however, attention was still focused on the stalemate on the ground, and on the implications that the Younis assassination would have for the future of the conflict. Meanwhile, in allied capitals, after initial hopes of a short war had been dispelled, the prevailing expectation was increasingly of a long struggle to dislodge Qaddafi from Tripoli. The rebels had been working to make inroads into the capital and prepare the way for an eventual assault, but the lengths to which Qaddafi might go to hold onto Tripoli were largely unknown. Serious concerns emerged that he might use chemical and other weapons against the population in a scorched-earth strategy.

The Fall of Tripoli

For a while, the assassination of Younis distracted attention from the gradual advance that rebels were making in the west. By August 15, however, it was clear that the advance that had started there the month before was gaining ground. On August 15, pushing east from the Nafusa Mountains, the rebels seized Zawiyah, an oil town with a key refinery only a half-hour by car from Tripoli. A back-and-forth battle with loyalist forces lodged in the refinery and regime snipers perched on rooftops continued for the next three days.[85]

---

[83] Trevor Mostyn, "Obituary: Gen Abdel Fatah Younis: Military Leader and Gaddafi's Trusted Aide Until He Defected to Libyan Rebel Forces," *The Guardian*, August 1, 2011, p. 32; David D. Kirkpatrick, "Gun Battle Disrupts Rebel Base in Libya," *New York Times*, August 1, 2011, p. A4.

[84] Interview with senior U.S. official, March 29, 2012.

[85] Kareem Fahim, "Refugees Flee Libya Oil City as Qaddafi's Forces Dig In," *New York Times*, August 18, 2011, p. A4; Kareem Fahim, "Libyan Rebels Gain Control of Key Oil Refinery as Qaddafi Forces Flee," *New York Times*, August 19, 2011, p. A6; Kareem Fahim, "Libya Rebels Threaten a Supply Line to the Capital," *New York Times*, August 15, 2011, p. A8.

On August 20, the rebels advanced with unexpected speed on the Libyan capital. Months of work had laid the ground for immediate defections from the regime as
the rebel forces advanced into Tripoli. NATO bombed heavily as the rebels advanced.
Within a few days, Qaddafi's compound was overrun and Qaddafi had fled (see
Figure 2.6). At nearly the same time, rebel forces took Brega, allowing them at long
last to connect the eastern half of the country with Tripoli. As a result, several militias
descended on the capital, taking control of key pieces of real estate that they would
hold long after the war was over.[86]

Qaddafi was still at large, but it was clear his rule was over. The pressure increased
proportionately on Russia and South Africa to back the intervention. At a meeting
of the Contact Group in Paris on September 1, Russia recognized the NTC. Soon

Figure 2.6
Approximate Territorial Control in Libya, August 2011

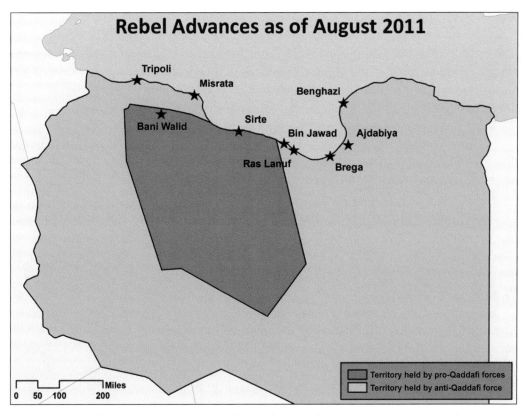

SOURCE: Adapted from NATO, "Evolution of the frontlines in Libya—March–Sept. 2011," online maps,
September 22, 2011.
RAND RR676-2.6

---

[86] Multiple news reports and interviews with White House officials, February 17, 2012.

thereafter, under enormous pressure at the U.N., South Africa, which had been holding up agreement on the sanctions committee to release the frozen funds to the rebels, relented, freeing up significant financing for the NTC.[87] Sarkozy, Cameron, and Secretary Clinton all visited Tripoli.

At this point, the United States was eager to bring the operation to a close, but some allies and the rebels themselves were more hesitant. Qaddafi and key members of his family, such as his son Saif, were still at large and could pose a risk to Libya's postwar stability.[88] NATO's authorization for OUP was scheduled to expire again at the end of September. With Tripoli in the hands of the rebels, the argument could be made that the Alliance's task was finished. The United States was eager to make a clear break, but the British, some other allies, and the rebels were concerned that if the operation ended, and the U.N. mandate ended with it, a reinsertion of forces in the event the situation deteriorated would have been difficult—if not impossible—to achieve. Moreover, the British argued, as long as civilians were threatened, the mission should continue, and as long as Qaddafi was at large, these threats were real. NATO thus renewed the authorization, and airstrikes continued into their seventh month.

The rebels eventually surrounded the holdout towns of Bani Walid and Sirte, where the remaining regime loyalists—and, presumably, Qaddafi—were holed up. After a failed attempt at negotiation, fighting resumed. The experience of the whole operation was then repeated on a smaller scale in subsequent weeks as rebels found their capabilities insufficient to take this last redoubt and NATO was unable to press the regime past the breaking point from the air.[89]

It was another month before the siege of Sirte and Bani Walid wore down Qaddafi. He attempted to flee on October 20, but a French fighter and a Predator struck the convoy in which he was traveling. Qaddafi sought cover in a drainpipe, but rebel troops found him, and he did not survive his capture. With the regime finished and the United States eager to call an end to the mission, NATO ended the operation on October 31.

The Impact on NATO

Afterward, several top officials hailed the intervention as a major triumph for the Alliance, especially the U.S. ambassador to NATO, Ivo Daalder, as well as NATO Secretary General Anders Fogh Rasmussen and SACEUR Admiral James Stavridis. There is good reason for this, as NATO had succeeded in protecting Libyan civilians and the

---

[87] Interviews with White House officials.

[88] Interview with senior U.S. official, July 9, 2012.

[89] Rod Nordland, "At Qaddafi Loyalists' Last Redoubts, A Struggle of Advances and Retreats," *New York Times*, September 18, 2011, p. A6.

rebels could not have won without NATO's involvement in the conflict. Whatever the long-term outcome in Libya, the intervention demonstrated Western support for the democratic movement across the region, and significantly increased Libyan citizens' future prospects.

As a means of achieving these goals, the Alliance functioned reasonably well. It moved relatively fast—indeed, much faster than in past interventions—to agree on operational plans. It was efficient at integrating important non-NATO partners into the operation, and thereby increasing the operation's overall legitimacy. While the operation might have been conducted under a coalition-of-the-willing arrangement, doing so would have been more difficult to command and control, and the challenges of integrating partners would have been significant, especially given that the United States had chosen not to play the central role.

Even though the United States contributed the most equipment and personnel to the operation, other allies also made large contributions, demonstrating that NATO has capabilities that transcend the U.S. military's, and is more than just a "political" Alliance. The intervention was an opportunity to reinvigorate the debate about NATO's utility and remind observers that, whatever NATO's shortcomings, it can still be an effective instrument for the international community.

As NATO looks beyond Afghanistan, Libya is one model that deserves attention from allied leaders and military planners. Nevertheless, these positive outcomes do not mean that NATO will find it easy to repeat the Libyan success. The operation also made clear a number of Alliance shortcomings. One was allied unity. Unified Protector had the lowest participation rate of any NATO intervention in history. It was effectively a coalition of states acting within NATO, and drawing on NATO assets, to carry out a mission that some key allies would have preferred not to see happen. Germany and Poland agreed to allow the operation to go forward, but their lack of material support was an important marker of underlying divergence within the Alliance. Some of the other states that did not participate simply could not do so, but overall, allied unity was clearly lacking—especially at the outset of operations. Non-U.S. military capabilities were showcased in Libya. Yet while the operation demonstrated NATO could undertake a mission without a dominant U.S. role, it also showed how challenging this was for the Alliance.

It is important to note, however, that most of the shortfalls in NATO capabilities identified during OUP were well known prior to the operation—overall, Libya did not reveal previously hidden weaknesses in the Alliance. Similarly, the "coalition within the alliance" format offers upsides, insofar as it is indicative of a more flexible Alliance that will be better able to serve the diverse interests of its members.

Whether NATO can repeat its performance in Libya will depend to a large degree on the type of crises that develop in the near future and the impact of the ongoing European financial crisis on members' defense budgets. Neither of these variables can be predicted with much certainty. If European states manage to emerge from their financial crisis with defense budgets relatively unharmed to the extent that they can complete existing and planned procurement orders—for the F-35 or new tankers, for example—there will be little question that they could repeat or perhaps even increase the role that they played, given similar circumstances. If, on the other hand, the euro-zone crisis accelerates the secular decline in European defense spending, or a more serious crisis arises requiring more of those capabilities that only the United States possesses, it will be difficult for NATO to employ the same model.[90] A NATO operation would still be possible under such conditions, but the United States will have to return to its traditional dominant role within the Alliance. French operations in Mali suggest that NATO still boasts capability and will, even without major U.S. support. The 2014 crisis in Ukraine could further nudge reluctant European leaders toward higher levels of defense spending.

Still, Libya was at the outer limits of what the United States can expect from its allies, at least in the next few years. Budgetary austerity will surely mean the list of items that European states would need to acquire to reduce the United States' role significantly from the one it played in Libya will remain long. Nevertheless, given the relative success of the operation, the experience of Libya is one the Alliance should reflect and seek to build upon.[91]

---

[90] For further discussion of NATO defense spending prospects, see F. Stephen Larrabee et al., *NATO and the Challenges of Austerity*, Santa Monica, Calif.: RAND Corporation, MG-1196-OSD, 2012.

[91] For elaboration on the reasons why the intervention was, on balance, a success, see Chivvis, *Toppling Qaddafi*.

CHAPTER THREE

The Libyan Experience

Frederic Wehrey

Introduction

On March 19, 2011, at about 4:45 p.m. local time, French fighter aircraft struck columns of Libyan tanks and vehicles advancing on Benghazi, beginning the coalition air campaign in Libya. Contrary to popular belief, the French pilots did not initiate air operations against loyalist forces in Libya. Rather, they joined a campaign that aircraft belonging to the newly formed Free Libya Air Force (*Quwwat al-Jawiya al-Libya al-Hurra*) already had started.

On February 21, shortly after the uprising began, Libyan air force officers at Benghazi's Banina Air Base declared their allegiance to the revolt. Nasser Air Base, in nearby Tobruk, quickly followed suit. The defection of these bases added an aging fleet of MiG-23s, MiG-21s, and Mi-24/35s to the anti-Qaddafi struggle.[1] On March 5, pilots from Banina began flying a variety of missions against Qaddafi forces near Ajdabiya and Ras Lanuf: close air support (CAS), maritime interdiction, reconnaissance, and at least one attempted air-to-air intercept of a loyalist fighter plane. By several accounts, they flew roughly 40 sorties from the start of the revolt until March 19.[2] Several lost their lives, including the pilots of two MiG-23s that were shot down in the early hours of March 19—prior to the French attack—in a last-ditch effort to stop the entry of Qaddafi forces into Benghazi.[3] In post-Qaddafi Libya, the saga of

---

[1] Prior to the civil war, the Libyan Arab Republic air force nominally included some 130 MiG-23 *Floggers* of various types, 45 MiG-21 *Fishbeds*, 100 MiG-25 *Foxbats*, 50 Su-17/-20 *Fitters*, 30 Mirage F1s, and a handful of Su-24 *Fencers* and Tu-22 *Blinder* bombers, as well as 35 Mi-25 and Mi-35 *Hind* helicopter gunships. However, training and maintenance shortfalls meant that many of these aircraft were unserviceable. See International Institute for Strategic Studies, *The Military Balance 2011*, London: Routledge, March 2011, p. 321; Lindsay Peacock and Eleanor Keymer, eds., *Jane's World Air Forces*, Issue 30, 2010.

[2] Interview with a Libyan air force officer who planned and led the anti-Qaddafi air strikes, Benghazi, Libya, March 11 and 12, 2012; interview with a Libyan Mirage F1 pilot, Tripoli, Libya, March 7, 2012.

[3] On March 19, Qaddafi forces shot down a two-seat MiG-23 on the outskirts of Benghazi. Later that day, a single-seat MiG-23 was shot down over Benghazi, possibly due to fratricide by anti-Qaddafi fighters inside the city. On April 9, an Mi-35 *Hind* was shot down 40 km west of Ajdabiya. A MiG-23 that was accompanying the *Hind* was escorted back to Banina Air Base and forced to land by NATO aircraft enforcing the no-fly zone. A

these aviators has been memorialized in billboards, museums, and numerous television tributes (see Figure 3.1).

While certainly romanticized and embellished, this early episode of the war nonetheless illustrates an important, oft-neglected aspect of the airpower story in Libya. Far from being passive beneficiaries of the NATO air campaign, Libya's opposition forces were active participants, displaying an understanding of airpower's effects and limitations that grew more sophisticated as the war progressed.

This chapter will explore Libyan perceptions of NATO airpower,[4] focusing on how opposition commanders viewed the strategic, operational, and tactical effects of the air campaign in the war's three critical fronts: the east, Misrata, and the Nafusa Mountains. It will begin by examining the important role played by former Libyan military officers, particularly air force officers, in staffing the command posts and operations rooms in Benghazi, Misrata, and Zintan. The presence of these individuals shaped the way that the opposition perceived NATO airpower. Particularly in Misrata, air force defectors played a critical role in liaising and coordinating with foreign special operations forces (described by interviewees as "advisors," "counselors," or "diplomats").[5]

Figure 3.1
"Falcons of the Revolution," a Billboard in Benghazi Paying Tribute to Fallen Opposition Aviators

SOURCE: Author's photograph.
RAND RR676-3.1

MiG-21 also crashed due to mechanical failure. Banina Air Base endured strikes by loyalist Su-24 aircraft flying from Ghurdabiya near Sirte, but the munitions missed the runway and there were no casualties.

[4]   Prior to March 31, air strikes were carried out by NATO member states rather than NATO per se; however, Libyan interlocutors referred to Western airpower both before and after that date by its Alliance affiliation, and their impressions are recounted here using that term.

[5]   The news media has reported that there were also private military contractors advising the Misrata opposition. Richard Norton-Taylor and Chris Stephen, "Libya: SAS Veterans Helping NATO Identify Al-Qadhafi Targets in Misurata," *The Guardian*, May 31, 2011.

This chapter draws heavily from interviews with a range of opposition commanders and fighters, defectors, and, to a lesser extent, loyalist officers in early March 2012 in Tripoli, Benghazi, Misrata, and Zintan. It generally was not possible to interview loyalist commanders—most were dead, in hiding, or in one of the militia-run prisons in Zintan or Misrata. For obvious reasons, those who remained in uniform during the war were reluctant to discuss their role in detail; retribution killings are still quite common.[6]

The next section will explore the opposition's perceptions in greater depth, focusing on the key mission areas of CAS, interdiction, suppression of enemy air defenses (SEAD), and strategic targeting. It will highlight the spectrum of opposition views regarding NATO's precision, persistence, and responsiveness, and it will assess how these dynamics affected morale and movement on the battlefield. The final section will focus more closely on the process of coordination and targeting between NATO and the opposition. It concludes with an examination of this process at work in Misrata during a pivotal moment in June 2011 when opposition forces, supported by NATO airpower and Western advisors, broke the siege and began their westward advance on Tripoli.

Libyan perspectives on the NATO campaign offer several instructive lessons. Air support frequently engendered much frustration from the opposition due to inflated expectations about what airpower could do; the limitations in NATO's mandate and capabilities (particularly ISR assets); and disarray within the opposition's ranks. That said, a process of operational learning occurred among opposition commanders that facilitated air-ground coordination as the war progressed.

By nearly every account, the arrival of foreign ground advisors had a transformational effect on air-ground coordination. They built trust, provided training, and corroborated targeting information provided by Libyan networks of spotters and informants that reported to the operations rooms. They helped smooth the political and regional divisions within the rebels' ranks. They proved instrumental in major breakthroughs on the Nafusa front, Misrata, and the liberation of Tripoli. Their effectiveness suggests a new variant of the Northern Alliance model that can amplify airpower's effects through the coordination of precision strikes, even when the military competence of indigenous forces is low or nil.

Libyan Airpower and Air Defenses: A Hollow and Marginalized Force

Qaddafi long had marginalized the Libyan Arab air force (LARAF). With the exception of a so-called "Guard Squadron" of MiG-23s based at Sirte, the Libyan leader

---

6   The author is grateful for the assistance of the U.S. defense attaché in Tripoli, LTC Brian Linvill, and the numerous Libyans who shared their insights. Any mistakes or omissions are the sole responsibility of the author.

distrusted his air force.[7] As a result of this suspicion, and the cumulative effect of sanctions, its aircraft were antiquated and decrepit, its budget meager, its training unrealistic and irregular, and its facilities run down. This marginalization had important implications for understanding not only Qaddafi's reaction to the allied air campaign, but the defection of numerous LARAF officers to the revolutionaries' ranks, which had a far-reaching effect on air-to-ground coordination.

A Nonexistent IADS

Although NATO commanders ruled out infrastructure targeting, the coalition mounted a concerted effort to take down the regime's C2, integrated air defense system (IADS) in Tripoli, and other strategic targets. However, in many respects, the Libyan IADS was almost nonexistent even before the campaign. "In 12 days, our air defenses were gone. We were completely blind," conceded a Libyan air defense officer, based throughout the war at the Bir Usta al-Milad air defense site, 15 kilometers south of Tripoli. "The S-200 (SA-5) was our only effective system. We reported a 60 percent readiness on the S-200; in fact, it was only 10 percent. We were all afraid of being shot," the officer stated.

The only real early-warning radar capability the regime possessed at the time that the air campaign began was a civilian ARSR-103D radar at Tripoli International Airport that fed data to the air defense operations room at nearby Mitiga Air Base via microwave or very high frequency (VHF). "It was not a very complete picture. And NATO eventually struck this. This was the technology of the 1960s warning against the 21st century," said the Libyan air defense officer. In late March, shortly after the initial NATO salvo, the Qaddafi regime began trying to mobilize the entire military to confront an impending ground invasion. Even air defense officers assigned to research and logistics sections were trained in the use of rocket-propelled grenades and AK-47s. "We were told that the U.S. Marines were coming to take Qaddafi," noted the officer.

Once the regime's fixed air-defense sites were destroyed, it was left with 14.5mm and 23mm anti-aircraft guns and man-portable surface-to-air missiles (MANPADS) including the SA-7 Strela and SA-24 (Igla). Several of these were organic to elite units such as the 32nd Brigade. An SA-7 gunner with the 32nd Brigade, captured in the assault on Misrata, noted that once NATO had taken out the 32nd Brigade's radar, they were effectively blind. He never fired a shot, although there were reports in Misrata of loyalist forces trying to use heat-seeking MANPADS against opposition vehicles. The 32nd Brigade also possessed a few UAVs that it used in Zawaiya and Brega. By June, these had all been lost due to malfunction or ground fire.

---

[7] Interview with a Libyan air force officer and former Mirage F1 pilot, Tripoli, Libya, March 7, 2012. Much of this suspicion began after the U.S. strike on Tripoli and Benghazi in 1986, when Qaddafi blamed the Libyan air force for not protecting the country.

To confound NATO, the regime tried a number of denial and deception strategies. Its air defense operations room reportedly switched locations to a succession of civilian sites. In one instance, it moved to a hotel in Dhara, a suburb of Tripoli, which NATO struck. According to one source, the regime brought in frozen dead bodies, part of a propaganda ploy to convince the international media of collateral damage. "We all knew they were frozen bodies because the eyes were frozen out," the source said. After the air defense site at Bir Usta al-Milad was struck, regime TV condemned it as a strike on a civilian hospital. A military hospital is located there, but the only targets struck were the logistics stores, launchers, and vehicles.

In general, observers in Tripoli were impressed with the NATO coalition's efforts to avoid collateral damage in striking strategic and air defense targets. The air defense officer pointed out on Google Earth the damaged headquarters of the 77th Brigade near Bab al-Azaziyah, highlighting the lack of damage to nearby civilian structures. Elsewhere, at Tajura Air Defense Overhaul Center in northeast Tripoli, NATO struck a depot of short-range "Qadrat" rockets, which started firing off into neighboring housing areas. NATO quickly restruck the area, dropping the entire roof on top of the rockets. Mistakes occurred, however. The commander of Banina Air Base wondered why the base's early warning radar had been struck on March 20, since the base was already under opposition control and had publicly declared its allegiance to the revolution on February 21 in a televised announcement. Moreover, NATO knew that opposition planes were flying from the base because it was monitoring pilots' flying sorties.

A "Revolt by the Air Force"

Perhaps more than is commonly recognized, the Libyan revolution was a civil war. Towns and tribes that enjoyed patronage from Qaddafi remained loyal: key examples include Bani Walid, Sirte, the Tawergha, the Warshafana, the Mashashiya, and certain neighborhoods of Tripoli such as Abu Slim. Those that had been marginalized—Misrata, Benghazi, Zawiya, Zintan, and the Suq al-Juma' neighborhood—formed the core of the opposition. Qaddafi had long neglected and underfunded the Libyan army, fearing its potential for a coup, and it either stood on the sidelines or defected to the opposition.[8] A key defection that tipped the scales in the east was that of the Benghazi-based Special Forces, the "Sa'iqa" or Lightning Brigade under General Abdel Fatah Younis. With the loss of this force, Qaddafi was left with a handful of elite praetorian units that either his sons (the 32d Brigade under Khamis al-Qaddafi) or diehard supporters commanded.

A common picture of the anti-Qaddafi rebellion is that it was a largely ad hoc, fractured, and disorganized movement, filled with enthusiastic volunteers, many with

---

[8]   Qaddafi applied the classic model of "coup proofing" by creating competition among security institutions and ensuring that the most capable and elite units were commanded by his sons. See James T. Quinlivan, "Coup-Proofing: Its Practice and Consequences in the Middle East," *International Security*, Vol. 24, No. 2, Fall 1999, pp. 131–165.

little or no military experience—students, day laborers, mechanics, volunteers from the Libyan diaspora, and the unemployed. To a large extent, this was the case. In the initial stages of the war, many were little more than neighborhood guard forces, organized into loose *kata'ib* ("brigades," singular: *katiba*), ranging from 20 to 200 youths.[9] What has not been widely recognized, however, is the role of former military officers in attempting to impart coherence, organization, and discipline into the armed opposition. In each of the key fronts of the war—Benghazi, Misrata, and Zintan—the opposition formed makeshift "command centers," or "operations rooms," which, as time progressed, grew more sophisticated and established greater command and control over frontline forces. Former military officers and, in many cases, former LARAF officers and pilots staffed and led these centers.

In retrospect, it is easy to see why so many air force officers joined the rebels' ranks. Air force officers' salaries and benefits paled in comparison to elite ground units like the vaunted 32nd Brigade commanded by Khamis al-Qaddafi, the 77th Brigade guarding Qaddafi's compound at Bab al-Azaziyah, or the "Hamza" Brigade, garrisoned near Sirte. As a former Mirage F1 pilot based at Mitiga Air Base, who defected to Zintan early in the revolution, noted: "I have a master's degree in aeronautics and am a Mirage pilot. Why should I make less than a truck driver in the Khamis Brigade?"[10] In other cases, the grievances ran much deeper. The brother of the commander of Banina Air Base was publicly executed in Benghazi in the 1980s for alleged anti-regime activity.[11] Fathi Ali Bashaagha, a Misratan opposition leader and former instructor pilot at the Misrata Air Force Academy, recalled an instance in the 1990s in which he and his pilot comrades were prevented for five days from using a helicopter to retrieve the body of a fellow pilot who had crashed on a training flight into a marsh near Misrata. Qaddafi had grounded all flying in the country during an Arab dignitary's state visit to Libya.[12]

Shortly after the uprising in Misrata started, officers at the Misrata Air Force Academy defected to the opposition *en masse*, sabotaging the Galeb trainer aircraft and *Hind* helicopters at the base. As noted, Banina Air Base defected as well. In the

---

[9] The disorganization and fractured nature of the opposition has been widely reported in the press. C. J. Chivers has called the Nafusa-based opposition "a guerrilla force that acts less like a coherent structure than a network of pickup fighting clubs." ("Lack of Coordination Hampers Libya's Rebels," *The New York Times*, July 21, 2011.) In Misrata, a member of the opposition noted: "In the beginning it was just total chaos. There were three hundred fronts. Three guys would form a neighborhood *Katiba*; they were just shooting at whatever was in front of them. Finally in June, there were three fronts or sectors (West, South and East). The *kata'ib* reported to a sector commander, which reported to the operations center, where the French and British were." In Benghazi, there was similar disorganization early in the conflict.

[10] Interview with a Libyan air force officer and Zintan-based opposition commander, Tripoli, March 10, 2012.

[11] Interview with a Libyan air force officer based at Banina who planned and led anti-Qaddafi strikes, March 12, 2012.

[12] Interview with a Misrata-based opposition planner and field commander, Misrata, Libya, March 13, 2012.

west, many officers at Tripoli's Mitiga Air Base fled to the Nafusa Mountains.[13] Many Misratans recalled the story of 'Ali Hadith al-Obeidi, an air force general who defected from Mitiga Air Base and walked for nearly two weeks to join the opposition in Misrata; he was later killed in the assault on Zlitan.[14] As a result, it is not surprising that for many interviewees, the February 17 uprising was, in many respects, a revolt by the air force.[15]

A number of ex-LARAF officers played pivotal roles in the opposition. Salah Badi, who helped form the first military committee inside Misrata in the early days of the war and who later became an operational commander, was a former pilot.[16] The commander of the Misrata opposition's operations room, Colonel Muhammad 'Abd al-Jawad, was a former operations room chief at the Misrata Air Base. Bashaagha was the main interlocutor between NATO and the Misratan opposition.[17] Roughly 100 other ex-military officers and soldiers augmented these officers, including Salim Juwha, a former artillery officer, who played a critical role in commanding the western sector of Misrata.

In the Nafusa Mountains, the air force officers had a similarly robust presence. In early March, the region's various militias coalesced under the umbrella of the Western Region Military Council, which the National Transitional Council and General Younis had recognized. Led by General Mukhtar Fernana, a former army logistics officer, its "operations centers" in Zintan and Nalut were staffed by roughly a dozen former air force officers who played a similarly important role in liaising with coalition advisors.[18] Among the most important was Colonel Jumma' Mdhakim, a former pilot, who coordinated all airstrikes with the advisors.[19]

In the east, as noted above, the opposition benefited from the presence of the Banina Air Base. Officers from Banina filled the staff of Younis and helped coordinate requests for air support from opposition forces in Ajdabiya, before start of the NATO campaign.[20] Once the liberation of the east was complete, Banina Air Base played an important role as a collection point for shipments of relief aid, weapons, and mate-

[13] Interview with a Libyan air force officer and Zintan-based opposition commander, Tripoli, Libya, March 10, 2012.

[14] Interview with a Malta- and Misrata-based opposition coordinator, Tripoli, Libya, March 8, 2012.

[15] Interviews with former oppositionists in Benghazi and Zintan, March 2012.

[16] Interview with a Malta- and Misrata-based opposition coordinator, Tripoli, Libya, March 8, 2012.

[17] Interview with a Misrata-based opposition planner and field commander, Misrata, Libya, March 13, 2012.

[18] Interview with a Libyan air force officer and Zintan-based opposition commander, Tripoli, Libya, March 10, 2012.

[19] Interview with the chief of the Zintan Military Council, Zintan, Libya, March 15, 2012.

[20] Interview with a Libyan air force officer based at Banina who planned and led anti-Qaddafi strikes, March 12, 2012.

rial to the besieged city of Misrata.[21] Given these varied roles, it earned the nickname among several interlocutors as the "Fourth Wheel of the Revolution"—the other three being Benghazi, Misrata, and Zintan.[22]

As NATO increased its air-to-ground coordination, particularly after the arrival of foreign advisors at Misrata and Zintan, these individuals were in a unique position to shape the application of airpower by interfacing with NATO member states and informing frontline troops about what airpower could and couldn't do. In managing the opposition's battlespace, they reconnoitered targets, as the war progressed, and worked closely with foreign advisors on the ground to call in airstrikes and conduct battle damage assessment (BDA). As will be discussed below at length, these dynamics were especially apparent in Misrata, which mounted the most effective and coordinated opposition to Qaddafi's military.

It is also important to note that the Western allies had longstanding relationships with several of these defecting officers—from both the air force and army—through attaché and security cooperation activities. In the United States' case, the Department of Defense had established an Office of Security Cooperation (OSC) at the Defense Attaché Office (DAO) in the U.S. Embassy in Tripoli starting in 2008, following Qaddafi's rapprochement with the West. The scope of the cooperation between Libyan armed forces and the United States should not be overstated; much of it was focused on exchange visits, English-language instruction, spare parts, and very rudimentary professional military education (PME). In several cases, this outreach was conducted with individuals who would fight to the very end for Qaddafi. Despite this, the personal relationships established between DAO personnel and several of these officers who defected to the opposition ranks would prove crucial to coordinating NATO operations with opposition ground forces.

Between Awe and Exasperation: Perceptions of NATO Airpower

Impressions of NATO's airpower spanned a broad gamut among the Libyan opposition. For many, bereft of military experience or an understanding of modern warfare, airstrikes assumed a mystical, otherworldly quality. "It was like magic for them, especially when the advisors were on the ground," noted a Western military officer who interfaced extensively with opposition leaders. "Some guy talks into a radio or pushes a button, and the tank in front of them goes 'boom!'"[23] A Misratan commander stated:

---

[21] Interview with a Libyan air force officer based at Banina who planned and led anti-Qaddafi strikes, March 12, 2012.

[22] Interview with a Libyan air force officer and Zintan-based opposition commander, Tripoli, Libya, March 10, 2012.

[23] Interview with a Western military officer involved with NATO operations, Tripoli, Libya, March 5, 2012.

"Many of our young fighters didn't believe it was NATO that was causing the explosions because they never heard the jet."[24] Consequently, inflated expectations arose about what airpower could achieve, as well as excessive frustration with what it wasn't achieving. Helicopter support against ground forces was in high demand, and many interviewees were frustrated that the platform was not deployed more frequently, particularly in the Nafusa and in Misrata.

That said, as the war progressed, the opposition developed a more nuanced understanding of airpower, as well as the limitations placed on NATO because of its mandate. As Misrata's military planner noted:

> We knew NATO was slow for several reasons. It didn't trust us, because early on it didn't have people on the ground. NATO was under tremendous pressure not to make a mistake. It had too much data and information from across the country. And it had to balance strategic and tactical targets. Finally, we knew that NATO is a committee. We had to explain to our youth the nature of [UNSCR] 1973 ... that it was meant to protect civilians. And if you have a gun in your hand, you are not a civilian.[25]

In general, though, the opposition perceived NATO airpower with a mix of awe, appreciation, ambivalence, and exasperation. This was particularly evident in each of NATO's mission roles throughout the campaign, particularly CAS and interdiction. Due to inflated expectations about NATO acting as the "rebels' air force," opposition commanders expected strikes against dynamic and mobile targets to be more responsive and timely. In the Nafusa, there was particularly criticism regarding the interdiction of loyalist forces early in the campaign. Despite this, a unifying thread throughout the interviews was the enormous psychological boost provided by NATO support and the transformative effect of ground advisors on facilitating precision strikes.

Close Air Support and Interdiction

Many interlocutors across Libya held enormous respect and admiration for NATO's precision, at the level of both CAS[26] and interdiction. An opposition commander fighting near Brega recalled the pinpoint destruction of enemy tanks outside the city: "It

---

[24] Interview with a Misratan opposition commander, Tripoli, Libya, June 30, 2012. With few exceptions, none of the interviewees in this study could identify types of aircraft or specific munitions, nor could they distinguish between fixed-wing and helicopter strikes, with the exception of the Misratan assault through Dafniya, when Apaches were present.

[25] Interview with a Misrata-based opposition planner and field commander, Misrata, Libya, March 13, 2012.

[26] In Operation Unified Protector "close air support" missions were flown against Libyan regime forces that were firing into civilian areas, rather than in direct support of Libyan rebel forces per se.

was like somebody had opened the hatch of the tank and dropped a bomb in."[27] In the Nafusa, a fighter manning a defensive trench in southern Zintan marveled at the destruction of Qaddafi troops and equipment less than one hundred meters away, "as if somebody was drawing a line through them with a pencil."[28]

In Misrata, a key opposition commander—and a former artillery officer— pointed to three important effects of the NATO campaign in not only saving the city, but enabling the Misratans to break the siege and push toward Tripoli:

1. **Disrupting command and control.** He noted that the early disruption of the Libyan command and control facilities meant that Qaddafi was unable to effectively organize and mass his forces. Qaddafi could not coordinate concentrated firepower at key junctures in the battle for the city. This was particularly true for his armored forces.

2. **Interdicting reinforcements.** There was general frustration in Misrata about the ability of NATO to provide close air support in the early days of the urban fight, when Qaddafi had entered the city and was controlling its key thoroughfare, Tripoli Street. That said, the commander praised NATO's interdiction of reinforcements to Misrata, arriving from Sirte, Sabha, Zlitan, and Bani Walid. This proved crucial in leveling the playing field in Misrata, particularly after artillery and Grad rockets arrived to the opposition-controlled Misrata port via Benghazi.

3. **Keeping Misrata's port open.** On this note, many Misratans praised NATO for keeping the port open; this was a crucial outlet for Misratans to receive reinforcements, artillery, and much-needed humanitarian supplies.[29]

A participant in the June offensive toward Dafniya that broke the siege described rolling airstrikes that moved with advancing rebels, with Western advisors providing careful guidance. Pointing to a map, he showed how NATO support enabled the right flank of the Misratan assault to encircle and envelop Qaddafi forces.[30] In other instances, airpower proved decisive in shifting the tide of a tactical engagement in the city. In Misrata, an opposition commander recalled the destruction of a 155mm howitzer as enabling the defeat of loyalist troops and auxiliaries from Tawherga attempting to seize control of a flour granary in the industrial, northeastern part of the city. According to many eyewitnesses, this was a key intervention that enabled the Misratans to seize a critical target that was essential to sustaining their fighters and civilian

---

[27] Interview with a commander of a Benghazi-based *Katiba Shuhada' Zawiya* (Zawiya's Martyrs' Brigade), Benghazi, Libya, March 11, 2012.

[28] Interview with a Zintan-based opposition fighter, Zintan, Libya, March 15, 2012.

[29] Interview with a Misratan opposition commander, Misrata, Libya, June 29, 2012.

[30] Interview with a Misrata-based opposition planner, Misrata, Libya, March 13, 2012.

population.[31] One commander speculated that the strike was completely ad hoc and unplanned—an example of dynamic targeting in which the pilot spotted a target of opportunity.[32]

Some targets acquired an almost-legendary status because of the precise degree of destruction. Virtually every Misratan knows about the *Suk Afriqi* (African Market), a covered market on Tripoli Street where loyalist forces had camouflaged three T-72 tanks. NATO struck the tanks through the roof of the market, eliciting awe from many observers. "Three tanks and three holes," marveled one fighter (Figure 3.2).[33]

In Libya's west, however, the picture was different. From February through late May, NATO deployed few assets to this theater, which elicited frequent protestations and anger from opposition commanders. In an interview, the commander of Nafusa opposition forces, General Mukhtar Fernana, angrily demanded to know why Apache helicopters or A-10s were not deployed to the west for close air support and, especially, interdiction.[34] This was particularly frustrating for the Nafusa opposition, since Qaddafi had few military units in the region prior to the revolution. According to one

Figure 3.2
Destroyed T-72 Tanks in the African Market, Misrata

SOURCE: Author's photograph.
RAND *RR676-3.2*

---

[31] Interview with a Misrata-based opposition planner and field commander, Misrata, Libya, March 13, 2012.

[32] Interview with the head of Misrata's Engineer Support Unit, Tripoli, Libya, June 30, 2012.

[33] Interview with a former opposition fighter based in Abu Slim neighborhood, Tripoli, Libya, March 13, 2012.

[34] Interview with General Mukhtar Milad Fernana, Tripoli, Libya, March 14, 2012.

source, only one Grad rocket unit and a security brigade were garrisoned at Gharyan.[35] Throughout the early stages of the revolt, Qaddafi was able to reinforce these units with impunity, ferrying troops and armor from Tripoli and accessing ammunition depots in the area that were untouched by NATO strikes. According to Fernana's operations officer, the head of the Jadu Military Council:

> NATO waited too long to destroy the depots . . . Qaddafi was able to resupply. It was killing our people. In the East, NATO was attacking convoys, but not in the West. Why? If NATO had hit the storage depots at Zintan, Mizdah, Gharyan and Azaziyah earlier, it would have lowered our casualty rate.[36]

According to Fernana, the scarcity of NATO airpower effectively stalled the Nafusa offensive once it had liberated the mountain towns of Zintan, Yafran, Wazin, Nalut, and Kikla. Without airpower, the opposition was unable to move out of the foothills and into the plains north of the Nafusa. Instead, it began fortifying its positions, digging an elaborate, 75-kilometer trench network that stretched from Zintan to Rajban and Jadu.[37] Of course, there were other reasons as well for the stalemate, not the least of which was the opposition's own logistical problems, lack of organization, and shortage of ammunition. Another member of the Western Region Military Council effectively acknowledged this, stating that the pause in the offensive was necessary to regroup and train many of the volunteers with no military background. It was during this period that Arab and western advisors arrived, along with shipments of air-dropped weapons and equipment.[38] As the next section will discuss, NATO stepped up its CAS during the next phase of the opposition advance into the lowland towns and villages below the Nafusa.

At the same time, there was recognition of the limits of NATO's airpower, particularly in densely populated urban areas. This understanding was particularly evident among the planners and coordinators with military backgrounds. General Younis told Banina Air Base that Qaddafi forces had to be stopped before Benghazi; once inside the city, airpower would be useless against the loyalists.[39] The commander of Misrata's

---

[35] Interview with the chief of the Jadu Military Council, Tripoli, Libya, March 14, 2012.

[36] Interview with the chief of the Jadu Military Council, Tripoli, Libya, March 14, 2012.

[37] Interview with the chief of the Zintan Military Council, Zintan, Libya, March 15, 2012.

[38] For a discussion of foreign advisory contributions in the Nafusa, see Mark Phillips, "The Ground Offensive: The Role of Special Forces," in Saqeb Mueen and Grant Turnbull, eds., *Accidental Heroes: Britain, France, and the Libya Operation*, an Interim RUSI Campaign Report, London: Royal United Services Institute, September 2011. Some participants involved in the Nafusa campaign allege hoarding by rival militias. A fighter based in Jadu never saw the weapons shipments and speculated that only 10 percent made their way past the distribution point in Nalut. Interview with a Jadu-based opposition fighter, Tripoli, Libya, March 6, 2012.

[39] Interview with a Libyan air force officer based at Banina who planned and led anti-Qaddafi strikes, March 12, 2012.

Military Council exhorted his colleagues to push the enemy outside the city's environs, "otherwise we will be just like Zawiya"—a reference to a coastal city west of Tripoli that Qaddafi forces had occupied *en masse*, negating the application of airpower.

The problem was compounded when loyalists began using civilian vehicles and "technicals" (civilian truck–mounted weapons) identical to those that the opposition deployed. In the later stages of the Misrata campaign, opposition commanders realized NATO was powerless to stop the shelling of the harbor from nearby Tawergha because Qaddafi forces, camouflaged in civilian vehicles, had ensconced their artillery teams near a mosque and inside schools.[40] In the Nafusa, a commander involved in the initial assault on al-Azaziyah—known as the "key to Tripoli"—noted that the presence of loyalist forces disguised as civilians meant that "NATO couldn't help. It was our problem, and we had to do it on our own."[41]

This recognition, however, did not dampen the frequent frustration with what some opposition sources perceived as an excessively cautious, risk averse strategy. A senior Misratan commander criticized NATO's aversion to striking mobile targets within the city itself, particularly at the height of close-quarter fighting. In particular, he referred to the repeated but unsuccessful rebel pleas for NATO to strike the Tamin Building (Figure 3.3). This building, the highest point in Misrata overlooking the frontline zone of Tripoli Street, was a notorious sniper's nest and the most contested structure in the city. During a single day, snipers from the building reportedly killed 20 Misratan civilians and fighters.[42]

Persistence and Responsiveness

One of the most common criticisms in discussing close air support or interdiction was NATO's sporadic operations tempo and its inability to respond quickly to fast-moving events on the ground. At the strategic level, the fluctuation in tempo was particularly acute in Tripoli. One observer argued the shift from Odyssey Dawn to Unified Protector created a lull in airstrikes that left many Tripoli residents confused and angry. "Everyone thought the regime would be finished if you had just kept going," said a Libyan air defense officer. "Libyan state TV was saying that the regime had reached a deal with the U.S. over oil and that Washington had pulled out of the war."[43] Another interlocutor noted that early in the campaign, NATO was bombing Tripoli two to three times a day. "Then it stopped, and we were angry."[44]

---

[40] Interview with a Misrata-based opposition planner and field commander, Misrata, Libya, March 13, 2012.

[41] Interview with a Libyan air force officer and Zintan-based opposition commander, Tripoli, Libya, March 10, 2012.

[42] Interview with a Western military officer involved with NATO operations, Tripoli, Libya, March 5, 2012.

[43] Interview with a Libyan air defense officer, Tripoli, Libya, March 6, 2012.

[44] Interview with a Libyan air defense officer, Tripoli, Libya, March 6, 2012.

Figure 3.3
The Tamin Building, Tripoli Street, Misrata

SOURCE: Author's photograph.
RAND RR676-3.3

In the West, people frequently expressed frustration that NATO would strike one or two targets of opportunity—tanks or artillery—and then disappear for days. "The Qaddafi forces would scatter and then reappear," noted the head of the Jadu Military Council. "We were very angry. There were 40 or 50 Grads, and tanks—all out in the open. We were very upset."[45]

Similar concerns were heard in Misrata about NATO's tempo and, especially, its ability to restrike targets and adapt to a fluid and dynamic situation. In general, Misratans believed that the effectiveness of Qaddafi's artillery and Grad barrages against the city was limited because of NATO's overflight. In many cases, the barrages were not adjusted for accuracy because, fearing airstrikes, loyalist troops would "shoot and scoot." That said, Misratans perceived NATO was only targeting artillery or heavy weaponry that was suspected of shelling civilians; it did not intervene when opposition forces were directly engaged with loyalist forces. At least one commander noted the Misratans used short, probing actions to provoke Qaddafi's forces into firing sustained barrages so that NATO would have enough time to acquire the target.

In other instances, it appeared that Qaddafi's artillery units were able to adjust their barrages to the rhythm of NATO flights. "Their artillery salvos would come in 30- to 40-minute bursts," said a Misrata-based opposition planner and field com-

---

[45] Interview with the chief of the Jadu Military Council, Tripoli, Libya, March 14, 2012.

mander. "They seemed to know when NATO wasn't there."[46] A commander of the city's defenses pointed out that defending and holding captured territory from counterattack was exceedingly difficult. His forces lacked heavy weapons, possessing only 80mm mortars, 14.5mm and 23mm anti-aircraft guns, recoilless rifles, and a few MILAN anti-tank weapons. The planner said that as a result of these shortages:

> A big problem was defending our positions from counter-attack. We would drive away Qaddafi forces with the help of NATO airpower. And then the Qaddafi units would quickly regroup and counterattack. Most of our casualties were from the Qaddafi counter-offensives, when NATO didn't re-attack to support us.[47]

In the east, the picture was different. Opposition forces converging on Sirte after the fall of Tripoli were quick to praise NATO's relentless, "day-and-night" bombing of Sirte's Neighborhood Two, where Qaddafi was (correctly) suspected of hiding.[48] The commander of a *katiba* from Benghazi noted that sustained helicopter strikes on Brega "shifted the balance" for the opposition forces.[49]

Collateral Damage and Friendly Fire

Opposition perceptions of collateral damage from NATO strikes present a mixed picture. In multiple instances, opposition interlocutors admitted mistakes. The indiscipline and overzealousness of young volunteers, combined with poor communication or ineffective lines of command, frequently resulted in *kata'ib* straying into NATO's line of fire. On the eastern front of Misrata, after the loyalist Hamza Brigade starting using "technicals," or improvised fighting vehicles, to harass the city's defenders, French warplanes began striking near the Qasr al-Ahmed harbor. Misrata's operations room warned the *kata'ib* about the no-go zone, but several crossed this line, directly disobeying orders. French strikes killed eight troops.[50] A similar dynamic was at work in the Nafusa Mountains. In the battle for Ghazaya, a strategic town in the foothills that was regarded as the "key to Gharyan," a group of *kata'ib* breached the opposition front and were killed by a NATO strike. According to one planner, their action was a blatant violation of orders.[51]

---

[46] Interview with a Misrata-based opposition planner and field commander, Misrata, Libya, March 13, 2012.

[47] Interview with a Misrata-based opposition planner and field commander, Misrata, Libya, March 13, 2012.

[48] Interview with a commander of the Benghazi-based *Quwwa Himaya Thawrat 17 Fibrāyir* (Protection Force of the February 17 Revolution), Benghazi, Libya, March 11, 2012.

[49] Interview with a commander of a Benghazi-based *Katiba Shuhada' Zawiya,* March 11, 2012.

[50] Interview with a Misrata-based opposition planner and field commander, Misrata, Libya, March 13, 2012.

[51] Interview with a Libyan air force officer and Zintan-based opposition commander, Tripoli, Libya, March 10, 2012.

In several cases, young fighters believed a rumor circulating that NATO was deliberately allowing Qaddafi forces to flee with their vehicles and tanks. Full of exuberance, they crossed the front lines into the no-go zones to attempt to capture the equipment and cut off the loyalists' escape.[52] In the western mountain region, one interlocutor attributed a cultural component to this dynamic, rooted in the Nafusa's tribal code of warfare. "In our culture, you have to capture your enemy's weapons or he will use them again against you," he said.[53] In one case, an opposition fighter captured a tank and drove it back toward the opposition lines with the gun turret still facing forward toward his comrades. NATO quickly struck the tank.[54] In other cases, command and control was a problem. Simply not enough radios or phones were available to control the scattershot movements of dispersed *kata'ib*.[55]

When Qaddafi forces starting using technical vehicles, friendly-fire casualties increased. Western advisors and interlocutors advised the rebels to begin marking the hoods and roofs of their vehicles. In the early stages of this tactic, it was simply a painted "N." When Qaddafi's troops started copying this, the opposition switched to painting their hoods with a yellow or orange fluorescent paint.[56] Later, when regime forces began copying these colors, the opposition used flags fastened to the hoods of their vehicles, with the colors of these flags announced hours before an assault. Later, the British gave a laser beacon to *kata'ib* commanders, usually the lead vehicle in a group of ten or so.[57]

In the wake of these strikes, opposition commanders often were reluctant to publicize mistakes. In some cases, they never told NATO about an errant strike for fear that NATO would stand down operations for the next three or four days.[58] In others, fears arose that the regime would exploit the mistake for propaganda purposes. In Tripoli, for example, a *katiba* commander described an instance in which a NATO strike had demolished an apartment bloc in Tripoli's Suq al-Jumma' neighborhood. The residents, guided by an underground *katiba*, quickly hid the bomb fragments.[59]

---

[52]   Interview with a Zintan-based opposition fighter, Zintan, Libya, March 15, 2012.

[53]   Interview with a Zintan-based opposition fighter, Zintan, Libya, March 15, 2012.

[54]   Interview with the chief of the Zintan Military Council, Zintan, Libya, March 15, 2012.

[55]   Interview with a commander of the Benghazi-based *Quwwa Himaya Thawrat 17 Fibrāyir*, March 11, 2012.

[56]   Interview with a commander of the Benghazi-based, *Quwwa Himaya Thawrat 17 Fibrāyir*, March 11, 2012; interview with a Misrata-based opposition planner and field commander, Misrata, Libya, March 13, 2012.

[57]   Interview with a commander of a Benghazi-based *Katiba Shuhada' Zawiya*, March 11, 2012.

[58]   Interview with a Malta- and Misrata-based opposition coordinator, Tripoli, Libya, March 8, 2012.

[59]   Interview with a Malta- and Misrata-based opposition coordinator, Tripoli, Libya, March 8, 2012.

The Psychological Impact of Airpower

Aside from the kinetic effects of CAS, interdiction, and SEAD, NATO airpower exerted a powerful psychological impact on both opposition and loyalist morale, though it is difficult to measure its effects. At critical points in the battle, NATO airpower had a fortifying effect on opposition resolve. Although Misratans frequently complained about the lack of airpower support in the city, they nonetheless felt that NATO's airpower would enable them to eventually triumph; several interlocutors predicted that it would be only a matter of time. A Misratan military planner tearfully recalled the first NATO strike outside the city:

> Throughout March, NATO was not active. There were tanks moving everywhere, shelling us. I thought, "What the hell are these people [NATO] doing?" But then on March 19th, NATO hit the Misrata Air Base. It was a sign that we were not forgotten, that our children might live. It was a lifejacket thrown to a drowning man.[60]

Similar sentiments were heard in Zintan. With the passage of the U.N. Security Council resolution authorizing the no-fly zone, a Nafusa-based fighter recalled his *kata'ib* firing precious ammunition into the night sky. "We knew that once Qaddafi no longer had planes, we would win, eventually," he said. "We are mountain fighters, after all."[61]

Airpower also had an apparently deleterious effect on loyalist morale and cohesion, although this, too, is difficult to gauge precisely. In Misrata and Brega, oppositionists reported on the frayed nerves of captured artillery crews due to NATO's persistent bombardment and overflight. At an observation post in Jadu, the highest point in the Nafusa, one recalled seeing Qaddafi artillery and armor crews scattering at the sound of a jet.[62] A Tomahawk strike on Ghurdabiya reportedly caused several loyalist pilots to defect to Benghazi. Even within the "elite" 32nd Brigade, morale appears to have faltered under the pressure of NATO's airstrikes. Soldiers were deprived of contact from the outside world; their cell phones and satellite phones were taken away.[63] Many refused to fire during the sieges of Misrata and Zintan, and later were found executed inside their tanks or lined up beside their artillery pieces.[64]

NATO psychological operations (PSYOP) were generally viewed with favor, although it again was difficult to assess actual effects. A Libyan military officer described the experience of a relative who fled his house near the SA-6 battery at Ayn

---

[60] Interview with a Misrata-based opposition planner and field commander, Misrata, Libya, March 13, 2012.

[61] Interview with the chief of the Jadu Military Council, Tripoli, Libya, March 14, 2012.

[62] Interview with a Jadu-based opposition fighter, Tripoli, Libya, March 6, 2012.

[63] Interview with a former Libyan air defense gunner with the 32nd Brigade, Misrata, Libya, March 13, 2012.

[64] Interview with the chief of the Zintan Military Council, Zintan, Libya, March 15, 2012.

Zara after seeing leaflets emblazoned with attacking helicopters descend on the area. In Tripoli, residents recalled hearing a radio program from NATO "with some guy with an Iraqi accent speaking beautiful Arabic." Misratans pointed to leaflets distributed in regime holdouts in Sirte as inducing defections, although it is difficult to corroborate this (Figure 3.4).

Aside from these psychological effects, a number of myths arose among Libyans regarding NATO. First, as noted, they believed that NATO was deliberately not targeting Qaddafi personnel, only equipment and armor. Much of this, undoubtedly, had to do with the perception that NATO was trying to calibrate its operations with its mandate under UNSCR 1973. Added to this, the rumor persisted that NATO had developed a special "sound missile" (*sarukh sawti*) that would scare Qaddafi forces into leaving their artillery pieces and armor, without actually destroying

**Figure 3.4
A NATO PSYOP Leaflet Dropped on Sirte**

SOURCE: Author's photograph from the Misrata Military Museum.
NOTE: Text warns loyalist holdouts that the "previous regime of Qaddafi no longer rules Libya. There are now two choices before you: fighting or peace."
RAND RR676-3.4

equipment.[65] Similarly, many interlocutors in Misrata believed NATO was dropping fuel-air explosives on African mercenaries fighting for Qaddafi. Finally, nearly every Misratan remains convinced that NATO or the United States shot down *Scud* missiles fired into Misrata from Sirte in late August, despite official denials from the Department of Defense.[66]

Targeting and Coordination with NATO

It is important to note that opposition forces did not merely try to adapt their strategies and movements to NATO's air campaign, but rather tried to directly influence its targeting process. What is not widely known is that oppositionists across the country formed a complex network of spotters, informants, forward observers, and battle damage assessors. Anyone with a cell phone, Google Earth, Skype, Twitter, or email was in a position to report—and all of these conduits were used to pass coordinates, pictures, and other data. As the war progressed, the quality of the reporting improved. According to one Misratan observer, "First it was the general area, then GPS, and then Google Earth. I personally never reported anything unless I had someone put eyes on the target."[67] The problem that mission planners faced, therefore, was not a shortage of targeting information, but a flood of it. The challenge was vetting the sources, corroborating the data with other collection platforms, transforming it into intelligence, and then determining what was actionable.

This learning was evident in the "operations rooms" set up in the war's major fronts—Benghazi, Misrata, and the western Nafusa Mountains—and frequently staffed by officers who had defected from the Libyan armed forces. These facilities managed the collection of intelligence on both fixed and mobile targets from networks of Libyan informants, tracked the movement of rebel forces via relatively sophisticated order-of-battle displays, and passed target coordinates to NATO member states. That said, divisions and competition within the rebels' ranks hindered their effectiveness: In Benghazi, for instance, Qatari and Emirati forces' separate operations rooms reportedly did not communicate or share information with one another, or with a rear-area operations cell in Dubai, UAE, that British personnel created and that AFRICOM later staffed.

The path of data often took a convoluted course. As an example, early in the campaign, frustrated observers in Zintan were passing the coordinates of ammunition

---

[65] Interview with a Malta- and Misrata-based opposition coordinator, Tripoli, Libya, March 8, 2012.

[66] Interview with a Malta- and Misrata-based opposition coordinator, Tripoli, Libya, March 8, 2012. For the Department of Defense denial, see Philip Ewing, "DoD Denies Reports Navy Shot Down Libyan Scuds," *DoDBUZZ*, August 31, 2011.

[67] Interview with a Malta- and Misrata-based opposition coordinator, Tripoli, Libya, March 8, 2012.

depots via SMS to a Misratan intermediary based in Malta, who then Skyped the coordinates and images to NATO member personnel in Germany or Italy.[68] At the same time, these Zintani observers were sending the data to the operations room in Benghazi. But according to several interviewees, Zintan and Benghazi deeply distrusted each other, with the belief among many in the Nafusa that Benghazi was trying to monopolize its access to NATO assets and communication lines.[69] Similar distrust was evident between the operations rooms in Misrata and the Nafusa.

Among Libyan spotters and observers, individual NATO member countries developed reputations for the responsiveness to targeting inputs. For example, the impression of one Libyan rebel forward observer in Misrata was that "the French were everywhere and the easiest to work with. They never asked questions like, 'Where did you get this?' They just took the data and said 'Thank you.' The British were the best. The people who worked with the British had 50 to 60 percent of their targets hit."[70]

Given this cycle, it is not surprising that many targets of opportunity were missed. It would typically take four to five days for action to be taken in response to information from a Libyan informant.[71] In some cases, the ponderousness of the process and convoluted chain had dire consequences for operational movements of opposition forces. This was particularly true early in the war, when Benghazi was the only conduit to the NATO powers. As Mukhtar Fernana, the commander of opposition forces in the Nafusa, related:

> Early in the war, I had planned attack on Zintan storage depot . . . The NTC in Benghazi said go ahead. Then, when I was a few kilometers away, they said 'Turn back. NATO will strike this.' I couldn't just turn around everyone so quickly. Then NATO never struck it—only three months later. The thuwwar (opposition fighters) came back to me angry, saying I was a traitor, I failed them.[72]

The lack of trust and communication between the intervening countries and the opposition became clear during these early weeks and months. This was felt especially in the Nafusa. Several interlocutors believed NATO's hesitation was because the Alliance was unsure of the opposition's composition, particularly with regard to the possible inclusion of al Qaeda elements. With the arrival of foreign advisors, much of this suspicion seems to have dissipated. A Zintan-based fighter noted that "once [they] came over to see us from Tunisia, that all changed. They found out who we were, and

---

[68] Interview with a Malta- and Misrata-based opposition coordinator, Tripoli, Libya, March 8, 2012.

[69] Interview with General Mukhtar Milad Fernana, Tripoli, Libya, March 14, 2012.

[70] Interview with a Malta- and Misrata-based opposition coordinator, Tripoli, Libya, March 8, 2012.

[71] Interview with a Libyan air force officer and Zintan-based opposition commander, Tripoli, Libya, March 10, 2012.

[72] Interview with General Mukhtar Milad Fernana, Tripoli, Libya, March 14, 2012.

things got better." [73] The targeting picture in the Nafusa also improved immeasurably once foreign advisors arrived; for the first time, the region had a direct line to Alliance members. "Once [they] arrived, we started hitting 80 to 90 percent of the targets we identified."[74]

This is not to say that the relationship with the foreign advisors was without friction or miscommunication. According to Mukhtar Fernana, the advisors "delayed us more than helped us. They were always imposing a line, saying 'stop here, don't go here.' They never gave us a reason. Meanwhile, Qaddafi's troops were retreating or withdrawing."[75] That said, other sources from Zintan described NATO airpower as a critical component in the offensive on Bir Ghanim, a town strategically located midway between Zawiyah and al-Aziziyah. Once the offensive reached Bir Ghanim, it moved forward to al-Azaziyah, to Zawiyah, and then on to Tripoli. Advisors reportedly moved with the opposition as it seized these strategic, lowland towns. At the same time, by late 2011, NATO had finally struck the ammo and storage depots in Gharyan, Mizdah, and al-Azaziyah, which further depleted the loyalist forces' capabilities.

In Misrata, sources describe the arrival of foreign advisors in the besieged city as having an even greater transformative effect on the target-coordination process. Although much of the details remain unknown, a period of intense collaboration reportedly occurred between NATO members and the opposition that preceded the actual arrival of Western advisors to Libya. According to several sources, the leadership of the Misratan opposition met with a senior NATO commander on board the French aircraft carrier *Charles de Gaulle* sometime in May. "The first thing he told us," recalled one participant, "is that we are not attacking the Libyan people."[76]

In April, the first advisors arrived, staying only for a short period. By mid-May, three or four additional advisors had arrived, maintaining a constant presence.[77] According to one planner, they reportedly traveled around the front lines incessantly, exposing themselves on numerous occasions to fire. Despite this, trust-building was still a lengthy process. "They didn't trust us at first," said a Misrata-based opposition planner and field commander. "They were always double-checking our data against their maps. We started taking our informants directly to [them] or letting them talk to them via Skype."[78] According to a Misratan commander, these advisors were focused primarily on the eastern front and the Misratan assault on Tawergha. Their role was

---

[73] Interview with the chief of the Zintan Military Council, Zintan, Libya, March 15, 2012.

[74] Interview with a Libyan air force officer and Zintan-based opposition commander, Tripoli, Libya, March 10, 2012.

[75] Interview with General Mukhtar Milad Fernana, Tripoli, Libya, March 14, 2012.

[76] Interview with a Misrata opposition commander, Misrata, Libya, June 29, 2012.

[77] Interview with a Misrata-based opposition planner and field commander, Misrata, Libya, March 13, 2012.

[78] Interview with a Misrata-based opposition planner and field commander, Misrata, Libya, March 13, 2012.

described as three-fold: "to coordinate NATO attacks on fixed targets before a Misratan assault; to prevent reinforcements from flowing in to the area; and to provide air cover."[79]

By early June, more advisors arrived, focusing on the western/Dafniya front. Misratans had a more favorable first impression of them. "We became friends in two or three days; they were eating our food with us and always traveling with us to the front," noted a Misrata-based opposition commander.[80] They also were the most proactive in planning for an offensive out of the city. "When [they] came, we started to act," said the commander. "We had a meeting with them in June and they told us, 'You must start your offensive [out of the city] before Ramadan'" in July. During this period, other advisors were in the city's operations room, coordinating logistics. By September, when Misratans joined in the assault on Sirte, at least four nations had small numbers of advisors on the ground. According to a Misratan present in the assault, the countries' teams were "competing" with each other for strikes; "they each had their own program and priorities."[81]

According to Misratan accounts, the advisors were using a range-finding device "like a video camera," with a large, touch-screen viewfinder that provided range and coordinates. The coordinates subsequently were called in to command centers via radio or satellite phone—Misratan witnesses stated the advisors did not have direct links to aircraft. In many cases, though, the response time between the ground observers' fixing on a particular target and a strike was described as "minutes." In describing ground-to-air coordination in the breakout toward Dafniya, a Misratan commander stated, "NATO was covering our advance."[82] At the same time, a perception existed that advisors were working directly with their planes, because the response time was so much more rapid than during early NATO operations in the siege of Misrata.

For their part, the opposition relied on an order-of-battle planning tool it had begun developing and populating shortly after the start of hostilities in early March. By the time the advisors arrived, Misrata already had a fairly sophisticated picture of the battlespace and, compared to Benghazi or the Nafusa, a well-defined system of command and control. This invariably helped NATO airstrikes support the western offensive of Misratan forces—a decisive turning point that would shift the tide of the entire war. The screenshot in Figure 3.5 depicts that pivotal moment when opposition forces broke through loyalist lines west of Misrata and began advancing through an area of farmlands known as Dafniya. The white figures represent opposition *kata'ib* (brigades). Red markers denote hostile forces, including troop concentrations, artillery,

---

[79] Interview with a Misrata opposition commander, Misrata, Libya, June 29, 2012.

[80] Interview with a Misrata opposition commander, Misrata, Libya, June 29, 2012.

[81] Interview with a Misrata opposition commander, Misrata, Libya, June 29, 2012.

[82] Interview with a Misrata opposition commander, Misrata, Libya, June 29, 2012. NATO air commanders, however, characterize the situation differently, since their mandate was one of protecting civilians.

Figure 3.5
The Order of Battle for Dafniya, Mid-June, 2011

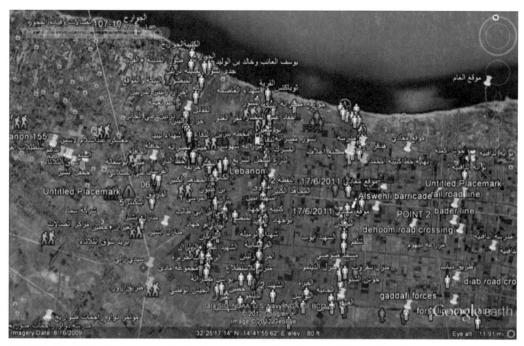

SOURCE: Google Earth data provided to the author by the Misrata Military Council.
NOTE: A Google Earth battle-space management tool developed by Misrata's defenders.
RAND RR676-3.5

Grad rockets, radar, anti-aircraft artillery (AAA), and armor. The map also plots civilian sites such as mosques, schools, and residences. The yellow markers denote targets that were reported via informants, verified with the Global Positioning System (GPS) by Misrata's operations room, and passed to NATO at first via Skype/email/Twitter and later through the foreign advisors. The blue line represents the westernmost front of Misrata's defenses prior to June. Road barricades and checkpoints are clearly marked. West of the red line adjacent to the blue line was a no-go zone prior to the June offensive, denoting an area of NATO strikes. The elongated area outlined in red just west of that line, in the area of open fields, was described as a free-fire zone.[83]

The actual flow of forces in the offensive was not always precisely coordinated with airpower. According to the commander of the Dafniya front, the advance from Misrata, across Dafniya, to Zlitan took nearly three months, with the opposing forces arrayed across a 7-kilometer-long front, sometimes no more than 300 meters apart. He

---

[83] Chris Stephen, "Libya Rebels Advance into Nato Bombing Path," *The Guardian*, June 14, 2011. The article notes that rebel commanders "say NATO has told them to treat the existing frontline as a 'red line' beyond which they should not move, so that the alliance can bomb anything it sees in the territory beyond."

recalled several instances of poor communication, even with the advisors present. He noted that in mid-June, a typical opposition assault would be preceded by the following pattern of air and artillery support: from 0200 to 0500, helicopters would attack; from 0500 to 0700, fighter aircraft would strike; from 0700 to 0730, the opposition would fire Grad salvos. Then the Misratans would move. On one occasion, having prepared for a morning assault, the helicopter and fighter support never arrived, and instead the Hamza Brigade subjected opposition positions to withering artillery and Grad salvos. The three-story observation post where the Misratan commanders and their advisors were based came under attack from artillery rounds; its occupants had to beat a hasty retreat. One advisor "was very upset and started cursing at NATO," the commander recalled.[84]

Press reports suggest further problems in coordinating the advance. In mid-June, errant PSYOP leaflets bearing the picture of an attacking Apache helicopter fell directly on opposition forces in Dafniya when they were clearly meant for Qaddafi forces based in neighboring Zlitan. The opposition reportedly had halted its advance, pulling back from their positions 10 kilometers east of Zlitan. A young field commander whom Reuters interviewed wondered, "Qaddafi's forces are far away. Is it logical that NATO has no idea we took those positions?" A fighter further west radioed in: "They dropped the leaflets right on us." At the command post, the opposition leader wondered, "Do I go back or do I go forward? Is it [the leaflet] for Qaddafi or for us?"[85]

Conclusion

This chapter has canvassed a broad spectrum of Libyan voices to assess Libyan perceptions of coalition and NATO airpower. It started with the premise that the country's anti-Qaddafi fighters were more active participants and collaborators in the air campaign than is commonly assumed. Much of this was rooted in defectors from the Libyan army and air force playing a pivotal role in shaping the opposition's strategy and interaction with NATO—a role that has not been widely acknowledged.

Based on these observations, a number of findings emerge. First, opposition interlocutors were nearly unanimous in their appreciation for the campaign's strategic impact. Interviewees from a broad range of backgrounds—frontline fighters, air defense officers, commanders, and civilian bystanders—spoke of NATO's capabilities with awe. Intervention from the air proved crucial to stopping Qaddafi's advance into Benghazi, enabling the opposition to establish a base of operations. In the war's

---

[84] Interview with a Misrata-based opposition planner and field commander, Misrata, Libya, March 13, 2012. Eric Schmitt and Steven Lee Meyers, "Surveillance and Coordination with NATO Aided Rebels," *The New York Times*, August 21, 2011; Chris Stephen, "Libyan Rebels in Misrata Accuse NATO of Ignoring Requests for Air Support," *The Guardian*, June 10, 2011.

[85] Matt Robinson, "Libyan Rebel Advance Checked by NATO Strike Leaflets," *Reuters*, June 14, 2011.

pivotal battle—the siege of Misrata—airpower had a limited direct effect on the street fighting that raged when Qaddafi's forces occupied nearly three-quarters of the city from March to late May. But airpower proved essential to limiting the effectiveness of loyalist artillery barrages, preventing loyalist reinforcements from flowing into the city, and keeping the port open, which enabled humanitarian supplies and weapons to be shipped in to the opposition from Benghazi. Once Qaddafi's forces were pushed beyond the city's environs, NATO airpower—guided by foreign advisors—proved crucial in aiding the opposition breakout toward Tawergha in the south and Dafniya/Zlitan in the west. This dynamic continued in the Misratan assault on Sirte.

The campaign had a profound psychological impact in fortifying the opposition's resolve that is difficult to measure. Opposition commanders and planners were also acutely aware of the tension between dynamic and strategic targeting, and especially how NATO's mandate under UNSCR 1973 limited its ability to provide responsive CAS. Regarding collateral damage, many were quick to acknowledge their own inexperience, disorganization, and poor command and control, as well as NATO's mistakes and, most commonly, the fog of war.

This nuanced understanding, however, did not lessen their frustration at the lack of strategic support during critical stages of the campaign. This was especially evident in the Nafusa campaign, where early interdiction against loyalist reinforcements from Tripoli and strikes against the area's ammunition depots might have hastened the opposition's advance and saved lives. In Misrata, similar exasperation was expressed with the lack of air support early in the war, but those interviewed expressed appreciation for the difficulties NATO faced in conducting CAS in the city's densely populated, urban battlespace.

In both the Nafusa and Misrata fronts, however, much of the consternation was eased with the arrival of French and British advisors. Although NATO member states have said little in public about these activities, Libyan sources were quite forthcoming about the details and the effect of these advisors on the battlefield. Of course, much of their narrative cannot be corroborated, but it offers important insights. By every account, the presence of foreign special operations forces in the command posts of Misrata, Zintan, and Benghazi had a transformative effect—it built trust between NATO members and the opposition, improved the targeting cycle, and bolstered the general coordination ground with air operations. As noted, the presence of former Libyan military officers inside the opposition ranks aided this, along with the presence of a liberated zone—Benghazi—from which the opposition could coordinate support to Misrata and the west in the early stages of the war. The behind-the-scenes presence of these defectors in the various "operations rooms"—managing sophisticated networks of spotters, order-of-battle display, and passing target coordinates to NATO—also paints a different picture from the common portrayal of the Libyan rebels as ragtag youths in pickup trucks.

In many respects, though, this coordination was as successful as it was because of factors that were exogenous to either NATO's or the opposition's capabilities: the decrepit state of Qaddafi's forces, the relatively open topography of the war's principal fronts, and the massive Libyan disenchantment with the dictator's 42 years of rule. Added to this was the relative homogeneity of Libyan society and the near-unanimous international resolve against Qaddafi. It seems unlikely that such a "perfect storm" of conditions will be replicated.

CHAPTER FOUR

The U.S. Experience: National Strategy and Campaign Support

Robert C. Owen

Introduction

There can be no doubt that airpower decisively shaped the outcome of the 2011 Libyan civil war. A coalition of NATO and partner states provided airpower that robbed the Libyan military of its ability to conduct sustained offensives, undermined its ability to coerce its citizens, and gave the Libyan rebels time to prepare for successful offensives. Had coalition states chosen not to act, the outcome of the conflict would have been quite different. Instead of a celebrating crowd of rebels executing the tyrant, it likely would have ended months earlier with the slaughter of thousands—rebel combatants and unarmed civilians alike—by Qaddafi's relatively better-trained and equipped army and air force. Even if the Libyan revolt somehow had organized itself and taken the country without external support, the butcher's bill and physical destruction of Libya's economic infrastructure would have been far more devastating than it was in 2011.

But the air war over Libya also revealed significant shortfalls in the readiness of the contributing air forces to conduct future operations. Perhaps most troubling, the "hollowness" of some air forces—their inadequate logistical provisions and limited capabilities in critical areas—became public knowledge almost as soon as strike operations began. Less obvious to the public, the United States also found that its air force and naval aviation arm were stressed to cover this relatively small-scale operation in addition to their existing docket: fighting wars in Iraq and Afghanistan; conducting engagement operations in a half-dozen other regions; responding to an earthquake and tsunami in Japan; worldwide training operations; and the need to give tired units an opportunity to maintain equipment and rest personnel. For the USAF, international and domestic political divisions over the need for—and even the legality of—the war also slowed the development of strategic plans, constrained the mobilization of reserve forces, and complicated C2 arrangements early in the operation. The NATO alliance's maturity in fostering staff and operational cooperation helped the participating air forces mitigate their shortcomings and political challenges to conduct effective operations over Libya. But the various challenges they had to overcome also left nagging impressions that many of the partner air forces were operating at the limits of their capabilities, and that their ability to take on larger challenges elsewhere in the near future should not be taken for granted.

These issues of hollowing air forces, shaky political foundations, and uncertainty set the stage for this examination of the strategic-level experiences and implications of the Libyan conflict for the United States, and particularly the USAF. It begins with an examination of the United States' decision to intervene, especially the influence of its historical relationship with Libya, domestic political divisions, and intercommand military relations. The chapter then examines the strategic elements of the American intervention. These elements include forces deployed, command relations, operations by "common-user" forces based in the continental United States (CONUS), and the long-term impact of those operations on the management of Air Force forces and capabilities. This discussion will be followed by enumeration of the salient implications of the Libyan air campaign for the USAF. The next chapter in this volume (Chapter Five, "The U.S. Experience: Operational"), by Deborah Kidwell, provides detailed discussions of the deployment, basing, organization, operations, and accomplishments of U.S. forces within the area of operations that were supported by the efforts described in this chapter. Consequently, a useful plan for apprehending the full scope of the American experience would be to begin by reading the "Intervention" and "Deployment and Operations" sections below, then shifting to read the entire companion chapter and, finally, returning to this chapter to examine its ultimate findings.

Intervention

The United States had reasons to get involved in Libya, as well as reasons to stay clear. Colonel Muammar Qaddafi's response to the outbreak of political unrest in the city of Benghazi on February 16, 2011 presented the United States with a moral imperative to intervene and an opportunity to close a festering political sore. The Libyan president's threat to put down the rebellion with "no mercy and no pity" had credibility, given his history of crushing dissent with violence. Aware of what had been the humanitarian costs of delay in places such as Rwanda (1994) and Bosnia (1995), many in the U.S. government saw no alternative to quick action to prevent another mass atrocity. Qaddafi's long sponsorship of international terrorism strengthened the impetus to become involved. An intervention resulting in Qaddafi's people overthrowing him, therefore, offered an opportunity to bring a just closure to the career of a criminal tyrant whose head-of-state status had protected him. But sharp domestic political divisions and the strained condition of American military forces raised concerns. In the month of debate leading up to military action, voices from many directions argued that the United States lacked the legal right, national interests, and military capabilities to add another commitment. The necessity of balancing this peculiar mix of moral imperative and political constraint would define many of the strategic features of the American intervention into Libyan politics.

The nature of Qaddafi and his government set the stage not only for the popular revolt, but for the role and effectiveness of intervention airpower. Qaddafi took control of Libya in a bloodless coup in 1969. Standing on the populist pillars of Arab nationalism and a paternalistic vision of government he named the *Jamahiriya*, or "State of the Masses," Qaddafi soon revealed himself as a mercurial and unpredictable autocrat. He accepted no resistance to his authority or his political vision. Within Libya, his network of informers fingered disaffected individuals and groups for brutal repression. His enemies who fled Libya often knew the terror of having Qaddafi's agents track down and kill dissenters as well as members of their families. Qaddafi built his political base by funneling power and opportunities for great wealth to his extended family, important loyalists, and his home tribe, the Qadhadhfa, generally situated around the coastal city of Sirte.[1] He had founded what analysts of the Middle East sometimes call a modern sultanate—a regime featuring an implacable focus on retaining power, nepotism, zealous repression of opponents, and a cult of personality. As Qaddafi aged, his rule became increasingly arbitrary and delusional, marked by a buffoonery of self-designed costumes, "Amazon Guards," and faux Bedouin lifestyle posturing.[2] So thorough and convincing was all this theater that even the outside world missed the reality that many, perhaps most Libyans, chafed under his rule. Perhaps no moment captures Qaddafi's self-delusion more than the plaintive "What did I ever do to you?" that he whimpered to his captors moments before they executed him on the road outside of Sirte.[3]

Directing or sponsoring murder across international borders was a central ingredient of Qaddafi's sultanic agenda. To demonstrate his leadership of pan-Arab nationalism and to satisfy his own ego, he believed that he had to kill outsiders. As soon as he came to power, Qaddafi aligned himself with Egypt in its confrontation with Israel and publically announced his material support for groups such as Al Fatah, Black September, the Provisional Irish Republican Army, and the Japanese Red Army Faction. Meanwhile, Qaddafi's hit squads tracked down and killed at least 25 of his most notable opponents in exile in the West.

The result, of course, was enmity and prolonged conflict with the United States, which suspended diplomatic relations with Libya in 1979. During the next decade, U.S. naval forces maneuvered frequently in the Gulf of Sidra in defiance of Libya's claim to

[1]   Lisa Anderson, "Demystifying the Arab Spring: Parsing the Differences Between Tunisia, Egypt, and Libya," *Foreign Affairs*, May/June 2011, pp. 2–7.

[2]   Jack Goldstone, "Understanding the Revolutions of 2011: Weakness and Resilience in Middle Eastern Autocracies," *Foreign Affairs*, May/June 2011, pp. 8–16.

[3]   Peter Beaumont and Chris Stephen, "Gaddafi's Last Words as He Begged For Mercy: 'What Did I Do to You?'" *The Guardian*, October 22, 2011.

exclusive navigation rights there. Two of these confrontations resulted in the downing of Libyan fighters, in 1981 and 1989. On April 5, 1986, Libyan agents planted a bomb in West Berlin's La Belle nightclub, killing three and wounding over 200 people. Two Americans were among the dead and 79 were among the injured. In retaliation, U.S. Air Force and Navy jets struck targets in Libya ten days later in Operation El Dorado Canyon, killing about 60 Libyan soldiers and civilians. After U.S. and French support helped the government of Chad eject Libyan military forces from its northern regions, Qaddafi retaliated by having agents plant bombs on Pan Am Flight 103 in December 1988 and on UTA Flight 772 in September 1989. Together these bombings resulted in the deaths of 352 people.

Then, following the disintegration of the Soviet Union, the United States and Libya began a period of gradual rapprochement as Qaddafi sought to ease tensions. In 1994, he entered into prolonged negotiations to release two suspects in the Pan Am 103 bombings to Scottish courts. Ultimately he did release them, and one was convicted in 2001. Following the 2003 invasion of Iraq, Qaddafi expanded his efforts to placate the West. Faced with the implications of Saddam Hussein's execution, Qaddafi allowed his government in 2003 to admit complicity in both airline bombings and began the process of compensating the families of the victims. In return, the United Nations lifted its sanctions against Libya. Meanwhile, Western intelligence agencies, including the CIA, began collaborating with their Libyan counterparts against Islamic militant groups, particularly al Qaeda.[4] The rapprochement continued, with Libya also renouncing its weapons of mass destruction ambitions in 2003 and entering into a host of economic and counterterrorism agreements with the United States, Great Britain, France, Italy, Russia, and other states.

The foundation of these expanded contacts was uneasy pragmatism, never friendship or respect. Few believed that his ongoing rehabilitation was more than a device to lift painful sanctions and strengthen Libya's economy, upon which his power depended. Another factor was his personal oddness: U.S. Secretary of State Condoleezza Rice discovered in 2008 his "eerie obsession" with her, which included keeping a scrapbook of his "African Princess" and having a song written about her. Despite her unease, Rice stayed focused on getting along with the aging tyrant, who seemed entrenched in power.[5]

However, even as Qaddafi's head-of-state status obliged the United States and many other countries to accommodate his criminality, the context of international practice and law was changing in ways that would untie their hands when he moved against his own people. "Conscience-shocking events" such as the massacres of civilians in Bosnia, Kosovo, and Rwanda in the 1990s drove the United Nations to host

---

[4]   Amy Davidson, "Eighty-Nine Questions: What Did Libya Do for the CIA?" *New Yorker Online*, September 3, 2011.

[5]   Condoleezza Rice, *No Higher Honor,* New York: Crown, 2011, pp. 701–703.

a process to elevate the responsibility of governments to protect their peoples from mass atrocities to the status of international law. Numerous private and civil organizations rose around the world to participate and to convince their own governments to embrace the "responsibility to protect" (R2P) doctrine.[6] The U.N.'s 2005 Millennium Summit was a milestone in the R2P process. One of the summit's outcomes was the nations' endorsement of two key R2P principles. First, they agreed that "each individual State has the responsibility to protect its populations from genocide, war crimes, ethnic cleansing and crimes against humanity." Second, they said that if governments refused or were unable to honor those responsibilities, the U.N. member states endorsed their obligation to "encourage and help States to exercise this responsibility"—by peaceful means, if possible, but through collective, timely, and decisive military actions if necessary.[7] Four years later, Secretary General Ban Ki-moon urged the General Assembly to consider "the strategy for implementing the responsibility to protect" and pledged to make the issue a primary focus of his tenure.[8]

In the United States, Harvard University's Carr Center for Human Rights Policy, under the leadership of Dr. Sarah Sewall, became one of the more influential organizations engaged in the effort to prevent future mass atrocities. Partnering with the U.S. Army War College's Peacekeeping and Stability Operations Institute in 2007, it set out to lay the foundations for "operationalizing" the R2P concept within the U.S. military and government. After a lengthy collaboration, the two organizations published *MARO—Mass Atrocity Response Operations: A Military Planning Handbook* in 2010. The document was a key element of the MARO team's effort to "enable the United States and the international community to stop genocide and mass atrocity," by developing "a widely shared understanding of the specific and unique aspects of mass atrocities and genocide and to create a common military approach to addressing these challenges." Prior to publishing the *Handbook*, the team tested its concepts during tabletop exercises at the U.S. European Command (EUCOM). The result was a highly detailed guide to the political, military, economic, and other factors involved in quickly planning MARO operations in a whole-of-government context.[9]

Thus, when Qaddafi announced that he was going to slaughter his citizens without mercy, his timing could not have been worse. The global community's determination to prevent mass atrocities had just coalesced in U.N. policies that linked the

---

6   U.N. Secretary General Ban Ki-Moon provides an authoritative history of the R2P process in United Nations General Assembly, *Implementing the Responsibility to Protect: Report of the Secretary General*, document A/60/L.1, January 12, 2009, pp. 4–10.

7   United Nations General Assembly, *2005 World Summit Outcome*, document A/60/L.1, September 15, 2005, outcomes 138–139.

8   Ban Ki-Moon, *Implementing the Responsibility to Protect*, pp. 4 and 29.

9   Sarah Sewell, Dwight Raymond, Sally Chin, et al., *MARO—Mass Atrocity Response Operations: A Military Planning Handbook*, Cambridge, Mass.: The President and Fellows of Harvard College, 2010, pp. 5, 9, and 132–135.

institution's credibility to making timely and decisive responses to such events. Many organizations and consequential individuals had rallied around the R2P idea. Likewise, in the United States, powerful individuals had engaged the issue and produced the will and guidelines for quick interventions in the face of just the kinds of threats Qaddafi was making.

In the weeks following the outbreak of fighting in Benghazi, support for intervention began to build in many centers, including the United States—slowly at first and then with a rush in mid-March. Samantha Power, an aide on the National Security Council, and Susan Rice, U.S. Ambassador to the United Nations, were early and outspoken advocates of intervention within the U.S. government. Michèle Flournoy, the Under Secretary of Defense for Policy, worked more quietly behind the scenes to counter initial DoD reluctance to endorse intervention. Driven by their memories of the consequences of delay in Bosnia and Rwanda, Power and Rice pushed their superiors to block Qaddafi. They gained traction with Secretary of State Hillary Clinton during the second week of March, when Libyan government forces began to push back toward Benghazi.[10]

Though cautious, President Obama agreed to authorize action, if the three officials could obtain an appropriate resolution from the U.N. Security Council and could convince at least some Arab states to commit forces to an intervention. When Clinton won commitments from several Arab states, and Power successfully brokered the tough provisions of UNSCR 1973 on March 17, the President authorized intervention. But he stipulated that there would be no American "boots on the ground" in Libya, and that American involvement would be only for a matter of days.[11] Addressing the American people the next day, he reaffirmed that "the United States is not going to deploy ground troops into Libya . . . [or] use force to go beyond a well-defined goal—specifically, the protection of civilians."[12]

Despite the caution of his rhetoric, the willingness of the President and important European allies to assist with the overthrow of Qaddafi was clear well before his March 18 speech. From the start, outside critics focused their concerns on the actions of "Qaddafi's government"—recognizing that nothing happened there without at least the tacit approval of the dictator. Commenting on the U.N. Security Council's imposition of an arms embargo on February 26, British Prime Minister David Cameron stated clearly that Qaddafi had to go, a position that Obama had also taken publicly.[13]

---

[10] Massimo Calabresi, "Susan Rice: A Voice for Intervention," *Time*, March 24, 2011.

[11] Helene Cooper and Steven Lee Meyers, "Obama Takes Hard Line with Libya After Shift by Clinton," *New York Times*, March 18, 2011.

[12] Jesse Lee, "The President on Libya: 'Our Goal Is Focused, Our Cause Is Just, and Our Coalition Is Strong,'" The White House blog, March 18, 2011.

[13] Rosa Prince and Richard Spencer, "Libya: Col Gaddafi 'Must Go Now,' Says PM amid Mounting Pressure on Dictator," *The Telegraph*, February 27, 2012; Lee, "The President on Libya."

On March 28, Obama raised Qaddafi's downfall to the level of public policy when he announced, "We remain committed to the broader goal of a Libya that belongs not to a dictator, but to the Libyan people."[14] A few weeks later, in response to concerns that the air campaign was exceeding the defensive charter of UNSCR 1973, Obama, Cameron, and French President Nicolas Sarkozy jointly declared: "It is unthinkable that someone who has tried to massacre his own people can play a part in their future government."[15]

These leaders' repeated statements in support of the intervention, and on removing Qaddafi, reflected the stiff domestic and international opposition they faced in prosecuting the conflict. In the United States' case, the administration came under sharp criticism from the start. Constitutional scholar Bruce Ackerman raked the President for having violated the Constitution and the War Powers Act by circumventing Congress to commit the country to a conflict that did not involve an immediate threat to the country or its military forces.[16] From the Congress, involvement in Libya came under attack from a gallery of powerful Republicans, including Senators Mitch McConnell of Kentucky, John Ensign of Nevada, and Richard Lugar of Indiana, as well as and Rep. Ron Paul of Texas. In various ways, they and many others echoed Ackerman's charge that the President had committed the country without congressional approval into a conflict not involving national interests and carrying the danger of expanding into another large-scale war in the Middle East.[17]

For Obama, the potentially looming war made for unexpected allies and opponents. Although Republicans led the charge against the actions, the House revealed bipartisan concerns by voting 268 to 145 to direct the President to not "deploy, establish, or maintain the presence of units and members of the United States Armed Forces on the ground in Libya unless the purpose of the presence is to rescue a member of the Armed Forces from imminent danger."[18] The complex political battle reached its apex in mid-June, when the Libyan conflict appeared to be mired in stalemate. At that point, Senator John McCain, a conservative Republican from Arizona, filed a resolution supporting continued involvement in Libya in response to a suit filed by a bipartisan group of ten representatives led by Congressman Dennis Kucinich, a liberal Democrat from Ohio, to prevent the President from continuing his "unlawful" war.[19]

Congress never broke its deadlock over Libya policy. Opponents of intervention failed to muster enough support to force a crisis under the War Powers Act, while the

---

[14] The White House, White House Press Office, "President Obama's Speech on Libya," March 28, 2011.

[15] Jim Garamone, "Leaders Describe Path to Peace in Libya," *American Forces Press Service*, April 15, 2011.

[16] Bruce Ackerman, "Obama's Unconstitutional War," *Foreign Policy*, March 24, 2011.

[17] Senator Mitch McConnell, "Military Action in Libya," *Congressional Record*, 112 (2), Senate, March 28, 2011, p. S1880; Richard Lugar, "Lugar Says Costly, Ill-Defined War in Libya Looms," Washington, D.C.: United States Senate Committee on Foreign Relations, press release, April 6, 2011.

[18] U.S. House of Representatives, H.Res. 292, June 3, 2011.

[19] U.S. Senate, S.J.Res. 20, June 21, 2011.

President's allies were unable to carry through any statements of support. More importantly, Congress never voted to authorize or fund the action. Military leaders and planners, consequently, were obliged to follow the President's orders to begin operations without clear guidance on what they were to do and without stipulated resources of personnel, units, and funding. About the only genuinely clear guidance they had on the eve of hostilities was that the intervention would have to be based on air and sea power only, with no U.S. ground forces planned for Libya.

Although the ebb and flow of the domestic political debate had little direct impact on the conduct of the campaign, the political division over the intervention infused it with several distinctive characteristics. Most importantly, it sharply limited the forces available for Libyan operations. With no funding, and mindful of Secretary of Defense Robert Gates's public reluctance to intervene, Joint Staff leaders told their American counterparts in Europe that they would have to fight mainly with the forces at hand. No large-scale deployment from the United States to the operational area would occur.[20] This left the U.S. Air Forces in Europe (USAFE) and the U.S. Sixth Fleet to provide whatever U.S. forces would be involved. But, like the rest of the U.S. military, other commitments and ongoing operations already had stretched thin their combat units. They could fight for a little while, but any prolonged involvement in Libya would undermine their general readiness and availability.

For American diplomats, the shortage of forces made gaining additional commitments from other states an imperative. Britain and France were already leading the movement toward engagement. But the attitudes of other NATO states initially ranged from cautious support to flat refusal. The willingness of Arab states was even more of an unknown, though U.S. strategists strongly wished to have at least a few of their air forces involved. So, American diplomats worked secretly in mid-March to encourage other partner states to get involved. Most importantly and as quickly as possible, the United States needed NATO to take over the operation—to legitimize the involvement of other states and to avoid any appearance that America was leading an intervention into yet another Arab state. When the rush of events forced the start of operations before the necessary political arrangements for a NATO takeover could be completed, the United States exercised informal leadership of the intervention until March 31, when the Alliance assumed responsibility for all operations.

---

[20] Major General Harold W. "Punch" Moulton II, interview by Robert C. Owen, September 17–18, 2012. During the period covered by this report, General Moulton was the director of U.S. European Command, J-3 Plans and Operations.

Deployment and Operations

This section examines the deployment and operations of the USAF's "global" forces participating in the international intervention in the Libyan civil war.[21] These included Air Force personnel and units drawn mainly from Air Mobility Command (AMC), Air Combat Command (ACC), USAFE, and Air Force Space Command (AFSPC). This intervention had two phases for the United States. The first was Operation Odyssey Dawn, conducted March 3–31, 2011, which was the code name for U.S. operations in support of U.N. Security Council Resolutions 1970 and 1973.[22] On March 31, NATO assumed full command of the campaign against Qaddafi's government, and integrated all separate national operations into Operation Unified Protector.

The term "global" bears some clarification. In a broad sense, all USAF forces are global, in that the service has commitments to support U.S. combatant commands (CCMDs) in every region of the world, and virtually all of its units or at least their capabilities are available for deployment to, or application in support of, any of those commitments. But this study uses "global" more narrowly, to indicate forces organized and operated to provide support to any and all CCMDs at the same time in accordance with the priorities set by the Secretary of Defense. In general, U.S. Transportation Command (TRANSCOM) and U.S. Strategic Command (STRATCOM) operate their respective Air Force components, AMC and AFSPC, on a "common user" basis, meaning that they present them or their capabilities to supported CCMDs as directed by the Secretary of Defense, but retain full combatant command authority over them. Retaining command authority over their forces allows the service components to support their people and units logistically, and the CCMDs to shift their capabilities rapidly between users as the ebb and flow of operations require. But when actual units are deployed to an area of operations for significant periods of time, the Secretary of Defense usually will transfer, or "chop," some level of command authority over them to the "gaining" CCMD. Such chops occur sometimes when AMC expeditionary tanker or airlift units are deployed, and almost always when ACC assets are moved. For obvious reasons, AFSPC on-orbit systems never transfer to another command, though some personnel or support teams may do so. Thus these commands are the most "global" elements of a global Air Force, in that they operate an interconnected network of forces and capabilities to provide simultaneous support to as many CCMDs as circumstances require and resources permit. USAFE normally is considered a "theater" air force, but its provision of forces to OOD and OUP put it in the "global" camp for the purposes of this analysis.

---

[21] For discussion of "theater" forces, see Chapter Five.

[22] Britain, France, and Canada conducted parallel but independent operations during this period; named Operation Ellamy, Operation Harmattan, and Operation Mobile, respectively.

As is usual in operational histories and assessments, this discussion of command authorities and relations makes for extremely dry reading. But command relations are almost always an important element in the conduct and understanding of operational events. This particularly was the case for OOD and OUP. The circumstances of these operations—political gridlock in Congress, the rush of military preparations, and pressure to get the most out of scarce assets—pressed the involved commands into relationships that were complicated, innovative, and at times problematic. These relationships influenced the operational and logistical details of OOD and OUP and carried noteworthy implications for future policy. Command relations and their contexts, therefore, must be at the heart of any discussion of the deployment and employment of AMC, ACC, and AFSPC forces in Odyssey Dawn and Unified Protector.[23]

Air Mobility Command

Air Mobility Command planners described the challenges facing them in March 2011 as "March Madness," borrowing a term from American college basketball's hectic tournament schedule. Twenty years of near-continual conflict since 1990 had normalized a high pace of operations for mobility forces. But March 2011 presented planners with an exceptional load of predictable as well as unpredictable challenges. By the middle of the month, every available aircraft and unit was taken up with ongoing operations, training, maintenance, and periods of mandatory or at least hoped-for rest. Those ongoing operations included supporting wars in Afghanistan and Iraq; providing lift and air refueling for the largest rotation of forces to date between those theaters and the U.S. homeland; participating in contingencies and exercises in support of every combatant command; assisting with the relief of Japan following the earthquake and great tsunami of March 11 (Operation Tomodachi); transporting the President and his large entourage around Latin America (a "Banner" mission); and performing the daily web work of missions linking the components of America's global military establishment. Routine training operations and heavy maintenance also tied down significant portions of the fleet.

When it came to Libya, the command had no spare airlift or air refueling capacity in reserve to handle a new tasking. Whatever AMC sent to that fight would have to come at the expense of other commitments or the training, maintenance, or rest activities of any units tapped for the mission. In other words, the new requirement potentially would put the command into a state of "surge"—a pace of operation not allowing normal levels of training, repair, and rest—although it never was officially declared as

---

[23] This report will discuss command relations only to the extent needed to understand the specific arrangements of OOD and OUP. Readers wishing to understand the full context of U.S. command relations terms and arrangements should begin by reading Joint Publication 1 (JP-1), *Doctrine for the Armed Forces of the United States*, Chapter Four, "Doctrine for Joint Command and Control," May 2, 2007, Incorporating Change 1, March 20, 2009.

such.[24] Nevertheless, as soon as things began to heat up in March, AMC began sending tanker-planning specialists to USAFE and U.S. Air Forces Africa (AFAFRICA). Two Air National Guard tankers were already operating from Morón Air Base, Spain, in support of the ongoing rotation of combat aircraft to and from the Middle East. Then, with the passage of UNSCR 1973 on March 18, but before issuance of a Joint Chiefs of Staff (JCS) "execution" order, AMC leaders made what one called "the risky decision" of starting the movement of seven active-duty tankers to Morón from Puerto Rico, where they had been supporting the Presidential Banner mission. This preliminary move risked getting the tankers to Morón without authorization or funding. But AMC leaders saw the risk as necessary to ensure that tankers would be available to support initial operations.[25]

Brigadier General Roy E. Uptegraff III, commander of the Pennsylvania Air National Guard's 171st Air Refueling Wing (ARW) at Pittsburgh, was given the job of putting together an expeditionary wing at Morón Air Base to support Operation Odyssey Dawn. While driving home from work on March 17, he received a call from a staffer at AMC who passed on a request from the AMC commander, General Raymond E. Johns, to consider "going somewhere far, sometime soon." Over the next two days, Uptegraff and his staff prepared his wing for deployment. On the afternoon of the 19th, Uptegraff received his orders: Take as many planes and crews as he could to Morón as quickly as possible. He left that night in the first of four aircraft and arrived at Morón on the morning of the 20th in a plane packed with people, baggage, equipment, and spare parts. As he arrived, a mix of four air reserve component (ARC) and active-duty tankers sent to Morón earlier was returning from having supported the first B-2 strikes against Libyan air force targets. Other aircraft and hundreds of personnel arrived in short order. In less than 72 hours from receiving his initial orders, Uptegraff found himself in command of an expeditionary wing containing as many as 15 KC-135s, 4 KC-10s, and almost 800 personnel drawn from as many as 14 wings from the ARC (the Air National Guard and Air Force Reserve) and the active duty Air Force.[26] Uptegraff named it the "Calico Wing" in reflection of the multicolored array of fin flashes on the Morón ramp.

[24] Major General Frederick H. "Rick" Martin, AMC Director of Operations (A3), interview by Robert C. Owen, February 29, 2012; and Dave Merrill, interview by Robert C. Owen, February 27, 2012. Mr. Merrill is the AMC A9.

[25] Major Mark McLean, "Talking Paper on Operation Odyssey Dawn MAF Support," 18 AF staff paper, May 12, 2011; interview with senior AMC officer by Robert C. Owen, February 27, 2012; Brigadier General Bryan J. Benson, interview by Robert C. Owen, March 13, 2012. General Benson was the 18 AF Vice Commander during the Libyan campaign. General Benson assessed the preemptive deployment as "risky," since, had Libyan operations not been authorized, TRANSCOM would have been responsible for stressing the fleet further for an operation that ultimately was not authorized or funded.

[26] Brigadier General Roy E. Uptegraff III, interview by Robert C. Owen, March 26, 2012; Major Andra Higgs, "Maintainers 'Dance' Ensured NATO Success for OUP," 313th AEW Air Expeditionary Group, January 3, 2012; Air Mobility Command Office of Public Affairs, "'Calico' Wing Serves as Representation of Total Force Team Supporting World-Wide Operations," April 15, 2011.

The U.S. field commanders for air refueling operations: Brigadier General Roy E. Uptegraff III, commander of the 313th Air Expeditionary Wing (left) briefs Colonel Ted Metzgar, commander of the Wisconsin Air National Guard's 128th Air Refueling Wing, at Morón AB prior to Metzgar taking command of the 313th AEW on June 14, 2011.
Courtesy of the U.S. Air Force, photo by Captain John P. Capra.

The availability of Morón AB greatly facilitated the stand up of the Calico Wing. Morón's isolated location in southern Spain, nearly 12,000-foot-long runway, huge parking ramp, large hangars, and robust personnel support facilities made it an unduplicated base in the region for tanker operations into Libya. Morón's suitability was not an accident; USAFE and AMC had invested heavily in it for years to maintain it as a "warm" base, ready to host a rapid influx of air mobility aircraft and personnel during contingencies. A USAFE unit, the 496th Air Base Squadron, ran the base with a cadre of about 100 active-duty personnel and up to 600 contract personnel, mostly Spanish nationals.

The arriving airmen did find some shortfalls in Morón's readiness to host such a large contingent. Most importantly, the base had released most of the Spanish contract personnel in a cost-cutting move. Morón's connectivity to the outside world also was inadequate to the demands of such a large unit. The tanker wing's initial communications were limited to public phone lines, sporadic unclassified email service, only one classified U.S. email line (SIPRNET), and no access to NATO's Battlefield Information Coordination and Exploitation System (BICES). Maintenance personnel, meanwhile, found that much of the available floor space in Morón's hangars was being used for storage. The main dining facility also was under construction.[27]

---

[27] Brigadier General Richard J. Evans, III, interview by Robert C. Owen, November 9, 2012. Colonel Evans served briefly as General Uptegraff's deputy commander at Morón and then as the Director of Mobility Forces (DIRMOBFOR), Allied Air Component (AAC), Izmir, during Operation Unified Protector.

The incoming and permanent party personnel solved all of these problems in short order. The contractor company rounded up as many of its former local employees as possible and quickly covered most services requirements. A combat communications squadron's visit soon cleared up the connectivity shortfalls, and Maintenance gained access to at least some hangar space.[28] Finally, the 496th expanded the kitchen staff at the Combined Officer/Enlisted Club to meet the messing challenge.

The greatest challenge to getting tankers into the fight was the absence of congressional authorization or funding. Although the Defense Department named the U.S. intervention Operation Odyssey Dawn, Congress never endorsed the intervention. Congress also did not give official recognition or authorization for U.S. participation in NATO's Operation Unified Protector. The Air Force found itself ordered into an overseas intervention that was "unnamed" by Congress and that came with neither a supplemental appropriation nor authorization to mobilize reservists. As a consequence, AMC and other commands had to call for volunteers to fill the new requirement and pay them with military personnel appropriation (MPA) funds. This was awkward, since Congress appropriated MPA funds to pay reservists for the days they spent in routine training activities, not in contingency operations.

Volunteerism and MPA "days" constituted a weak foundation upon which to build a long-term operation. The absence of a mobilization order left it up to individual reservists to decide if they wanted to become involved, and it potentially weakened the case they could make to their employers and families that they needed to be away for long periods. MPA funds were a limited resource and did not cover operating expenses, such as maintenance spares and fuel. Money for those had to come from supplemental appropriations from Congress—which weren't forthcoming—or the operation and maintenance (O&M) accounts of the Air Force, AMC, and individual units. Diverting O&M funds, in turn, immediately hampered unit-level efforts to keep planes ready for extended operations and their personnel fully trained for war.[29] From the start, then, Congress's inaction left AMC and its units to depend on a limited pool of volunteers and painful diversions of funds needed elsewhere. In other words, it put the command in a state of at least moderate surge.

AMC and AMC-gained reservists overcame the mobilization challenge through several actions. Most directly, AMC plundered its MPA accounts to pay deployed volunteers, though this presented what were regarded as large problems in long-term financial and training management.[30] Indirectly, General Johns selected General Uptegraff as the expeditionary wing commander, because he was well qualified for the job and because he had the professional standing and social connections to draw vol-

---

[28] Uptegraff interview, March 26, 2012; interview with senior member of Lieutenant General Ralph J. Jodice II's staff by Dr. Deborah Kidwell, May 24, 2012.

[29] Scott Fontaine, "Libya Causing Cuts in Training, Other Programs," *Air Force Times*, June 17, 2011.

[30] Merrill interview, February 27, 2012.

unteers to Morón.[31] His seniority and experience as a Guard leader gave him credibility to ask units and individuals to give their best efforts to keep Morón supplied with sufficient aircraft, crews, and ground support personnel for an indefinite period. His membership on the Air National Guard KC-135 Weapons System Council, composed of all KC-135 wing commanders, gave him a conduit for reaching out. To strengthen his recruiting efforts, Uptegraff asked Colonel Richard J. Evans III to join him at Morón as his vice commander. In addition to being the commander of the Nebraska ANG's 155th Air Refueling Wing at Lincoln, Evans was the chair of the Weapons System Council and the ANG's representative on AMC's Mobility Air Forces Council. He already had played a pivotal role in gathering up volunteers for the initial deployment to Morón, and Uptegraff expected him to continue in that role during deployment. Evans served in that position for a few days, until AMC replaced him with active duty officer Colonel David Cohen, vice commander of the 6th Air Mobility Wing at Florida's MacDill Air Force Base. AMC wanted an active duty officer to share the command echelon with Uptegraff, since the Morón wing would consist of both ARC and active aircraft. Having released Evans from the vice commander position, General Johns asked him to stay in Europe as his liaison to Allied Air Command Izmir, and to guide mobility preparations for NATO's takeover of the war.[32]

Another necessary task in getting operations underway was setting up the chain of command for Uptegraff's wing, a job that at least doctrinally should have been simple. Under normal doctrinal guidance, the Secretary of Defense would have directed TRANSCOM to transfer operational control (OPCON) of the deploying tankers to AFRICOM. For prolonged deployments, OPCON had the advantage of centralizing authority over the operations and logistical support of deployed units. Having received OPCON of the tankers, the commander of AFRICOM, Army General Carter F. Ham, would have pushed it down to the commander of his Air Force component, AFAFRICA, Major General Margaret H. Woodward, whose headquarters was at Ramstein AB, Germany.[33] Woodward was an ideal recipient of OPCON authority, since she was experienced in the entire range of air mobility operations and had just completed an assignment as vice commander of TRANSCOM's air component, the 18th Air Force (18 AF).

The fly in the command-relations ointment was that AMC leaders did not believe that the AFRICOM and AFAFRICA staffs were capable of exercising the full range of responsibilities incumbent in OPCON for a large tanker force, particularly one being financed out of AMC's MPA funds and manned by a rapid rotation of vol-

---

[31]   Benson interview, March 13, 2012.

[32]   Richard J. Evans to Robert C. Owen, email, "Subject: OUP Information," November 8, 2012.

[33]   Joint Publication 1 (JP-1), *Doctrine for the Armed Forces of the United States*, 2009, pp. IV-7 and IV-8.

Operation Odyssey Dawn Air Component Commander Major General Margaret Woodward.
Courtesy of the U.S. Air Force.

unteer personnel.[34] Organized only in 2007, AFRICOM's primary mission was to conduct political-military outreach, or "engagement," operations in Africa, including military-to-military training activities, humanitarian relief operations, and small-scale counterpiracy and counterterrorism activities. Fighting regional conflicts was on AFRICOM's list of missions, but General Woodward's air component staff never received personnel in the numbers and expertise that were needed to fight a "full-spectrum" air war. Indeed, Woodward's air operations center, the 617 AOC, was staffed partly on a "matrix" basis, meaning that many of its key members were drawn from other staff positions and available only on a part-time basis.[35]

Given these limitations, General Raymond Johns, Commander, AMC, had pressed Air Force General Duncan McNabb, Commander in Chief of TRANSCOM, to retain OPCON of the Morón tankers and give AFRICOM only tactical control (TACON) over them. TACON would allow General Woodward to direct the operations of the tankers at Morón, but leave logistics support and personnel management responsibilities in the hands of their parent wings and the AMC staff. TRANSCOM's effort to coordinate this OPCON/TACON split with the Joint Staff at the Pentagon, AFRICOM, and EUCOM took some time, since it would be a first for a deployed tanker unit. During the coordination process, the Defense Department issued orders

---

[34] Major General Rowayne A. "Wayne" Schatz Jr., AMC Director of Strategic Plans, Requirements and Programs (A5/8), interview by Robert C. Owen, February 28, 2012.

[35] Group interview with personnel serving in 603 AOC Air Mobility Division and USAFE/A9 during the Libyan campaign, by Robert C. Owen, March 21, 2012. Hereafter cited as "USAFE interview."

directing the usual OPCON transfer to AFRICOM. But with the agreement of General Woodward, Major General Moulton at EUCOM, USAFE Commander General Mark A. Welsh III, and their combatant commanders, General Johns was ultimately successful, and the principal air commanders' desire for a split arrangement soon superseded the initial JCS execution order's assignment of OPCON to AFRICOM.[36]

To address her staffing shortfalls, General Woodward amalgamated her 617 AOC staff with that of the 603 AOC, also located at Ramstein. As the AOC of USAFE's Third Air Force (3 AF), the 603rd was staffed to conduct a major, full-spectrum air war. In contrast to the 617 AOC's 115 billets, the 603rd had a staff of more than 400, which was experienced in the day-to-day oversight of the command's three fighter wings (the 31st, 48th, and 52nd), the 86th Air Mobility Wing, and 100th Air Refueling Wing. This expertise became available to General Woodward as soon as she moved into what became known as the 603/617 AOC. Woodward also took counsel from General Welsh and the 3 AF commander, Lieutenant General Frank Gorenc, both experienced combat air force commanders.[37] Taking advantage of all the assets at her command, General Woodward was able to put together the initial air campaign on the fly, going from a cold start to a full range of combat and support operations in a matter of a few days.

After NATO assumed control of intervention operations as Operation Unified Protector on March 31, command arrangements for the AMC-provided air refueling force changed at the higher levels. AFRICOM relinquished control of the operation to U.S. Navy Admiral Samuel J. Locklear III, commander of Allied Joint Force Command Naples (JFC Naples). Admiral Locklear's deputy, Royal Canadian Air Force (RCAF) Lieutenant-General Charles Bouchard, took direct control of operations as the Combined Joint Task Force Commander of Operation Unified Protector. Bouchard's air commander was USAF Lieutenant General Ralph J. Jodice II, commander of Allied Air Command Izmir (AAC Izmir). By the last week of March, Colonel Rich Evans had moved from Morón as AMC's liaison to AAC. For all practical purposes, he also served as Jodice's Director of Mobility Forces (DIRMOBFOR), supervising a staff of about 19 mobility specialists to plan and monitor tanker operations.[38] Evans accompanied General Jodice, when the latter shifted his combined force air component (CFAC) headquarters from Izmir to Poggio Renatico, Italy, around March 9, to take advantage of the better C2 facilities provided by NATO CAOC 5.[39]

---

[36] Interview with senior AMC officer, February 27, 2012; Benson interview, March 13, 2012; and Moulton interview, September 17–18, 2012.

[37] Moulton interview, September 17–18, 2012.

[38] Evans interview, November 9, 2012; and Evans, "OUP Information."

[39] Technically, General Jodice was the commander of the CFAC, the staff of which he moved to the CAOC to centralize planning and expedite his decisionmaking by getting "closer" to the flow of ISR and other information coming in from the Joint-Combined Operational Area. The CAOC was a separate, service-providing

Unified Protector CFACC Lieutenant General Ralph J. Jodice II receives a briefing on the Swedish JAS 39 Gripen fighter at Sigonella, Sicily, September 13, 2011.

Courtesy of the U.S. Navy, photo by PO2 Gary Prill.

The laydown of command authority over the Morón and USAFE tankers also did not change in its essentials. In response to General Jodice's combined statement of operational requirements, which was his list of the forces he needed for the operation, the U.S. Joint Chiefs of Staff made a transfer of authority (TOA) of the Morón and appropriate Mildenhall tankers to NATO.[40] This TOA specified that TRANSCOM and USAFE would retain U.S. OPCON over the Morón tankers, while General Jodice received NATO OPCON.[41] The difference was that U.S. OPCON included logistical responsibilities, while its NATO equivalent did not.[42] Thus the parent commands of the tankers remained responsible for their "care and feeding," while the forward air component commander assumed full power to plan and direct their operations in support of the campaign.

Within the U.S. command structure, arrangements were more convoluted than those of NATO. Technically, AFRICOM remained the supported combatant command, since the war was in its U.S.-designated area of responsibility. But, with no air forces assigned or attached to the command once NATO took over the campaign, AFRICOM had "no further role in the campaign . . . though [it] continued to 'flight

---

organization and, even during OUP, continued to plan and control other, completely separate NATO operations on behalf of other commands. See Lieutenant General Ralph J. Jodice II, interview by Robert C. Owen, November 14, 2012.

[40] Jodice interview, November 14, 2012.

[41] Lieutenant General Ralph J. Jodice II to Robert C. Owen, email, "Subject: Redacted interview outline notes," November 15, 2012.

[42] North Atlantic Treaty Organization, *NATO Glossary of Terms and Definitions*, AAP-06, 2010, March 22, 2010, p. 2-O-3; and interview with USAF officer from OUP CAOC by Robert C. Owen, November 1, 2012.

follow' many events and managed U.S. planning for tangential contingencies outside the scope of OUP."[43] Also, since both EUCOM/USAFE and TRANSCOM/AMC retained OPCON of their mobility forces, the two commands remained involved in their support and, consequently, highly interested in how NATO was employing them. Officers at the 100 ARW at Royal Air Force (RAF) Mildenhall, Great Britain, and in the 603/617 AOC's Air Mobility Division remained responsible for arranging for the "care and feeding" of tankers deployed from Mildenhall to Souda Bay, Crete, and then to France's Istres Air Force Base. They also tried to keep track of operational taskings coming out of the CFAC at CAOC 5. AMC, meanwhile, sent mobility planners to the combined 603/617 AOC and CAOC 5, and a EUCOM theater DIRMOBFOR, Brigadier General Scott P. Goodwin, to Ramstein. Goodwin was the commander of the 21st Expeditionary Mobility Task Force, stationed at Joint Base McGuire-Dix-Lakehurst, New Jersey, but covered the EUCOM DIRMOBFOR position as a core responsibility. He would stay at Ramstein until NATO and Colonel Evans were in firm control of tanker operations. Thus, the command relations picture had come to include a NATO air component in control of operations, and three U.S. combatant commands—TRANSCOM, EUCOM, and AFRICOM—with responsibilities or at least intense interest in tracking the employment of tanker forces and organizing their support.

Meanwhile, back at Morón, General Uptegraff was caught in the middle of the command relations imbroglio. He arrived at Morón fully expecting USAFE to be in charge of his unit, and was surprised to learn TRANSCOM/AMC intended to retain OPCON and that AFAFRICA would issue his daily operating orders. Recognizing the sensitivity and importance of the issue, Uptegraff took advantage of USAFE Commander General Welsh's visit on March 22 to urge him to issue written orders for the unit as quickly as possible.[44] The issue was still on the table two days later when the AMC commander, General Johns, visited Morón and told Uptegraff he still didn't have valid orders from either command. To that, the Guard General simply responded that he was from Pittsburgh and, therefore, was comfortable being a "Pirate."[45] Things got no less confusing on March 30, when USAFE and AMC simultaneously issued "G-Series" orders establishing Uptegraff's wing as the 406 AEW under USAFE OPCON and the 313 AEW under 18 AF OPCON, respectively.[46]

---

[43] Email from USAF officer in OUP CAOC to Karl Mueller, October 29, 2012.

[44] Email from officer in 521 Air Mobility Operations Wing, to Lieutenant General Robert Allardice, Vice Commander, Air Mobility Command, SUBJECT: DV Notes/Comments, March 25, 2011. In a later interview, General Moulton, the EUCOM/J3, suggested General Welsh had "fully agreed with TRANSCOM retaining OPCON," from the beginning of Odyssey Dawn and probably had come to Morón, which fell under his command, only to ensure that the base was ready to support Uptegraff's operations; Moulton interview, September 17–18, 2012.

[45] Uptegraff interview, March 26, 2012. Pittsburgh's National League baseball team is the "Pirates."

[46] Department of the Air Force, Headquarters United States Air Forces Europe, Special Order GD-25, March 30, 2011; and Department of the Air Force, Headquarters Air Mobility Command, Special Order GAA1-11, March 30, 2011.

Uptegraff was pressed from all directions by resource shortfalls, arriving aircraft and crews, problems with the setup of air space allocations and routes for tanker operations, and myriad other operational concerns. He decided that command relations weren't his biggest problem. As long as he had fuel, serviced aircraft, rested crews, and a minimal ability to coordinate his operations with the fighter units needing support, he decided to get into the fight and let higher echelons figure out who owned his wing. Over the next couple of weeks, he pragmatically reported up both of his command chains—to USAFE and AMC—and made specific requests for support to whichever command he felt was best placed to satisfy them. By the time the issue was settled in AMC's favor, the 313th AEW was engaged fully in the air war over Libya.

General Uptegraff's adroit handling of the OPCON issue was appropriate to his situation. Since no one questioned that General Woodward held TACON and, later, that General Jodice had NATO OPCON, he knew his operational guidance would come from those sources, and that AMC had the stick on logistical and personnel support. Logistics was never a major problem, since USAFE energetically worked his local base support issues, while AMC handled personnel, aircraft, and supply issues. The arrangement also allowed AMC to rotate personnel and aircraft with greater agility and rationality within the global tanker fleet than might have been possible to coordinate through USAFE and NATO. AMC also was left to pay for all of those MPA days—an item of great importance to AFRICOM and EUCOM, given the absence of supplemental funding from Congress.

Not surprisingly, AMC leaders consistently endorsed the OPCON/TACON split as essential to AMC's ability to conduct rapid global mobility.[47] They argued that, particularly in a period of "deep surge," global cognizance and access to the tanker fleet allowed the command to extract maximum productivity from its assets and cover as many of its assigned missions as possible. During OUP, for example, AMC's retention of OPCON less TACON, and the presence of Colonel Evans at CAOC 5, facilitated the occasional application of unused OUP tankers to other AMC and USAFE missions. With the approval of General Jodice, Colonel Evans or his later replacement, Colonel Kenneth D. Lewis, would notify 18 AF or USAFE of available aircraft as soon as the CFAC published the daily air tasking order. The home commands might then task their aircraft against another requirement, as long as they did not impact the OUP mission.[48] This flexibility had limits, of course. When General Jodice caught wind of "another command wanting our tankers," he reminded AMC that "you can't do that, they're TOAed to NATO by a SECDEF order . . . You can take them back; but you

---

[47] Major General Martin interview, February 29, 2012.

[48] Evans interview, November 9, 2012; Major General Martin interview, February 29, 2012; Brigadier General Lawrence Martin, Jr., Vice Commander, 18th Air Force, interview by Robert C. Owen, February 29, 2012.

have to go through the formal process."[49] Despite this, the tanker "swings" worked well, allowing AMC to manage them in the global system, while NATO retained first refusal on their capacity.

Some USAFE operations managers did identify logistics and force management challenges created by the OPCON/TACON split.[50] AMC's retention of the logistics responsibilities of OPCON, the managers felt, confused and slowed requests for logistics support. This was particularly the case at Istres, France, where multi-point refueling system (MPRS)–equipped tankers from USAFE's 100th Air Refueling Group and the 313 AEW collocated later in the operation. In one case, obtaining a simple one-time flight waiver for a Morón tanker from the 92nd Wing at Fairchild AFB, Washington, required a meandering, seven-phase coordination effort involving Fairchild, the 313 AEW, the 100 ARG, the 603/617 AOC, 18 AF, and a group of unhappy sergeants in between. This was a consistent problem, and led General Johns in August to rate communication between USAFE and AMC regarding Istres maintenance issues as "poor."[51] USAFE staffers reported that giving NATO OPCON authority to the Combined Forces Air Component at Poggio complicated their own ability to monitor the maintenance status of airborne aircraft and manage USAFE's tanker operations as a whole. Because they "never had a coherent mobility picture in NATO," the USAFE staffers felt that they lacked the ability to make timely logistical and aircraft scheduling adjustments to maintenance problems, changes in ongoing Libyan missions, or reallocations of sorties among the other missions they were trying to cover.[52]

Beyond the sometimes-heated dispute over command relations, air-refueling operations in the Libyan conflict were fairly ordinary. For the most part, tankers flew out of Morón and Istres, crossed the Mediterranean, orbited for long hours off the coast, and offloaded fuel as required. These missions tended to be unusually long, even for tanker operations. The flight time between the two tanker bases and Libya was between two and two and a half hours each way. Tankers often remained in or near their orbits for another five or six hours, depending on when and how many fighters pulled up to take on fuel. KC-135s departing the area often transferred unused fuel to KC-10s standing by in reliability orbits to cover unexpected requirements or emergencies. Since the Libyan army and air force presented some localized air defense threats until well into the summer, tankers stayed offshore until the last few weeks of the campaign.

---

[49] Jodice interview, November 14, 2012. "TOA" refers to the U.S.-NATO transfer of authority giving control of the tankers to NATO.

[50] Benson interview, March 13, 2012. General Benson believed there was good understanding and acceptance of the arrangement at the 3- and 4-star levels, but the problem was "getting field graders to accept it."

[51] Lieutenant Colonel Barbara M. Claunch, 100th Air Refueling Group, "OUP Organization and Air Force Doctrine—Tanker Perspective," briefing, November, 2011, slide 9; AMC History Office, "AOR Trip Discussion Points," notes of discussion of AMC/CC, General Raymond Johns' trip to Europe and Middle East, August 23, 2011.

[52] USAFE interview.

Mission planning and command and control for the AMC contributions to both the humanitarian relief efforts in Japan and Operation Odyssey Dawn were led by AMC's Tanker Airlift Control Center at Scott AFB, Ill. As AMC's hub for global operations, the TACC plans, schedules, and directs a fleet of nearly 1,300 mobility aircraft in support of strategic airlift, air refueling, and aeromedical evacuation operations around the world.
Courtesy of the U.S. Air Force, photo by Captain Justin Brockhoff.

Despite the routine nature of tanker operations during OOD and OUP, the distances involved and the near-absence of other suitable airfields available for KC-135 operations provide some insights useful to Air Force planning. Compared to the Southwest Asian and Pacific areas of operation, the Libyan AOR was relatively compact. Even then, air-refueling support was critical, and the size of the tanker fleet determined the scale and tempo of combat operations. In the rush to begin initial operations, AFAFRICA asked USAFE and AMC for as many tankers as they could provide, then planned combat operations accordingly. The same situation persisted during the NATO phase, where tanker availability was the main limiting factor for the pace of air operations.[53] Given the distances between fighter bases and the combat zone, combat air patrols and on-call strike packages could not be maintained without robust tanker support. To increase efficiency, General Jodice and Colonel Evans spent considerable energy looking for tanker bases closer to the fight. However, even in the developed environment of the Mediterranean region, this proved impractical. Airfields with the requisite 10,000-foot runways either lacked the fuel capacity required to support

---

[53] Evans interview, November 9, 2012.

tanker operations, were civil airports unavailable for military flights, or did not have ramp space available to park tankers.[54]

During this study, the KC-135R's performance limitations naturally led to discussions of the KC-46 that is currently under development. Unquestionably, the KC-46 compares well with the older aircraft it will replace. Benefiting from a half-century of aeronautical development since the Stratotanker was designed, the KC-46 will be substantially more reliable and operationally flexible.[55] With a much larger design than the KC-135R, the KC-46 will carry more than twice as many cargo pallets, sixteen compared to six, and its engines also will be significantly more fuel efficient.[56] Further, all KC-46s will be air-refuelable to extend their range and flexibility. The power of the KC-46's engines also shortens its takeoff rolls compared to the KC-135, with significant impact on the bigger plane's basing flexibility and productivity. On a standard day (sea level and 59°F), for example, a KC-46 could have flown fully loaded from the 8,000-foot runways at Sigonella Naval Air Station during the Libyan conflict, while the KC-135R could not.[57]

Another lesson from the Libyan air campaign was that it was a valid test of the limits of ARC volunteerism, but not of the long-term viability of the present mix of ARC and active units in the tanker force. The willingness of so many reservists to come forward over a period of months without a formal mobilization testified to their patriotism and unit loyalty. But by mid-July, the volunteer pool was drying up. To keep things going, the Air Force took the innovative step of diverting active person-

---

[54] Uptegraff interview, March 26, 2012; Evans interview, November 9, 2012.

[55] As a consequence of Boeing and USAF proprietary restrictions, there is no single, publically available source of comparative performance data for the KC-135 and KC-46. Consequently, the author extracted and derived the following data and comparisons from several sources including: Boeing, "767 Airplane Characteristics for Airport Planning," September, 2005; Air Force Pamphlet 10-1403, *Air Mobility Planning Factors*, December 18, 2003; Paul Jackson, ed., *Janes All the World's Aircraft 2012–13*, "Boeing 767-300ER," London: HIS Global, 2012, p. 998; and the USAF's fact sheets on the KC-135R and KC-46. The findings in this section, therefore, should be understood as derivative, but probably within a few percentage points of the actual numbers.

[56] The KC-46's two Pratt and Whitney 4062 engines will produce a total of 124,000 pounds of thrust and together burn about 10,000 pounds of fuel per hour at cruise. With its four CFM-56 engines, the KC-135 burns about 12,000 pounds per hour to produce some 86,000 pounds of thrust at cruise.

[57] For all its modernity, the KC-46's general performance specifications in some circumstances will offer only a marginal improvement over those of the KC-135R. The newer aircraft's derivation from a twin-aisle commercial design means that it will carry around a lot of structural weight in relation to the amount of fuel it will bring to the fight. At 412,000 pounds maximum takeoff weight, the KC-46 will carry 207,000 pounds of offload fuel. The 322,000-pound takeoff weight of the KC-135R includes 200,000 pounds of fuel. Thus, at the point of takeoff, the two aircraft are nearly equal in capacity. As distances increase, however, the KC-46's more efficient engines gradually give it an advantage. In a Libya-like operating profile (two hours out, four hours holding on a tanker track, two hours back), the KC-135R would have about 100,000 pounds of fuel to offload, while the KC-46 would offer around 120,000 pounds. If they had been permitted to operate from Sigonella, however, the KC-135R's payload would have decreased by as much as 60,000 pounds, depending on ambient temperatures, while the KC-46's would not have changed.

nel and aircraft from the Middle East to Morón, and mobilizing ARC units to back-fill the vacated positions in "the desert." The move was expedient, since U.S. Central Command had mobilization authority and money to pay for its operations, whether active or ARC personnel performed them. In contrast, AMC was running out of MPA money but had to pay the active personnel anyway. If anything, the ARC-active swap exemplified the deep integration of the ARC and active components of the USAF. While it did little to reduce the total stress on the air mobility system, it did at least buy time for the Libyan campaign to continue.

Air Combat Command

Often misunderstood even within the Air Force, Air Combat Command is a global force provider in much the same way as AMC or Air Force Space Command. Within the command's directorate of operations (A3), the Operations Division (A3O) manages the tasking of all Air Force conventional forces, regardless of their owning combatant command, except for airlift, air refueling, and special operations. This oversight authority includes the tasking of theater-assigned forces to support operations in other theaters. When the Joint Staff receives a Request for Forces (RFF) from a combatant command for conventional forces, the Operations Division recommends which units can fill the request. Its criteria for selection include the condition of the units, the degree to which they have been tasked for deployed operations already, and Air Force commitments elsewhere. Presuming that all echelons agree with A3O's recommendations, the Air Force Operations Group cuts the general, or "G-series," orders for units to deploy. Since virtually every unit in ACC and the overseas Air Force component commands is embedded in the ongoing rotation of air expeditionary forces (AEFs), any unexpected calls for forces necessitate far-reaching "reworks of apportionments and taskings." These usually involve painful trade-offs that can increase the risks of current or planned operations in other CCMDs. These decisions have become increasingly difficult in the last decade, as the Air Force has constricted in size and budget without proportional reduction in its commitments and taskings.[58]

Uncertainty over the Libyan mission made an already complicated force management problem even more so. As Libya heated up in late February and early March, AFAFRICA Commander General Woodward began issuing requests for forces. ACC began identifying the appropriate units and personnel for deployment. But political uncertainty surrounding the likelihood and scope of American intervention, and the impact that premature deployments would have on other operations, meant that actual movement orders were slow to emerge from the Joint Staff and the Air Force. Then, when EUCOM covered UNSCR 1970's no-fly zone with forces in-theater already, ACC's planning for immediate deployments went by the boards. Instead, the command began building deployment lists for the possibility that Libyan operations might

---

[58] ACC Operations Division (A3O) interview by Deborah H. Kidwell and Robert C. Owen, March 12, 2012.

extend beyond 45 days. Only a handful of ISR aircraft initially went forward. As a result, when the abrupt passage of UNSCR 1973 prompted a flurry of new RFFs from EUCOM, ACC had to rebuild its force management plan anew and coordinate it with the commands that would be losing support to free up assets to go to Europe. This imposed delays on the process, as did initial confusion over how much other air forces would carry the combat effort. These unexpected delays irritated and confused local commanders, particularly General Woodward, and theater operational planning staffs. But, at least from the perspective of ACC, the delays were unavoidable under the circumstances.[59]

Fortunately for the USAF, its NATO allies, Sweden, and Arab partner states provided significant combat and combat support forces that greatly reduced ACC's necessary contribution to Unified Protector. With partner air forces providing most of the counterair, strike, and much of the combat support assets for the campaign, ACC's presentation of forces to AFAFRICA was much smaller proportionately than that of AMC. Throughout Unified Protector, ACC presented a flight of six F-16CJs from the 77th and 55th squadrons of the 20th Fighter Wing, based at Shaw AFB, South Carolina, to USAFE's 31st Fighter Wing at Aviano AB, Italy. In conjunction with a similar number of U.S. Navy EF-18G Growlers and Italian Air Force Tornado ECR aircraft, these planes provided the bulk of the coalition's suppression/destruction of enemy air defenses (SEAD/DEAD) capabilities.[60] Additionally, ACC dispatched ISR assets from the 9th and 55th Reconnaissance Wings at Beale AFB, California, and Offutt AFB, Nebraska, respectively. These included TR-1/U-2s, at least two MQ-1B Predators, and E-8 Joint STARS and RC-135 Rivet Joint aircraft. It also dispatched E-3 Sentry AWACS aircraft from the 552nd Air Control Wing, Tinker AFB, Oklahoma. Finally, ACC provided several hundred active, Guard, and Reserve members to augment various headquarters and staff units at AFAFRICA, USAFE, CAOC 5, and on the command ship USS *Mount Whitney*.[61]

These deployments, small as they were in relation to ACC's overall capabilities, strained the command and placed several units in "surge." Qualitatively, the Air Force identifies units in surge whenever their operational commitments force them to delay personnel leaves, training, and or maintenance actions in order to handle immediate operational tasks. Quantitatively, the service measures surge by the dwell-to-deployment ratios of its units. These ratios reflect the amount of time that units and individuals spend at and away from their home stations, families, and normal routines.

---

[59] ACC Operations Division (A3O) interview, March 12, 2012; USAFE interview; and General Margaret Woodward, interview by Deborah Kidwell, March 7, 2012. Woodward pointed out in this interview that only four of her 94 RFFs had been filled by the start of Odyssey Dawn.

[60] Senior Airman Daniel Phelps, "NATO Called—Shaw Responded: Part 1 of 4," Shaw Air Force Base, S.C.: 20th Fighter Wing Public Affairs, online, February 3, 2012; Aeronautica Militare, "Libya (2011): 'Odyssey Dawn' and 'Unified Protector' Operations," online, undated.

[61] See Appendix B for overall orders of battle.

As a target for active forces, the Air Force aims at deployment-to-dwell ratios of 1:2 (.33), meaning one-third of the time deployed and two-thirds at home station. The established minimum ratio is 1:1 (.50). For ARC units, the targets are 1:5 (.16) normal and 1:4 (.20) minimum. In ACC's case, Unified Protector pushed some active units well below their normal dwell ratios, with at least one unit hitting 2:1 (.67) and others obliged to defer some training.[62]

United States Air Forces Europe

The boundaries delineating the areas of operation of U.S. geographic combatant commands are considered nearly sacred. That put USAFE in an interesting position as a global force provider during Odyssey Dawn and Unified Protector. As the air component of U.S. European Command, its area of operations extended southward across the Mediterranean to the territorial waters of Libya, twelve miles from the North African coast. Thus, many of the major battles of the Libyan civil war occurred within sight of USAFE's operational boundaries. But Libya was in U.S. Africa Command's AOR (see Figure 4.1). So AFAFRICA had the job of fighting the air war, even though its opera-

Figure 4.1
U.S. Combatant Command Areas of Responsibility

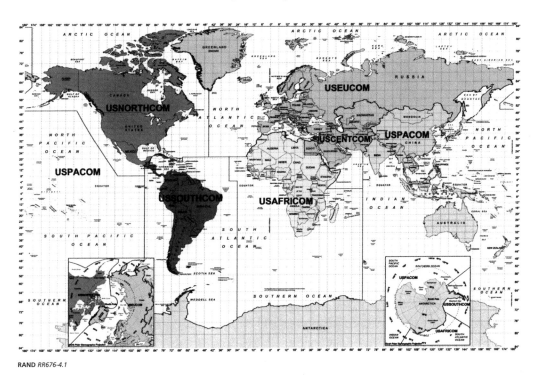

RAND RR676-4.1

---

[62] ACC Operations Division (A3O) interview, March 12, 2012; Fontaine, "Libya Causing Cuts in Training, Other Programs."

tional component, 17th Air Force (17 AF), had minimal capability to plan and conduct combat air operations. It had no assigned operational units, and its 617th AOC was small. The personnel in the 617th were as trained and ready as those in any other AOC, but many of the 617 AOC's 115 billets were empty and others were manned on a split-duty or "matrix" basis. By comparison, around 400 personnel manned USAFE's 603rd Air Operations Center, and they were experienced in the day-to-day oversight of the command's three fighter wings (the 31st, 48th, and 52nd), the 86th Air Mobility Wing and the 100th Air Refueling Wing. So, during the war in Libya, USAFE found itself as a sort of airpower Gulliver supporting AFAFRICA's Lilliputian joust with an ogre at the edge of its own operational back yard.

USAFE did whatever it could to underpin AFAFRICA's success. During Odyssey Dawn and for the first week or so of Unified Protector, USAFE presented the bulk of all USAF forces made available to AFRICOM. The 48th Fighter Wing (FW) at RAF Lakenheath sent F-15Es to Sigonella Naval Air Station and Aviano Air Base, Italy. The 52nd FW sent A-10s and defense suppression F-16CJs to Aviano. The F-16–equipped 31st FW basically fought in place at Aviano. Even the tankers at RAF Mildenhall moved forward, initially to Hellenic Air Force Base Souda, Crete, and then to Istres, France. During Odyssey Dawn, the 603/617 AOC enabled more than 2,000 sorties and identified more than 1,400 targets.[63] By the first week or so of Operation Unified Protector, the combined commitments of the various non-U.S. allied air forces grew to approximately 120 to 130 fighter, 13 air refueling, and 20–25 support aircraft.[64] By that time, U.S. air units were conducting air patrol and strike sorties only on an exceptional basis. Most deployed USAFE units were returning or preparing to return to their home fields.

As in the case of the other Air Force major commands involved, the relatively small commitment of forces to OOD and OUP pushed some USAFE units to the edge of their available capabilities. The 480th Fighter Squadron, for example, repositioned to Aviano even though it was in its final weeks of preparation for a rotation to Afghanistan. The 100th Air Refueling Wing was under particular stress, since it remained heavily committed throughout OOD and OUP. At the beginning of Odyssey Dawn, the Wing received verbal orders to generate as many tankers as possible for Libyan operations. With around 15 KC-135s on hand, the Wing's 351st Air Refueling Squadron committed to eight sorties per day, leaving its other aircraft in maintenance or covering the unit's training, aeromedical evacuation, and transatlantic mission support taskings. Even this load was unsupportable over the long run and, when the 351st

---

[63] Major Paul D. Baldwin, "That's a Wrap for 603rd AOC in 2011," USAFE-AFAFRICA: 3rd Air Force Public Affairs, January 3, 2012.

[64] These numbers are based on several sources, and the total number of aircraft involved in the operation varied frequently. The NATO fact sheet reports 260 aircraft were involved in OUP. In that case, the non-U.S. commitment would have been about 60 percent of the general effort and much more than that of the fighter effort.

shifted from Souda to Istres on April 20, the Wing reduced its commitment to six sorties per day. Conducting "split operations" from both Mildenhall and Istres put the Wing's staff and unit personnel at the limits of what they could do, left some wing offices empty, and pushed its dwell-to-deployment ratio to 1:1.27 (.56 deployment).[65]

As in the case of AMC and its tankers, EUCOM retained U.S. OPCON of its OOD/OUP-committed KC-135Rs. This arrangement spared AFAFRICA and CFAC significant logistical and management burdens, and empowered the experts at the 100th ARW and the 617/603 AOC to get the most from the tankers at Istres and Mildenhall. Still, the arrangement unquestionably further complicated the flow of information and decisions within the air refueling effort. As the commander of the 100th Operations Group pointed out in regard to the amalgamation of USAFE and AMC MPRSs-equipped tankers at Istres, "We had aircraft responding to two different combatant chains of command in response to orders from a combined headquarters in support of a third combatant command operating from the base of a foreign air force." Also, as discussed above, the arrangement was fraught with the possibility of crossed signals and delayed actions, particularly in the realms of air space control, mission planning, and logistics.[66]

Air Force Space Command

As components of the U.S. Strategic Command (STRATCOM), Air Force Space Command (AFSPC) and its various elements provided vital—though often unseen—support to war fighters in the European and African theaters during Operations Odyssey Dawn and Unified Protector. Space planners and controllers generally agreed that Libya represented what one described as "a pretty standard inventory of space support requirements," but the conflict nevertheless raised caution flags regarding resource limitations and future capabilities.[67]

An understanding of Air Force space support to Odyssey Dawn and Unified Protector begins with an appreciation of its organizational context. U.S. Strategic Command exercises command authority over virtually all U.S. military space assets. As a service component of STRATCOM, AFSPC trains, organizes, and equips Air Force forces for "presentation" to STRATCOM for operations. To actually conduct operations, the STRATCOM commander assigns OPCON of space forces to the Joint Functional Component Command for Space (JFCC Space), headquartered at Vandenberg AFB, California, and under the command of Lieutenant General Susan Helms

---

[65] 100th Operations Group interview by Robert C. Owen, March 20, 2012.

[66] 100th Operations Group interview; 100th Maintenance Group, "100 MXG OOD/OUP Lessons Learned," sometime in November, 2011, slide 6; and 100th Operations Group, "100 OG OOD/OUP Lessons Learned," also sometime in November, 2011, slides 6-14, 28-31, and 40-2.

[67] Group interview with 614 AOC and JSpOC officers by Deborah Kidwell and Robert C. Owen, April 24, 2012. Hereafter referenced as "JSpOC group interview."

during the Libya campaign. General Helms, in turn, executed her OPCON authority through the Joint Space Operations Center (JSpOC), also at Vandenberg, to provide combat effects in and through space in direct support to combatant commanders in their areas of responsibility.

Overseas, combatant commanders usually interface with JFCC Space and the JSpOC through their space coordination authorities. During the Libyan campaign, Major General Woodward acted as AFRICOM's Space Coordination Authority and delegated the associated responsibilities to the commander of her 603 Air Operations Center. Within the 603 AOC, a single space weapons officer in the Strategy Division and a small group of space controllers in the Combat Operations Division, led by Major Justin Littig, did the legwork of planning, directing, and supervising space operations and coordinating access to space capabilities with the JSpOC. A final but critical member of the space team at AFAFRICA was the Director of Space Forces (DS4), Colonel Vincent Jefferson, who served as the principal space adviser to General Woodward and provided senior-level access into the space community.[68]

Fortunately for the success of initial Odyssey Dawn operations, Generals Woodward and Helms did not wait for formal direction to begin the integration of their staffs and planning. In mid-February, General Woodward directed Colonel Jefferson and her AOC staff to begin planning for possible operations in Libya. Fully aware of increasing tensions in the area, General Helms simultaneously directed the JSpOC to keep an eye on the region and pushed STRATCOM to begin full-scale planning. The JSpOC director, Colonel Chris Moss, told his Strategy Division chief, Colonel Miguel Colon, and his lead planner, Lieutenant Colonel Kevin Carlson, to begin planning support for AFAFRICA operations with the 603 AOC.[69] They immediately began collaborating with Colonel Jefferson and the space weapons officer in the Strategy Cell, Captain Andrew Emslie, to develop a supportable space plan. Carlson and Emslie, as strategists, constituted the main line of coordination.

Carlson and Emslie had recently participated in a Joint Crisis Action Planning Conference for a EUCOM Tier 1 exercise that facilitated their collaboration. It included features such as maintaining a no-fly zone and interdicting enemy road convoys that presaged events to come in Libya.[70] That conference and the parallel organizational structures of the two operations centers allowed their staffs to communicate easily and

---

[68] Interview with JSpOC officers by Robert C. Owen, July 24, 2012.

[69] Lieutenant General John E. Hyten, Vice Commander, Air Force Space Command, email to Thomas E. Erhard, Special Assistant, Air Force Chief of Staff, "Air Force Space Command with examples v6.docx," July 19, 2012. Based on reviews by AFSPC personnel of an earlier draft of this section, General Hyten provided consolidated recommendations for changes and expansions.

[70] Within the National Exercise Plan (NEP), Tier I exercises are centered on White House directed, government-wide strategy and policy-related issues and require participation by all appropriate government departments and agencies. See Department of Defense Instruction 3020.47, *DoD Participation in the National Exercise Program (NEP)*, January 29, 2009, for further discussion of these policies and definitions.

to anticipate one another's planning deadlines and information needs throughout the forthcoming conflict. Indeed, Emslie and other officers in the 603rd had produced a draft campaign plan by early March, which became the basis for the actual OOD-OUP plan. This was fortunate, since the gap between receipt of the formal execution order for planning and the start of operations was 24 hours, or no longer for space leaders and planners than for anyone else in the Air Force. Had they waited for formal clearance to begin planning, they would have been hard-pressed to have the necessary effects in place to support early operations.[71]

AFAFRICA's planners had access to the capabilities of a formidable space order of battle. STRATCOM controlled a large fleet of satellites and their support systems—about 63 at the end of 2011. These satellites included the ubiquitously important GPS; the Defense Support Program (DSP); Space Based Infrared System (SBIRS); the Defense Meteorological Satellite Program (DMSP); and communications satellites such as Milstar, Defense Satellite Communications System (DSCS), and Wideband Global SATCOM (WGS). It also happened that the military lineup in 2011 included Tactical Satellite (TACSAT) III, a developmental hyperspectral imaging system.

In addition to these systems, U.S. leaders, planners, and organizations in Europe had access to systems and capabilities provided by other space operators. These included the output of National Oceanographic and Atmospheric Administration (NOAA) weather satellites, and systems operated by the National Reconnaissance Office (NRO), the National Geospatial-Intelligence Agency (NGA), and the National Security Agency (NSA). The satellite constellations and products of these organizations generally are classified, but are noted for their high quality and breadth of coverage in visual and electronic formats. Also, two commercial companies, GeoEye and Digital-Globe, operated five satellites between them and sold images and data to the military that were only marginally less detailed in some formats than those that government systems provided.[72]

Each of the military systems brought invaluable capabilities to the tasks of building a comprehensive picture of Libyan forces and following the progress of events on the ground. The 2nd Space Operations Squadron operated GPS, which enhanced the planning of virtually every operation, from airdrops, air refueling, search and rescue, reconnaissance, and precision weapons delivery to airmen using GPS data on their personal phones to find hotels, restaurants, and navigate the roads back to their deployment bases in unfamiliar places. NOAA spacecraft's weather information was of obvious and similarly widespread utility. The DSP and SBIRS systems were particularly important to planners and commanders, since they detected and characterized the infrared signals of events such as missile launches, artillery fire, explosions, and aircraft crashes. TACSAT II's ability to scan a wide electromagnetic spectrum provided

---

[71] JSpOC group interview and interview with JSpOC officers.

[72] James Risen, "A Military and Intelligence Clash over Spy Satellites," *New York Times*, April 19, 2012.

unprecedented capabilities to analyze potential targets. For example, the system could tell whether the grass in a soccer stadium was real atop dirt or plastic on concrete and whether a structure might be hidden underneath.[73] It also could distinguish whether a vehicle was civilian or military based upon its paint.[74]

The products of the GeoEye and DigitalGlobe commercial systems filled valuable functions as well. Most importantly, they provided information that the USAF could pass on to any partner without encountering classification issues. In general, no coalition space operator, including the United States, was willing to share information that would reveal the full capabilities or operational characteristics of its military space systems. As a result, U.S. intelligence analysts in the CAOC could look at imagery from the NRO, but could not share it with their counterparts from other nations. All coalition partners used the GPS system, of course. But the Space Cell in the 603 AOC could not warn them of pending degradations of the system due to the ever-changing positions of individual satellites. So, through a program called Eagle Vision, the Air Force relied on the commercial operators to provide some 75 "products," which augmented U.S. organic capabilities and which could be passed on to partner air forces to support planning and operations.[75]

The short straw in American capabilities to provide space support to the European and African theaters was manpower—there simply weren't enough space professionals in the system to fully exploit all the capabilities available all the time. Within the 603 AOC Space Cell, only one officer and four noncommissioned officers (NCOs) were available to execute space operations, and one of the NCOs was not yet certified for the task. Problematically, the Space Cell saw its workload increase from single-shift, peacetime routine to supporting sustained combat operations without reinforcement, except for one officer that Colonel Jefferson dragooned from AFSPC. This augmentation allowed the Space Cell to operate on a 24/7 basis with the rest of the AOC staff until May 4, when the exhaustion of its members required a return to single-shift operation. The pressure remained equally high on the other two space specialists available, who operated without backup in their critical positions.[76] Meanwhile, the JSpOC felt comfortable with the space support team it established to liaise with the 603 AOC, but acknowledged it would have been hard-pressed to set up another team for another contingency or cover an expansion of Libyan operations.[77]

The generally tight manning of space forces emerged as a root cause of several disconnects between theater and global operators. On one side of the issue, the space

---

[73] Air Force Space Command Public Affairs, "Space Command TacSat 3 burns up in atmosphere," May 5, 2012.

[74] Hyten comments.

[75] Hyten comments.

[76] Interview with JSpOC officers.

[77] JSpOC group interview.

team at Ramstein voiced several concerns regarding the support they received from CONUS. First, they emphasized the challenge of getting augmentation personnel in a timely manner. While they perceived that other commands, such as ACC and AMC, sent out planners on a preemptive basis, they felt that STRATCOM and AFSPC held fast to formal RFF procedures that were too slow for the pace of events. Some Ramstein team members also reported their sense that JFCC Space and the JSpOC were neither as sensitive to their specific support requirements nor as flexible in providing the support they needed. When, for example, the Space Cell requested that the JSpOC tailor its daily report on GPS availability to the theater's specific needs, it received a response that they would have to take the general report sent to all theaters and do its own analysis. Also, when the JSpOC seemed slow in adjusting its overhead persistent infrared (OPIR) watch boxes over Libya to match unfolding operations, the Space Cell felt obliged to make an end run directly to the unit operating the system. This serious violation of JFCC Space procedures resulted in further friction with the JSpOC.[78]

On the other side of the issue, the JSpOC pointed out that its manning was no less stringent than that of the 603/617 AOC. Like the rest of the Air Force, the JSpOC was fully employed, covering a global spread of commitments and its training obligations when the Japanese earthquake relief effort and then Odyssey Dawn fell on it in the same month. Moreover, the JSpOC was not manned or chartered to send out augmenters to the theaters. JSpOC leaders, however, were willing to send out some personnel to Ramstein or CAOC 5, but never received a validated request from STRATCOM. When all of these limitations were considered, they acknowledged, the JSpOC's capacity to provide 15-person space support teams for different operations and to cover special requests for tailored reports and OPIR watch box adjustments likely fell short of theater desires.[79]

Regardless of the obstacles they faced, however, the space practitioners in CONUS and Europe ensured that the war fighters received as much support as possible. Their first order of business was to ensure that general services—mainly GPS, communications, and weather support—were running and connected to the necessary nodes.[80] Next, Air Force space elements contributed to the frantic effort to update the overall intelligence picture of what was going on in Libya. This was a formidable task, given the lack of attention that U.S. intelligence agencies had allotted to the country during the preceding decade of rapprochement with Libya and wars in Iraq and Afghanistan. Still, with access to the outputs of dozens of satellites, numerous ISR aircraft, and human sources from within Libya itself, the United States and then NATO quickly created a comprehensive and persistent mosaic of the situation. Air Force space sys-

---

[78] Interview with JSpOC officers.

[79] JSpOC group interview.

[80] JSpOC group interview.

tems, particularly DSP, SBIRS, and TACSAT, contributed importantly to building that mosaic and supporting targeting and other planning efforts.

The Air Force space team's ability to pool the "feeds" from its individual systems into a cohesive "battlespace characterization" that drew Major General Woodward into the 603 AOC's Space Cell on OOD's first night. Working together, the 603rd, the 2nd Space Warning Squadron, the JSpOC, and national agencies provided the best and, in some cases, the only awareness of the overall situation in the theater and of the results of specific strikes. This situational awareness allowed General Woodward and other leaders from the first night of Odyssey Dawn to watch many air strikes and other operations in real time.

Space capabilities thus were integrated into every mission conducted in support of the Libya operation. They were so reliably and transparently provided at the time that some users and later analysts might miss the great resource investments and human efforts required to make them available. That would be an unfortunate oversight, since the Libyan experience reinforced the necessity of managing and capitalizing space forces energetically and astutely.

Allies

Other sections of this report describe the contributions of individual national air forces in great detail, so this section will examine allied contributions only in terms of their implications for USAF policy and future operations. During the conflict, the main concerns were with the interoperability of forces, particularly in their ability to share classified information, and with shortages of precision munitions in the arsenals of some air forces.

The condition of allied air forces in 2011 was a consequence of two decades of shrinking budgets and strategic transformation that constrained decisionmaking. Following the fall of the Soviet Union, all NATO states sought to reduce military spending and apply the resulting "peace dividends" to social programs. By 2005, the CIA estimated that Britain was spending about 2.7 percent of its gross domestic product on its military forces. The other two major NATO military powers, France and Germany, were spending 2.6 and 1.5 percent, respectively. By comparison, the United States was spending 4.06 percent.[81] Military forces shrank accordingly. By 2011, most NATO and other European air forces presented personnel rosters and combat aircraft strengths that were only about one-third to one-half of their 1990 levels. Moreover, in their efforts to keep as many combat aircraft on line as possible, non-U.S. NATO air forces funded other capability areas and their logistics support only sparsely. Despite the development of national strategies to increase their "out of area" capabilities, most

---

[81]   CIA, "Country Comparison: Military Expenditures," *The World Factbook*.

NATO air forces consequently were deficient in their on-hand munitions stocks, air mobility capabilities, and C4ISR (command, control, communications, computers, intelligence, surveillance, and reconnaissance) assets by the time they decided to deploy to Libya.[82] Indeed, while the non-U.S. Alliance members and partners between them came up with about 120 fighters for Libyan operations, they supplied only about a dozen tankers, a similar number of surveillance aircraft of various types, and some of them ran low on precision munitions during the campaign.

In the overall context of operations and their implications for the future of the USAF, the scale and details of the contributions of non-U.S. NATO states to the air refueling force have particular significance.[83] The most obvious issue was scale: The entirety of NATO was able to contribute only about 12 to 15 tankers to the fight at any particular time. France led the way, deploying six C-135FRs and a tanker C-130 to Crete. Britain sent two VC-10s or Tristars to Decimomannu AB, Sardinia, and several others to Cyprus. Canada deployed two Polaris tankers to Trapani AB, Sicily. The Dutch sent a KDC-10 to Sardinia until April 4, when they had to pull it away from OUP to cover other commitments. The Swedes brought a C-130T and the Italians made a KC-767 available. Thus, apart from the United States, the Alliance was only able to establish on the order of a 1:10 tanker/shooter force ratio, and contribute about one-quarter of the overall air refueling effort. The 25 or so USAF tankers at Morón and Istres contributed the rest of the effort, though even their addition only brought the tanker/shooter ratio to 1:4. The near-term impacts of the limited number of tankers available were that the Air Mobility Command had to scrape its buckets of MPA funds and reserve volunteerism to make up some of the shortfall, and CFAC planners had to ration tanker support in ways that restricted the productivity of some air units.

The limited number of tankers involved tended to reinforce the advantages to smaller air forces of bringing their own refuelers to the fight. All of the tanker operators found that owning their own aircraft gave them a reliable and familiar capacity to deploy and support expeditionary combat forces. In possession of relatively more robust tanker elements, the French and the British provided most of their own refueling requirements thereby gaining a degree of predictability and operational efficiency that the operators of only one or two tankers did not enjoy. All operators, of course, had access to the tankers made available to NATO for Libyan operations. But, even though the CFAC basically operated the tanker fleet as a pool, air forces providing tankers had an easier time getting access to them and, if they desired, could withhold some of their tankers for their own use. The Turkish Air Force, for example, reserved its tankers for its operations. Upon discovering that its JAS 39 Gripens could not obtain

---

[82] Christian F. Anrig, *The Quest for Relevant Air Power: Continental European Responses to the Air Power Challenges of the Post–Cold War Era*, Maxwell AFB, Ala.: Air University Press, 2011.

[83] The material and examples of this and the next two paragraphs are an encapsulation of air refueling information found in the other chapters in this volume.

JP-4 fuel at Sigonella Naval Air Station, where they were based, the Swedes used their lone C-130T to pick up fuel at other bases for transfer to the Gripens on the ground or in flight. Moreover, despite preconflict exercises, the crews of refueler and receiver aircraft from different air forces sometimes experienced difficulties with communications and procedural disconnects. Unquestionably, then, owning at least enough tankers to support some level of expeditionary operations is a gateway to strategic and operational independence and credibility for even smaller air forces.

Conclusions and Lessons

For the U.S. Air Force, the strategic implications of the 2011 Libyan civil war spring more from its political than its military characteristics. Politically, the influence of the responsibility to protect (R2P) doctrine on many states' decisions to get involved in Libya certainly carries implications for the likelihood of the United States engaging in future wars for humanitarian purposes. Conversely, the deep divisions within the government over the Libyan intervention suggest that the Air Force's role in such conflicts may be shaped as much by domestic political considerations as by its demonstrated ability to exert strategic influence at minimum cost and risk. Militarily, little was in the details of Odyssey Dawn and Unified Protector that the USAF and its people had not already experienced to a greater or lesser degree during the preceding twenty years of wars and short-notice humanitarian and military expeditions. In a matter of hours, the institution went from a cold start to dropping bombs on targets, even as more forces were flowing into the theater and senior leaders were working through some unique command-relations problems. Glitches occurred in the USAF's conduct of Libyan operations, of course. But, in general, the institution and its people rose to the challenge, performed their missions expertly and, as a consequence, underwrote the overall cohesion and success of the intervention. This virtuoso operational record leaves Air Force visionaries and planners to consider mainly logistical matters. The management of the air reserve components, basing issues, limitations in the current and future tanker force, and the limited capabilities of allied air forces in key areas raise questions about the future structure and management of USAF forces.

The emergence of a formalized and internationally endorsed R2P doctrine likely will have a profound influence on future USAF involvement in humanitarian conflicts. Its existence in early 2011 was the diplomatic and political lubricant that slid the United States into the Libyan intervention. Although legally no more than an expression of international opinion at the time, R2P still represented the moral sense of an influential body of government and private citizens in many countries. Thus, when Britain, France, and other European states began to move toward blocking Qaddafi's threatened actions, R2P gave them motivation, justification, bases of domestic political support, and energetic encouragement from the U.N. These developments did much to encourage President Obama to act before attaining the political and financial support of Congress. It remains to be seen whether resulting political gridlock and its many impacts on Air Force finances and operations will become a pattern. But, given the forward progress of the R2P doctrine over the last decade, Air Force leaders are advised to think about what they will do if it does.

For U.S. strategists, perhaps the most troubling revelation of this experience was that this conflict, in combination with ongoing operations elsewhere in the world, pushed its military forces to their limits of sustainable, unmobilized management. Entire brigades of armor and infantry were in garrison, wings of fighters on their ramps, and carrier strike groups at sea or in their bases during this short-lived war. But to break from their established schedules of deployment-reconstitution-preparation-deployment would have unhinged the long-term readiness of American military forces to a disproportionate degree. Squadrons and battalions broken out of their schedules to fight in Libya would have been unavailable for other contingencies or potentially shifted in the rotation schedule, with a cascading effect on other units and missions. So, if American long-term military "capabilities" and "standing commitments" were plotted on a graph, Libya marked a moment when those lines crossed. Sustaining what amounted to a single major regional contingency (MRC) in Southwest Asia, homeland defense, the nuclear deterrent, and other routine commitments had left the United States unable to take on a minor fight in North Africa without putting units in surge, cajoling allies to get involved, and exploiting the patriotism of its reservists. Libya demonstrated that maintaining a single-MRC military might necessitate hard strategic choices for a country with global interests and involvements.

Nowhere were the incumbent risks of overstretched forces more evident during the Libyan conflict than in the management of the air refueling fleet. Coming up with around 25 tanker "tails" to support Libyan air operations placed AMC and USAFE refueler units under stress and would have been beyond the capacity of the Air Force to produce, had ARC volunteers not saved the day. But reliance on ARC volunteerism was unsustainable over time, financially and in terms of personnel stress. So, when the volunteer pool began to run dry, AMC pulled the sleight-of-hand of shifting the ARC commitment to CENTCOM missions, where they could be mobilized and paid from contingency funds, and covering Morón with active duty crews freed from "the desert" by the ARC swap. These initiatives kept the tanker effort at full strength throughout Unified Protector. But, pragmatically successful as they were in dealing with immediate demands, they did nothing to ease the overall strain on the Air Force tanker fleet, which soldiers on fully committed every day and with a primary aircraft that was in design in 1953, the year in which the present Air Force Chief of Staff, General Mark A. Welsh III, was born.

The stress on the overall air refueling fleet and the age of the KC-135 fleet reaffirms the need to energetically pursue its modernization. Acquiring the new KC-46 Pegasus will be the essential first step. Its greatly improved reliability, lower operating costs, and shorter runway requirements in comparison to the KC-135R will enhance the productivity and flexibility of the Air Force refueler fleet. The KC-46 also will bring marginally improved range/offload capacity per aircraft over the KC-135, although its capabilities will be qualitatively similar to those of its predecessor. In theaters characterized by greater distances, sparse basing facilities, and/or contested skies, the limitations of such tankers will be more salient than they were in the Libyan conflict, however. Air Force leaders, consequently, should consider whether dealing with such conflict scenarios would be best served simply by the acquisition of more KC-46s or perhaps by a more diverse tanker fleet including some number of other types to provide greater flexibility and efficiency in a wider variety of situations. These could include a class of "heavy" tankers optimized for offload at great distances and/or "tactical" tankers optimized for forward basing and quick-response support. AMC planners are fully engaged, of course, in assessing the options for later phases of the refueling fleet modernization. Their studies must be creative and far-sighted because, if the longevity of the KC-135 is instructive, they may be conceptualizing fleet elements that will still be on the line in the year 2100.

In concert with its own tanker modernization planning, the USAF would be well served to encourage and help allied air forces to expand their air refueling capabilities. As revealed clearly in this study, the weakness or absence of tanker capacity in all other air forces during Libyan operations limited the intervention's ability to project force and put the success of the whole effort at risk. Had the United States not been able to scrape up the tankers it did, the pace and scope of air operations would have been reduced drastically. In General Jodice's estimate, "If you took the U.S. tankers from NATO, we could not have done this operation."[84] But, in bigger wars or other scenarios, even its unequalled tanker fleet may be inadequate to support U.S. operations, let alone make it possible for allies to participate. So, as the United States strains its budget to maintain its unique strength and expertise in aerial refueling, it remains imperative that even small air forces balance their "shooter," refueler, and other support forces in keeping with their expectations for expeditionary operations.

Mitigating the stress on the air refueling fleet also shaped the noteworthy setup of tanker command relations during the conflict. In the cases of both USAFE and AMC tankers, the Defense Department left operational control in the hands of their parent combatant commands, transferring TACON only to AFRICOM/AFAFRICA. Given the war fighting limitations of the AFRICOM and AFAFRICA staffs in comparison to those of the bigger commands, the move made imminent sense and they worked well, overall. The obvious question for Air Force and Joint leaders, consequently, is whether or not such command authority splits should become a norm for tanker and other types of force transfers in the future.

---

[84] Jodice interview, November 14, 2012.

As a final implication for Air Force planning, Morón Air Base's vital role during the Libyan conflict suggests a need to lower the costs of maintaining "warm" bases wherever the United States anticipates large-scale operations. In addition to the infrastructure investments that AMC and USAFE sunk into the base, the huge expense of keeping hundreds of contract services and support personnel on strength is a daunting budget challenge for the latter command. Informally, this study heard estimates of $11 million to $17 million per year simply to keep Morón ready. In other theaters, particularly the Asia-Pacific region, a better answer might be to maintain far-flung bases in "lukewarm" status, manned by very small cadres of USAF or trusted contract personnel to support limited transient activities, if any, and ensure the security of logistics supplies in storage and facilities in mothballs. Coupled with robust mobility forces and base opening and services units, such a concept would allow the United States to bring lukewarm bases into operation in short order, without the necessity of keeping large cohorts of local contract personnel on hand.

CHAPTER FIVE

The U.S. Experience: Operational

Deborah C. Kidwell

Introduction

U.S. forces successfully conducted military operations in Libya from March 19 to October 31, 2011, first in a coalition and later under the command and control of NATO. The magnitude of this accomplishment, given the constraints and limitations of Operations Odyssey Dawn and Unified Protector, should not be underestimated. U.S. forces overcame resource, time, and other constraints to accomplish objectives that international priorities had defined. They responded quickly, planned comprehensive military operations, and coordinated an increasingly complex battlespace. The use of airpower during this intervention presents an attractive model for achieving limited goals without committing U.S. ground troops, with limited financial and time commitments, and with no casualties and little collateral damage. Both military operations relied heavily on the expertise and dedication of individual airmen, and clear communications between allies and partners to maintain consensus of action. While the discussion may just be beginning regarding the applicability of the experience to future air operations, it is clear that U.S. forces made particularly significant contributions to the air component of both operations through effective planning, communication, and coordination, and by committing specialized expertise, particularly in the areas of air operations and targeting, ISR, airlift and logistics, and refueling.

This chapter examines the theater-level actions of the United States' armed forces during the intervention, centering on ISR, strike, and command and control. It also discusses the leadership and management of the campaign in the air operations centers (AOCs) from which it was commanded. A coalition and an alliance in which the United States deliberately sought to play a nondominant role respectively conducted Operations Odyssey Dawn and Unified Protector. However, U.S. personnel represented by far the largest contingent of strategists, targeteers, and other directors and managers of the campaign, so as a practical matter, these activities are well suited to inclusion in this chapter in spite of their highly multinational nature.

U.S. Military Planning and Considerations

In February 2011, U.S. government officials observed the events in Libya with growing concern, although continuing economic problems, an already stretched-thin military, and the public's reluctance to become involved in additional foreign interventions argued against conducting military operations. However, President Barack Obama noted toward the end of February that a national security team had been monitoring the situation and coordinating with international partners to identify "a way forward." By February 25, the U.S. Department of State had suspended all embassy operations in Libya and prepared for the orderly evacuation of U.S. personnel from that country. That same day, the chartered ferry *Maria Delores* departed from Tripoli, completing U.S. citizens' evacuation from Libya. President Obama invoked sanctions targeted against the Qaddafi government, noting in his executive order that the "violation of human rights, brutalization of its people, and the outrageous threats have rightly drawn the strong and broad condemnation of the international community."[1]

Beginning in late February, Secretary of Defense Robert Gates, through the Joint Chiefs of Staff (JCS), issued a series of planning orders. Two issues soon became paramount: to define the area of operations and to establish effective command and control relationships within the assigned combatant command. A third challenge would occur later, as military leaders attempted to acquire the necessary resources for the operation. As Operation Odyssey Dawn developed, U.S. Africa Command (AFRICOM) became the supported command, and commanders established various supporting command relationships within the defined area of operations.[2] Changing strategic guidance and the unclear desired end state described in the planning orders made the process of conducting a mission analysis, developing a concept of operations, and obtaining the necessary resources to execute the plans problematic. The U.N. Security Council resolutions provided military planners with a clearer picture of the purpose; however, the question of end state was never fully resolved and became simply to prepare to transition command and control of operations to another (unnamed) organization, while also achieving the goals identified in the Security Council resolutions.[3]

---

[1]   Executive Order 13566, Executive Order Blocking Property and Prohibiting Certain Transactions Related to Libya, Washington, D.C.: The White House, February 25, 2011.

[2]   As will be described later, U.S. Africa Command became the supported command; U.S. European Command, U.S. Central Command, U.S. Transportation Command, and U.S. Strategic Command were supporting commands during OOD. Several U.S. Air Force major commands contributed forces, including Air Combat Command (ACC), Air Mobility Command (AMC), and Global Strike Command (GSC). See "Units Participating in Operation Odyssey Dawn," *Air Force Times*, April 4, 2011, for a list of units.

[3]   This ambiguity continued into Operation Unified Protector, where Lieutenant General Ralph J. Jodice II, the air component commander, described the desired end state informally as to protect civilians, essentially until our (NATO) services were no longer needed. Ralph J. Jodice, oral history interview with Deborah Kidwell, Washington, D.C.: Joint Base Anacostia Bolling, February 28, 2012.

Africa Command and the Evolution of a Command and Control Structure

Libya fell into the area of responsibility (AOR) of AFRICOM, under the command of General William E. Ward and his headquarters staff at Stuttgart, Germany. General Carter F. Ham would succeed Ward as commander just days before the coalition intervention began. AFRICOM had been established in 2008, primarily to conduct diplomatic, humanitarian, and training missions. AFRICOM's personnel structure reflected these priorities; more than half of the command's manning derived from civilian employees, non–Defense Department agencies, and contractors.[4] AFRICOM's air component, 17th Air Force (or AFAFRICA), which Major General Margaret Woodward commanded with headquarters at Ramstein Air Base in Germany, was responsible for executing air and space operations in support of theater objectives.[5] Although 17th Air Force's mission statement included maintaining the ability to conduct the full range of military options, personnel assignments and manpower levels did not reflect the numbers and skillsets required to conduct extensive sustained combat operations. AFRICOM planners simply did not anticipate being tasked to perform full-spectrum military operations in early 2011.[6] Although the initial assignment of crisis planning was given to U.S. European Command due to AFRICOM's lack of assigned forces and reliance on shared resources, eventually a consensus supported the assignment of the mission to the newly arrived General Ham as the geographic combatant commander.[7]

Thus, the planning orders AFRICOM received to develop potential courses of action for full-scale military operations came at a time of vulnerability: The command was relatively new, it had not anticipated managing a major air campaign, and events were moving quickly to suggest a rapid response would be required. As General Ham assumed command on March 9, planning efforts were well under way to conduct full-scale military operations under his command. Although the Air Force had established the 17th Air Force and its 617th AOC to support AFRICOM's anticipated mission, it required augmentation to execute a major offensive mission.[8] With no permanently assigned air

---

[4] Supporting service commands to AFRICOM include: U.S. Army Africa (USARAF) based in Vicenza, Italy; U.S. Naval Forces Africa (NAVAF) based in Naples, Italy; U.S. Air Forces Africa (AFAFRICA) based at Ramstein Air Base, Germany; U.S. Marine Corps Forces Africa (MARFORAF) based in Stuttgart, Germany; Combined Joint Task Force—Horn of Africa (CJTF-HOA) Camp Lemonnier, Djibouti; and Special Operations Command-Africa (SOCAFRICA) based in Stuttgart, Germany. U.S. Africa Command Fact Sheet, accessed at http://www.africom.mil, February 9, 2012.

[5] 17th Air Force Fact Sheet, February 29, 2012.

[6] General Woodward later noted that AFRICOM had unexpectedly become (after U.S. Central Command) the second "most kinetic" theater of operations at the time.

[7] Joint and Coalition Operational Analysis, *Libya: Operation ODYSSEY DAWN (OOD)—Executive Summary*, Suffolk, Va.: JCOA, September 21, 2011.

[8] AOCs are not generally staffed to conduct full-spectrum operations on a large scale without augmentation. This was typical and by design; however, it is mentioned here not because of a lack of capability or confidence within any AOC, but rather as a factor that had to be addressed at the beginning of operations. As it happened, an Air Force reorganization to combine the 603rd (supporting EUCOM) and 617th AOCs within six months of

forces, 17th Air Force relied on reachback, Request for Forces (RFF), and Global Force Management (GFM) processes, which could take up to 120 days to complete.

Command and Control for the Air Component

During Operation Odyssey Dawn, theater commanders and staff personnel developed a unique command and control structure and improvised creative measures that included close coordination for basing, staging, and forces within the U.S. European Command (EUCOM) AOR. General Woodward was in an unusual position as a commander with no permanently assigned air forces, an Air Operations Center in transition, and without the necessary manpower to conduct full-spectrum military operations. The 617th AOC originally was stood up as a tailored Falconer AOC, limited in scope and primarily focused on conducting daily ISR activities, and controlling mobility assets supporting AFRICOM missions.[9] With no assigned air forces (and little time to obtain them), it became apparent that many of the required forces would necessarily derive from Third Air Force—the air component of U.S. Air Forces in Europe (USAFE)—commanded by Lieutenant General Frank Gorenc. As the JCS guidance allowed the supporting and supported commanders to work out specific command relationships, USAFE's commander, General Mark A. Welsh III, decided that regardless of established doctrine and experience, the Commander, Air Force Forces (COMAFFOR), and the Joint Force Air Component Commander (JFACC) duties would be divided between General Gorenc and General Woodward.[10] General Woodward, as JFACC, coordinated closely with General Gorenc, who acted as the COMAFFOR, while General Woodward had tactical control of forces assigned to OOD. A joint force commander with operational control authority (OPCON) could task-organize and establish support relationships between assigned forces, while tactical control authority (TACON) would allow the commander to receive the requested

---

the beginning of OOD was already in progress. These were totally different organizations structurally, and in the types of support they provided two very different Combatant Commands (U.S. European Command and U.S. Africa Command). Merging the two organizations, while seemingly fraught with difficulties, actually went fairly smoothly, due in large part to the leadership of junior officers and senior NCOs.

[9] For a description of Air Expeditionary Task Force command and control mechanisms including the Falconer and Tailored Falconer, see Air Force Doctrine Directive (AFDD) 2, p. 105: USAF Operations and Organization, April 3, 2007, pp. 54–56. "The AOC [Air Operations Center] weapon system (AN/USQ-163) is also known as the 'Falconer.' It is the operations command center of the JFACC and provides the capability to plan, task, execute, monitor, and assess the activities of assigned or attached forces. The Falconer AOC is the senior C2 element of the TACS [Theater Air Control System] and includes personnel and equipment from many necessary disciplines to ensure the effective conduct of air and space operations (e.g., communications, operations, intelligence, etc.)."

[10] Unclassified information from Headquarters United States Air Forces in Europe and 3 AF Lessons Learned (HQ USAFE/A9AL & 3 AF/A9O), *Operation ODYSSEY DAWN: Lessons Learned from a USAFE Perspective*, Ramstein Air Base, Germany: HQ USAFE, December 8, 2011, not available to the general public.

number of units or sorties without regard to maintenance, training, administration, or unit replacement concerns.[11]

As JFACC, General Woodward was authorized tactical or operational command of the forces used, while General Gorenc, as COMAFFOR, retained operational control of all USAF forces used in the operation but assigned to EUCOM. A study later noted that this command arrangement generally worked well. However, two problems were associated with the approach: It complicated efforts to align operational control of all USAF forces under a single commander and created some confusion among the staff. The forces assigned to AFRICOM remained under its administrative control, while those forces assigned to EUCOM remained under its administrative control. Generally, EUCOM-provided forces were under the operational command authority of General Gorenc, as the COMAFFOR, and tactical command authority was given to General Woodward as JFACC. At the same time, some forces provided from outside EUCOM were under the operational control of General Gorenc, while others were under the operational or tactical control of General Woodward due to the combatant commands to which they were assigned (see Table 5.1).[12]

The three commanders—Generals Woodward, Gorenc, and Welsh—provided sufficient manning for General Woodward's air operations center by combining the 617th AOC from 17th Air Force and the 603rd AOC from Third Air Force, and through augmentation from Air National Guard (ANG) units of the 217th Air Operations Group

Table 5.1
Comparison of OOD and OUP Command and Control Arrangements

	Operation Odyssey Dawn	Operation Unified Protector
Mandate	UNSCR 1970 & 1973	UNSCR 1970 & 1973
Framework	Coalition	NATO alliance
Authority	National governments	North Atlantic Council
Supported command	AFRICOM	Joint Force Command Naples
Commander	General Carter F. Ham, USA	Admiral Samuel J. Locklear, USN
JTF commander	Admiral Samuel J. Locklear, USN	Lieutenant-General Charles Bouchard, RCAF
JFACC/CFACC	Major General Margaret Woodward, USAF	Lieutenant General Ralph J. Jodice II, USAF
CAOC	617 AOC, Ramstein AB, GER	CFAC, Poggio Renatico, ITA

NOTE: For OOD, only U.S. command arrangements shown.

---

[11] Joe Quartararo, Sr., Michael Rovenolt, and Randy White, "Libya's Operation Odyssey Dawn: Command and Control," *Prism: A Journal of the Center for Complex Operations*, Vol. 3, No. 2, 2012, pp. 141–156.

[12] Unclassified information from HQ USAFE/A9AL & 3 AF/A9O, 2011.

(AOG) and the 152nd AOG.[13] One study later noted, "Perhaps just as important as the manpower provided by the ANG units was the fact that the AOCs and those ANG units were intimately familiar with one another due to the long-standing relationships (11 years for 603 AOC/152 AOG and two years for 617 AOC/217 AOG)."[14]

In addition to the unique command structure, staff members developed an improvised system of knowledge management. The volume of information requested through the request for information (RFI) process initially overwhelmed the AOC.[15] The fact that not everyone understood the unique command structure compounded the confusion.[16] The Component Numbered Air Force Operations Center (C-NOC) managed this problem for Third Air Force, and the Odyssey Dawn Air Operations Center stood up a two-man RFI response cell to manage information requests on a 24-hour basis.[17] In addition, a study later noted a recommendation from senior commanders that the JFACC "be prepared to share targeting video, provide anecdotes to the Joint Staff, and release statements to the press" as a standard practice.[18]

Obtaining manpower for the operation was initially difficult, in no small part due to the absence of congressional authorization (amid controversy) and subsequent contingency funding. Given these circumstances, the military services were unable to activate National Guard and Reserve forces, and thus relied on volunteers. Some units were able to deploy personnel on (already planned) exercise orders.[19] Obtaining forces under the reachback and the Global Force Management (GFM)/RFF processes did not always produce the needed forces within the requested time frame.[20]

---

[13] General Woodward noted that the 217th AOG organization unit routinely supported 17th Air Force (617th AOC) from Battle Creek, Michigan, and that the 152nd AOG supported the Third Air Force (603rd AOC) from Syracuse, New York. Major General Margaret H. Woodward, oral history interview with Deborah Kidwell, Washington, D.C.: Joint Base Anacostia Bolling, March 7, 2012.

[14] Unclassified information from HQ USAFE/A9AL & 3 AF/A9O, 2011, p. 5

[15] RFI refers to any specific time-critical request for information needed to support an ongoing crisis or operation.

[16] Unclassified information from HQ USAFE/A9AL & 3 AF/A9O, 2011. However, many officers are experienced in the U.S. Central Command area of operations where the COMAFFOR and the JFACC often were the same officer. With these duties divided between two commanders, many were unsure where to send specific information requests.

[17] The C-NOC is a dedicated group led by a battle captain that includes representatives from most staff directorates. This group is staffed on a 24-hour basis and is a centralized location responsible for the collection of and response to information requests.

[18] Unclassified information from HQ USAFE/A9AL & 3 AF/A9O, 2011.

[19] HQ USAF/A9 email to Deborah Kidwell, "OOD draft—USAFE," April 2, 2012. Several staff members contacted believed the operation went much more smoothly due to the competency and experience of the 152nd AOG. See Chapter Four for additional discussion of these issues.

[20] Notable exceptions include the 217th and 152nd Air Operations Groups (Air National Guard Units), and the 92nd Air Refueling Wing stationed at Fairchild AFB, Washington. Some respondents consulted as sources for this report noted that the lack of resources was more likely due to the overall resource limitations of the operations, rather than the processes used to request and assemble forces, while others believed that the processes were

An additional issue for the planners was that surprisingly little current information existed on the Qaddafi regime's military capabilities—years had passed since Libya's rapprochement with the West ended its status as a high-priority potential adversary calling for intensive military intelligence collection. Reuters reporters noted, "On paper, Libya's military has some 100,000 troops, more than 2,000 tanks, 374 aircraft and a navy and [sic] includes two patrol submarines."[21] The reporters estimated that perhaps only 10,000 to 12,000 loyal troops remained by the beginning of March, much of the available equipment was "poorly maintained or unusable," and that many human rights groups had alleged that the regime relied heavily on African mercenaries as reinforcements. In testimony before the U.S. Senate Committee on Armed Services on March 17, Air Force Chief of Staff General Norton Schwartz stated that the Libyan air force consisted of "multiple tens of combat aircraft."[22] Most of Libya's air defense assets were believed to be located along the Mediterranean coast, with unknown capabilities in the country's sparsely populated interior desert areas.[23]

The lack of intelligence preparation challenged the staff throughout both OOD and OUP. Planners continued to learn about Libya's geography, demographics, and regime military capabilities well after the start of operations, but the lack of information about the state of Libyan military capabilities increased demand for offensive counterair missions at the beginning of the campaign. In the absence of reliable intelligence, planners had to make conservative initial assumptions—for example, that the integrated air defense system was fully functioning (it actually was decrepit), and that essentially all regime troops remained loyal. Red-team analysis was difficult in the absence of information about the various factions in the conflict and their objectives and possible actions. The net effect was to delay effective campaign planning until the joint intelligence preparation of the operational environment (JIPOE) was complete, particularly after the beginning of OUP, as will be explained later in this chapter.[24]

---

not able to produce needed resources within the needed time frames. See also Jason R. Greenleaf, "The Air War in Libya," *Air and Space Power Journal*, Vol. 27, No. 2, 2013, pp. 28–54.

[21] Peter Apps and William Maclean, "Factbox: Libya's Military: What Does Gaddafi Have Left?" *Reuters* online, March 1, 2011.

[22] General Norton Schwartz, U.S. Senate Committee on Armed Services, "Testimony on the Department of the Air Force in review of the Defense Authorization, 112th Congress," March 17, 2011.

[23] For a discussion of the Libyan air defenses and forces see Florence Gaub, "The North Atlantic Treaty Organization and Libya: Reviewing Operation Unified Protector," The Letort Papers, Carlisle, Penn.: U.S. Army College Papers, June 2013, especially pp. 6, 8–11. See also Jeremiah Gertler, *Operation Odyssey Dawn (Libya): Background and Issues for Congress*, Washington, D.C.: Congressional Research Service, CRS R41725, March 28, 2011.

[24] See Gregory K. James, Larry Holcomb, and Chad T. Manske, "Joint Task Force Odyssey Dawn: A Model for Joint Experience, Training, and Education," *Joint Force Quarterly*, No. 64, January 2012, pp. 24–29. JIPOE includes defining the operational environment; describing the impact of the operational environment; evaluating the adversary; and determining adversary courses of action. In Red Team analysis, an organizational element or "red team" is formed to research enemy and other perspectives within a specific operational environment. See Joint Publication 1-02, *Department of Defense Dictionary of Military and Associated Terms,* January 15, 2012.

Joint Task Force Odyssey Dawn

Even before plans had been finalized, on March 3, AFRICOM established Joint Task Force Odyssey Dawn (JTF-OD) under Admiral Samuel J. Locklear III. Locklear served jointly as commander of U.S. Naval Forces Europe and Africa, and as commander of Allied Joint Force Command, Naples, which had operational responsibility for NATO missions in the Mediterranean. Admiral Locklear conducted tactical operations from the U.S. Sixth Fleet's flagship, the command ship USS *Mount Whitney*, in conjunction with liaison officers representing a number of allied countries. General Woodward became the JFACC; Vice Admiral Harry B. Harris, Sixth Fleet commander, served as the Joint Force Maritime Component commander (JFMCC); Brigadier General Christopher Haas, U.S. Army, of Special Operations Command Africa, served as the joint special operations task force commander; and Brigadier General Michael Callan, 17th Air Force vice commander, led the air component coordination element; all served under the theater commander, General Ham (see Figure 5.1). No joint force land component commander (JFLCC) was assigned, as the United States had decided not to commit ground troops to the operation. The J-staff for Odyssey Dawn was tailored to include J1 through J7, J9, public affairs, judge advocate, surgeon, comptroller, and chaplain. Twenty-eight U.S. and ten foreign liaison officers (from Italy, France, and the United Kingdom) supported the J-staff. The Navy's Red Crown system provided airspace deconfliction and the airborne command and control platform for the first five days of the operation. USS *Mount*

Figure 5.1
Operation Odyssey Dawn Organization

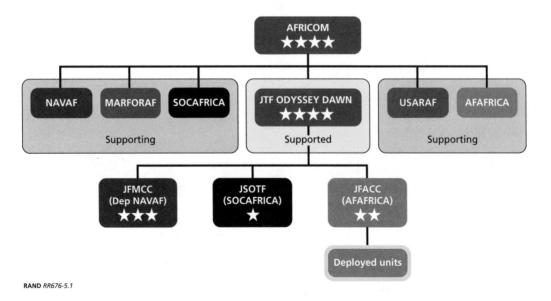

Whitney deployed on March 14 and prepared to conduct military operations, but without exact mission orders in hand, other than the humanitarian and evacuation operations already under way.[25]

Evolving Strategic Guidance

The most important questions now facing the military planners included the type of mission required, the desired end state, and how to obtain the forces necessary to accomplish the plans once they were approved. General Woodward later noted that in the 21 days from the start of crisis action planning to the first strikes, "almost every day brought new planning guidance with new objectives, approaches and priorities."[26] For example, as will be explained in detail, the earliest plans called for noncombatant evacuations under uncertain conditions and humanitarian relief missions. Later, the JCS requested options to establish a no-fly zone under a variety of constraints—without any kinetic strikes to eliminate threats from Libya's air defenses; with only one kinetic strike; and, finally, the approved concept of operations that treated disabling the air defense system as an integral component of establishing the no-fly zone. Moreover, UNSCR 1973 added the mandate to take military action to protect civilians from attacks perpetrated by regime troops. This required planning direct action against regime troops advancing on Libyan cities, as well as degrading the regime's ability to continue such attacks by damaging or destroying military facilities, equipment, and communications capabilities.

Not only did the type of requested mission planning frequently shift, political leaders' and the military chain of command's desired end state was unclear. For their part, U.S. policymakers seemed to prefer ambiguity to preserve their freedom to maneuver. The no-fly zone appeared to provide a low-risk, low-cost potential solution to the problem of using the military option under very limited conditions. In spite of their need for specific guidance to make plans to achieve the desired effects, military planners needed to become comfortable with this ambiguity by planning action on intermediate objectives with a number of constraints and limitations, while remaining flexible enough to change course with the political winds that would determine the desired end state at a later date. While each side believed their position to be necessary under the circumstances, the positions were clearly out of sync with each other.[27]

---

[25] James, Holcomb, and Manske, "Joint Task Force Odyssey Dawn." The authors note that the majority of the directors and deputies of the J-staff directorates were Air Force and Navy officers.

[26] Major General Margaret H. Woodward, "Defending America's Vital National Interests in Africa," prepared remarks before the 2011 Air & Space Conference & Technology Exposition, September 21, 2011.

[27] The author wishes to thank Michael Kometer for his insightful comments regarding this section. Although the tasking orders remain classified, there is ample evidence to suggest that the orders process was less formal and specific than is generally the case, as is explained throughout this chapter. For example, B-2 bombers were several

The first order of business included military assistance to close the U.S. Embassy in Tripoli and later other types of humanitarian assistance. Because of the increasingly violent nature of events, and because no one could accurately predict Qaddafi's reaction, the first planning efforts considered conducting a noncombatant evacuation under hostile or uncertain conditions. Such a mission can be complicated and risky, and one that planners would definitely prefer to avoid by obtaining more information, resources, or by isolating or limiting constraints.[28]

In addition to the efforts to evacuate American citizens and embassy personnel, the United States conducted a variety of humanitarian relief operations beginning in early March. Defense Secretary Gates ordered USS *Kearsarge*, USS *Ponce*, and 400 Marines of the 26th Marine Expeditionary Unit (MEU) to the area to provide a capability for emergency evacuations and to provide humanitarian relief.[29] Airmen from the 86th Air Wing, flying C-130Js from Ramstein, and members of the 435th Contingency Response Group collectively delivered 18,000 pounds of supplies to refugee camps in Tunisia. Over the next 11 days, Marine KC-130s returned more than 1,100 displaced Egyptians to their homeland.[30] The U.S. Agency for International Development (USAID) provided an initial $10 million in emergency assistance in support of international organizations, nongovernmental organizations, and the Libyan Red Crescent, and prepared to provide food resources where needed. As the U.S. State Department noted at the time: "We are deeply concerned about how the current situation is affecting the Libyan People and others in the country and are working intensely with the international community to meet their urgent humanitarian needs."[31] However, as Secretary Gates pointed out:

> I would note that the U.N. Security Council resolution [1970] provides no authorization for the use of armed force. There is no unanimity within NATO for the use of armed force . . . Our job is to give the president the broadest possible decision space and options . . . [however] all of the options beyond the humanitarian assistance and evacuation are complex.[32]

---

hours into their flight to Libya before receiving a signed air tasking order. See also Quartararo, Rovenolt, and White, "Libya's Operation Odyssey Dawn."

28 Kirit Radia, "US Evacuates Embassy in Libya," *ABCNews.com*, February 25, 2011; Consulate General of the United States, "U.S. Citizens Evacuated Libya," February 25, 2012.

29 OASD (PA), "DOD News Briefing with Secretary Gates and Adm. Mullen from the Pentagon," Washington, D.C.: U.S. Department of Defense, March 1, 2011.

30 Woodward, "Defending America's Vital National Interests in Africa."

31 U.S. Department of State Fact Sheet, "Humanitarian Assistance for Libya," Washington, D.C., February 28, 2011.

32 OASD (PA), "DOD News Briefing with Secretary Gates and Adm. Mullen from the Pentagon."

Although the mandate to conduct military operations did not exist until the passage of UNSC Resolution 1973 on March 17, U.S. forces continued to prepare for a range of possible options.

With the area of operations and command responsibilities defined, AFRICOM issued a planning order on February 26 that required 17th Air Force planners, as the air component command, to produce and deliver plans for a no-fly zone to the theater command and the Joint Staff within 36 hours. General Woodward noted:

> Almost immediately, it was evident to our planners that any course of action involving a No-Fly Zone would require establishing Air Superiority and freedom of maneuver. To achieve these things, we needed to eliminate the threats posed by a fairly robust Libyan integrated Air Defense System and a relatively incapable but still lethal Libyan Air Force . . . Our view of the mission led us to believe that sustained precision engagement with regime ground forces as well as counter-air operations would be required. This fundamental perspective and our subsequent analysis of objectives were the foundations for our first Course of Action; the one we eventually executed.[33]

This course of action became controversial, for both the resources it would require and the operations or types of mission it implied. As a result, 17th Air Force planners were asked to provide options to establish and maintain a no-fly zone without any kinetic strikes. Although a paucity of information existed on Libyan military capabilities, it was known that regime officials had constructed an integrated air defense system (IADS) from older Soviet technology. Pentagon briefer Vice Admiral William Gortney later evaluated the system as having "still good capability."[34] General Woodward observed that a consequence of the first tasking would be that a majority of operations would take place within range of multiple and highly capable surface-to-air missile (SAM) systems. "We developed this plan as directed," she remarked, "but assessed it as extremely high risk and offered our original COA [course of action] as an alternative."[35] On March 2, General Woodward's planners submitted a Request for Forces consistent with the operational approach they had initially proposed; although Africa Command and the Joint Staff endorsed this concept, the approval for resources did not occur before the operation began.[36]

Planning guidance for possible military action continued to develop even as humanitarian missions continued. 17th Air Force planners were asked, for example,

---

[33] Woodward, "Defending America's Vital National Interests in Africa."

[34] OASD (PA), "DOD News Briefing with Vice Adm. Gortney from the Pentagon on Libya Operation Odyssey Dawn," Washington, D.C.: U.S. Department of Defense, March 19, 2011.

[35] Woodward, "Defending America's Vital National Interests in Africa."

[36] General Woodward noted that out of 94 requests for resources, only four were provided by March 5. Woodward, oral history interview, March 7, 2012.

to plan to execute one initial strike aimed at preventing Libyan regime aircraft from flying, with only limited defensive counterair (DCA) and SEAD. General Woodward noted that some planning guidance to develop courses of action occurred during video teleconferences (VTCs) and arrived via email. Some planning requests described what were essentially tactical tasks—to damage runways, for example—rather than comprehensive planning objectives for military operations.[37] The sheer number and nature of planning requests reflected the difficulty of the policy decision to intervene militarily, and often, a lack of understanding between military and political decisionmakers.

As General Woodward recalled, "Throughout this planning cycle, the situation in Libya continued to deteriorate. It appeared that unless the world acted, nothing would prevent Colonel Qaddafi and his lieutenants from committing mass murder in Benghazi."[38] White House officials continued to state publicly that they were considering a range of options. When planners received a draft version of UNSC Resolution 1973 on March 16, they were surprised to note an additional mandate—protecting civilians. As planners contemplated the implications of conducting air-to-ground strikes not only against military assets and facilities to establish the no-fly zone, but also against advancing regime troops, they realized they would have to consider atypical sources and methods to acquire the resources, combat support, and specific skill sets required.

The Coalition Coalesces

As the violence in Libya escalated, three events paved the way for U.S. military operations: the Arab League expressed support for a no-fly zone, a growing political consensus developed within Congress and the Obama administration to take action, and the passage of UNSCR 1973 provided the international authorization to use military force. As individual nations and Alliance organizations considered their support, Obama administration officials also weighed the possibility of military intervention. U.S. Ambassador to the United Nations Susan Rice stated as early as February 28 that "we have been very clear that we have a range of options . . . that we're considering."[39] A few days later, President Obama added: "The violence must stop; Muammar Qaddafi has lost the legitimacy to lead and he must leave; those who perpetrate violence against the Libyan people will be held accountable."[40]

---

[37] Woodward, oral history interview, March 7, 2012. Eventually, the plans tasked multiple units to provide the necessary forces (from 17th Air Force, 3rd Air Force, 18th Air Force, and eventually the 313th AEW, for example).

[38] Woodward, "Defending America's Vital National Interests in Africa."

[39] Press briefing by Press Secretary Jay Carney and U.S. Permanent Representative to the United Nations Susan Rice, February 28, 2011.

[40] Jesse Lee, "The President on Libya: 'We Have Already Saved Lives,'" The White House blog, March 22, 2011.

Defense Secretary Gates and other military officials continued a dialogue with Congress regarding possible military options, the resources required, and the potential consequences to U.S. interests and foreign policy. Initially, Congress appeared to show little understanding of the kinetic aspects and complexity of establishing a no-fly zone and even less of a consensus regarding the will to act. Secretary Gates testified bluntly before Congress, "A no-fly zone begins with an attack on Libya to destroy the air defenses. That's the way you do a no-fly zone. And then you can fly planes around the country and not worry about our guys being shot down. But that's the way it starts."[41] Air Force Chief of Staff General Norton Schwartz testified before the Senate Committee on Armed Services that it "would take upwards of a week to establish a no-fly zone and would require U.S. forces to first neutralize Libyan ground to air anti-aircraft sites" and that a no-fly zone itself "would not be sufficient" to defeat loyalist forces' possible counterattack.[42]

By passing UNSCR 1973 on March 17, authorizing member states to employ "all necessary means" to protect civilians in Libya, the U.N. Security Council provided support for military intervention. The planning was complete, the resolution affirmed international consensus, and the political will existed, setting the stage for U.S. military intervention in Libya.

Concept of Operations

As the AOC and C2 structure evolved, the basic concept of operations emerged. Planners co-located the headquarters for Third Air Force, 17th Air Force, and USAFE at Ramstein Air Base, Germany, with a primary forward operating location at Aviano, Italy. Three U.S.-based B-2 Spirit bombers were to conduct initial strikes against Libyan regime aircraft and facilities. Additional aircraft and sea-launched cruise missiles would attack other hard targets—regime military assets and facilities such as radars, missile launch sites, and communications nodes. Aggressive counterair missions, suppression or destruction of enemy air defenses (SEAD/DEAD), and electronic warfare activities were to precede and accompany the secondary strikes to defeat threats such as missile and radar warning sites, neutralize any regime aircraft that managed to survive, and render regime assets vulnerable to attack, while protecting the attackers. Strike aircraft included B-2 Spirit (and later B-1B Lancer) heavy bombers; F-15E Strike Eagles, F-16 Fighting Falcons; A-10 Thunderbolt IIs; and AC-130U Spectre gunship aircraft. Navy and Marine EA-18G Growler aircraft, along with Air Force F-16CJs, would conduct both offensive and defensive counterair missions, including SEAD and

---

[41] David E. Sanger and Thom Shanker, "Gates Warns of Risks of a No-Flight Zone," *New York Times*, March 2, 2011.

[42] Gertler, *Operation Odyssey Dawn (Libya)*, p. 3.

reactive and preemptive jamming. Base support and logistics activity, global mobility (refueling, cargo, and combat support), and ISR assets were the critical enablers of the planned missions. Global mobility assets included C-130 Hercules and C-17 Globemaster transport aircraft, and KC-10 Extender and KC-135 Stratotanker refuelers. ISR assets included RC-135 Rivet Joint and E-8C JSTARS (Joint Surveillance Target Attack Radar System) aircraft. E-3 Sentry AWACS aircraft provided a C2 platform. Marine strike aircraft—six AV-8B Harrier IIs launched from the amphibious assault ship USS *Kearsarge*—were to conduct additional air-to-ground strikes to protect Libyan civilians.[43]

Logistics and combat support units embraced the entire effort to support the rapid influx of personnel and equipment at various forward operating bases, primarily in southern Europe.[44] U.S. Air Force units were located in Greece (Souda Bay and Kalamata), Italy (Sigonella and Aviano), Spain (Rota and Morón), and Istres, France.[45] Some aircraft, such as the B-2 stealth bombers, operated from their home stations.[46] Planners initially decided to locate specific units at facilities according to the type of air asset, the base's existing capability, capacity to conduct operations, and historical precedent, although sheer necessity also factored into the initial laydown of forces. General Woodward noted the uncertain approval for the start of operations and the time required to obtain clearances for weapons into Italy delayed aircraft generation, which required some units to originate from their home stations and recover elsewhere in Europe before continuing on to Aviano Air Base in Italy for continuing operations. As coalition members arrived, they were bedded down where space was available and where contributing nations could obtain permission from host countries. Moreover, the pace of operations was so fluid that U.S. forces could do little more than deconflict the actions of allies and partners in real time, until they could be later incorporated into the air tasking orders.

---

[43] OASD (PA), "DOD News Briefing with Vice Adm. Gortney," March 19, 2011.

[44] For a complete list of facilities outside the continental U.S. see NATO website, "Operation Unified Protector Map," accessed March 27, 2012, and Appendix B, below.

[45] W. Butler, "Operation Odyssey Dawn/Operation Unified Protector," USAFE History Office list, March 27, 2012. In general, U.S. fighter aircraft generated from Aviano; electronic warfare and ISR aircraft from Souda Bay and Sigonella; E-3 AWACS and E-8C JSTARS aircraft from Rota; and U-2 reconnaissance aircraft from Akrotiri in Cyprus. (See Appendix B.)

[46] The B-2 aircraft generated and returned to their home base, Whiteman Air Force Base, Missouri. F-16 and F-15E squadrons, on the first night of operations, generated from RAF Lakenheath and recovered in theater. Woodward, oral history interview, March 7, 2012.

U.S. Forces Assigned

The services deployed the air forces as appropriate to conduct the concept of operations. Planners tasked B-2 Spirit bombers from the 509th Bomb Wing at Whiteman AFB in Missouri to conduct air-to-ground strikes on combat aircraft shelters at Ghardabiya Airfield in the initial hours of the operation. The 31st Fighter Wing at Aviano AB, Italy eventually deployed expeditionary fighter squadrons from Spangdahlem AB, Shaw AFB, and RAF Lakenheath; these aircraft conducted combat air patrols, SEAD and DEAD, and air strikes on regime ground forces advancing on opposition forces in Benghazi from their home stations on the first night of operations.[47] The 510th and 555th Fighter Squadrons from Aviano would conduct aerial interdiction (AI) and strike coordination and reconnaissance (SCAR) missions.[48] A-10s and AC-130 gunships supplemented the fighter aircraft in conducting air-to-ground attacks on regime ground forces. C-130J aircraft from the 37th Airlift Squadron at Ramstein Air Base, Germany, which theater-based C-17 cargo planes supplemented, moved ground equipment and personnel to forward bases. KC-135 aircraft from the 100th Air Refueling Wing at RAF Mildenhall and the 92nd Air Refueling Wing from Fairchild AFB, Washington refueled the strike aircraft en route to forward staging bases and while conducting operations.[49] EC-130J Commando Solo aircraft from the 193rd Special Operations Wing of the Pennsylvania ANG conducted information operations that included broadcasting messages.

The U.S Navy assigned forces and assets to provide electronic warfare support, embargo enforcement, ISR support, and amphibious landing and rescue capabilities. USS *Mount Whitney* functioned as the command ship, along with USS *Lewis and Clark, Robert E. Peary*, and *Kanawha* in support. The *Arleigh Burke*–class guided-missile destroyers USS *Stout* (DDG 55) and USS *Barry* (DDG 52), along with submarines USS *Providence* (SSN 719), USS *Scranton* (SSN 756), and USS *Florida* (SSGN 728), conducted initial Tomahawk land-attack missile (TLAM) strikes along with the British submarine HMS *Triumph*. Four Navy P-3C and one EP-3E Orion aircraft conducted maritime patrol duties, with the capability to perform C2, reconnaissance,

---

[47] 480th Expeditionary Fighter Squadron (Spangdahlem); 492nd Expeditionary Fighter Squadron (Lakenheath); the 510th and 555th Fighter Squadrons (Aviano); Butler, "Operation Odyssey Dawn/Operation Unified Protector."

[48] According to Joint Publication 3-03, *Joint Interdiction*, SCAR missions are flown to identify targets and coordinate attack or reconnaissance efforts on those targets. SCAR aircrews perform a role similar to that of a forward air controller during close air support, in support of aerial interdiction missions. All of the fighter squadrons essentially performed the SCAR mission at one point or another, due to the fluid nature of the operation. See Butler, "Operation Odyssey Dawn/Operation Unified Protector."

[49] John A. Tirpak, "Odyssey Dawn Units Identified," *Air Force Association Daily Report*, March 22, 2011. For more detail on the air mobility and refueling effort, see Chapter Four. See Appendix B for a list of assets deployed from each contributor and their locations.

F-16CJ pilots from the 480th Fighter Squadron receive a briefing at Spangdahlem AB, Germany, before deploying to Aviano AB, Italy, for Operation Odyssey Dawn, March 19, 2011.
Courtesy of the U.S. Air Force, photo by Staff Sergeant Benjamin Wilson.

anti-surface, and anti-submarine warfare functions when necessary.[50] Marine aviation assets conducted air interdiction missions and provided Tactical Recovery of Aircraft and Personnel (TRAP) mission capability.[51] AV-8B Harrier pilots assigned to Marine Medium Tiltrotor Squadron (VMM-) 266 participated in the initial strikes on regime air defenses, and continued to conduct air strikes on loyalist ground forces advancing on opposition strongholds and populated areas. Marine KC-130J Hercules provided aerial refueling when needed.[52]

---

[50] On March 28, a P-3C Orion, along with a USAF A-10 and guided missile destroyer USS *Barry,* fired on the Libyan coast guard vessel *Vittoria*, after the vessel and two smaller craft fired on merchant ships in the port of Misrata. The *Vittoria* was beached, another vessel destroyed, and a third abandoned. Joint Task Force Odyssey Dawn Public Affairs, "US Navy P-3C, USAF A-10 and USS *Barry* Engage Libyan Vessels," March 29, 2011. See also "Navy Accomplishes Several Firsts During Operation Odyssey Dawn," Targeted News Service, Washington, D.C. April 1, 2011.

[51] Tom Baughn, "U.S. Marine Corps Operations During Libya Crisis," unpublished manuscript, February 3, 2012. Units included Battalion Landing Teams 1/2 and 3/8; Marine Medium Tiltrotor Squadron 266 of the 2nd Marine Aircraft wing reinforced with elements of Marine Attack Squadron 542; Light Attack Helicopter Squadron 467; Heavy Helicopter Squadron 461; Aerial Refueler Transport Squadron 252; and Combat Logistics Battalion 26.

[52] Baughn, "U.S. Marine Corps Operations During Libya Crisis."

By March 18, Libyan regime troops had advanced to within kilometers of Benghazi. Early the next morning, they began shelling the city.[53] As opposition and regime forces battled for control of the city's outskirts, intense fighting resulted in numerous civilian casualties until opposition forces compelled regime forces to retreat. French aircraft destroyed several targets with air-to-ground strikes beginning at 1645 GMT.[54]

U.S. forces initiated Operation Odyssey Dawn with a full range of military operations on March 19. The first phase focused on two goals: to protect civilians and to degrade the regime's capability to resist the no-fly zone. The first 24 hours of the operation included strike, counterair, SEAD/DEAD, ISR, electronic warfare, and support (airlift and refueling) missions. Vice Admiral Bill Gortney, director of the Joint Staff and Pentagon spokesman, stated that U.S. action was intended to "shape the battle space in such a way that our partners may take the lead in . . . execution. As the President has said, we are not going to use force to go beyond a well-defined goal, specifically the protection of the civilians."[55]

Initial strike missions began at 3 p.m. EST, when U.S. and British surface ships and submarines fired Tomahawk cruise missiles (TLAMs) at air defense (IADS) targets, including SA-5 sites, early warning radar sites, key communication nodes, and other military facilities primarily along the Libyan coast (see Figure 5.2). On the first day of Operation Odyssey Dawn, two U.S. guided missile destroyers and four submarines fired more than 120 Tomahawk missiles at more than 20 targets. The heaviest concentration of Tomahawk strikes took place near Tripoli and Misrata, although the coalition also struck areas near Sirte and Zuwarah. Admiral Gortney reported that the strikes were "very effective in significantly degrading the regime's air defense capability to include their ability to launch many of their SA-5s which are the long-range surface-to-air missiles, the SA-3s and the SA-2s."[56] Additional air-to-ground strikes from 15 USAF F-15Es and F-16s, and AV-8Bs from USS *Kearsarge*, along with coalition partners and U.S. Navy EA-18G Growlers providing electronic warfare support, took place some 10 miles south of Benghazi, where the Libyan regime forces targeted by the initial French attack had not yet completely halted their advance on the city. Initial weapons system video from a Harrier indicated that the attacks halted regime ground troops, leading Admiral Gortney to comment, "Benghazi is not completely safe from attack, but it is certainly under less threat than it was yesterday. We believe [Qaddafi's] forces are under significant stress and suffering from both isolation and a

---

[53] Aljazeera English Video Report, accessed via YouTube on February 9, 2012 (video no longer exists). See also Barbara Jones and Ian Mcilgorm, "The Battle of Benghazi: City Seemed Lost to Gaddafi Forces But Was Retaken by Rebels," *The Daily Mail Online*, March 20, 2011; Aljazeera, "French Jets Attack Gaddafi Targets," March 19, 2011.

[54] "Libya: French Plane Fires on Military Vehicle," *Bbc.co.uk*, March 19, 2011.

[55] OASD (PA), "DOD News Briefing with Vice Adm. Gortney," March 19, 2011.

[56] OASD (PA), "DOD News Briefing with Vice Adm. Gortney," March 20, 2011.

Figure 5.2
Operation Odyssey Dawn Initial Strikes and No-Fly Zone

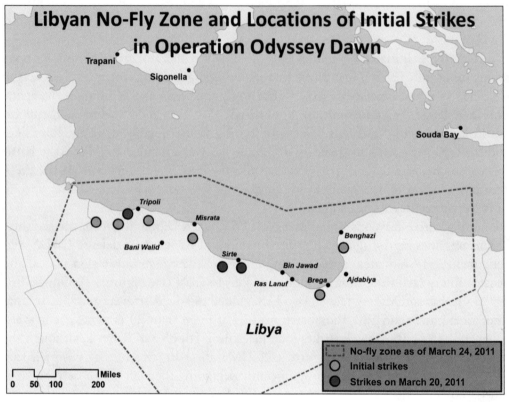

RAND *RR676-5.2*

good deal of confusion."[57] Within a few hours, combat air patrols began operating in a wedge-shaped preliminary no-fly zone that extended along the entire coast of Libya.

In the early hours of March 20, three B-2 Spirit bombers flying from White-man AFB targeted 45 hardened aircraft shelters near Sirte. The urgency of the mission prompted officers to use atypical orders and staff processes: Pilots launched without a written execution order, and six hours into the flight, they received orders to continue to the targets as planned. The air tasking order called for Joint Direct Attack Munitions (JDAMs) capable of penetrating aircraft shelters and destroying the aircraft inside. Brigadier General Scott Vander Hamm of the 509th Bomb Wing reported that the strikes had limited the regime's ability to fly combat missions.[58] There were no

---

[57] OASD (PA), "DOD News Briefing with Vice Adm. Gortney," March 19, 2011.

[58] NPR Morning Edition, "B-2 Bombers from Missouri Hit Libyan Targets," March 21, 2011.

reports of any Libyan fighters attempting to intercept the attacking aircraft once the campaign was under way.

The next day, Air Force F-15E Strike Eagles from the 492nd and 494th Fighter Squadrons, flying from RAF Lakenheath, conducted strikes against C2, air defenses and other fixed targets near Sirte, and against maneuver forces advancing on Benghazi, while also patrolling the skies to intercept any Libyan aircraft that might have survived the attacks. F-16CJ defense-suppression aircraft from the 480th Fighter Squadron at Spangdahlem Air Base, Germany, armed with AGM-88 High-speed Anti-Radiation Missiles (HARMs) flew in air packages to protect strike aircraft from potential missile launches or other threats. Aviano-based Navy EA-18G Growler aircraft conducted electronic warfare support, SEAD, and DEAD missions—the Growler's first-ever combat mission.[59]

Several factors complicated the operation in its early hours. First, because OOD was hastily planned as a unilateral action, little strategic guidance or planning existed to incorporate coalition partners into the operation. General Woodward, her British counterpart, and the numerous liaison officers and their staffs worked hard to coordinate activities. In the beginning, they could do little more than deconflict flight activities in real time; later, they incorporated allies and partners into a comprehensive Master Air Attack Plan (MAAP), air tasking orders, and battle damage and intelligence analysis activities. The piecemeal and ad hoc yet rapid arrival of allies, and the limitations each nation placed on the use of their forces, made this coordination diffi-

F-15E Strike Eagle preparing to depart RAF Lakenheath, March 19, 2011.
Courtesy of the U.S. Air Force, photo by Technical Sergeant Lee A. Osberry Jr.

---

[59] "Navy Accomplishes Several Firsts During Operation Odyssey Dawn," *Targeted News Service*, Washington, D.C., April 1, 2011; "Units Participating in Operation Odyssey Dawn," *Air Force Times*.

cult, although the fact that many officers had previously worked together during train-ing exercises helped to mitigate the situation, particularly at the operational and tacti-cal levels. The initial coalition (on March 19) comprised the United States, France, and the United Kingdom, which were joined in operations over Libya by Italy and Den-mark on March 20. The next day Spanish, Canadian, and Belgian aircraft began flying combat missions,[60] and within a week fighters from Norway, the United Arab Emir-ates, Qatar, and the Netherlands were also pariticipating. Moreover, few ISR resources were available; AWACS was not available for the first five days, JSTARS was not used during the first seven days, and full-motion video assets (MQ-1 Predator UAVs) were not used during OOD. Finally, the lack of knowledge regarding the capability and functionality of the Libyan IADS meant that planners had to assume that the system was fully capable—and thus to potentially waste precious resources preparing for the worst-case scenario.[61]

Targeting During Odyssey Dawn

Air Force Targeting Center (AFTC) expertise was crucial to the success of Odyssey Dawn. Increased demand for precision effects has resulted in a commensurate need for more complex target intelligence. The electronic targeting folders necessary to con-duct precision effects comprise five basic elements: target characterization (imagery), precision coordinates, collateral damage estimates, weaponeering data, and target sig-nificance. In 2009, Air Force leadership redesignated the Air Combat Targeting and Intelligence Group as the AFTC, with a mission to "provide targeting and geospatial products and services, expertise and advocacy to Air Force and Joint Warfighters."[62] Headquartered at Langley AFB, Virginia, AFTC's active duty squadrons included the 15th and 36th Intelligence Squadrons (ISs) (Langley); the 20th IS (Offutt); and the 120th Intelligence Group (Great Falls, Montana). The AFTC Air National Guard units included the 150th IS (Albuquerque, New Mexico), the 194th IS (Tacoma, Washington), and the 236th IS (Nashville, Tennessee). The AFTC deployed ANG personnel on a volunteer basis, to complement active duty personnel serving as liaison officers to provide targeting expertise during Odyssey Dawn.[63]

The AFTC provided 78 percent of all target materials produced during Odyssey Dawn.[64] The reachback concept adequately provided personnel, even though the quick

---

[60] See USAFE, "OOD Fast Facts," PowerPoint slides provided by Billy Harris, USAFE historian. Coalition partners were also integrated into the Special Instructions to Pilots (SPINS), other planning and execution docu-ments, and intelligence products.

[61] Woodward, oral history interview, March 7, 2012.

[62] Air Force Historical Research Agency, "Air Force Targeting Center (ACC)," online fact sheet, posted January 15, 2010.

[63] Air Force Historical Research Agency, "Air Force Targeting Center."

[64] Wayne Larsen, "The Air Force Targeting Center Unit Mission Brief," June 15, 2012.

response and operational environment presented significant challenges. In the absence of a congressional authorization, obtaining sufficient manpower depended heavily on volunteers within the ANG units. Although it was judged that sufficient personnel volunteered in this case, the process was cumbersome to enact quickly, and given the limited number of trained professionals, could rapidly reach maximum capacity, particularly during sustained operations or larger conflicts. Targeteers generally spend up to 14 to 16 months in training, and require frequent exercise participation to maintain proficiency. Moreover, properly producing and vetting a target is time-consuming— approximately 133 man-hours.[65] Thus, the Air Force could scarcely provide the targeting expertise needed without tasking ANG units.

A particular challenge was that U.S. targeting capability had been allowed to atrophy in terms of manpower and training. However, even less targeting capability resided with allies and partners, so the bulk of this effort fell on AFTC personnel. Some of the problems encountered caused the AFTC to propose a plan to train more targeting professionals, rewrite battle damage assessment (BDA) procedures to standardize requirements across combatant commands and perhaps international partners, and to reinvigorate training programs.[66]

Pilots and targeting professionals used dynamic targeting and SCAR tactics to search for and destroy enemy forces.[67] General Woodward recounted that as one of the first SCAR packages approached Benghazi on March 19, a HARM missile fired from an F-16CJ aircraft employing the advanced avionics/launcher interface computer (ALIC) destroyed an activated SA-8 tactical SAM system.[68] "In addition, the location of the SAM provided a superb 'mark' for our Sniper pods, helping our Strike Eagles locate and slam Qaddafi's elite 32nd Brigade with over 12,000 pounds of munitions," General Woodward said.[69] SCAR tactics placed more responsibility for positive identification on aircrew members, and thus required a great deal of diligence and fire discipline; moreover, pilots were reluctant to initiate missions without well-defined

---

[65] Larsen, "Air Force Targeting Center Unit Mission Brief."

[66] Larsen, "Air Force Targeting Center Unit Mission Brief." Battle damage assessment is an estimate of damage that consists of three phases: physical, functional, and target system assessment. See United States Joint Forces Command Joint Warfighting Center and Office of the Secretary of Defense Joint Battle Damage Assessment Joint Test and Evaluation, *Commander's Handbook for Joint Battle Damage Assessment*, June 1, 2004.

[67] Dynamic targeting is a process used to prosecute targets identified too late, or not selected in time to be included in deliberate targeting, according to Joint Publication 3-60. SCAR missions employ reconnaissance and strike assets during dynamic targeting, to perform positive identification and targeting control, especially when a forward air controller (FAC) is not available on the ground.

[68] Woodward, "Defending America's Vital National Interests in Africa."

[69] The package consisted of F-15E Strike Eagles from the 48th Fighter Wing and F-16CJ aircraft from the 52nd Fighter Wing. Woodward, "Defending America's Vital National Interests in Africa."

targets.[70] However, these tactics, especially when used in combination, had the advantages of more precise targeting and reduced collateral damage.

A Strategy of Limited Objectives

The U.S. military articulated a strategy characterized by limited objectives, declining U.S. participation, and preparations to transition C2 responsibilities to another group with coalition support, preferably NATO. When asked about "mission creep" after the start of operations, Pentagon briefers carefully specified U.S. objectives: establish the no-fly zone, sustain the arms embargo, and conduct tactical aircraft strikes against elements of the regime threatening populated areas. Secretary Gates stressed that "common agreement on . . . the terms set forth in the Security Council resolution [1973]" primarily guided the coalition.[71] As early as the second day of operations, Admiral Gortney noted that "General Ham is working diligently to effect a smooth transition to a coalition command structure in the next few days . . . We remain committed to creating, and then sustaining, the conditions under which our allies and partners can take the lead in implementing the no-fly zone."[72] From the beginning, then, the U.S. strategy was one of front-loaded, declining participation; initially, U.S. forces were to provide a large share of the resources and capabilities—with specific contributions to the strike, ISR, air mobility, and munitions supply efforts. Over time, U.S. officials anticipated a decline in tactical strike sorties and the command and control of operations, until their contribution dwindled to airlift, refueling, electronic warfare, ISR, and other support missions, which would remain constant or decrease over time as the coalition and its capabilities grew. Looking forward, Secretary Gates added, "This is basically going to have to be resolved by the Libyans themselves . . . We will have a military role in the coalition, but we will not have the preeminent role."[73]

What was absent from this strategic discipline was a clearly defined end state, which politicians complicated with their tendency to suggest what amounted to tactical military action.[74] However, in this case, the ambiguous desired end state—generally undesirable to planners attempting to achieve broad effects—created an unintended consequence that allowed Libyan opposition forces to be the determining factor

---

[70] Brigadier General Roy Uptegraff et al., "U.S. Air Force Contingency Operations," unprepared remarks before the 2011 Air & Space Conference & Technology Exposition, September 21, 2011.

[71] OASD (PA), "Media Availability with Secretary Gates Enroute to Russia, from Andrews Air Force Base," Washington, D.C.: U.S. Department of Defense, March 20, 2011. The reliance on areas of consensus, rather than waiting to act until a comprehensive agreement addressed all contentious points (how to conduct the air-to-ground strikes, for example) was extremely significant throughout both operations.

[72] OASD (PA), "DOD News Briefing with Vice Adm. Gortney," March 20, 2011.

[73] OASD (PA), "Media Availability with Secretary Gates."

[74] Recall General Woodward's statement that during the planning period before operations "almost every day brought new planning guidance with new objectives, approaches and priorities," as discussed earlier in this chapter.

in the conflict. Because U.S. planners were not committed to a particular outcome, they were more open to achieving immediate objectives, while allowing time for political decisions to develop and the operation to transition to NATO command and control. While the coalition did much to damage regime assets, it was still for the Libyan opposition to decide if an uncertain outcome was worth fighting for.

Planners carefully adhered to targeting priorities throughout OOD and clearly articulated these priorities to the news media. In setting up the no-fly zone, priority was given to efforts to destroy or degrade Libyan air defenses, destroy regime aircraft on the ground, and enable freedom of movement in the air. Admiral Gerard P. Hueber succinctly listed targeting priorities for interdiction missions as "mechanized forces, artillery . . . mobile surface-to-air missile sites, interdicting their lines of communications . . . their command and control and any opportunities for sustainment of that activity."[75] Air strikes were carefully tied to the desired effects—that is to say, they were limited to regime facilities, equipment, and personnel being used to attack civilians or that could be used to attack coalition forces enforcing the no-fly zone or arms embargo. This was illustrated on the second day of operations, when Admiral Gortney provided BDAs that showed no damage observed to the civilian-use areas of the dual-purpose Ghardabiya airfield. Post-strike photographs, when compared to prestrike images, noted that military aircraft shelters struck by TLAMs or precision-guided munitions (PGMs) released by B-2 bombers suffered extensive damage, while the civilian infrastructure was not targeted and no damage to it was visible.[76]

Avoidance of collateral damage was a strictly observed priority.[77] When asked how coalition forces distinguished regime from opposition forces, DoD briefers observed that mechanized forces had to be positively identified as advancing on population centers. Lieutenant-General Charles Bouchard, commander of Operation Unified Protector, later noted that this positive identification was extremely important in building trust and confidence in the coalition's good intentions. Making even one mistake could have disastrous consequences.[78] Many aircrews consulted for this report noted that precision weapons, fire discipline, and tactical skills were applied to reduce collateral damage and the negative press it would engender.

---

[75] OASD (PA), "DOD News Briefing with Rear Adm. Hueber via Telephone from USS *Mount Whitney*," Washington, D.C.: U.S. Department of Defense, March 23, 2011. DoD briefers noted that they had no contact or coordination with opposition forces, and referred to interdiction rather than close air support (CAS) missions.

[76] OASD (PA), "DOD News Briefing with Vice Adm. Gortney," March 20, 2011.

[77] OASD (PA), "DOD News Briefing with Gen. Ham via teleconference from Germany," Washington, D.C.: U.S. Department of Defense, March 21, 2011.

[78] For this reason, targeting second-tier regime forces compensated for the difficulty of positive identification. See Lieutenant-General Charles Bouchard (Royal Canadian Air Force), "Coalition Building and the Future of NATO Operations: 2/14/2012—Transcript," remarks presented at Atlantic Council of the United States, Washington, D.C., February 14, 2012.

Specific targeting priorities continued to evolve, even though they remained consistent with initial guidance. At the beginning of the planning process, as Woodward later said, "we made some pretty big assumptions," as JTF Commander Admiral Locklear and General Ham identified the constraints and restraints to guide target selection.[79] Targeteers were reluctant, for example, to plan strikes near Tripoli or attack C2 structures, primarily to avoid the appearance that they were trying to kill Qaddafi to achieve regime change. Woodward also sought to avoid strikes targeting Libyan infrastructure, such as water lines, to provide for an easier postwar transition to civilian control. By the end of Odyssey Dawn, however, the list of possible targets had vastly expanded to include sites near Tripoli, regime C2 facilities, ammunition sites, and other tactical and strategic targets, many of them identified through dynamic targeting methods.

By the second day of conflict, U.S. Admiral Mike Mullen, Chairman of the Joint Chiefs of Staff, reported that the no-fly zone was effectively in place.[80] Battle damage assessments confirmed the B-2 strikes against military facilities and aircraft were successful, and that the Tomahawk missile strikes had inflicted heavy damage on the regime's fixed air-defense capabilities, including SA-5, SA-3, and SA-2 surface-to-air missile batteries, and the early warning radars that could potentially target coalition aircraft. At issue, however, were mobile SAM capabilities and a large number of handheld SAMs (MANPADS). While this threat was reduced, CFAC Commander Lieutenant General Jodice II noted the threat of attack by mobile air defenses continued as late as August, when regime troops tried to reconstitute enough capability to menace Alliance aircraft. Navy EA-18G Growler and USAF F-16CJ aircraft conducted counterair missions as components of complete air packages, as described in the air tasking orders produced every 24 hours.[81] Admiral Gortney noted: "We now have the . . . capability to patrol the air space over Libya and we are doing just that, shifting to a more consistent and persistent air presence."[82]

U.S. Marine Air Operations

While General Woodward focused on the operational fight, the 26th MEU, under the command of Colonel Mark Desens, turned its attention to the protection of civilians

---

[79] Woodward, oral history interview, March 7, 2012.

[80] Michael J. Carden, "Mullen Says No-Fly Zone 'Effectively in Place,'" *American Forces Press Service*, March 20, 2011.

[81] An air tasking order is a method used to task and disseminate to components, subordinate units, and C2 agencies projected sorties, capabilities and/or forces to targets and specific missions, which normally include general and specific instructions and call signs, targets, C2 relationships, and other pertinent information as per Joint Publication 1-02. Air tasking orders are produced every 24 hours. The air tasking cycle takes 72 hours to produce an air tasking order (96 including battle damage assessment), although the 72-hour cycle can be adjusted as required by the conditions and situation.

[82] OASD (PA), "DOD News Briefing with Vice Adm. Gortney," March 20, 2011.

near Benghazi. The *Kearsarge* Amphibious Ready Group (ARG) operated about 100 miles offshore, and conducted operations in Libya from the first week in March until April 27. As Marine assets were positioned close to the battlespace, an effective cultural collaboration developed between the services. Although Marine aircraft lacked the armament and range of other assets, their proximity to the battlespace gave them a quick-response capability that made them especially effective during dynamic targeting of highly mobile enemy assets. Flying mostly at night, their training to conduct CAS missions closely correlated with the mission to protect civilians, and the Harriers' Litening integrated targeting pods provided target imagery in the absence of full motion video. The absence of forward air controllers challenged the operations, although the positive identification of regime troops was made easier by the regime's use of standard military equipment, while opposition forces operated primarily from pickup trucks with machine guns or other improvised equipment.

MEU commander Colonel Desens stated that because the JFACC was more than 350 nautical miles away from potential targets, hours factored into the decision cycle, while the MEU decision cycle took mere minutes.[83] The Marines' capability to generate high sortie rates with limited logistical assets validated not only their tactical airpower role, but also underscored the utility of the ARG. The TRAP mission illustrated the rapid response capabilities of the Osprey, and the organic air assets of the *Kearsarge* conducted responsive interdiction missions of regime forces with its six Harrier aircraft.[84] During Odyssey Dawn, Harriers destroyed 35 T-72 tanks, 25 armored personnel carriers, four heavy equipment transporters, two self-propelled artillery pieces, two multiple rocket launchers, and a *Scud* missile.[85]

The rescue of an Air Force pilot illustrated how Marine capabilities from an amphibious group could be used on the tactical level. As the operation continued into the evening of March 21, an Air Force F-15E crashed while conducting a mission near Benghazi. As the pilot and weapons system officer (WSO) ejected from the aircraft, USS *Kearsarge* was approximately 200 miles off the Libyan coast. Local opposition forces assisted the WSO to safety, but unidentified forces pursued the pilot, and the Air Force dispatched an F-16 to provide cover for the downed pilot to escape. The *Kearsarge* responded with a section of two AV-8B Harrier II fighters just after midnight.[86] The Harrier pilots rushed to the scene, and as they identified approaching enemy vehicles searching the area, one Harrier released two GBU-12 laser-guided 500-pound

---

[83] Colonel Mark Desens, "Forward Deployed Marines," excerpts from 26th Marine Expeditionary Unit Post Deployment Brief, December 6, 2011.

[84] Baughn, "U.S. Marine Corps Operations During Libya Crisis."

[85] Desens, "Forward Deployed Marines."

[86] Baughn, "U.S. Marine Corps Operations During Libya Crisis."

CH-53E Super Stallions loaded with quick reaction force Marines of Company B, 1st Battalion, 2nd Marine Regiment, 26th MEU, aboard USS *Kearsarge* (LHD-3), March 22, 2011.
Courtesy of the U.S. Marine Corps, photo by Lance Corporal Michael S. Lockett.

bombs on the vehicles.[87] As the Harriers provided close air support, at 1:22 a.m., the *Kearsarge* launched a TRAP team consisting of two MV-22 Ospreys, each carrying 15 Marines of 3rd Battalion, 8th Marine Landing Team, flying at 200 feet above ground level to evade radar detection. Two CH-53E Super Stallion helicopters launched at 1:51 a.m. carrying 46 additional Marines. As the Ospreys approached, the crew chief obtained a visual location on the downed pilot, and an F-16 marked the location with a laser indicator. The second Osprey landed less than 50 yards from the downed pilot, and a Marine reconnaissance team deployed to establish a defensive perimeter as the pilot climbed aboard, the team reboarded, and the aircraft took off, all in less than a minute. The entire flight returned to the *Kearsarge*, without the need for the CH-53s and their quick reaction landing team to respond. One Osprey pilot credited the aircraft's avionics and speed for the success of the rescue operation, noting that the aircraft made the difference between "having a smart phone and a dial telephone."[88]

---

[87] Baughn, "U.S. Marine Corps Operations During Libya Crisis." As Dr. Baughn noted, there are differing accounts of the details; however, two bombs were reportedly dropped on two different passes over the vehicles. The AV-8Bs were not carrying gun pods, so were unable to strafe. (Interview with Major General Margaret Woodward at the Pentagon, January 16, 2013.)

[88] Baughn, "U.S. Marine Corps Operations During Libya Crisis." See also USAF Aircraft Accident Investigation Board Report, F/15E Strike Eagle, T/N 91-000304, March 21, 2011, and Otto Kreisher, "Strike Eagle Rescue," *Air Force Magazine*, March 2013, Vol. 96, No. 3.

From Odyssey Dawn to Unified Protector

AFRICOM commander General Ham reported on March 21 that as the coalition continued to grow, BDAs from tactical and strategic air strikes showed they had achieved measurable desired effects, and coalition aircraft were gradually extending the no-fly zone. Coalition naval vessels continued maritime patrols to enforce the arms embargo and facilitate humanitarian support. There was concern that Libyans in Brega, Misrata, and Tripoli had fallen victim to regime attacks; however, concerns over possible collateral damage in urban areas limited tactical airstrikes.[89] Although U.S. military operations had contributed significantly to achieving intermediate objectives, regime forces had not yet complied with the UNSC resolution.[90]

Rear Admiral Gerard P. Hueber, chief of staff for JTF OOD, stated that military operations continued to inflict significant damage on regime forces. By March 23, the JTF had degraded fixed surface-to-air missile systems to "a negligible threat" and was "putting pressure" on Qaddafi's ground forces in Ajdabiya, and in Misrata to the west, although significant fighting continued in many areas. As operations continued, the focus shifted to the interdiction of regime forces intending to enter populated areas, C2 nodes, and lines of communication.[91]

The battle lines had shifted to the west and south by March 24. Admiral Gortney reported that naval and air forces had executed additional strikes on fixed targets and maneuver forces along the coastline and near the cities of Tripoli, Misrata, Zintan, and Ajdabiya. It seemed that U.S. forces had passed important milestones in terms of their participation. Substantial talks were under way to pass command and control of operations to other leadership, and other coalition forces were conducting roughly half of the strike missions and 75 percent of the combat air patrol missions in support of the no-fly zone. Admiral Gortney also noted that of the more than 350 aircraft dedicated to military operations in Libya, "Only slightly more than half belong to the United States."[92] An additional 14 Tomahawk cruise missiles had struck at an air-defense site near Sebha in the south and a *Scud* missile garrison near Tripoli. As the no-fly zone expanded further south, so did the naval presence of the coalition, as two aircraft carriers from France and Italy joined the maritime effort.[93]

As operations continued, U.S. and coalition forces shifted their attacks westward to Tripoli, southward near Sebha, and began to emphasize dynamic targeting. The targets of opportunity were primarily regime forces that posed threats to population centers. As coalition participation increased, JTF OOD came closer to achieving the

---

[89] OASD (PA), "DOD News Briefing with Gen. Ham."

[90] OASD (PA), "DOD News Briefing with Adm. Locklear via Telephone from USS *Mount Whitney*," Washington, D.C.: U.S. Department of Defense, March 22, 2011.

[91] OASD (PA), "DOD News Briefing with Rear Adm. Hueber via Telephone from USS *Mount Whitney*."

[92] OASD (PA), "DOD News Briefing with Vice Adm. Gortney," March 24, 2011.

[93] OASD (PA), "DOD News Briefing with Vice Adm. Gortney," March 24, 2011.

third leg of its strategy—to transition C2 of operations to other leadership. NATO assumed the lead for the maritime embargo mission, under the command of Vice Admiral Rinaldo Veri of the Italian Navy, on March 23,[94] and NATO Secretary General Anders Fogh Rasmussen announced that the Alliance would also assume responsibility for the no-fly zone within the next few days.[95] U.S. officials began to talk of the "unique capabilities" that U.S. forces would provide to the Alliance; however, no clear option seemed to exist regarding who would assume the air interdiction strike missions. Admiral Gortney said, "Whichever way the third mission goes, whoever ends up taking it over, I can assure you that we will continue to support our allies and partners with our unique capabilities and that we will continue to work hard to make sure that transition is seamless. Job one is to protect the Libyan people, and the job doesn't change just because we get a new boss."[96]

As the fighting continued, U.S. officials prepared to transition leadership of military operations in Libya to NATO. Secretary of Defense Gates and Secretary of State Clinton shared their conception of the continuing American role in a series of press conferences on March 27. Secretary Gates assessed that coalition forces had implemented the no-fly zone, which could be sustained with much less effort in the future, and had "prevented the large scale slaughter that was beginning to take place, has taken place in some places." Secretary Clinton added:

> What is quite remarkable here is that NATO assuming the responsibility for the entire mission means that the United States will move to a supporting role . . . We are supporting a mission through NATO that was very much initiated by European requests joined by Arab requests . . . This is a watershed moment in international decision making.[97]

Talks were still ongoing regarding the responsibility for tactical air strikes against regime forces. *Washington Post* reporters quoted a Western diplomat as saying that Turkish officials "had balked on reaching a final agreement because of their uneasiness with the coalition's ground attacks, which have raised concerns in the Arab world over possible civilian deaths."[98]

---

[94] From March 23 to October 31, 2011, Admiral Veri was the commander of the Maritime Forces for Operation Unified Protector. NATO Allied Maritime Command Naples website, "Commander Allied Maritime Command," accessed February 24, 2012.

[95] NATO, "Statement by the NATO Secretary General on Libya Arms Embargo," March 22, 2011. NATO command and control of the no-fly mission occurred on March 24.

[96] OSD (PA), "DOD News Briefing with Vice Adm. Gortney," March 25, 2011.

[97] OASD (PA), "ABC's *This Week* Interview with Secretary Gates and Secretary Clinton on Libya," Washington, D.C.: U.S. Department of Defense, March 27, 2011.

[98] Mary Beth Sheridan and Greg Jaffe, "Coalition Agrees to Put NATO in Charge of No-Fly Zone in Libya," *Washington Post*, March 24, 2011.

In the last few days under coalition (JTF-OOD) control, coalition forces conducted additional TLAM strikes and flew 178 sorties in the 24-hour period ending March 28. AC-130 gunships joined A-10s in the efforts against regime forces in fiercely contested areas. Opposition forces gained control of Ajdabiya and moved westward to within 80 miles of Sirte. Admiral Gortney noted that regime troops appeared to be preparing defensive positions around Sirte. Coalition aircraft continued to attack regime forces near Misrata, and where heavy fighting had taken place over the last few days in Sirte and Ras Lanuf. Six TLAMs struck the headquarters facility of Qaddafi's 32nd Brigade, and strikes continued to attack ammunition stores and bunkers near Tripoli and Sebha.[99] Two B-1B Lancer bombers of the 28th Bomb Wing left Ellsworth AFB, South Dakota, early on March 27 to strike additional fixed targets that included ammunition depots, aircraft and vehicle maintenance facilities, and buildings related to C2 and air defense systems. The B-1Bs recovered at bases in Europe after striking nearly 100 targets with JDAMs. The crews had two days to plan the mission, which included 24 hours of flight time. This marked the first time the B-1 fleet had launched combat sorties from U.S. bases to strike overseas targets.[100]

As coalition capabilities grew throughout OOD, the percentage of U.S. sorties declined. Pentagon spokesmen acknowledged that U.S. forces had expended more than 455 air-delivered PGMs and 199 TLAMs, 93 of the latter having been launched from the *Ohio*-class guided-missile submarine USS *Florida*. In a final press conference on March 28, Admiral Gortney noted that of a total of 1,602 sorties thus far, U.S. forces had flown 983, which included fighters, strike aircraft, tankers, surveillance, and C2 missions and aircraft. Of 735 strike sorties, U.S. forces had flown roughly half—370 compared to 365 strike sorties flown by other coalition members.[101] General Schwartz, then Air Force Chief of Staff, later noted that U.S. airmen had conducted 99 percent of operational airlift, 79 percent of inflight refueling, 50 percent of airborne reconnaissance, and 40 percent of strike missions during Odyssey Dawn.[102]

U.S. forces had overcome significant challenges. Airmen had extended C2 relationships across combatant commands and developed work-arounds for AFRICOM's lack of manpower, capabilities, and assets. Airmen adapted staff processes and used improvised orders processes (verbal orders, PowerPoint, email, video conferencing) to produce the needed resources and equipment. General Ham, Admiral Locklear, General Welsh, General Gorenc, and General Woodward had worked through ambiguous

---

[99] OASD (PA), "DOD News Briefing with Vice Adm. Gortney," March 28, 2011; John A Tirpak, "Bombers over Libya," *Air Force Magazine*, July 2011, pp. 36–39.

[100] Scott Fontaine, "B-1B Crew Recalls Epic Mission to Libya," *Air Force Times*, April 2, 2011; David Axe, "Two Bombers, 24 Hours, 100 Libyan Targets Destroyed," Wired Danger Room online, July 13, 2011.

[101] OASD (PA), "DOD News Briefing with Vice Adm. Gortney," March 28, 2011.

[102] General Norton Schwartz, "Air Force Contributions to Our Military and Our Nation," prepared remarks delivered at the World Affairs Council, Wilmington, Del., undated.

strategic guidance and the lack of a clear end state to develop constraints (right and left limits), intermediate objectives and tactical objectives, and had planned for the handover to NATO.

General Welsh, the USAFE commander, described the operation as a definite success story for airmen. As many as 3,132 USAF personnel and 153 aircraft deployed to support OOD; those aircraft flew 13,930 flight hours during 2,132 sorties. U.S. aircraft had employed 764 weapons and fired an additional 2,169 rounds of ammunition. Support aircraft flew 311 air-refueling missions and distributed 17.3 million pounds of fuel. In addition, U.S. forces flew 151 airlift missions that transported 3,177 passengers and carried 2,371 tons of cargo.[103] With the transition of all missions to NATO leadership on March 31, Odyssey Dawn drew to a close, and military operations in Libya continued under Operation Unified Protector.

Operation Unified Protector

On March 27, NATO leaders agreed to assume control of all military operations in Libya under UNSC Resolutions 1970 and 1973.[104] Royal Canadian Air Force Lieutenant-General Charles Bouchard, the deputy commander, Joint Force Command, NATO, and the commander of Operation Unified Protector, noted that three characteristics described the operation: it was quickly made, cheap, and flexible. He characterized the transition of military operations from the Odyssey Dawn coalition to the Alliance structure as a "hail Mary pass" because of the rapid response required, and the fact that some observers may have been skeptical about the chances for the success of such an undertaking. Unified Protector and NATO member nations faced significant fiscal and political constraints, which made efficient, precise, and coordinated operations essential. Moreover, the integration of non-NATO nations into operations increased their complexity; in particular, challenges in the areas of equipment interoperability and standard security procedures quickly became apparent. General Bouchard observed that communication—using doctrine rather than dogma as a guide—and flexibility in other areas were the keys to operational success.[105]

Although OUP headquarters was a true multinational organization, the United States provided a large share of its personnel. Staffing levels were smaller than during Odyssey Dawn, and the total manning in NATO billets in the combined force air

---

[103] Unclassified information from Headquarters United States Air Forces in Europe/Office of History, *The United States Air Forces in Europe in Operation Odyssey Dawn*, Ramstein Air Base, Germany: HQ USAFE/HO, February 28, 2012, not available to the general public.

[104] NATO, "NATO and Libya," online, last updated March 28, 2012 (accessed December 5, 2011).

[105] Lt.-Gen. Bouchard, "Coalition Building and the Future of NATO Operations: 2/14/2012—Transcript."

component continued to build throughout the first few months.[106] By comparison, while 900 people were on board USS *Mount Whitney* during Odyssey Dawn, approximately 300 personnel from the NATO command structure and another 220 national representatives, weapons system experts, and liaison officers worked in the air component headquarters in Poggio Renatico Air Base near Ferrara, Italy. For most personnel, rotations lasted 45 to 60 days.[107] Admiral James Stavridis, Supreme Allied Commander, Europe, discharged his duties from NATO headquarters in Mons, Belgium. General Jodice served as CFACC, initially from his headquarters in Izmir, Turkey, and later from NATO's Combined Air Operations Center (CAOC 5) facility at Poggio Renatico.[108] Italian Vice Admiral Rinaldo Veri served as maritime component commander from his headquarters at Nissita, Italy. Admiral Locklear continued to serve as commander, Allied Joint Forces Command Naples.[109]

The Transition to NATO

General Jodice's headquarters staff conducted planning activities beginning in mid-March to prepare for the transition to NATO C2 under Unified Protector. When asked how he would characterize the transition, General Jodice used the analogy of a "planned play with some risk, but preparation" because of the coordination conducted between the upcoming NATO CFACC and Odyssey Dawn's JFACC, General Woodward, during the transition period.[110] Together, Generals Jodice and Woodward developed a deliberate plan for the handoff of the air component command. The CAOC 5 staff at Poggio Renatico, under the CFAC director, USAF Colonel Ancel B. Yarbrough II, prepared to conduct air operations approximately two weeks before the transition to NATO began. As they expanded the operations floor, augmentees (approximately 45 Italian nationals, and ten personnel from CAOC 7 in Greece) received the call to assemble as they had trained for NATO Response Force activation. The CFAC enterprise was initially split by function—air tasking order planning, execution, and mission analysis personnel were located at Poggio, while General Jodice's headquarters staff remained at Izmir. The headquarters staff performed the strategy development and provided written guidance to shape planning decisions. Initial shortages occurred in some disciplines, such as subject matter experts in the Intelligence, Surveillance

---

[106]"Coalition Building and the Future of NATO Operations."

[107]Email from USAF officer from OUP CAOC to Deborah Kidwell, "OUP stats," April 6, 2012.

[108]NATO website fact sheet, "Operation Unified Protector Command and Control," accessed March 7, 2012. CAOC 5 was one of the five operations centers under the Southern Europe commander of NATO air forces Component Command Air (CC-Air), located in Izmir, Turkey, and was staffed with personnel assigned from 13 Alliance member nations. See "NATO CAOC Five," accessed March 26, 2012.

[109]Karen Parrish, "Locklear Nominated as Next PACOM Commander," American Forces Press Service, December 30, 201.

[110]General Jodice, oral history interview, February 28, 2012.

and Reconnaissance Division and targeting capability.[111] The planning section initially lacked sufficient manning, equipment, and facilities to execute a 24-hour continuous planning production process, which altered the planning cycle, at times compressing it and extending execution days. General Jodice soon realized that to conduct the type of dynamic targeting required for successful operations, the two functional areas should be collocated, and so all personnel deployed to Poggio Renatico by early April.[112]

At the combined air operations center, which eventually evolved to resemble its U.S. counterpart Joint Air Operations Center (JAOC), staff members progressively developed processes and organizations to develop strategy, select targets, and control operations. Center personnel built a strong strategy division capability during the first two weeks of the operation. The CAOC director guided the development of the organizational structure to provide the functions that were initially lacking or understaffed. This included a Guidance/Apportionment/Targeting branch within the strategy division to enhance the formulation of strategy and guidance provided to air tasking order planners. U.S. doctrine and practice influenced the ISRD, which started with available manning levels and facilities. The division continued to expand its capabilities until it achieved maturity in midsummer. This effort required a division chief who possessed a comprehensive knowledge based in deep experience, as many personnel in both the strategy and ISR divisions lacked the required background and were trained on site as the operation progressed. Innovation also was necessary. During the first two weeks, the operations floor shifted several times to find the optimum capabilities pairing and to enhance communication on the floor. Although NATO procedures were modified to meet operational challenges, the most significant difference was that new components were added to meet mission requirements: "There were so many 'new' parts added to our CAOC that by the end of the operation, we didn't look anything like we do during peacetime."[113] Although doctrine and practice served as a baseline for operations, most personnel interviewed for this report stated that flexibility, agility and tailoring functions and organizations to meet mission requirements in an innovative manner were essential.

---

[111] Email and attachment from USAF officer in OUP CAOC to Deborah Kidwell, "RE: referral from General Jodice," March 19, 20, 21, 2012. Intelligence, Surveillance and Reconnaissance Division (ISRD), composed of members from USAF's five AN/USQ-163 Falconer AOCs, the Distributed Ground Station community, USAF major commands and subordinate units, and coalition and joint partners, provides the Combined Force Air Component Commander, air operations center, and subordinate units with intelligence, operations, and targeting to meet military objectives. See United States Air Forces Central Command, "Intelligence, Surveillance and Reconnaissance Division (ISRD)," Fact Sheet, posted online September 7, 2009.

[112] General Jodice, oral history interview, February 28, 2012.

[113] Email from USAF officer in OUP CAOC to Deborah Kidwell, March 19, 2012. It is important to remember that NATO peacetime CAOCs (CAOC 5 before Unified Protector) are not equivalent (as comprehensively staffed) to USAF AOCs that support combatant commanders.

Order of Battle

U.S. military forces continued to support all three elements of the NATO mission and assigned forces and assets as necessary. The bulk of the air forces generated from U.S. European Command, including the 406th Air Expeditionary Wing, Expeditionary Fighter Squadrons, an Airborne Air Control Squadron, an Expeditionary Airborne Command and Control Squadron, an Air Base Squadron, and several Rescue Squadrons attached or assigned to either permanent party units at the forward operating bases, the numbered air forces, or the air expeditionary wing.[114] The 22nd MEU, reinforced with attack, helicopter, aerial refueler transport, logistics, and electronic warfare elements, replaced the 26th MEU in late April.[115] U.S. naval assets included the cruiser USS *Monterey*; destroyers USS *Barry, Stout*, and *Roosevelt*; the USS *Bataan* ARG including USS *Ponce, Mesa Verde*, and *Whidbey Island;* and support ships USS *Kanawha, Laramie*, and *Robert E. Peary.*[116] U.S. forces remained distributed throughout the Operation Unified Protector area of operations, as they had during Odyssey Dawn.[117]

U.S. air assets provided to Unified Protector included a broad range of aircraft types. Manned aircraft provided refueling, ISR, electronic warfare, and SEAD/DEAD. The USAF provided E-3 Sentry aircraft to cover one of the four lines in the 24-hour AWACS orbit maintained by NATO, and limited surveillance and reconnaissance sorties from a U-2 aircraft. President Obama approved the use of two armed MQ-1B Predator drones to provide ISR and offensive counterair (OCA) strike capability. General Cartwright, Vice Chairman of the Joint Chiefs of Staff, explained that this was necessary because of the change in the character of the fight—"the intermixing of the lines"—and the need for more precision identification, although news sources noted the apparent strategy shift

---

[114] Essentially, the 31st Fighter Wing at Aviano with supporting expeditionary fighter squadrons from Spangdahlem, Shaw, and Lakenheath; the 100th Air Refueling Wing serving initially at Morón for OOD then shifting some assets to Istres, France, to support OUP; ISR elements at Sigonella and Souda Bay; and the rescue elements at initially Sigonella and later Kalamata. The 406th AEW only existed for a very brief time.

[115] Daily News Staff, "22nd MEU relieves 26th MEU," *The Daily News*, Jacksonville, N.C., April 29, 2011. The 22nd MEU remained deployed until February 2012 aboard the Bataan ARG. See "22nd MEU to Return This Week," *The Daily News*, Jacksonville, N.C., February 2, 2012.

[116] Henry Boyd, "Operation Unified Protector—Allied Assets Deployed to Libya," *IISS Voices*, online. Coalition assets as of June 10, 2011. USAF HH-60G Pave Hawk combat search-and-rescue (CSAR) helicopters deployed on French and British amphibious assault vessels during Operation Unified Protector, the first such occurrence. This forward deployment similarly enabled reduced transit time and allowed them to better support theater missions.

[117] Butler, "Operation Odyssey Dawn/Operation Unified Protector." Specific units included: 406th Air Expeditionary Wing (with assigned Operations and Maintenance Groups and Medical Squadron), 77th Expeditionary Fighter Squadron (EFS), 55th EFS, 965th Expeditionary Airborne Air Control Squadron, 16th Expeditionary Airborne Command and Control Squadron, 776th Expeditionary Air Base Squadron, 347th Air Expeditionary Group, 38th Expeditionary Rescue Squadron (ERS), 56th ERS, 71st ERS, 48th ERS, 55th ERS, and 58th ERS, attached to the 406th Air Expeditionary Wing, Third Air Force, 17th Air Force, the 347th or 322nd Air Expeditionary Group at Souda Bay, the 31st Operations Group at Aviano, or the 48th Mission Support Group at Kalamata.

from a strictly support role to again providing lethal strike capability.[118] Three MQ-4 Block 30 Global Hawk remotely piloted aircraft (RPA) flew more than 335 hours of ISR missions in support of operations in Libya through mid-April.[119] E-8 JSTARS and RC-135V/W Rivet Joint aircraft provided airborne battle management, C2, and ISR functions on a limited daily basis. Navy EA-18G Growler (later EA-6B Prowler) and Air Force F16CJ aircraft continued to fly electronic warfare and SEAD/DEAD missions from Aviano Air Base. Information operations personnel conducted psychological operations and dropped leaflets from tactical fighters and other aircraft in an attempt to influence regime troops to cease fighting. KC-10 and KC-135 aircraft assigned to Unified Protector conducted refueling operations, while C-17 and C-130 transport aircraft provided airlift and other combat support capabilities.[120]

In early April, however, the United States made a decision to reduce its contribution of strike assets to OUP. The U.S. strike aircraft, including A-10 and AC-130 ground-attack planes, were placed on standby, to be called if requested by General Bouchard, according to Admiral Mullen.[121] The commander of the U.S. Sixth Fleet (the AFRICOM Naval Component commander) maintained operational control of the 22nd MEU, which arrived during the transition period to Unified Protector. The Bataan ARG (BATARG)/22nd MEU team was tasked with four possible mission sets: 24/7 TRAP response for flights over Libya and the Department of State team in Benghazi; strike; humanitarian assistance; and possible securing of sensitive sites. The MEU operated from the NATO air tasking order and special instructions (SPINS) for airspace management; if NATO required support, the request flowed up to AFRICOM in Stuttgart and through the commander, Sixth Fleet, to the MEU. The complete BATARG/22nd MEU team supported Unified Protector from late April through the end of July. From August through November, detachments of the 22nd MEU from the USS *Mesa Verde*, USS *Bataan,* and USS *Whidbey Island* variously supported OUP and then Operation Odyssey Guard, the opening of the U.S. Embassy in Tripoli.[122]

---

[118] OASD (PA), "DOD News Briefing with Secretary Gates and Gen. Cartwright from the Pentagon," Washington, D.C.: U.S. Department of Defense, April 21, 2011.

[119] Flown from Sigonella Air Base from March 1 to April 14 according to Northrop Grumman, "Global Hawk—Global ISR Operations! 'March Madness,'" accessed online March 28, 2012.

[120] See Christopher M. Blanchard, *Libya: Unrest and U.S. Policy*, Washington, D.C.: Congressional Research Service, July 6, 2011, p. 5, for a general description of operations, and Chapter 3. U.S. cargo aircraft were not assigned to NATO.

[121] David S. Cloud, "Region in Turmoil; U.S. Cutting Its Craft from Libya Sorties," *Los Angeles Times*, April 1, 2011, p. AA5.

[122] The TRAP mission required continuous planning that included rehearsals, chat rooms, liaison officer visits to various personnel recovery cells and NATO maritime assets, and daily contact with the U.S. State Department team. Email from 22nd MEU officer to Deborah Kidwell, "OOD and OUP Project," May 30, 2012.

A 931st Air Refueling Group KC-135 Stratotanker, deployed with the 313th AEW, prepares to refuel a C-17 Globemaster over the Atlantic Ocean at the end of Operation Unified Protector, October 29, 2011. The C-17, from the 172nd Airlift Wing, Mississippi Air National Guard, was en route from Tripoli to Boston to deliver 22 Libyan rebel fighters for medical care.
Courtesy of the U.S. Air Force, photo by Major Andra Higgs.

Changes to the Concept of Operations

By the time NATO assumed responsibility for military operations, the regime forces had regained momentum and prepared to counterattack. Throughout April, poor weather conditions hampered ongoing operations and intelligence collection (particularly battle damage reports and monitoring troop movements). To make matters more difficult, regime forces had adopted new tactics—in many cases, they abandoned military equipment and discarded their uniforms to blend in with opposition forces. For much of the fighting that followed, Libyan military assets changed hands so often that troop identification became difficult. However, General Bouchard noted that the threats against civilians were very real—Qaddafi had initially ordered his loyal troops to kill all males between the ages of 17 and 40 upon entering Benghazi, and continued to issue orders to behead civilians as late as October.[123] As regime troops closed the gap between themselves and heavily populated areas where opposition forces gathered, it often became difficult to distinguish clear battle lines. As a result, NATO focused on conducting strikes against ground troops in the second echelon areas, and targeting lines of communications, depots, C2 nodes, and military facilities.

When Unified Protector began, military planners focused their efforts to protect civilians by attempting to stabilize areas near Benghazi and Ajdabiya. Regime troops had entrenched near Brega, and NATO planners realized that the close proximity

---

[123]Lt.-Gen. Bouchard, "Coalition Building and the Future of NATO Operations," February 14, 2012.

of oil and water pipelines would make interdiction of these forces difficult if regime troops managed to advance further than Ajdabiya in their efforts to reach the opposition stronghold of Benghazi. Other concerns during the first three months included efforts to keep the port of Misrata open, stabilize operations in the western mountains, and ensure that the oil and water pipelines so close to Benghazi, and so critical to Libya's economic recovery, were preserved. As NATO operations began to stabilize large opposition-held areas in the western and eastern portions of Libya, opposition troops began to organize and train, and the Libyan National Transitional Council (NTC) sought political recognition.[124]

While the goals and objectives of the U.N. Security Council resolutions remained consistent into Operation Unified Protector, the concept of operations shifted focus to fit the operational environment. The targeting process placed progressively greater emphasis on dynamic targeting, which was the primary reason to collocate General Jodice's staff (from Izmir) and CAOC 5 personnel at Poggio Renatico.[125] Air tasking orders focused on destroying regime C2 nodes, logistics, and ammunition storage facilities. Planners shifted their focus from destroying or degrading enemy air defenses to maintaining air supremacy. This required continued monitoring of the IADS remnants, and of mobile air defenses in particular. For example, as late as July, regime forces attempted to relocate and reconstitute air defense weapons located near Sebha in the defense of Tripoli. Conducting BDA was sometimes problematic, as personnel and equipment shortages rendered assessments above phase 1 level difficult.[126] As an integral partner within the NATO alliance, U.S. forces continued to provide air refueling, ISR assets, defense suppression capabilities, and munitions, which were all precision-guided. As in Odyssey Dawn, the desired strategic end state remained imprecise, and General Jodice described it as essentially "until your services are no longer needed."[127]

A new consensus model emerged slowly on the CAOC floor. Instead of a comprehensive agreement on all missions that were considered necessary to achieve Alliance goals, the NATO command structure incorporated the resources each member or partner was willing to commit to certain missions on a piecemeal basis.[128] Under these circumstances, liaison officers (LNOs) were crucial to the success of the Alliance C2 structure and the production of air tasking orders. Liaisons coordinated action between individual air and naval components of NATO and their respective countries' national

---

[124]"Coalition Building and the Future of NATO Operations."

[125]General Jodice, oral history interview, February 28, 2011.

[126]General Jodice, oral history interview, February 28, 2011.

[127]General Jodice, oral history interview, February 28, 2011.

[128]This level of coordination represents a distinct departure from previous NATO and coalition efforts, which may become more common. If contributors can agree on the need to act to protect civilians, for example, they may not all allow their aircraft to be used in strike missions against the enemy. Where this was the case, allies were given alternative tasks.

command authority, in addition to their more general role as subject matter experts on weapons and targeting. As links between the use of weapons systems, intelligence platforms, and planners, LNOs continually revised special instructions to pilots (SPINS). Without customary levels of C2 and intelligence preparation, some pilots initially were uncomfortable with more fluid special instructions. As LNOs revised the SPINS to provide the guidance for dynamic targeting (quantifying the standards for positive identification of targets, for example), pilots and weapons officers became proficient in developing the language, procedures, and instructions necessary to complete the missions. Nearly every person contacted in the course of this study listed the performance of LNOs as one of the best practices of both military operations, and one that particularly allowed the NATO alliance to coordinate operations effectively.[129]

The senior national liaison officers at the Combined Forces Air Component Headquarters, often identified as red-card holders, performed an especially important function for the Alliance. As previously discussed, the urgency to act to protect civilians precluded a definitive resolution of all the issues regarding the desired strategic end state and the exact use of national assets. This time pressure left the Alliance vulnerable to disagreement unless a workable process could be found to resolve discrepancies on a case-by-case basis. Red-card holders are an element of NATO doctrine used to resolve areas in which consensus does not exist on each issue within the Alliance and to ensure mission accomplishment. Red-card holders exercised the rights of each contributor of forces by ensuring that the missions they were assigned met their national policy, and had the power to veto the use of their national assets for a particular mission. Red-card holders met regularly as a group with the air operations center director, and when the air component commander required it. Through these meetings, Alliance members and partners were kept informed not only of each nation's policy regarding the acceptable use of its military assets, but also the operational assessments and intentions of air tasking officials. During ongoing kinetic operations, red-card holders or their designated alternates observed operations from the air operations center floor. During dynamic targeting they were a component of the decision tree that determined whether or not to strike a particular target; as the air operations center floor learned mission requirements, red-card holders ensured no reservations existed regarding the use of each asset provided by their countries. Even though the asset in question was tasked to conduct a NATO mission, the liaison process maintained Alliance consensus and ensured that each nation's tasking also satisfied internal guidance. This coordination process was more difficult to assimilate into the air tasking orders in the early days of the operation; however, the air operations center floor staff quickly learned each nation's caveats and avoided areas where conflict could hamper operations.[130]

---

[129] Email from USAF officer in OUP CAOC to Deborah Kidwell, March 20, 2012. General Jodice noted the effort to coordinate the use of resources was one of the most difficult challenges of Unified Protector.

[130] Email from USAF officer in OUP CAOC to Deborah Kidwell, March 20, 2012.

The NATO effort also included nonkinetic operations. While some airborne assets migrated seamlessly from Operation Odyssey Dawn—the capability to conduct radio broadcasts, for example—other capabilities such as leaflet drops were not initially available, and staff spent the first several months focused on finding suitable alternatives.[131] General Jodice and his staff were committed to the value of nonkinetic operations; however, available assets, processes, and personnel initially proved to be limitations. Although the first leaflet drop occurred in early May, it was not until July that the elements to more fully employ nonkinetic operations became fully available. Staff spent the first few months (April to June) determining which aircraft were capable of dropping leaflets within the constraints provided, the weapons to deliver the leaflets, and developing a process to obtain approval for the drops.[132]

U.S. tactical fighters and other assets delivered leaflets from medium altitude, typically concentrated in one or two locations in an attempt to influence regime forces to surrender or cease hostilities. These efforts evoked fear of lethal kinetic strikes and ensured that regime forces knew they were under surveillance, according to senior CAOC officers.[133] U.S. forces released approximately nine million leaflets from F-16 aircraft throughout the campaign, which were designed to reach multiple audiences that included regime forces and mercenaries, opposition groups, and civilians.[134] During the first four months, F-16CJ aircraft from Aviano were tasked to perform the leaflet drops, which left fewer aircraft to accomplish the primary SEAD/DEAD mission. Beginning in August, however, U.S. authorities dedicated three F-16CMs from the Aviano wing for the sole purpose of leaflet dropping, which allowed F-16CJ aircraft to concentrate on the SEAD/DEAD mission.[135]

Simultaneously, U.S. EC-130H Compass Call aircraft provided more than 4,500 hours of sustained radio broadcasts on multiple tactical and approved commercial frequencies to inform Libyan audiences of NATO's mission and to persuade combatants to lay down their arms.[136] Measures of performance and effect indicated that the target audiences received these radio broadcasts, which in some cases inspired listeners to seek additional information from nonregime sources. Airborne electronic warfare

---

[131] Email from AAC Izmir officer, "Re: Non Kinetic Actions in Libya," to Deborah Kidwell, May 21, 2012. See also Geoffrey Childs, "Military Information Support to Contingency Operations in Libya." *Special Warfare,* Vol. 26, No. 1, January 2013, pp. 14–17, for a discussion of Military Information Support Operations during both operations.

[132] Email from AAC Izmir officer, "Re: Non Kinetic Actions in Libya."

[133] Email from USAF officer in OUP CAOC to Deborah Kidwell, March 20, 2012.

[134] Email from USAF officer in OUP CAOC to Deborah Kidwell, April 3, 2012; the F-16CMs delivered up to 650,000 leaflets to multiple locations in a single mission. E-mail, "Re: Non Kinetic Actions in Libya."

[135] Email from USAF officer in OUP CAOC to Deborah Kidwell, April 3, 2012.

[136] Email from AAC Izmir officer, "Re: Non Kinetic Actions in Libya." See also Childs, "Military Information Support."

A U.S. Air Force F-16CJ from the 20th Fighter Wing on a leaflet-dropping mission over Libya on July 13, 2011. Under its right wing is a PDU-5/B leaflet dispenser.
Courtesy of the U.S. Air Force.

assets were employed in some required places to disrupt regime communications and prevent regime forces from attacking or threatening to attack civilians and civilian populated areas. Indications suggested that these efforts, particularly at late stages in the campaign, were highly effective and prevented regime forces from attacking civilians. Finally, the CFAC worked to employ shows of presence/shows of force when appropriate to influence target audiences to give up the fight and to ensure audiences knew NATO was present to protect civilians as necessary.[137] To enhance the coordination (and thus the synergistic effect) of these nonkinetic and kinetic effects, the CJTF developed a synchronization matrix, which General Jodice later noted had significantly contributed to the effectiveness of the air campaign.[138]

As the war continued, opposition forces began to organize and train to defeat regime troops. Finally, opposition forces conducted offensives originating from three areas: forces in the western mountain areas moved eastward to Tripoli; forces in Misrata moved both westward toward Tripoli as well as toward Brega to the east; and forces from Benghazi organized and moved to the west.[139] The key turning points for opposition forces came when forces in the Berber highlands gained access to the coastal road from Tripoli to Tunisia, and when opposition forces broke out from Misrata. Subsequently, regime troops suffered severe operational difficulties that restricted

---

[137] Email from AAC Izmir officer, "Re: Non Kinetic Actions in Libya."

[138] General Jodice, oral history interview, February 28, 2012.

[139] Lt.-Gen. Bouchard, "Coalition Building and the Future of NATO Operations," February 14, 2012.

their logistics and freedom of movement. Opposition forces occupied Qaddafi's compound in Tripoli by mid-August; however, the leader and his family were not found, and Qaddafi remained defiant.[140] Reuters reported that through August, U.S. aircraft had flown 5,316 sorties, including 1,210 strike sorties, of which 262 had dropped ordnance on targets, and that 101 U.S. Predator drone strikes had occurred.[141] By September, opposition forces occupied the airport and citadel areas of the southern desert town of Sebha, although heavy fighting continued near Tripoli.[142] Regime forces finally collapsed with the death of Qaddafi on October 20 in Sirte, as that city fell to opposition forces.[143] After seven months of air and sea operations, NATO ended its mission in Libya on October 31, 2011. NATO Secretary General Rasmussen said, "NATO answered the call. We launched our operation faster than ever before. More than 8,000 servicemen and women took part in our mission for Libya. We were effective, flexible and precise."[144]

U.S. forces flew more than 7,100 total sorties during Operation Unified Protector, which represented nearly 27 percent of the total sorties flown during the operation. The U.S. Air Force flew approximately 25 percent of the total OUP sorties, while the U.S. Navy and Marine Corps completed more than 2 percent of the sorties flown. Of the U.S. sorties, more than 4,200 refueling; more than 1,500 SEAD/DEAD/EW; and approximately 100 offensive counterair, 450 remotely piloted aircraft, 200 reconnaissance, and 250 information operations missions were conducted.[145]

Conclusions

Despite the political, economic, and military complexities involved, U.S. forces led a successful coalition effort that established a no-fly zone, enforced an embargo, protected civilians, and transitioned operations to NATO command and control. Subsequently, U.S. forces contributed to a fully functioning Alliance that reacted quickly

---

[140] David D. Kirkpatrick, "Qaddafi Defiant After Rebel Takeover," *The New York Times*, August 23, 2011.

[141] "Factbox: Pentagon Says U.S. Stepped Up Pace of Libya Air Strikes," *Reuters*, August 22, 2011. Unified Protector was the first time the U.S. Air Force had used the Predator aircraft in the DEAD role.

[142] Ian Black and Chris Stephen, "Libya: Gaddafi Son Spotted in Bani Walid as Heavy Fighting Continues," *The Guardian*, September 19, 2011.

[143] Rania El Gamal and Tim Gaynor, "Gaddafi Killed as Libya's Revolt Claims Hometown," *Reuters Africa*, October 20, 2011.

[144] NATO Press Office, "'We Answered the Call'—The End of Operation Unified Protector," October 31, 2011.

[145] Email from USAF officer in OUP CAOC to Deborah Kidwell, "OUP stats," April 6, 2012. General Jodice reported that 26 nations were represented in the CFAC, which produced 218 air tasking orders, and that 16 nations flew over 25,000 sorties, with more than 9,000 of those sorties as offensive counterair missions. Ralph J. Jodice II, "Operation Unified Protector (OUP) Mission Brief," presented at the Atlantic Council, Washington, D.C., June 4, 2012.

and built and maintained a consensus for action that gave Libyans the opportunity to decide their own fate without suffering mass civilian casualties. General Welsh, then commander of U.S. Air Forces in Europe, noted the two operations were unique, because the primary responsibility during Odyssey Dawn fell to a less mature combatant command and because of the atypical coalition that participated in Unified Protector.[146] The significance of this achievement should not be underestimated.

Airmen worked together to find creative solutions to the structural challenges they faced, including C2 arrangements, scarce resources, and planning ambiguities. Doctrine guided, but did not prescribe appropriate C2 structures; when presented with an unusual situation, commanders devised a unique solution. Planners overcame ambiguous strategic guidance and time constraints through coordination between service planning staffs and joint staffs to produce sound military options. Although AFRICOM's responsibility to conduct kinetic operations through JTF-OOD came at a vulnerable time in many respects, staff personnel used their training, expertise, and relationships to overcome the challenges of the impending change of command, unexpected mission, and limited resources. Air component commanders correctly identified unity of action and maintenance of a consensus as important overarching priorities. If a single lesson were to be learned from military operations in Libya, it would be that this consensus model is a central component of smoothly functioning coalition and Alliance military operations.

Liaison officers were particularly critical to Alliance cohesion. They provided the crucial information that air tasking order production personnel needed to match the tasking, weaponeering, and politically acceptable uses of assets with the missions required to achieve operational objectives.[147] Senior commanders drew on their working relationships with their national and international peers to forge solutions to challenges that included command authority, manpower and capability needs, cumbersome security practices, and limitations of equipment interoperability. This coordination and innovation occurred across the range of levels and staffs. Moreover, high levels of trust developed between Alliance members. Partly this stemmed from their commitment to each other and to the purpose and success of the mission, but it also came because of common NATO mission and training standards, which allowed each member nation to understand and be confident of each contributor's capabilities.[148] In short, the people made the operation successful through flexibility, training, and dedication.

---

[146] General Mark A. Welsh III, notes from oral history interview, Deborah Kidwell, May 14, 2012.

[147] The weapon system liaisons communicated what the aircraft and pilots could do; the political liaisons communicated what the national command authorities would allow their nations' aircraft to do. The air tasking order production team assimilated and coordinated this information into a comprehensive air campaign that produced a workable air tasking order every 24 hours.

[148] Interview with senior member of Lieutenant General Jodice's staff by Deborah Kidwell, "Outline Transcript," May 24, 2012. Ongoing military-to-military exchanges, established relationships, and common exercises allowed Alliance members and partner nations to understand NATO targeting data, and the capabilities of allies and

Both Odyssey Dawn and Unified Protector relied heavily on U.S.-trained expertise and resources. U.S. forces made up the bulk of manpower and assets for ISR, targeting, airlift, and logistics and refueling efforts.[149] Moreover, U.S. contributions in terms of munitions, combat service support logistics, and SEAD missions also were preeminent, although this should not be taken to suggest that the contributions of allies were either unimportant or less capable. Manpower, equipment, and capability within the CAOC and its specific component capabilities such as the ISRD especially limited OUP during its first two months. A comprehensive intelligence collection plan was key, and it was important not only to task various ISR assets to gather information, but also to actively plan to hunt for the most relevant information. The primary intelligence expertise necessary to produce targeting folders also resided within U.S. forces. Fusion intelligence was particularly crucial to conducting dynamic targeting, maintaining positive control of targets, and reducing collateral damage.[150] Moreover, many U.S.-produced target folders were initially not releasable to NATO, as they contained classified images or products. Coordination efforts were crucial in order to create comprehensive effects.

One question remains to be answered: Does the experience in Libya serve as a model for the future use of U.S. airpower? This chapter has shown that Operations Odyssey Dawn and Unified Protector were examples of comparatively lower cost, multinational aerial interventions.[151] No coalition personnel were killed or seriously injured, and the concerted action achieved the three goals listed in the U.N. Security Council resolutions within the constraints applied. However, each situation must be evaluated on its own merits, and the specific working arrangements used in Libya may not apply to the next scenario.[152] The context in which the two operations occurred may be unlikely to reoccur. The Qaddafi regime was not as formidable an adversary as others might be. Its command and control structure was flawed, its communications

---

partners. For example, the close relationships between some U.S. and UAE units, and between French and Qatari units contributed to the confidence and understanding of allied and partner nation forces' capabilities and assets.

[149] See Greenleaf, who states, "The operation has made visible that the Europeans lack a number of essential military capabilities."

[150] Fusion intelligence is generally considered to be more reliable as it derives from multiple sources reinforcing a consistent description of the situation or target. The most preferred fusion intelligence derives simultaneously from human, signal, and full-motion video intelligence sources.

[151] Kevin Baron, "For the U.S., War Against Qaddafi Cost Relatively Little: $1.1 Billion," *The Atlantic* online, October 21, 2011; Z. Byron Wolf, "Cost of Libya Intervention $600 Million for First Week, Pentagon Says," ABCNews blog, March 28, 2011. The U.S. Congress did not authorize, nor did the Obama administration, through the Defense Department, ask for contingency funding for military operations in Libya during 2011. See also Jeremy Lemer and Christine Spolar, "U.S. Military Operations in Libya Hit Spending Rate of $2m a Day," *Financial Times*, June 9, 2011.

[152] Interview with senior member of Lieutenant General Jodice's staff by Deborah Kidwell, "Outline Transcript," May 24, 2012. Both General Welsh and General Woodward cautioned against making (in particular) doctrinal changes solely from the Libyan experience.

were poor, and initial strikes virtually eliminated its ability to mount a meaningful defense against coalition airpower.

On the United States' side, the operations strained the force structure in significant ways—the dwell time ratio decreased, essential training activities were upended, and other disruptions occurred as personnel and resources shifted to meet operational requirements. Forward basing allowed for the scope of operations; Odyssey Dawn, General Woodward said, was a "wake-up call . . . If we didn't have forward basing, I feel very confident that we would not have prevented" Qaddafi's troops from entering Benghazi.[153] The reaction time of U.S. forces certainly would have been longer, along with fewer capabilities available for logistical and combat support duty.

In some ways, these operations were a come-as-you-are war in that commanders used available resources, rather than appropriated resources. The approach relied heavily on developing and retaining centralized specialized capabilities (such as targeteering, weaponeering, airspace control, and intelligence) and ensuring that these capabilities were available whenever and wherever needed. Although military organizations cannot always be prepared and staffed for every potential mission, the processes to acquire needed forces and resources, especially to staff and organize the AOC with the necessary specialized expertise, will need to be configured to respond quickly.

While the conversation is just beginning regarding the implications of the use of airpower given the U.S. experience in Libya, many contributors of information to this study identified topics for further study. The most noted suggestions included: establishing baseline contingency planning documents (SPINS, air operations directives, a mission command checklist, rules of engagement); studying the effectiveness of nonkinetic operations; increasing manpower at the targeting center; and assessing reachback and other force presentation issues.[154]

The stress on U.S. forces accumulated risk, which did not prevent successful operations in this case, but could easily have done so. Some career fields, such as targeteers, airspace controllers, and AOC-qualified personnel, often were in short supply. General Woodward noted, "There is danger in relying too much on 'reachback.'"[155] Additionally, the availability of refueling assets limited operations, especially during the first few days, and airspace planning for tankers was not optimal. Some pilots reported a heavy reliance on the Traffic Collision Avoidance System (TCAS) to avoid midair col-

---

[153] General Margaret Woodward, quoted in John A. Tirpak, "Lessons from Libya," *Air Force Magazine*, December 2011, pp 34–38.

[154] Other suggestions for further study included airspace control, the duties and effectiveness of liaison officers, tanker utilization, airspace structure, facilities, and training. See also Susan J. Helms, "Global Space Operations," *Hampton Roads International Security Quarterly*, July 1, 2011, p. 16.

[155] General Margaret Woodward as quoted in Tirpak, "Lessons from Libya."

lisions.[156] Increased use of irregular staff processes (VOCO, PowerPoint, and email) could introduce opportunities for misunderstanding. Planners receiving unclear guidance could erode positive control of the military or lead to other changes in the traditional civil-military relationship.[157] Releasing intelligence products to partners was often encumbered by equipment interoperability and standards such as "need to know" versus what General Bouchard called "need to share."[158] As one tallies these risk factors, Winston Churchill's observation of the failure of the Gallipoli invasion comes to mind: "The terrible 'ifs' accumulate."[159]

General Welsh noted that the Libyan experience indicated that airpower will "continue to be 'on call,' a short-notice response will be expected, and decision makers may not readily understand the implications."[160] The decision to contribute specific capabilities to NATO and coalition activities suggests a need for significant changes to future force shaping programs. The U.S. military role clearly shifted from C2 of full spectrum operations during Odyssey Dawn to providing what some officials called unique capabilities or combat enablers such as logistics support, ISR, SEAD, refueling, and airlift functions.[161] Thus, more emphasis may be placed on these force multiplier capabilities and Alliance requirements. For example, U.S. personnel and assets necessarily would concentrate disproportionately into areas such as intelligence production and gathering, targeting folder production, and battle damage assessment. Production of replacement refueling aircraft may take on greater urgency. More emphasis will be placed on developing and supporting the technology and equipment that provide ISR activity and intelligence analysis, and to reducing the invisible tail of producing precision military operations to prevent losses and collateral damage.[162] Maintenance of this

---

[156] The TCAS system is an onboard system that provides airspace situational awareness by monitoring airspace around an aircraft independently from air traffic control, and warning pilots of the presence of other similarly equipped aircraft.

[157] Heavy reliance on general political statements (such as general North Atlantic Council ministerial objectives, U.N. Security Council resolutions, statements made by political leaders) by air component commanders to derive missions, commander's intent, and commander's estimates in the absence of specific guidance (definition of end state, for example) from civilian authorities could potentially (though not in this case) result in misunderstanding of authority or responsibility and could alter traditional civil-military relations in the United States. Moreover, unclear strategic guidance (or the absence of strategy) has historically been a cause or extenuating factor in stalemated military operations.

[158] Lieutenant-General Bouchard, "Coalition Building and the Future of NATO Operations," transcript from prepared remarks delivered at the Atlantic Council, Washington, D.C., February 14, 2012.

[159] Winston Churchill, as quoted in Geoffrey Parker, ed., *The Cambridge Illustrated History of Warfare*, Cambridge, UK: Cambridge University Press, 1995, p. 276.

[160] General Mark Welsh, interview with Deborah Kidwell, "Outline Transcript," May 14, 2012.

[161] OASD (PA), "DOD News Briefing with Vice Adm. Gortney from the Pentagon on Libya Operation Odyssey Dawn," Washington, D.C.: U.S. Department of Defense, March 25, 2011.

[162] It may take as many as 186 personnel to support a single full-time MQ-1/-9 combat air patrol (CAP). Estimated requirements included 45 people in the mission control element (MCE), 82 processing, exploitation, and

model would necessitate continuing warm-base facilities, even when the need for their services was not anticipated. Expenses incurred to retain these capabilities for potential operations could be difficult to justify given sequestration cuts and likely austere military budgets.

As Unified Protector ended, issues remained for the U.S. participation as an integral member of the NATO alliance. General Jodice noted that coordinating full spectrum operations in a challenging fiscal environment, within the NATO Smart Defense strategy and command structure, will be one of the most difficult tasks facing future Alliance commanders.[163] Member nations may benefit from coordinated resource allocation to provide specific mission capabilities in an effort to avoid costly duplication of capabilities within the Alliance.[164] Releasing intelligence products to Alliance and future coalition members may require a formulated "need to share" policy, rather than the current existing U.S. forces' "need to know" standard. The interoperability of alliance equipment and systems also may become an important factor in U.S. participation in future operations.[165]

U.S. military forces contributed to a successful allied military campaign in Libya in 2011, and airpower was the dominant combat arm. Understanding the U.S. contribution at the operational level illustrated that the United States can lead or participate in multinational military operations and can provide specialized capabilities. U.S. forces completed the mission even though the operations were resource constrained. Planners had to work through ambiguous and dynamic strategic guidance, endure unsteady domestic political support, and work to provide the career specialties in short supply. Commanders and staff devised effective theater command-and-control arrangements that reached across combatant commands and incorporated allies and partners. The professionalism and dedication of personnel, along with practiced working relationships, allowed U.S. forces to conduct operations under Odyssey Dawn, transition to an effective alliance command structure, and, ultimately, achieve the goals of the U.N. Security Council through coordinated military action.

---

dissemination (PED), and 59 launch recovery element (LRE) personnel. (Briefing slide, "Not 'Unmanned' Single 24/7/365 MQ-1/9 CAP Requirements," provided by Mike Dugree, Air Combat Command Deputy Historian, Langley AFB.)

[163] General Jodice, oral history interview, February 28, 2012.

[164] However, the fact that some member nations declined participation in the intervention or in certain missions (and lacked necessary resources) during OUP suggests that this concept may ultimately be unsatisfactory. While a designated backup force could perform missions objected to by specific members but sanctioned by the Alliance, this arrangement may run counter to maintaining the cohesiveness and will of the Alliance. (Kidwell notes from General Jodice, prepared remarks given at the Atlantic Council, Washington D.C., June 4, 2012.)

[165] Lt.-Gen. Bouchard, "Coalition Building and the Future of NATO Operations," February 14, 2012.

CHAPTER SIX

The British Experience: Operation Ellamy*

Christina Goulter

Introduction

Operation Unified Protector was a clear demonstration of the flexibility and effectiveness of airpower as a tool of policy. After nearly a decade of counterinsurgency campaigns in Iraq and Afghanistan, it provided a useful corrective to those who have argued that counterinsurgency warfare will be the only military commitment for the foreseeable future. It also was a salutary reminder that contingency operations will make demands on national resources, usually at the most inconvenient times. For the UK, the Libyan operation[1] had to be performed while engaged in the "main effort" (Afghanistan) and suffering the force-reduction impact of the 2010 Strategic Defence and Security Review (SDSR), which meant that already seriously overburdened defense manpower and materiel had to work even harder.

As the crisis deepened in Libya, only airpower and prepositioned maritime power could be deployed quickly enough to deal with the situation. For a variety of understandable political and operational reasons, the decision was made not to deploy allied land forces to Libya. This was set against the backdrop of the United States' decision to limit its role in Libya; a new UK-French bilateral defense agreement, which saw the two nations adopting the diplomatic and military lead; and a handing-over of the operation to NATO command. So, not only did events on the ground move rapidly, but the political and strategic context also proved to be fluid, and, as a result, airmen had to think innovatively and adapt existing structures, doctrine, tactics, and procedures. Indeed, one of the defining features of the British contribution to Operation Unified Protector was how the full spread of airpower effect was flexed in a highly responsive manner to meet changing political and operational requirements. Even before the main commitment began, there was a "textbook" airlift to evacuate British and

---

* This chapter draws on numerous nonattributable interviews with British military and government personnel conducted by the author in 2012 and 2013. It was reviewed by several senior Royal Air Force officers prior to publication.

[1] The Libyan operation was referred to as Op ELLAMY in the UK. "Ellamy" was a randomly generated codename.

entitled personnel, many of whom were located deep in the desert. Then, as the air campaign against Qaddafi's fielded forces developed, "dynamic targeting" procedures were adapted to address increasingly urgent tactical requirements. One of the key factors in creating "battle shock" among regime forces was the precision of air attacks, and when particular concerns arose over collateral damage risks, Royal Air Force crews were called on to perform some of the most demanding strikes. Attacks on preplanned targets also undermined regime forces' morale, and British personnel played a central role in strategic effect targeting during the NATO campaign. However, the transition to NATO command was less than smooth for Britain, as it had disinvested in its support for NATO for nearly a decade and found it challenging to operate with partners other than the United States. This was particularly true in relation to intelligence sharing. Operation Ellamy was the first "standing start" campaign the UK had engaged in for three decades, and it tested the RAF's rapid reaction capability to the maximum. It made the UK uncomfortably aware of the extent to which it had become dependent upon allies for several key capabilities.

Intervention and Initial UK Air Operations

When open protests against the Qaddafi regime began in Libya on February 15, 2011, and then escalated into a general civil war, the British government's immediate concern was for the safety of British nationals in the country. The suddenness with which anti-Qaddafi protests spread and escalated across Libya caught Britain by surprise. Because of a prioritization of the intelligence effort on Iraq and then Afghanistan, coverage of Libya was very limited, and both the Foreign and Commonwealth Office (FCO) and the Ministry of Defence had a poor understanding of the situation in the country. The way in which geography determined Qaddafi's power base, coupled with the fact that the Libyan regime centered on a cult of personality, explains the rapidity of the revolution's success.[2] However, Whitehall officials had little appreciation of many of these factors in the opening stages of the Libyan operation, and much of the early contingency planning was done with minimal intelligence understanding. Most of the intelligence on Libya was at least five years out of date. As urgent political and military analy-

---

[2]   One of the main reasons the Qaddafi regime lost power so quickly is because most of the country is desert and the Libyan population is concentrated in only two places, the Jafara Plain around Tripoli and the Jabal Akhdar in Cyrenaica, which contains Benghazi and was a traditional anti-regime stronghold. So when Qaddafi lost control over Benghazi in March, he lost control over eastern Libya, and when the rebels took Tripoli in August, he lost control over the other half of the country. The only places remaining loyal to him were Bani Walid and Sirte, the family's seat.

Hercules with RAF Regiment Protection Team during Operation Deference.
Courtesy of the UK Ministry of Defence. Used under Open Government License provisions.

ses of the instability in Libya got under way, the military priority became contingency planning to support the FCO in the evacuation of British and entitled personnel.[3]

The Qaddafi regime's military effort focused on securing Tripoli, so this is where some of the most violent clashes between protesters and security forces occurred. On the night of February 21, British Embassy personnel and dependents came under fire while sheltering in the Radisson Hotel. Options for evacuating all nonessential staff and dependents were limited, especially as the situation at Tripoli's airport deteriorated. Therefore, on February 24, the Royal Air Force and the Royal Navy were called upon to start the evacuation of British and entitled personnel. Over subsequent days, RAF Hercules aircraft, helicopters, and the frigate HMS *Cumberland* evacuated some 800 UK nationals and about 1,000 personnel from 50 other countries, under the auspices of Operation Deference.

In the course of this activity, it became apparent that several hundred UK nationals, principally oil workers, were stranded in the more remote parts of the Libyan desert, prompting the employment of RAF Hercules aircraft in several long-range missions to rescue them. The first such mission was performed on February 26, when C-130s were flown from Malta to two separate locations: Nafoora and Waha (300 miles southeast and 370 miles south-southeast of Benghazi, respectively). A total of 176 evacuees were airlifted back to Malta. The following day, February 27, a second oilfield mission was launched, involving three Hercules flying to various sites south of Benghazi, includ-

---

3   UK House of Commons, Defence Committee, "UK Contribution to the Operation," February 2012; JSCSC, *Operational Lessons Identified*, December 12, 2011; Dr. Saul Kelly, lecture ACSC, JSCSC, Defence Academy, 2011.

ing Zillah, some 600 miles from the coast. A total of 189 civilians were evacuated and the flights returned to Malta without casualty, although one aircraft did sustain hits from ground fire and a bullet grazed the pilot's helmet. In this case, the local opposition forces had misidentified the C-130 as a regime asset. Accompanying the flights were members of the RAF Regiment, who were tasked with securing the airstrips and protecting the civilian personnel from threats of violence. Operation Deference was supported from the outset by airborne C2 and intelligence, surveillance, target acquisition, and reconnaissance (ISTAR) assets, including an E-3D Sentry, and the role of such aircraft became even more crucial when the nature of the operation shifted from a noncombatant evacuation effort to combat.[4]

By the beginning of March, it was apparent that Qaddafi's military and security machinery was brutalizing the Libyan civilian population in an effort to quash the rebellion, especially in zones that the regime had retaken. A conservative estimate made at the time suggested that some 400 civilians had been killed in the violence, and thousands more had been arrested and tortured. Brega, at the base of the Gulf of Sidra, found itself in the middle of numerous engagements between the rebels and regime forces, and Qaddafi's armor and airpower heavily pounded it in the middle of March. To the west, Zawiya witnessed a rapid escalation in violence from March 6. Qaddafi used some 50 tanks and airpower to destroy most of its residential areas and the central mosque, which was being used as a makeshift hospital. Elite military units with close family ties to Qaddafi perpetrated some of the worst atrocities, in particular those commanded by his sons, Khamis and Saadi.[5] In response, the International Criminal Court (ICC) announced it would investigate alleged crimes against the Libyan people. While undoubtedly appropriate, this also served to stiffen the regime's resolve to stay in power; Qaddafi was now backed into a corner, and the violence continued to escalate.

The violence prompted multiple calls throughout the international community for the imposition of a no-fly zone (NFZ) over Libya in order to protect the civilian populace, but the Obama administration was reluctant to contemplate intervention. The African Union, Russia, and China also were vocal in their opposition to any intervention, so the probability of a U.N. Security Council authorization for an NFZ seemed remote. However, the tide turned in the second week of March when the Gulf Cooperation Council (GCC) affirmed its support for an NFZ; the Organization of the Islamic Conference (OIC) and then the Arab League quickly followed suit. These

---

[4]   UK House of Commons, Defence Committee, "UK Contribution to the Operation," pp. 10–11; Mark Urban, "Inside Story of the UK's Secret Mission to Beat Gaddafi," *BBC News Magazine*, January 19, 2012; Ministry of Defence, "The Royal Air Force Post-SDSR," undated.

[5]   32nd Brigade, commanded by Khamis, quickly developed a reputation for its brutality and vindictiveness. See also UK House of Commons, Defence Committee, "UK Contribution to the Operation," pp. 1–4; Saqeb Mueen and Grant Turnbull, eds., *Accidental Heroes: Britain, France, and the Libya Operation*, an Interim RUSI Campaign Report, London: Royal United Services Institute, September 2011, pp. 2–3; "Libya: Gaddafi Troops 'Force Rebels out of Brega,'" *BBC News*, March 13, 2011.

declarations provided the United States, Britain, and France, as the leading partners in the forthcoming coalition, with the legitimacy for action they sought.

The British Decision to Intervene

Neither the newly created National Security Council, nor the British military, anticipated the UK's decision to intervene in Libya. The exception was the RAF, which had engaged in some contingency planning since February. The National Security Strategy, unveiled some five months earlier, listed some fifteen "priority tasks" in the defense and promotion of British interests.[6] Not only did Libya not feature in the Tier One set of priorities, the coalition government, under David Cameron, also had indicated it was opposed to the type of "liberal interventionism" that it attributed to the previous Labour government, especially during Tony Blair's tenure as prime minister. So, when Cameron stated that he was determined not to let Benghazi turn into "another Srebrenica," it caught most of Whitehall by surprise.[7] This decision was not based on extensive intelligence assessments or the usual level of political or military staff work; it reflected the prime minister's desire to demonstrate that "something had to be done." Nor did he have universal backing within his own party. Liam Fox, when he was still Minister of Defence, cautioned against military action for a number of reasons, not least because of the UK's large commitment in Afghanistan and because he felt that Libyan intervention represented an open-ended commitment for comparatively little strategic gain. The Chief of the Defence Staff (CDS), General Sir David Richards, echoed this view. While he was happy to support the evacuation of entitled personnel during February, he reminded Cameron and the service chiefs that Afghanistan had to be considered the "main effort" and cautioned against Britain taking the military lead in Libya. While the prime minister accepted the point about Afghanistan, he instructed both Fox and CDS to develop plans for military intervention in Libya, starting with the imposition of a naval blockade and a no-fly zone, with potential to expand the operation if required but short of a commitment of land forces.[8]

Between March 12 and March 16, Britain and France took the initiative in drafting a U.N. resolution to impose an NFZ. Secretary of State Hillary Clinton endorsed it on March 16, but, on this occasion, Prime Minister Cameron and President Sarkozy were the ones in the forefront of a steadily cohering group of like-minded nations determined to take action. The resolve of Britain's and France's leaders undoubtedly helped the passing of U.N. Security Council Resolution 1973 on March 17, but, within

---

[6]   Her Majesty's Government, *A Strong Britain in an Age of Uncertainty: The National Security Strategy*, London: The Stationery Office, CM7953, October 2010, p. 27.

[7]   Patrick Wintour and Nicholas Watt, "David Cameron's Libyan War: Why the PM Felt Gaddafi Had to Be Stopped," *The Guardian*, October 2, 2011.

[8]   Michael Clarke, "The Making of Britain's Libya Strategy," in Adrian Johnson and Saqeb Mueen, eds., *Short War, Long Shadow: The Political and Military Legacies of the 2011 Libya Campaign*, London: Royal United Services Institute (RUSI), Whitehall Report 1–12, 2012, pp. 8–9.

the UK, a clear mandate also emerged for the use of force, with a vote on the resolution being passed in the House of Commons by 557 votes to 13 in favor of using UK military assets and personnel in support of UNSCR 1973. This was surprising, not least because of the robustness of the resolution's language. It called for member states to "take *all necessary measures* to protect civilians and civilian populated areas under threat of attack in Libya," while excluding a foreign occupation force of any form on any part of Libyan territory. The words "all necessary measures" gave the coalition an unusual degree of latitude, and the way in which the resolution was interpreted did give rise to inevitable tensions. Some nations chose to interpret the imposition of an NFZ narrowly, limiting action to countering regime aircraft engaged in hitting civilian targets, while others, including the UK and France, saw the "protect" function as including allied strikes on Qaddafi's land forces. But, even within the UK, serious disagreements remained over the resolution's remit. General Sir David Richards was of the opinion that it did not authorize the direct targeting of Qaddafi. This put him at loggerheads with Liam Fox and the prime minister, who asserted in public that targeting the Libyan leadership was not ruled out and went on to publish the attorney general's advice on the subject.[9]

Tensions among the principal allies implementing the NFZ (Britain, France, and the United States) were almost inevitable, as no two countries can have perfectly aligned foreign policies. These tensions were most noticeable when countries engaged in perceived or actual unilateral action. For example, on March 19, at the end of a summit between the three, President Sarkozy revealed in front of the world's press that French Rafale fighters had just undertaken attacks on Qaddafi's forces that were advancing on Benghazi. The British and U.S. delegations at the summit were concerned that France would be portrayed as having acted unilaterally ahead of the rest of the coalition, so an all-important demonstration of unity was conveyed to the world. In fact, in light of what we now know, the French attacks were vital to the campaign's success. Had there been a massacre in Benghazi, the coalition's primary justification for involvement (the protection of the local populace) would have been seriously undermined, and Qaddafi could have consolidated his position in the east of the country. Benghazi was the National Transitional Council's base, and it had become a symbol of the revolution.

In what was, in fact, a *largely* coordinated effort, British and U.S. submarines launched 112 Tomahawk Land Attack cruise missiles (TLAMs) at predetermined air defense and C2 targets throughout Libya a few hours after the French attacks, focusing primarily on air bases near Tripoli and Misrata. Shortly thereafter, three RAF Tornado GR4s launched from their base at Marham on a 3,000-mile round-trip sortie to perform Storm Shadow cruise missile attacks, also against Libyan air defense and C2 targets. It was the RAF's first bombing strike launched from the UK since the Second

---

9   Patrick Wintour and Ewen MacAskill, "Is Muammar Gaddafi a Target? PM and Military Split over War Aims," *The Guardian*, March 21, 2011.

World War and the longest British bombing mission since the "Black Buck" operations of the Falklands conflict. It involved multiple refuelings from two VC10s and a Tristar. The Storm Shadow provided a unique capability within the UK arsenal, as it enabled successful attacks on hardened installations and bunkered weapons storage facilities. As it is a "standoff" weapon, Storm Shadow also reduced substantially the threat that surface-to-air (SAM) systems posed to aircraft, an important consideration given that intelligence on Qaddafi's military capability was out of date.[10]

Assessment of Regime Capability

These initial attacks were considered vital prerequisites for the UNSCR 1973–mandated role of protecting the Libyan populace. Although Qaddafi's military was not regarded as the most capable in the region, efforts had to be made to limit its freedom to maneuver while allowing the coalition aircraft the freedom to perform their designated role. UNSCR 1973 was instituted primarily as a means of denying Qaddafi the use of his air force. The Libyan air force comprised a multiplicity of Soviet-era aircraft types, and although most of them were assessed as being of marginal airworthiness, a sufficient number of platforms remained to cause concern. For example, at least 30 Su-22 *Fitters* remained in service, and were considered capable ground-attack aircraft. Similar concerns existed over a significant number of Su-24 *Fencers*. While the Libyan air force was thought to be deficient in air-to-air capability, it was known that its MiG-23 *Floggers* had been upgraded recently. This was one of the prime reasons the main air base outside Tripoli (Metiga) was targeted on day one, as this housed at least one squadron of *Floggers*. However, one of the greatest threats to the civilian population was the Mi-24 *Hind* attack helicopter, of which the Libyan air force possessed at least 20. The fact that few reports surfaced of the regime using *Hinds* against the rebels remains a mystery. However, the extent of coalition partners' counterair activity from the beginning of the operation indicates that nothing was left to chance. It turns out this caution was warranted, because there was evidence that the Libyan air force attempted to regenerate some aerial capability out of Tripoli airport after its main bases were hit. As a result, the coalition maintained combat air patrols, and, on March 20, ten Typhoons deployed to Gioia del Colle, Italy, as part of the UK's contribution to the counterair effort. These flew their first combat air patrol two days later. Although the UK Air Contingent commander (UK ACC), Air Vice-Marshal Greg Bagwell, declared confi-

---

[10] Royal Aeronautical Society–International Institute for Strategic Learning (IISS) Libya Seminar, February 22, 2012; Mueen and Turnbull, *Accidental Heroes: Britain, France, and the Libya Operation*, pp. 4–5; JSCSC "Libya Crisis: Lessons Learned," paragraph 36; *Air Forces Monthly*, May 2011, p. 28; Ministry of Defence, "Libya: Operation ELLAMY: Background Briefing," undated; Alastair Cameron, "The Channel Axis: France, the UK and NATO," in Johnson and Mueen, *Short War, Long Shadow*, pp. 16–17.

dently in public on March 23 that the Libyan air force "no longer exists as a fighting force," much greater caution was expressed behind the scenes.[11]

The coalition also took the Libyan ground-based air defenses extremely seriously. Despite a U.N. arms embargo, Qaddafi was believed to have updated his SAM systems since the Soviet era, and still possessed numerous older but still potentially dangerous systems, such as the long-range SA-5 *Gammon* along with medium- and short-range SAMs including the SA-6 *Gainful*, SA-8 *Gecko*, SA-9 *Gaskin*, and the French Crotale. But one of the biggest threats to coalition air operations during the first phase of Ellamy was perceived to be the proliferation of man-portable SAMs (MANPADS) throughout Libya. One estimate suggested the presence of more than 20,000, including the SA-24 *Grinch*, which can reach altitudes up to 20,000 feet. In some places, this caused fast jets to operate above the threat altitude, constraining their flexibility. Further, the regime also had a wide range of anti-aircraft artillery (AAA) to complement the SAMs. Radar-guided SAMs and AAA were particularly heavily concentrated between the Tunisian border and Sirte, around Benghazi and Tobruk in the east of the country, and also around Ghat, in the southwestern desert. Although other parts of the desert had patchy early warning coverage, the coalition was facing its first integrated air defence system, albeit an outdated one, since the 2003 attack on Iraq. For aircrews accustomed to the relatively benign operating environment of Afghanistan, the prewar threat assessments for Libya called for significant psychological readjustment, and also exposed weaknesses in aircraft defensive inventories and electronic warfare (EW) training. One of the weapons to have gone out of service since the Iraq conflict was ALARM (Air Launched Anti-Radiation Missile), which was designed to destroy enemy radars. This meant that the RAF became even more dependent upon coalition partners for SEAD (suppression of enemy air defenses).[12]

Dependence Upon Airborne ISTAR

As the days passed, the campaign became more complex, both militarily and politically, and presented some unusual challenges. It was a war by proxy, with the anti-regime forces facing the same enemy as the UK, but in the initial stages the two friendly sides did little to coordinate. The absence of coalition land forces meant that commanders had to rely particularly heavily on air-derived intelligence and situational awareness. The United States provided approximately 27 percent of the ISTAR requirements, and continued to provide this level after taking a back seat in the campaign, prompting the NATO Secretary General later to comment that the campaign's success

---

[11] During this period, the standing UK ACC was located at Ramstein Air Base, Germany, but changed to Air Commodore Edward Stringer when the UK ACC was deployed forward to Gioia del Colle, Italy, *BBC News*, March 23, 2011. See also *Air Forces Monthly*, May 2011, pp. 28–33; "Parliament Honours UK Troops for Libya Operations," *Mod.UK*, April 25, 2012; Ministry of Defence, Defence News, "Libya: Operation ELLAMY: Background Briefing."

[12] *Air Forces Monthly*, May 2011, pp. 28–33; "Parliament Honours UK Troops for Libya Operations," *Mod.UK*; Ministry of Defence, Defence News, "Libya: Operation ELLAMY: Background Briefing."

RAF Typhoon during Operation Ellamy.
Courtesy of the UK Ministry of Defence. Used under Open Government License provisions.

had been dependent upon this U.S. capability. However, the UK's contribution also was significant. The RAF's E-3D Sentry AWACS aircraft, operating from Akrotiri in Cyprus, provided airborne C2 and battlespace management. Two Sentinel R1s, also based in Cyprus, offered wide area surveillance, as well as the ability to detect and track multiple vehicles through their moving target indicator radar. Royal Navy Sea King helicopters augmented this ability to track vehicles along the coastal zones. One of the RAF's Nimrod R1s, scheduled to be retired at the end of March, was given a 90-day extension to its service to be able to contribute to Ellamy, and provided exceptional signals and communications intelligence (SIGINT and COMINT) capability. Meanwhile, Tornado GR4 strike aircraft proved their multirole credentials by using the Raptor reconnaissance pod to collect imagery that ultimately was used to support coalition intelligence and targeting (including missions that Typhoons performed later in the campaign after they, too, assumed a ground attack role). Even the Tornados' and Typhoons' Litening III targeting pods provided useful imagery that could be analyzed and shared with other assets while aircraft were still in the air.[13] Therefore, although the concept of combat ISTAR was derided in some defense circles when first discussed in 2005 as nothing more than a cynical Air Force attempt to peg its slice of the defence budget by claiming that all aircraft were potential ISTAR platforms, Ellamy tended to validate the idea. Further, the manned platforms turned out to be vital because of the shortfall in availability of unmanned aerial vehicles (UAVs). As a consequence of the primacy given to the campaign in Afghanistan, only a modest number of UAV assets

---

[13] This included feeds to Apache crews embarked on HMS *Ocean* later on in the campaign.

were made available for the Libyan campaign. Although UAVs can provide valuable "pattern-of-life" intelligence once on station, the limited number of UAVs and the vast distances between areas of interest limited their ability to monitor what was a very fluid battlespace.[14]

Between March 23 and March 31, before NATO assumed command of the Libyan campaign, RAF aircraft were engaged in numerous strikes against regime land forces in Misrata and Ajdabiya, with priority given to protecting civilians against regime violence. Tornado GR4s destroyed at least 32 tanks and numerous other fighting vehicles during the week, and the combined effects of the imposition of an NFZ and the coalition air strikes targeting regime forces resulted in the stabilization of the front line and allowed the rebels to push back Qaddafi's forces from Ajdabiya. The RAF also launched another long-range Tornado strike from Marham using Storm Shadow against bunkers around Sebha in the southern Libyan desert. This was the site of Libya's former nuclear program, which had also been used for testing missiles and was known to contain large stocks of ammunition. In the course of these attacks, it became clear that ISTAR was, indeed, the key capability, not just because it facilitated timely and responsive targeting, but primarily because it minimized the risk of civilian casualties.

The overriding imperative for UK (and later NATO) forces was to protect civilian life, so aircraft were under strict instructions to minimize collateral damage. Air Chief Marshal Sir Stephen Dalton, Chief of the Air Staff, revealed that many targets were rejected because of the risk to civilians, and aircraft often failed to release their weapons in the process of dynamic targeting when the ground environment became ambiguous. For much of March, pro-Qaddafi forces were still fairly distinct from the opposition because of the armored and other fighting vehicles they used. However, by the end of the month, Qaddafi's troops started to abandon vulnerable tanks and other regime vehicles, and increasingly made use of technicals and other 4X4s, which the anti-Qaddafi fighters also used, making positive identification difficult.[15]

Political Sensitivities and Fears over Stalemate

During March, a variety of factors pointed to the need for British liaison with the National Transitional Council (NTC) and the anti-Qaddafi fighters, not least to assist in the targeting process, battle damage assessment, and for feedback on the effect on

---

[14] House of Commons, Defence Committee, "Operations in Libya," Section 3, NATO, pp. 4–6; Royal Aeronautical Society–IISS Libya Seminar; Elizabeth Quintana, "The RAF and Expeditionary Operations," *RUSI Defence Systems*, Summer 2011, p. 53.

[15] *Storm Shadow* attacks were still being performed from RAF Marham at this stage of the campaign, due to difficulties deploying the weapon to Italy. House of Commons, Defence Committee, "Operations in Libya," Section 3, NATO, pp. 4–6; Royal Aeronautical Society–IISS Libya Seminar; Ministry of Defence, "Operational Update on Libya," March 25, 2011; Ministry of Defence, "Brimstone Missiles Destroy Armoured Vehicles in Libya," March 26, 2011; Ministry of Defence, "RAF Strikes Further Targets on Libya," March 28, 2011.

morale of the coalition's attacks. Within Whitehall, skepticism also was expressed over whether air strikes would achieve the desired results in Libya, and the Chief of the Defence Staff, General Richards, and the Secretary of State for Defence, Liam Fox, both called for the provision of training and equipment to the forces of the NTC, using UK special advisors. However, the government's appetite for both open and covert contact with the NTC almost unraveled the Libyan campaign from the outset. At the beginning of the month, the Secret Intelligence Service (SIS) was given approval to develop its contacts with the opposition in Benghazi. To avoid using an obvious national symbol, such as a Royal Navy frigate in the area at the time, the decision was made to use an RAF Chinook to fly the SIS personnel from Malta. When the Chinook landed near Benghazi, it attracted an unhelpful level of attention, not least because the close protection team on board was wearing plain clothes, and the anti-Qaddafi fighters who took the UK personnel captive remained convinced for some time that they had stumbled upon foreign mercenaries. Nor did the debacle remain quiet. Britain was compelled to use diplomatic channels to plead for the release of the captives, but, worse, Qaddafi's internal security apparatus intercepted one of the telephone calls made by Foreign Secretary William Hague to the UK ambassador to Libya and broadcast it to the world, much to the British government's embarrassment. Thereafter, insertions of UK personnel were done with much greater care.

As relationships were developed with rebel fighters, assessments could be made about the efficacy of air attacks and the state of morale among regime units (as well as among rebel forces). By these means it was known, for example, that coercion of conscripts was endemic within Qaddafi's forces, with mass executions used to exert control. So while morale was assessed as fragile within many of the regime units, the mechanisms of state terror being applied meant that the defense of some towns and cities would be determined and attritional. This was witnessed in Ajdabiya, south of Benghazi, where control of the town changed several times during March. Indeed, as Qaddafi's forces went on the offensive during the first week of April, retaking significant centers such as Brega, politicians expressed increasing concern that the campaign in Libya was heading for a stalemate.[16]

Nervousness over a potential stalemate in the campaign coincided with the United States stepping back from a main combat role. It had been apparent since February that the United States was reluctant to take the lead role in the Libyan operation, and although the ultimate success of the campaign was due to the Americans providing most of the SEAD capability, 77 percent of the air-to-air refueling capacity, and just short of one-third of the ISTAR, the ramifications of its stance were felt immediately at the military-strategic planning level. In the absence of unequivocal U.S. support, it fell

---

[16] Mark Urban, "Inside Story of the UK's Secret Mission to Beat Gaddafi;" Mueen and Turnbull, *Accidental Heroes: Britain, France, and the Libya Operation*, pp. 10–12; Ministry of Defence, "UK Military Liaison Advisory Team to Be Sent to Libya," April 19, 2011.

on the European partners to generate and sustain the military capacity required. This represented a significant paradigm shift, and a variety of issues arose.

There were great hopes for the UK-French Defence and Security Co-operation Treaty, signed the previous November. But the infancy of this bilateral arrangement meant that few of its mechanisms were tried and tested. Not enough time had elapsed for the forging of working relationships between the two militaries, not least in the area of intelligence sharing. Therefore, Anglo-French management of the campaign would prove to be more one of deconfliction rather than true integration. Both countries continued to pursue their national interests, often not declaring their intentions before operations. For example, the French government eventually admitted to providing a unilateral supply of arms to Berber tribal fighters in the Nafusa Mountains, which ultimately facilitated a rebel thrust toward Tripoli.[17]

Meanwhile, in the UK, the National Security Council (NSC) also was in the process of finding its feet. One of its six assigned functions is "coordination with allies," and it had to work overtime to foster closer links between the United States, France, and Britain, as well as garnering regional support through intensive engagement with the Arab League and individual Arab states. The fact that the GCC, the Islamic Conference, and the Arab League all affirmed their support for the imposition of an NFZ through UNSCR 1973 is a testament to the success of the NSC (as well as French and American) lobbying behind the scenes. But in spite of its hard work, some European nations remained unmoved, including Germany, which abstained from voting on UNSCR 1973, while the African Union and the BRICs (Brazil, Russia, India and China) were vocal in disapproving of military action. Nor did it appear that the NSC members were of the same mind over national objectives in Libya. The NSC seemed to oscillate between prioritizing the protection of Libyan civilians on the one hand and regime change on the other. This had implications for military planning, which had to interpret political intent on a daily basis. And it was set against a backdrop of a clear directive from the military-strategic level to regard Operation Herrick (the campaign in Afghanistan) as the main effort.[18]

The Transition to NATO Command

While the early use of cruise missiles and rapid deployment of Typhoons and Tornados to Italy signaled the UK's commitment to the enforcement of UNSCR 1973, the political and strategic foundations of the Libyan campaign were less well defined.

---

[17] "French Confirm Arms Drops to Libyan Rebels," *Agence France-Presse*, June 29, 2011.

[18] Mueen and Turnbull, *Accidental Heroes: Britain, France, and the Libya Operation*, p. 6; Treaty Between the United Kingdom of Great Britain and Northern Ireland and the French Republic for Defence and Security Co-operation, London: The Stationery Office, November 2, 2010; House of Commons, Defence Committee, Operations in Libya, "UK Contribution to the Operation," pp. 1–2.

Command and control originally resided with the United States, under Africa Command's General Carter Ham. However, no formal process or evidence of U.S. intent was developed to include partner nations. Nor was there an obvious campaign plan shared among the allies. As a result, U.S., UK, and French aircraft operated in discrete national stovepipes, and this resulted in inefficiencies. For example, the British Sentinel aircraft often was airborne at the same time as the U.S. JSTARS, and the effort was duplicated because the RAF has had sufficient experience with the American system and could have used its products. Then the United States made a number of statements indicating that responsibility for the Libyan operation would be handed over "shortly," but it was unclear as to whether this meant to NATO or a European country. Negotiations between NATO members on March 23 and March 24 led to the conclusion that NATO should assume command of both the maritime embargo and the NFZ, and NATO formally assumed sole command of all military operations within Libyan territory on March 31. The NATO operation, now known as Operation Unified Protector, came under the command of Supreme Allied Commander, Europe, Admiral James Stavridis, with theater command exercised out of Allied Joint Force Command in Naples. Meanwhile, the Air Component Command was delegated from the NATO CAOC in Ramstein, Germany, to Poggio Renatico, in Italy.[19]

The British government placed a great deal of faith in NATO's ability to conduct the type of campaign it desired, and doubtless believed it would be able to exert a certain amount of influence over the direction taken. However, the UK was to suffer immediately from its previous disinvestment in southern NATO. There had been no senior British representation in NATO South for the previous eight months, and with no senior officers based in Naples, Poggio, or Izmir, Britain had limited input in the initial planning for OUP. The steady reduction particularly in RAF posts within NATO not only had damaged the UK's reputation, but it meant that RAF officers had a diminished understanding of NATO C2 constructs. They also found themselves at the back of the queue for office space, information technology (IT), and communications. The disinvestment had come about partially because of defense cuts, but mainly because of a focus on the Middle East and Afghanistan. The number of traditional NATO posts gapped rose sharply between 2003 and 2011, and a NATO tour was not seen as career-enhancing. Although the UK Air Contingent commander, Air Commodore Edward Stringer, would eventually be located forward at Poggio in April, much valuable time and potential for influence were lost as the UK hurriedly built up its NATO teams.[20]

While the UK had neglected its investment in NATO, it soon became apparent that NATO structures were themselves less than fit for the purpose, and required reworking according to the demands of the campaign. At the start of OUP, the CFAC was structured along NATO Response Force lines, but it was physically separated from

---

[19] House of Commons, Defence Committee, "Operations in Libya," Section 3, NATO, pp. 1–2.

[20] Royal Aeronautical Society–IISS Libya Seminar.

the CAOC in Italy. It quickly became clear that the two needed to be co-located in order to improve situational awareness and to respond to the dynamic battlespace in Libya. Initially, poor situational awareness made tactical and operational-level decision-making extremely difficult, and the Izmir-based CFACC, Lieutenant General Ralph J. Jodice II, was concerned that delays in the decisionmaking cycle or mistakes made as a result of poor situational awareness would have strategic implications. Therefore, the CFACC relocated to Poggio, and this move greatly enhanced the responsiveness of allied airpower in the campaign. A sluggish targeting decisionmaking cycle, often taking days, developed into one measured in hours. As impressive as this was, however, serious flaws remained within NATO structures for sharing national intelligence and targeting information, with national classifications and caveats preventing the timely sharing of intelligence on many occasions.[21]

Initial Difficulties in Operation Unified Protector

As OUP got under way, allied air assets were focused on stopping the advance of regime forces and preventing the shelling of Misrata. Backing this effort were strikes on regime forces' command and control, lines of communication, and logistics to degrade their ability to attack civilians. Air planners focused on developing a campaign that would separate Qaddafi from his power base, and reached the conclusion that Qaddafi's center of gravity was regime cohesion, which had allowed the regime to exercise the mechanisms of state power and harm civilian opponents. In the process of developing a campaign plan, however, several limiting factors arose. It quickly became apparent that NATO was heavily reliant on national reconnaissance platforms, most of which were committed to other operations (especially in Afghanistan). Second, NATO found itself short of qualified intelligence analysts and targeteers, and many RAF personnel were pulled from their posts in the UK to augment the analytical staffs in Italy. Third, a complex approval process hamstrung targeting within a NATO construct, with each member nation maintaining the right of veto. National "red cards" often were played, and considerable differences also arose about the rules of engagement (ROE) across the Alliance. All of these factors added unnecessary frictions during the first month of OUP.[22]

As challenging as the UK workup had proved to be, once the UK Air Contingent Commander was in place at Poggio, he helped to develop the CAOC, and General Jodice soon considered British staffs to be key in shaping NATO processes. Streamlining targeting clearance was the most urgent requirement, and as the UK became the principal trusted intelligence provider as the weeks advanced, the targeting process

---

[21] Royal Aeronautical Society–IISS Libya Seminar; Eric Schmitt, "NATO Sees Flaws in Air Campaign Against Gaddafi," *New York Times*, April 14, 2012, p. A1.

[22] House of Commons, Defence Committee, "Operations in Libya," Section 3, NATO; Schmitt, "NATO Sees Flaws in Air Campaign Against Gaddafi"; Royal Aeronautical Society–IISS Libya Seminar.

became easier. For the British contribution to OUP, most of the targeting approvals in the initial stages still had to be routed through the UK Permanent Joint Headquarters (PJHQ) in London, but PJHQ was useful for corroborating target intelligence and enabling All Source analytical assessments. Target verification and corroboration of sources ensured that the risk of collateral damage was reduced to a minimum. However, some of the target authorizations had to come from the ministerial level, and this inevitably added considerable delays to the targeting process.[23]

At OUP's outset, it was apparent that some mechanism was needed to enable aircraft patrolling an area to respond quickly against regime forces engaged in attacking civilians. It was impossible to preplan sorties against targets that were so mobile and that often adapted their tactics on a daily, if not hourly, basis. Therefore, a process of dynamic targeting was adopted, in which the UK ACC and aircrews were given far more responsibility for targeting decisions, and the ACC became the national "red card" holder for targeting decisions. National authority still was sought, but if legal and political advisors were satisfied that a positive identification of a regime target was available and that the risk of collateral damage was zero or very low, then approvals for strikes could be given almost instantaneously. But aircrews also learned that Qaddafi's forces continued to adapt their tactics, techniques, and procedures in order to counter air strikes. Through open sources, typically the broadcast media, the regime was quick to establish NATO's restrictions, and increasingly placed their assets in positions where collateral damage was a concern. This was one of the main reasons HUMINT (human intelligence) provided by either anti-Qaddafi rebels or other national sources was so crucial, because it gave the granularity of understanding required to be able to differentiate between regime and friendly forces. The UK ACCs (Edward Stringer and his successor, Gary Waterfall) found the overriding imperative to avoid collateral damage meant they had to get involved with a level of tactical detail that they had not anticipated.[24]

Weapons of Choice

Most of the fast jet aircrews involved in the Libyan operation had combat experience only in Afghanistan, and this proved problematic when the crews were called upon to perform attacks in urban areas. To begin with, crews adopted cautious lines of attack to minimize the risk of collateral damage, and other means of mitigating risk also were pursued. Among these was the employment of weapons with an extremely limited effects radius, and the precision-guided munition (PGM) that became the weapon of choice for Tornado crews was the recently developed Brimstone missile. This

---

[23] House of Commons, Defence Committee, "Operations in Libya," Section 3, NATO; Schmitt, "NATO Sees Flaws in Air Campaign Against Gaddafi"; Royal Aeronautical Society–IISS Libya Seminar.

[24] Royal Aeronautical Society–IISS Libya Seminar; interviews with author, February 22 and November 2–3, 2012.

50-kilogram PGM had been designed as an anti-armor weapon, and the latest variant (referred to as the Dual Mode Seeker Brimstone, or DMSB), which used laser guidance, proved to be an extremely reliable, accurate, and potent weapon for use against a wide variety of targets, including highly mobile ones. As armor and moving targets were the norm from the beginning of the campaign, the RAF quickly found its stocks of DMSB running low (down to single figures at one point). This was particularly so after it was realized that Brimstone gave the UK a unique capability to strike difficult targets with little or no collateral damage because of the small size of the weapon and its warhead.[25]

RAF Operations Intensify

During April and May, with Benghazi and eastern Libya in rebel hands, NATO aerial activity was concentrated in the west of the country. The focus was first on Misrata and Sirte, with some attacks also occurring in the Berber Highlands to the south and west of Tripoli. For the RAF, most of the strikes were against regime armor and field artillery near Misrata, although some attacks also were made on regime strongholds in Sirte. The tempo of RAF operations increased considerably during the first week of April, thanks in part to the augmentation of the Tornado force with an extra four aircraft (from eight to twelve). The following week saw the first-ever use of Typhoon fighters in a ground attack role, demonstrating their versatility as a multirole platform. Up to that point, Typhoons had been used in a control-of-the-air role to escort Tornados. But on April 12, Typhoons armed with Enhanced Paveway II bombs operated alongside Tornados armed with Paveway IV bombs and Brimstone, and a total of eight tanks were destroyed just outside of Misrata. The incident brought the RAF's total to more than 100 main battle tanks, armored vehicles, artillery pieces, and SAM installations up to that point in the campaign.[26] Another notable feature of this particular attack was that the destruction of the tanks caused regime personnel in surviving units to flee, and it was observed how near-misses also served to scare targeted individuals to such an extent that the C2 chain was broken. Deliberate near-misses often were used where potential existed for collateral damage, but they regularly had the desired psychological effect against regime personnel.

Some of the missions performed by the RAF were done in concert with other UK forces, reinforcing the point that OUP was a truly joint and combined operation. For example, on April 18, Royal Navy Tomahawk missiles were launched against regime C2 facilities in conjunction with precision strikes by Tornado, Typhoon, and other NATO aircraft. On the same day, HMS *Liverpool*, performing a blockade function as part of the ongoing arms embargo imposed under UNSCR 1970, intercepted

---

[25] House of Commons, "Operations in Libya," pp. 7–9.

[26] Typhoon operated with Enhanced Paveway II only. Ministry of Defence, "Typhoon Joins Tornado in Libya Ground Attack Operations," April 13, 2011.

a merchant vessel heading for Tripoli, and a boarding party found a significant cargo of military hardware. Such activity proved that NATO contingency operations could work well, within and across national stovepipes, despite considerable impediments.[27]

The RAF's strikes against Qaddafi's fielded forces continued in a similar vein into May, and the progress westward of the rebel campaign became obvious with an increasing number of attacks on regime targets in the cities of Sirte and Zlitan, and then in the capital, Tripoli. During the first two weeks of May, RAF Tornados and Typhoons both were used against regime field artillery, including a noteworthy strike on May 6, after imagery analysis had spotted 20 FROG-7 (9K52 Luna) long-range rocket launchers south of Sirte. The regime had 45 Soviet era FROG-7s in its inventory; half were concentrated around Sirte, indicating the significance Qaddafi had attached to the city and suggesting that he was likely to make his last stand there. Then, on May 12, a Typhoon destroyed Palmaria self-propelled 155mm howitzers near Sirte. Such artillery and mobile rocket launchers received priority in NATO's target list.[28]

For most of April and the early part of May, air strikes were directed primarily against the regime's fielded forces. But, from the second week of May, increasing attention was paid to strategic targets. This reflected strategic analysis that had been done in the UK, and marked the point at which RAF personnel, in particular, started to have a sizable influence on campaign design. As well as destroying Qaddafi's physical means of repression, NATO also targeted his internal security apparatus. On May 16, in conjunction with other NATO assets, RAF Tornados and RN Tomahawks were employed against the regime's intelligence agency in Tripoli and facilities used by Qaddafi's Executive Protection Force. The latter acted as a close protection team to the regime's inner circle. This particular strike was intended to degrade Qaddafi's ability to use the mechanisms of state terror against his population, but it also sent a clear message to those who continued to support the regime that NATO had the ability to find and hit them at will. It is no coincidence that a significant number of defections occurred after this attack, including that of Qaddafi's oil minister, Shokri Ghanem. Subsequent attacks on Qaddafi's Bab al-Aziziyah complex in the center of Tripoli reinforced this message. The complex was recognized as his home and the location of a major military barracks. But equally important was the impression that NATO was omnipresent in Libya, and could hit sites simultaneously at any time. On May 19, RAF Tornados attacked the naval base at Al Khums near Misrata, sinking two corvettes that had been used to shell coastal towns, and destroying dockyard facilities housing inflatable fast attack craft that the regime used to lay mines and interdict merchant ships carrying humanitarian relief. Between May 21 and May 24, RAF Tornados and Typhoons destroyed regime armored vehicles near Zlitan, and on the 23rd attacked a large military vehicle depot within the Bab al-Aziziyah complex. Then, on the 25th, RAF aircraft attacked

---

[27] Ministry of Defence, "Typhoon Joins Tornado in Libya Ground Attack Operations."

[28] Ministry of Defence, "Libya Operations: Updates."

British Army Apaches embarked on HMS *Ocean*.
Courtesy of the UK Ministry of Defence. Used under Open Government License provisions.

another large military vehicle depot at Tiji in the west, as this had been supporting regime assaults on the civilian population in the Djebel Nafusa region southwest of Tripoli. On May 27, RAF Typhoons, as well as other NATO assets, revisited the Bab al-Aziziyah complex and destroyed its guard towers. This latter attack was conducted with the specific aim of having a psychological impact on the regime.[29]

It was clear that NATO had ramped up the pressure on the regime, and Britain continued to demonstrate her commitment to the campaign by deploying five Army Air Corps Apache AH1 attack helicopters that embarked on HMS *Ocean*. Although some initially saw the decision to employ Apaches as a cynical attempt to "prove that Jointery works," the attack helicopters did make a genuine contribution to the campaign. The Apaches undertook a relatively modest number of attack sorties (22 in total), but the deployment had a significant psychological impact on regime forces, thanks to the Apache's reputation in Afghanistan. Pro-Qaddafi forces were reported to be in fear of Apache attacks, and sizable rewards were posted for the first successful shooting down of one. Armed with Hellfire missiles, rockets, and 30-millimeter cannon, the Apaches made short work of regime technicals (comprising half of the targets destroyed), as well as AAA sites and radar installations, and such attacks complemented those undertaken by French Tigre attack helicopters from the assault ship *Tonnerre*.

On a number of occasions, including their first operational sorties on June 3, Apaches operated in concert with RAF and U.S. SEAD aircraft, and this required the development of completely new tactics, techniques, and procedures. Among the suc-

---

[29] Ministry of Defence, "RAF Destroys Gaddafi's Rocket Launchers," *gov.uk*, May 9, 2011; Ministry of Defence, "Libya: Operations Updates."

cess stories was the provision of imagery that Tornados and Typhoons acquired and that was being fed to HMS *Ocean* to assist the Apache crews in their premission planning, before going into combat alongside the fast jets. Although NATO considered Libya to be a medium-threat environment for the attack helicopters, the risks were considered acceptable, and the UK military representative to NATO, Air Marshal Sir Christopher Harper, commented that their employment in this way was "jointery at its best."[30] However, the employment of Apaches was not without its issues. HMS *Ocean* could only accommodate five Apaches because of the helicopter's rotor size (the blades cannot be folded), so storing and retrieving Apaches became a major limiting factor on the extent of their contribution to the operation. In addition, the Apaches required a disproportionately large amount of ISR support to ensure their safety and the accuracy of their attacks. Finally, the UK's ROE meant the Apaches did not have the freedom of maneuver that the French Tigre crews enjoyed, and one of the reasons the Apache sortie total was comparatively small is because most of the "no-go" decisions were due to uncertainties over collateral damage risk. So, while the Apaches' attacks complemented those of the French Tigres, they could not match the French level of sortie generation, nor the effects achieved.

The tempo of UK air operations increased yet again during the first week of June. Strikes on Tripoli took place almost every day, with repeat attacks on Qaddafi's complex and other military depots, and a particular focus on the regime's intelligence apparatus. As a result of attacks on June 6 and June 7, it was reported that Qaddafi's domestic intelligence agency had been hit particularly hard. Evidence also surfaced that the regime's forces were running out of ammunition, as NATO's operations depleted stockpiles closer to the coast. Qaddafi was now dependent upon ammunition depots located deeper in the desert, and the RAF conducted successive strikes against one of the largest depots, located at Waddan, in the central region of Libya. After RAF attacks between June 12 and June 14, at least a half-dozen bunkers at Wadden were destroyed. The destruction of ammunition bunkers was seen as an important means of protecting the civilian populace, because regime forces still were engaged in attacks on towns associated with the opposition. Therefore, the RAF maintained its surveillance over the Djebel Nafusa highlands, southwest of Tripoli, where regime forces repeatedly had attacked Berber opposition groups. Between June 26 and June 28, RAF Tornados and Typhoons successfully struck regime tanks, armored vehicles and artillery in the area, and these attacks continued well into July. The value of Brimstone was amply demonstrated on July 2, when a regime T-55 tank attempted to shelter from air attack in a narrow alleyway in a town in the Djebel Nafusa, but was destroyed without damaging the surrounding buildings or causing any collateral damage. Other attacks on

---

[30] Ministry of Defence, "Libya: Operations Updates."

RAF Tornado GR4 refueling en route to Libya.
Courtesy of the UK Ministry of Defence. Used under Open Government License provisions.

Qaddafi's forces were performed using Paveway laser-guided bombs only after it had been established that civilians were not at risk.[31]

RAF Augmentation

In the middle of July, it became apparent to NATO that Qaddafi was attempting to secure a number of significant towns, and was concealing troops, equipment, and C2 infrastructure in populated areas, using the civilian population as human shields. The resulting intelligence and targeting demands on NATO became even more onerous. To address this, the RAF deployed an additional four Tornado GR4s to Gioia del Colle to act primarily in a reconnaissance role, but also significantly adding to NATO's strike capability. Over the next month, much of the RAF's fast-jet activity was focused on the towns of Brega and Zlitan. The former was, again, the focus of bitter fighting in the middle of July, and RAF aircraft were involved in attacks on regime armored vehicles and mobile artillery in the town between the 14th and 16th. As much of the fighting was in residential parts of Brega, aircrews found it challenging but resolved to do their utmost in the face of regime threats to turn the town "into hell." After three days of heavy fighting, which NATO bombing assisted, rebel forces were able to bypass Brega, cutting off the garrison's lines of communication. On the morning of July 18, Qaddafi's forces were in full retreat toward Ras Lanuf, and the NTC was claiming victory in the battle for Brega. The regime claimed to have inflicted more than 500 deaths

---

[31] Ministry of Defence, "Libya: Operations Updates."

among the rebel forces, but the total losses in Brega are likely to have been considerably higher, as it had been the focus of numerous clashes since February.[32]

Meanwhile, Zlitan, 99 miles east of Tripoli, was now on the front line as rebel forces advanced westward from Misrata. The military garrison had brutally crushed a rebel uprising there during June, and there were indications that regime forces again would repress the local civilians with extreme violence if they offered support to the rebels. A staged pro-Qaddafi rally in Zlitan in the middle of July signaled the beginning of a regime backlash as rebels attempted to take the town. Over the next three weeks, the RAF's Tornados and Typhoons were extremely active over Zlitan, destroying scores of regime tanks, armored vehicles, technicals, mobile rocket launchers, and C2 facilities inside the town. A number of days were notable for the type of activity undertaken. On July 19, RAF aircraft attacked some 29 buildings in and around Zlitan, which reconnaissance and intelligence analysis identified as C2, ammunition storage, and supply sites. They also struck mobile rocket launchers and a couple of artillery positions, which HMS *Iron Duke* also engaged with naval gunfire. Meanwhile, under cover of darkness, Apaches from HMS *Ocean* used Hellfire missiles against a variety of military targets between Zlitan and Al Khums, further down the coast. Joint actions of this type were now becoming the norm. Then, on July 31, as intelligence indicated that regime forces were about to go on the offensive, Tornados and Typhoons hit a regime staging post neat Zlitan, and a similar operation was mounted the next day to hit another staging post. Although regime forces were able to launch a counter-offensive, they were not able to capitalize on it, thanks to the ongoing aerial activity. On August 2, RAF Tornados and Typhoons conducted precision strikes on two buildings in Zlitan that had been confirmed as C2 facilities, making the regime units they supported largely "blind." Then, the following day, in another demonstration of joint, coordinated action, Tornados and Apaches hit buildings that housed most of Qaddafi's military personnel in the city. Attacks in and around Zlitan continued for another couple of weeks, and included a Tornado strike on August 11 on a staging post near the town that Qaddafi mercenaries were using, as well as the destruction of a psychological warfare facility. These attacks in the first half of August effectively unhinged the regime's hold over Zlitan, and unlocked the area surrounding Tripoli, just as Lieutenant General Jodice had intended in his campaign plan.[33]

Advance on Tripoli

NATO's air operations during the remainder of August were designed to accompany the rebels' advance on Tripoli and to address any other pockets of conflict within Libya with the aim of protecting the civilian population from any reprisals. Of concern was

---

[32] "Libya Rebels Say Gaddafi Forces in Retreat," *Reuters*, July 18, 2011; ""Libyan Rebels Claim Victory in Battle for Brega," *BBC News*, July 18, 2011; Ministry of Defence, "Libya: Operations Updates," p. 21.

[33] Ministry of Defence, "Libya: Operations Updates," pp. 14–21.

the status of Zawiya, the oil-refining city some 30 miles west of Tripoli, which had suffered almost complete devastation a few months earlier. Rebels had re-infiltrated into Zawiya in June, and had interdicted an arterial route in and out of the city shortly, but the regime's forces quickly reversed this success. At the start of August, anti-Qaddafi forces launched an offensive into the plain surrounding Zawiya, reaching as far as the outskirts of the city by the middle of the month. NATO was determined to see the regime neutralized in the city, and RAF aircraft were engaged in several attacks on pro-Qaddafi units in the area. On several occasions, to minimize the risk to civilians inside buildings, novel use was made of airburst weapons to deal with regime sniper positions on roofs, and a successful anti-shipping strike on August 17 in Zawiya harbor prevented the escape of regime personnel. The RAF's activity was undoubtedly one of the main contributory factors in Qaddafi's decision to abandon the city, because the rebels were incapable of taking Zawiya on their own.

Meanwhile, Tornados and Typhoons were active over Tripoli, maintaining constant pressure on the regime. Their activity over the city was made easier through the previous month's destruction of radar at the airport, effectively blinding the regime. In the early hours of August 20, Tornado GR4s conducted a precision attack on a communications facility that Qaddafi's intelligence apparatus used in the southwest of the city. Extreme care was taken in the planning of this mission to avoid collateral damage, and all the PGMs launched hit the facility. The aircraft were then retasked to hit some of Qaddafi's tanks on the city's southern edge. Over subsequent days, as rebel forces fought to overcome regime elements in Tripoli, the RAF maintained its surveillance effort and continued to attack Qaddafi's personnel and military hardware, claiming among the tally a FROG-7 missile launcher. By this stage, almost all the strikes were the result of dynamic targeting, and their tempo fatally dislocated pro-Qaddafi forces in and around the city. The rebels prevailed, and most of Tripoli was in their hands by the end of August 21, with just small pockets of resistance holding out until the end of the month.[34]

As Qaddafi lost his grip on Tripoli, he announced he had moved the capital to Sirte. NATO's attention followed suit, although Qaddafi's intent to fight on from a new base following the loss of his capital may have surprised some within NATO. But Sirte was home to many of the Qaddafi family and had great significance to the regime. The RAF mounted armed reconnaissance around Sirte, destroying armored vehicles, tanks, and artillery, and the Storm Shadow's bunker-busting capability was called upon to destroy facilities that Qaddafi could have used to continue the fight. On the night of August 25/26, Tornado GR4s launched from RAF Marham to fire Storm Shadow missiles against a large headquarters bunker in Sirte, then did the same against the complex at Sebha the following week.

---

[34] BBC News, "Libya Conflict: Rebels Battle Gaddafi Troops in Zawiya," August 14, 2011; Ministry of Defence, "Libya: Operations Updates," pp. 11–13, 20–21.

Sebha became the focus of Tornados' attention at dawn on September 15, after reports indicated that regime troops were shelling the local civilian population. This particular mission demonstrated the versatility of Brimstone as a weapon, because it could be fired in salvos. At Sebha, a large concentration of regime armored vehicles had been located, and the salvo firing technique was used for the first time.[35] Seven or eight vehicles were assessed as destroyed, with no collateral damage reported.

Rebel forces had now surrounded most of Sirte, and were embarking on an attritional, street-by-street campaign to dislodge Qaddafi. NATO tasked the RAF with strikes on C2 facilities, staging posts, and military hardware. Paveway and Brimstone PGMs were used throughout, and, in one instance over the weekend of September 24–25, an inert Paveway filled with concrete was employed to prevent collateral damage. RAF aircraft remained active over Sirte and Bani Walid to the southwest, where regime units were reported to be an ongoing threat to the safety of Libyan civilians. For the next two weeks, operations over Sirte and Bani Walid consumed almost all the RAF's capacity, and the targets attacked were typically tanks, armored vehicles, and technicals, although Tornado GR4s successfully struck two C2 facilities in Bani Walid on October 7, significantly degrading Qaddafi's ability to exert any authority over the town's remaining regime units. This would prove to be a significant result when Qaddafi attempted to connect with his forces a week later. As the days progressed, RAF Tornados were on constant lookout for regime technicals in and around Sirte and Bani Walid. Any such vehicles located by reconnaissance were attacked using either Paveway or Brimstone, including an attack on October 17 that destroyed a group of nine vehicles near Bani Walid that had been identified as belonging to Qaddafi's remnant forces. NATO's overwatch continued as NTC forces launched their final assault in Sirte on October 20. It was during this action that Qaddafi attempted to flee to the south, but rebel fighters captured him and he was dead less than an hour after being taken captive.[36]

Lessons and Conclusions

A number of conclusions can be drawn from Operation Unified Protector, as well noting some important general and UK-specific lessons. Airpower was critical in meeting the political requirements for an immediate and agile response to the highly fluid situation in Libya. For the UK, this began with Operation Deference, which proved to be an almost textbook example of crisis response undertaken at long range. Airpower was the only feasible means of quickly and safely evacuating several hundred UK civilians from sites deep within the Libyan desert. The way in which the RAF Regiment

---

[35] The Brimstone variant used in this case is referred to as "Legacy Brimstone," the older variant of the weapon.

[36] Ministry of Defence, "Libya: Operations Updates," pp. 1–8.

provided organic defense to aircraft and to the evacuees also is noteworthy, and reinforces the importance of having a dedicated force-protection element within the air force. Then, when the main campaign began, airpower achieved the decisive effect of removing most of the regime forces' advantages, especially in airpower and heavy weapons. This helped to even the playing field, and bought the anti-Qaddafi forces sufficient time to achieve a minimal level of organization, training, and equipment. Further, post-campaign analysis has revealed that while most regime personnel had little fear of or respect for the anti-Qaddafi forces, they genuinely feared air attack, and concluded that this was their decisive disadvantage.

"Dynamic targeting" (referred to as deliberate dynamic targeting, or DDT) was particularly significant in this respect. Initially adopted as a means of responding to urgent tactical targets, the high operational tempo it created proved to be a potent force multiplier. It was extraordinarily successful in creating "battle shock" among regime forces, and the morale effect of NATO's broad-ranging and simultaneous attacks was particularly significant against the regime's non-Libyan mercenaries. After the heavy and sustained air attacks on Misrata in April, many mercenaries fled into Niger and the Sudan. By the end of the campaign, more than 80 percent of targets fell into the category of DDTs, and the fact that weapon systems such as Brimstone achieved such high levels of accuracy (almost 99 percent of all Brimstones fired hit their intended targets) also would have played on the minds of regime forces. But attacks on preplanned targets also undermined regime morale. The repeated attacks on the Bab al-Aziziyah and Sebha complexes, in particular, demonstrated to the senior regime figures that nowhere in Libya was safe and that fleeing into the desert was pointless. But these sites also were major symbols of the regime's authority, and NATO's ability to hit them with impunity sent important signals about Qaddafi's military impotence.[37]

In spite of the fact that the Libyan battlespace became more ambiguous and congested as the months wore on, diligent intelligence analysis and rigorous adherence to ROEs kept "blue on blue" and "blue on green" incidents to a bare minimum.[38] This was doubly important. Not only was the preservation of human life the stated objective of UNSCR 1973, but NATO's care exercised was vital for campaign authority among the NTC rebels and for political support elsewhere. It proved that NATO and the other nations represented in the coalition kept their word. This is why intelligence was not just a key enabler; it underpinned the whole campaign, and, in many senses, drove the campaign.

OUP reinforced that analysis is always the bottleneck in the intelligence cycle, and that the UK, and NATO more widely, needs to develop more analysts, not least to increase global intelligence coverage. Libya also demonstrated how focusing on *the*

---

[37] House of Commons, Operations in Libya, "UK Contribution to the Operation," p. 7.

[38] "Green forces" referred to the anti-Qaddafi rebels in this case, but the term is used more generically for third-party friendly forces.

war (Afghanistan), as opposed to *a* war, had led to an erosion of targeting skills and electronic warfare training and equipment. Britain has a generation of more junior officers with no experience in high-end operations. The air-centric nature of the campaign exacerbated some of these shortcomings, putting a premium on airborne ISR and kinetic capabilities. To compensate for the lack of a land component, connections with the rebel forces had to be developed using special forces (SF), and it transpired that the most valuable SF presence in Libya came from non-NATO sources. The incorporation of non-NATO partners into the campaign design created new challenges, especially in the area of intelligence sharing. However, intelligence sharing among NATO nations also was problematic.

The Libyan campaign placed enormous demands on ISTAR capabilities across NATO, and resources remained tight throughout, mainly because many national assets were being employed in Afghanistan. Although the United States performed the preponderance of the ISR effort, the UK made a significant contribution using the Nimrod R1, Sentinel, and Tornado GR4 Raptor pod. The utility of the Nimrod R1 as a SIGINT platform was quickly demonstrated, and it received a very brief extension in service beyond its announced retirement date of 2011. The RAF will not regain a proper SIGINT capability until Air Seeker (Rivet Joint) comes into service. Similarly, the Sentinel proved to be exceptionally good at detecting movement on the ground, with fidelity of imagery that allowed for highly accurate targeting. Sentinels acquired intelligence and imagery that was passed on to fast jets, and without the precise intelligence and situational awareness they provided, strike aircraft would have spent far more time in armed reconnaissance without necessarily finding targets or hitting them with the precision demanded by the UNSCR 1973 remit. In other words, Sentinel proved to be one of the most important force multipliers. What made it particularly valuable was the fact that much of the basic intelligence analysis could be done on board, providing near real-time intelligence and not merely situational awareness. The Ministry of Defence in May 2012 reviewed the decision to take it out of service after the end of the campaign in Afghanistan, following the House of Commons Defence Committee's recommendation. This was a prudent decision, because the UK should not automatically assume the availability of adequate U.S. ISR support in future contingency operations.[39]

Indeed, Operation Ellamy proved to be extremely valuable for highlighting many of the flawed assumptions underpinning the Strategic Defence and Security Review (SDSR). One of David Cameron's first acts when he took over as prime minister in 2010 was to undertake a review of Britain's defense and security apparatus, with the intent of aligning financial resources with the newly formulated National Security Strategy (NSS). The NSS itself had come about as a result of concerns in Whitehall over

---

[39] House of Commons, Defence Committee, Operations in Libya, "UK Contribution to the Operation," pp. 4–5.

the deficit in strategic thinking that Britain's handling of both the Iraq and Afghanistan campaigns had exposed. It was felt that a National Security Strategy would assist government by outlining strategic priorities (using national capabilities to build Britain's prosperity, extending the nation's influence in the world, and strengthening the UK's security), and ensure a unity of purpose across Whitehall departments to achieve these objectives. SDSR was designed to provide additional guidance on the ways and means, specifically to ensure that UK forces in Afghanistan receive the equipment they need; to bring the defense budget deficit back into balance; and to guarantee that the UK possesses capable and agile armed forces sufficient to protect the UK in "an age of uncertainty." However, far from providing a remedy to short-term thinking, the SDSR not only proved that this still existed but, in many senses, exacerbated it. Priority given to Afghanistan equipment levels led to making hard and fast delineations between what was required for that theater of operations versus what would be required after Afghanistan. As a result, it was decided, among other things, to take Sentinel out of service in 2015.[40]

Similarly, SDSR led to retirement of the Nimrod MR2 maritime patrol aircraft (MPA) fleet in 2010 and cancellation of the new Nimrod MRA4 aircraft intended to replace it. The House of Commons Defence Committee concluded that the reason for canceling the Nimrod MRA4 program was purely financial, because of already prohibitively costly overruns and also to save more than £200 million in annual support costs. But no apparent urgency has resulted to find a replacement maritime surveillance platform, in spite of the fact this capability is central to UK defense and national security. The British government argued that protection of the nuclear deterrent, territorial waters and sea trade, the prevention of piracy, terrorism and global illicit transfers, as well as search-and-rescue functions, all could be met through the use of other assets, such as Type 23 Frigates, Merlin and Sea King helicopters, and the E-3D Sentry. While these may help mitigate the loss of the Nimrod MRA4, they are by no means a total solution, as the UK would still lack a wide-area surveillance and maritime patrol capability.[41] However, the government has decided that this represents a "tolerable risk," even though a succession of events since 2010, including Libya, has proven otherwise. During OUP, NATO had at its disposal only three maritime patrol aircraft (provided by Canada and Spain), an insufficient number to provide the required 24-hour surveillance of the North African littoral. The RAF's Chief of the Air Staff, Sir Stephen Dalton, acknowledged that

---

[40] Her Majesty's Government, *A Strong Britain in an Age of Uncertainty: The National Security Strategy*, London: The Stationery Office, CM7953, October 18, 2010; House of Commons, Public Administration Select Committee, *Who Does UK National Strategy? First Report of Session 2010–11*, London: The Stationery Office, HC435, October 2010.

[41] S. Austin, "To What Extent Should the Regeneration of a Wide-Area Maritime Patrol Capability Be a Priority for UK Defence and National Security?" Defence Research Paper, Advanced Command and Staff Course, UK Defence Academy, 2012, Annex E.

the availability of Nimrod would have helped in securing the northern coastal waters of [Libya]. It could have been deployed there very quickly. It could be maintained there, because it is a long-range, long-endurance aeroplane, and it had the sensor suite that would have allowed us to have the perfect picture.[42]

The Qaddafi regime used the Libyan Navy to mine harbors and threaten humanitarian shipping, and although a number of successful NATO air attacks occurred on regime vessels, some of these escaped any damage and managed to transit out of Libyan waters without detection. Regime fast attack craft were particularly active under cover of darkness, and this is when the wide-area 24-hour surveillance capability of a maritime patrol aircraft such as the Nimrod MRA4 would have been particularly useful.

In the face of capability gaps, the UK has become more dependent upon allies. The Chief of the Defence Staff, in his evidence to the House of Commons Defence Committee, stated that the UK has to rely on its allies "to compensate for areas that we might not have, but other countries have."[43] This was one of the main reasons the UK entered into the Anglo-French Treaty on Security and Defence so enthusiastically in November 2010. But such accords are not panaceas. Allies cannot be relied upon if their national interests widely diverge, and this is why niche role-playing within alliances can be dangerous. Using the MPA as an example, should the UK need to defend the Falklands Islands against Argentine aggression in a manner similar to the campaign in 1982, it is unlikely that any Alliance partner would be willing to provide such a capability for the pursuit of UK specific national interests.

One of the many lessons from Libya is that nations need to have realistic expectations of alliances, especially when partnerships are new. The Anglo-French accord is a good case in point. Several disconnects surfaced between the two allies, but this is not surprising, as the treaty had been in place scarcely three months when the Libyan campaign started. Most of the details as to how the two nations were going to pool equipment and develop a Combined Joint Expeditionary Force had not been worked out, and the Libyan operation preceded the first exercise (Southern Mistral) planned for March 2011. As a result, each country went into the Libyan campaign using its own command-and-control arrangements and information systems.[44] The simple fact was that the UK and France operated alongside each other, in a state of deconfliction rather

---

[42] Air Chief Marshal Sir Stephen Dalton, oral evidence to HCDC, May 11, 2011, House of Commons Defence Committee, *The Strategic Defence and Security Review and the National Security Strategy: Government Response to the Committee's Sixth Report of Session 2010–12, Ninth Special Report of Session 2010–12*, London: The Stationery Office Limited, HC 1639, November 10, 2011, p. 28. See also Lee Willett, "Don't Forget About the Ships," in Johnson and Mueen, *Short War, Long Shadow*, p. 42.

[43] General Sir David Richards, oral evidence to HCDC, "The Appointment of the Chief of Defence Staff," November 17, 2010.

[44] Kim Willsher, "Sarkozy Opposes NATO Taking Control of Libya Operation," March 22, 2012.

than true integration. Recognizing this, David Cameron decided to prioritize work in the "key area of command and control."[45]

Therefore, while maintaining existing levels of cooperation with the United States, Operation Unified Protector demonstrated the need for UK personnel to become more familiar with non–U.S. C2, not least because the main focus for U.S. defense is pivoting away from Europe and the Middle East to the western Pacific. Anglo-French interoperability at the beginning of the Libyan campaign proved to be difficult, but, as time went on, obstacles were bypassed, and liaison between the British and French maritime-based attack helicopter forces was considered to be one of the highlights of the new bilateral defense cooperation.

However, one of the greatest sources of embarrassment for UK defense was the realization it had ignored NATO for the best part of a decade and that the time had come to reinvest. In the early stages of OUP, British personnel had to work extremely hard to adapt to NATO constructs, and rapid augmentation of staffs had to occur by pulling people from their UK posts. But, overall, what the Libyan campaign demonstrated was the need for regular exercising with NATO (and especially non-NATO) partners to ensure commonality of tactics, techniques, and procedures, or at least the mechanisms to build these quickly as the need arises. The very nature of contingency operations means that no C2 construct will be fit for purpose in every instance, and regular exercising with a varying number of international partners ensures flexibility of mindset.[46]

Operation Ellamy was the first "standing start" campaign the UK had waged since the Falklands War of 1982, and it tested the RAF's rapidly deployable capacity to the maximum. It was evident that Afghanistan had reduced capability for contingency operations, and many people struggled to see the distinction between deployed operations, such as Afghanistan and Iraq, and contingent expeditionary operations. In the former, the planning lead-time usually allows for the prepositioning of infrastructure in a theater of operations, but the latter often demands building support infrastructure from scratch, and the rewriting of tactics, techniques, and procedures according to the specific operating environment. When two of the RAF's Expeditionary Air Wings (EAWs), 906 and 907, were called upon for Operation Ellamy, it quickly became apparent that Poggio had insufficient space and headquarters (HQ) staff to support the two wings, so they were merged under one commanding officer. This meant that a proportion of EAW personnel could provide administrative support to the UK Air Combat Command and his HQ staff, allowing them to focus on the mission and reducing their overall burden. This was just one example of adaptable C2 in action, because, under normal circumstances, the HQ staff would be supporting the

---

[45] "UK-France Declaration on Security and Defence," *10* (official site of the British Prime Minister's Office), February 17, 2012. See also Cameron in Johnson and Mueen, *Short War, Long Shadow*, pp. 19–22.

[46] House of Commons, *Operations in Libya*, "UK Contribution to the Operation," pp. 10–11.

EAW. However, 906th EAW had to operate in austere conditions, and much of the technical support was operated from tented accommodation. But, through the tenacity and hard work of personnel involved, especially the commanding officer, the EAW concept worked well in practice. Within 18 hours of Gioia del Colle being identified as the operating base for RAF fast jets, UK assets were launching missions from the base, and it is worth noting that the EAW received complete support from those UK stations that deployed squadrons to the Mediterranean. OUP demonstrated that the UK should think and prepare for both deployed and contingency operations, and to have exercises that address high-end contingency expeditionary warfare. One of the initiatives since Ellamy has been to establish a center for expeditionary capability training at RAF Leeming, and the aim is to ensure that future EAWs are efficient, scalable, and adaptable to whatever scenarios they face. The importance of this initiative lies in the fact that the center also will train partner nations in tandem, thus building up an interoperable international cadre.[47]

While it can be argued that contingency operations play to airpower's strengths because of its responsiveness and flexibility, the Libyan campaign also demonstrated the difficulties that nations face when those types of operations need to be sustained over longer periods. The UK's stocks of precision weapons, especially Brimstone, ran perilously short, and the United States had to step in to replenish NATO's supplies of other types of PGMs. This was because of the overarching requirement to safeguard the Libyan population and keep collateral damage to a bare minimum. Indeed, with only a few exceptions, precision weapons were employed in every instance during the campaign. The UK faced other potential areas of fragility in its sustainment of Operation Ellamy. Aging VC10s and Tristars, which also had to support ongoing operations in Afghanistan, performed air-to-air refueling. The refueling of Storm Shadow missions from the UK required eight-hour return flights, placing considerable strains on the already overburdened fleets. As the VC10s near their retirement, the Tristars will have to carry the load until the introduction of the A330 Voyager, and very little spare capacity is available to meet any other contingency operations in the near future. Indeed, the U.S. Defense Secretary heavily criticized UK and other European NATO members for failing to equip and sustain their forces adequately.[48]

Conflicts invariably result in tactical- and operational-level innovations, and OUP was no exception. Success in the campaign was due in no small part to people's preparedness to abandon accepted norms and existing structures. This was witnessed in a number of areas. The RAF procured the Typhoon as an air-to-air platform, but it was

---

[47] House of Commons, "UK Contribution to the Operation"; Royal Aeronautical Society–IISS Libya Seminar; Chief of the Air Staff's Air Power Conference, November 1, 2012.

[48] John Tirpak, "Lessons From Libya," *Air Force Magazine*, Vol. 94, No. 12, December 2011, p. 37; Neil Dunridge, "ELLAMY Enabler," *Air Forces Monthly*, January 2012, pp. 42–46; Royal Aeronautical Society–IISS Libya Seminar.

shown to be a capable ground-attack aircraft. The mixing of Tornados and Typhoons in strike packages was a pragmatic development that worked well. Typhoons acted as fighter escort to Tornados, then joined in the attack mission. The way in which fast jets provided imagery for the Apache attack helicopters and then operated in concert with them also was unique in the UK's experience. But perhaps the most interesting aspect was the dominance of deliberate dynamic targeting. While the concept of DDT had been in use since the main combat phase of Operation Iraqi Freedom in 2003,[49] when the requirement for "kill box interdiction" arose, the Libyan campaign was unusual because of the extremely high proportion of DDT attacks.

The combination of the UK's speed of response to the Libyan crisis, agility of mind, and tactical level excellence enhanced Britain's reputation within the coalition. More specifically, the CFACC, Lieutenant General Jodice, knew he could rely on the UK to strike swiftly and with precision against the most testing of targets, and given UNSCR 1973's overriding remit to protect the Libyan civilian population, precision equaled zero (or very low) collateral damage. The fact that the UK also brought unique capabilities to bear, such as Storm Shadow and Dual Mode Seeker Brimstone, further enhanced this reputation. By the end of the campaign in October 2011, the RAF, Royal Navy, and Army Air Corps had destroyed more than 1,000 regime targets that had presented a threat to the Libyan people. In order to achieve this, the UK had deployed 2,300 service personnel; 16 Tornado GR4s, 10 Typhoons, 5 Apache attack helicopters, AWACS Sentry E-3Ds, two Sentinel R1s, one Nimrod R1, VC10s, and one Tristar. No service personnel were killed in action, and Ellamy cost an incredibly small amount considering its achievements. It was initially estimated to cost £210 million, but a revised figure shows the total cost was closer to £150 million, making it one of the cheapest conflicts in British history. Operation Unified Protector was a unique campaign. Nothing remotely resembling it had been seen before. But OUP proved that airpower, focused and driven by ISR, can win a campaign when combined effectively with irregular ground forces.[50]

---

[49] The British designation for its participation in the invasion of Iraq was Operation Telic.

[50] Ministry of Defence, "Libya: Operations Updates," pp. 1–5; *Defence News*, "Cost of Libya," December 8, 2011; Treasury Brief, January 25, 2012.

CHAPTER SEVEN

The French Experience: Sarkozy's War?*

Camille Grand

Introduction

The Libyan campaign was unique in many respects among recent French military engagements, to the point that some commentators have called this operation "Sarkozy's War,"[1] a reference to the 2010 Bob Woodward book *Obama's Wars* about the U.S. president's efforts in Afghanistan and Pakistan. This emphasis on the Libya campaign in the narrative about Nicolas Sarkozy's presidency overshadows France's recent military endeavors elsewhere. After all, in 2011, France did send more troops and spent more money than the United States did in Afghanistan, and engaged its forces to facilitate a successful political transition in Ivory Coast. Yet several important factors make Libya stand out:

- A genuine French leadership (or co-leadership) in the diplomatic management of the crisis and the conduct of military operations, making France much more than a contributor to a U.S.-led operation.
- A strong moral, legal, and political case in the context of the Arab Spring, combining a clear mandate with a United Nations Security Council resolution (UNSCR 1973), the moral imperative of the responsibility to protect (R2P), and the support of many Arab countries.
- A successful military campaign combining an appropriate use of force, few civilian casualties, and a successful political outcome with the fall of Colonel Muammar Qaddafi.
- The personal involvement of Sarkozy, who decided very early in the crisis to take the lead and who was directly involved in the daily conduct of operations.

---

*This chapter draws on numerous interviews with French military and government personnel conducted by the author in 2012 and 2013.

[1] For example, Natalie Nougayrède, "La guerre de Nicolas Sarkozy," *Le Monde*, August 24, 2011.

Both during and after the campaign, the Sarkozy administration developed the storytelling[2] that places the emphasis on the central French (and to a lesser extent British) role while underplaying the United States' role. Separate from this narrative, however, the conflict offers some interesting lessons, both from an operational standpoint and from a political-military perspective, and which may prove relevant to future decisions about military interventions.

Why and How Did France Decide to Act?

Domestic politics, and the appeal in an election year of Sarkozy being perceived as a strong commander-in-chief, cannot explain alone the French decision to take the lead in the Libyan affair. Nor can the support of French "intellectuals" such as the popular author and media figure Bernard-Henri Lévy. In digging deeper into France's motivations, the memories of Srebrenica and other atrocities committed during the Balkan wars played an important role, as did the need to express clear support to the Arab revolts by not allowing the Qaddafi regime to crush the rebellion in the Arab Spring's first weeks.[3] From a strategic perspective, Libya also was an opportunity for some Europeans to demonstrate they could take the lead in managing a significant crisis in the Mediterranean at a time when the United States was perceived as reluctant to engage in another campaign when its strategic interests were not obviously involved.

In that context, Sarkozy's partnership with British Prime Minister David Cameron was interesting, as the Libyan conflict took place a couple of months after the signing in Lancaster House of a series of historic treaties expanding Franco-British defense cooperation.[4] For the two European leaders, it was an opportunity to make a point about the possible use of force in the management of international crises and signal they were still able to take part jointly in a crisis in the vicinity of Europe.

Libya and the Arab Spring

The Libyan crisis started when the protests began in Benghazi on February 15, 2011, prompting Qaddafi's security forces to begin a brutal crackdown. By February 20, protestors had taken control of Libya's second largest city, Benghazi, building a significant anti-Qaddafi force. These events were taking place weeks after protesters in Tunisia

---

[2]   Natalie Nougayrède, "La guerre de Libye et la tentation du 'storytelling' français," *Le Monde*, September 14, 2011. Such storytelling also exists in other capitals, as in the Obama administration's efforts to downplay the "leadership from behind" narrative during the 2012 election campaign demonstrate.

[3]   For a good assessment of the French debate at the time, see Pierre Tran, "Why Did France Move So Forcefully on Libya?" *Defense News*, March 28, 2011.

[4]   On the Franco-British nexus in the campaign, see Alastair Cameron, "The Channel Axis: France, the UK and NATO," in Adrian Johnson and Saqeb Mueen, eds., *Short War, Long Shadow: The Political and Military Legacies of the 2011 Libya Campaign*, London: Royal United Services Institute (RUSI), Whitehall Report 1–12, 2012.

and Egypt had successfully brought about the demise of local authoritarian regimes, with Zine El Abidine Ben Ali fleeing from Tunis and Hosni Mubarak withdrawing from power in Cairo.

During the first phase of the Arab Spring, France, along with most Western diplomacies, was slow to react with embarrassing initial support to Ben Ali and Mubarak, who were both key partners in French Mediterranean diplomacy (in particular on Sarkozy's Union for the Mediterranean project since 2008). When the Libyan crisis unfolded, France was in the midst of a rapid reappraisal of its diplomatic stance. Michèle Alliot-Marie resigned as foreign minister, and her replacement was Alain Juppé, who had been prime minister from 1995 to 1997 and foreign minister during the pivotal Bosnia events from 1993 to 1995. Sarkozy and Juppé quickly advocated a strong international response to the events in Libya, both as a genuine effort to address the Libyan crisis and as a way to end a perceived French political and diplomatic failure to address the Arab Spring.

France's Long and Complicated Relationship with Qaddafi's Libya

Libya was not a former French colony like other Maghreb countries such as Tunisia, Algeria, and Morocco, and the relationship between the two countries after Qaddafi's coup was tortuous. In the 1970s, France supported the new regime, which soon became a major customer for French weaponry. In the 1980s, however, France was in direct confrontation with Qaddafi's forces and proxies in Chad, and strongly supported the Chadian efforts to expel Libyan forces from their territory. Operation Epervier, which started in February 1986 to defend Chadian sovereignty, is still ongoing. France nevertheless distanced itself from the April 1986 U.S. Operation El Dorado Canyon by denying overflight to U.S. aircraft attacking Libya from British bases after a terrorist attack in Berlin. Later in the decade, France was directly confronted with Libyan state-sponsored terrorism with the bombing of UTA Flight 772, bound from Chad to Paris, in September 1989 (one year after Lockerbie), killing all 170 people aboard.

After a freeze in the 1990s, bilateral relations slowly resumed in 2003 and 2004 with a settlement on the past terrorist attacks. The strange state visit of Qaddafi to Paris in December 2007, during which the Libyan dictator embarrassed Sarkozy, was the high (or low) point of a French attempt to restore good relations and win commercial contracts with a normalized Libya, which many world leaders sought at the time. From that visit, Sarkozy is reputed to have learned that Qaddafi was "crazy and unreliable," an argument he often made during the 2011 crisis.

From this mixed experience with Qaddafi's Libya, France drew some harsh lessons that partially explain its rather hawkish stance. Because Qaddafi was a known international political figure, the French public was deemed ready to understand the need to intervene.

Assessment of the Humanitarian and Political Situation

A second key element in the decision to intervene was the humanitarian assessment and the perceived immediate risk that Qaddafi forces would crush the revolt in Benghazi. A strong sense of humanitarian urgency prevailed in the decision to act as well as in the later justification of the war. Throughout the war, the Qaddafi forces' violence against civilians served as a useful reminder of the fundamental reason behind intervention.

The decision to first strike Qaddafi's forces assaulting Benghazi as early as March 19 (less than 48 hours after the adoption of UNSCR 1973) was both a military and political choice aimed at avoiding that city's fall and the anticipated subsequent bloodbath. The Security Council resolution mandated protecting civilians from harm, an objective that subsequently drove political and military decisions. It also was a major military constraint, though NATO forces quite successfully responded to the intense pressure not to harm civilians.

The U.N. Process and the Decision to Act Militarily

It took more than two months after the Libyan upheaval in Benghazi to secure a decision to act. France played a major part in that process, although its position evolved throughout the process as the situation in Libya worsened and as international support grew for an operation under Chapter VII of the U.N. Charter.

At first, France emphasized sanctions, with Sarkozy proposing on February 23 that the European Union adopt sanctions on Libyan leaders. After U.N. Secretary-General Ban Ki-moon encouraged the U.N. Security Council to act on Libya, France and Britain called on the U.N. to approve an arms embargo as well as sanctions. At the time, French leaders were still excluding the military option. On February 26, the Security Council unanimously passed Resolution 1970, which called for an immediate end to the violence, leveled sanctions against Qaddafi and other figures of his regime, and referred Libya to the International Criminal Court, calling for a investigation by the body into "widespread and systematic attacks" against civilians. Later in the month, the EU adopted further sanctions, including an arms embargo.

When the discussion of a no-fly zone (NFZ) started in late February, France insisted on the need for regional support and a U.N. mandate, and appeared skeptical about NATO involvement. In this early stage, the diplomatic debate about the no-fly zone did not go into details about the military dimensions of its implementation. Furthermore, post-war accounts note the French were aware a no-fly zone would be insufficient, and that as early as March 1, they already were considering the option of targeted strikes as the only way to prevent massacres.[5] At the political level, an NFZ was primarily perceived as an option short of a full-fledged military intervention on the ground and an easier sell in the U.N. At the time, many had in mind some pre-

---

[5]   See the testimony of Jean-David Levite in Jean-Christophe Notin, *La vérité sur notre guerre en Libye*, Paris: Fayard, October 10, 2012, p. 62.

cise precedents, in particular the 1991–2003 NFZ over Northern and Southern Iraq preventing Saddam Hussein from using airpower against Kurdish and Shiite regions, and Operation Deny Flight over Bosnia-Herzegovina in 1993–1995, both pursuing humanitarian objectives. During this period of intense diplomatic activity, the French closely consulted with their British counterparts to build international support for additional pressure on Qaddafi, including military options. The Gulf Cooperation Council's calls for a no-fly zone unlocked the debate in early March by creating momentum for regional support. It was followed by the Organization of the Islamic Conference (OIC), which announced its support for a no-fly zone over Libya. At the time, NATO was divided, as the United States and Germany were reported to be opposed to a no-fly zone while Britain and France were working on a draft resolution at the U.N. calling for one. France's engagement took a new turn when on March 10 it became the first Western country to recognize the Libyan National Transition Council (NTC) as the sole legitimate representative of the Libyan people.

During a European Union summit on March 11, the EU reached agreement to consider "all necessary options" to protect civilians in Libya. The statement did not refer to recent French and British calls for a no-fly zone. It did note that any proposed military action would require a clear legal basis, regional support, and a clear objective. This statement sought to bridge divisions within the EU between Germany's open skepticism over the use of force and France's and Britain's clear contemplation of airstrikes.

On March 12, the League of Arab States called on the Security Council to impose a no-fly zone that could meet the condition that many had set for regional support. As France was pushing in New York in favor of a UNSC authorization for a no-fly zone, Qaddafi's forces regained most of the territory they had lost to rebel forces and began preparing an assault on the opposition stronghold of Benghazi. At this point, the Obama administration shifted policy and began to press the Security Council to authorize an international coalition featuring representation from Arab states to take military action.

The United States took the lead in the drafting of the UNSC resolution, which France and Britain supported. Three senior Obama administration officials (National Security Council staff member Samantha Power, U.N. Ambassador Susan Rice, and Secretary of State Hillary Clinton) played important roles in convincing the President to go beyond the more cautious approach being advocated by those reluctant to see America engaged in another war in a Muslim country. The UNSC voted on March 17 to authorize member nations to "take all necessary measures . . . to protect civilians and civilian populated areas" under Chapter VII of the U.N. Charter. UNSC Resolution 1973 passed with ten votes in favor and five abstentions—China, Russia, Brazil, India, and Germany. Together with the United States and Britain, France spared no effort to convince the members of the UNSC to vote in favor and not to veto the resolution. Juppé traveled to New York for the vote on Resolution 1973, and President Sarkozy personally engaged leaders of all the countries on the Security Council. The immediate threat to Benghazi and Qaddafi's frightening comments about the fate of insurgents helped persuade some countries to vote in favor and led both China and Russia not to use their veto powers.

This diplomatic campaign was successful for France, which had been at the forefront of the international debate. France worked closely with Britain and the United States, resolving some differences in the last days before the resolution was adopted. It also used its good relationships with Arab leaders in the Gulf (Qatar and the United Arab Emirates) to secure regional support and engagement. When operations started, France had secured all of its requirements for going to war: U.N. and regional support, a clear legal basis, and a mandate broad enough to allow some flexibility in conducting military operations. In spite of later quarrels about the scope of UNSCR 1973, the French legal reading was simple: Ground operations and occupation of Libya were prohibited, while air operations to protect civilians beyond a simple no-fly zone were authorized. From a French perspective, the debates in the drafting of the resolution left little ambiguity: The UNSC had accepted the use of airpower not only to enforce a no-fly zone, but also to protect civilians through targeted strikes on Qaddafi's forces.

EU, NATO, or Coalition of the Willing?

In the run-up to the first strikes, France was at first very reluctant to involve NATO and explored alternative options. The motivation was political, as Paris feared the political consequences of another NATO mission in a Muslim country. It sought to set up an operation involving regional players (which was later secured when Qatar, the UAE, and Jordan joined the coalition). Senior French officials publicly expressed criticism about a NATO involvement. Throughout the first period of the crisis and the first days of the conflict itself, France openly questioned the role of the Alliance, as the spokesperson of the Ministry of Foreign Affairs said on March 18: "We have always thought that a NATO operation was neither opportune nor appropriate in the [Libyan] context."[6]

If an EU operation quickly was ruled out, France hoped as operations were about to begin to set up an ad hoc Franco-British headquarters. Despite the close personal relationship between Sarkozy and Cameron and the Anglo-French spirit following the Lancaster House treaties, the British choice to start planning with the Americans in Ramstein led to some bitterness in Paris. As Alastair Cameron noted, "It remains unclear whether British political officials might have endorsed a form of bilateral France-UK command-and-control arrangement, which was then superseded by advice from the British military chain of command."[7] According to military historian Jean-

---

[6] Point du presse, "Adoption par le Conseil de sécurité des Nations unies de la résolution 1973 sur la situation en Libye," March 18, 2011. Translation by the author.

[7] Cameron, "The Channel Axis," in Johnson and Mueen, *Short War, Long Shadow.*

Christophe Notin, the French armed forces had in mind a different command structure with the French Air Force's Lyon-Montverdun air operation center serving as JFACC (it is NATO Response Force–certified up to 1,000 sorties per day), while the British Permanent Joint Headquarters at Northwood would serve as operations headquarters (OHQ). A French team even traveled to Northwood to prepare for such an arrangement, only to realize that their British counterparts already were preparing to deploy to Ramstein.[8] Senior French military officials continue to assess, from a military point of view, that a multinationalized French, British, or Franco-British chain of command (OHQ + JFACC) could have managed planning and C2 of the operation. From a political point of view, however, it seems doubtful that other contributors would have agreed to such a command arrangement, especially a non-U.S.-led one, an option that met no support from coalition partners. The decision to operate on an ad hoc basis from Ramstein nevertheless was swiftly accepted in Paris, and senior French officers quickly were inserted into the Ramstein air operations center.

France therefore went along with this coalition-of-the-willing logic under a U.S. HQ but continued to resist the handover to NATO, only accepting it under intense allied pressure. It took threats from Italians, Norwegians, and other NATO allies to impose NATO as the commanding structure, and Paris went along with this approach only when it became clear that Washington was unwilling to continue leading the coalition and that Britain had no intention of supporting the French view. Besides the political concerns about NATO being too Western, France feared that constraints from NATO allies that had been reluctant about the operation (namely, Germany and Turkey) would limit the Alliance's ability to act. Even after the handover to Operation Unified Protector began on March 25, Paris took the unusual step of trying to limit the political control of the North Atlantic Council, insisting the handover to NATO and the Naples JFC was a "technical" decision to use the NATO "machinery" and promoting the political role of the contact group versus NATO as a political forum. France also insisted on retaining some direct operational control of its forces. Interestingly, the French narrative has since evolved, as the French now insist that Libya was a success story in part because of their return to the integrated military structures (decided in 2009) that enabled them to play a major role in the conduct of operations.

Was France in the Driver's Seat?

France was undeniably a major player in the setting up of the Libyan operation. It was not alone in that endeavor, however. The roles played by Britain and the United States, which often were downplayed in Paris as well as by key Arab states, offer a more nuanced view than the notion of France in the driver's seat. For all of its high-profile leadership, France's views did not always unilaterally prevail and needed the support of others. It is nevertheless clear that Paris had a strong part in the diplomatic process

---

[8] On this strange episode, see Notin, *La vérité sur notre guerre en Libye*, pp. 191–193.

and could claim co-leadership of the management of the crisis. From that perspective, a strong nexus exists between the political engagement and the military role.

The French Military Engagement

The French engagement, labeled *Opération Harmattan*, started the air campaign, as Sarkozy announced to France's partners during the Libya summit on March 19 that he had ordered a first strike on Libyan forces in the suburbs of Benghazi. It continued until the last day of Operation Unified Protector.

Recent accounts point to a discreet but quite systematic French national ISR campaign focused on the coast of Libya in the preceding week using air, naval, and space assets to establish a more accurate order of battle of the Libyan forces and to assess their capabilities, in the logic of an intelligence preparation of the battlefield.[9] Even though this campaign was executed under serious political constraints—the French feared an incident that would jeopardize the chances of a robust U.N. resolution—it allowed a national assessment of the status of Libyan forces and the planning of the initial French strikes.

Even though it was relatively modest in size by U.S. standards, Operation Harmattan was nevertheless the largest engagement for the French Air Force and Navy at least since Kosovo. It actually was not modest for France at all when it came to the maximum operational contract given to the air force. At any given time, the French Air Force must be able to provide up to (and no more than) 70 combat aircraft in a coalition operation. But in addition to Libya, the French Air Force was already deployed in several other countries, including Afghanistan (with six combat aircraft), Chad (three aircraft), and the UAE (six aircraft). At the peak of the operation, with 39 combat aircraft engaged in Libya, the French Air Force almost reached its "operational contract" of 70 combat aircraft deployed in operations.

Operation Harmattan primarily involved the air force, but the navy and army also contributed. As detailed below, the French took—together with the British—the largest share of strike missions and allowed the United States to withdraw the bulk of their combat assets fairly quickly and "lead from behind," according to the famous phrase coined during the campaign. This was a very significant experience for the French forces, as they had not played such a central role in coalition operations in post–Cold War conflicts (Bosnia in 1995 came closest, at least on the ground with the Quick Reaction Force set up with London). During the 1991 Gulf War, the 1999 Kosovo campaign, or in Afghanistan since 2001, France always had taken a back seat to the United States in combat operations. This changed with Libya, as the non-U.S. members of the coalition were expected to produce the core military effect after the first few days.

---

[9] See Notin, *La vérité sur notre guerre en Libye*, pp. 81–85.

Before entering into the details of the French engagement, two observations are worth noting. First, the Libyan campaign was not the Battle of Britain; it was a limited and successful air campaign conducted by a relatively small force confronting a rather modest adversary that was in no position to engage superior and more modern air forces. Second, the French, compared with many coalition partners, did have a pre-Libya experience of managing operations with their own command-and-control assets. Much of that experience came through a series of national engagements in Africa, some of which were quite demanding.

Deployment and Command Structure

France deployed military assets from the first day of operations on March 19 until the end of the NATO operation on October 31. Up to 4,300 servicemen and women were deployed as part of Operation Harmattan (the national operation retained its name after the launch of NATO's Operation Unified Protector).

Even though it was a primarily an air campaign, Operation Harmattan involved all three services. France conducted the first strikes in Libyan territory with air force planes that originally operated from French bases, but then flew mostly from La Suda in Crete and Sigonella in Sicily to reduce transit. The Aircraft Carrier Battle Group (GAN) also was quickly involved in operations over Libya from the aircraft carrier *Charles de Gaulle*; the first operational flight by naval Rafale M multirole fighters occurred as early as March 22; and the first strike carried out by Super Étendard strike aircraft took place the following day.

Twenty-seven different ships were engaged for more than seven months to ensure continuity of maritime operations and control of sea and air space while conducting artillery strikes against land targets. With more than 1,500 days at sea, they allowed the deployment of a naval combat aircraft force, army attack helicopters, and air force helicopters dedicated to the recovery personnel in hostile territory. *Aéronavale* carrier aircraft accounted for 1,590 sorties (including 840 offensive sorties) from March 22 until August 12, roughly one-fourth of the French total. On May 18, the Army attack helicopter group (GAM), composed of 24 helicopters (20 Gazelles and 4 Tigres), went into action from the *Mistral*-class Projection and Command Ships (BPC) (*Tonnerre* followed by *Mistral*).

At the peak of the crisis, France committed more than 40 aircraft, 30 helicopters, and a dozen warships. Air force and navy planes totaled nearly 5,600 sorties and more than 27,000 flight hours, achieving 25 percent of sorties by the coalition, 35 percent of offensive missions, and 20 percent of strikes. This represents nearly 3,100 offensive sorties, 1,200 reconnaissance sorties, 400 air defense sorties, and 340 air traffic control and 580 air-to-air refueling missions. The Army's attack helicopter group conducted some 40 raids comprising more than 250 sorties.[10]

---

[10] Data from the *Dossier de presse* prepared for the end of air operations in Libya, November 10, 2011, p. 4.

The Choice of Bases

Libya was a special case of power projection from a French perspective, as operations could be conducted from airfields in France. Several air bases in continental France did take part in the air campaign: Avord, Dijon, Istres-Le Tubé, Nancy-Ochey, and Saint-Dizier-Robinson. The base in Corsica, Solenzara, played an important role as France's most southern military airfield.

The first strikes were launched from air bases in northeastern France (carried out by Mirage 2000Ds from Nancy, and Rafales from Saint Dizier). But it proved extremely useful to progressively shift the main bases closer to Libya, first by making extensive use of Solenzara, and then by forward-deploying air assets to Sigonella in Sicily and La Suda on Crete. This saved significant transit time and enabled French combat aircraft to spend more time in actual combat missions.

In this particular geographical context, the role of the aircraft carrier in the campaign was less important than it would have been in more distant engagements. Accordingly, after it played a significant role in the first months of the French engagement, the *Charles de Gaulle* was withdrawn from the operation.

The First Days of the Operation

France was the first coalition partner to strike, on March 19 at 6:00 p.m., a few hours before British and U.S. forces went into action. This decision was taken for a series of reasons. It was, of course, Sarkozy's highly political decision to demonstrate French resolve and take a leadership role. The fact that the strike was announced during the coalition senior-level meeting on Libya and took place immediately after the meeting maximized the political and media effects. The decision also was prompted by a sense of humanitarian emergency, as Qaddafi's armored forces were closing on Benghazi. The choice of military targets in the ground forces encircling Benghazi was consistent with that concern.

From a military perspective, this first strike did not go by the book according to standard U.S. practice, as SEAD operations or the confirmed destruction of Libyan airpower had not yet taken place. It was, therefore, a rather risky operation carried out successfully, and not merely a symbolic attack. It involved around 20 air force aircraft: eight multirole Rafales, two Mirage 2000-5s (for air superiority), two Mirage 2000Ds (for interdiction), six C-135FR tankers, and one E-3F AWACS, striking targets located some 1,500 kilometers from their bases. Four Libyan armored vehicles were reportedly destroyed during the mission, two by GBU-12 laser-guided bombs dropped by the Mirage 2000Ds and two by AASM guided weapons launched by Rafales. This was a rather small number by military standards, but it stopped the advance of Qaddafi's leading forces at the outskirts of Benghazi and probably helped prevent a massacre in the city. Had Benghazi fallen, the outcome of the war could have been quite different. As such, this initial strike served a critical political and strategic purpose.

As Christian Anrig has noted, this attack could point at a difference in "ways of war":

> Specifically, the United States musters overwhelming force to produce decisive results at the least cost of lives. In contrast, former European colonial powers have a history of fighting outgunned and outnumbered . . . This attitude is also reflected in the French air force's initial strikes on 19 March 2011. Some commentators were quick to play down the risks involved, arguing that the French had identified a gap in the fixed-site air defense system, but the threat of mobile surface-to air missiles undoubtedly remained.[11]

In their post-war assessment, the French point at this first strike to downplay their reliance on U.S. assets for SEAD. This assessment is correct for this particular raid, since no losses occurred. Libyan air defenses nonetheless identified the French raid and engaged it with an SA-8 surface-to-air missile system, which fortunately was out of range.[12] It is, however, questionable that such a risky tactic would have worked for the whole campaign, as the French were probably not ready to take significant risks of aircraft losses. Therefore, this opening move might denote a divergence of operational habits. The French, like the British, are used to making do with less.

Despite France's early accomplishment, the first days of operations relied heavily on U.S. assets, especially ones that the French were unable to provide, including SEAD aircraft and Tomahawk cruise missiles that conducted deep strikes against critical infrastructure. (Of the 199 sea-launched cruise missiles fired in the first ten days, 192 were American and seven were British. None of the missiles were French, as the French naval equivalent, SCALP Naval, had yet to enter service.) Some have criticized this coalition show of force as unnecessary overkill, with the potential for negative political impact among Arab states in particular. In the first three days of Operation Odyssey Dawn, the French conducted about 55 sorties (slightly more than one-quarter of the grand total, with U.S. forces conducting the bulk of the operations).

Who's in Charge?

Because the operation was swiftly launched, the command issue was not fully resolved when operations started. In the first three days, operations were primarily under national command. The JFACC in Ramstein focused on deconfliction among the three national U.S., UK, and French operations— Odyssey Dawn, Ellamy, and Harmattan. With a great deal of HQ work, operations evolved after a couple of days to a more integrated approach, allowing the JFACC to take a more classic command role involving "a hierarchy of objectives, distribution of tasks, daily generation of Air Task-

---

[11] Christian Anrig, "Allied Air Power over Libya: A Preliminary Assessment," *Air and Space Power Journal*, Winter 2011.

[12] See Notin, *La vérité sur notre guerre en Libye*, pp. 174–175.

ing Orders (ATO) orchestrating the whole operation, [and] introduction of opportunity targeting."[13]

During the first days of operations, according to Italian journalist David Cenciotti, the French still advocated a coalition-of-the-willing approach and seemed to "have clearly shown an interest to assume command of all air operations of Operation Odyssey Dawn while Italy threatened to cease supporting coalition planes on its airbases and close its airspace if NATO does not take over the unitary command of the air campaign, in clear contrast with the French position."[14] Jean-Christophe Notin's detailed account confirms this.[15]

At the time, U.S. Secretary of Defense Robert Gates was saying, "This isn't a NATO mission. This is a mission in which the NATO machinery may be used for command and control." The decision to move to NATO command was made on March 24, after France was put under intense pressure from allies (Britain, the United States, and Italy) to shift in that direction. The NATO structure was in place by March 31 with the formal launch of Operation Unified Protector and with JFC Naples taking over command. France only reluctantly endorsed this move, insisting that the operation should use NATO command assets without being placed under Alliance political control. France went along, but did not really get on board until it became clear that there were more forces engaged in the operation than NATO. France continued throughout the campaign to put the emphasis on the Contact Group as the prime forum for political consultations in the coalition. It is important to underscore General Bouchard's role in the difficult but successful transition from Odyssey Dawn to Unified Protector, from Ramstein to Naples.

Operations

As the campaign developed over seven months, it went through several distinct phases. Difficult transitions sometimes occurred, especially concerning C2. The first two to three days was the first phase, which actually was a collection of three independent national operations. The second phase was Operation Odyssey Dawn (OOD) under U.S. command, with other allies contributing significantly (France and the UK) or more modestly (Denmark, Norway, Canada, Qatar). During that first phase, U.S. airpower provided the bulk of all air missions and strikes. As coalition capabilities grew, the United States' participation declined. Of the 1,990 coalition sorties during OOD,

---

[13] For more on the first month of the operation, see Philippe Gros, "De Odyssey Dawn à Unified Protector: Bilan transitoire, perspectives et premiers enseignements de l'engagement en Libye," Paris: Fondation pour la Recherche Stratégique, Note No. 04/11, April 2011, p. 25.

[14] For a daily account of operations, one of the best open sources throughout the war was Italian journalist David Cenciotti's weblog "The Avionist."

[15] See the chapter "Autant l'Otan," in Notin, *La vérité sur notre guerre en Libye*, pp. 182–232.

French Air Force Mirage 2000D (center) and PGM-armed Rafale B (left) and C (right).
Courtesy of NATO.

AFRICOM reported that U.S. forces flew 1,206 sorties, including almost precisely half of the strike missions (463 out of 952).[16]

During that first phase, the French order of battle evolved. The BA 116 air base at Solenzara, Corsica, became the main forward operating base with the deployment of six of eight Rafales, eight Mirage 2000Ds, and six Mirage F-1CR reconnaissance fighters. Three Mirage 2000-5s started operating from Suda to conduct air-superiority missions with their counterparts from Qatar. The navy deployed the aircraft carrier *Charles de Gaulle* with its battle group of 14 Rafales and modernized Super Étendards and two E-2 Hawkeyes, expanding the potential number of sorties.

French forces used many capabilities not previously employed in combat. The navy and the air force for the first time fired SCALP cruise missiles (the French version of the British Storm Shadow), with the first raid carried out jointly by the air force (Mirages and Rafales) and the navy (Rafales), firing a total of seven cruise missiles against Al-Joufra air base 250 kilometers into Libya in order to demonstrate there was no safe haven for pro-Qaddafi forces.[17] French fighter-bombers also used an IR imagery version of the AASM-guided munition (Armement Air-Sol Modulaire, or modular air-to-surface armament, an all-weather stand-off PGM propelled by a rocket booster) that had not previously been used in Afghanistan. Libya also was France's first opportunity to deploy new pods on the Rafale, with the Reco NG reconnaissance pod and the Damocles MP targeting pod seeing their first operational use.

---

[16] Amy McCullough, "The Libya Mission," *Air Force Magazine*, Vol. 94, No. 8, August 2011.

[17] On this mission, see Notin, *La vérité sur notre guerre en Libye*, pp. 213–218.

After the NATO takeover, the United States withdrew most of its combat assets after April 4 in keeping with its unprecedented decision to play a more modest role. The pace of operations was markedly reduced after peaking in late March at 180 daily sorties. French and British forces suddenly were at the forefront and had to take over a larger share of combat missions with only a handful of partners; only Italy, Canada, Denmark, Norway, and Belgium then were engaged in strike missions, while others remained focused on enforcing the no-fly zone. The U.S. decision to "lead from behind" also showed the Europeans' weaknesses. U.S. assets remained vital to the conduct of operations, as tankers and advanced ISTAR capabilities (including UAVs) proved indispensible to sustaining and continuing the operations, even at the slower pace that characterized the campaign after its initial days. The slow pace, combined with the fact that fewer deliberate targets appeared as regular Libyan forces became scattered and dismounted, significantly slowed down the number of sorties and strikes.

Allies also had to adjust their forces to evolving Libyan tactics. France and the UK decided to deploy attack helicopters offshore to add a capability focused on targeted air support for the rebel forces engaged in ground combat. As far as France was concerned, Sarkozy decided on this deployment of army helicopters, which began on May 18, and started conducting daily raids from the *Mistral*-class BPC ships on June 3. This force of 24 helicopters combined four modern Tigres and 20 older Gazelles and successfully conducted more than 250 sorties in 37 raids. French helicopters destroyed 614 targets, including 400 vehicles, with coalition helicopters carrying out nearly 90 percent of strikes. The UK was the only other nation to employ attack helicopters; the imbalance with the British engagement can be explained by different tactics. British Apaches were used only to attack predesignated targets and did not engage in opportunity targeting. In complicated and demanding missions, the French helicopters were able to attack targets at close range that would have been too risky or to difficult to attack with fixed-wing combat aircraft, given NATO's rules of engagement. French Army helicopters took real and significant risks and served an important purpose at a time when the operation seemed a bit stalled.

The French prepared and promoted the engagement of attack helicopters early in the conflict as an additional tactic aimed at producing tactical effects on the ground. General Bouchard's background as a helicopter pilot helped the French make a convincing case to NATO. Their engagement required careful planning, as the army Gazelle and Tigre attack helicopters were operating for the first time from a naval platform.[18] Drastic security measures also were taken to limit as much as possible the risks for the crews, with air support and a combat search-and-rescue (CSAR) helicopter attached to each raid. Most of the targets destroyed were light vehicles (pickup trucks) that planes found more difficult to target, given the constraints imposed on altitude. These targets also were less important from a strategic standpoint compared to the heavy vehicles,

---

[18] On this engagement, see Notin, *La vérité sur notre guerre en Libye*, pp. 368–380 and 406–415.

Amphibious assault ships HMS *Ocean* (foreground) and FS *Tonnerre* (background) in company off the Libyan coast, August 2011.
Courtesy of the UK Ministry of Defence. Used under Open Government License provisions.

the depots, and C2 that fixed-wing aircraft targeted. Helicopter operations nevertheless played an important tactical role in Brega and Misrata.

For the air combat force, the French operation also evolved over time. Six Mirage 2000Ds were redeployed to Souda, which is 900 kilometers from Misrata versus the more than 1,200 kilometers from Solenzara. This redeployment reduced transit time and the need for refueling, and increased time on station in the theater, thus improving the force's reactivity. The force could perform between 15 and 20 daily interdiction sorties, most often comprising mixed patrols of Rafales and Mirage 2000s or Rafales and Super Étendards, with three more counterair sorties by Mirage 2000-5s from Souda, supported by ten refueling sorties, air control (performed by AWACS or E-2), and reconnaissance (Mirage F-1CR or Rafale with Reco NG pod). When the mission of the *Charles de Gaulle* ended in August, air operations continued under the sole responsibility of the air force, whose updated force included six Mirage 2000Ns (the nuclear-capable version of Mirage 2000, which since the 1990s also has performed conventional missions), partially compensating for the withdrawal of French Navy aircraft. The French commitment remained altogether relatively modest in size, as the number of combat aircraft engaged in the Libyan theater never exceeded 39. As far as munitions were concerned, the French chief of staff said in a Senate hearing in October 2011 that 1,000 bombs, 600 missiles, 1,500 rockets, and thousands of various ammunition rounds were fired by early September. France did not face significant ammunition shortages and could manage with its stockpile throughout the seven months of operations.[19]

---

[19] Testimony by Amiral Edouard Guillaud, chef d'état-major des Armées, Hearings of the French CHOD, Senate Foreign Affairs and Defense Committee, October 12, 2011.

Finally, it is important to note that in many respects, the French experience in Libya was a joint experience. Beyond the role of the army attack helicopters, the naval interdiction mission, and the contribution of carrier-based aircraft, the navy also was directly involved in onshore operations. After May 4, French frigates used their guns to fire at land targets, something the French Navy had not done in decades. The navy altogether fired 3,000 100-mm and 76-mm rounds, which reportedly helped damage the morale of besieged anti-Qaddafi forces. Naval assets also were used as intelligence tools; the *Rubis*-class French nuclear attack submarine (SNA) is said to have performed a number of reconnaissance missions in Libyan waters.[20]

The Role of Ground Forces

Even though many commentators have compared Libya with Kosovo, this parallel may be partly inaccurate. A better precedent might well be the air operations supporting the Northern Alliance in Afghanistan in 2001, as ground operations under the leadership of Libyan "rebels" proved essential in the efforts leading to the fall of Qaddafi. In many ways, and beyond the first weeks, the coalition acted in support of the opposition rebalancing the situation and enabling it first to resist pro-Qaddafi forces, then to take over Libyan cities until the Qaddafi regime finally fell apart. In that context, the French political resolve to do the job was important, especially when the coalition and the international community started to show concern over the risk of stalemate.

French land forces, except for some very limited numbers of special forces, were not deployed in Libya at any point during Operation Harmattan. But France admitted to having parachuted some armaments to the rebels and also facilitated Arab countries' similar activities. The small numbers of special forces deployed by France, the UK and Arab countries played a role in advising and training Libyan rebels, helping them gain confidence and professionalism. Jean-Christophe Notin offers a detailed account of their role in several key moments of the campaign, which to this date has not been officially confirmed.[21] In a nutshell, it seems the targeted engagement of selected forces of the *Commandement des opérations spéciales* (COS, equivalent of the U.S. Special Operations Command) in Libya was mostly about intelligence as well as providing mentoring and assistance to anti-Qaddafi forces.

Cooperation with Allies

Cooperation among allies was essential throughout the entire campaign. France benefited in particular from basing facilities provided by Italy at Sigonella and by Greece at Souda Bay.

Despite some political differences and distinctive military postures, cooperation with the United States and United Kingdom proved extremely successful on both the

---

[20] See Notin, *La vérité sur notre guerre en Libye*, pp. 358–360.

[21] See Notin, *La vérité sur notre guerre en Libye*.

political and military levels. As the three air force chiefs explained after the conflict: "As Libya reminded us, there are great advantages in our collective ability to provide airpower for the defense of our nations. Long before that campaign started, the three of us, and our staffs, had been working closely to improve strategic-level collaboration. This investment has improved understanding between our headquarters staffs and identified areas of mutual interest. Our early participation over Libya both justified this vision and motivated us to make yet more progress."[22]

The cooperation with the UK was extremely close, as both the RAF and the *Armée de l'Air* engaged Franco-British crews (as part of pilot-exchange programs) on Mirage 2000 and Tornado strike aircraft. The two air forces employed similar-sized forces and played broadly comparable roles. This cooperation among equals confirmed the validity of the Anglo-French agreements of November 2010, even though it was too early to benefit from the new, enhanced bilateral cooperation because none of the decisions taken in 2010 about joint procurement or training had yet been implemented.

Cooperation with the United States was essential to the success of OUP, even beyond the withdrawal of most U.S. combat assets. The choice to provide key enablers that were either unavailable in Europe or not available in sufficient numbers was crucial to fulfill the mission. This filled European gaps in air-to-air refueling, SEAD, and ISTAR. U.S. tankers and UAVs proved to be indispensible assets in the conduct of even a fairly limited operation and allowed the coalition to perform reasonably well, even though the force did not follow the so-called "American way of war" because of limited capabilities. European dependency on U.S. capabilities notwithstanding, France was one of the few other partners able to provide some of these key enablers: tankers, ISR assets with the engagement of a UAV (Harfang), and other reconnaissance planes (Mirage F-1CR, Rafale with Reco NG, and C-160 Gabriel ELINT aircraft), and the use of national space imagery and human intelligence. The French nevertheless recognized the extremely important role that U.S. assets played throughout the conflict.

Learning from Libya

Even though it was a lengthy but relatively small air campaign, Libya demonstrated both the capabilities of the Atlantic Alliance and the depth of the capability shortfalls of the European allies in NATO.

Military Lessons

Two points have been rightfully highlighted. Air-to-air refueling capabilities were too limited to allow the coalition to conduct the operation without a massive U.S. involve-

---

[22] General Norton Schwartz, Air Chief Marshal Sir Stephen Dalton, and Général Jean-Paul Paloméros, "Libyan Air Ops Showcase French, UK, U.S. Partnership," *Jane's Defence Weekly*, March 21, 2012, p. 19.

ment during the entire conflict. This point has been well taken, and France intends to accelerate the replacement of its aging KC-135 fleet. Conducted in conjunction with the national decision to acquire more modern tankers (Airbus MRTT), efforts are under way to work on a European acquisition of a fleet of modern tankers as a response to this particular shortfall.

The French also have fully acknowledged shortfalls in the area of ISR. They plan to procure jointly with the UK a new generation of medium-altitude, long-endurance (MALE) UAVs. The French also joined with the United States in a cooperative initiative to improve NATO's ISR in the preparation for the NATO Chicago summit in 2012. The initiative will go beyond the acquisition of the Air Ground Surveillance (AGS) system, as it will build a NATO ISR capability in Sigonella that is able to use all ISR assets of NATO nations beyond the AGS itself.

Libya also has led to debates about the need for more long-range deep-strike capabilities, as the lack of French participation in the first days' sea-launched cruise missile campaign underscored. Tactically, the value of precision munitions such as the British Brimstone has been highlighted as well. In spite of severe financial constraints, many of these lessons learned should have an impact on the decisions to come in the next procurement bill covering the years 2014 to 2019.

The fact remains that military planning across Europe has for decades been built on the assumption that the United States would perform some functions and would provide some key enablers. Based on this assumption, all European governments, including those that have preserved a small but more or less full-spectrum force (France and the UK) have capability gaps that Libya highlighted. Besides those already mentioned, SEAD and CAS come to mind as far as airpower is involved.

There is a legitimate pride in France about the positive outcome of the Libya campaign. Even though NATO's use of force was quite restrained, NATO forces achieved their political objectives through an air campaign that caused very limited collateral damage. Even with the United States only "leading from behind," the operation demonstrated that Western military power still was able to deliver and did not have to put boots on the ground (except for a very limited number of special forces) to do so. Having taken a significant part in this effort, France deserves its share of this success, especially as far as the high readiness of its forces was concerned. The key issue for the future is the ability of Europeans to deliver budgets allowing the preservation of significant military capabilities in key European countries. This should not be taken for granted, given the deepening of the economic crisis in Europe and the fiscal constraints associated with it.

With respect to command and control, it surprised many French officials that all other allies (excluding the United States, but including the UK) were not really in a position to engage in an operation without NATO's support for planning and commanding the operation. This dependence on NATO's military structure surprised the French military, which has preserved a strategic culture of autonomy if and when necessary. For their part, the French were only just coming back into NATO's integrated military structure after the 2009 Sarkozy decision to do so, and will have to reinvest in NATO to gain a better understanding of NATO's procedures and culture.

Political-Military Lessons

In spite of its reluctance to act through NATO, France now recognizes that the Alliance performed reasonably well as a military structure and proved altogether useful from a military standpoint. It was noticeably successful in integrating non-NATO allies in operations. From a French perspective, some important political-military issues remain to be addressed for the future of the Alliance. First, the Alliance was, initially, not united and had a hard time finding a common position. A major ally (Germany) abstained on UNSCR 1973 and was not only reluctant to use force but not ready to allow the use of force for a mission combining a sound legal basis, a serious security challenge in the vicinity of Europe, and a good moral and political case. Strong political divisions existed on the Libyan crisis within the Alliance and were never completely ironed out.

Second, the military contribution of NATO allies was unequal. Some did not take part in OUP (Germany, Central Europeans, and the Baltic States). Only a handful (eight of 28) took an active part in the strikes (United States, Britain, France, Italy, Belgium, Canada, Norway, Denmark), while others took part in OUP but limited their commitments to naval operations or enforcement of the no-fly zone. This tendency of some nations carrying the bulk of the effort while others abstain is damaging to the Alliance over the long term.

Moreover, this proves the limits of specialization within the Alliance. How can allies rely on unreliable partners for key capabilities when they could decline to participate in a military engagement? An essential lesson is to be learned, especially at the present time, when the "smart defense" narrative at times insists on such specialization as a way to address European capability shortfalls.

Third, the American choice to lead from behind also came as a shock to many Europeans. All previous major NATO operations, such as Bosnia, Kosovo, and Afghanistan, saw the United States taking the lead and providing the bulk of forces. The Libyan case is a challenge to the European allies (and Canada) as it could open a new era in which U.S. leadership in the management of a crisis should not be taken for granted. If Libya signals the way of the future for U.S. leadership, Europeans would consider it a major change. It does question directly the ability of the Europeans to act on their own or with limited U.S. support to address security challenges and crises. The issue could shift from the challenges of interoperability with U.S. forces to the need to be able to act alone. If confirmed, this would dramatically alter the capability requirements for the Europeans, and also could have very significant political implications for NATO and the EU.

Finally, the limited U.S. engagement partially explains the length of the conflict. It led the coalition to pursue a longer and more constrained air campaign than what originally was expected and planned. Many rightfully suggest that a full-fledged U.S. commitment probably could have shortened the duration of the conflict by achieving decisive results earlier. Other constraints, such as carefully avoiding collateral damage or allowing the NTC to better organize its ground forces, nevertheless suggest that the conduct of operations and the final outcome might not have been that different.

Libya and the Future of Warfare: A Model for Future Conflicts?

A year after the campaign was completed in Libya, many seemed to have forgotten the operation and the lessons learned from the conflict. The 2012 Chicago summit could have been an opportunity to take stock of a successful NATO operation, but the emphasis was put on ongoing operations, starting with Afghanistan.

It is, nevertheless, worthwhile to explore some of the important positive future lessons learned:

- Airpower allowed achieving the political objectives that UNSCR 1973 assigned without losses on the Alliance side and with very limited collateral damage from the operation itself (as the U.N. and Amnesty International acknowledged). However, the human costs and consequences of seven months of civil war should not be underestimated.
- The operation proved to be relatively affordable despite budget constraints, certainly compared to Afghanistan but also relative to its effects, and was conducted in a relatively short time frame. It thus met the challenges associated with "war fatigue" in Western democracies, the growing aversion to casualties, boots on the ground, and high financial costs.
- A long-term and difficult engagement on the ground in Libyan territory was avoided (and even prohibited under UNSCR 1973). This military constraint restricted options, but ultimately led to choosing a less ambitious and demanding path, which presumably took longer but ultimately was successful. The lack of direct control over Libyan territory also had some significant disadvantages, with the difficult stabilization of post-war Libya and the spread of light weapons to the Sahel having a negative impact on the region's stability. Several years after the end of NATO operations, the final assessment is now darker. It is, however, not clear that a more classic land operation (had such an operation been allowed) would have been much more successful in addressing these complex side effects of regime change in Libya.
- Western military superiority can still make the difference. A limited use of airpower had a decisive effect and not only allowed the operation to address a

humanitarian crisis associated with the logic of "responsibility to protect," but allowed regime change after 42 years of Qaddafi to take place.

- NATO taking the lead of an operation involving regional partners with a U.N. mandate was a politically sound approach. This has led NATO to put a new emphasis on partnerships, as the ability to act with non-NATO partners was politically essential and militarily useful.
- Intense cooperation among the air forces of key partners (United States, Britain, and France in particular) proved to be extremely useful during the campaign.

Can the Libyan model be applied elsewhere? From a political perspective, the conditions were unique and will be difficult to reproduce, as proven by difficult debates about Syria in the UNSC in 2012 and 2013. From a military standpoint, and given the war fatigue in many Western societies, this approach combining local allies and airpower might have more traction than protracted land wars. It is also important to note that ongoing budget cuts in Europe could have a significant effect on the ability of Europeans to conduct such an operation in the future, as it seems that not only the reduction of capability shortfalls will become more difficult, but that European allies might well scrap some capabilities that proved useful in Libya.

Although no conflict is ever replayed in the future, the operations in Libya certainly could serve as a model for a variety of future contingencies. It was, in any case, a major experience for France as it allowed the country to successfully test a generation of new equipment. President Sarkozy's political choice to move to the forefront of the international debate was backed by the more-than-significant commitment of French forces, with airpower playing the major role.

CHAPTER EIGHT

The Italian Experience: Pivotal and Underestimated

Gregory Alegi

Introduction

In 1911–1912, the Italian Army's fledgling air component, reinforced by a handful of naval aviators and civilian volunteer pilots, pioneered in Libya the applications of airpower in real operations. Flying a single-seat, 50-horsepower Blériot XI monoplane, on October 23, 1911, Capitano Carlo M. Piazza carried out the world's first operational sortie by a heavier-than-air aircraft, a 61-minute reconnaissance over territory at once unknown, inhospitable, and unfriendly.[1] Piazza flew his Blériot for other notable flights, including the first naval artillery ranging (October 28), the first photoreconnaissance (February 23, 1912), and the first operational night flight (March 4, 1912); his colleague, Tenente Giulio Gavotti, dropped the first bombs on November 1, 1911, striking Ain Zara and Tagiura.[2] Yet on October 23, 2011, the Italian Air Force (ITAF) did not celebrate the 100th anniversary of these milestone events. The omission was not due to a lapse of memory, but to ITAF involvement in its largest operation since the end of the Second World War,[3] which absorbed a large amount of resources and enhanced the anniversary's political sensitivity. Celebrating what historians see as the turning point in the metamorphosis of the airplane from sporting implement to practical military machine, and what the ITAF considers its informal birthday, seemed inappropriate, for the Italian Air Force had just fought another war in the skies above Libya.

For almost eight months in 2011, Italy employed the full spectrum of airpower capabilities, which had now expanded to roles and types unthinkable a century before—such as SEAD, air-to-air refueling, electronic warfare, and signals intelligence

---

[1] For a recent succinct summary of the 1911–1912 air campaign, see Gregory Alegi, "Nei cieli della Libia. Colonialismo e i primi impieghi bellici dell'aeroplano," in R. H. Rainero and P. Alberini, eds., *Le Forze Armate e la Nazione Italiana (1861–1914)*, Rome: CISM, 2003, pp. 247–263.

[2] The Libyan operation also prompted thoughts about establishing a transport service (mainly for mail service) and air-to-air combat (using the standard side arms issued to officers, as would indeed happen in the opening stages of the First World War)—and it brought about the first combat aircrew casualties (pilot Carlo Montù was wounded on January 31, 1912, and Tenente Manzini died on August 25, 1912).

[3] Gen. s.a. Giuseppe Bernardis, email communication to all ITAF personnel, November 1, 2011.

(SIGINT), some of which were unique or in very scarce supply among the air forces intervening against the Qaddafi regime. About 85 percent of the Italian contribution came from the ITAF, with the navy providing the rest. The ITAF put its direct contribution at over 7 percent of the sorties flown, directly involving some 4,800 personnel on seven bases.[4] In addition to air assets, the navy contributed 16 ships with about 3,500 crew members.[5] Former Chief of Defense Staff Mario Arpino ventured that the inclusion of surveillance and reconnaissance sorties would make the Italian contribution the largest after that of the United States.[6] For the first time in its history, the ITAF dropped only precision-guided munitions (PGMs), achieving a 97 percent success rate.[7]

Crucially, Italy made seven ITAF bases available to NATO for Operation Unified Protector and—less visibly, but perhaps more importantly—provided the comprehensive connecting tissue of infrastructure, logistics, consumables, and services that Italy was asked to provide as host nation. The number of aircraft supported from Italian bases averaged about 200, with peaks around 250. Trapani air base alone witnessed a ten-fold increase in flying activities that eventually amounted to 14 percent of all coalition sorties. ITAF Logistics Command faced, in terms of both quantity and expenditure, an immediate 2,000 percent increase in fuel consumption. According to Arpino, the military campaign cost Italy some €150 million, to which increased costs and lower revenue should be added. National air traffic service provider ENAV witnessed a 22-percent drop in air traffic to Africa, translating into 8 percent less (€42 million) turnover on an annual basis.[8]

Mere numbers, however, do not provide a complete picture of the Italian involvement. A qualitative evaluation, including its enabling role and capacity multiplication, is necessary. There is little doubt, however, that the lack of Italian bases would have made the participation of many coalition members virtually impossible in practical terms, particularly considering the severe shortage in coalition air-to-air refueling assets. A third dimension, even harder to measure but largely unperceived outside the country, concerns the additional security risks (and associated burdens) that Italy took

---

[4]   Stefano Cosci, "Missione conclusa," *Rivista Aeronautica*, June 2011, pp. 7–9; for an English language summary, see Aeronautica Militare, *The Italian Air Force in Operations Odyssey Dawn and Unified Protector,* undated.

[5]   Italian Navy Press Release 20, November 2, 2011, hereafter quoted as PR20; Italian Navy press office, email to author, July 12, 2012, hereafter quoted as ITN email. The latter is more detailed than PR20, because it addresses specific questions arising from the combined reading of PR20 and other sources.

[6]   Gen. Mario Arpino, "L'Italia nelle operazioni in Libia," *AffarInternazionali*, December 6, 2011. Now a member of the executive board of Istituto Affari Internazionali (IAI), Arpino is the former Chief of the Defense Staff (1999–2001) and Air Staff (1995–1999).

[7]   Stato Maggiore Aeronautica—3° Reparto—Sala Situazioni (ITAF Staff, 3rd Department, Situation Room; hereafter quoted as "SMA3 summary"), attachment D. Except where noted, all ITAF statistics are from this SMA3 summary.

[8]   Isabella Stifani, "Campagna d'Africa," *Volare*, May 2012, p. 43.

on by turning its territory into a springboard against Libya, including the possibility of terrorists infiltrating among the illegal immigrants that poured into Italy.

This chapter comprises four sections, beginning with the political scenario, continuing with the ITAF situation and doctrine, an operational summary, and a brief discussion with conclusions. To provide an understanding of the specific Italian perspective, it describes Italian events through Italian sources, often overlooked due to limited circulation, language barriers, or simply lack of familiarity.[9] The narrative is based on unclassified military material and press reports, supplemented by extensive (albeit not-for-attribution) personal interviews and private conversations with decisionmakers and direct participants. Many of these took place during the crisis, helping to shape the retrospective understanding of issues and attitudes.

The Political Scenario

Despite Qaddafi's posturing, Italy and Libya traditionally have had a close relationship based on historical ties, regional outlook, and commercial interests. Whatever their party affiliation, Italian prime ministers consistently treated Libya with respect and aimed to mediate with other Western countries to alleviate its long isolation. In 2010, as in previous years, Italy and Libya were each other's leading trading partners, with Italy buying 31.6 percent of the commodities exported by Libya and Libya receiving 16.3 percent of its imports from Italy.

Building upon treaties signed in 2000 and 2007 to cooperate to curb illegal immigration,[10] which is always a hot domestic issue in Italy (see Table 8.1), the two countries in August 2008 signed a comprehensive Treaty of Friendship, Partnership and Cooperation in Benghazi.[11] Its 23 articles covered topics ranging from resolving past controversies to annual consultations between the heads of government and foreign ministers, and from scholarships to cultural cooperation. From an international perspective, the most controversial clauses arguably were Articles 3, 4, and 5, by which the signatories "in agreement with international law" undertook "not to threaten or

---

[9] Confirming the strong interest in the political consequences of the conflict for its national interests, in Italy the Libyan crisis quickly resulted in a record number of books on Libya and Qaddafi, albeit with limited attention to actual military operations. These include Farid Adly, *La rivoluzione libica,* Milan: Il Saggiatore, 2012; Alessandro Aruffo, *Qaddafi. Storia di una dittatura rivoluzionaria,* Urbino: Catelvecchi, 2011; Antonello Biagini, ed., *C'era una volta la Libia: 1911–2011. Storia e cronaca,* Torino: Miraggi, 2011; Federico Cresti and Massimiliano Cricco, *Qaddafi. I volti del potere,* Rome:, Carocci, 2011; Federico Cresti and Massimiliano Cricco, *Storia della Libia contemporanea: dal dominio ottomano alla morte di Qaddafi,* Rome: Carocci, 2012; Vincenzo Ruggero Manca, *Italia-Libia stranamore,* Rome: Koiné, 2011; Karim Mezran and Arturo Varvelli, *Libia. Fine o rinascita di una rivoluzione?* Rome: Donzelli, 2012; Paolo Sensini, *Libia 2011,* Milan: Jaca Book, 2011.

[10] "Immigrazione, accordo Italia-Libia," *Corriere della Sera.it,* December 29, 2007.

[11] This replaced and superseded the Joint Declaration of July 4, 1998 and the Verbal Process of Operating Conclusions of October 28, 2002.

Table 8.1
Illegal Immigration to Italy from Libya, 2008–2011

Year	Immigrants	Landings	Immigrants per Landing
2008	31,838	428	74
2009	6,290	55	114
2010	346	9	38
2011	28,431	101	282

SOURCE: Ministero degli Interni, Direzione Generale dell'Immigrazione e della Polizia delle Frontiere, email, July 11, 2012.

use force," "not to use [their] territories, nor allow them to be used, in hostile acts of whatever kind" against each other, and to seek the peaceful resolution of controversies. Some saw the combined effect of the three articles as a nonaggression pact limiting obligations that Italy already held with NATO; in fact, it merely reiterated a principle established in the 1998–2002 agreements. Either party could be reasonably expected to invoke "international law" (presumably to include formal U.N. and EU decisions) to be released from its obligations.[12]

This treaty drove an expansion in business relationships, accelerating from the traditional oil and gas business to aerospace, defense and security contracts, and banking.[13] The cumulative effect of Libyan-Italian engagement helps explain why, on the eve of the so-called Arab Spring, the annual National Security report issued on February 28, 2011 mentioned Libya only once, in a positive assessment of the reduction of the flow of illegal immigrants.[14] Italian think tanks and nongovernmental reports similarly ignored or failed to detect the mounting storm.[15] It also is possible that business links and in-country presence endowed the Italians with a nuanced and nonideological understanding of the general state of affairs in the country. Prime Minister Silvio Berlusconi made no secret of his closeness to Qaddafi. For Belusconi, personal misgivings, fears for the weakness of his government, and an instinctive understanding of the shallow support that the

---

[12] For a balanced commentary see Natalino Ronzitti, *Il trattato Italia-Libia di Amicizia, partenariato e cooperazione*, Senato della Repubblica, Servizio Studi, series Contributi di Istituti di ricerca specializzati, n. 108, January 2009. The treaty is now in limbo; see Natalino Ronzitti, "Il futuro dei trattati tra Italia e Libia," *AffarInternazionali*, February 2, 2012.

[13] The main deals included the LIATEC joint venture to recommission Libyan aircraft fleets (January 2006), the purchase of an ATR42 Surveyor maritime patrol aircraft (January 2008) and of a Selex Sistemi Integrati border surveillance and protection system (October 2009), the refurbishment of 800 miles of Libyan railways by Ansaldo STS (July 2009), and the LIATEC helicopter assembly line at Abou Aisha (April 2010).

[14] Presidenza del Consiglio dei Ministri/Sistema di informazione per la sicurezza della Repubblica, *Relazione sulla politica dell'informazione per la sicurezza 2010*, p. 53.

[15] The Stato Maggiore Difesa (SMD)–sponsored *Panorama su scenari internazionali e di crisi* yearbook ignored Libya in 2010 and concentrated on the Islamist threat in 2011 (pp. 31–32); in his introduction to the Nomisma 2010–2011 *Nomos & Khaos* report, Gen. c.a. Giuseppe Cucchi, former military advisor to prime ministers Romano Prodi and Massimo D'Alema, candidly admitted that the events "took everyone by surprise" (p. 28).

insurgents enjoyed were summed up by his often-misunderstood February 19 remark about "not disturbing" Qaddafi with phone calls at that difficult juncture.

ITAF Situation and Doctrine

As in many other Western countries, by 2011 the Italian defense establishment was showing the cumulative effects of repeated budget cuts.[16] ITAF reductions between 2004 and 2009 translated into cutting 28 percent of units, 49 percent of staff, and 57 percent of aircraft, though efficiency measures allowed it in 2008 to fly 66 percent of its 1995 activity with 45 percent of the budget.[17] The €275 million allocated for fuel in 2009 was planned to drop to €100 million in 2010 and only €14 million in 2011.

Despite this, the extensive technological and doctrinal overhaul of the Italian Air Force that was launched based on the lessons of the first Gulf War in 1991 had transformed the service, and some 20 years of almost continuous operations had allowed the ITAF to hone its skills and acquire new capabilities. Whereas in 1991 only a small fraction of the force had taken part in major training exercises abroad, by 2011 a sizable proportion had real operational experience, both from home bases (particularly in the extended late-1990s Balkans operations cycle) and in expeditionary operations (including Iraq and Afghanistan, the latter still fully active during the Libyan crisis).

In 2005, the ITAF carried out a comprehensive review of its organization and assets to identify priorities. The pragmatic approach included giving up Boeing MMA and C-17 acquisitions, still in the planning phase, to defend participation in JSF as its next-generation attack aircraft. It also reexamined Italian airfields, many of which still belonged to the Ministry of Defense despite having been turned over to civilian use decades ago. Those to be retained included two main operating bases (MOBs) for air defense (at Grosseto and Gioia del Colle, reducing Trapani to Deployment Operating Base (DOB) status), three for tactical units (Ghedi, Istrana, Amendola), four for support (Pisa, Pratica di Mare, Cervia, and Grazzanise), and three for training (Lecce, Latina, and Frosinone).[18]

The period also witnessed two major changes in personnel, with the introduction of voluntary military service for women (1999) and the suspension of compulsory male service (in effect from January 1, 2005). Although air forces by nature are highly

---

[16] The ITAF budget for operating costs—excluding personnel and investment expenditure—declined from just over 1 billion Euros in 2005 to 499 million in 2006. To make things worse, cuts were often made midyear, negating the benefits of careful planning. See "A.M.: L'organismo è Allo Stremo. Ora è Urgente Ripristinare le Funzioni Vitali," *Dedalonenews*, April 28, 2006.

[17] "I Tagli al Bilancio Metteranno l'Aeronautica a Terra nel 2010? Gli Scenari Preoccupanti Emersi dal Seminario CESMA," *Dedalonews.it*, March 29, 2009.

[18] The list and division by category (MOB, DOB, and transfer to civil aviation) were sanctioned by ministerial decree on April 20, 2006; see *La Trasformazione*, p. 30.

technical organizations with limited use for draftees, these changes went hand in hand with severe personnel cuts that halved staffed levels. Thus the 79,000-man, draftee, peacetime organization of 1990 shrank to the 44,000-person, professional, operational ITAF of 2011.

Reorganization proceeded in parallel with a revival of doctrinal studies that rapidly moved away from late Cold War complacency.[19] This included an effort to define a national airpower doctrine, both to support the development of a relevant force and to imbue personnel with a coherent view of their service. The initial document was published in late 1997 under Gen. s.a. (Lieutenant General) Mario Arpino, followed by another in 2007 under Gen. s.a. Vincenzo Camporini.[20] In 2006 the ITAF launched a new publication, the *Quaderni della Rivista Aeronautica,* specifically aimed at reviving airpower debate. The rethinking culminated in a formal doctrine statement, *Potere Aereo-Spaziale—Fondamenti,* roughly equivalent to the U.S. Air Force Doctrine Document 1 (AFDD-1) and coincidentally approved for publication on June 14, 2011, in the midst of the Libyan crisis. In the foreword, General Bernardis declared, "To leave the debate on Aerospace Power to the academic domain, to relegate it inside General Staff offices or to isolate them in some lecture hall, is the mistake we have made for years."[21] From 2009 there followed regular closed-door airpower seminars for middle-level officers, many of which could bring to bear significant levels of operational experience in joint and out-of-area environments.

Yet despite this clear vision and the significant overall progress, when the Libyan crisis broke out, many crucial programs were in a state of flux that resulted in a number of short-term challenges. Combat Forces Command (CFC), under Gen. d.a. (Major General) Enzo Vecciarelli (whom Gen. b.a. [Brigadier General] Roberto Nordio later replaced), saw its Eurofighter Typhoon force rapidly maturing, with two two-squadron wings operational and a growing confidence in its deployability. On the other hand, the very successful "Peace Caesar" program, under which Italy leased F-16As from the United States for air defense pending the Typhoons' delayed arrival, already had entered the phase-out mode, with activity scaled back in accordance with the planned disbanding of 18th Squadron in late 2011.[22] At the outbreak of the crisis, this dictated an immediate review of remaining fleet hours, maintenance plans, and foreseeable commitments, which in turn led to purchasing additional F-16 flying hours from the

---

[19] For somewhat exaggerated examples of 1970s mentality, see the memoirs of Bruno Servadei, a former A3/2 staff officer. *Ali di travertino. Un cacciabombardiere allo Stato Maggiore,* SBC Edizioni, Ravenna, 2012, *passim.*

[20] *La dottrina dell'Aeronautica Militare,* supplement to *Rivista Aeronautica,* No. 1, 1998; *La trasformazione,* supplement to *Rivista Aeronautica* (2007).

[21] Italian Air Force, *Potere Aereo-Spaziale—Fondamenti* (SMA 9), June 2011 edition.

[22] The F-16 force was stood down on May 23, 2012. The original FMS contract, later extended, provided for 45,000 hours between 2003 and 2010, with a minimum of 48 daily sorties.

United States.[23] The continuously upgraded Tornado fleet, including the unique electronic combat reconnaissance (ECR) defense suppression variant and the IDS (interdictor strike) variant that recently had acquired Storm Shadow standoff missile capability, formed the backbone of the attack forces. It was supplemented by single-engine, single-seat AMXs at the latest Aggiornamento Capacità Operative e Logistiche standard (Updated Operational and Logistic Capabilities, or ACOL).

Mobility and Support Forces Command (CFMS), under Gen. b.a. Vincenzo Parma, showed an equally mixed situation. The transport element sported two Lockheed Martin C-130J squadrons and an Alenia C-27J squadron, both recent platforms. After retiring its last Boeing 707 Tanker/Transport, the ITAF had just received the first of its four KC-767A tankers on January 27, 2011, some five years behind schedule.[24] Despite having formidable capabilities (including both boom and hose-and-drogue), when the crisis broke out, the single KC-767A available had not achieved its initial operational capability. On the other hand, the search-and-rescue (SAR) and combat-search-and-rescue (CSAR) helicopter component was severely aged in terms of both 1960s vintage platforms and airframe life. The AB.212 (equivalent to the UH-1N) was taxed by intensive operations in Afghanistan, while the HH-3F had suffered a string of accidents that cast doubts on its reliability. Contracts for new AW139 and EH101 helicopters had been signed, but replacement lay a few years ahead. The Bréguet BR1150 Atlantic maritime patrol aircraft fleet faced a similar, albeit less dramatic, aging aircraft problem.

On January 18, 2011, Italian Army General Vincenzo Camporini, who had been Capo di Stato Maggiore della Difesa (Chief of the Defense Staff, CSMD) for almost three years, was succeeded by General Biagio Abrate, the former Secretary General of Defense.[25] General Abrate thus became the highest Italian operational military authority, in charge of, among other things, transferring authority over Italian forces to NATO. The Italian national chain of command ran from CSMD to the Comando Operativo di Vertice Interforze (Joint Operational High Command, [COI]), initially under Italian Army Gen. c.a. (Lieutenant General) Giuseppe Valotto and then Gen. c.a. Giorgio Cornacchione. By coincidence, COI had an air force officer as Chief of Staff, Gen. d.a. Roberto Corsini, who left in early September 2011 to take office as Deputy Chief at ITAF Staff.

General Abrate reported to Minister of Defense Ignazio La Russa, a Sicilian lawyer whose political career had started with the neo-Fascist MSI party and contin-

---

[23] S. Durante, L. Ricci, and E. Salvati, ". . . l'impegno continua . . . ," *Rivista Aeronautica,* May 2011, p. 14.

[24] Italy selected the KC-767 in July 2001 and signed the contract in December 2002. Boeing unveiled the prototype on February 24, 2005. Administrative acceptance of the first KC-767A took place in Wichita on December 29, 2010, but the aircraft only arrived in Italy on January 27. The second aircraft was accepted on March 10 and arrived about three months later.

[25] "Abrate subentra a Camporini al vertice della Difesa. In Afghanistan un soldato viene ucciso e uno ferito," *Dedalonews.it,* January 18, 2011.

ued with its various transformations through its merger into the Partito della Libertà (Freedom Party). The other key cabinet figure in the handling of the war was Foreign Minister Franco Frattini, a former government lawyer and Berlusconi stalwart; interestingly, Frattini selected Camporini as national security advisor, despite knowing that the highly respected officer had a strained relationship with La Russa.

Operational Summary

The 2011 Libyan campaign can be divided into three main periods, starting with the humanitarian crisis that the spreading Arab Spring and associated political developments precipitated, followed by a brief deployment phase, and culminating in an extended phase of operations.[26] For Italy, the latter was further subdivided into an initial six-week period, during which no bombing was authorized, and the remaining 24 weeks, during which 704 munitions were expended in 483 sorties.

The Road to War

By late January, the situation in Egypt had degraded to the point at which it no longer was considered safe to land at Cairo West airport. On January 29, two ITAF Eurofighter Typhoons about to leave for the Aero India show in Bangalore were forced to re-route at short notice, together with their associated supporting C-130Js, via Souda Bay (Crete) and Al-Azraq (Jordan) before continuing to Doha and Jamnagar, in northern India.[27] The next day, a C-130J was tasked with evacuating civilians from Egypt.

By February 16, revolts had broken out in Benghazi, with a bloody repression following the next day. With the situation in Libya fast degrading, and with the recent experience from Tunisia and Egypt in mind, Western nations within a few days began evacuating their citizens from Libya. By February 22, both Portuguese and Dutch C-130s deployed to Sigonella, in eastern Sicily, for this purpose.[28] In what now appears as an indication of the ambiguous international legal status of the crisis, the first Italian C-130Js were hastily dispatched without diplomatic clearance and the Libyans forced them to turn back.[29] On February 24, an ITAF C-130J without diplomatic clearance entered Libyan airspace to evacuate some 50 Italians from Sebha. After spending some

---

[26] The basic political chronology is provided by Germano Dottori, "La drole de guerre all'italiana," *Limes* special issue *La guerra di Libia,* pp. 17–24. For an open source military chronology of the first three weeks see "La non-guerra di Libia," *JP4 Mensile di aeronautica,* pp. 40–45. ITAF figures from SMA3; ITN figures from PR20.

[27] Lt. Col. Marco Bertoli, "Appunti di viaggio," *Rivista Aeronautica,* February 2011, pp. 26–29; M. Morelli, "Mille anime, un solo spirito," in Gregory Alegi and Alessandro Cornacchini, *Al Lupo! Al Lupo! Il 4° Stormo Caccia da Gorizia a Grosseto, 1931–2011,* Rome: Aviator Edizioni/Rivista Aeronautica, 2011.

[28] S. Durante, L. Ricci, and E. Salvati, "Nel 'cuore' della missione italiana," *Rivista Aeronautica,* March 2011, p. 21.

[29] Interview with Italian general, March 2012.

three hours on the ground surrounded by armed Libyan troops, the aircraft took off with more than 90 evacuees, well beyond its nominal capacity, due to the decision to embark 41 British, French, Germans, Austrians, and Slovenians, who had pointed out to the Italian crew the lack of alternative means of rescue.[30] Evacuation flights continued until March 18.

With tension mounting, La Russa announced the mobilization of a number of ships, including destroyer *Mimbelli* (D461), amphibious transport docks (LPDs) *San Giorgio* and *San Marco* (L9892 and L9893), and supply ship *Vesuvio* (A5329).[31] On February 24, La Russa added to the list "the *Cavour* aircraft carrier," the Navy's newest and largest ship, which did not participate in the operation.[32] Other ships would be added in March, in part as replacements for the first group; the most crucial addition was the air-defense destroyer *Andrea Doria* (D553). On March 5, *Mimbelli* and patrol vessel *Libra* (P402) moored in Benghazi, ostensibly to deliver supplies, but Libya classified the mission an unauthorized armed violation of its borders.

On February 26, the U.N. Security Council passed Resolution 1970 (UNSCR 1970). La Russa immediately announced a legally ambiguous "suspension" of the friendship treaty, adding that Italian Guardia di Finanza (Treasury Police) personnel serving in Libya on anti-immigration duties had been withdrawn to the embassy compound.[33] The verbal banter persisted throughout the crisis, which Italian politicians continued to view from a short-term domestic perspective, ignoring reports indicating that French aircraft were making dry-run rehearsals for an attack.[34]

The rapidly evolving situation surprised everyone, with an emotional Berlusconi unable to react swiftly with either a quick about-face or a decisive mediation.[35] Despite its misgivings, the Italian government made seven air bases available in the event of a U.N.-sanctioned intervention, which it firmly believed (or gambled) to be unlikely. The bases included Birgi (near Trapani, Sicily), Gioia del Colle (near Bari, in Apulia), Sigonella (near Catania, in Sicily), Decimomannu (near Cagliari, Sardinia), Amendola (near Foggia, in Apulia), and Pantelleria (a small island between Sicily and Tunisia). Quite apart from the potential breach of Friendship Treaty obligations, this represented a significant political concession. Simply put, the "basing rights" mentioned by the First Sea Lord to defend the British government's 2010 decision to scrap its carrier

---

[30] Gen. b.a. Stefano Fort email to author.

[31] PR20.

[32] ANSA newswire, February 24, quoted in Dottori, "La drole de guerre." The Navy did not include *Cavour* in PR20; in fact, it was not declared operational until early 2012.

[33] Carlo Marroni, "Italia-Libia, trattato sospeso, *Il Sole 24 Ore,* February 27, 2011.

[34] Interview with Italian general, February 14, 2012.

[35] Karim Mezran, "Piccolo glossarietto delle bufale belliche," in *La guerra di Libia,* special issue of *Limes,* April 2011, pp. 70–71.

and decommission its Harrier force do not apply to Italian bases.[36] Although specific treaties have allowed Aviano and Sigonella to host U.S. Air Force (since 1954)[37] and U.S. Navy (since 1959) units, they remain under full Italian sovereignty and cannot be used for non-NATO purposes without Italian consent.[38]

When France proposed the use of airpower in Libya on March 10, La Russa replied that Italy would follow NATO, which Italy was beginning to see as an important tool to buy time and moderation.[39] While details of Italian diplomatic efforts to influence decisionmaking by the U.N. Security Council (UNSC) are unavailable, Berlusconi probably thought that Russia, with whose prime minister he had forged close personal links, would veto the resolution. It was also probably hoped that Germany, a temporary member of the UNSC, would vote against the armed intervention that it publicly opposed. Some believe Berlusconi also hoped that, on account of his excellent relations with Qaddafi, the international community eventually would ask him to broker the dictator's exit.[40] None of these events materialized, leaving his government facing the very real possibility of a direct military intervention, difficult for any Italian administration to deal with. The difficulty is partly linked to the explicit ban on "war as a tool to infringe the freedom of other peoples and means to resolve international controversies" enshrined in the Italian Constitution, only partly tempered by its provision for "limitations of sovereignty required by a framework to ensure peace and justice among nations."[41] To further add to Italian discomfort, in the background loomed the colonial past for which Italy had apologized to Libya in 2009.[42]

On March 17, the Security Council passed Resolution 1973 (UNSCR 1973), the document that became the immediate legal framework for the attack on Libya. Although the expansive interpretation of the freshly minted no-fly zone clashed with less aggressive implementations in other crises, including Operation Deny Flight in 1993–1995,[43] UNSCR 1973 compelled Italy to make good on its promise to provide

---

[36] The answer is quoted in United Kingdom House of Commons, Defence Committee, "UK Contribution to the Operation," prepared February 8, 2012.

[37] The agreement was ratified on October 20, 1954, and the first military arrived shortly thereafter; a recent account of local attitudes to the presence is provided by Ermanno Furlanis, "Aviano, Oh-Ahio," *Limes*, No. 4, 1999, pp. 107–124.

[38] Sigonella and Aviano have each had high profile jurisdiction incidents, respectively in 1985 (during the *Achille Lauro* hijacking crisis) and 1998 (the Cermis cable car accident).

[39] Ignazio La Russa, March 11, 2011, quoted in *Limes*, No. 3, 2011, p. 194.

[40] Author's interview with leading opposition MP.

[41] Constitution of the Italian Republic, Article 11. The lack of congressional approval posed a significant challenge to USAF operations as well—see Chapter Four in this volume.

[42] Franco Frattini, March 3, 2011, quoted in *Limes*, March 2011, p. 194.

[43] The no-fly zone over Bosnia was first established on October 9, 1992 by UNSCR 781, and was expanded on March 31, 1993 by UNSCR 816 to cover all flights. From April 12, 1993 to December 20, 1995 over 100,000

bases and forced the government to decide how to participate in operations. President Giorgio Napolitano was widely reported to have weighed in heavily in the final decision, overcoming doubts that cut across party lines and Berlusconi's personal misgivings. A top-level government meeting certainly was held at 10.45 a.m. on March 17, possibly followed by an informal update with Napolitano and cabinet ministers in the evening at a special performance of *Nabucco* to celebrate the centennial of Italian unification.[44] The first Tornados redeployed to Trapani in the early morning of March 18;[45] the antisubmarine support carrier *Giuseppe Garibaldi* (C551) sailed from Taranto the same day.[46]

At 2:15 p.m. on the 17th, the Cabinet was urgently convened to discuss UNSCR 1973 and ensure "an active role in the protection of civilians and areas threatened with attacks, including providing the use of existing military bases on [Italian] domestic territory."[47] Just over an hour later, ministers Frattini and La Russa appeared before a joint session of the Senate and House Foreign Affairs and Defense committees to explain the government's position, the undertakings (including both bases and SEAD aircraft), and the exclusions (particularly mentioning land forces) and to seek parliamentary approval before proceeding.[48] Even then, the government did not hide its concerns and its hope that a negotiated solution might still be reached. Although Parliament approved, these occasions brought to light serious splits in both the majority and opposition. In this case, predictable Catholic pacifism and left-wing antimilitarism joined with Lega Nord (Northern League) isolationism and Berlusconi reluctance, resulting in lukewarm political support.[49] On April 30, the Lega Nord went as far as to ask for a time limit on Italian participation and a guarantee against funding the campaign with additional taxes.[50] This dictated the use of already limited ordinary funds.[51]

---

missions were flown. Offensive counterair sorties were flown only in August–September 1995 under operation Deliberate Force.

[44] Dottori dates the event to the 16th (p. 18). The concert, however, was actually held on the evening of the 17th. See Rosario Amato, "Muti dirige Nabucco per i 150 anni dell'Unità Leo Nucci: 'Un inno alla Patria e alla libertà,'" *La Repubblica* online, March 10, 2011.

[45] Gen. s.a. Giuseppe Bernardis, interview with Gregory Alegi, July 26, 2011 (hereafter "Bernardis interview"). Quotes from the published version in *La grande storia dell'Aeronautica Militare,* Milan: Fabbri, 2012, p. 698.

[46] Andrea Tani, "La crisi libica," in *Rivista Marittima,* June 2011, p. 31.

[47] Governo italiano, Presidenza del Consiglio dei Ministri, Consiglio dei Ministri n. 131 (press release), March 18, 2011.

[48] Senato della Repubblica, Giunte e Commissioni, Resoconto Stenografico n. 5.

[49] For the Lega position see Marco Reguzzoni, "Speriamo finisca presto: la pace non è una parola priva di valore" and Maria Elena Ribezzo, "Libia. Maggioranza compatta a Montecitorio," in *La Padania*, March 25, 2011, pp. 8–9.

[50] *La Padania*, April 30, 2011.

[51] Gen. s.a. Giuseppe Marani, interview with Lt. Col. Alessandro Cornacchini, *Rivista Aeronautica*, No. 3, 2011, p. 59.

Despite this and the moral suasion of President Napolitano, the possibility of coercive action remained singularly unattractive for most political forces. An immediate consequence of these difficulties was the centralization of all communication and media activities under the direct control of the Minister of Defense, which, in turn, resulted in significant limitations in releasing to the general public a transparent narrative of the ITAF role in Odyssey Dawn and Unified Protector activities.[52] As in all previous engagements from the Gulf War onward, the Italian public would be kept in the dark about the activities of its armed forces, while the latter were left to deal with the extensive needs of a large and technologically sophisticated multinational coalition. ITAF Chief of Staff Bernardis summed up the situation tersely with, "We have been given a role which is not easy to play."[53] This referred, presumably, to having to stay a course between the Scylla of domestic politics and the Charybdis of international commitments.

On March 19, the Paris summit ended with the unilateral announcement that French aircraft had gone into action over Benghazi. Although in the past days the military had corroborated French press reports about imminent action in Libya, the Italian government was taken by surprise as much as everyone else.[54] The unilateral French action is said to have made American and British leadership "privately furious."[55] While the recently retired Camporini pointed out on national TV that the target was more than two hours away from the nearest French base, Italian political analysts widely perceived it to be a French bid for Mediterranean hegemony and to replace the influence France was poised to lose with regimes in the Maghreb as a result of the Arab Spring.[56] More pointedly, the French were seen to aim overtly at replacing Italy as partner of choice and main broker for Libya's reentry into the international community.[57] This attitude, which to some extent predated the 2011 crisis, was in evidence in Italy throughout the campaign and seen by many to explain the creation of an otherwise incongruous non-NATO chain of command based on NATO assets in a NATO operation. In the Italian military, many felt a difference from past campaigns, but

---

[52] Particularly after the Scolari incident described below, the ITAF severely restricted Italian reporters' access. Those who were invited by other coalition countries to fly on their tankers or interview personnel on Italian bases were kept separate from Italian staff.

[53] Bernardis to ITAF personnel, November 1, 2011.

[54] For one such report, see "Libye: les alliés mettent au point leur dispositif militaire," *Le Figaro*, March 18, 2011. Andrea Tani, "La crisi libica," *Rivista Marittima*, June 2011 p. 15, claims that armed Rafales entered Italian airspace without warning.

[55] Saqeb Mueen and Grant Turnbull, eds., *Accidental Heroes: Britain, France, and the Libya Operation*, an Interim RUSI Campaign Report, London: Royal United Services Institute, September 2011, p. 4.

[56] See *La guerra di Libia*; Karim Mezran, "Come l'Italia ha perso la Libia," *Limes*, No. 2, 2011; K. Mezran, "Ora costringiamo Bengasi a rispettare i tripolitani," *Limes*, No. 3, 2011, July 2011; M. Arpino, "L'Italia nelle operazioni in Libia."

[57] For an immediate and explicit interpretation, see Franco Bechis, "Ma quale Gheddafi Sarko ha dichiarato Guerra all'Italia," March 22, 2011 blog post.

this only became public in late October 2011 when former ITAF Chief of Staff Gen. s.a. Leonardo Tricarico (ret.) publicly returned the Légion d'Honneur that French President Jacques Chirac awarded him in recognition of the ITAF's support during the 78-day Kosovo air campaign.[58] The "collaborative spirit" which had characterized the Kosovo campaign "in the name of harmony and dialogue—sometimes heated but always loyal—among participating countries," he wrote in the letter delivered to the French ambassador and the newswires, had been overtaken by the "unruly behavior" and "cynical" and "ugly" motives displayed by his successor Nicolas Sarkozy. When *Corriere della Sera* published a preview of Bernard-Henri Lévy's "war diary," few were surprised to read that on June 30, Sarkozy had boasted in private that "when this war is won the world will see that it was won by us and the Libyans, period."[59]

The ITAF quickly established its Task Group Air (TGA) "Birgi" as the Italian National Component—Air, under Col. Mauro Gabetta and leveraging his local 37th Fighter Wing, augmented with aircraft detached from other units and staff from CFC. NATO and non-NATO members of the "coalition of the willing" began to flow in. From the beginning, Trapani hosted the main Canadian contingent (Task Force Libeccio) and a British VC10 tanker detachment, in addition to its habitual NATO Airborne Early Warning (NAEW) E-3A AWACS component.[60] Beginning on March 18, further international contingents poured into Sigonella, which eventually would include the Danish, Canadian (CP-140 Auroras, leveraging commonality with U.S. Navy P-3 Orions), French (Rafale fighters, Atlantique 2 military patrol aircraft, and the Harfang UAV), Swedish (JAS 39 Gripen, from April 2), Turkish (F-16 fighters and a KC-135 tanker) and UAE (F-16 and Mirage 2000, both relocated from their initial deployment to Decimomannu) air forces.[61] (See Figure 2.4 and Appendix B.)

The RAF deployed its 906th Expeditionary Air Wing to Gioia del Colle (near Bari), in part to leverage the Eurofighter logistics provided by the similarly equipped ITAF 36th Wing. The Spanish arrived at Decimomannu on March 19, followed by the United Arab Emirates contingent on March 27; the latter eventually moved to Sigonella. Training activities on the air range continued throughout the cycle, as did non-OUP national airspace defense patrols. A Jordanian F-16 unit deployed to Aviano, while the U.S. increased its presence at both bases. Pantelleria provided general support to coalition air traffic, including potential unscheduled landings.

---

[58] For a selection of media reports, see bibliography.

[59] Bernard-Henri Lévy, "Quando Sarkozy mi disse 'Usa assenti, Italia senza testa,'" *Corriere della Sera,* November 9, 2011, pp. 42–43.

[60] Riccardo Niccoli, interview with Gen. b.a. Roberto Nordio, CFC commander from July 2011, in *Coccarde Tricolori 2012*, pp. 42–47, hereafter quoted as "Nordio interview."

[61] All dates from Durante, Ricci, and Salvati, "Nel 'cuore' della missione italiana," pp. 20–21. The Canadian task force was very appropriately named: "Libeccio" is the Italian name for a hot and humid southwesterly wind originating from Libya.

Compared to the protracted Balkan operational cycles of the late 1990s, the ITAF approached the upcoming operation in a broader and more comprehensive fashion.[62] In addition to the customary reinforcing of air defenses, which involved relocating to Trapani the Spada point-defense missile system from 2nd Wing at Rivolto (near Udine, in the northeast), the ITAF deployed extensive force protection assets drawn from 9th Wing (from Grazzanise, near Naples) and 16th Wing (from Martina Franca, near Bari). Drawing on the experiences in Iraq and Afghanistan, the ITAF used protection measures that included long-range thermal cameras, GPS locators on patrol vehicles, and various emission-control procedures.

With the creation of TGA Birgi and the arrival of the foreign contingents, Trapani and Sigonella rapidly became saturated. Airline service at Trapani was suspended on March 18, but local politicians exerted pressures that led to a compromise allowing 18 (from March 29) and then 20 daily flights (from April 8) in and out of Trapani.[63] Coexistence with airline traffic also was a challenge at Sigonella, mainly because the airfield hosted American and French unmanned systems whose operations needed harmonizing with nearby Fontanarossa, one of Italy's busiest commercial airports. Although Italy had implemented rules for unmanned aircraft systems (UAS) operations in controlled airspace years before, in practical terms these were put to severe tests. Commercial traffic proximity, different approach speeds (from under 100 knots for UAS to more than 200 knots for fighters) and sheer volume of activity (192 UAS movements in August alone) constituted a severe test, albeit one passed with flying colors upon switching as many as possible to the 2200/0700Z time frame.

CFMS immediately decided to outfit for the AAR role as many C-130Js as possible, but to wait as long as possible to fit the central tank to avoid compromising short-term transport capabilities.[64] It also reinforced the 46th Brigade's maintenance resources, increased the Piaggio P.180 liaison fleet readiness to shuttle crews and possible casualties, planned logistics areas at Sigonella and studied how to put the new KC-767A in action as soon as possible. By February 22, Trapani was providing a SAR helicopter on 30-minute readiness around the clock, later increasing to two.

Logistics Command (COMLOG) stepped up maintenance of air defense infrastructure, advancing or postponing radar maintenance as needed to limit the risk of malfunctions or unscheduled downtime which might have created gaps in coverage and exposed Italian territory to attacks.[65] This was another example of the unique burden shouldered by the ITAF specifically, and Italy in general, as a result of the attack on

---

[62] Durante, Ricci, and Salvati, "Nel 'cuore' della missione italiana," p. 19.

[63] Gen. b.a. Giacomo De Ponti, "Il coordinamento civile-militare nella gestione dello spazio aereo," *Rivista Aeronautica*, March 2011, pp. 40 ff.

[64] Gen. b.a. Vincenzo Parma, "Il ruolo del Comando Forze Mobilità e Supporto," *Rivista Aeronautica*, March 2011, pp. 37–38.

[65] Marani interview, p. 61.

AMI Tornado ECR at Trapani, Air Base, Sicily, carrying HARM anti-radiation missiles on its fuselage hardpoints for a SEAD mission.
Courtesy of NATO.

Libya. As former NATO Military Committee chairman Amm. (Adm.) Giampaolo Di Paola would reflect after becoming Minister of Defense, what to some is the "Middle" East is the "Near" East to others; from Rome, Tel Aviv is closer than Dublin and Kabul no farther than the North Cape.[66]

Odyssey Dawn

Within two hours of the first French raid on March 19, ITAF wing commanders were asked to double their contribution to operations.[67] The rules of engagement under which they were called to operate might perhaps be summarized as the ultimate effect-based operations. The Italian government stuck to the letter of UNSCR 1973, steering well clear of France's implicit goal of regime change. In keeping with the official NATO goals, this designed a "zero CIVCAS" framework that translated into the highest level of protection of civilians, property, and civilian infrastructure.[68] While this automatically excluded targets of indirect military benefit (such as aqueducts) or close to urban centers, from the very beginning Italian aircraft explicitly were allowed to open fire for self-defense or in defense of coalition assets.[69] National "red card holders,"

---

[66] Amm. Giampaolo Di Paola to all ranks, undated letter, March 27, 2012, p. 1. Author's archive.

[67] "Michele, those numbers we asked for . . . double them!": Gen. d.a. Enzo Vecciarelli, quoted by M. Morelli, "Mille anime, un solo spirito," p. 22.

[68] Nordio interview.

[69] Nordio interview. A similar situation existed for Italian ships, which unlike their French equivalents were not allowed to use their guns against shore targets. See A. Tani, "Valutazioni politico-militari della campagna libica," *Rivista Marittima*, October 2011, p. 31.

the popular designation of what were more properly known as senior National Liaison Officers, voiced additional limitations or caveats, as well as individual national interpretations of UNSCR 1973. A further constraint in mission planning was the range of the personnel recovery envelope, which limited penetration into Libyan territory.

Italian forces were placed under U.S. authority, with a line of command comprising JFCC on USS *Mount Whitney* (LCC20) and the AOC at Ramstein Air Base, Germany, both of which included Italian officers. But the U.S.-led nature of the operation meant that while the air tasking order could be shared with the Italians and other coalition partners, it could only be transmitted over U.S. networks and would thus never reach deployed non-U.S. units, including NATO assets.[70] The solution eventually was found in transferring the information to the NATO Secret Wide Area Network (WAN).

The first Italian air assets placed under U.S. authority for Odyssey Dawn were four F-16ADFs from the 18th Squadron at Trapani for air defense and four 155th Squadron Tornado ECRs, promptly relocated from Piacenza to Trapani. Configured for a defense suppression (SEAD) role, the latter provided the coalition with a unique capability that only the United States possessed otherwise, including canvassing known civilian emitters to avoid erroneous attacks.[71] Four Tornado ECRs flew the first Italian operational sorties on March 20, escorted by 18th Squadron F-16s and supported by two Tornado IDSs (6th Wing) performing "buddy" in-flight refueling.[72] The SEAD component aimed to protect other aircraft (particularly tankers and airborne radar) from possible surface-to-air threats. The Tornado ECRs used their emitter locator systems (ELS) to find emissions and identify sources (including "radar which potentially would not represent a direct threat [but] which might hide an indirect danger")[73] and—if necessary—hit them with AGM-88B HARMs. Meanwhile, Italian Navy AV-8B Harriers aboard the *Garibaldi* made their first flights of the campaign on March 21 in the DCA role.[74]

The nature of Italian involvement in the campaign quickly became an issue, with both domestic and international audiences perceiving the dropping of ordnance as the

---

[70] Stefano Cosci, "A Poggio Renatico, centro di comando e controllo di 'UP,'" in *Rivista Aeronautica*, March 2011, p. 47.

[71] Although the Luftwaffe at Lechfeld possessed similar capabilities with its Tornado-equipped JaboG 32, the rigid neutrality policy followed by Germany denied the coalition its use. (*Rivista Aeronautica*, No. 3, 2011, p. 12). RAF Tornado GR.4s equipped with the Air Launched Anti-Radiation Missile (ALARM) could also conduct SEAD, but their inability to localize electromagnetic emissions made ALARMs difficult to use in a "zero CIVCAS" environment.

[72] *Rivista Aeronautica*, No. 2, 2011, pp. 2–3. It should be noted that, although functionally linked to the U.S. operation, the Tornados used in the buddy tanker role remained at all times under Italian authority, as did other assets throughout the crisis (including KC-130J tankers, a C-130J transport, and a G.222VS SIGINT platform).

[73] Durante, Ricci, and Salvati, "Nel 'cuore' della missione italiana," p. 16.

[74] ITN email.

sole measure of whether a state was truly participating. The early missions soon generated controversy over the dropping of ordnance, particularly after the news media ambushed Tornado ECR navigator Maggiore (Maj.) Nicola Scolari at Trapani following a mission and he muttered something about a "positive outcome." The media translated this as indicating that missiles had been launched against Libyan air defenses, but actually it meant that strike forces had been successfully protected from potential threats. The domestic flap spilled into the international media circuit and was interpreted as evidence of halfhearted Italian support; in fact, the ITAF SEAD component was in high demand, flying 38 sorties during OOD and 170 during OUP.

The lack of NATO involvement in Odyssey Dawn denied the ITAF contingent access to the Alliance's NAEW AWACS force, which was doubly annoying given that Trapani-Birgi is an NAEW base. Each of the parallel U.S., British and French air operations used its own AWACS platforms, sharing only the minimum amount of information required. Without its own national airborne control assets, Italy relied on the radar of the air defense destroyer *Andrea Doria* (D553) to generate the Recognized Air and Surface Picture (RASP) applicable to the area of operation; ITAF pilots were attached to the ship to coordinate air activities and communicate directly with aircrews with the confidence made possible by Link-16 capability.[75] In addition to escorting fighter-bombers and protecting "High Value Airborne Assets" (such as tankers and E-3s) during the following days, the F-16s carried out low-level "show of presence" overflights of Libyan cities.[76] The Eurofighter Typhoon made its ITAF operational debut in the early hours of March 30.[77] Mission Titan 25 comprised two fully armed 4th Wing aircraft tasked with monitoring Umm'Aitiqah and Okba bin Nafa airfields; another pair of 4th Wing Eurofighters relieved them.

Agreement was reached on March 23 to transfer control of naval operations to NATO, which would exercise them from Naples through Amm. Sq. (Vice Admiral) Rinaldo Veri as Maritime Component Commander (MCC). Two days later, Italy placed under NATO command for naval embargo purposes the *Garibaldi* (including its AV-8B+ Harrier II jump jets, four of which were transferred under NATO authority and made their no-fly zone debut three days later),[78] frigate *Libeccio* (F572), patrol ship *Comandante Bettica* (P492), and supply ship *Etna* (A5326). C. Amm. (Cdre) Gualtiero Mattesi, already in charge of Standing NATO Maritime Group 1 (SNMG1), took command of the newly formed Task Group 455.01 (TG 455.01).[79] Ship-based helicop-

---

[75] Col. (OF.5) Loris Giusti, quoted in Stefano Cosci, "A Poggio Renatico," p. 47.

[76] Federico Anselmino and Giancarlo Gastaldi, *F-16A Air Defence Fighter*, Turin, Aviation Collectables, 2011, p. 53.

[77] Morelli, "Mille anime, un solo spirito," p. 26.

[78] ITN email.

[79] Tani, "La crisi libica," p. 17. The initial TG 455.01 command ship was Etna (A5326).

ters provided search and rescue (SAR), combat SAR, maritime patrol (MP), and ISR duties, as well as shuttle services with ground-based infrastructures.[80]

Although the naval element played a secondary role in the NATO campaign, placing it under an Italian admiral helped assuage fears of being marginalized and allowed the Italian government to trumpet the success of its diplomacy. According to media reports, "The French grudgingly accepted that command be passed to NATO and that the allied fleet be under Italian leadership."[81] To support this interpretation, analysts pointed out that French ships, including the aircraft carrier *Charles de Gaulle*, operated under the French-only Task Force 473 (TF 473).

Operation Unified Protector

Operation Unified Protector officially began on March 31.[82] The transfer of authority brought about a unified chain of command and helped clear up the initial overlap of disjointed national operations. The chain of command ran from the Supreme Allied Commander, Europe (SACEUR) to JFC in Naples, which had operational control and under which Combined Joint Task Force 445 was formed, headed by Canadian Lt.-Gen. Charles Bouchard. While the CJTF 445 MCC was in Naples, the corresponding Air Component Commander was located at Izmir, in Turkey, under USAF Lt. Gen. Ralph J. Jodice II. Lt. Gen. Jodice worked through CAOC 5 in Poggio Renatico, near Ferrara, under Gen. s.a. Mario Renzo Ottone. Air tasking orders were materially issued by CAOC 5, and eventually Lt. Gen. Jodice relocated to Poggio Renatico to simplify activity. Gen. s.a. Leandro De Vincenti was the senior Italian representative at JFC and Gen. s.a. Ottone at ACC.

The general NATO rules of engagement included dynamic targeting, to respond quickly to emerging or fleeting targets on the ground.[83] Despite this, dynamic targeting was still subjected to individual national caveats and required specific approval from national C2 command chains.[84] The targeting division, which Gen. s.a. De Vincenti specifically requested, was the only element of the CJTF command structure headed

---

[80] ITN email reports 253 MP/ISR flying hours out of a total of 1,830 hours for the campaign, slightly more than half of the 3,311 helicopter hours given in PR20, which did not specify by type or function.

[81] Gianandrea Gaiani, "Uno sguardo alle lezioni apprese (e non) nel conflitto libico," *Rivista Marittima*, October 2011, p. 18.

[82] Col. Roberto Di Marco, "'Odyssey Dawn' e 'Unified Protector': l'impiego del Potere Aerospaziale e delle capacità operative dell'Aeronautica Militare," in *Rivista Aeronautica*, March 2011, p. 23.

[83] Dynamic targeting prosecutes targets of opportunity that are identified too late or not selected for action in time to be included in deliberate targeting but, when detected or located, meet criteria specific to achieving objectives. When plans change and planned targets must be adjusted, dynamic targeting can also manage those changes. See Joint Publication (JP) 3–60, *Joint Targeting*, Washington, D.C.: Joint Chiefs of Staff, April 2007, p. viii.

[84] Di Marco, "'Odyssey Dawn' e 'Unified Protector'," p. 25.

by an Italian, first Gen. b.a. Claudio Gabellini and then Gen. b.a. Silvano Frigerio.[85] In support of the stated NATO goal of no civilian casualties, it normally worked on a 72-hour planning cycle, much to the chagrin of the French who complained privately about the British "needing to get advice from three law firms before dropping a bomb," while Sarkozy simply would ask his chief of staff "and if my chief of staff says I can go, I go."[86] Some high-ranking coalition staff made no secret of considering Italian targeting responsibilities hard to reconcile with abstaining from actual strikes, but in fact, political considerations do not appear to have influenced the Italian staff and its work.[87] Libyan television, for instance, was kept off the target list by the shared over-arching preoccupation with avoiding collateral damage and casualties, allowing Qaddafi to broadcast his messages and arguably bolstering resistance. Similar constraints militated against striking refineries, stocks, and much of the oil industry, which in turn fueled (literally) the Libyan armed forces.[88]

The first ITAF missions over Libya were carried out, again from Trapani, by 6th Wing Tornado IDS fighter-bombers, in conjunction with 50th Wing Tornado ECRs. While 50th Wing continued to fly in the specialized SEAD role, 6th Wing saw its range of missions evolve as the Italian role expanded. Its 156th Squadron, previously used as buddy tankers, were fitted with RecceLite pods and immediately began flying ISR sorties over Libya "where not everyone reaches, meaning deep inside where the threat of Colonel Qaddafi's Surface-to-Air Missiles (SAMs) is still present and active."[89] Italian Navy AV-8Bs made their Unified Protector debut on April 1, with two air defense and reconnaissance missions, each flown by a pair of aircraft.[90] Operating under the same restrictions as their air force colleagues and alternating with the Eurofighters, the naval aircraft orbited about 65 nautical miles north of Tripoli.[91]

On April 5, Gen. Tricarico, the former ITAF Chief of Staff, advocated the deployment of the Italian Predator force.[92] He was greatly ahead of events, for their use would

---

[85] Organizational chart in Gen. b.a. Silvano Frigerio, "Targeting Lessons from Libyan Air Operations and the Impact on Future Requirements," presentation at the International Fighter Conference, London, November 9, 2011 (hereafter IFC 2011), slide 8.

[86] B-H. Lévy, p. 43.

[87] Author's interviews.

[88] Author's interviews. Oil stocks were carefully monitored by the Swedish Flygvapnet contingent, whose measuring techniques were greatly appreciated.

[89] *156° Gruppo. Le Linci. 70 anni di storia*, Rome, Edizioni Rivista Aeronautica, 2011, p. 170.

[90] ITN email; SMD press release, April 1, 2011. All Harrier reconnaissance sorties were flown with Litening II pods which, when within range, relayed the raw imagery to the interpretation unit aboard *Garibaldi* for onward transmission to CAOC 5.

[91] ITN email.

[92] "Gen. Tricarico: in Libia centrale il potere aereo. Le polemiche su Trapani danneggiano le aspirazioni di altri aeroporti," *Dedalonews.it*, May 4, 2011. See also Gianandrea Gaiani, "Ma quanto mi costi," *Volare*, June 2011, pp. 8–13, and interview on p. 13.

be approved only in August. Three days later, two 46th Air Brigade C-130Js airlifted wounded Libyans from Benghazi to Italy.[93]

Meanwhile, a threat unique to Italy had materialized. As a direct consequence of the attack on Libya, the country had become the target of a massive inflow of illegal immigrants. It was fed in part by the collapse of Libyan government structures and to a much greater extent by a Qaddafi strategy to turn illegal immigrants into a tool of unconventional warfare against Italy, hoping this would drive a wedge in the PDL-Lega coalition supporting the Berlusconi government, diminishing its ability to support what was becoming an open-ended commitment. After five consecutive months without illegal immigration from Libya, in March 2011 the flow resumed at full strength and grew quickly into a humanitarian crisis (see Table 8.2). The total number of illegal immigrants landed in Italy from January to July 2011 eventually would be recorded as 51,881 (almost 12 times as many as in the entire previous year and 1.4 times higher than any other year in the 2005–2011 period);[94] by the end of the year, Libyan illegals would number 28,431 (82 times more than in 2010).[95] Every day, the makeshift fleet laden with ragged people, including children and pregnant women,

Table 8.2
Illegal Immigration to Italy from Libya in 2011

Month	Immigrants	Landings	Immigrants per Landing
January	0	0	0
February	0	0	0
March	1,467	6	245
April	5,759	21	274
May	9,396	29	324
June	4,573	18	254
July	2,055	8	257
August	5,006	16	313
September	62	1	62
October	0	0	0
November	44	1	44
December	69	1	69

SOURCE: Ministero degli Interni, Direzione Generale dell'Immigrazione e della Polizia delle Frontiere, email, July 11, 2012.

---

[93] R. Gentilli, *sub data*.

[94] Antonella Rampino, "La Libia: clandestini in arrivo," *La Stampa*, May 13, 2012, p. 15, and accompanying chart, which does not distinguish by country of origin.

[95] Immigration data provided by Ministero degli Interni, Direzione Generale dell'Immigrazione e della Polizia delle Frontiere, email, July 11, 2012 (hereafter DGIPF email).

dominated Italian TV news and strained the population of the 20.2-square-kilometer island of Lampedusa, as well as carrying an added risk of terrorist infiltration. The arrivals led the Lega Nord to invoke ending operations and withdrawing support from OUP, in the hope that Libya would reinstate the 2007 treaty provisions. Although Frontex, the European Union frontier agency, used Pantelleria as base for its monitoring fleet, the international community's refusal to develop a multilateral answer to the immigrant crisis boosted the effectiveness of the Libyan strategy.[96] Reflecting the acute domestic political concerns, on April 10, SMD changed the heading of its daily news releases to include the "Emergenza immigrazione" (Immigration Emergency). An agreement eventually was brokered with the new Tunisian government, providing much needed naval patrols that mitigated the collapse of the Italo-Libyan treaty. In addition to the national tasking of Atlantic MPAs from Sigonella, ITAF's own initiative combat jets monitored the flow on the return leg of raids, passing the results to the appropriate authorities.[97]

Operating as close as 60 nautical miles from the Libyan coast, from April 15 onward *Garibaldi* provided a combat SAR capability at three-hour readiness, based on two SH-3D helicopters in the personnel recovery role, an EH.101 as airborne mission coordinator, and two AV-8Bs to escort and protect them.[98] The package alternated every 12 hours with that provided by USS *Bataan* with its CH-53s, V-22s, and AV-8Bs.

At this time, the initial operational success in arresting the Qaddafi onslaught was beginning to translate into a stalemate or, at the very least, lack of obvious progress on the ground. The withdrawal of U.S. attack forces reduced the coalition's striking power, which the British aggravated by their determination to proceed with the planned June 1 disbanding of two RAF Tornado squadrons, including one actively participating in operations over Libya.[99] At the time of the April 14 Atlantic Council meeting in Berlin, NATO Secretary General Anders Fogh Rasmussen pleaded openly for additional combat aircraft to continue OUP air strikes.[100] With Germany resolutely opposed, the pressure increased on the Italian government to authorize air strikes against Libya. Berlusconi relented in late April, calling U.S. President Barack Obama to inform him that Italy would change its position.[101] On April 27, Frattini and La Russa informed Parliament that the government had decided to "broaden the options

---

[96] Durante, Ricci, and Salvati, "Nel 'cuore' della missione italiana," p. 21.

[97] Author's interviews.

[98] ITN email.

[99] For the UK reaction to the quixotic decision, see "Armed Forces Set Out Plans for First Redundancies," BBC News, March 1, 2011.

[100] Helen Pidd, "NATO commander of Libya mission pleads for specialised fighter jets," *Guardian*, April 14, 2011.

[101] The White House, Office of the Press Secretary, "Readout of the President's call with Prime Minister Berlusconi of Italy," press release, Washington, D.C., April 25, 2011.

for its contribution to Operation Unified Protector."[102] While the overall aircraft allotment remained unchanged, new roles were added. ITAF was given the opportunity to employ its Tornado IDS strike aircraft as bombers "using laser or satellite-guided precision armament systems for actions against selected military targets or even for straightforward reconnaissance tasks." The naval Harrier force was given a similarly expanded brief. What was not disclosed was that the Italian government had not authorized dynamic targeting, a position that later would change as the campaign evolved. La Russa claimed that in terms of ethics things remained unchanged, there being no difference between those who took part in a given military action, regardless of their role, "like midfielders and forwards in a soccer team." In addition, Italy soon would be sending ten "military instructors, which, together with an equal number of instructors supplied by France and Great Britain, will be inserted in the military command structure to be created by the National Transition Council in Benghazi."[103] The announcements led to immediate questions in Parliament, both against and for the government.[104] It is perhaps no coincidence that the Ministry of Defense immediately switched its news updates to a single weekly summary.[105]

Under the new rules, 6th Wing Tornado IDS now was allowed to carry out strikes, albeit with very narrow rules of engagement adhering strictly to the letter of UNSCR 1973 and that initially contemplated only deliberate targeting.[106] The load-out comprised only precision munitions, including laser-guided GBU-16 Paveway IIs and GPS-guided GBU-32 JDAMs. Despite these limitations, the situation was already markedly different from the previous deployment to Afghanistan, when political sensitivity limited the unit's "Red Devil" detachment to acquiring imagery and target

---

[102]"Comunicazioni del governo su recenti sviluppi della situazione in Libia," April 27, 2012, in Camera dei Deputati. The document is incorrectly dated to March 26, 2011 in some recent publications.

[103]Christened "Operation Cyrene," the mission began on April 28 in Benghazi and moved to Tripoli on November 21, and is listed as a "wide-ranging bilateral cooperative assistance operation" in the Italian MOD 2012 *Nota aggiuntiva* (supplement to the annual budget), Attachment B, p. 1–B/18. Its 2011 duties were listed as "supporting the Libyan staff of the Benghazi operations center (OC) in acquiring autonomous capabilities in planning, organizing and carrying out military operations." This should not be confused with the role played by Italian intelligence and Special Forces, which several Italian authors (e.g., Gaiani, p. 21, and Tani, "Valutazioni," p. 30) claim to have been very successful and much appreciated. Perhaps understandably, details are lacking.

[104]Franceschini et al., question with immediate reply 3–01616, April 27, 2011; Baldelli and Cicu, question with immediate reply 3–01617, April 27, 2011.

[105]In March SMD published five releases for nine days of operations, rising to 18 in April (of which 17 were issued in the first 22 days) and dropping to five each in May and July, four each in June and August, six in September (including one describing solely a staff visit), and three in October. There was no official end-of-operations release or recapitulation.

[106]Deliberate targeting prosecutes planned targets. These are targets that are known to exist in the operational environment with engagement actions scheduled against them to create the effects desired to support achievement of JFC objectives. (JP 3–60, 2007, p. viii.)

Giuseppe Garibaldi, flagship of NATO Task Group 455.1,
under way in the Mediterranean on June 2, 2011, with
AV-8B+ Harriers and SH-3D helicopters ranged on deck.
Courtesy of NATO.

information with RecceLite pods.[107] Tornado IDS strikes were routinely escorted by 155th Squadron/50th Wing Tornado ECRs. Navy Harriers flew their first attack sorties over Libya on the morning of April 28, with loadouts comprising GBU-12s, -16s, and -32s.[108]

The KC-767A was rushed into service in May by using the temporary Operational Certification procedure under Logistics Command responsibility while simultaneously engaging in the necessary receiver clearance and pilot qualification flights.[109] This allowed the two tankers to be used, albeit with receivers restricted to Italian aircraft and hose-and-drogue systems only. The second tanker arrived in late March and immediately was put into service. By mid-May, the KC-767As had been cleared to refuel Eurofighter and Tornado, alleviating the need for buddy tanking and KC-130J

---

[107] Durante, Ricci, and Salvati, "Nel 'cuore' della missione italiana," p. 9.

[108] ITN email.

[109] "KC-767 ufficilmente in servizo con l'Aernautica Militare," *Dedalonews.it*, May 17, 2011; Durante, Ricci, and Salvati, " . . . l'impegno continua . . . ," p. 15. Operational certification was introduced by Decree of the President of the Republic (DPR) No. 556 of October 25, 1999.

operations. Given the dependence on U.S. tanker support, which represented about one-seventh of the total coalition sorties, this was a crucial result. Excluding buddy tanking refueling, the Italian tanker effort for the campaign included 57 KC-767A and 63 KC-130J sorties, totaling 599 hours.

The different in-flight refueling systems ruled out mixed formations between F-16 and Eurofighters.[110] Both types were the subjects of undisclosed improvements during the campaign, again by recourse to operational certification.[111] By mid-May, Euro-fighters also were deployed on night sorties, sometimes up to six hours long, with occasional extensions and changes of area of responsibility.[112] The Eurofighters operated up to 200 nautical miles south Tripoli, about 510 nautical miles from Trapani.[113] Their typical counterair configuration included three external fuel tanks, four active radar-guided AIM-120 Advanced Medium-Range Air-to-Air Missiles (AMRAAMs) under the fuselage and four infrared-guided IRIS-T short-range missiles.

In mid-May, the Tornado IDS fired the first of a total of 25 Storm Shadow stand-off missiles, long-range weapons which allowed hitting targets deep inside Libya.[114] The results were considered uniformly excellent, but once again, political directives resulted in the capability remaining unreported. Over the first two months, Italy flew about 1,200 OUP sorties, slightly over one-fourth of the 4,600 flown in total for the period.[115] On 17 May the media reported a 46th Air Brigade C-130J had dropped anti-Qaddafi leaflets over Tripoli, marking the only confirmed Italian PSYOPS of the campaign.[116] On the same day, ITAF unveiled to the media its KC-767A tankers, revealing it had achieved an initial capability in record time.

On June 1, *Garibaldi* (C551) became the flagship of the NATO naval Task Group 455.01 (TG 455.01). Four days later, the F-16 fleet achieved 45,000 hours, completing the original Peace Caesar program. On June 14, the Eurofighter component achieved 1,000 flying hours.[117] The Tornado ECR SEAD component returned to its base at Piacenza–San Damiano on June 21, having completed a total of 208 sorties and more than 860 flying hours.

---

[110] *Rivista Aeronautica*, March 2011, p. 13.

[111] Marani interview, pp. 60–61.

[112] *Rivista Aeronautica*, No. 3, 2011, p. 16. According to *Eurofighter World*, the manufacturer's house organ, some missions lasted "up to eight hours, including up to three in-flight refuellings" (No. 1, 2012, p. 8).

[113] *Eurofighter World*, p. 8.

[114] *Rivista Aeronautica*, No. 5, 2011, p. 12; Bernardis interview, July 26, 2011.

[115] Gen. s.a. Tiziano Tosi, "La Dimensione Aerospaziale della risposta," *Rivista Aeronautica*, March 2011, p. 27.

[116] "I tagli al bilancio metteranno l'Aeronautica a terra nel 2010? Gli scenari preoccupanti emersi dal seminario CESMA," *Dedalonews.it*, March 29, 2009.

[117] In addition, between June 2 and June 10, the two wings had deployed four aircraft to Iceland for exercise Northern Viking 2011, in preparation for providing air policing duties to the country in 2013.

Media reports variously registered French optimism, venturing as far as to imagine that the end of the campaign might be celebrated on July 14. In fact, progress was slow and the drawn-out campaign was beginning to wear on the "willing," some of which began to recall aircraft. At the biennial Paris Air Show, the French media reported that 60 percent of the Rafale crews were involved in Operation Harmattan, and that some pilots already had flown 130 hours of the 180 allotted them for the year.[118] Coupled with the June 1 disbanding of No. 13 RAF Squadron, this again brought pressure on the remaining coalition members to step up their contributions.

Two further controversies erupted in June, respectively regarding CAOC 5 and UAVs. The first spilled into the media on June 16 when Gen. Tricarico revealed that at a recent meeting in Brussels on NATO restructuring, La Russa had unquestioningly surrendered to a Spanish proposal to turn CAOC 5 into a Deployable Air Command Center (DACC) and relinquish its other responsibilities to CAOC 8 at Torrejon.[119] Tricarico added a wealth of details about the minister's six-hour delay at the crucial meeting and his lack of understanding of military issues, prompting La Russa to reply a week later during a news conference at the Paris air show.[120] On this occasion, he waved a thank-you letter from NATO Secetary General Rasmussen and claimed to actually have won an upgrade because when the DACC was activated, it would have a staff of 280, versus 180 for the permanent staff. The second round of polemics arose from the showcasing of ITAF UAV capabilities at Amendola air base.[121] The 32nd Wing commander went on record not only with his unit's readiness to field the new MQ-9 Predator B, but also with political unwillingness to arm the drones. This caused complaints from the opposition. While the politicians dithered, other drones arrived.[122]

On July 25, four AMX attack aircraft were assigned to the TGA with both ISTAR and close air support (CAS) duties. The aircraft were drawn equally from 51st Wing at Istrana (Treviso) and 32nd Wing at Amendola (Foggia). Their arrival coincided substantially with the return of the Italian Eurofighters to their bases at Grosseto and Gioia del Colle.[123] Many speculated that ITAF had replaced its latest high-end twin-engine fighter with an inexpensive single-engine type, but in fact the AMX were offensive counterair replacements for Navy AV-8Bs.[124] The latter flew their final sorties on

---

[118] Bernard Bombeau, "Afghanistan et Libye, l'arme aérienne au coeur des combats," *Air & Cosmos*, No. 2270, June 17, 2011, p. 78.

[119] ANSA newswire, June 16, 2011; Vincenzo Nigro, "La Russa 'buca' la riunione Nato e la Spagna ci soffia la base radar," *La Repubblica*, June 19, 2011.

[120] "La Russa a Parigi: 'Nessun taglio sugli investimenti della Difesa, manutenzione in sofferenza,'" June 20, 2011.

[121] "Nella tana dei Predator, operativi in Afghanistan e pronti per la Libia," *Dedalonews.it*, June 29, 2011.

[122] Lt. Col. Stefano Cosci, "Sigonella: missione supporto," *Rivista Aeronautica*, May 2011, p. 20.

[123] Durante, Ricci, and Salvati, ". . . l'impegno continua . . . ," p. 4.

[124] Nordio interview. In 2008 an AMX flying hour cost 105 percent of an F-16 hour (SMA3, table "Onerosità per ora di volo dei velivoli A.M.," 2008 ed.); the cost of Eurofighter flying hours is not at hand.

July 17 and were withdrawn on July 26 together with *Garibaldi* (C551), with C. Amm. Filippo Foffi transferring command of TG 455.01 to the amphibious transport dock ship *San Giusto* (L9894), which continued to support the CSAR capability until the end of the campaign.[125] Total AV-8B activity stood then at 1,218 flying hours, including 1,030 hours and 504 sorties for OUP.[126]

By July 30, NATO forces had flown 17,023 sorties, including 1,645 by Italian aircraft. The AMX flew their first ISR sortie over Libya on August 10, but their employment was noteworthy for several reasons. In the first place, unlike the similarly equipped "Black Cats" detachment in Afghanistan, the AMX would not be confined to the RecceLite pod, but could use GBU-12 Paveway, GBU-38 JDAM, and Lizard bombs; second, dynamic engagements also were approved.[127] A third reason was the deployment of the Litening III pod, a few of which had been received just a few weeks earlier.[128] As a result, only a handful of pilots were qualified to use it and it was necessary to train others at Trapani in parallel with operations. The AMX flew a total of 550 hours in 150 sorties, including 72 OCA sorties with 128 munitions released.

A single MQ-9 Predator B eventually was assigned to OUP on August 8, and 28th Squadron flew its first ISR mission over Libya two days later.[129] The Predator B operated from Amendola and was controlled via satellite link for the entire 12-hour sortie. Thirty-one other sorties followed, an average of about one every three days and an average duration of about 11.5 hours, with more than five hours on station for both local, border, and aerial surveillance.[130]

The unexpectedly rapid fall of Tripoli on August 22 helped mitigate the general sense of fatigue that was beginning to set in among coalition members who found it difficult to sustain what had become an open-ended commitment. This situation was in part addressed on September 16 by the U.N. Security Council through a third resolution, UNSCR 2009, which eased the Libyan asset freeze and undertook to keep the measures introduced with UNSCR 1973 "under continuous review" and to "terminate" the authorization to use "all appropriate measures," albeit without establishing a firm deadline. Of direct importance to Italy, the fall of Tripoli immediately cut arrivals from Libya: Immigrants fell from 5,006 in August to 62 in September, hovered around

---

[125] NATO Allied Maritime Command Naples, "OUP Maritime Operations: Mission Accomplished," News Release 53, November 1, 2011; ITN email.

[126] ITN email; PR20 gives 1,223 hours total, without further details. The SMA3 summary quotes 994 hours in 375 sorties, breaking down these slightly lower figures into 54.5 percent offensive counter air (541.5 hours in 173 OCA sorties with 145 ordnance released), 31.4 percent recce, and 9 percent CAP.

[127] Lt. Col. Alessandro Cornacchini, editorial, *Rivista Aeronautica*, No. 5, 2011, p. 2.

[128] Nordio interview.

[129] Alegi, "I Predator italiani debuttano nei cieli della Libia," *Dedalonews.it*, August 12, 2011.

[130] Statistics based on SMA3 summary; Nordio interview.

that number in the following months, and returned to zero in February 2012.[131] But it was still necessary to deal with previous immigrants, and as late as September 21, ITAF C-130Js were required to shuttle to Sigonella some 150 immigrants who had set fire to the crowded Lampedusa Identification and Expulsion Center.[132]

The final Italian sorties over Libya were flown in the afternoon of October 31 by a pair of 37th Wing F-16s, which landed at 1550L while the Tornados and AMXs were beginning to head back to their home bases.[133] An NAEW AWACS landed at midnight, at exactly the same time as the official end of OUP. On November 1, Gen. Bernardis issued his "well done" message to all ranks. Amm. Sq. Veri addressed crews at sea by radio.[134] In the following days, the international contingents returned home, gradually bringing the situation in Italy to normality.

Discussion and Conclusions

To the historian, the Italian political debate and gradual expansion of the mission in Libya bear more than a passing resemblance to the Italian participation in the first Gulf War and the events surrounding it. In 2011, the ITAF was on par with its coalition partners in terms of equipment (platforms, systems, and ordnance), procedures, and training. The ITAF destroyed 534 (86 percent) of its 618 Designated Mean Points of Impact (DMPIs) and 97 percent of engaged targets.[135] Its shortcomings were circumscribed or were shared with most of its partners, and were balanced by areas of unique expertise or equipment. Coupled with the provision of coalition-enabling logistic support and the difficult political and budgetary circumstances, the overall assessment was one of success and satisfaction.

The "lessons identified" and "lessons learned" process was launched immediately after the end of operations, with the closed-door airpower workshop held in November 2011. It included a "Lessons of Libya" panel that was chaired by Gen. b.a. Gabellini, the original head of the targeting division.[136] The first broad lesson that the ITAF drew in public from the Libyan crisis was the need for interdiction, air defense and SEAD, the very capabilities that protracted counterinsurgency engagements in Iraq

---

[131] DGIPF email.

[132] *Rivista Aeronautica*, May 2011, p. 21.

[133] Lt. Col. Stefano Cosci, "Missione conclusa," p. 5.

[134] NATO Allied Maritime Command Naples, "OUP Maritime Operations: Mission Accomplished," News Release 53, November 1, 2011.

[135] SMA3 summary, attachment D.

[136] Nordio interview; *Rivista Aeronautica*, June 2011, p. 13.

and Afghanistan had sidelined.[137] This, in fact, merely underscored the long-held ITAF belief in the need for a balanced service centered upon an effective capability to carry out complex operations throughout the aerial domain, beyond the grand-scale logistics requested (or implied) by surface forces.[138] Air superiority's enabling role with regard to surface operations is often forgotten or misunderstood by services whose use of aircraft is limited in quantity, breadth, and scope. The assumption that C2, ISTAR, AAR, air dominance, air transport command and management, logistics (including ordnance), and training are available (or that the lead nation, coalition partners, or other national services will provide them) is unrealistic and does not form a basis for autonomous complex air operations.

Immediate Lessons

In practical terms, the most immediate consequence regards the need for Trapani to remain a full-fledged ITAF major operating base due to its strategic location close to North Africa, with a role far beyond the mere protection of the local NAEW operation. Given the intense internal debate that had surrounded the controversial decision to consolidate the air defense force much farther north around Grosseto (in Tuscany) and Gioia del Colle alone, this was hardly surprising. The means by which Trapani might be preserved beyond the F-16 withdrawal ceremony held on May 23, 2012 still is unclear, particularly after the new round of cuts announced by Di Paola, who took on a new role as Minister of Defense in the new Mario Monti cabinet sworn in on November 16, 2011 after Berlusconi's resignation. ITAF, however, is adamant about keeping Trapani open with a Wing "capable of expressing autonomous operational capabilities"[139] and has not disbanded 37th Wing—despite leaving it temporarily without aircraft.

Although Airgest turned out to be not much more than a nuisance,[140] it underlined the lack of a legal framework to ensure the full availability of infrastructures crucial for military or security operations, particularly given the prevalent lack of military and security culture. Some observers have pointed out this will weigh negatively against the dual-use aspirations of communities hosting the few remaining air bases. The ITAF might as a result take a more cautious approach to base closures, which would in turn translate into increased costs or, at least, smaller savings.

---

[137] Francesco Saverio Agresti, "Potere aereo e strategia nell'era della 'guerra al terrore' . . . e oltre," *Rivista Aeronautica*, April 2011, p. 11; Nordio interview.

[138] The philosophy for a modern, relevant ITAF had been publicly described as early as 1997 in terms not vastly different from that currently applied. See *La dottrina dell'Aeronautica Militare*, pp. 54–59.

[139] Nordio interview.

[140] By August 17, Airgest, the company operating the commercial side of Trapani airport, had been promised 10 million Euros in damages by the national government and a further 2 million by the Sicilian regional government in "support of route development and continuation of existing routes." (Salvatore Ombra to ministries of Transportation and Defense, plus 35 other addressees, No. 1340/11, August 17, 2011.)

In terms of equipment, the nonavailability of the NAEW component in Operation Odyssey Dawn, compounded by the German decision to withdraw their personnel from the multinational unit, reinforced the ITAF's long-held belief in the need of an autonomous ISTAR capability, comprising both airborne early warning and Joint Asset Movement Management.[141] Originally framed in a purely national perspective, the desired asset came to be seen over the years as a potential high-value contribution to multinational, regional, or ad hoc coalitions. After considering in 1993–2003 the Grumman E-2C Hawkeye and failing in 2007 to select a mixed airborne early warning and control/multimission maritime aircraft force to establish a Joint Surveillance Wing due to a mixture of inter-service, funding, and industrial issues, the ITAF now is set to receive a number of Gulfstream 550 Eitam systems in a complex deal that will see Israel acquire Alenia Aermacchi M-346 advanced/lead-in fighter trainers.[142]

The Litening III pod proved a resounding success and soon will be integrated on ITAF Tornados and eventually Typhoons, providing the latter with additional means of visual target identification for airspace surveillance and no-fly zone enforcement.[143] The integration of Litening and RecceLite data was found particularly effective. The ITAF was quite impressed with Brimstone effectiveness and it would hardly be surprising to learn of its acquisition, funds permitting.

Moving from systems to platforms, Gen. b.a. Frigerio, the second head of the targeting division, asked whether a need might exist for low-cost platforms for low intensity operations, a consideration directly tied to European coalition members' fiscal constraints.[144] The use of unmanned systems met expectations and confirmed long-held beliefs in their permanent value and role in modern operations.

Operational certification, previously used in a developmental mode only, made a direct impact on capabilities by making it possible to field the new tankers in a very short time. This dovetailed with the ability of the Electronic Warfare Technical-Operational Support Unit (ReSTOGE), which specializes in updating and developing software libraries, to offer flexibility through daily field reprogramming work.[145]

---

[141] Col. Sandro Sampaoli, quoted in *Rivista Aeronautica*, March 2011, p. 35. Ironically, the requirement had been first highlighted in April 1986 by an earlier Libyan crisis, when NATO had turned down an Italian request for an urgent NAEW redeployment to Sicily despite the firing of Libyan *Scud* missiles.

[142] At the time of this writing, the ITAF has made no official announcements regarding its intention to procure the Eitam. When the system made its international debut during the Vega 2010 exercise in Sardinia, it was described in glowing terms in the ITAF magazine. See Emanuele Salvati, "Gulfstream 550 Eitam. Il piccolo CAEW," in *Rivista Aeronautica*, February 2011, pp. 82–85; in addition an Italian contract to procure NATO-compatible communications, navigation, and identification for two Eitams was signed on July 19, 2012. See "Finmeccanica: contratti con Israele per 850 mln di dollari, compresi i 30 M-346," *Dedalonews.it*, July 19, 2012.

[143] Nordio interview.

[144] Gen. b.a. Frigerio, IFC 2011 presentation, slide 23.

[145] *Rivista Aeronautica*, March 2011, p. 16; *Rivista Aeronautica*, May 2011, pp. 12–13. ReSTOGE stands for *Reparto Supporto Tecnico Operativo per la Guerra Elettronica*.

Naval analysts concentrated on the role of carrier-based naval aviation, including the novel basing of attack helicopters on ships. The simultaneous attention devoted to the predicament of the newly carrier- and Harrier-less Royal Navy suggests these conclusions were closely connected to broader concerns about the role of naval aviation, particularly considering that the "Italian Navy is without equal in Europe in LHD procurement, intending to acquire up to 3 new 20,000-ton helicopter carriers."[146] In all likelihood, the ongoing debate over the ITAF commitment to procuring the F-35B short take-off and vertical landing (STOVL) wing also contributed to shape the conclusion. At an early stage the official navy magazine proclaimed, and repeated later, that the crisis had confirmed the need for carriers, variously arguing that proximity to the target area allowed shorter transit times, that this translated into lower costs, and that it made it impossible for reporters to determine the level of activity by monitoring aircraft movements from airports.[147] In fact, with some exaggeration in October, the navy proclaimed its single Harrier squadron, the Gruppo Aerei Imbarcati, to be "the only national multirole tactical aviation component, perfectly integrated with the world's most advanced Air Forces."[148]

Broader Considerations

As might be expected in the contemporary 24/7 news cycle, the refusal to shape the discourse in an attempt to muzzle political debate actually backfired.[149] Maintaining a low profile and political ambiguity helped hide Italy's qualitative and quantitative role throughout the crisis, which was largely unreported or underestimated in the first wave of English-language narratives about the Libya intervention. It also allowed President Obama to include Denmark, but not Italy, among the countries whose role he acknowledged in his remarks at the United Nations on September 20, 2011.[150] Although Italian opinion is divided as to whether the slight was intentional, it is clear that the pain was only in part mitigated the next month when Secretary of Defense Leon Panetta told a

---

[146]Cfr. C.V. Michele Cosentino, "La saga dell'aviazione navale britannica," and Pietro Batacchi, "Il futuro della Royal Navy," both in *Rivista Marittima*, October 2011; "Le unità d'assalto anfibio e gli elicotteri d'attacco in Libia," in *Rivista Marittima*, November 2011.

[147]Tani, "La crisi," p. 32; Tani, "Valutazioni," p. 32; these conclusions are endorsed by the Navy staff in ITN email, cit., which adds the reduced need for tanker aircraft and safe take-off and landing outside enemy range. Tani does not appear to take into account the cost of the ship, the cost of the required escort group, the number of aircraft actually carried, and the time necessary for ships to reach their operating area. With regard to the latter, Libya is probably the closest imaginable area from the Italian Navy's homeport in Taranto.

[148]Italian Navy press release No. 19, October 25, 2011 (PR 19).

[149]For a blunt assessment see G. Gaiani, p. 20.

[150]The White House, Office of the Press Secretary, "Remarks by President Obama at High-Level Meeting on Libya," Washington, D.C., September 20, 2011.

media conference at the Italian embassy in Washington: "In Libya, frankly, if it were not for the Italians, we really don't feel that we could have completed this mission."[151]

Internally, the overall lack of visibility and recognition also had a negative impact on the Italian military's ability to maintain funding levels, force levels, and structure. The cuts to planned F-35 procurement levels were certainly fueled by reduced budgets and program delays. But the nonrecognition of the kinetic role played by the ITAF and Navy air assets helped make the cuts easier.

In many ways, this situation was hardly surprising. The ITAF had chafed under the restrictions imposed by La Russa, who centralized all external communication under his direct control and likely originated the restriction on even ordinary news releases from April onward. "There is turmoil, activity is heavy under whatever point of view and clashes with the business as usual atmosphere felt everywhere," said Gen. s.a. Marani, head of COMLOG, three months into the campaign. "Although our fighters and those of the coalition are carrying out continuous real sorties over Libyan territory, there is minimal perception of the seriousness of the situation, and not only among ordinary people."[152] When the Berlusconi government resigned in November 2011, La Russa did not include Libya (or, for that reason, any other real operation) among his proudest ministerial achievements, which he listed as the military-familiarization program for youths, the celebrations for the 150th anniversary of Italian unification, and the use of soldiers for police patrols.[153]

To some extent, the Italian government appears to view closer European defense integration as a way of compensating for an overall reduction in its defense spending. In fact, Di Paola held out the possibility of Italy helping drive this initiative when, in February 2012, he announced a further round of major defense cuts.[154] Even without this budgetary pressure, the benefits of closer integration are very clear. It has been noted, not without irony, that Italy and the United Kingdom fielded two Tornado IDS variants in Desert Storm in 1991 (GR1 and PA200) and three in 2011 (GR4, IT-MLU, and IT-ECR) "despite having taken part in exactly the same operational situation since 1991."[155] Had Germany participated, it would have added its own variants. Still, it remains to be seen whether the *"vincolo esterno"* (external constraint) strategy, which often has succeeded in coercing Italian politicians into action, will work in this case. Also, the prospects and time frame for meaningful progress remain

---

[151] Italian Embassy in Washington, D.C., "Media Availability with Secretary Panetta and Minister La Russa," October 17, 2011.

[152] Marani interview, p. 61.

[153] "Difesa: Bilancio La Russa, è stato onore guidare ministero," ANSA newswire November 10, 2011, 10.57; November 16, 2011, 18.18.

[154] Minister of Defense G. Di Paola, House and Senate Defense Committee testimony, February 15, 2012; letter, p. 2.

[155] Gen. b.a. Frigerio, IFC 2011 presentation, slide 44.

uncertain. In 1997–1998 Gen. s.a. Arpino, then Chief of Air Staff, addressed the issue in public on at least two occasions, concluding that specializing European air forces through "areas of excellence in which to develop autonomously, in a way coherent and complementary with the policies of other nations" would require the "political consolidation of the European Union which is still a long way away."[156] Political unity appeared to Arpino as a precondition for a nation to renounce "essential components of its Air Force [and] accept to remain in certain respects completely subordinate to the contribution and willingness of others." Arpino described "air defense" as closely approximating "national sovereignty," hence not renounceable. In July 2011, his successor Bernardis noted no European armed forces were still in sight and saw "greater compatibility with allies" as a more realistic goal in a 20-year time frame.[157]

While it is generally accepted that coalition warfare will remain the prevalent model for the foreseeable future, some critical thinking about its implications clearly is required. At one level, if the need to avoid political backlash in coalition countries and defend their legitimacy in the eyes of the population by minimizing collateral damage is expected to become a standard feature in future interventions, it follows that Italy and the rest of NATO will have to address present shortfalls in Alliance intelligence and targeting capabilities.[158] This would include adopting a NATO Collateral Damage Estimate (CDE) methodology and a permanent NATO Targeting Center from which to draw to establish the dedicated Targeting Directorate of future Joint Task Forces. At another, widespread concern remains that the divided political agendas damaged both the image and substance of NATO and the EU. NATO can be expected to continue to provide the necessary common operational doctrine, training, and language (both literally and metaphorically), but it cannot be expected to act as a collective "lead nation." The EU also appears ill suited for the task, particularly until the various components of political action are viewed severally (rather than synergistically) and domestically (rather than federally, for want of a better word). This was very much in evidence during the Libyan campaign, when the Franco-Anglo-American-driven coalition leaned heavily on Italy to increase its already sizable contribution and, simultaneously, the EU withdrew from the immigration crisis. In fact, it fueled Italian resentment by simultaneously demanding high standards of treatment and refusing to accept individual refugees, with France actually expelling into Italy those crossing its borders. This threatened to destabilize an important ally, with potentially disastrous immediate consequences on operations.

---

[156] Gen. s.a. Mario Arpino, "L'Aeronautica Militare alle soglie del terzo millennio. Uno sguardo al futuro," lecture at the Centro Alti Studi Difesa, Rome, June 19, 1998, p. 16; a similar viewpoint in *La dottrina*, pp. 56–57.

[157] Bernardis interview, p. 704.

[158] Gen. b.a. Frigerio, IFC 2011 presentation, slide 35; Col. Francesco S. Agresti, p. 4.

Implications for Airpower in General

More than 90 years have passed since Giulio Douhet first publicly formulated his ideas about airpower, but it still is customary to analyze conflicts in relation to his prediction that future wars would be won through "command of the air." Thus Douhet famously has been proclaimed "alive and well in the Gulf," but largely wrong in Libya.[159] In fact, sweeping differences in technology, politics, and social structures, together with the deep misunderstanding of the scope and goals that Douhet set for his writings, have made both readings irrelevant.[160] It should suffice that the strict targeting guidelines, the severely limited assets, and effective lack of unity of command (or, perhaps more accurately, of singleness of purpose) that prevailed throughout OUP all were in such direct contradiction with basic Douhetian tenets as to make a reading through this perspective meaningless.

The British observation that "the number of self-imposed constraints gave the initiative to the forces and events on the ground rather than to an aggressive air strategy" and turned OUP into "effectively comprising the air wing of the National Transition Council (NTC) land component"[161] points to the fact that proper assessment of the effectiveness of airpower in the campaign needs to examine the level of preliminary analysis carried out,[162] the assessment of the opponent (not merely in terms of military hardware),[163] the assets and financial resources available for the campaign, the political conditions and constraints, and so on. One Italian observer has gone as far as saying that "for once, arms have surprised and made up, at least in the short term, for what lacked in political vision."[164]

Insofar as this is true, it begs the question of the degree to which proponents of the intervention thought it through in terms of strategy and outcome. Among Italian analysts, little doubt exists that the prevalent conclusion is deep skepticism about these issues, regardless of their political or military background. This consensus arises partly from practical considerations, such at the disappearance of a huge number of Libyan surface-to-air missiles, and the contrast between the "responsibility to protect"

---

[159] Oberst Wolfgang Pusztai, "Die militärstrategischen Lehren aus der Intervention in Libyen," in Johann Pucher and Johann Frank, eds., *Strategie und Sicherheit 2012*, Vienna-Köln-Weimar, Böhlau, 2012, p. 265.

[160] Giulio Douhet, "Riepilogando" (1929), reprinted in Giulio Douhet, *Il dominio dell'aria e altri scritti*, Luciano Bozzo ed., Roma, Stato Maggiore Aeronautica/Ufficio Storico, 2002, p. 272.

[161] Wing Commander R. A. C. Wells, "One swallow maketh not a summer. What success in Libya means for NATO," *JAPCC Journal*, No. 15, Spring/Summer 2012, p. 70. If this observation is true, it follows that airpower did not achieve the end state alone but rather that the coalition outsourced land operations to the NTC.

[162] B. Bombeau mentions "tens of days of planning" in order to "propose all possibilities of intervention" to the French Joint Chief of Staff (p. 76).

[163] B.-H. Lévy apparently promised Sarkozy that the war would have lasted only three days because "the Qaddafi army consists of 300 ill-equipped losers." "Scènes de la vie dans la Libye libre," in *Le Point*, March 10, 2011, quoted in P. Sensini, p. 86.

[164] Tani, "Valutazioni," p. 26.

invoked in February and March 2011 and the bloody post-conflict anarchy. Perhaps more importantly, it reflects a nearly universal Italian reading of the motivation and prospective outcome (versus Libya, domestic issues, other coalition partners). Gani best summarized the former view, saying: "It is evident that the cavalier and aggressive penetration in Libya aims to replace the Italians in terms of influence, trading position and energy and construction projects."[165] Tani cynically described the latter as replacing the "consolidated kleptocracy of the Qaddafi family with a new pervasive kleptocracy" and "a stable lay autocracy with an Islamic-flavored chaos whose outlines cannot be mapped yet."[166] Even the official SMD magazine concluded its analysis of the post-Qaddafi prospects with an eloquent "Inshallah" ("God willing").[167] The Italian operational success, in other words, is not considered to have contributed to the overarching goal of stabilizing NATO and the Mediterranean; in fact, quite the contrary.[168] If it were proved that the governments substituted action for analysis, the implication of the Libyan campaign would be that airpower is shaped by history (and, therefore, politics) rather than the contrary.[169]

---

[165] G. Gaiani, p. 20.

[166] Tani, "Valutazioni," p. 25. Several Italian analysists have commented that under Qaddafi Libya had the highest per capita income in Africa and provided aid to other African countries.

[167] Arcangelo Marucci, "Il post-Gheddafi tra estremismo fondamentalista e minaccia terroristica," *Informazioni della Difesa*, January 2012, pp. 14–21; similar concerns in Matteo Capasso, "La crisi in Libia," in N. Pedde, K. Mezran, and V. Cassar, eds., Panorama 2012, Rome: GAN, 2011, pp. 75–82.

[168] As other chapters in this volume indicate, this "glass half empty" perspective notably contrasts with post-conflict assessments of the interventions effects that appear dominant in a number of the other participating countries.

[169] This concept is elaborated upon in Gregory Alegi, "L'influenza della storia sul Potere Aereo," *Rivista Aeronautica*, No. 5, 2009, pp. 168–175.

CHAPTER NINE

The Canadian Experience: Operation Mobile

Richard O. Mayne

Introduction

It was a heroes' welcome. The roar of a CP-140 Aurora long-range patrol aircraft, followed by CF-188 tactical fighters, a CC-150 Polaris tanker, and other key aircraft flying in formation over the Canadian Parliament on November 24, 2011, marked the last act in Canada's successful involvement in the NATO mission Operation Unified Protector. This fly-past, as well as a special event on Parliament Hill dedicated to the Canadian Forces personnel involved in the mission, was recognition for a job well done. The government wanted Canada to play a significant and leading role in Libya through Operation Mobile (the Canadian designation for the mission to protect civilians from Muammar Qaddafi's regime), and the Royal Canadian Air Force (RCAF) helped deliver those effects. One of the RCAF's key mandates is to provide Canada and NATO with relevant, responsive, and effective airpower,[1] yet it is not always easy for it to do so. Smaller NATO nations such as Canada do not have the same resources as their larger allies, and often have to struggle to find the right balance of equipment, training, personnel, and doctrine that will allow them to provide the readiness, agility, flexibility, and versatility required to respond to unforeseen situations.[2]

The RCAF has recently developed a new capability centered on an independent Air Expeditionary Wing (AEW). Supported by new air expeditionary doctrine, this wing is designed to provide a mechanism for rapidly deploying Canadian airpower and delivering strategic effects around the world without causing major disruptions to the air force's existing capabilities.[3] Although the AEW did not become operational until 2013, Libya nevertheless served as a test of the concept. A number of accounts suggest that this concept served Op Mobile well in Libya, as one NATO official argued that

---

[1] Testimony of RCAF Commander Lieutenant-General A. Deschamps to Senate Committee on National Security and Defence, February 27, 2012. For more information on current RCAF doctrine see: *Canadian Forces Aerospace Doctrine*, Government of Canada, December 2010, pp. 1–5.

[2] Peter Diekmeyer interview with Lieutenant-General Andre Deschamps, *Canadian Defence Review*, June 2010, p. 9.

[3] David Pugliese, "Development of Expeditionary Unit a Priority for RCAF," *Ottawa Citizen*, May 24, 2012.

Canada had clearly "punched beyond its weight" during the conflict in terms of both the leadership and capabilities it provided. Former U.S. Secretary of Defense Robert Gates expressed a similar sentiment, and it is understandable why Canada received these types of accolades.[4] Not only did a Canadian (Lieutenant-General Charles Bouchard) command the NATO mission, but when compared to its overall size, the Canadian Forces (CF) made a significant contribution by rapidly deploying seven CF-188 fighters, two CC-150 Polaris tankers, two CC-177 and two CC-130 transports, two CP-140 Aurora long-range patrol aircraft, and a CH-124 Sea King helicopter as well as a Royal Canadian Navy frigate.[5] Yet some scholars and pundits claim that upon closer examination, their nation's military, humanitarian and diplomatic efforts were "flying under the radar" of international opinion, which suggested that Canada overestimated its role in the conflict.[6] As a result, the aim of this chapter is to determine whether and how Canadian expeditionary airpower allowed the government to achieve its foreign policy aims in Libya through the delivery of fast, effective, agile, and flexible strategic effects. Put another way, did Canada truly "punch above its weight" during Op Mobile, and what lessons, if any, did the RCAF learn from the mission?

Beyond Rhetoric, Taking Action

The Canadian government was quick to condemn the Qaddafi regime's violent crackdown on the protests that erupted within Libya in early 2011. Minister of Foreign Affairs Lawrence Cannon in mid-February made it clear in statements that Canada was deeply concerned with the events unfolding in Libya, emphasizing that Qaddafi had to "respect the rights and freedoms of [his] people and engage in peaceful dialogue of their legitimate concerns." While Canada observed that it was watching the situation closely and made strongly worded appeals to the Libyan government to stop the use of violence against its own people, its first priority was placed on the safety of Canadian nationals. Working closely with "like-minded countries," the Department

---

[4]   Peter O'Neil, "Canada Punching Above Its Weight in Military Alliance, Gates Tells Officials," *Winnipeg Free Press*, June 11, 2011; Tom Blackwell, "Canada Contributed a Disproportionate Amount to Libya Air Strikes: Sources," *The National Post*, August 25, 2011.

[5]   Canadian military aircraft carry three-digit designations that are sometimes but not always based on corresponding U.S. designations. Thus the Boeing F/A-18 Hornet became the CF-188 (commonly referred to informally as the CF18 Hornet), the CC-177 is the Boeing C-17 Globemaster, and Canadian Lockheed C-130 Hercules are designated CC-130. The CP-140 Aurora is a derivative of the Lockheed P-3C Orion, and the recently acquired CC-150 Polaris is an Airbus A330-based tanker.

[6]   Carl Meyer, "Extent of Canadian Involvement in Libya Flying Under the Radar," *Embassy Magazine*, June 8, 2011; Douglas MacKinnon, "Canada, the Forgotten Ally," *Baltimore Sun*, May 29, 2012.

Seven CF-188 fighters led by a CC-150 Polaris flying over the Candian Parliament during the welcome home ceremony to mark the end of Operation Mobile.
Courtesy of the Canadian Department of National Defence, photo by Master Corporal Julie Bélisle. Used in accordance with Crown Copyright provisions.

of Foreign Affairs and International Trade (DFAIT) looked at various means to secure passage out of Libya for the 331 registered Canadians living there.[7]

It did not take long before concerns emerged about DFAIT's efforts; so much so, in fact, that members of the Official Opposition in parliament as well as the press were quick to jump on claims that the initial evacuation was a confused affair.[8] The RCAF was in a good position to help. On February 25, a CC-177 from 429 Transport Squadron en route to Kandahar, Afghanistan, was redirected to Rome and then Malta in anticipation of supporting the evacuation from Tripoli. Canadian Expeditionary Force Command (CEFCOM), which was the organization responsible for CF operations outside of North America, authorized the mission on the following day, marking the beginning of Operation Mobile.[9]

The RCAF moved quickly to provide the necessary support for what was described as a DFAIT-led, whole-of-government, multinational effort to evacuate Canadian dip-

[7] Foreign Affairs and International Trade Canada, "Statement by Minister Cannon on Situation in Libya," No. 72, February 19, 2011; "Statement by Minister Cannon on Situation in Libya," No. 73, February 21, 2011; and "Ministerial Statement on Libya," No. 76, February 22, 2011.

[8] "Libya-Canada Diplomatic Relationship Halted," *CBC News*, February 26, 2011; House of Commons Debates, Hansard, 40th Parliament, 3rd Sess., No. 135, February 28, 2011.

[9] Major General Yvan Blondin, "Assisting Canadians—Making History!" *Prairie Flyer II*, Spring 2011; Captain Tim Stokes, "CC-177 Aassists in Moving Civilians Out of Libya," Royal Canadian Air Force: 429 Transport Squadron, March 1, 2011.

lomatic staff, citizens, and foreign nationals from Libya. Other RCAF assets that would join Joint Task Force (JTF) Malta, the name given to the forces allocated to this phase of Op Mobile, included a second CC-177 (which, like the first, was retasked from Afghanistan) and two CC-130J Hercules aircraft from 8 Wing in Trenton, Ontario, along with the CF's Operational Liaison and Reconnaissance Team (OLRT), a maintenance team, medical staff, military police, and an air component C2 team. Preparations at Trenton were completed within 24 hours, and once in-theater they joined a military assistance team of CF members already serving in the area on other assignments. Based in Valletta, this military assistance team, which became the JTF Malta HQ, established links with regional allies as well as personnel from other Canadian departments and partners.[10] The entire contingent integrated quickly with DFAIT's diplomatic staff and multinational agencies, resulting in the safe evacuation from Libya of 4,431 people from 24 nations.[11] Of this total, the 80 CF personnel of JTF Malta were responsible for evacuating 191 individuals (61 Canadian and 130 foreign nationals) from 23 countries by the time of its last flight on March 8.[12]

Having reached its full operating capacity two days after deploying, the RCAF flew six evacuation missions (two by CC-177 and four by CC-130J) over an 11-day period. It was not an easy mission: The presence of Canadians across the vast country and Libyan authorities' occasional refusals to grant landing rights both added to its complexity.[13] Nevertheless, for Major General Yvan Blondin, then serving as the commander of 1 Canadian Air Division in Winnipeg, Manitoba, the RCAF's contribution to JTF Malta "highlighted the agility and responsiveness of airpower and the professionalism of our airmen and air women." Canadian Prime Minister Stephen Harper agreed. He said the RCAF's transport aircraft had given the government a "flexible capability" to respond to the growing crisis. The Chief of the Defence Staff, Lieutenant-General Walt Natynczyk, indicated that it also displayed Canada's "ability and willingness to help those in need."[14] Yet officials had little time to enjoy the evacuation's success, as the Canadian government already was considering the appropriate politi-

---

[10] Blondin, "Assisting Canadians—Making History!"; "TF Libeccio Op Mobile Brief," October 29, 2011.

[11] Major Bernard Dionne, "1st Canadian Division HQ personnel return from Op Mobile," undated.

[12] TF Libeccio Post Op Brief, November 11 [2011], TF LIB CEFCOM and 1 CAD brief; "TF Libeccio Op Mobile Brief," October 29, 2011.

[13] Murray Brewster, "More Canadians Flee Libya as Dutch Commandos Captured," March 3, 2011, *Toronto Star*, March 3, 2011; interview with Peter MacKay by Beverly Thomson, March 2, 2011, *CTV News*, March 2, 2011.

[14] Blondin, "Assisting Canadians—Making History!"; Office of the Prime Minister of Canada, "Statement by the Prime Minister of Canada on Implementing Sanctions Against Libya;" February 27, 2011; "Minister MacKay Salutes Evacuation Operations in Malta," *National Defence and the Canadian Forces*, mobile verison, March 12, 2011.

Sergeant Stephen Miller returns passports to Canadian evacuees after they board a CC-130J Hercules aircraft at Tripoli International Airport, March 2, 2011.
Courtesy of the Canadian Department of National Defence, photo by Corporal Jax Kennedy. Used in accordance with Crown Copyright provisions.

cal and diplomatic response to the worsening situation in Libya, as well as a potential military intervention.[15]

The government took great pride in its reaction to the crisis. Its support for U.N. Security Council Resolution (UNSCR) 1970—which challenged Qaddafi's violence against his own people through an arms embargo, travel ban, asset freeze, and the establishment of new sanctions—was firm and unequivocal.[16] After suspending Canada's diplomatic presence in Libya and evacuating the ambassador and his staff on February 26, both the prime minister and the Foreign Affairs minister emphasized that the nation "supports the demands of the Libyan people for freedom, democracy, human rights and the rule of law."[17] In fact, the Conservative government went beyond UNSCR 1970 by imposing additional asset freezes as well as a prohibition on financial transactions with the Libyan government and its central bank. By doing so, the gov-

---

[15] Office of the Prime Minister of Canada, "Statement by the Prime Minister of Canada on the Current Situation in Libya," February 25, 2011

[16] U.N. Security Council, Resolution 1970, February 26, 2011.

[17] Foreign Affairs and International Trade Canada, "Statement by Minister Cannon on Situation in Libya," No. 85, February 26, 2011; "Statement by Minister Cannon on Situation in Libya," No. 86, February 26, 2011; Office of the Prime Minister of Canada, "Statement by the Prime Minister of Canada on Implementing Sanctions Against Libya."

ernment emphasized it was trying to further prevent the Qaddafi regime from gaining access to money that could be used to perpetrate additional acts of violence against its people.[18] It also was designed to show that Canada's support to the Libyan people was not mere rhetoric; the Harper government later observed that Canada was among the first nations to impose heavy sanctions on the Qaddafi regime.[19] The decision to deploy the frigate HMCS *Charlottetown* to the region on March 1 achieved a similar effect, as did a government pledge of $5 million in humanitarian aid to the Libyan people for medical care, food, and shelter. But exactly how Canada was going to help Libya achieve a free and more democratic society was less clear.[20]

Ready to Act, but Awaiting Consensus

Foreign Affairs Minister Cannon made initial comments that Qaddafi should be brought before the International Criminal Court to answer for his attacks on his own people, while Government House leader John Baird called for regime change in Libya. But those declarations soon were muted by the reality that the international community was far from united on what next to do.[21] While some nations, notably Great Britain and France, were hankering for a no-fly zone over Libya, others, such as the United States, were advising caution.[22] For Canada, this uncertainty meant the government had to mark time. Observing that the talk of a no-fly zone "had abated somewhat," Minister of National Defence Peter MacKay cautiously warned that, while all NATO nations were participating in discussions, no decision had been made.[23] The lack of consensus within NATO ensured that the Canadian government's messaging remained the same for the next two weeks, explaining why MacKay later told the press that "Canada is standing with our allies to monitor the current situation in North Africa and will keep working with our allies as the situation continues to develop."[24] Various members of the government already had hinted that Canada wanted to act

---

[18] Office of the Prime Minister of Canada, "Statement by the Prime Minister of Canada on Implementing Sanctions Against Libya."

[19] Allan Woods, "Gadhafi: All My People Love Me," *Toronto Star*, March 1, 2011.

[20] Campbell Clark and Steven Chase, "Canada Girds for Substantial Military Role in North Africa," *Globe and Mail*, March 1, 2011; House of Commons Debates, Hansard, 40th Parliament, 3rd Sess., No. 137, March 2, 2011; Office of the Prime Minister of Canada, "Statement by the Prime Minister of Canada on the Situation in Libya," March 18, 2011.

[21] Woods, "Gadhafi: All My People Love Me."

[22] Clark and Chase, "Canada Girds for Substantial Military Role"; "Obama Continues to Caution for Libya No-Fly Zone," *Ottawa Citizen*, March 12, 2011.

[23] "MND Peter Mackay Discusses Situation in Libya," interview by Evan Solomon, *CBC Power and Politics*, March 1, 2011.

[24] "Obama Continues to Caution for Libya No-Fly Zone."

more forcefully, but as a NATO partner, it was clear that Canadian intervention was tied to what the Alliance was willing to do.

Comments in the Canadian parliament indicated that the government was hoping the popular uprising in Libya would follow a path similar to those in Tunisia and Egypt, where the ruling elite eventually bowed to the popular will, negating the need for foreign intervention.[25] Other Alliance members undoubtedly felt the same way, but with the once-confident Libyan rebels on the run, and Qaddafi vowing to crush his opposition, it was obvious events were not transpiring in a similar manner. Worse yet, as the regime's forces closed to within 130 kilometers of the rebels' bastion in Benghazi, Qaddafi's promises of a bloodbath were backed with action. Faced with this unpleasant prospect, President Barack Obama's administration came out in support of a no-fly zone over Libya.[26] As a result, on March 17, UNSCR 1973—to protect civilians as well as impose a no-fly zone and strengthen the arms embargo on Libya— was passed with ten nations in favor and five abstentions.[27]

Speculation began about the type of military commitment that Canada would make to Libya. Some journalists wondered whether Canada could participate in a substantial combat role, given its heavy involvement in Afghanistan. Others expected a deployment that was similar to Kosovo, where, it was observed, the RCAF shouldered "a disproportionate share of the mission's burden . . . to help stop Serbian ethnic cleansing."[28] It did not take long before they had their answer. After announcing that CF-188 fighters and other RCAF assets would be joining the Royal Canadian Navy (RCN) frigate that was already on-station off the coast of Libya, Prime Minister Harper then framed the reasons for Canadian intervention in Libya. After explaining that the situation "remains intolerable," he said urgent action was required to support the U.N. resolution because "the Libyan people have shown by their sacrifices that they believe in [democracy]. Assisting them is a moral obligation upon those of us who profess this great ideal . . . One either believes in freedom or one just says one believes in freedom."[29] In addition to the moral imperative to act, the Prime Minister also framed Canada's decision to intervene on the grounds of it being an active member of both the U.N. and NATO. As an international steward and Alliance partner, Canada had

---

[25] House of Commons Debates, Hansard, March 21, 2011.

[26] "UN OKs Action Against Ghadhafi," *Waterloo Region Record*, March 18, 2011; "US Changes Diplomatic Tune," *Vancouver Sun*, March 17, 2011.

[27] UN Security Council Resolution 1973 (2011), March 17, 2011. The five abstentions were Brazil, China, Germany, India, and the Russian Federation.

[28] "The West Takes a Stand," *Ottawa Citizen*, March 18, 2011; "Canada May Take on Large Share of Libya Mission," *The National Post*, March 21, 2011.

[29] "Libya: Canada to Send Fighter Jets for No-Fly Zone," March 18, 2011, *BBC News*; Office of the Prime Minister of Canada, "Statement by the Prime Minister of Canada on the Situation in Libya," March 18, 2011.

not only worked hard to gain support for UNSCR 1973, but also had engaged "like-minded states to ensure that it could be enforced."[30]

Defence Minister MacKay was even more direct. Rising in the Canadian parliament on March 21 to explain the government's position on Libya, MacKay announced that Canada was in a strong position to play an active role in protecting the lives of Libyan civilians and enforcing both the Security Council's mandated no-fly zone and the arms embargo. He reminded his fellow parliamentarians that the deployment of the RCAF to this particular mission was not without precedent. In 1999, Canada's CF-188s were involved in the NATO mission in Kosovo (Operation Allied Force), where they flew 678 sorties and logged more than 2,600 flying hours from March to June while carrying out 10 percent of NATO's strike missions. As in that situation, MacKay reiterated, the Prime Minister's message that Canada was "compelled to intervene, both in a moral duty and by duty of NATO and the United Nations, which, as members would know, are institutions that we helped found. In this situation, deploying the Canadian Forces is the right thing to do, and I expect that Canadians and members of the House clearly recognize that fact."[31]

In reality, the outcome of the vote in the House of Commons was never in doubt. Having used the weekend to work the phones with the leaders of the opposition parties, Harper's actions meant Parliament's support for Canadian intervention was unanimous. As a result, all parties agreed with a mission that one opposition member described as "a perfectly legitimate operation since it is being carried out as a multilateral effort and its purpose is to protect civilian populations." Concerns remained, however. During the debate on the motion, the opposition asked some tough questions, such as how long the mission would last and whether the government had an exit strategy in case it dragged on. Some wondered if any metrics existed to determine when the mission could be considered a success, while yet others feared that the government was rushing into a war without knowing if its true purpose was to protect civilians or create the conditions for regime change in Libya. Fears that a commitment to Libya eventually would lead to the employment of Canadian ground troops caused further anxiety to some opposition members, who, in looking at Canada's ten-year involvement in Afghanistan with a bit of trepidation, worried that their country might be entangled in a prolonged engagement. Although Canada was making an important contribution to the war in Afghanistan, the length of that commitment led to some heated and bitter debates in the House of Commons. As a result, the opposition insisted that Parliament maintain a strong oversight role on Canada's intervention in Libya as well as calling

---

30 Office of the Prime Minister of Canada, "Statement by the Prime Minister of Canada at an Emergency Meeting on Libya," March 19, 2011.

31 House of Commons Debates, Hansard, March 21, 2011.

for an approach that was both military and diplomatic in nature.[32] Harper agreed with many of these points. Although he was in a minority government situation—meaning that the Conservatives' motions easily could be defeated through the cooperation of all opposition parties—the prime minister long had argued that any Canadian military intervention should be brought before Parliament for its blessing. He was further willing to put a three-month limit on the mission, at which time Parliament would have to approve any extension.

An Opportunity to Lead

There were, of course, other reasons for the government's decision to intervene. Ever since his Conservative government was first elected in 2006, Harper set upon an active foreign policy that one pundit described as "muscular pragmatism."[33] Replacing the Liberal Party's "Pearsonian" diplomacy, which depicted Canada as an "honest broker" that relied on soft power to help defuse international situations and conflicts, Harper's foreign policy took more definitive positions. For instance, while the previous Liberal governments had taken a neutral approach to the question of Palestinian statehood, the Conservatives left no doubt they were willing to support Israel. Critics have observed that this new approach cost Canada. Some cited Portugal's selection over Canada to obtain a seat on the U.N. Security Council in October 2010—upsetting Canada's record of winning a seat on the Council at least once per decade since 1945—as evidence that Canada had lost influence on the international scene.[34]

For proponents, however, the mission in Libya, in conjunction with its role in Afghanistan, offered another chance to show how Canada was "a potent force for good." According to this view, Canada's quick reaction and willingness to provide military and diplomatic support not only added credibility to "the mission but to Canada itself." With tongue in cheek, it was further observed that, despite gaining the Security Council seat, Portugal was not sending any forces to enforce the no-fly zone. That led to claims that Canada's actions were speaking louder than words.[35] In many ways,

---

[32] Murray Brewster, "Canadian CF 18s Enforce No-Fly Zone," *The Chronicle Herald*, March 22, 2011; House of Commons Debates, Hansard, March 21, 2011; "CF 18 Head into No-Fly Zone," *Red Deer Advocate*, March 22, 2011; John Ibbitson, "Crisis in Libya," *The Globe and Mail*, March 22, 2011.

[33] "National Post Editorial Board: A Better, Prouder Canadian Foreign Policy," *The National Post*, January 1, 2012.

[34] "Canada's Actions Speak Volumes; Role in Libya Gives Heft to United Nations' Words," *Calgary Herald*, editorial page, March 24, 2011.

[35] "Canada's Actions Speak Volumes."

therefore, the Canadian decision to get involved in Libya served as a test of the government's larger foreign policy objectives.[36]

The Libyan mission also tested another Canadian-inspired U.N. concept, "the responsibility to protect" (R2P). Born from the international community's inability to stop the slaughter of hundreds of thousands of Tutsis during the 1994 Rwandan genocide, as well as its late and somewhat limited success in Kosovo five years later, the R2P doctrine is based on a set of principles designed to protect civilian populations from acts of genocide, war crimes, ethnic cleansing, and crimes against humanity.[37] Simply put, this doctrine, which the U.N. unanimously adopted in 2005, claims that sovereignty is a responsibility and not a right, meaning that the international community has a "moral obligation" to intervene when nations turn their guns on their fellow citizens. Although many Canadian commentators argued that Qaddafi's actions against his people fit the doctrine perfectly, others found it odd that Western nations were paying so little attention to the R2P doctrine when framing their intervention in Libya. Stranger still was the fact that even the Canadian government was not using the doctrine to explain the role it was planning to play, particularly since the Libyan mission appeared as an ideal situation that finally could give the doctrine some teeth.[38]

Explaining why the government did not place much emphasis on R2P is not easy. After all, Canada played a key role in the doctrine's creation and as one newspaper noted, "It is only about stopping the strong from slaughtering the weak. What could be more Canadian?"[39] Politics was one possible reason. Through a vote of no confidence, the opposition parties defeated the government over a domestic issue, resulting in an election campaign that began on March 26. Yet neither the government nor the opposition made R2P (or even the mission in Libya) a campaign issue. In all likelihood, the opposition avoided the topic because it portrayed the prime minister as a statesman who was taking a leading role along other NATO allies. As international affairs expert Aurel Braun observed, "It is difficult to attack the prime minister on something most Canadians support . . . there is a wide consensus across the political spectrum that Canada is doing something just."[40] As for the government, it appears there was no desire to use the mission to score political points.[41] No matter the reason, however,

[36] For an appreciation of Canada's current foreign policy, see Paul Heinbecker, *Getting Back in the Game: A Foreign Policy Playbook for Canada*, Toronto: Dundurn Press, 2011.

[37] Lloyd Axworthy and Allan Rock, "World Leaders Must Call R2P What It Is," *Ottawa Citizen*, March 2, 2011.

[38] For the best account of the U.N.'s failure in Rwanda, see Roméo Dallaire, *Shake Hands with the Devil: The Failure of Humanity in Rwanda*, Toronto: Random House Canada, 2003.

[39] Dan Gardner, "Why No One's Talking About Libya on the Campaign Trail," *Ottawa Citizen*, April 1, 2011.

[40] "The Look Ahead: March 21–25, Election: Can PM Cast off the Grime, Regain Moment," *Globe and Mail*, March 21, 2011.

[41] Interview with Peter MacKay by Craig Oliver, *CTV Question Period*, March 20, 2011; Stephen Bede Scharper, "Libyan Intervention: A Just War or Just a War," *Toronto Star*, March 28, 2011; Campbell Clark, "Crisis in Libya:

Canada's involvement in both the development of the R2P doctrine and the intervention in Libya essentially was portrayed the same way. The intervention was framed on Canada's belief in a "moral imperative" to protect civilians as well as its desire to play a key role as a global steward through the U.N. and a reliable and active member of the NATO alliance.[42]

Adaptability and Impact

The RCAF responded rapidly to the government's order to deploy. Less than a day after the passage of UNSCR 1973, seven CF-188 fighters and two CC-150T tanker aircraft were on their way to join Operation Odyssey Dawn (the name given to the U.S.-led coalition to enforce the no-fly zone and arms embargo).[43] They arrived in Italy on March 19 and were in combat a little less than 48 hours later. Conseqently, the Defence Minister was able to tell the House of Commons: "We are fortunate to have an air force with capabilities . . . that takes mere hours to deploy six [sic] highly-sophisticated fighter aircraft and necessary support to depart for a theatre of operations nearly 7,000 kilometres away."[44] The RCAF had demonstrated its agility and readiness, but preparing for the mission was not easy, since prior to March 17 no one had been certain exactly what, if any, military action would be taken in Libya.

The RCAF had done what it could in the meantime. With the situation in Libya obviously spiraling out of control, a staff check was conducted to assess readiness and determine what types of roles and aircraft the RCAF could send to Libya if called upon by the government to do so. The fact that the RCAF was about to deploy a combat-ready contingent of CF-188s (along with 140 support personnel) as part of Canada's commitment to NATO's Icelandic air policing program offered a unique opportunity. Although the battle order would require some modification from air policing to combat operations, Operation Ignition (the code name for the Iceland deployment) meant that the RCAF had a contingent of CF-188s that already was prepared at the NATO quick-reaction alert standard. This, it has been estimated, allowed the RCAF to respond 24 to 48 hours faster than it otherwise would have. Moreover, in a further display of its agility and readiness, the RCAF was able to send CF-188s to both com-

---

Foreign Policy Little Talk on the Hustings of Canada's Role," *Globe and Mail*, March 31, 2011; Gardner, "Why No One's Talking About Libya on the Campaign Trail."

[42] Tony Gentile, "Canada's Role? Opportunity to Lead Regime Change," *London Free Press*, March 26, 2011.

[43] "TF Libeccio Op Mobile Brief," October 29, 2011.

[44] House of Commons Debates, Hansard, March 21, 2011; "Statement by Minister MacKay on the Deployment of CF-18s to Enforce No-Fly Zone over Libya," March 18, 2011.

Task Force Libeccio Avionics Technician Corporal Desire McCormick salutes a CF-188 Hornet pilot before he departs for Canada from Trapani, Italy, on November 2, 2011, at the conclusion of Operation Mobile.
Courtesy of the Canadian Department of National Defence. Used in accordance with Crown Copyright provisions.

mitments, as the aircraft redeployed to Mobile were replaced by others that arrived in Iceland later in the month.[45]

Six CF-188s (plus one spare) is the RCAF standard deployment package, as it permits a four-aircraft sortie (or a minimum of four sorties per day) mission set, while the "spare" serves as a backup that covers the detachment's maintenance requirements and improves its serviceability rate. On the other hand, the RCAF originally sent both of its Airbus CC-150 Polaris refueling aircraft because it allowed all seven CF-188s to cross the Atlantic at the same time, meaning that the entire detachment reached the theater of operations quicker and as a composite unit. It is interesting to note that the original intent was to return one CC-150 to Canada after the initial deployment. However, that plan was quickly altered once it was realized that the mission faced a shortage of tankers. The fact that aerial refueling would prove one of the most sought-after commodities of the campaign also explains why the RCAF deployed two CC-130T Hercules tankers to replace one of the CC-150s that had returned to Canada for scheduled maintenance in May.

Arriving in Sicily on March 25—their warning order to move being issued on March 18 and their first mission being flown ten days later—the two deployed CP-140

---

[45] RCAF officer email to the author, June 28, 2012; "Operation Ignition," *Crew Brief*, Vol. 9, No. 1, pp. 8–9; news conference transcript with Peter MacKay and Assistant Chief of the Air Staff Major General Tom Larson, Ottawa, March 21, 2011.

Auroras also were much in demand due to their modernized sensors suite, making them another invaluable asset. However, while the Alliance faced a shortage of ISR and MPA throughout the mission, the RCAF would not have found it easy to send more due to the ongoing concurrent modernization of the aircraft, which already was stretching the fleet's operational capacity. As a result, it was determined that two aircraft would give the CP-140s a 100 percent availability rate without pushing this capability beyond its limits.[46]

Aircraft were not the only RCAF assets deployed. On the same day that the CF-188s and CC-150s were landing in Sicily, the leading element of Task Force Libeccio's headquarters arrived at Ramstein Air Base, Germany, to start the process of coordinating the RCAF's involvement in Operation Odyssey Dawn. Named after the strong southwesterly wind that blows all year in the Mediterranean, Task Force Libeccio (TFL), which initially comprised the CF-188 and CC-150 detachment at Trapani and the CP-140 detachment at Sigonella, was one of three original Canadian task forces assigned to the mission. TFL, for instance, was the national command and support element that led, directed, and managed the RCAF's assets. It also was home to the commander of TFL and Air Component Commander Colonel Alain Pelletier, who exercised operational control over all Canadian air assets and was entrusted with ensuring they acted in accordance with national objectives and goals. Task Force Charlottetown (TF CHA), on the other hand, consisted of the frigate HMCS *Charlottetown*, as well as an RCAF CH-124 Sea King helicopter that was embarked onboard. Its primary function was to enforce the arms embargo on Libya, which it had been doing since it was officially "CHOPed" to CEFCOM and Standing NATO Maritime Group 1 on March 14.[47] The final unit was Task Forces Naples (TFN). Having emerged while JTF Malta was wrapping up, TFN originally consisted of the liaison and reconnaissance team that deployed to NATO Joint Forces Command HQ. As the Minister of National Defence announced on March 22, TFN also performed the function of a National Coordination Centre and Support Contingent (NCCSC), and as such was responsible for all support and administrative issues related to the mission.[48]

While the RCAF was quick to get into the air on operations, it did take time to settle into its new homes in Italy. Much of this delay was the product of deploying so quickly. This meant that the Mission Support Flight, an expeditionary unit designed to provide air operations and bases with essential infrastructure and services, could

---

[46] RCAF officer email to the author, June 28, 2012.

[47] Email from HMCS *Charlottetown* officer to author, July 5, 2011, email; "Operation Mobile," *Crew Brief*, Vol. 9, No.1, pp. 8–9; National Defence and the Canadian Forces, "Operation MOBILE: National Defence and Canadian Forces Response to the Situation in Libya," online, undated.

[48] *End of Tour Report*, Annex A, November 7, 2011, 1630-1 (Comd TF LIB); TF Libeccio Post Op Brief, Nov 11 [2011], TF LIB CEFCOM and 1 CAD brief. For updates on CF Operations in Libya, see National Defence and the Canadian Forces, "Operation MOBILE: National Defence and Canadian Forces Response to the Situation in Libya," online, undated.

not arrive in theater until days after air operations had already commenced—a price of achieving rapid tactical and operational effect with very little warning time. It also faced a daunting challenge because much of the infrastructure to support wartime operations was not present at most locations.[49] Over time, both the Mobile Strikers Force (MSF) and engineers built up the Canadian footprint at these locations, and the RCAF was quite fortunate to get the bases it did. Despite restricted ramp space, which resulted in the need to locate the CP-140s at Sigonella, the base at Trapani was one of the closest to Libya, which cut down considerably on flight times. Although the RCAF would have preferred to have all its air assets at one location for command and logistical reasons, Sigonella also was close to the action and had the benefit of being familiar to CP-140 personnel (who had previous experience operating from this long-range patrol base).[50]

Issues at the bases did not appear to have any significant effect on RCAF operations during the ten days in which they served under *Odyssey Dawn*. It was a busy period. The distance they had to travel from Canada to Italy meant the RCAF was not part of the initial assault on Libya. Under the command of U.S. Africa Command, American and British forces pounded air defense, communication, and command locations with approximately 110 Tomahawk cruise missiles. This paved the way for coalition aircraft, which turned their attention to cutting off the regime forces' logistical support. They also stopped the regime's assault on Benghazi with French aircraft leading the way, and stalled the advances on Ajdabiya and Misrata.[51] The RCAF first joined these efforts on March 21, when four CF-188s, refueled by the two CC-150s, conducted escort and air interdiction patrols off Libya's coastline. It was an important moment for the Canadian government, as Defence Minister MacKay saw tremendous significance in an inaugural mission that "demonstrates our government's intent and Canada's ability and willingness to play an active role in Libya."[52] The RCAF's second mission was equally symbolic. Canadian officials were determined to maintain a policy of zero civilian casualties, and a decision by the CF-188 pilots not to release their weap-

---

[49] Captain Jill Strelieff, "17 Mission Support Flight Rolls into Mobile," Royal Canadian Air Force, October 27, 2011; Alain Pelletier, "Canadian Forces: Op Mobile Lessons Observed, Brief," TFL Lessons Learned Symposium, June 6, 2012, Winnipeg, Manitoba.

[50] Notes from author meeting with TF LIB personnel, Naples, Italy, November 2, 2011; Alain Pelletier, "Canada Forces: Op Mobile Lessons Observed," TFL Lessons Learned Symposium, June 6, 2012, Winnipeg, Manitoba; "Operation Mobile," *Crew Brief*, Vol. 9, No. 1, pp. 8–9; RCAF officer email to author, June 11, 2012.

[51] "TF Libeccio Op Mobile Brief," October 29, 2011; "Gaddafi Vows Long War," *National Post*, March 21, 2011; "Missiles Rain on Gadhafi," *Edmonton Journal*, March 21, 2011; "Western Military Action over Libya," *London Free Press*, March 23, 2011.

[52] News conference transcript with Peter MacKay and Assistant Chief of the Air Staff Major General Tom Larson, Ottawa, March 21, 2011.

ons on a targeted Libyan airfield because of fears of collateral damage immediately underscored that the RCAF was taking this responsibility quite seriously.[53]

The RCAF was next in action over Misrata, where CF-188s destroyed an ammunition depot with four laser-guided bombs as part of the coalition's attempt to push regime forces' back from that besieged city.[54] CF-188 targets and operations over the rest of the week ranged from air interdiction patrols over Libya to attacks on other ammunition dumps, reinforced bunkers, and reportedly an electronic-warfare site. The RCAF's contribution to Odyssey Dawn also was spread over a wide expanse of the country, covering an area from just outside of Tripoli to Brega and as far south as the Jufrah Airfield. From the available evidence, it appears the RCAF's greatest concentration of strikes was in the Misrata region, as the area between this city and the strategic crossroads at Ajdabiya reported some of the regime forces' worst cases of violence in Libya.[55] The CC-150s, which operated over the Mediterranean, also were extremely active during their involvement with Odyssey Dawn as they refueled RCAF and coalition aircraft alike. Having accomplished the type's first transoceanic refueling mission to get the CF-188 into theater, the CC-150s quickly were certified on a variety of different receiver aircraft from various nations, and from then onward, they were one of the preferred refueling platforms within the coalition.[56] The CP-140s, on the other hand, only had the chance to fly 20 hours during Odyssey Dawn in which they performed maritime reconnaissance and limited psychological warfare ops (using radio transmissions) as well as ISR flights before the mission was turned over to NATO.[57]

Although it took some time for NATO to sort out a suitable C2 arrangement, the transition from the U.S.-led Operation Odyssey Dawn to Unified Protector on March 31 did not significantly impact the RCAF. Perhaps the most notable change was the relocation of the TFL HQ. Having already moved once from the U.S. CAOC to the NATO HQ building in Ramstein on April 1—which was done to allow better communications with CEFCOM and the air detachments at Trapani and Sigonella—the

[53] Eric Reguly, "Crisis in Libya: Inside the Cockpit of a CF-18," *Globe and Mail*, April 4, 2011; "Canadian Pilots Abort Bombing over Risk to Civilians," *CTV News*, March 22, 2011.

[54] "Gadhafi's Guns Silenced," *The Star Phoenix*, March 24, 2011; "Canadian Jets Destroy Libyan Arms Depot," *Ottawa Citizen*, March 24, 2011; "NATO Pushes Gadhafi Forces," *Waterloo Region Record*, March 24, 2011.

[55] Rear Admiral Russ Harding, "NATO Determined to Protect the People of Libya," text of speech delivered at press conference in Naples, April 6, 2011; "Gadhafi's Guns Silenced"; "Canadian Jets Destroy Libyan Arms Depot"; "NATO Pushes Gadhafi Forces"; "Canadian Jets Bomb Second Libyan Ammo Dump," *The Whitehorse Star*, March 29, 2011; National Defence and the Canadian Forces, "Operation MOBILE: National Defence and Canadian Forces Response to the Situation in Libya," online, undated.

[56] National Defence and the Canadian Forces, "Operation MOBILE: National Defence and Canadian Forces Response to the Situation in Libya," online, undated; *End of Tour Report*, November 7, 2011, 1630-1 (Comd TF LIB).

[57] "Libyan Rebels Retreat to Brega," CBC News, March 30, 2011; *End of Tour Report*, Annex A, November 7, 2011, 1630-1 (Comd TF LIB).

TFL HQ again was uprooted to Poggio Renatico six days later.[58] This move made perfect sense, as NATO's CAOC 5—the Alliance's C2 center responsible for planning, directing, and coordinating all air activities over Libya—was a key operational nerve center. In the end, the Canadian Air Component HQ's quick deployment and attainment of full operational capability as well as its integration into the NATO CAOC went extremely well—so well, in fact, that one senior Canadian officer observed that it "demonstrated the ability of the RCAF to quickly and seamlessly integrate into a multi-national coalition command structure, enabling near immediate employment of RCAF aircraft in the conduct and support of combat operations."[59]

The transition from Odyssey Dawn was even more significant for Canada because a Canadian commanded Unified Protector. Lieutenant-General Charles Bouchard was considered a good choice to head the NATO mission; Canada's Minister of National Defence described him as a "formidable leader, with tremendous character and ability."[60] Having served as the deputy commander of Allied Joint Force Command in Naples since 2009, Bouchard was familiar with the area and had much experience in NATO and coalition environments. As a result, the transition from U.S. Admiral Samuel J. Locklear (who was the commander, Allied Joint Force Command Naples, and responsible for Odyssey Dawn) to Lieutenant-General Bouchard represented a natural progression. Moreover, Lieutenant-General Bouchard immediately put his NATO experience to good use. When summoned to Admiral Locklear's command ship (the USS *Mount Whitney*) and effectively given seven days to establish a Combined Joint Task Force HQ within the constraints of JFC Naples, Bouchard was able to quickly pick much of OUP's leadership team from the officers who had previously helped him prepare the NATO Reaction Force.[61]

Perhaps the greatest challenge Lieutenant-General Bouchard and the forces under his command faced during Unified Protector was operating in a highly dynamic environment where it often was difficult to identify belligerents.[62] Yet thanks to extensive upgrades in 2005, as well as the addition of the Sniper Advanced Targeting Pod (ATP) and laser designators, the RCAF's CF-188s were in a good position to play an important role in fulfilling the Canadian Forces' mandate to "integrate into the NATO C2 structure under NATO OUP to enforce UNSCRs 1970 and 1973 . . . and protect

---

[58] RCAF officer email to author, June 11, 2012.

[59] *End of Tour Report*, November 7, 2011, 1630-1 (Comd TF LIB). On April 12, the Canadian flag was raised in Poggio Renatico, and it officially became home to the Air Component Commander and TFL Command.

[60] "Canadian to Lead NATO's Libya Mission," *CBC News*, March 25, 2011.

[61] Telephone conversation with RCAF officer, July 4, 2012 and follow-up correspondence, November 12, 2013.

[62] Dean Black, "Lieutenant General Charles Bouchard, Three Tenets of Allied Air Power Operations," *Air Force Magazine*, Vol. 35, No. 4, 2012, p. 23.

CP-140 Aurora returning from Operation Mobile, arriving at Greenwood, Nova Scotia, November 5, 2011.
Courtesy of the Canadian Department of National Defence, photo by Corporal Laura Brophy. Used in accordance with Crown Copyright provisions.

civilian populated areas in Libya."[63] The CF-188 contribution to this mandate would consist of a mixture of dynamic and deliberate targeting as well as defensive counter-air operations. Also known as Strike Coordination and Reconnaissance (SCAR) and consisting of searches for targets of opportunity, most of the RCAF's strike sorties (680 out of 944) during Op Mobile were dynamic in nature. Air Interdiction, or deliberate targeting, accounted for 212 sorties, while DCA was performed on four other occasions. The remaining 48 sorties were classified as deliberate-dynamic targeting (DDT); a relatively new concept developed during Mobile in which pilots were prepared for a specific mission but could be retasked while airborne.[64]

Having flown combat missions every day for the first 40 days of the mission, the CF-188s were most active in the Misrata, Ajdabiya, Brega, Zintan, Tripoli, and Waddan areas throughout April and May.[65] While the majority of targets were dynamic and consisted of main battle tanks and other vehicles, the RCAF did conduct a number of deliberate sorties on ammunition, vehicle, and communication facilities as well as bunkers. Much of this effort was directed at disrupting the regime forces' lines of communication and supply, particularly around Misrata, whose civilian population was

[63] *End of Tour Report*, November 7, 2011, 1630-1 (Comd TF LIB); Colonel Eric Kenny, Op Mobile/ TF Libeccio Lessons Learned Symposium Brief, June 6, 2012, Winnipeg, Manitoba.

[64] Colonel Eric Kenny, "Op Mobile/ TF Libeccio Lessons Learned Symposium Brief," June 6, 2012, Winnipeg, Manitoba.

[65] Colonel Alain Pelletier, Task Force Libeccio—TF Lessons Learned on C2 and Intel Supt Commander TFL Brief to 1 Cdn Air Div.

under heavy barrage.[66] Zintan, in western Libya, also was a source of concern, since it was the focus of a large regime assault. Although the RCAF would continue to assist with curtailing the regime forces' attacks on Misrata, as well as hitting some targets around Brega, many of the CF-188s' missions in June were flown in support of NATO operations in the Tripoli area, with successful strikes reported on various command and vehicle facilities as well as barracks and logistical nodes.[67] The operational tempo for the CF-188s continued to increase over the summer months. Peaking in July, the RCAF's seven CF-188s were flying an average of six sorties per day, although surges to eight sorties also occurred. This tempo later was reduced to an average of four per day to keep within the allocated flying rate for the operation.[68]

This active pace continued into August and did not begin to abate until mid-September, when regime forces had been confined to area between Sirte, Bani Walid, and Sebha. It was at this time that the RCAF flew its deepest strike into Libya. On September 11, the RCAF became one of the first OUP air forces to operate below the personnel recovery line when its CF-188s participated in a mission that was reported to be in the Sebha area.[69] Some accounts even suggest that no other aircraft ever flew as far south as the RCAF did on that day, but the true measure of the CF-188s' overall proficiency during this period was recognized by the fact that they often served as mission commanders for a number of multination strike packages. More importantly, however, serving in this role demonstrated their interoperability as the CF-188s easily integrated into coalition and alliance operations.[70] Individual pilots also were making major achievements; among them was Major James "Buca" Kettles, who flew his 50th combat mission on October 2, 2011 to become the first RCAF pilot to do so since the Korean War.[71]

Early October brought an important new capability to the CF-188s, which added to the RCAF's flexibility and versatility as a whole. In many instances poor weather, in combination with the mission's extremely strict rules against collateral damage, had limited the use of the RCAF's GBU-10 and GBU-12 laser-guided bombs. By using GPS guidance systems, GBU-31 and GBU-38 Joint Direct Attack Munitions (JDAMs) could be dropped under all conditions, and Canada began making inquiries about acquiring these weapons from American sources as early as April 2011. With help from the USAF, USN, and Boeing, Canadian officials managed to streamline a complicated

---

[66] TF Libeccio Post Op Brief, Nov 11 [2011], file TF LIB CEFCOM and 1 CAD brief.

[67] "Gaddafi Defiant as NATO Intensifies Tripoli Strikes," *Reuters*, June 7, 2011.

[68] RCAF officer email to author, July 17, 2012.

[69] TF Libeccio Post Op Brief, Nov 11 [2011], TF LIB CEFCOM and 1 CAD brief. Locations south of the personnel recovery line were out of range of CSAR helicopters operating from vessels in the Mediterranean.

[70] TF Libeccio Post Op Brief, Nov 11 [2011], TF LIB CEFCOM and 1 CAD brief.

[71] TF Libeccio Post Op Brief, Nov 11 [2011], TF LIB CEFCOM and 1 CAD brief.

and normally lengthy procurement and testing process, enabling the RCAF to receive its first JDAMs within four months. The result was that CF-188s were able to successfully deploy two GBU-31 and two GBU-38 JDAMs against the Bani Walid ammo storage area on October 1.[72] Brigadier General Derek Joyce, who directly commanded the RCAF's efforts in Op Mobile at this time, described that attack as an "unmitigated success." Joyce later recalled how the introduction of JDAMs "showcased the CF's capacity to respond rapidly to operational requirements in time of war."[73] Indeed, Canadian JDAMs were employed to great effect throughout the last weeks of the mission, considerably increasing the RCAF's future flexibility. Op Mobile also allowed the CF-188 community to combat-test other capabilities. Thanks to the earlier acquisition of the Sniper Advanced Targeting Pod and laser designator, the RCAF's CF-188s were able to drop GBU-10 2,000-lb bombs for the first time in this operation on May 7 while leading a 16-aircraft strike on a vehicle storage facility.[74]

Air Refueling and Long-Range Patrol

The CF-188s and their pilots certainly did their part throughout Mobile, as they were responsible for more than 10 percent of NATO's strike missions.[75] None of these achievements for the CF-188 community would have been possible without the CC-150Ts and CC-130Ts as well as other allied refueling aircraft. The CC-150s and CC-130Ts were the true enablers, as NATO strike aircraft required refueling at least once per mission. Of the two, the CC-150s were far better suited for this role. Not only did they provide a greater degree of flexibility, but they also possessed higher speeds and greater fuel capacity as well as an ability to remain on station longer than the CC-130Ts. Indeed, the CC-130s often were pushed to their limits.[76] Yet their deployment into theater nevertheless demonstrated their agility, as these aircraft were originally intended to provide a domestic air-to-air refueling capability. As a result, they were a welcome addition and filled a key gap during the period when one CC-150 under-

---

[72] TF Libeccio CF-188 JDAM Employment Brief, November 1, 2011; "TF Libeccio Op Mobile Brief," October 29, 2011.

[73] *End of Tour Report*, November 7, 2011, 1630-1 (Comd TF Lib); *JDAM End of Tour Report*, Annex A, November 2011, 1630-1 (Comd TF LIB).

[74] *End of Tour Report*, Annex A, November 2011, 1630-1 (Comd TF LIB); *End of Tour Report*, November 7, 2011, 1630-1 (Comd TF Lib); "TF Libeccio Op Mobile Brief," October 29, 2011.

[75] Colonel Alain Pelletier, Task Force Libeccio—TF Lessons Learned on C2 and Intel Supt Commander TFL Brief; Colonel Eric Kenny, Op Mobile/ Task Force Libeccio Lessons Learned Symposium, Winnipeg, Manitoba, June 6, 2012.

[76] Paul Koring, "Canada's Hercs Star in Dangerous Ballet of Mid-Air Refuelling," *The Globe and Mail*, June 14, 2011. It was reported the CC-130s had to throttle close to full power (and reportedly go into a shallow dive) to make refueling easier, while the strike aircraft had to fly much slower than normal.

went required maintenance by offloading close to four million pounds of fuel between May 23 and September 12. The CC-150s, on the other hand, were responsible for the delivery of 14 million pounds of fuel during the conflict. This feat was all the more significant given that this was a relatively new role for an aircraft that only had recently acquired an AAR capability. These types of results were the product of an extremely hectic operational tempo in which the RCAF's CC-150s and -130s were sometimes flying two missions per day and responsible for 4.1 percent of all NATO refueling sorties.[77] Their serviceability rate, which stood at 96 percent, was impressive, as was their ability to refuel almost every type of allied aircraft (including some unique experiences, such as when a CC-150 topped up a Swedish Air Force JAS 39 Gripen for the first time on May 18).[78] They also achieved some key operational distinctions, most notably the authorization in September to fly overland in support of the CF-188's deep strikes, as well as providing fuel to the French aircraft that stopped Qaddafi's convoy while it was fleeing Sirte in October.[79]

The RCAF's two CP-140s were similarly active. Providing a strategic picture of both the ground war and the situation at sea, the CP-140 detachment flew almost every day and ended the mission with a 99 percent serviceability rate, logging 179 missions and 1,403.1 hours in the air. Most of that time was divided between ISR and MPA missions, but the CP-140s displayed their versatility by performing psychological-warfare operations with radio broadcasts over Libya as well as forward control for NATO attack helicopters and naval gun support to British and French warships.[80] These latter roles were new to a platform that was designed to hunt Soviet submarines during the Cold War, and conducting these operations drew the CP-140s progressively closer to shore. Originally authorized to operate at least 21 miles from Libya's coast, the CP-140s were cleared to close to within four miles on September 18, followed by their first "dry" (over land) mission four days later.[81]

Yet it was the adoption of a SCAR capability that brought the CP-140s their greatest acclaim. Although SCAR remained a CF-188 mission set, the CP-140s were tasked in the SCAR coordinator (SCAR-C) role. The CP-140 would carry a Fire Support Team (FST) or Forward Air Controller (FAC) (also known as Joint Terminal Attack Controller [JTAC]), which, after using the aircraft's powerful package of sensors and cameras to locate targets, then would coordinate with the CAOC and direct

---

[77] "TF Libeccio Op Mobile Brief," October 29, 2011.

[78] Colonel Alain Pelletier, Task Force Libeccio—TF Lessons Learned on C2 and Intel Supt Commander TFL Brief to 1 Cdn Air Div.

[79] "TF Libeccio Op Mobile Brief," October 29, 2011.

[80] "Canada Joins Propaganda War Aimed at Gadhafi Forces," *CTV News*, July 29, 2011; Tim Ripley, "US and Canadian Orions Direct UK Naval Gunfire off Libya," *Jane's Defence Weekly*; email from HMCS *Charlottetown* officer to author, July 5, 2011.

[81] "TF Libeccio Op Mobile Brief," October 29, 2011.

Crew members of U.S. fleet replenishment oiler USNS *Big Horn* secure palettes of cargo to HMCS *Vancouver's* CH-124 Sea King helicopter in a vertical replenishment during Operation Unified Protector, October 13, 2011.
Courtesy of the Canadian Department of National Defence, photo by Corporal Brandon O'Connell. Used in accordance with Crown Copyright provisions.

suitable strike aircraft to the area in question.[82] Having an airborne JTAC capability also was new to the RCAF. As a result, FST personnel from the UK carried out FAC duties during the CP-140's first SCAR-C mission on October 1. However, the RCAF quickly deployed its own JTAC team to Sigonella, which, having a British Fire Support Team's certification, produced the first all-Canadian CP-140 SCAR-C mission on October 17.[83] In total, the Auroras would fly 12 SCAR-C missions, three of which were flown by all-Canadian crews. Not only was this enough to "properly map out and codify" this new capability, according to a post-operation report, it showed how the CP-140 was "extremely capable in this role" and was a preferred platform by many FSTs "because of its enhanced capabilities and mission suite."[84] Indeed, the CP-140s proved so agile and flexible that one source characterized them as Mobile's "Cinderella stars of the show."[85]

The RCAF had developed a number of new capabilities during Mobile, and on October 5, most of them were brought together over Bani Walid in a display of air-to-

---

[82] "TF Libeccio Op Mobile Brief," October 29, 2011.

[83] *End of Tour Report*, November 7, 2011, 1630-1 (Comd TF LIB).

[84] *End of Tour Report*, November 7, 2011, 1630-1 (Comd TF LIB); *End of Tour Report*, Annex A, November 2011, 1630-1 (Comd TF LIB).

[85] Peter Pigott, "Answering the Call," *Frontline Defence*, Issue 6, 2011, p. 30; Colonel Alain Pelletier, Task Force Libeccio—TF Lessons Learned on C2 and Intel Supt Commander TFL Brief to 1 Cdn Air Div.

air integration that one subsequent analysis described as a "great day for the RCAF."[86] It was at that time that the CP-140 detachment, flying back-to-back sorties, managed to support NATO aircraft prosecuting seven targets over the course of three separate missions. The key from a Canadian perspective, however, was the CP-140s' ability to provide prestrike, full-motion video coverage and post-strike battle assessment of the four targets that were hit by the six CF-188s using their new JDAM capability. Moreover, a CC-150T handled the CF-188s' refueling prior to the strike. It was a defining moment during the mission; the Combined Joint Task Force Unified Protector (CJTFUP) Combined Force Air Component Commander, at his morning brief on October 6, commented on "the outstanding contribution of Canada's efforts the previous day."[87]

Although the CF-188s, CC-150s, CC-130s, and CP-140s collectively represented the RCAF's main contribution to Mobile, a word must be said about its other important operational commitments. Canadian personnel on NATO's E-3A AWACS aircraft, for instance, played an active part in directing the battle space over Libya. Some involved numerous Canadian assets, such as a dynamic targeting event on April 26. Having detected evidence of a regime attack near Misrata, the frigate HMCS *Charlottetown* forwarded this information to a Canadian weapons controller on an AWACS aircraft; the controller quickly assigned air assets to confirm this threat to a civilian-populated area. The result was that two Royal Air Force Tornados and four CF-188s successfully prosecuted these regime forces threatening Misrata.[88] A similar event occurred on May 30 when *Charlottetown* once again identified a threat to Misrata, this time from a loyalist vehicle firing rockets into the city. Much like the earlier occurrence a Canadian AWACS controller orbiting in a NATO Boeing E-3A successfully vectored two CF-188s onto the target.[89]

Nor should the CH-124 Sea King's part be overlooked. While control of the CH-124 Sea Kings aboard HMCS *Charlottetown* and that ship's replacement, HMCS *Vancouver*, rested with the Maritime Component Commander (MCC), these RCAF helicopters represented a force multiplier that helped the RCN enforce the arms embargo. Although serviceability and airframe limitations were problematic for *Charlottetown*'s aircraft, the aging CH-124s (first acquired in 1963) nevertheless proved particularly useful for tracking smaller vessels as well as extending both frigates' over-the-horizon radar capability. Yet, the CH-124's main strength lay in its ability to build situational awareness along Libya's coast for the RCN and other NATO navies. Provid-

---

[86] "TF Libeccio Op Mobile Brief," October 29, 2011.

[87] "TF Libeccio Op Mobile Brief," October 29, 2011; *End of Tour Report*, November 7, 2011, 1630-1 (Comd TF LIB).

[88] "TF Libeccio Op Mobile Brief," October 29, 2011.

[89] *End of Tour Report*, November 2011, Appendix 1 to Annex K, 22/25.

ing "top cover" for naval boarding parties was another function that rounded out the RCAF's multi-capable and flexible contribution.[90]

Canadians also were found in other key Alliance roles. For instance, the director of Strategic Plans within the Supreme Headquarters Allied Powers Europe (SHAPE), Brigadier General Pierre St-Amand, was a Canadian. So, too, were some members of his staff, most notably the lead planner. Strategic Plans was responsible for monitoring security situations that had the potential to impact NATO. It was in charge of the standup and staffing of the OUP planning group, ensuring that Canadians were involved with their Alliance partners from the mission's earliest formation. As such, this team was instrumental in determining the contingencies that NATO potentially would face over Libya as well as the requirements needed to deal with such situations.[91] Finally, many Canadian personnel served in direct support of Lieutenant-General Bouchard and in various positions at the CJTF HQ, as well as the Canadian contingent posted to JFC Naples.[92]

Assessing Operation Mobile

A great many things clearly went right for the RCAF during Operation Mobile—particularly at the tactical level—but challenges naturally surfaced to provide lessons observed. Command and control was one such issue. Largely because of the speed at which the RCAF deployed, the lines of authority between the organization with administrative control over the mission, Task Force Naples, and the operational level staff at TFL HQ were not always clear.[93] The logistical support element (mission support flight) and four detachments that were deployed separately (rather than as a composite force) and in two separate locations with a limited communication network was something that further muddied the waters.[94] The solution to these growing pains was found in the draft Air Expeditionary Wing doctrine, and the new command arrangement, which took effect on August 7, 2011. It grouped the detachments, the MSF (logistical, administrative, and engineering services), and an Operational Support Flight (coordination of the employment of operational resources) together into the Sicily Air Wing. This wing, in turn, was responsible to TF Libeccio (TF LIB), which itself had been created by consolidating TFN and TFL into a single organization. The

---

[90] Terrance Chenard, "Everyday HMCS Vancouver's Sea King Gets the Job Done," National Defence and the Canadian Forces website, October 19, 2011.

[91] I am indebted to Major General Pierre St-Amand for this information.

[92] Email from RCAF officer to author, November 12, 2013.

[93] *End of Tour Report—Task Force Libeccio*, Annex A, November 7, 2010, 1630-1 (Comd TF LIB); interview with RCAF officer, July 13, 2012.

[94] *End of Tour Report—Task Force Libeccio*, November 7, 2010, 1630-1 (Comd TF LIB).

Members of the Sicily Air Wing board a CC-150 Polaris transport/tanker aircraft
for their departure back to Canada from Trapani, Italy, on November 4, 2011.
*Courtesy of the Canadian Department of National Defence, photo by Corporal Mathieu St-Amour. Used in
accordance with Crown Copyright provisions.*

commander of this force, newly appointed Brigadier General Derek Joyce, reported
directly to CEFCOM in Ottawa.[95]

This arrangement supported the RCAF's AEW concept and doctrine—a number
of logistical issues were resolved, given the single command layer and clearer delinea-
tion of authority, stronger communication between the detachments and the HQ, as
well as improved support management. But a few concerns remained. One was that
Brigadier General Joyce was stationed in Naples, meaning that the senior Canadian
commander no longer resided with the NATO CFACC in Poggio Renatico. While a
Canadian presence was retained in the CAOC as an Air Coordination Element (ACE),
the result of this transition was that direct support to kinetic air operations became
somewhat complex. Of course, in some measure this was offset by the relocation to
Naples, which put Brigadier General Joyce in close proximity to JTF OUP and allowed
him to provide some level of support to Lieutenant-General Bouchard and his staff.[96] In
any event, an ideal C2 structure for Op Mobile was recommended after the mission:
"TF LIB should have been comprised of a Joint Task Force Commander ACE, MCE
[Maritime Coordination Element], and TF LIB HQ, co-located in Naples with the

---

[95] *End of Tour Report—Task Force Libeccio*, November 7, 2010, 1630-1 (Comd TF LIB).

[96] Email from RCAF officer to author, November 12, 2013.

CJTFUP HQ, leaving an [Air Component Commander] in Poggio Renatico and an MCC on the CHA/VAN" (with clear tactical control authority on tactical sub-units).[97]

Logistics and support requirements led to other important lessons for the RCAF, particularly because the speed of the deployment and its distance from Canada meant that it took time to position essential support aspects in theater. The MSF's arrival after the CF-188s and CC-150s was one challenge; another was supporting a force that was operating from four distinct and separate geographical locations.[98] The RCAF also identified manning as a subject worthy of closer analysis, particularly since some units faced personnel shortages, while others reported cases in which relatively junior members were employed in positions beyond their rank level. It was suggested, therefore, that headquarters and unit establishments in future deployments should be "as robust as possible, both in terms of personnel and experience level," as well as flexible so they can adapt to unexpected situations.[99] Moreover, it was further recommended that an entire MSF should be fully deployed and eventually reduced "as the mission evolves."[100]

Targeting and intelligence were other aspects of the mission that provided a number of observations for future Libya-like operations. The precision of targeting during Mobile was unparalleled and was the product of the strict no-civilian casualty policy, good intelligence, a careful targeting process, and the technical capabilities of the weapons used. Canadians were heavily involved in the targeting process; however, intelligence often was a challenge.[101] National security restrictions among states, as well as a lack of connectivity to classified information networks, meant that not all nations were in a position to see each other's raw data. Without firsthand access it was, at times, difficult for some countries, such as Canada, to determine whether a nominated target met national requirements. The introduction of improved connectivity at Poggio Renatico, as well as the provision of a Canadian targeteer in the U.S./UK "targeting shop," certainly helped to identify the value of developing intelligence enablers for future missions.[102] It also resulted in suggestions to develop a purely RCAF targeting capability.

A similar conclusion was drawn regarding the RCAF's communication requirements. While communications during Op Mobile generally were good, individuals

---

[97] *End of Tour Report—Task Force Libeccio*, November 7, 2010, 1630-1 (Comd TF LIB).

[98] *End of Tour Report—Task Force Libeccio*, November 7, 2010, 1630-1 (Comd TF LIB); *End of Tour Report— Task Force Libeccio*, Annex G, November 7, 2010, 1630-1 (Comd TF LIB).

[99] *End of Tour Report—Task Force Libeccio*, Annex A, November 7, 2010, 1630-1 (Comd TF LIB); Colonel Mike Barker, RCAF LL—Op Mobile/TF Libeccio Brief, OP MOBILE Lessons Learned Symposium Brief, June 6, 2012, Winnipeg, Manitoba; phone interview with RCAF officer, July 13, 2012.

[100] *End of Tour Report—Task Force Libeccio*, Annex G, November 7, 2010, 1630-1 (Comd TF LIB).

[101] Colonel Eric Kenny, Op Mobile/ TF Libeccio, June 6, 2012, LL Symposium Brief, Winnipeg, Manitoba.

[102] *End of Tour Report—Task Force Libeccio*, November 7, 2010, 1630-1 (Comd TF LIB); Task Force Libeccio TF Lessons Learned on C2 and Intel Supt Commander TFL, Brief to 1 Cdn Air Div.

in the early stages of the operation often used BlackBerries as their primary source of contact with others. A suitable communication infrastructure, created literally from the ground up, naturally took time to establish; this led to a desire within the RCAF to develop a more robust communication suite that could be deployed at short notice.[103]

RCAF and NATO: Lessons Observed

While most of the analysis related to the RCAF's lessons observed naturally focused on specific Canadian issues, some conclusions could apply to the Alliance as a whole. The usefulness of developing a NATO joint-targeting cell and an increased intelligence-sharing capability among allies certainly was one important takeaway from the mission. The shortage of AAR, ISR, and long-range patrol aircraft assets also was keenly felt, as the tankers experienced a hectic operational tempo to keep up with demand, while the CP-140 and other Alliance surveillance aircraft often were split between the need to provide essential support to maritime tasks and ground situational awareness. Conversely, the value of innovative thinking and rapidly adapting to circumstances to produce either new capabilities or strategic affects was a common characteristic that should be repeated and specifically fostered during future missions. (For the RCAF, this manifested in the streamlining of JDAM procurement and evaluation process; adapting to the requirements of deliberate-dynamic targeting; the rapid certification for the CC-150 to fuel allied aircraft; and following the French and British example by using the CP-140 in the SCAR-C role as well as a naval gunfire support platform.) The same is true for the advice General Bouchard provided on the key to successful NATO operations, such as OUP: "When working within a complex alliance . . . it's important to 'play nice with all others in the playground [and] share your toys.'"[104]

Op Mobile undoubtedly was a success for the RCAF, particularly since it demonstrated the effectiveness of various Canadian airpower concepts and capabilities. It indicated that the recently developed Air Expeditionary Wing doctrine not only will give the RCAF a considerable capability, but also should help solve a number of challenges that the air force faced during Op Mobile. Although Op Mobile was only able to partially validate this concept (many aspects of the future air expeditionary capability were still under development and could not be stood up), it did show how Canadian airpower was capable of providing the government and the Alliance with flexible, responsive, and agile effects. Moreover, it further suggested that anticipatory collective training of a deployable "skeleton" C2 team could prove its worth in the quick

---

[103] *End of Tour Report—Task Force Libeccio*, Annex L, November 7, 2010, 1630-1 (Comd TF LIB); Col Alain Pelletier, Task Force Libeccio TF Lessons Learned on C2 and Intel Supt Commander TFL, Brief to 1 Cdn Air Div; TF Libeccio Op Mobile, October 29, 2011.

[104] Dean Black, "Lieutenant General Charles Bouchard: Three Tenets of Allied Air Power Operations," *Air Force Magazine*, Vol. 35, No. 4, p. 23.

establishment of effective airpower in an expeditionary role while using the AEW elements to fully support the rapid onset of operations. Indeed, the emphasis being placed on expeditionary operations, along with the experience gained during Op Mobile, will help the RCAF prepare for other administrative and logistical issues—such as the nuances of support contracting outside of Canada, as well as ammunition storage restrictions and shortages—that it faced when operating in Italy.

Another key to the RCAF's success rested in its high level of air-to-air integration and interoperability, as was demonstrated through the CC-150s' and CC-130s' ability to provide fuel to almost every coalition nation; the CF-188s' joint strike missions; the CP-140s' ISR, MPA, and SCAR-C sorties; and the ACE's work with the CAOC. Finally, Op Mobile showed that the RCAF had achieved a good mix of multipurpose capabilities through the acquisition and modernization programs of the previous decade. Certainly, the conversion of CC-150s into strategic refuelers, the upgrading of the CF-188s and CP-140s with either new weapons or sensors suites, and the addition of the CC-177 for a greater strategic airlift role have acted not only as force multipliers and strategic enablers, but will allow the RCAF to continue to provide responsive, flexible expeditionary effects for the Canadian government and NATO in the years to come.[105] More specifically, however, it was the balance of capabilities contained within this force structure, along with the training and dedication of the air personnel involved, which allowed the RCAF to punch above its weight during Op Mobile. Of course, the same can be said of many other participating NATO nations, and as a result the strength of working and integrating seamlessly with Alliance partners was one of the key elements behind the RCAF's success.

Unprecedented acts of gratitude—such as flypasts and special tributes—left little doubt that the government saw the RCAF as an effective part in its Libyan foreign policy. The RCAF answered Canadian government calls for a quick response to protect Libyan civilians through its international and NATO commitments. Despite its size relative to its larger partners, Canada made contributions in areas in which NATO faced shortages (such as AAR and ISR roles) as well as in delivering kinetic effects in OUP. General Bouchard's leadership also was a key factor to the success of OUP, as was the RCAF's ability to adopt new capabilities and roles as the mission evolved. That this was achieved in a particularly busy operational year—the RCAF also was involved in many domestic and international operations as diverse as Afghanistan, Haiti, and the Arctic—was the product of being able to provide what one analysis described as a "mix of the right people, with the right training at the right time, with the right equipment."[106]

---

[105]RCAF officer email to author; Task Force Libeccio TF Lessons Learned on C2 and Intel Supt Commander TFL, Brief to 1 Cdn Air Div.

[106]Lieutenant-General Andre Deschamps, *Crew Brief*, Vol. 9, No. 1.

Op Mobile indicates the RCAF has found a good balance to meet Canada's domestic and international needs, but a word of caution is required. While OUP provides some excellent lessons observed for both Canada and NATO, no two conflicts are ever exactly the same. It would be a mistake for Canadian policymakers to assume the mission sets that worked so well for the RCAF and RCN in Libya should automatically be applied to all future conflicts. Instead, each new global situation will come with its own unique requirements. The final lesson from Operation Mobile, therefore, is that its success should not place unrealistic political expectations on either the RCAF or on Canadian airpower.

CHAPTER TEN

The Belgian, Danish, Dutch, and Norwegian Experiences

Christian F. Anrig

Introduction

This chapter examines the roles that four NATO member states—Belgium, Denmark, the Netherlands, and Norway—played in the Libyan air campaign. Not only did the air forces of these countries deploy similar forces and make contributions out of proportion to their size to the campaign, they also share a number of basic commonalities that makes it natural to examine them together. The foremost of these commonalities is that they are the air arms of relatively small- to medium-sized Alliance member states and that the main weapon system of each is the F-16AM fighter-bomber. The latter connection extends beyond equipment *per se*—operating the same weapon system, which the four countries purchased and then upgraded collaboratively, has fostered cooperative arrangements among them pertaining to procurement, training, and deployment.

Due to their limited size, the four air forces cannot effectively wage autonomous air operations, and instead are postured to plug into multinational air campaigns. While their air forces structurally are quite similar, the four countries pursue distinct defense policies with, at times, marked differences. Yet their common strategic denominator is their ambition to appear as reliable allies. As such, their goal has not so much been to proactively shape a campaign at the operational and strategic level, but to make useful and noticeable contributions at the tactical level.

In the course of the Libya campaign, the four air forces' performance was indeed impressive. The number of PGMs expended by Belgian, Danish, and Norwegian fighter-bombers corresponded to approximately three-quarters of the weapons that British and French fixed-wing aircraft combined delivered.[1] In particular, Denmark and Norway were singled out as the most flexible nations throughout April 2011 when it came to engaging certain targets. As such, their air forces proved critical to maintain pressure on Muammar Qaddafi's regime after U.S. forces had ceased offensive opera-

---

[1] The total number of PGMs expended by Belgian, Danish, and Norwegian fighter-bombers was 1,984. The Royal Air Force was reported to have dropped approximately 1,400 PGMs (including air-launched cruise missiles) by October 24, 2011, and French Air Force and Navy aircraft in excess of 1,140 PGMs (including air-launched cruise missiles) by the end of September 2011 ["UK, France Detail Sorties Mounted, Ordnance Expended," *Jane's Defence Weekly*, November 2, 2011, p. 5].

tions. While political restraints prevented Dutch pilots from conducting air-to-ground strikes, they used their targeting pods in unorthodox ways to corroborate the ISR picture—a contribution that did not go unnoticed by Unified Protector's CFACC. On the negative side, the four countries failed to leverage their cooperative arrangements for deployed operations.

Background

To contextualize the reactions of Belgium, Denmark, the Netherlands, and Norway to the Libya crisis, it is essential to understand the origins and evolution of their roles in NATO. This section first provides a basic background on the four countries' Cold War defense policies. It then examines post–Cold War air operations and the growing cooperation between the four countries' air forces.

NATO's First Four Decades

All four countries became original signatories to the North Atlantic Treaty in 1949. However, Denmark and Norway integrated into NATO's defense structure only with certain limitations. Even prior to signing the treaty, Oslo declared that foreign military bases would not be allowed on Norwegian territory in peacetime, with Copenhagen following suit in 1953. Similarly, both Norway and Denmark prohibited the storage of nuclear weapons on their soil in peacetime. Yet while Oslo undertook sizable defense efforts, Copenhagen kept Danish defense spending quite low for most of the Cold War. Consequently, Copenhagen repeatedly received criticism for its below-average military efforts, particularly from its U.S. ally.[2] Yet with deployed operations coming to the fore in the post–Cold War era, Denmark's Alliance profile would completely change.

In 1985, a Dutch scholar observed: "The failure of neutrality in 1940 enhanced the tendency toward alignment after World War II in the same way as the success of neutrality in 1914 had fostered the continuation of that policy during the interbellum period."[3] After the Netherlands signed the North Atlantic Treaty in 1949, Dutch decision-makers viewed the country's security exclusively in transatlantic terms.[4]

In Brussels, the Belgian parliament ratified the North Atlantic Treaty by a large majority in May 1949. This decision largely rested on the country's historical experi-

---

[2]   Magnus Petersson and Håkon Lunde Saxi, "Shifted Roles: Explaining Danish and Norwegian Alliance Strategy 1949–2009," *Journal of Strategic Studies, iFirst* article, 2012, pp. 5–7.

[3]   Jan G. Siccama, "The Netherlands Depillarized: Security Policy in a New Domestic Context," in Gregory Flynn, ed., *NATO's Northern Allies: The National Security Policies of Belgium, Denmark, the Netherlands, and Norway*, Totowa, N.J.: Rowman & Allanheld, 1985, p. 117.

[4]   Siccama, "The Netherlands Depillarized," p. 117.

ence that neutrality had failed Belgium twice in the preceding half-century. Henceforth, Belgium's ambition was to tailor its defense policy to be in line with the Alliance as a whole—or, more specifically, with the United States.[5] In the last decade of the Cold War, Brussels still viewed NATO as the central pillar of Belgium's military security, though Belgian decisionmakers also began to support the idea of a more genuine European pillar within NATO.[6] In contrast, attempts at establishing European—as opposed to transatlantic—defense structures were viewed in the Netherlands as likely to undermine NATO alliance cohesion. This stance changed only during the presidency of Bill Clinton, who—unlike his predecessor—encouraged such cooperation.[7]

The most conspicuous defense cooperation among Belgium, Denmark, the Netherlands, and Norway was their collaboration to procure a common multirole fighter aircraft, an effort that began in 1974.[8] Following a hotly contested international competition, they opted for the U.S.-made F-16A Fighting Falcon as the next-generation fighter-bomber for all four air forces.[9] The partners expected industrial advantages through this joint acquisition program, but the commonality of equipment also would form the basis for further programmatic and operational cooperation.

After the Cold War: The Balkans and Afghanistan

The Royal Netherlands Air Force (RNLAF) was the driving force behind cooperative arrangements in the domain of European F-16 operations. The culmination of these efforts was the creation of the European Participating Air Forces' (EPAF) Expeditionary Air Wing (EEAW), a multinational European F-16 wing. The EPAF concept originally was conceived as a means of pooling national procurement requirements. In the 1990s, EPAF specified a common requirement for the midlife update (MLU) of Belgian, Danish, Dutch, and Norwegian F-16A/B Block 15 fighter-bombers.[10]

The RNLAF also was in the vanguard in the air operations over both Bosnia and Kosovo. During Operation Deliberate Force in 1995, the RNLAF was the only EPAF contributor, and Dutch F-16s made a significant contribution to NATO's air

---

[5] Luc Reychler, "The Passive Constrained: Belgian Security Policy in the 1980s," in Flynn, 1985, pp. 6–7.

[6] Reychler, "The Passive Constrained," p. 50.

[7] Alfred van Staden, "The Netherlands," in Jolyon Howorth and Anand Menon, eds., *The European Union and National Defence Policy*, London: Routledge, 1997, pp. 96–98.

[8] All four air forces operated, and needed to replace, the aging F-104G Starfighter; the new fighter would also supplant Dutch NF-5s, Norwegian F-5As, Danish F-100s, and Belgian Mirage 5s.

[9] Serge Van Heertum and Marc Arys, *F-16 Fighting Falcon: 30 Years in Action with the Belgian Air Force*, Brussels: Belgian Defence Composair IPR, 2009, p. 6.

[10] Christian F. Anrig, *The Quest for Relevant Air Power: Continental European Responses to the Air Power Challenges of the Post-Cold War Era*, Maxwell Air Force Base, Ala.: Air University Press, August 2011, pp. 235–236, 255.

campaign, which was instrumental in bringing about the Dayton Accords and peace to Bosnia-Herzegovina.[11]

For Operation Allied Force—NATO's 1999 air campaign for Kosovo—the Netherlands made available 20 F-16s and two KDC-10 tanker aircraft. Since 1995, it had become the only European F-16 force capable of employing laser-guided bombs (LGBs) autonomously. RNLAF fighter-bombers delivered in excess of 850 air-to-ground weapons against Serbia and the Serb armed forces in Kosovo, including 246 LGBs and 32 Maverick missiles. To put the figures in perspective, the RNLAF released slightly more PGMs during the campaign than the larger Royal Air Force (RAF) contingent, which delivered 244 LGBs and six ALARM antiradiation missiles. In addition, an RNLAF F-16 downed one of three Serb MiG-29s that NATO forces destroyed during the first night of Operation Allied Force—the only European air-to-air kill in major air campaigns throughout the 1990s.[12] The RNLAF clearly stood out as the leading operator of European F-16s.

Operating alongside their Dutch counterparts in 1999, in the framework of the Deployable Air Task Force (DATF), Belgian Air Force (BAF) fighter-bombers dropped air-to-ground munitions for the first time in a post–Cold War air campaign. Belgian F-16s released 271 weapons, including 32 PGMs.[13]

Although Norway made F-16s available for Operation Allied Force in 1999, little political appetite existed in Oslo to conduct offensive air-to-ground strikes. Moreover, since the completion of the midlife update was still pending, the Royal Norwegian Air Force (RNoAF) F-16 fleet was not perceived to be ready for precision air-to-ground engagements at the time.[14] In 1999, the Royal Danish Air Force (RDAF) was a few steps ahead of its Norwegian counterpart. While initially flying only air-to-air sorties, the RDAF conducted a limited number of offensive missions in the second half of Operation Allied Force. It dropped only unguided bombs, however.[15]

Against the backdrop of Operation Enduring Freedom, a combined Danish, Dutch, and Norwegian detachment of 18 F-16s, supported by an RNLAF KDC-10 tanker aircraft, deployed to Manas International Airport in Kyrgyzstan in Autumn 2002. While participating in air operations over Afghanistan, the detachment regularly provided CAS to ground troops. Despite some legal and procedural obstacles, the EPAF arrangement proved effective. For example, the RNLAF and RDAF provided

---

[11] The RNLAF delivered approximately 13 percent of the munitions in Operation Deliberate Force. See Anrig, *The Quest for Relevant Air Power*, pp. 240–241.

[12] Anrig, *The Quest for Relevant Air Power*, pp. 242–243, 256.

[13] Rolf de Winter and Erwin van Loo (RNLAF History Unit, The Hague), interview by the author, June 24, 2004.

[14] Dr. Dag Henriksen, RNoAF Academy, email to the author, June 6, 2012.

[15] Maj Jacob Barfoed, Expeditionary Air Staff, RDAF, Karup, Denmark, email to the author, February 29, 2012. Information provided was cleared by the RDAF Headquarters.

targeting pods for common use, while Norway provided a deployable communication module and a hangar.[16]

To further enhance cooperation among European F-16 operators, Lt. Gen. D. L. Berlijn, the RNLAF commander-in-chief, approached his counterparts and asked their views on a common deployable air wing. His efforts resulted in the establishment of the EEAW. The ministers of defense of Belgium, Denmark, the Netherlands, Norway, and Portugal—now also an F-16AM operator—signed the corresponding memorandum of understanding during the NATO summit in Istanbul on June 28, 2004. The goal was to make optimum use of available and complementary assets in deployed operations.[17] In 2005, for instance, an EEAW F-16 detachment deployed to Kabul International Airport to support ISAF.[18] In addition to common deployed operations, EPAF member states set up the Fighter Weapons Instructor Training program, in which nationalities and even airframes are completely mixed, resulting in a very high level of standardization among the EPAF air forces.[19]

In light of the operational experience and continuing improvement of their air forces, decisionmakers in Brussels, Copenhagen, Oslo, and The Hague could count on airpower in 2011. The following sections will examine in turn each country's decision to commit to Libya air operations and its air force's role in Operations Odyssey Dawn and Unified Protector.

The Royal Danish Air Force

In the post–Cold War era, Denmark has been above average for its size in its involvement in deployed military operations. Behind this involvement are three pillars that have remained constant. Danish security and defense strategy documents repeatedly and formally refer to two of the pillars—the U.N. and NATO.[20] The third pillar, referred to implicitly, is Denmark's strong partnership with the United States. According to Danish scholars, Denmark's ambition is "to support and demonstrate relevance and trustworthiness to its great power allies in NATO, especially the United States, in

---

[16] Anrig, *The Quest for Relevant Air Power*, pp. 235–236, 243.

[17] Anrig, *The Quest for Relevant Air Power*, p. 236.

[18] Anrig, *The Quest for Relevant Air Power*, p. 243.

[19] Lt. Col. Jeroen Poesen, Belgian Defence Air Component, Brussels, Belgium, email to the author, May 22, 2012.

[20] The Danish Defence Agreement 2005–2009, preliminary translation, Copenhagen: Danish Ministry of Defence, June 2004; and Danish Defence Agreement 2010–2014, Copenhagen: Danish Ministry of Defence, June 24, 2009.

order to preserve the security guarantee that they provide."[21] In March 2011, all three pillars aligned themselves to provide the impetus for Denmark's proactive role in the air operations against Qaddafi's military machine, and once again allowed Denmark to play a role out of proportion to its size.

Intervention

The Danish decisionmaking process that paved the way for Danish military intervention was swift by European standards. Prior to the adoption of UNSCR 1973, a possible Danish contribution to operations over Libya already had been discussed among the leaders of the political parties, because Copenhagen wanted to be part of a possible military operation from the start if France, the United Kingdom, and the United States decided to act.[22] Thus, when the international community reached a consensus on military action, the process of gaining broad political support for a Danish military contribution was almost complete, and the Danish government was in the process of drafting a proposal for a parliamentary resolution. This proposal was presented to the Danish parliament on the evening of March 18, 2011 and was passed unanimously shortly after midnight on March 19—the day that French fighter-bombers opened the campaign. Historically, the unanimous parliamentary decision to use military force was a first for Denmark in the post–World War II era.[23] What made Libya different was the perceived need to act swiftly to prevent genocide and the fact that ground forces were ruled out from the start. Libya thus presented a perfect opportunity for doing good with U.N. support in a way that presented few risks to Danish personnel.[24] Key political actors were the ministers of Foreign Affairs and Defense and the members of the Parliamentary Defence Committee.[25] Denmark's swift and proactive involvement was a natural continuation of its defense and foreign political ambitions of the last decade, providing Copenhagen—in relation to its size—with a large silhouette on the international stage.

Deployment and Operations

The tight parallelism of the political decisionmaking and military preparations expedited a swift Danish response. Fighter Wing Skrydstrup received notice to prepare for deployment at the same time that Danish politicians started to deliberate about a pos-

---

[21] Peter Viggo Jakobsen and Karsten Jakob Møller, "Good News: Libya and the Danish Way of War," in Nanna Hvidt and Hans Mouritzen, eds., *Danish Foreign Policy Yearbook 2012*, Copenhagen: Danish Institute for International Studies, 2012, p. 109.

[22] Jakobsen and Møller, "Good News," p. 114; and Barfoed, email to the author, February 29, 2012.

[23] Barfoed, email to the author, February 29, 2012.

[24] Jakobsen and Møller, "Good News," pp. 111–112; and Dr. Peter Viggo Jakobsen, Associate Professor, Institute for Strategy, Royal Danish Defence College, Copenhagen, email to the author, May 21, 2012.

[25] Barfoed, email to the author, February 29.

sible Danish contribution to a forthcoming military operation. The other operational wings of the Royal Danish Air Force were ordered on standby to provide immediate direct or indirect support to the Danish detachment. Simultaneously with the parliamentary debate on the evening of March 18, a so-called site survey team and an initial operations enabling team landed at Sigonella Air Base in Italy to facilitate a deployment if the Danish government made the political decision to intervene. Immediately after parliamentary approval, and after examining the suitability of the air base, the team in Sigonella was able to give the go-ahead.[26] Sigonella was at the top of the site survey team's priority list, and the fast Danish decisionmaking process allowed the RDAF to use its No. 1 choice as its forward base. Given Sigonella's proximity to Libya, some missions were flown without air-to-air refueling.[27] Throughout the deployment phase, the Ministry of Defence, the Defence Command Denmark, and the Tactical Air Command were in constant dialogue about such issues as the size and composition of the contribution, the national rules of engagement, and any caveats.[28] As will be examined later in this chapter, the political domestic decisionmaking processes in Brussels, Copenhagen, Oslo, and The Hague all proceeded quickly but at different paces, which was not conducive for a common EEAW deployment. Thus, the various European F-16 deployments were domestically driven.

The Danish fighters took off from Skrydstrup Air Base (Denmark) en route to Sigonella at 6:00 a.m. on March 19. In the afternoon of March 20, they flew their first mission over Libya under the command of U.S. AFRICOM's AOC located at Ramstein Air Base, Germany.[29] After this mission, Denmark's Minister of Defence, Gitte Lillelund Bech, underlined the air force's capabilities to quickly respond to an emerging crisis:

> It is proof of professionalism and good will that within three days the Danish Defence is ready to present fighter jets for operational deployment ... I am proud of the speed with which we have been able to suit the action to the UN resolution and the parliamentary resolution.[30]

From a military vantage point, no hesitation was perceived at the political decisionmaking level regarding the detachment's swift integration into a U.S.-led operation. The only Danish caveat was to place a national "red card holder" into the Ameri-

---

[26] Barfoed, email to the author, February 29.

[27] Maj Per Harding Svarre, Expeditionary Air Staff, RDAF, Karup, Denmark, telephone interview, May 21, 2012.

[28] Svarre, email to the author, February 29, 2012. Information provided was cleared by the RDAF Headquarters.

[29] Barfoed, email to the author, February 29, 2012.

[30] "Danish Fighter Jets Deployed to Libya," Copenhagen: Danish Ministry of Defence, news release, March 21, 2011.

can chain of command. This official had the authority to cancel any Danish mission at any time if he judged a specific mission to be outside of the Danish mandate or UNSCR 1973.[31]

The Danish detachment consisted of six F-16AM fighter-bombers, two of which were kept in reserve. To comply with maintenance requirements, or if technical faults could not be fixed on site, Danish F-16s were rotated between Denmark and Sigonella. While the number of jets deployed did not change, the number of sorties did. The Danish detachment normally conducted eight sorties a day, except for a three-week period in July, when the number was reduced to four. During this period, Danish personnel at Sigonella were reduced by 30 percent. At SACEUR's request to all NATO nations for an increased effort, Denmark subsequently returned to eight sorties a day from the beginning of August, and the contingent again was ramped up to the original 112 personnel. The eight daily sorties continued until early September, when the rate again was reduced to four.[32] The Danish commitment to the air campaign never wavered. Indeed, Denmark was one of the few nations that sustained an operational tempo of two sorties per aircraft and per day with its four aircraft assigned to tasking. While the majority of force contributors had a weekly no-fly day, the RDAF F-16s flew every day for the first 26 days of the air operations (March 20 to April 14), surging to 10 or 12 sorties per day several times as the operational situation dictated. The reduction in sortie rate in July only was implemented because the development of the conflict made it possible. If the operational tempo had been higher, the RDAF would have stayed at eight sorties a day. In this regard, easing the strain on financial resources was a secondary concern. In light of an impending cessation of NATO operations by the end of September, Denmark's Minister of Defence deliberately intended to surge RDAF operations applying massive pressure throughout August.[33] The Danish detachment conducted its last fighter mission on the very last day of Operation Unified Protector. To resupply the detachment and rotate personnel, the RDAF drew upon its own aircraft—a C-130J Hercules and a Bombardier CL-604—as well as civilian chartered aircraft.[34]

The RDAF also dispatched personnel to planning cells. During Operation Odyssey Dawn, the RDAF's national liaison team at the AOC consisted of a senior national representative in the rank of a colonel, a red-card holder in the rank of lieutenant colonel, a legal advisor, an air tasking order planner, two unit representatives, and an intelligence specialist. The senior national representative participated in a host of meetings to coordinate and obtain information about the operations at higher levels. The red-card holder—together with the legal advisor—checked all preplanned targets and

---

[31] Svarre, email to the author, February 29.

[32] Svarre, email to the author, February 29.

[33] Bg Gen Steen Harboe Hartov, Chief of Staff, RDAF, Karup, Denmark, email to the author, May 16, 2013.

[34] Svarre, email to the author, February 29.

was present in the operations room at all times during Danish missions. The air tasking order planner worked in close cooperation with the AOC planning staff, worked out the plan for the RDAF fighter-bombers, and requested AAR for Danish missions. The two unit representatives were in direct contact with the Danish detachment at Sigonella and ensured that the unit understood its mission. The intelligence specialist worked closely with intelligence specialists from other coalition nations to make sure the detachment received all relevant documents and information.[35]

When the operation was about to be transferred to NATO's authority after the initial attacks, Denmark stood up a shadow liaison team at the CAOC in Poggio Renatico, Italy, to prepare for the transfer. At the time, it was unclear exactly when the transfer would occur. Preparing a shadow team proved to be a sound idea, as the transfer took place after a delay of 24 hours. The original team then quickly traveled from Ramstein to Poggio Renatico to relieve the shadow team. This enabled the RDAF to secure a seamless transition in terms of planning from Operation Odyssey Dawn to Operation Unified Protector.[36] To keep up operational momentum, the RDAF deliberately delayed its transition to NATO command until the last moment.[37]

In the ensuing weeks, the senior national representative was relieved and the red-card holder assumed his responsibilities and was temporarily promoted to colonel.[38] During Operation Odyssey Dawn, the Danish red-card holder was only presented with the targets that appeared on the approved joint integrated prioritized target list and that RDAF fighter-bombers were supposed to strike. This changed in the early stages of Operation Unified Protector, when the red-card holders were invited to sit in on the joint targeting working group. This allowed them to observe the various targets being developed at an early stage.[39] In addition to the national liaison team, the RDAF volunteered to send additional staff to augment the multinational planning effort. The RDAF planning staff assumed functions and positions that included providing offensive plans; ISR plans; dynamic targeting in the current operations cell; and an assistant to the chief of the current operations cell.[40]

During Operation Odyssey Dawn, RDAF F-16s flew a roughly equal mix of dynamic and deliberate missions, during which they engaged all types of ground targets. The target set for fielded forces also included moving targets. In general, tanks and armored personnel carriers were attacked, as well as multiple rocket launchers and artillery positions. In an offensive counterair role, RDAF fighters engaged ground-

---

[35] Svarre, email to the author, February 29.

[36] Svarre, email to the author, February 29.

[37] Hartov, email to the author, May 16.

[38] Svarre, email to the author, February 29.

[39] Svarre, telephone interview, May 21.

[40] Svarre, email to the author, February 29.

Royal Danish Air Force F-16AM on a SCAR mission west of Sirte on
August 30, 2011, armed with GBU-49 500-lb PGMs.
Courtesy of the Royal Danish Air Force.

based air defense positions and air bases. Beyond fielded forces and counterair-related targets, the RDAF struck at C2 nodes and munitions depots.[41]

After the transition from Operation Odyssey Dawn to Operation Unified Protector, the number of deliberate targets decreased, and the majority of RDAF missions became dynamic.[42] The fact that the RDAF was prepared to take on a large degree of dynamic targets again testifies to its proficiency.[43] The increase of dynamic missions during Operation Unified Protector also can be interpreted as the result of NATO's too-rigid air tasking order cycle. During Operation Odyssey Dawn, operations were run through a 48-hour air tasking order production cycle, including execution. This compressed cycle supported a safe and manageable air tasking order production that was flexible enough to deal with the fluid ground situation. This produced the maximum amount of relevant deliberate targets. Of course, even with a compressed 48-hour cycle, some targets—particularly mobile targets—emerged suddenly, and dynamic targeting had to address those. In contrast, throughout the NATO-led Operation Unified Protector, the CAOC used the conventional 72-hour air tasking order production cycle, which proved slow and inflexible in reacting to the situation on the ground. As a consequence, dynamic targeting increased. While dynamic targeting allowed the

---

[41] Svarre, email to the author, February 29.

[42] Svarre, email to the author, February 29.

[43] During Operation Unified Protector, British Royal Air Force sources underlined the more challenging nature of dynamic strikes as opposed to preplanned deliberate missions. See Gareth Jennings, "Royal Air Force Downplays Carrier Aviation," *Jane's Defence Weekly,* Vol. 48, No. 30, July 27, 2011, p. 12.

striking of targets within hours or even minutes, it came at a price. The effective use of available resources decreased, including fewer optimized munitions, less efficient use of AAR capacities, or poorer coordination of assets in general.[44]

With regard to deliberate targets, two attack missions illustrate the RDAF aircrews' level of proficiency. The first was an attack on a C2 complex in Tripoli. The complex consisted of several buildings and an underground, two-story bunker. The attack on the bunker was particularly challenging because, to ensure total destruction of its functionality, it was necessary to detonate bombs at each level. A composite air operations (COMAO) mission with participation from four nations conducted the attack, and the task of attacking the bunker fell to the Danes. It was solved by employing GPS-guided 2,000-pound bunker-buster bombs in tandem, one bomb to break through the roof to detonate at the upper level and another to go through the hole made by the first bomb, penetrate the floor, and detonate at the lower level. RDAF fighter-bombers delivered eight bombs through four holes. The Danish attack received special attention from Lieutenant General Ralph J. Jodice II, the CFACC, and it singled out the RDAF detachment as one of the most reliable that could be entrusted with the most challenging tasks. The second example was an attack on a military C2 and storage facility situated in a mountain range. The target consisted of a maze of deep caves, above-ground buildings, storage warehouses, and other structures. A multinational, 20-strong COMAO package carried out the attack, with each formation assigned their individual targets. The most complicated targets were the caves. The entrances were covered with reinforced doors and almost fully concealed in narrow valleys, offering only very narrow attack angles and small release windows due to the steep surrounding slopes. The only way to attack them was to use the GBU-24 laser-guided 2,000-pound PGM, which is able to glide long distances at a shallow angle. This task also fell to RDAF fighter-bombers successfully employing a combination of bunker-buster and general-purpose warheads.[45]

The RDAF employed the full array of its air-to-ground armaments inventory over Libya, amounting to 923 released PGMs, 102 employed during Operation Odyssey Dawn and 821 during Operation Unified Protector.[46] This included GBU-12 laser-guided 500-pound, GBU-24 laser-guided 2,000-pound, GBU-31 GPS-guided 2,000-pound, and GBU-49 laser- and GPS-guided 500-pound PGMs. The GBU-49 was particularly suited for dynamic targeting, as it could be programmed in flight. The possibility of changing target parameters in flight provided great flexibility, especially in the fluid environment of the Libyan conflict. The RDAF F-16s' ability both to receive target coordinates generated by external sensors and to self-generate coordinates with

---

[44] Maj. Per Harding Svarre, RDAF, "Lessons from the Libya Conflict," briefing, Brussels: Air Operations Working, Group, November 16, 2011.

[45] Hartov, email to the author, May 16.

[46] Hartov, email to the author, May 16.

the aircrafts' own targeting pods enhanced flexibility. All RDAF F-16 fighter-bombers flying missions over Libya were equipped with LANTIRN ER (Extended Range) targeting pods. The RDAF conducted exactly 600 combat missions, two of which were DCA and the remainder offensive missions.[47] Danish aircraft accounted for more than 12 percent of the total number of strike sorties flown in Operations Odyssey Dawn and Unified Protector together.[48]

On June 27, a *Defense News* report highlighted the RDAF's shortage of PGMs and discussions between the Danish, U.S., and Dutch government on procuring additional munitions.[49] After the RDAF had all but depleted its own PGM stocks, Denmark did indeed borrow a number of weapons from allied nations through bilateral arrangements. Furthermore, toward the very end of Operation Unified Protector, the RDAF received a shipment of factory-fresh GBU-54s from the manufacturer through a sped-up procurement process. By this point, however, no longer was there a need to employ these bombs.[50] While resupply efforts were intense at times, the RDAF never ran out of weapons during the conflict.[51]

With regard to fighter escort, the midlife-updated RDAF F-16s proved their versatility. With their advanced air-to-air armament, consisting of AIM-9X Sidewinder, AIM-120B AMRAAM, or both, Danish F-16 strikes did not require a coalition fighter aircraft escort. Given the potential air-to-air threat in the early stages, RDAF fighter-bombers, with their air-to-ground armament jettisoned, would have been perfectly capable of dealing with a Libyan air-to-air threat on their own.[52]

RDAF two-ships regularly were paired with other two-ship formations, with one pair being appointed the mission lead. In the latter half of Operation Unified Protector, COMAO missions became more common to strike larger target complexes simultaneously.[53] These included force contributions from four to six nations based at as many different air bases. As such, they represented a particular feat by all parties involved. While planning and briefing such missions face-to-face would have been the aircrews' natural choice, this had to be done by telephone instead. The high success rate can be ascribed to the combined training and exercises conducted regularly before the conflict, such as the EPAF's Fighter Weapons Instructor Training, the NATO Tactical

---

[47] Svarre, email to the author, February 29.

[48] Hartov, email to the author, May 16.

[49] Tom Kington, "Small Bombs Loom Big as Libya War Grinds On," *Defense News,* Vol. 26, No. 25, June 27, 2011, p. 1.

[50] Svarre, email to the author, February 29.

[51] Hartov, email to the author, May 16. As examined below in the section on the Royal Netherlands Air Force, bomb bodies and fuzes were transferred from Dutch munitions stocks to the RDAF. In the course of the conflict, Denmark also acquired bomb fuzes from a commercial Israeli company.

[52] Svarre, email to the author, February 29.

[53] Svarre, telephone interview, May 21.

Leadership Program, and U.S. Red Flag exercises. Many of the pilots from different nations had trained together so long that they recognized each other's voices in the air.[54]

Since dedicated SEAD assets were very scarce, missions perceived as most threatened were given priority. As a consequence, RDAF fighter-bombers most often flew without dedicated SEAD escort. The aircrafts' targeting pods also played a vital part in ISR gathering. By means of targeting pod-generated images, the Danish detachment could enhance its mission reports. These reports, describing all observations during a specific mission, provided a large part of the battle damage assessment.[55]

For AAR, any capable and certified refueling tanker supported the Danish F-16s. Since the majority of AAR assets were American, Danish missions were primarily supported by USAF tankers. Canadian tankers also provided support on a regular basis.[56]

The RDAF made a contribution to Libya operations out of proportion to its size, both quantitatively and qualitatively. When doubts about a successful outcome for the operation started to emerge in June 2011, Lene Espersen, Denmark's Minister of Foreign Affairs, emphasized the importance of Denmark's ongoing commitment. "We went into this operation in Libya with open eyes and knew that it could cost us," Espersen proclaimed. "The important thing is that Denmark has been at the forefront, and helped to keep civilians safe and ensure that the UN resolution is carried out."[57] In a similar vein, Bech, Denmark's defense minister, remained steadfast in her commitment to Libya operations when her Norwegian counterpart announced Oslo's intention to draw down its fighter-bombers by August 1.[58] Thus, Denmark's political support for the mission never wavered.

The Royal Norwegian Air Force

While major NATO allies were gearing up for out-of-area operations in the post–Cold War era, Norway found itself on a "forgotten alliance flank."[59] Throughout the 1990s, Russia's military decline seemed to ease the situation. From a Norwegian vantage point, however, a long-term uncertainty remained.[60] With the country's continu-

---

[54] Hartov, email to the author, May 16.

[55] Svarre, email to the author, February 29.

[56] Svarre, email to the author, February 29.

[57] Gerard O'Dwyer, "Libya Operations Threaten Nordic Budgets," *Defense News,* Vol. 26, No. 24, June 20, 2011, p. 8.

[58] "Danmark Bliver i Libyen Trods Norsk Exit" [Denmark Stays in Libya Despite Norway's Exit], *Avisen.dk,* June 10, 2011.

[59] Petersson and Saxi, "Shifted Roles," p. 17.

[60] Olav Riste, *Norway's Foreign Relations: A History,* Oslo: Universitetsforlaget, 2001, p. 278.

ing focus on its "High North" region and neighboring Russia, Norway's increasing commitment to out-of-area operations in the wake of the 1999 Kosovo campaign also must be seen as its effort to secure Alliance security guarantees in case of an emerging crisis in Norway's vicinity.[61]

Given the importance Oslo attaches to its good relations with the United States, the Norwegian armed forces participated in the U.S.-led Operation Enduring Freedom in Afghanistan from 2002 to 2006.[62] After having drawn down its contribution to Enduring Freedom, Norway focused on the seemingly less intense and less controversial ISAF mission in Afghanistan.[63]

Still, securing U.S. commitment to Norway's territorial integrity has remained a policy cornerstone. As such, the recent Norwegian defense white paper, published in March 2012, explicitly singled out the United States as Norway's most important bilateral partner in defense matters. At the same time, Norway attaches great importance to multilateral security cooperation in northern Europe.[64]

In line with this security rationale, the fulcrums of Oslo's military and foreign policy strategies are NATO's Article V, which provides for collective territorial defense, and the U.N., which—from a Norwegian vantage point—is crucial for securing a global world order where international law, conventions, and norms regulate interstate affairs.[65] Hence making relevant contributions to U.N.-mandated and U.S./NATO-led operations as in Libya serves both to strengthen the international legal system and to preserve the security guarantees by NATO allies, especially the United States.

Intervention

Norwegian Prime Minister Jens Stoltenberg attended the Paris Libya summit on March 19, 2011. Espen Barth Eide,[66] who accompanied the prime minister to the Elysée Palace, described the atmosphere at the summit as being infused with a sense of urgency. This urgency could be met only by airpower's swift response time and

---

[61] Petersson and Saxi, "Shifted Roles," p. 17.

[62] Minister of Defence Grete Faremo, "Fullmakt til Deltakelse Med Norske Militære Bidrag i Operasjoner til Gjennomføring av FNs Sikkerhetsrådsresolusjon 1973 (2011)" [Authorization for the Participation of a Norwegian Military Contribution in Operations for the Implementation of U.N. Security Council Resolution 1973 (2011)], *Kongelig Resolusjon* [Royal Decree], March 23, 2011, Section 5.

[63] Petersson and Saxi, "Shifted Roles," p. 20.

[64] Det Kongelige Forsvarsdepartement [The Royal Ministry of Defence (Norway)], *Et Forsvar for Vår Tid* [A Defense for Our Time], *Prop. 73 S (2011–2012): Proposisjon til Stortinget (Forslag til Stortingsvedtak)* [Proposition to Parliament (A Proposal for a Parliamentary Decision)], Oslo: Ministry of Defence, March 23, 2012, p. 28.

[65] Norwegian Ministry of Defence, *Capable Force: Strategic Concept for the Norwegian Armed Forces*, Oslo: Ministry of Defence, November 2009, pp. 4–5.

[66] At the time, Espen Barth Eide was state secretary in the Ministry of Foreign Affairs. In November 2011, he succeeded Grete Faremo as Minister of Defence.

flexibility.[67] While the Royal Norwegian Air Force detachment deployed to Souda Air Base, Greece, on March 21, the formal political decisionmaking process was ongoing for an eventual participation in the Libya campaign.[68]

On March 23, the Norwegian prime minister adopted a royal decree authorizing the RNoAF to contribute to the enforcement of UNSCR 1973 and participate in the American-led Operation Odyssey Dawn.[69] The decree explicitly highlighted the legal foundations for Norway's participation in the Libya campaign. As such, it referred not only to UNSCR 1973, but also to the Arab League's March 12 decision to request the U.N. Security Council to establish a no-fly zone and safe havens to protect the civilian population. Norwegian decisionmakers viewed UNSCR 1973, based on Chapter VII of the U.N. Charter, as the ultimate legal authorization for the use and necessity of military force. On March 21, the Norwegian government formally notified the U.N. Secretary General and the Secretary General of the Arab League of Norway's intention to contribute to the implementation of UNSCR 1973. Moreover, the royal decree explicitly mentioned that UNSCR 1973 excluded Norwegian forces from any form of foreign occupation.[70]

The decree also explicitly referred to the United States as leading Operation Odyssey Dawn and alluded to the possibility of a future command transfer to NATO, yet expressed uncertainty as to whether and to what extent NATO would have a specific role in this regard.[71] Furthermore, the decree defined the size and duration of the Norwegian military contribution. It foresaw the deployment of six fighter-bombers, along with the necessary logistical support, for a limited period of up to three months.[72]

Speaking at a January 2012 airpower conference, the Minister of Defence emphasized that, from a Norwegian vantage point, the United Nations' central role was crucial. He underlined that, as a small state, Norway has a particular interest in a smoothly functioning international legal order enshrined in the U.N. Given the clear U.N. mandate for Libya air operations, it was in Norway's interest to participate. In a similar vein, the Arab League's providing of regional backing was central—very much in contrast to operations in Afghanistan. The Minister of Defence also welcomed the support that Nigeria,

---

[67] Minister of Defence Espen Barth Eide, "Innledning" [Introduction], *Luftforsvarets Luftmaktseminar: Internasjonal Krisehåndtering Under Og Etter Libya* [Air Force Air Power Seminar: International Crisis Management During and After Libya], Trondheim, Norway, January 31, 2012.

[68] Faremo, "Fullmakt til deltakelse med norske militære bidrag," March 23, Section 3.

[69] Statsministerens Kontor [Prime Minister's Office], "Norge Med i Operasjoner i Libya" [Norway Participates in Operations in Libya], *Pressemelding* [press release], March 23, 2011.

[70] Faremo, "Fullmakt til deltakelse med norske militære bidrag," March 23, Sections 1, 2.

[71] Faremo, "Fullmakt til deltakelse med norske militære bidrag," March 23, Section 2.

[72] Faremo, "Fullmakt til deltakelse med norske militære bidrag," March 23, Section 3.

A Norwegian fighter pilot performing a final check of his F-16AM shortly before take-off from Souda Air Base, Crete. In addition to AIM-120B AMRAAM missiles, the aircraft is armed with GBU-31(V)1/B and GBU-31(V)3/B PGMs, the latter designed to penetrate hard targets such as bunkers.
Courtesy of the Royal Norwegian Air Force.

Lebanon, Gabon, and South Africa gave to UNSCR 1973; as members of the Security Council, their backing diverted criticism of Western hegemonic interests.[73]

Deployment and Operations

The Norwegian detachment commander and a site survey team preceding the main force met with their Belgian counterparts in Brussels on, March 20. The same day, both parties traveled together to Araxos Air Base in western Greece, where a Belgian F-16 detachment already was deployed for an exercise. A point of discussion was whether the RNoAF and the Belgian Air Force (BAF) could conduct common operations from Araxos. Yet because ongoing construction work on the airstrip inhibited night missions, neither appears to have perceived Araxos Air Base as particularly suitable. Subsequently, the Norwegian and Belgian teams continued their journey to Souda Air Base in Crete. A cooperative arrangement between the two nations within the framework of the EEAW was discussed, but it appears both parties concluded that the available facilities at Souda Bay were too small for both a Belgian and a Norwegian detachment. Since the BAF already was established at Araxos Air Base, and the RNoAF needed to find a base without further delay on March 21—the RNoAF fighter-bombers were already in the air en

---

[73] Eide, "Innledning," January 31.

route to their potential forward base—it was agreed that the RNoAF would operate from Souda Air Base.[74]

The deployed F-16s came from all of the RNoAF's fighter squadrons—331 Squadron and 332 Squadron (132 Air Wing at Bodø Main Air Station) as well as 338 Squadron (138 Air Wing at Ørland Main Air Station).[75] RNoAF fighter-bombers flew their first combat sorties over Libya on March 24, three days after their deployment to Souda Bay and one day after the Norwegian prime minister had adopted the royal decree authorizing RNoAF operations in Libya.[76]

RNoAF operations out of Souda required approximately 110 personnel in Crete.[77] To deploy this detachment in the early stages of Operation Odyssey Dawn, the RNoAF could—in addition to its own C-130J Hercules aircraft and land transport—draw upon the NATO Heavy Airlift Wing. One C-17A Globemaster flight thus supported the deployment.[78]

To meet the conditions set in the royal decree of March 23, Norway dispatched national red-card holders to the planning cells of Operation Odyssey Dawn and later Operation Unified Protector. In particular, the Norwegian Minister of Defence under-lined the robust rules of engagement in both operations, a prerequisite for Norwegian participation in combat missions.[79] Swift integration into Operation Odyssey Dawn required a great deal of flexibility and liaising with AFRICOM through Ramstein Air Base and with U.S. forces collocated at Souda.[80] For Espen Barth Eide, Norwegian Minister of Defence from late 2011 to 2012 and later Minister of Foreign Affairs, the fact that Norwegian aircraft were capable of delivering an effect within five days after the Paris summit of March 19 exemplified a unique politico-military interaction ability. He also pointed to the high percentage of PGMs dropped by Norwegian and Danish fighter-bombers.[81]

---

[74] Henriksen, email to the author, June 6.

[75] Henriksen, email to the author, June 6.

[76] Forsvarsdepartementet [Ministry of Defence (Norway)], "Forsvarsministerens Redegjørelse for Stortinget 9. Mai" [Defence Minister's Statement to Parliament on May 9], *Artikkel* [article], May 9, 2011.

[77] Forsvaret [Defence (Norway)], "Sluttrapport Libya" [Final Report on Libya Operations], December 2, 2011.

[78] Brigadier Per Egil Rygg, RNoAF, Commander 132 Air Wing, Bodø, Norway, email to the author, March 27, 2012. The NATO Heavy Airlift Wing works within the framework of NATO's Strategic Airlift Capability. It is a cooperative NATO arrangement to commonly operate three Boeing C-17 strategic transport aircraft out of Pápa Air Base in Hungary. In addition to ten NATO member countries—including the United States—Sweden and Finland also participate in this arrangement. See NATO, "Strategic Airlift Capability (SAC): A Key Capability for the Alliance," online, last updated August 7, 2012.

[79] Forsvarsdepartementet [Ministry of Defence (Norway)], "Kommandooverføring til Nato" [Transfer of Command to NATO], *Nyheter* [News], March 30, 2011.

[80] Rygg, email to the author, March 27.

[81] Eide, "Innledning," January 31.

Yet Norway's efforts also had limits. Approaching the end of the three-month deployment period as stipulated in the royal decree of March 23, Minister of Defence Grete Faremo on June 10 announced Norway's intention to withdraw its fighter-bomber contribution by August 1. In particular, she asked Norway's allies for understanding, since an air force of the RNoAF's size could not maintain such a large fighter contribution over a prolonged period.[82] In the interim, a reduction from six F-16 aircraft to four was to be implemented by June 24.[83] Norwegian combat aircraft flew their last operational mission on July 30; Norway formally ceased fighter operations in the framework of Operation Unified Protector on July 31, and the bulk of the RNoAF detachment left Souda on August 1. In addition to its contribution to the NATO Airborne Early Warning and Control Force, the RNoAF subsequently continued to support the Alliance efforts against Qaddafi's regime with ten staff officers in NATO's air planning cells.[84]

Other than the strain of Libya air operations, no public or formal explanation was given for the RNoAF ceasing Libya air operations at the end of July. Multiple explanations for the government's decision not to extend Norway's participation in the campaign have been informally offered within Norwegian security policy circles, but the issue has yet to be thoroughly researched.[85]

During Operation Odyssey Dawn, RNoAF F-16 fighter-bombers flew 32 sorties and dropped a total of 19 PGMs. In the subsequent NATO-led Operation Unified Protector, Norwegian aircraft carried out 583 sorties and released 569 PGMs. Overall, the RNoAF detachment flew a total of 615 sorties, totaling 3,121.6 flying hours.[86] The Norwegian operational tempo right after the transition from Operation Odyssey Dawn to Operation Unified Protector was outstanding. As of May 1, 2011, it was reported that the RNoAF detachment had released a total of 266 PGMs.[87] In a May 9 statement, Minister of Defence Grete Faremo confirmed to Parliament that Norwegian fighter-bombers had been striking a broad array of regime targets, taking a

---

[82] Forsvarsdepartementet [Ministry of Defence (Norway)], "Viderefører Kampflybidraget til 1.August" [Continuing the Fighter Jet Contribution til August 1], *Pressemelding* [News Release], June 10, 2011.

[83] Gerard O'Dwyer, "Libya Operations Threaten Nordic Budgets," *Defense News*, June 20, 2011, p. 8.

[84] Forsvaret, "Sluttrapport Libya," December 2; and Forsvarsdepartementet [Ministry of Defence (Norway)], "Norge Med i Nato-Ledet Våpenembargo" [Norway Participates in NATO-Led Arms Embargo], *Nyheter*, March 24, 2011.

[85] Henriksen, email to the author, June 6.

[86] Forsvaret, "Sluttrapport Libya," December 2.

[87] Gunn Evy Auestad, "Held Tett om Norsk Role i Drapet På Gaddafi-Son" [Stays Silent on the Norwegian Role in the Killing of Gadhafi's Son], *NRK* [Norwegian Broadcasting Corporation] (May 1, 2011).

central role in the air attack missions.[88] Given that the RNoAF had previously released only a handful of PGMs in Afghanistan, this operational pace is even more impressive.[89]

In a publicly released December 2, 2011, report, Norwegian officials provided figures on weapons deliveries (see Table 10.1). Approximately 20 percent of the targets were dynamic, and the remaining 80 percent were deliberate targets. To deliver this precision firepower, all Norwegian strikers were equipped with state-of-the art Pantera targeting pods.[90] Alongside the RDAF, the RNoAF stood out as one of the air forces to keep up the operational momentum after the transition from Operation Odyssey Dawn to Operation Unified Protector. At some point in April, once the red-card holders were invited to sit in on the daily joint targeting working group, saw the targets being developed, and got increased access to adequate intelligence information, they had even fewer deliberations to strike targets presented on the prioritized target list (PTL). Prior to this, the national red-card holders only saw the proposed targets when they were approved on the PTL.[91] At an airpower seminar at the Norwegian Air Force Academy, Operation Unified Protector's JTF Commander, Lt.-Gen. Charles Bouchard, reemphasized Norway's willingness to act decisively: "You [Norway] were

Table 10.1
RNoAF Weapons Deliveries During Operations Odyssey Dawn and Unified Protector

Target Category	Number of PGMs	Distribution (%)
Tanks	45	8
Aircraft shelters	11	2
Artillery	29	5
Munitions depots	248	42
Scud missiles	1	0
Command and control facilities	113	19
Land lines of communication	12	2
Armored personnel vehicles	19	3
Ground-based air defense	12	2
Other vehicles	28	5
Infrastructure (storage, etc.)	70	12
Total	588	100

SOURCE: Forsvaret [Defense (Norway)], "Sluttrapport Libya" [Final Report on Libya Operations], December 2, 2012.

---

[88] Forsvarsdepartementet [Ministry of Defence (Norway)], "Forsvarsministerens Redegjørelse for Stortinget 9. Mai" [Defence Minister's Statement to Parliament on May 9], *Artikkel*, May 9, 2011.

[89] Henriksen, email to the author, May 16, 2012.

[90] Col. Geir Wiik RNoAF, Chief J3 Air, Norwegian Joint Headquarters, Bodø, Norway, email to the author, April 11, 2012.

[91] Henriksen, email to the author, May 16.

one of the go-to countries when we needed to get things done . . . You did some stuff the others did not want to do. Norway flew well, and flew very precise."[92] A senior USAF member of the CFACC's staff reiterated Norway's determination, especially in the early stage of Operation Unified Protector: "Norway took some of the most challenging missions and performed in a superb manner."[93]

In addition to national formations, Norwegian F-16 fighter-bombers flew alongside combat aircraft from the United States, Belgium, Denmark, France, Canada, and the United Arab Emirates. In particular, RNoAF F-16s had an extended cooperation with American F-16CJs and EA-18G Growlers. In terms of COMAOs, the Norwegians primarily joined with Belgian, Danish, French, and Canadian aircraft. The common Fighter Weapons Instructor Training is considered to significantly have increased the RNoAF aircrews' overall level of proficiency in air-to-air and air-to-ground missions and enhanced combined missions with other EPAF F-16 operators, as well as other contributing nations in Operation Unified Protector.[94]

The Belgian Air Force[95]

Belgium's 1994 defense white paper identified five main axes of Belgian defense policy: "developing the European Union, maintaining the transatlantic link, broadening cooperation with other countries, reinforcing the United Nations' role, and participating in arms control." In particular, Belgian decisionmakers supported an "armed wing" of the EU as well as strengthening NATO's European pillar. They also perceived this emerging pillar as in line with, and not in contradiction to, a transatlantic partnership; it was understood as committing European NATO partners to assume more responsibilities and thus contribute to transatlantic burden sharing.[96] Since the 1990s, successive governments have upheld, with slight differences in style, this dual-track policy of simultaneously supporting a thrust toward more integrated European defense and

---

[92] Lt.-Gen. Charles Bouchard, JTF Commander of Operation Unified Protector, at the annual Norwegian Chief of the Air Staff Air Power Seminar, Norwegian Air Force Academy, February 2, 2012.

[93] Email from senior member of Lt. Gen. Jodice's staff to Dr. Dag Henriksen, April 27, 2012, forwarded to the author, May 16, 2012.

[94] Henriksen, email to the author, June 21, 2012.

[95] The Belgian Air Force as the air intervention component of the Belgian Armed Forces is formally called the Belgian Defense Air Component. In an international context, it is still referred to as the Belgian Air Force. The transition from a single-service structure to a component structure was enacted by the *Arrêté Royal Déterminant la Structure Générale du Ministère de la Défense et Fixant les Attributions de Certaines Autorités* [Royal Decree Determining the General Structure of the Ministry of Defence and Defining Certain Authorities' Fields of Responsibility], Brussels: Ministry of Defence, December 21, 2001, Chapter IV, Section 1, Paragraph 2.

[96] *White Paper '94*, Brussels: Ministry of Defence, 1994, pp. 22–23.

emphasizing the transatlantic partnership with NATO.[97] It was reiterated in June 2008 by Minister of Defence Pieter De Crem, who underlined both Belgium's support of a more integrated European defense in the framework of the EU and enhanced cooperation within NATO. In the same vein, he supported better coordination and cooperation between the EU, NATO, and the United Nations, viewing the three organizations as complementary.[98]

While Belgium's decisionmakers have been able to reconcile their EU and NATO defense ambitions, they have appeared to have more trouble in reconciling their country's historically determined pacifism with their support for collective security within the EU and NATO. Collective security requires the ability to engage in operations across the spectrum of military force. At the same time, Belgium's pacifism is rooted in the country's historical experience as Europe's battlefield.[99] Thus, De Crem argued in mid-2008 that Belgium's ambition to be a responsible and dependable partner required taking a fair share of the risks involved in current military operations. In line with this policy, the armed forces' ability to participate effectively in international operations would be prioritized and enhanced, despite budgetary constraints.[100] None of the government parties actively opposed De Crem's goals.[101]

Intervention

Belgium's Libya intervention drew upon airpower as the main element and included a small naval component consisting of a minehunter.[102] According to Belgian scholar Sven Biscop, an operation designed around air and naval power is less controversial for Belgian decisionmakers than one hinging on army forces. While it is Belgium's ambition to engage in operations across the spectrum of military force, debates have arisen about the army's actual ability to operate in high-intensity warfare. In contrast, deploying air and naval components for combat operations is regarded as less controversial, partly because of the relatively low risk entailed for the Belgian military.[103]

---

[97] Sven Biscop, "Belgian Defence Policy: The Fight Goes On," *Security Policy Brief*, No. 32, December 2011, pp. 1–2.

[98] Pieter De Crem, *Note d'Orientation Politique* [Note of Political Orientation], Brussels: Ministry of Defence, June 2008, pp. 13, 15.

[99] Biscop, "Belgian Defence Policy," pp. 1, 4.

[100] De Crem, *Note d'orientation politique*, pp. 2, 9.

[101] Prof. Dr. Sven Biscop, Royal Institute for International Relations, Brussels, Belgium, email to the author, May 23, 2012.

[102] On March 23, 2011, the minehunter *Narcis* started operating in the framework of Operation Unified Protector. La Défense [Defence (Belgium)], "Aperçu Hebdomadaire des Opérations Extérieures" [Weekly Report on Deployed Operations], March 17, 2011–March 23, 2011, p. 2.

[103] Biscop, "Belgian Defence Policy," p. 3.

This reality also can be observed in the context of operations in Afghanistan. Belgian ground troops initially were relegated to logistical tasks and the protection of Kabul International Airport.[104] Later, they added efforts to the support of the Kunduz Provincial Reconstruction Team (PRT) in the north of Afghanistan.[105] In contrast, Belgian politicians preferred airpower to do the "heavy" fighting. In early 2008, the government decided to deploy F-16 fighter-bombers to the south of Afghanistan.[106] Beginning in September 2008, six Belgian Air Force F-16s operated out of Kandahar, taking on demanding combat tasks such as ground alert CAS.[107] At the Chicago NATO Summit in May 2012, De Crem confirmed this ongoing fighter deployment until the end of 2014. At the same time, the overall Belgian defense commitment in support of ISAF was to be decreased.[108]

Throughout the entire Libya crisis, Belgium was undergoing a protracted period of political stalemate. The political deadlock originated from tensions between the Flemish- and French-speaking communities. In April 2010, the government resigned. The outgoing government subsequently ran the country for 541 days as a "caretaker" executive with reduced authorities. Not until December 6, 2011 was a new government sworn in.[109] This particular circumstance resulted in a situation in which Parliament, fully functional, became exceptionally strong vis-à-vis the executive branch.[110]

Outside of Belgium's national decisionmaking process, Belgian EU parliamentarians had become quite concerned about events unfolding in North Africa by mid-March 2011. Across party and linguistic boundaries, former Belgian ministers Guy Verhofstadt, Louis Michel, and Isabelle Durant were united in their views and lobbied for a proactive role for the EU in the Libya crisis, including a military one. At the same time, the Belgian media closely followed the popular uprising in Libya, which began in Benghazi in mid-February, unambiguously highlighting the Qaddafi regime's atrocities against civilians. The Belgian media also underlined the importance of a military intervention in stopping imminent carnage.[111]

Against this backdrop, on March 18, the Belgian Parliament unanimously voted in favor of a military contribution to solve the Libya crisis—one day after the U.N.

---

[104]Dr. Joseph Henrotin, senior researcher at the Centre d'analyse et de prévision des risques internationaux and Institut de stratégie et des conflits, email to the author, March 8, 2012.

[105]Biscop, "Belgian Defence Policy," p. 3.

[106]De Crem, *Note d'orientation politique*, p. 10.

[107]Poesen, email to the author, March 22, 2012. Information provided was screened and endorsed by the Chief of Staff, Deputy Air Component Commander.

[108]Poesen, email to the author, May 22.

[109]"Belgium Swears in New Government Headed by Elio di Rupo," *BBC News*, December 6, 2011.

[110]Henrotin, email to the author, March 8.

[111]Henrotin, email to the author, March 8.

Security Council had adopted Resolution 1973 and one day prior to the beginning of combat operations.[112] Not only did Parliament's backing give the Belgian military contribution a solid foundation and justification, but it also was necessary—the "caretaker" government, which initiated the parliamentary vote, lacked the constitutional authority to take this decision.[113]

Three political conditions had to be met for a Belgian military intervention in Libya: a demonstrable necessity, regional support, and a U.N. mandate.[114] In the case of Libya, all three stipulations were seen as having been met in mid-March 2011. Parliament's unanimous vote in favor of a military participation is indeed a rare occurrence in Belgian politics. According to Belgian scholars, three factors principally made it possible: UNSCR 1973, which was widely regarded as a solid foundation for action, the widespread media coverage, which created a sense of necessity, and the public antipathy toward Qaddafi.[115]

The various parties' motives converged for different reasons. For instance, Green Party members, who are in principle against the use of force, saw humanitarian issues at stake. For the liberals, both Flemish- and French-speaking, it was an issue of supporting a seemingly liberal revolution in North Africa. Moreover, the French-speaking liberals saw an opportunity to indirectly criticize the former Minister of Defence, André Flahaut, a French-speaking socialist, and his perceived weak posture when it came to military deployments. In contrast, his successor De Crem, a member of the Christian Democratic and Flemish (CD&V) party, had a more hawkish image.[116]

It also seems that French President Nicolas Sarkozy's proactive stance regarding Libya influenced a number of Belgian decisionmakers, particularly among the French-speaking liberals. In Belgian politics, France is widely considered as a power whose actions generally inspire confidence. Both countries also share an ambition to strengthen European defense.[117]

Deployment and Operations

On March 21, two days after the start of Operation Odyssey Dawn, the Belgian government decided to contribute actively to this operation. On the same day, four BAF F-16s conducted their first combat air patrol mission.[118] Six days later, on March 27, the

---

[112] Poesen, email to the author, March 22.

[113] Biscop, email to the author, April 20, 2012.

[114] Poesen, email to the author, March 22.

[115] Henrotin, email to the author, March 8; and Biscop, email to the author, April 20.

[116] Henrotin, email, March 8.

[117] Henrotin, email, March 8.

[118] La Défense [Defence (Belgium)], "Aperçu hebdomadaire des opérations extérieures" [Weekly Report on Deployed Operations], March 17, 2011–March 23, 2011, pp. 1, 3.

A BAF F-16AM overflies Tripoli on transit toward the air refueling tracks on April 28, 2011, after conducting a SCAR mission in the Zintan area, southwest of Tripoli. During this stage of the conflict, few NATO resources were dedicated to support the emerging third rebel front in the Nafusa mountains. To engage moving ground targets, this aircraft was armed with two GBU-12 laser-guided 500-lb bombs, in addition to medium-range AIM-120B AMRAAM and short-range AIM-9M-9 Sidewinder missiles.
Courtesy of the Belgian Air Force, photo by Vador.

Belgian detachment conducted its first air-to-ground strikes. During three consecutive days, the Belgian detachment carried out offensive counterair strikes against Libyan air force installations. On March 27 and March 28, a total of four attacks were conducted, each involving two aircraft. Four BAF F-16s flew one larger attack mission on the next day.[119] In late March, Minister of Defence De Crem publicly released images of a Beligan forces' airfield attack, showing the destruction of a Libyan Sukhoi Su-22 on the ground.[120]

The BAF detachment operated out of Araxos Air Base in western Greece by coincidence rather than design. One of the BAF's units already was conducting a deployment exercise at this Greek base, and when Operation Odyssey Dawn started, it remained in place to make up the initial Belgian detachment.[121] The detachment at Araxos consisted of six F-16 fighter-bombers and, initially, 130 deployed personnel. BAF operations in support of UNSCR 1973, and in the framework of Operation Odyssey Dawn

[119] La Défense, "Aperçu hebdomadaire des opérations extérieures" [Weekly Report on Deployed Operations] (March 24, 2011–March 30, 2011), p. 3.

[120] "De Crem geeft beelden bombardementen vrij" [De Crem releases bombing images for publication], *De Standaard*, March 30, 2011.

[121] Poesen, email to the author, March 22.

and later Operation Unified Protector, formally were referred to as Operation Freedom Falcon. Belgian decisionmakers already had anticipated coalition air operations would soon be handed over to NATO.[122] Consistent with this emphasis on multinational cooperation, the BAF detachment regularly contributed to missions combining aircraft from different countries. BAF two-ships smoothly combined with national elements from other EPAF partner nations and easily operated alongside French or British combat aircraft using common NATO standards and procedures.[123]

The Belgian government approved national rules of engagement on March 21, the first day of Belgian air operations in the framework of Operation Odyssey Dawn. In particular, it anticipated the use of Belgian F-16s' entire array of weapons. Moreover, it did not exclude a later redeployment from Araxos Air Base to another air base.[124] To retain national discretion and compliance with national rules of engagement, a Belgian red-card holder was based at Ramstein Air Base.[125] Swift integration into the American-led Operation Odyssey Dawn was made possible because of experience drawn from recent operations and routine peacetime cooperation with the United States and other allies, particularly at NATO headquarters Allied Air Command, Ramstein.[126] After Libya air operations had been handed over to NATO, Belgian red-card holders, like their Danish and Norwegian counterparts at Poggio Renatico, Italy, were invited to sit in on the daily joint targeting working group and saw targets prior to the release of the prioritized target list. This early integration in the targeting process did not remove national restrictions on certain targets, but it allowed Belgian red-card holders to provide a quicker approval, with their questions and concerns being addressed at an early stage.[127]

Until May 13, BAF fighter-bombers did not conduct night missions over Libya. The reason was related to maintenance work on the runway at Araxos, which had not allowed for night sorties prior to this date. The Belgian Minister of Defence personally contacted Evangelos Venizelos, his Greek counterpart, to ask for completion

---

[122]La Défense [Defence (Belgium)], "Aperçu Hebdomadaire des Opérations Extérieures" [Weekly Report on Deployed Operations], March 17, 2011–March 23, 2011, pp. 1–2.

[123]Poesen, email to the author, May 22.

[124]La Défense [Defence (Belgium)], "Aperçu Hebdomadaire des Opérations Extérieures" [Weekly Report on Deployed Operations], March 17, 2011—March 23, 2011, p. 2.

[125]La Défense [Defence (Belgium)], "Aperçu Hebdomadaire des Opérations Extérieures" [Weekly Report on Deployed Operations], March 17, 2011—March 23, 2011, p. 2.

[126]Poesen, email to the author, March 22.

[127]Poesen, email to the author, May 25, 2012.

of the maintenance work.[128] After May 13, Belgian F-16s regularly conducted night missions.[129]

Unlike the RDAF or the RNLAF, the BAF no longer formally splits its detachments into operational and reserve aircraft. Rather, commitments are expressed in numbers of flying hours and the sortie rate per day. In the case of Operation Freedom Falcon, the goal was to fly 360 hours per month at a rate of between two and four sorties per day. To efficiently generate these numbers, Belgian F-16s were rotated between Belgium and Araxos Air Base throughout the campaign. In contrast to fighter rotations for operations in Afghanistan, which require in-flight refueling, en-route staging, and numerous diplomatic clearances, rotations between Araxos and Belgium occurred in a single flight without external support.[130]

Throughout Operation Unified Protector, six BAF personnel were continuously assigned to Poggio Renatico. The Belgian personnel included a red-card holder, who also acted as the senior national representative and was assisted by a legal advisor. In addition to assisting the Belgian red-card holder, the legal advisor supported the planning team on request. During the transition phase from American-led Operation Odyssey Dawn to NATO taking on full responsibilities for all air operations, the BAF had red-card holders both at Ramstein Air Base and at the NATO CAOC in Italy. This secured a seamless continuation of Belgian air operations. In general, the remaining BAF personnel dispatched to CAOC 5 came either from NATO CAOC 2 in Uedem, Germany, or from Allied Air Command, Ramstein.[131]

Up to October 18, Belgian fighter-bombers spent approximately 2,500 hours in the air and released 473 PGMs.[132] When the Belgian Minister of Defence visited the BAF detachment at Araxos Air Base on October 29, BAF fighter-bombers conducted their last mission over Libya, but had no need to engage ground targets. On the same day, two of the six F-16s redeployed to Belgium. The following day, a four-hour standby by Belgian aircrews constituted the final NATO combat tasking before the remaining four F-16s and the bulk of the Belgian detachment returned home on October 31.[133]

When Operation Freedom Falcon ceased on October 31, BAF F-16s had flown 620 sorties, including 236 night sorties. Typically, two to four sorties per day were conducted during six days out of seven. Flight duration varied from 2.5 to 6.5 hours. In

---

[128]La Défense [Defence (Belgium)], "Vols de Nuit pour Nos F-16 en Libye" [Night Flights by Our F-16s over Libya], May 19, 2011.

[129]La Défense [Defence (Belgium)], "Aperçu Hebdomadaire des Opérations Extérieures" [Weekly Report on Deployed Operations], May 12, 2011 – May 18, 2011, p. 2.

[130]Poesen, email to the author, March 22.

[131]Poesen, email to the author, March 22.

[132]La Défense [Defence (Belgium)], "Khadafi et son régime neutralisés," October 20, 2011.

[133]La Défense [Defence (Belgium)], "Aperçu Hebdomadaire des Opérations Extérieures" [Weekly Report on Deployed Operations], October 27, 2011–November 2, 2011, p. 2.

total, Belgian fighter-bombers spent 2,589 hours airborne throughout Operation Freedom Falcon. Five percent of their missions were DCA, 30 percent were deliberate targeting missions, and the majority—65 percent—were dynamic targeting missions. The latter were primarily armed strike-coordination and reconnaissance (SCAR) missions. So-called SCAR boxes were established over specific areas or "hot spots," depending on the evolution of the tactical situation.[134]

The Belgian fighter-bombers released a broad array of laser- or GPS-guided PGMs. These included 21 GBU-10 laser-guided, 110 GBU-12 laser-guided, 11 GBU-24 laser-guided, 146 GBU-31(V)1/B GPS-guided, 35 GBU-31(V)3/B GPS-guided, and 150 GBU-38 GPS-guided bombs. Due to limited stocks and the lead times for replenishment, Mk-84 general-purpose bomb bodies, rather than BLU-109 hardened penetration bomb bodies, had to be used in some instances. All Belgian F-16 strike aircraft flying missions over Libya were equipped with targeting pods.[135] The state-of-the-art AN/AAQ-33 Sniper was the BAF detachment's standard targeting pod.[136]

Regarding AAR, Belgian F-16s are qualified to receive fuel from any boom-type NATO tanker. Based on availability, Belgian fighter aircraft were refueled by tankers from the USAF, the RNLAF, or the French Air Force. Although compatible Turkish Air Force tankers operated in the vicinity, they were under a national caveat to support only Turkish missions. Each Belgian offensive sortie required prestrike and often post-strike AAR support.[137] That AAR was a scarce commodity was demonstrated on October 7, when two Belgian missions were canceled due to the unavailability of allied tanker aircraft.[138]

As in the case of the RNLAF detachment at Decimomannu Air Base in Sardinia, the European Air Transport Command (EATC) coordinated the airlift to support the BAF detachment at Araxos. BAF C-130 Hercules aircraft, if available, were the first choice for resupplying the Belgian contingent. When this was not possible, the EATC had full authority to task transport aircraft from other partner nations.[139] German transport aircraft also reportedly supported the Belgian detachment in Greece.

---

[134]Poesen, email to the author, March 22.

[135]Poesen, email to the author, March 22.

[136]Serge Van Heertum, freelance aeronautical journalist and SBAP editor, email to the author, February 13, 2012.

[137]Poesen, email to the author, March 22.

[138]La Défense [Defence (Belgium)], "Aperçu Hebdomadaire des Opérations Extérieures" [Weekly Report on Deployed Operations], October 6, 2011–October 12, 2011, p. 2.

[139]Poesen email, March 22. Founding nations of the EATC—besides Belgium—are Germany, France, and the Netherlands. The EATC began operations in the second half of 2010.

The Royal Netherlands Air Force

Over the last decade, the Netherlands had been a staunch supporter of American for-eign and security policy goals. Like Denmark, it became a member of the U.S.-led "coalition of the willing" against Iraq in 2003. After the invasion was completed, it deployed troops to help stabilize the country. Dutch forces pulled out of Iraq in the spring of 2005, with the focus redirected to Afghanistan.[140] Minister of Defence Henk Kamp underlined Dutch defense political goals in 2004. In his view, allied solidar-ity must be demonstrated not only by a country's military capabilities, but also by its willingness to share risk. In accordance with this view, the Netherlands Armed Forces' ability to engage at the higher end of the military spectrum became an important pillar of Dutch foreign and defense policy.[141] From a transatlantic vantage point, the Netherlands was a dependable ally, willing to shoulder significant responsibilities, and airpower always was in the vanguard of Dutch military contributions. As discussed in the introduction, the Royal Netherlands Air Force proved throughout the Balkan wars and beyond to be an asset out of proportion to its size.

The issue of fragile political support for military operations came to the fore in early 2010. After the release of the Davids report in January 2010, strong tensions developed among the Netherlands ruling coalition parties. Prime Minister Jan Peter Balkenende had only reluctantly and under political pressure established the Davids Committee, named after and headed by a former president of the Supreme Court. The committee's task was to critically examine Netherlands decisionmaking in con-nection with Operation Iraqi Freedom. It concluded that no proper legal mandate existed for the invasion of Iraq, which had been supported by the first Balkenende cabinet. Balkenende initially disagreed with several findings of the Davids Committee. To smother a political crisis with the Labor Party (PvdA), one of his coalition allies, he then revised his response. Yet one month later, the issue of extending the Netherlands military presence in Afghanistan laid bare the irreconcilable fissures among the coali-tion parties. The Labor Party did not back a further extension of operations there.[142] As a consequence, withdrawal of the Netherlands Armed Forces from Afghanistan was scheduled to start in August 2010.[143] (The drawing-down of Dutch troops and the Netherlands giving up its ISAF lead nation role in the province of Uruzgan did not result in the country's complete disengagement from Afghanistan. In 2011, the Netherlands established a police-training mission in Kunduz. A detachment of four

---

[140] Anrig, *The Quest for Relevant Air Power*, 246.

[141] Henk Kamp, Minister of Defence, address, Royal Netherlands Association of Military Science, Nieuwspoort Press Centre, The Hague, March 1, 2004.

[142] Dr. Gustaaf Reerink, attorney-at-law, Amsterdam, email to the author, March 28, 2012.

[143] David Charter and Tom Coghlan, "Dutch Confirm Afghan Troop Pullout Sparking Fears of Domino Effect," *The Times*, February 22, 2010.

RNLAF F-16s was kept in Afghanistan as a protection force and for supporting ISAF operations.[144])

Disagreements over Afghanistan operations in February 2010 finally led to the fall of Balkenende's fourth cabinet, with Queen Beatrix accepting the resignation of the Labor Party ministers on February 23, 2010. The ensuing Dutch general election on June 9 resulted in the formation of the Rutte cabinet. Prime Minister Mark Rutte headed a minority cabinet formed by the People's Party for Freedom and Democracy (VVD), a liberal conservative party, and the Christian Democratic Appeal (CDA), a Christian conservative party. Its political decisionmaking power hinged significantly upon the support of the far right-wing Freedom Party (PVV), headed by Geert Wilders. Queen Beatrix installed the Rutte cabinet on October 14, 2010.[145] Thus, very much in contrast to previous post–Cold War operations, when the Netherlands played a proactive role, the political constellation was less favorable and conducive to robust military operations than it had been prior to 2010.

Intervention

On March 18, the day after the U.N. Security Council had adopted UNSCR 1973, Minister of Foreign Affairs Dr. U. Rosenthal and Minister of Defence J. S. J. Hillen informed Parliament of a forthcoming military contribution to support the resolution's implementation.[146] Prime Minister Rutte participated in the following day's Libya crisis summit at the Elysée Palace. After the adoption of UNSCR 1973 and the crisis summit in Paris, the RNLAF started to prepare substantively for participation in the Libya campaign.[147]

Finally, on March 22, the ministers of Foreign Affairs and Defence presented the planned Netherlands military contribution to Parliament. While the contribution included a naval component, consisting of one minehunter, the Netherlands decisionmakers primarily drew upon airpower. The air component consisted of six RNLAF F-16 fighter aircraft, including two reserve aircraft, in the air-to-air role. In addition, the RNLAF was detailed to support the NATO AWACS effort and augment NATO's operational headquarters. Overall, the Netherlands contribution was planned to amount to 200 deployed military personnel for an initial period of three months. The only asset to be deployed for a very limited period, until April 4, was one

---

[144] Erwin van Loo, Netherlands Institute for Military History, The Hague, email to the author, June 22, 2013.

[145] Reerink, email, March 28.

[146] "Betreft Kennisgevingsbrief over Uitvoering Veiligheidsraad Resolutie 1973 Inzake Libië" [Letter of Information Relating to the Implementation of Security Council Resolution 1973 Concerning Libya] by the Minister of Foreign Affairs Dr. U. Rosenthal and the Minister of Defense J.S.J. Hillen to the Chairman of the Senate, The Hague, March 18, 2011.

[147] Air Commodore Paul Mulder, RNLAF, Director Operations Air Staff, Breda, Netherlands, telephone interview by the author, January 31, 2012.

of the RNLAF's two KDC-10 tanker aircraft. Netherlands air assets were intended for NATO operations only and not authorized to conduct air-to-ground strikes.[148]

According to Article 100 of the Netherlands Constitution, the government is formally required only to inform Parliament about deployed military operations, not seek its approval.[149] Yet to secure broad political support, Parliament *de facto* regularly approves of the Netherlands Armed Forces' contributions to deployed military operations. In the case of Libya operations, it granted approval on March 23.[150] Yet in contrast to their counterparts in Brussels, Copenhagen, or Oslo, decisionmakers in The Hague put a premium on the Netherlands Armed Forces operating exclusively under established NATO command structures.[151] As such, RNLAF F-16 fighter aircraft were not to be tasked by AFRICOM's AOC, but by NATO CAOC 5 in Poggio Renatico, Italy. On March 25, NATO extended Operation Unified Protector, launched two days previously as an arms-embargo operation, to include NFZ operations.[152]

Deployment and Operations

On March 24, one day after parliamentary approval was granted, the RNLAF detachment deployed to Sardinia. The Netherlands defense attaché in Italy secured Decimomannu Air Base as a forward operating base for the RNLAF contingent. As the width of the available taxiways at Decimomannu was too limited, however, the KDC-10 had to be diverted to Sardinia's Cagliari-Elmas International Airport.The following day, the aircraft were ready to contribute to NATO air operations. Yet since CAOC 5 at Poggio Renatico was not in a position to task missions in the NATO framework of Operation Unified Protector until three days later, the RNLAF detachment's first mission took place on March 28.[153]

Throughout operations, RNLAF aircraft regularly were rotated between Decimomannu and the Netherlands, as higher-level maintenance could be provided more efficiently in the Netherlands. In particular, the inspection time frame of 300 hours set the deployment limit for individual aircraft. Simultaneously with the Libya operations, the RNLAF F-16 fleet underwent a software upgrade. As a result, aircraft with

---

[148] "Betreft Nederlandse Bijdrage aan Uitvoering VN Veiligheidsraad Resolutie 1973 Inzake Libië" [Letter of Information Relating to a Netherlands Contribution to the Implementation of Security Council Resolution 1973 Concerning Libya], by the Minister of Foreign Affairs, Dr. U. Rosenthal, and the Minister of Defense, J.S.J. Hillen, to the Chairman of the Senate, The Hague, March 22, 2011, p. 1.

[149] "Artikel 100: Handhaving of Bevordering Internationale Rechtsorde" [Article 100: Maintain or Advance International Legal Order], *Nederlandse Grondwet* [Netherlands Constitution].

[150] Air Commodore Ralph W. Reefman, RNLAF, Deputy Director Operations Defence Staff, The Hague, Netherlands, telephone interview by the author, February 3, 2012.

[151] Mulder, telephone interview, January 31.

[152] NATO Media Operations Centre, "Operation Unified Protector Final Mission Stats," November 2, 2011.

[153] Mulder, telephone interview.

Royal Netherlands Air Force F-16AM taxiing at Decimomannu Air Base, Sardinia, on April 21, 2011. It carries the standard Dutch armament for OUP comprising one short-range AIM-9L and three medium-range AIM-120B AMRAAM air-to-air missiles. All RNLAF F-16s flying missions over Libya were equipped with the Litening Advanced Targeting Pod (ATP), enabling them to conduct so-called non-traditional ISR missions. In the background are UAE F-16E/Fs.
Courtesy of the Netherlands Ministry of Defence, photo by Dave de Vaal.

upgraded software were deployed to Decimomannu in the course of Operation Unified Protector. Through this rotation cycle, the RNLAF was able to maintain its detachment at high readiness throughout the operation.[154]

The RNLAF detachment at Decimomannu amounted to as many as 125 personnel.[155] It also received support from the Italian and German air forces, which have used the Decimomannu Air Base for aerial combat training since 1959. For instance, German air force personnel provided catering.[156]

RNLAF missions over Libya did not require dedicated SEAD escort. By the time Netherlands fighter aircraft were flying missions over North Africa, Libya's air defenses had ceased to exist as a substantial threat. Thus, RNLAF F-16s relied on evasive maneuvers, the AN/ALQ-131 electronic countermeasures pod, and chaff and flares for self-protection. For air-to-air armament, Dutch aircraft carried a mix of short-range AIM-9L and medium-range AIM-120B AMRAAM missiles; the standard armament configuration consisted of three of the latter and one of the former. In addition to the

---

[154] Mulder, telephone interview.

[155] "Betreft Uw Verzoek Inzake Nederlandse Bijdrage aan Uitvoering VN Veiligheidsraad Resolutie 1973—Libië" [Relating to Your Request for a Netherlands Contribution to the Implementation of Security Council Resolution 1973—Libya], letter by the Minister of Foreign Affairs, Dr. U. Rosenthal, and the Minister of Defense, J.S.J. Hillen, to the Chairman of the House of Representatives, The Hague, March 31, 2011.

[156] Mulder, telephone interview, January 31; and Anrig, *The Quest for Relevant Air Power*, p. 174.

self-protection suite and the air-to-air armament, all RNLAF F-16s flying missions over Libya were equipped with the Litening Advanced Targeting Pod (ATP). With the use of this pod, the RNLAF detachment was able to conduct nontraditional ISR missions (ISR without the specific means to perform these tasks), while the RNLAF's dedicated RecceLite reconnaissance pods had been prioritized for missions in Afghanistan.[157]

In mid-May 2011, the RNLAF detachment's mandate was extended to perform missions over land, and the information subsequently transmitted to the CAOC made the air planners aware of the RNLAF detachment's nontraditional ISR capabilities. Immediately, they started to include nontraditional ISR tasks into the air tasking order. Initially, the Misrata harbor area, as well as nearby airbases, airfields, and ground-based air defense positions, were of particular interest to the CAOC. After the siege of Misrata was lifted, nontraditional ISR tasking followed the "front lines," both to the west and to the south (especially the Tripoli area and south of that city). The nontraditional ISR missions included observing front lines, specific locations, and suspected installations by means of the ATP. These observations were transmitted during the flight via voice (description) and Link-16 (geographic positions) to AWACS aircraft. After the flight, the same information was completed, amplified, and directed via appropriate channels to the CAOC. This information included mission reports and video material.[158] RNLAF F-16 fighter aircraft thus made a contribution to the campaign that went well beyond their initial task of enforcing the NFZ.

Flying from Decimomannu, which was significantly farther from Libya than Sigonella, for instance, Dutch missions resulted in exhausting sorties, which took five and a half hours of flying time on average.[159] The RNLAF detachment conducted most of its missions using national two-ship formations. As Operation Unified Protector progressed, RNLAF F-16s regularly participated in COMAO missions fulfilling the air-to-air escort role. During these missions, Dutch combat aircraft also used nontraditional ISR to gather information. Besides the air-to-air and ISR roles, the RNLAF detachment regularly was tasked to perform "show of presence" (SOP) missions above front lines, cities, and other specific areas.[160]

In a letter dated March 31, the day when NATO assumed full responsibility for all operations over Libya, the ministers of Foreign Affairs and Defence informed Parliament of specific national rules of engagement. They clearly stated that RNLAF F-16 fighter aircraft were not to react offensively to potential ground-based air defense threats, but only defensively. When asked whether Netherlands F-16s were collecting information to prepare air-to-ground strikes, the ministers replied that RNLAF F-16

---

[157] Mulder, telephone interview, January 31; and Pieter Baastiens, "Going Dutch," *Air Forces Monthly*, No. 287, February 2012, p. 79.

[158] Mulder, telephone interview, January 31, and email to the author, June 4, 2012.

[159] Baastiens, "Going Dutch," p. 79.

[160] Mulder, emails to the author, June 4 and June 9, 2012.

fighter aircraft could gather information on both air and ground targets. Yet they also added that a national red-card holder retained decisionmaking authority over any RNLAF F-16 mission.[161]

The RNLAF supported the international planning effort with approximately five to ten staff officers. They supported the production of the Master Air Operations Plan, psychological warfare operations, and the current operations cell.[162] RNLAF staff officers normally are attached to CAOC 2 in Uedem, Germany. Because CAOC 5 at Poggio Renatico lacked a number of experts, augmentation of CAOC 5 by CAOC 2 was vital.[163]

In the initial stages, the Netherlands' contribution also included tanker operations. The RNLAF's KDC-10 at Cagliari-Elmas International Airport was swiftly integrated into NATO's tanker plan. It not only refueled Dutch fighter aircraft, but also began to support Belgian, Danish, Norwegian, and USAF F-16s—the latter toward the very end of Operation Odyssey Dawn, when NATO was simultaneously assuming full responsibilities for the air operations.[164] Yet the KDC-10 was involved only for a limited period, until April 4.[165] Dutch tanker operations required 33 deployed personnel in Sardinia.[166] After the KDC-10 had redeployed to the Netherlands, USAF tankers provided most AAR for Dutch fighter aircraft. Because the RNLAF's second KDC-10 tanker was undergoing an overhaul, and as RNLAF-16s had to be ferried back and forth from operations in Afghanistan, the remaining Dutch tanker could be made available only for a short period.[167]

Logistical support was provided by all available means (air, ship, train, and road). The European Air Transport Command tasked air transport missions and, in general, Netherlands transport aircraft supported the detachment at Decimomannu Air Base.[168] On only one occasion did a German A-310 transport aircraft support the Netherlands detachment with a partial load.[169]

---

[161] "Betreft Uw verzoek," March 31, 2011.

[162] Mulder, telephone interview, January 31.

[163] Lt. Col. Guus de Koster, RNLAF, Netherlands Defence Academy, Breda, telephone interview by the author, February 3, 2012.

[164] Mulder, telephone interview, January 31.

[165] "Betreft Nederlandse bijdrage," March 22, 2011, p. 1.

[166] "Betreft Uw verzoek," March 31, 2011.

[167] Mulder, telephone interview, January 31.

[168] After its brief appearance in Operation Unified Protector, the Dutch KDC-10 also was tasked with ferrying surplus F-16s to Chile. (Mulder, telephone interview, January 31.)

[169] Mulder, email to the author, February 6, 2012.

In total, the RNLAF F-16 detachment conducted 591 sorties and accumulated 2,845.4 flying hours.[170] All six aircraft returned home on November 2.[171] It is notable that—despite the politically restricted contribution to Operation Unified Protector—the Netherlands government twice decided to extend the Dutch contribution by three-month periods.[172] Drawing down the RNLAF detachment at Decimomannu Air Base prior to the cessation of Operation Unified Protector never was seriously considered.

While no multinational F-16 deployment took place within the framework of the EEAW, the existing structures and networks played a minor role by facilitating the transfer of bomb bodies and fuzes from Netherlands stocks to the RDAF when the latter was running low on PGMs in the midst of the campaign.[173] According to the RNLAF Air Staff, the transfer did not include the delivery of guidance kits to turn unguided bombs into PGMs.

Lessons and Conclusions

Although the smaller European F-16 operators were much less in the spotlight than the larger USAF, RAF, or French Air Force, some commentators noticed their outstanding performance. An October 2011 *Financial Times* article, quoting Pentagon sources, highlighted the readiness of the Belgian detachment to take on virtually any mission, however hazardous.[174] In a similar vein, the *Times* reported in late September 2011 that the RDAF had hit almost as many targets as the much larger RAF contingent.[175] According to Col. Rachel A. McCaffrey, chief of the ISR Division during Operation Unified Protector, Denmark and Norway were the most flexible nations in April 2011, the first month NATO took on full responsibility of the air campaign. While other nations might eventually have gotten approval to engage certain targets, these nations' clear national guidance on acceptable targets, coupled with their decision to delegate target approval to their red-card holders, allowed the RDAF and the RNoAF

---

[170] Mulder, email to the author, May 1, 2012.

[171] Pieter Baastiens, "Going Dutch," *Air Forces Monthly,* No. 287, February 2012, p. 79.

[172] "Betreft Verlenging van de Nederlandse Bijdrage aan Operatie Unified Protector—Libië" [Relating to the Extension of the Netherlands Contribution to Operation Unified Protector Concerning—Libya], letter by the Minister of Foreign Affairs Dr. U. Rosenthal and the Minister of Defense J.S.J. Hillen to the Chairman of the House of Representatives and the Chairman of the Senate, The Hague, June 10, 2011, p. 1; and "Betreft Besluit Verlenging Nederlandse Inzet NAVO Mandaat Operatie *Unified Protector*" [Relating to the Decision of Extending the Netherlands Mission Within the Framework of NATO Operation Unified Protector], letter by the Minister of Foreign Affairs Dr. U. Rosenthal to the Chairman of the House of Representatives (The Hague, September 22, 2011), p. 1.

[173] Mulder, telephone interview, January 31.

[174] Gideon Rachman, "The Libyan War and the Gallant Belgians," *Financial Times*, October 28, 2011.

[175] Deborah Haynes, "Denmark's Tøp Guns Trump RAF in Libya," *The Times*, September 29, 2011, p. 13.

to act rapidly and decisively. Norway and Denmark's flexibility proved especially critical during the initial stages of the campaign to successfully implement the JTF Commander's strategy of maintaining constant pressure on the Libyan regime.[176]

The comparisons in Table 10.2 clearly reveal that the European F-16 operators punched significantly above their weight. Despite their small defense expenditures, they made a disproportionate contribution to the campaign. In particular, the RDAF accumulated a strike volume approaching those of the French forces and of the RAF. The latter was reported to have dropped approximately 1,400 PGMs (including air-launched cruise missiles) by October 24 and French Air Force and Navy aircraft in excess of 1,140 PGMs (including air-launched cruise missiles) by the end of September.[177] While—among the EPAF nations—Denmark came out on top in terms of strike missions conducted and PGMs dropped, this was a reflection of the different political conditions that shaped each country's contribution to the campaign, according to the RDAF chief of staff, Bg Gen Steen Harboe Hartov. Belgian, Dutch, or Norwegian pilots could have paralled the results that Denmark achieved had they been given the same opportunity.[178] While the number of PGMs that Belgium, Denmark, and Norway delivered speaks for itself, these nations contributed not only in quantity, but also very much in quality.

Table 10.2
Comparison of Belgian, Danish, Dutch, and Norwegian F-16 Operations During Operations Odyssey Dawn and Unified Protector

	Defense Expenditure	F-16s Deployed	PGMs Released	Mission Sorties	Flying Hours
Belgium	5.5	6	473	620	2,589[a]
Denmark	4.5	6	923	1,288	4,716[b]
Netherlands	11.3	6	—	591	2,845[c]
Norway	7.2	6	588	615	3,122[d]

[a] Poesen, email to the author, March 22, 2012.

[b] Svarre, emails to the author, February 29 and May 2, 2012.

[c] Mulder, email to the author, May 1.

[d] Forsvaret, "Sluttrapport Libya," December 2.

NOTE: Defense expenditures for 2011 are given in billions of U.S. dollars (International Institute for Strategic Studies, *The Military Balance 2013*, London: Routledge, March 2013, pp. 115, 125, 158, 160). The figures tend to be approximate, enabling a comparison across the states. Since 2011, the Netherlands defense expenditures in particular have experienced significant reductions.

---

[176] Col Rachel A. McCaffrey, Head of the Intelligence Division at NATO's Air Component Ramstein, email to the author, May 17, 2013.

[177] "UK, France Detail Sorties Mounted, Ordnance Expended," p. 5. The figures do not include missiles and rockets fired by French and British attack helicopters. In particular, the former fired in excess of 430 HOT anti-tank missiles.

[178] Hartov, email to the author, May 16.

While the smaller Nordic air forces seem to have outclassed Belgium and the Netherlands in this particular campaign, it should be mentioned that neither Norway nor Denmark deployed F-16 fighter-bombers to Afghanistan in 2011—in contrast to the Benelux air forces. Since September 2008, six BAF F-16s had been operating out of Kandahar. This effort continued unchanged throughout the Libya campaign.[179] Likewise, the RNLAF deployed four F-16s to Afghanistan during the whole of 2011.[180] Undoubtedly, the RNLAF would have been ready to carry out difficult air attack missions in Libya, had political restraints not prevented the detachment at Decimomannu from doing so. Nevertheless, the RNLAF detachment's ability to conduct nontraditional ISR missions over "hot spots" received attention from air planners. The CFACC, Lieutenant General Jodice, later judged that the scarcity of tactical reconnaissance assets meant the Dutch F-16s were worth more to the campaign as ISR collectors than they would have been as bombers.[181]

Examining the costs of the various national contributions, the European F-16 forces provided good value for money. The RDAF's total cost for the operation was 621 million Danish kroner ($109 million). Of this amount, 297 million kroner ($52 million) would have been spent on training, salaries, and maintenance in any case. Thus, the added cost for the RDAF's Libya operations was 324 million kroner ($57 million). This added cost primarily covered the munitions expended.[182] In January 2012, the Norwegian Minister of Defence stated that the cost of Norwegian Libya operations amounted to approximately 320 million Norwegian kroner ($55 million), which turned out to be lower than a May 2011 estimate.[183]

The total cost of the Belgian participation in Operations Odyssey Dawn and Unified Protector amounted to €44.7 million ($58.4 million). This figure includes replenishing PGM stocks as well as minesweeper operations by the Belgian Navy. The net cost was €33 million ($43.2 million).[184] The Netherlands, for its part, estimated additional costs for air and maritime operations at approximately €15 million ($19.6 million) for a three-month period.[185] Given that the Netherlands Armed Forces were involved for slightly more than seven months, the additional costs must have amounted to approximately $45 million. In summary, the costs for Belgian, Danish, Dutch, and

---

[179] Poesen, email to the author, March 22.

[180] Mulder, telephone interview, January 31.

[181] Ralph J. Jodice II, remarks on Operation Unified Protector at the Atlantic Council, Washington, D.C., June 4, 2012.

[182] Barfoed, email to the author, February 29.

[183] Forsvarsdepartementet [Ministry of Defense (Norway)], "Libya-Operasjonen: Billigere enn Forventet" [Libya Operations: Cheaper Than Expected], *Nyheter* [news], January 23, 2012.

[184] Poesen email to the author, March 22.

[185] "Betreft Nederlandse bijdrage," March 22, 2011, pp. 8–9; and "Betreft Verlenging," June 10, 2011, p. 8.

Norwegian air operations over Libya were extremely modest, in relation to both the output and national defense expenditure of each country.

Cooperative Frameworks

All four of these European F-16 deployments were domestically driven and hurried, and the EEAW concept was not activated as a framework for a combined deployment. With all four F-16 detachments ending up at different locations, it would have been very difficult to coordinate the individual national efforts. Being based at the same forward base would have helped considerably in making better use of the EEAW concept, and as such would have helped reduce the logistical footprint.[186] Co-location is an essential prerequisite for the concept to function smoothly. Given the time pressures involved and the requirements for rapid national decisionmaking processes, it proved difficult to coordinate a multinational F-16 deployment and find enough ramp space and adequate infrastructure for a combined F-16 force.

An EEAW steering committee meeting in Lisbon on June 6, 2012 acknowledged the shortcomings of the EEAW in Operations Odyssey Dawn and Unified Protector. The failure to co-locate the EPAF detachments was, among other things, due to the lack of a permanent EEAW coordination element and the unavailability of a Greek or Italian base absorbing four EPAF detachments in a compressed time frame. The steering committee put forward a number of potential improvements. In particular, it identified a need to raise the visibility of the EEAW at all levels, specifically the political, within NATO and the EU. To that end, the appointment of the Belgian military representative at the EU as the chairman of the EEAW steering committee was expected to further increase the EEAW's profile on a European level. Furthermore, more common training exercises were suggested, structurally integrated into each nation's exercise planning starting in 2014.[187] In April 2014, live-flying exercise Frisian Flag at Leeuwarden Air Base in the Netherlands occurred in an EEAW context with F-16s from all five member air forces participating.[188]

Although the EEAW did not play a direct role in the Libya campaign, the experience of engaging in multinational European F-16 operations proved extremely valuable. According to Danish sources, the EPAF Fighter Weapons Instructor Training course was instrumental in providing RDAF pilots with the required skills for Operations Odyssey Dawn and Unified Protector.[189] The Norwegian Minister of Defence reiterated this conclusion. In his view, the EPAF framework had played a key role in enhancing the RNoAF's performance since Operation Allied Force. Moreover, he

---

[186] Mulder, telephone interview, January 31.

[187] Poesen, email to the author, June 18, 2012.

[188] Poesen, email to the author, September 23, 2014. Frisian Flag also included German, Spanish, and Finnish fighters.

[189] Barfoed, email to the author, February 29.

expected this European partnership to move forward through the procurement of the F-35 Lightning.[190]

In the context of Libya operations, the BAF, RDAF, RNLAF, and RNoAF also contributed to the NATO Airborne Early Warning and Control Force. In general, operations ran with the allocated peacetime personnel, and no substantial number of augmentees was needed.[191]

Regarding European airlift cooperation, the European Air Transport Command had full authority to task transport aircraft from any partner nations. Thus, German airlifters ended up resupplying the BAF detachment at Araxos Air Base and the RNLAF detachment at Decimomannu Air Base. Given Germany's abstention when UNSCR 1973 was adopted, this is a particularly interesting aspect, and leads to a further conclusion not directly pertaining to the European F-16 operators. Because of Germany's historical legacy, the use of military force is likely to remain a sensitive issue for the German constituency in the foreseeable future. Thus, Germany could be encouraged to gear up its efforts in the supporting aspects of military power, such as airlift.

As a member country of the NATO Heavy Airlift Wing, another cooperative arrangement in the domain of military airlift, the RNoAF benefited from a C-17 lift during the deployment phase to Crete. Since Operation Allied Force in 1999, cooperative arrangements gradually have increased European airlift volumes.

National Lessons

In general, Operations Odyssey Dawn and Unified Protector proved the success of Denmark's recent reforms. According to RDAF sources, the successful Danish contribution hinged significantly on Danish forces' being used to making do with few resources. The F-16 wing in Denmark must struggle to make ends meet, and this has made the deployed Danish F-16 force very lean and efficient. The Danish F-16 technical crews were able to reconfigure the jets with remarkable speed, and no sortie was canceled due to maintenance issues during the entire campaign. Maintaining six jets at the forward base, including two reserve aircraft, and executing eight daily sorties two-thirds of the time and four during the remaining one-third is quite an achievement.[192] On top of that, as examined in the chapter on the Swedish contribution to Operation Unified Protector, the RDAF detachment at Sigonella was crucial in integrating the neighboring Swedish detachment into NATO air operations.

After Operation Unified Protector, the RDAF offered to NATO a number of initial lessons identified. In particular, it highlighted the privileged sharing of intelli-

---

[190] Eide, "Innledning," January 31.

[191] La Défense [Defence (Belgium)], "Libye: six F16 et un navire," March 25, 2011; Svarre, email to the author, February 29; Mulder, telephone interview, January 31; and Forsvarsdepartementet, "Norge med i Nato-ledet våpenembargo," *Nyheter*, March 24, 2011.

[192] Svarre, email to the author, February 29.

gence among the Anglo-American partners to the exclusion of other NATO members as detrimental to the smooth running of operations. Moreover, the RDAF concluded that the conventional 72-hour air tasking order planning cycle that NATO used had proven to lack the required adaptability and flexibility. Also, the transition from Operation Odyssey Dawn to Operation Unified Protector initially had a negative impact on the planning side. In particular, NATO's ability to swiftly take over full C2 for the air campaign was somewhat limited, which led to a perceived initial decrease in operational tempo. As to the management of PGM resupply, appointing a lead nation responsible for coordination would have improved the munitions flow, particularly for the smaller nations.[193]

Since the lessons-identified process was still ongoing within the RNoAF at the time of writing, no specific operational lessons identified could be released publicly.[194] Yet the head of the Airpower Department at the RNoAF Academy indicated that Norway ought to rethink its role in terms of influencing a campaign, if it continues to make substantial contributions as in Libya. Although these were extraordinary circumstances, providing a significant portion of the initial strike missions in Operation Unified Protector indicated Norway's role exceeded simply being a player at the tactical level. Yet Norway did not seek influence at the operational level. If Norway's contribution to Operations Odyssey Dawn and Unified Protector does not remain an exception to the rule of future contributions, linking means to ends deserves a more prominent place in Norwegian military thinking.[195]

The Norwegian Minister of Defence cautioned about drawing general lessons from the Libya crisis, as the circumstances were quite specific. For instance, Libya's proximity allowed the Alliance to operate from NATO air bases. As a result, logistical requirements could be kept at a minimum.[196] A more distant theater might prove much more challenging, particularly for European NATO allies.

Like the RDAF, the BAF identified a number of concrete lessons. On the positive side, the multirole concept for operating Belgian fighter-bombers proved very efficient—an important aspect for a small defense establishment. While smaller European air forces could and did make a substantial contribution to Operations Odyssey Dawn and Unified Protector, NATO still relied in large part on U.S. personnel and equipment. This was particularly the case in the domains of C2 and combat support, particularly AAR. On the negative side, events and political decisions overtook the EEAW concept—a missed opportunity, since all documents and procedures were available

---

[193] Svarre, email to the author, February 29.

[194] Rygg, email to the author, March 27.

[195] Henriksen, email to the author, June 6.

[196] Eide, "Innledning," January 31.

and proven. Similar to the RDAF, the BAF identified the need for sufficient PGM stocks and an efficient and established resupply scheme.[197]

RNLAF air staff concluded that restricted national rules of engagement and the intensity of flying hours during Operation Unified Protector had a negative impact on the swing-role capability, which requires RNLAF pilots to be proficient in three roles (air-to-air, air-to-ground, and reconnaissance). Because RNLAF pilots were not allowed to engage in air-to-ground missions, their training standards in this particular role tended to deteriorate over time. Against the backdrop of the first and second extensions of the campaign, approval was granted to provide extra funds to compensate for the lack of training in air-to-ground missions. This was not the case during Allied Force, for instance, when the RNLAF contingent flew all mission types and was fully proficient in all tasks.[198]

Assessment

At a political and military-strategic level, air operations over Libya again revealed no carved-in-stone patterns regarding particular national behaviors. A few years earlier, it hardly could have been foreseen that the RNLAF would not exploit its full operational potential. National historical experiences, as well as the context of a particular campaign as determined by both domestic and foreign policies, are likely to determine national European contributions, rules of engagement, and the resulting force mix.[199] Thus, it is not possible to anticipate the European force providers for a future campaign with certainty, and flexibility is a prerequisite in dealing with this specific European reality. All of the four air forces examined have very flexible fighter-bomber fleets at their disposal, which allows them to respond to specific political circumstances.

Since Operation Allied Force in 1999, the BAF, the RDAF, the RNLAF, and the RNoAF have undergone significant improvements. For instance, their precision firepower has been enhanced significantly, both qualitatively and quantitatively. All European F-16 fighter-bombers operating over Libya were equipped with state-of-the-art targeting pods. In 1999, only a few RNLAF F-16s carried targeting pods, and these were needed to provide "buddy-lasing" for other aircraft. While they primarily dropped unguided bombs in the Balkan wars, they only employed PGMs in 2011. All four air forces examined now have achieved great proficiency and proved flexible enough to swiftly integrate into a multinational air campaign. Through cooperation in the framework of the EPAF, the less-advanced partners were able to catch up and reach the same standards as their more advanced counterparts.

---

[197] Poesen, email to the author, March 22.

[198] Mulder, telephone interview, January 31.

[199] Christian F. Anrig, "Allied Air Power over Libya: A Preliminary Assessment," *Air and Space Power Journal* XXV, No. 4, Winter 2011, p. 94.

The four air forces time and again have proven their ability to conduct offensive missions, but they are largely dependent on their larger NATO partners in the domain of combat support. Air-to-air refueling is probably the most obvious case. Without AAR support—particularly from the USAF—the European F-16 fighter-bomber detachments could not have operated the way they did. As noted above, even in this case some missions had to be canceled due to AAR scarcity.

Despite these deficits, Libya proved that the European F-16 forces offer political decisionmakers flexible tools that can operate across the spectrum of military force. The BAF, the RDAF, the RNLAF, and the RNoAF proved to be proficient and combat-proven forces that have taken their places firmly in the vanguard of NATO air forces.

CHAPTER ELEVEN

The Swedish Experience: Overcoming the Non–NATO-Member Conundrum

Robert Egnell

Introduction

On April 2, 2011, Sweden deployed eight JAS 39 Gripen (Griffon) fighters to partici-pate in the NATO-led Operation Unified Protector (OUP) in Libya. This was the first Swedish international deployment of combat aircraft since the early 1960s, when Swed-ish J 29 "Tunnan" fighter-bombers supported U.N. operations in the former Belgian Congo.[1] The time span since the last international combat deployment of the Swedish Air Force is not the only remarkable aspect of the Swedish contribution to OUP. More interesting is that Sweden, as a traditionally nonaligned country, chose to contribute to a NATO air campaign in Northern Africa with little hesitation or debate, and that it did so very successfully and made a substantial contribution to the operation.

The Swedish political process leading up to the deployment was handled at a record pace. The formal request for a Swedish contribution to the operation in Libya was presented on March 29. That same day, the Prime Minister presented a govern-ment bill to Parliament, which reached a decision on April 1 to contribute eight JAS 39C Gripens and a C-130H Hercules for aerial refueling. It entailed a national caveat not to engage ground targets. The Swedish Air Force started deploying to Sigonella, Italy, the day after the decision and flew its first mission on April 7 upon reaching ini-tial operational capability.

The Swedish mission was divided into two rotations. The first covered the period from April 1 to June 26, during which the unit had the formal task only to defend the no-fly zone through DCA operations and tactical air reconnaissance (TAR). The second rotation covered the period between June 27 and October 24 and involved a mandate that covered TAR across the full spectrum of U.N.-mandated tasks—going beyond the NFZ by including the enforcement of the arms embargo and, most impor-tantly, the protection of civilians. During the second rotation, the Swedish unit con-

---

[1] From 1961 to 1963, Swedish Air Force J 29 fighters (nicknamed "Tunnan" or "Flying Barrel") flew reconnais-sance and strike missions as part of the air component of the United Nations Operation in the Congo (ONUC), along with Ethiopian and Italian F-86 Sabres and Indian Canberra bombers.

ducted one-third of all the tactical reconnaissance within the operation. While the Swedish contingent faced a number of serious challenges and difficulties described in this chapter, the operation as a whole has been described as a success from a Swedish perspective. This was true not only in terms of protecting civilians but also in removing Qaddafi from power, although the latter was, for Sweden, an uncomfortable addition to the aim after the Berlin Summit. It also was seen as a success with respect to Sweden's relationships with NATO and the United States, as well as a tremendous boost in experience for the Swedish Air Force and the personnel involved in the operation, including more than 30 pilots.[2]

From an international perspective, the Swedish contribution initially was seen as politically useful, but there was skepticism regarding its military significance. This skepticism nevertheless was quickly transformed into praise after the reconnaissance missions and photos provided by the Gripens and the Swedish analysts proved highly useful. A Royal United Services Institute for Defence and Security Studies (RUSI) report on the international intervention in Libya concluded that the Swedish contribution was seen within the international coalition in a very positive light. The political benefits stemming from receiving the support of a traditionally nonaligned nation were expected, but the substantial contribution in an initial defensive air combat role, and then, much more so in a tactical reconnaissance role, favorably surprised the coalition, the report said:

> The Gripen aircraft and the Swedish pilots and support staff proved outstanding in [the reconnaissance] role and outstripped other combat assets with the quality of its tactical ISR (intelligence, surveillance and reconnaissance). Moreover, despite participating in its very first NATO air operation, the expected interoperability and integration problems turned out to be remarkably limited.[3]

As a nonmember of NATO, Sweden's perspective on the operation can provide a valuable source of lessons for future operations. How was the partner country received and integrated within the operational structure? How did the Swedish contribution perform, and to what extent did it contribute to the international coalition? Understanding why the Swedish unit achieved such relative success, as well highlighting the main problems Sweden faced as a nonmember, provides important lessons for future NATO operations involving broad international coalitions.

The key lesson of this chapter is that nonmember coalition partners can make valuable operational contributions if they have the interoperability that comes from technical integration as well as extensive experience from joint training and exercises. However, the chapter also reveals that, while the Swedish contribution to OUP as a

---

[2]   Interview with senior civil servant, Swedish Foreign Ministry, March 23, 2012.

[3]   Johnson and Mueen, 2012, p. 32.

nonmember was in many ways a success for both NATO and Sweden, the operation highlighted a number of important challenges that need to be addressed for improved operational effectiveness of broad coalitions in the future. Not the least of these were the procedures for providing partner access to secure networks, and for fully integrating partner communication systems into NATO command and control systems. Many of these challenges are to be found at the strategic and political levels, and will require improved policies and procedures within NATO HQ. Importantly, to properly develop and test new procedures, these cumbersome steps should ideally be made part of training exercises with nonmembers in order to replicate the challenges of real operations.

The Swedish Decision to Participate in the Intervention

While many countries, members and nonmembers of NATO alike, experienced substantial debate regarding a potential intervention in Libya, the Swedish decision to contribute was surprisingly uncontroversial. In fact, there was almost a collective euphoria regarding the prospects of intervening in Libya and toppling the regime of Muammar Qaddafi. All parties in the Swedish Parliament approved the decision except the Sweden Democrats, a right-wing populist party with an isolationist security policy. An exception to the euphoria was an op-ed in one of the biggest newspapers that stirred debate within the political left and the peace movement by raising issues about the nature of the intervention, the potential consequences, and the appropriateness of Swedish participation.[4] However, this debate remained quite limited, and public-opinion surveys showed great support for an international intervention and Swedish participation.[5] An example is the German Marshall Fund's yearly survey, *Transatlantic Trends*, the 2011 version of which (conducted between May and June 2011) included a number of questions regarding the intervention in Libya. The survey highlighted that Sweden stood out in a number of ways—not least in its support for the intervention in Libya. Some 69 percent of Swedes approved of international forces' military action in Libya—the highest percentage among all nations surveyed—and only 28 percent disapproved, the lowest in the survey. About 89 percent supported the Swedish government intervening to protect civilians, 79 percent answered that they would support the Swedish government in removing Qaddafi, and 73 percent even supported the hypothetical idea of Sweden sending military advisors to assist the rebels who opposed Qaddafi—again, in each case, the highest percentages for any country in the survey.[6]

---

4   Robert Egnell, "Är Vi Beredda på att ta Ansvar för Libyens Framtid?" [Are We Ready to Take Responsibility for the Future of Sweden?], *Dagens Nyheter*, March 22, 2011; Anne-Li Lehnberg, "Vänstern Oenig om Libyenattacken" [The Left Cannot Agree on Attacking Libya], March 3, 2011.

5   German Marshall Fund, *Transatlantic Trends 2011: Topline Data July 2011*, Brussels, 2011.

6   German Marshall Fund, *Transatlantic Trends 2011*.

This raises the following questions: Why were Swedish policymakers, as well as the public in general, so keen on intervening in Libya, and why did the fact that it was an air campaign led by NATO not create more debate? Four important factors played a role:

- the perception that this was a near-perfect case of intervention, based on pure humanitarian ideals and aims.
- the presence of strong U.N. backing through UNSCR 1973.
- a continuation of a policy of Swedish participation in most international operations since the turn of the millennium.
- a strong and "militant" Swedish support for promotion of democracy and human rights internationally.

Regarding the first factor, public outrage and humanitarian concerns about the situation in Libya in general, and the fear of air attacks and cleansing in Benghazi in particular, cannot be overestimated. The impact of the media coverage was enormous; the contrast between the Libyan situation and the successful democratic regime changes in Tunisia and Egypt perhaps helped to fuel it.[7] The Libyan uprising, somewhat naively, was interpreted in the light of the recent revolutions in Tunisia and Egypt as a completely benign and legitimate democratic and popular movement against a terrible dictator. A genuine humanitarian concern and a perceived need to protect civilians, therefore, were the primary basis for the Swedish support of the intervention.[8] The United States' decision not to take the lead perhaps also strengthened the perception of a genuinely humanitarian international intervention. The usual, almost intuitive Swedish popular suspicions regarding the only remaining superpower's intentions in international interventions were thereby left out of the equation.

The second factor was the U.N. Security Council Resolution 1973 that backed the intervention. This is not only a policy requirement for Swedish participation in international operations; it also reflects a strong Swedish tradition of support for, and belief in, the U.N. From the organization's earliest days, Sweden has taken great pride in being an active member, as well as in contributing substantially to U.N. peacekeeping operations.[9] The importance of U.N. peace operations has shifted, however, in favor of the European Union's (EU) crisis management activities, as well as, to a more limited extent, NATO. This trend is clear in official policy documents and

---

[7]   Alexander Gabelic and Linda Nordin Thorslund, "Nu Måste Omvärlden Ingripa" [Now You Need the Outside World to Intervene], *SvD OPINION*, March 15, 2012; Inger Österdahl, and Ylva L. Hartmann, "Omvärlden Bär ett Stort Ansvar" [The Outside World Has a Great Responsibility], *SvD OPINION*, March 2, 2012; Kristina Bolme Kühn and Johan Mast, "Dags att ta ansvar," *Medecins San Frontieres*, May 19, 2011.

[8]   Swedish Government, "Svenskt Deltagande i Den Internationella Militära Insatsen i Libyen" [Swedish Participation in the International Military Operation in Libya], Prop. 2010/11:111, March 29, 2011.

[9]   German Marshall Fund, *Transatlantic Trends 2011.*

also is reflected in the fact that substantial Swedish contributions beyond observers in U.N.-led peace operations are rare today. Instead, the organizational framework of preference seems to be operations within the framework of the Common Security and Defence Policy (CSDP).[10] Nevertheless, while other countries often have a rather cynical view of the U.N. and its role as the primary international guarantor of international peace and security, this is not the case in Sweden. The belief in the appropriateness of the U.N. Security Council as the moral compass of international politics is still strong and seldom questioned. The intervention in Kosovo was an important exception—the Swedish government supported it despite the deadlock within the U.N.[11]

The third factor is the view of a Swedish contribution in Libya as the continuation of a Swedish policy of active participation in international crisis management and peace operations. As Ann-Sofie Dahl observed, "Sweden has participated in every single NATO operation since the end of the Cold War, and has been a regular 'blue-helmet' peacekeeper—and later, peace enforcer—under the U.N. flag since the very early days of that organization."[12] Dahl accurately notes that not participating in a clear mission with a U.N. mandate, with NATO taking the lead of a strong coalition, would have been more unusual and surprising. The only really unusual aspect of Swedish participation in Libya was that it was an air campaign.[13] NATO Secretary General Anders Fogh Rasmussen's visit in Stockholm the day before the parliamentary vote on the contribution to Operation Unified Protector also provided important support for the political processes. He gave a much-appreciated briefing to the Swedish Parliament and removed many of the potential doubts through thorough answers and explanations to the concerns of the parliamentarians. It is believed that this meeting contributed to the surprisingly strong support in the parliamentary vote the following day.[14]

The fourth factor is more surprising given Sweden's traditional, yet now discarded, policy of neutrality. It seems that a long tradition of democracy and human-rights promotion as part of Swedish development cooperation, on the one hand, and a strong belief in international crisis management and peace support operations, on the other, together have created a rather hawkish approach to intervention and democracy promotion. Sweden's first year in the transatlantic survey revealed that the country's public opinion stood out among the other EU countries on a number of issues. Compared

---

[10] Utrikesdepartementet, "Sveriges Säkerhetspolitik" [Swedish Security Policy], online, updated March 24, 2011.

[11] See as an example, FN-Förbundet, "Inställningen till FN Och Internationella Frågor Bland Gymnasieungdomar i Sverige" [Attitudes Toward the U.N. and International Questions Among High School Students in Sweden], undated.

[12] Ann-Sofie Dahl, "Sweden and NATO: More than a Partner? Reflections Post-Libya," NATO Defence College Paper, June 2012, p. 8.

[13] Dahl, "Sweden and NATO: More than a Partner?"

[14] Interview with Ambassador Veronika Wand-Danielsson, September 10, 2012.

to other Europeans, the Swedes were more willing to maintain troops in Afghanistan, expressed more support of the intervention in Libya, and showed more inclination to promote democracy in the Middle East and North Africa. A significant finding was that 83 percent of Swedes in one survey said that democracy should be promoted in conflict situations such as in North Africa and the Middle East, even if it leads to instability.[15] The hawkish tendency is perhaps exaggerated by a lack of memory and understanding of the horrors of all armed conflicts—it has been almost 200 years since Sweden directly experienced war.

These factors help enhance our understanding of Swedish participation in this specific operation. But what does this mean for the future? Has the Swedish contribution to Operation Unified Protector changed the nature of the NATO debate in Sweden? Can Sweden, with or without membership, be counted on in future NATO operations?

Membership in NATO has long been a nonissue in Swedish politics. The traditional Swedish policy of nonalignment with the purpose of neutrality in case of war is a deeply embedded part of the Swedish self-image, despite its having been discarded for almost two decades.[16] Because of Sweden's history of neutrality policy and nonalignment, the active promotion of NATO membership is politically risky, which also means that virtually no debate occurs about this issue in Sweden. Has OUP changed the tone of the (non-) debate? The operation in Libya again clearly displayed the convergence of interests between Sweden and NATO allies in international crisis management. It also displayed the Swedish preference for operating under the NATO or EU banner—something that has changed dramatically since the era of Swedish U.N. peacekeeping. Charlotte Wagnsson highlights deeply rooted "discursive differences" between the Swedish idealistic frame of reference and NATO's realist way of describing and dealing with international security. However, she also notes that NATO's operation in Libya, justified on humanitarian grounds rather than national interests, certainly suited the Swedish political context. Thus, a continued NATO movement toward a more global, humanitarian, and cosmopolitan outlook would, in Wagnsson's view, remove some of the political risks in moving toward NATO membership.[17]

At the same time, OUP displayed the mutual benefits of nonmembership in operations. By contributing as a partner country to the operation, Sweden received tremendous good will despite the national caveats. It is unlikely the enthusiasm would have been as substantial if Sweden were a member of the Alliance. At the same time, from a NATO perspective, the political legitimacy that Sweden—as a traditionally neutral

---

[15] German Marshall Fund, *Transatlantic Trends 2011.*

[16] For a discussion regarding the popular perception of NATO, as well as the mental linkage between peace and neutrality, see Ann-Sofie Dahl, *Svenskarna och NATO* [The Swedes and NATO], Stockholm: Timbro, 1999.

[17] Charlotte Wagnsson, "A Security Community in the Making? Sweden and NATO post-Libya," *European Security* 20:4, December 2011, p. 598.

country—could add to the operation would have been lost with Swedish membership. Thus, while the nonmember status caused integration problems in the early weeks of the operation, it is probably fair to say that both Sweden and NATO benefited from Sweden's non-membership in the case of Libya. Moreover, OUP does little to influence the key question of whether membership is necessary to remain a credible international actor and to protect the territorial integrity of Sweden. It is, therefore, unlikely the operation will change the nature of the Swedish debate regarding membership.

Given the policy of active international engagement through diplomacy and participation in international crisis management, and the preference for Swedish operations within the NATO and EU frameworks, Sweden nevertheless is highly likely to continue contributing to future NATO operations—as long as a U.N. mandate backs them. The question, then, is how to make this special partnership as mutually beneficial and effective as possible. Before discussing that further, let us take a closer look at the Swedish contribution to OUP.

The Swedish Contribution: "Operation Karakal"

As briefly noted in the introduction, the Swedish operation in Libya was divided into two rotations with different political mandates. The first covered the period from April 1 to June 26, during which the unit had the formal task only to defend the no-fly zone through DCA operations and TAR using the politically mandated eight JAS 39C Gripens. Beyond the Gripens, the deployment also involved about 130 personnel, a Tp 84 (C-130H) Hercules for air-to-air refueling, and an S102 Korpen (Gulfstream IV)—a signals-intelligence aircraft only under Swedish command that was used for intelligence-gathering and to update national databases. It should, however, be noted that the Swedish contingent flew only six DCA missions and 66 swing-role missions involving TAR and DCA early in the operation, and that the vast majority of missions involved pure reconnaissance. This type of mission was most needed and appreciated within the coalition. The second rotation covered the period between June 27 and October 24, and involved a mandate that covered TAR across the full spectrum of U.N.-mandated tasks, not only supporting the NFZ, but also enforcement of the arms embargo and—most importantly—the mission to protect Libyan civilians. During this period, the political mandate included only five Gripens instead of eight, but as the mandate said nothing of the number of missions that should be flown, the Swedish unit continued flying the same amount over Libya, with an increased frequency of maintenance rotations of the aircraft.

In total, the Swedish operation included more than 570 missions and about 1,770 flight hours. In the reconnaissance role, about 2,770 reconnaissance exploitations reports (RECCEEXREPs) were sent to higher command. As already noted, the main contribution of the Swedish unit—beyond the political support of the operation—was in TAR. At the height of operations during the summer, the Swedish contingent flew roughly 30 percent of all TAR missions within the operation. As Lt.-Gen. Charles Bouchard repeatedly expressed regarding the Swedish contribution: "The Gripens have a strategic importance for the operation. They have a spectacular capability."[18]

Preparations and Initial Deployment

The decision to participate in Operation Unified Protector was made in the Swedish Parliament on April 1. On April 2, the Swedish Air Force started deploying to Sigonella Air Base in Sicily. After less than a week, all eight Gripens and most of the support organization were in place, and the unit reached Initial Operational Capability (IOC). The speed of this process is remarkable in comparison with previous international deployments of Swedish troops.

The most important reason that the Swedish Air Force was able to deploy so quickly in support of OUP was that an EAW was on standby within the EU Nordic Battle Group. The European Union constantly has two battle groups on standby, and during the first half of 2011 the Swedish-led Nordic Battle Group 11 had this responsibility. The EAW was a completely self-sufficient unit that involved all the necessary command structures, logistics, ground staff, and mission support elements, including the all-important photo interpreters.[19] The unit also had a complete set of standing orders, standard operating procedures, and months of training behind it. Thus, when the political decision was made, the unit simply had to take off and apply the systems already in place. Only one important asset had to be added to the EAW upon deployment, the Hercules C-130 for aerial refueling—an asset that proved essential, given the challenging fuel situation at Sigonella Naval Air Station. In short, the coincidence that the EAW was on standby this particular spring meant that the Swedish Armed Forces had the perfect tool for immediate deployment upon the political leadership's request. The positive lessons and policy implications are self-evident.

The second factor was the political process in tandem with predeployment preparations at all levels. Without a quick political process in Sweden, as well as the reconnaissance and negotiations in Italy for a suitable base (discussed below), the speed of EAW readiness would have been in vain. Informal discussions regarding a Swedish contribution were ongoing from the start of international operations in Libya with a dialogue between the Ministry of Defence and the armed forces regarding the nature of a possible contribution. On March 23, this dialogue was formalized as a ministerial request and was sent to the armed forces asking about possible resources for contributions. The reply came the same day that eight Gripen fighter jets stood ready.[20] It

---

[18] Lt.-Gen. Charles Bouchard, cited in Eddy de la Motte (V.P., head of Gripen Export, Saab Aeronautics), "Gripen: When logic is part of the equation," briefing, July 11, 2012.

[19] Interview with Lt. Col. Stefan Wilson, Contingent Commander FL01, March 7 and 20, 2012.

[20] Swedish Government, "Svenskt deltagande i den internationella militära insatsen i Libyen."

should be noted that the procedure of formal requests to individual members or part-ners, although common within U.N. operations, is unfamiliar to the NATO structure. This was nevertheless needed for the Swedish domestic debate, and NATO therefore provided such a request specifically to Sweden. The request obviously also was drafted to suit the Swedish debate by not asking for what was really needed—strike fighters with air-to-ground capability.[21]

The third factor was the fact that the Swedish Air Force, in February and March, had operated a C-130 over Libya for noncombatant evacuation operations and human-itarian relief operations. This meant that the Air Tactical Command staff and orga-nization at HQ had built up competence of the area of operations and was on high readiness—factors that proved highly useful during the quick predeployment phase in late March.[22]

The foreign minister nevertheless made it clear from the beginning that a Swedish contribution only would be possible if NATO took full command of operations. NATO reached an agreement to do so on March 27. The next day, Swedish media reported that an official NATO request for Swedish participation had arrived, although this was not confirmed officially until March 29.[23] Nonetheless, on the 28th, the Swedish government met with the opposition in order to discuss the Swedish contribution. As highlighted above, broad consensus existed regarding the ambition to contribute with fighters at this stage, and the main discussion point was the nature of the Swedish con-tribution and the specific national caveats.[24] On March 29, an agreement was reached and a government decision to participate was made before lunch. The same afternoon, the prime minister presented a government bill to the Parliament. The Parliament also dealt with the issue in record time, leading to the April 1 decision.[25]

The short time frame for deployment meant that the military predeployment planning and preparations had to take place in parallel with the political negotiations in Sweden. This was nevertheless a sensitive matter, as it risked giving the impression of an inevitable political decision. However, the strong support from all of the major political parties eased that tension.[26]

One challenge of the planning process was that the formal procedure for includ-ing partnership countries in operations was not followed.[27] In the context of specific

---

[21] Interview with Swedish civil servant, September 12, 2012.

[22] "I Backspegeln—Hur Flygvapnets Libyeninsats 2011 Startade" [Looking Back—How the Air Campaign in Libya 2011 Started], *Flygvapenbloggen*, March 26, 2012.

[23] Love Benigh and Örjan Magnusson, "Nato har frågat Sverige om Jas-plan till Libyen," *SVT.SE*, March 28, 2011.

[24] Interview with senior civil servant, Ministry of Foreign Affairs, March 23, 2012.

[25] Interview with senior civil servant, Ministry of Foreign Affairs.

[26] "Bred majoritet för Libyeninsats" [Broad majority for Libyan operation], Svenska Dagbladet, April 1, 2011.

[27] Ambassador Veronika Wand Danielsson, interview with author, March 2012.

operations, the North Atlantic Council (NAC) is supposed to decide on the recognition of a non-NATO country as an operational partner, on the basis of Military Committee advice, after the successful completion of the following measures as required:

- a formal statement of intent by the country that it is prepared to offer a contribution in support of a NATO-led operation.
- provisional recognition by the NAC of the country as a potential operational partner.
- completion of proper security arrangements with the potential operational partner to allow the sharing of classified operational information.
- completion of participation and detailed financial arrangements with the potential operational partner.
- the signature, if required, of a technical memorandum of understanding between the relevant military authorities of NATO and of the potential operational partner.
- a certification by NATO military headquarters (SHAPE) of the potential operational partner's contribution.[28]

The urgency of the process of forming the coalition meant that these formal steps were replaced by ad hoc measures.[29] The problem for non-NATO members is that they lack access to meetings and information until a commitment to contribute is formally made. Thus, the status of Swedish officials and officers within the organization was constantly a problem, as they were not allowed to participate in OUP meetings and therefore had limited insight into operational planning and operations during the Swedish predeployment phase.[30] This was solved informally through bilateral meetings between the Delegation of Sweden to NATO and member states. However, it substantially increased the workload and time that had to be invested to gain access to information. A politically difficult, yet important, lesson is the need for a way to provide access for the likely contributing partners before formal commitments are made.

While negotiations and deliberations were ongoing in Stockholm, the armed forces were tasked to conduct reconnaissance trips to Italy to find an appropriate base for the Swedish jets. As the armed forces did not have the mandate or the authority to negotiate directly with NATO, a representative from the Delegation of Sweden to NATO in Brussels also joined the trip to Italy. As a representative of the Swedish government, this person could conduct the formal negotiations in Italy, which turned out

---

[28] NATO, "Political Military Framework for Partner Involvement in NATO-led Operations," undated.

[29] Wand Danielsson, interview with author.

[30] Danielsson interview.

to be quite useful, as it substantively shortened the deployment time when the parliamentary decision was finally made.[31]

A number of challenges were identified during the reconnaissance trip, some of which were rather pressing—not least the issue of dealing with the Italian concerns about Swedish Gripens deploying to Sigonella. Italy expressed some concerns about the Swedish contribution—especially regarding logistics issues related to the fact that no other contributing nation used the JAS 39 fighter.[32] The recce team, which U.S. contacts helped support through some arm-twisting, nevertheless successfully resolved most of these issues in time. It should be noted, however, that when the first planes took off from Sweden, they still did not have permission from the Italians to land at Sigonella. While the Swedish contingent was hoping for clearance to Sigonella at take-off, the formal flight plan was to Sardinia. The planes flew via Hungary before they received the final positive decision from the Italians regarding Sigonella.[33]

Another important lesson from the predeployment phase is, therefore, the importance of close contacts and bilateral discussions with a key ally. In this case, contacts with U.S. officials in both Brussels and at the Pentagon in Washington turned out to be absolutely central in the negotiations with Italy and in gaining access to operational information before the formal commitment to contribute forces was made.[34] This relationship deepened during the operation and served as an important entry point for Sweden to NATO as a partnership country. In a similar vein, the deployment of liaison officers within the NATO command structure at an early stage proved to be important and created the foundation for later successes during the operation. Finally, the support of diplomatic staff at the Delegation of Sweden to NATO in Brussels, as well as within the reconnaissance delegation to Italy, was instrumental in resolving concerns and building good relations with the United States' NATO delegation for access to the necessary command structures.[35]

A Typical Gripen Mission During OUP[36]

The JAS 39C Gripen is a Swedish-built, lightweight multirole fighter, comparable in capabilities to advanced versions of the slightly larger F-16. It can perform a wide vari-

---

[31] Interview with officials at the Delegation of Sweden to NATO, March 5, 2012.

[32] Interview with Lt. Col. Stefan Wilson, March 2012.

[33] Interview with Ministry of Foreign Affairs official, February 25, 2012. Interview with Lt. Col. Tommy Petersson, July 17, 2012.

[34] Interviews with officials at the Delegation of Sweden to NATO and the Embassy of Sweden in Washington, D.C., April 2012.

[35] Interview with officials at the Delegation of Sweden to NATO, March 5, 2012.

[36] The information in this section is based on interviews with Lt. Col. Hans Einerth, Chief Operations, CO A 3/5 branch, FL 02, and Lt. Col. Tommy Petersson, Chief Operations, CO A 3/5 branch, FL 02, July 17 and 20, 2012.

Swedish Air Force JAS 39C Gripen refueling from Tp 84 (C-130H) Hercules over the Mediterranean, April 8, 2011. Aircraft is carrying IRIS-T and AMRAAM air-to-air missiles and a Rafael RecceLite pod. *Courtesy of the Swedish Armed Forces.*

ety of counterair missions, air interdiction and CAS, antishipping attacks, and strategic and tactical air reconnaissance. During OUP, the Gripens were equipped with AMRAAM and IRIS-T missiles for self-defense. On the centerline, the Gripen carried a reconnaissance pod with an electro-optical sensor in the visual range that took 24-megapixel slides in a mosaic pattern and could cover vast areas with high resolution. The imagery was stored on an 80-gigabyte memory flash hard drive that, upon landing, was directly inserted into an analysis system. The pod was new to the Swedish Air Force, whose pilots and maintenance crews never had previously used the version used over Libya. Many of the pods were delivered directly from the factory to Sigonella, requiring adjustments by technical support staff from SAAB that were deployed with the Swedish unit for that purpose during the operation. The Gripens also carried a Litening 3 laser-designating targeting pod, with a high resolution infrared-video camera. The imagery from this pod was used for in-flight information and also after landing in the production of the RECCEXREP.

CAOC 5 in Poggio Renatico, Italy, tasked all missions. CAOC 5 was responsible for the tactical level of the air campaign during OUP. A number of Swedish liaison and staff officers worked at CAOC 5 during the operation and they proved absolutely essential for the correct tasking of the Swedish unit. Beyond the everyday tasks of any staff officers in different functions at CAOC 5, the Swedish personnel in the staff therefore also had two main tasks in relation to the Swedish unit: First, they served as a "red card" holder—an asset all contributing nations used to coordinate the targeting and tasking processes with the specific national mandates and caveats. Second, they supported the staff in making sure the tasking suited the specific capabilities of the unit, helping to optimize the effectiveness of the missions.

The tasking was formulated in an air tasking order that was issued to the unit at least 12 hours prior to takeoff. In the air tasking order, the unit found all mission details such as details of the recce targets, time on targets, air-to-air refueling areas and assets, airspace corridors, and communications (frequencies and crypto keys). Since the air tasking order covered all air missions in the operation, it also provided the pilots with a good general picture of the situation in their airspace.

When the air tasking order reached the Swedish unit and was extracted from the NATO Secret network (initially via the Danish unit and later on via a terminal provided by the Italian base at Sigonella), the intelligence and planning officers made an initial analysis and started the mission planning by entering the intended route and targets in the planning system. Four hours before takeoff, the detailed planning continued, now with the involvement of pilots and all other relevant personnel. Two hours prior to takeoff, the two-ship leader held a mission brief, in which all details and contingency plans of the missions were covered. The pilots entered the cockpit 30 minutes prior to takeoff and initiated the start-up procedures and system checks on the aircraft.

The missions always consisted of two Gripens; one aircraft was the main reconnaissance asset and also the flight lead, while the other was the supporting aircraft with the primary tasks of providing situational awareness and searching for potential threats. After takeoff, the two flew along a predefined route along special corridors. They passed Malta, and thereafter contacted an E-3 AWACS (U.S., NATO, or French) on their way to their first AAR. The AWACS were responsible for informing the crew of threats and friendly air traffic, coordinating refueling, and also forwarding in-flight reports and any new targets (dynamic targets) to the crew. The AAR took place in a predefined area beyond the Libyan coastline. Near the end of OUP, it was possible to refuel over Libya itself, and this was required to provide imagery of targets further south in Libya. The Gripens initially used the Swedish C-130 Hercules for refueling, but later refueled from U.S., French, and Canadian tankers as well. After refueling, the aircraft flew to their reconnaissance targets, which were overflown several times to get imagery from different sensors and angles. Much consideration was required when collecting imagery, such as if vertical or oblique angles were to be used, and the direction of the target in relation to the sun and clouds. On some missions, several AARs were needed to be able to cover all of the recce targets.

The missions were flown at altitudes above 20,000 feet to stay well above ground-based air defense threats, such as anti-aircraft guns, small-arms fire, and man-portable infrared-guided missiles. This behavior required air superiority, something that was obviously achieved early in the conflict. Even so, the Swedish Gripens detected a number of more-advanced missile systems with their electronic warfare suites and the radar warning receivers. Normally, a flight covered ten targets during a mission. Limitations on the number of targets included aircraft endurance and available memory capacity. The most important limitation, however, was the time it took to analyze the imagery back at Sigonella Air Base on Sicily. After the Gripens had collected imagery from all the tasked targets they often remained in the air waiting for so-called dynamic targeting—additional, time-sensitive reconnaissance targets.

Upon each mission's completion, the aircraft returned to Sigonella. After landing, the memory units from the sensors were rushed to the image analysis systems and the analysis personnel immediately started to go through the immense amount of data. Beyond looking at the tasked information, such as locations of military materiel, they marked locations of schools and mosques to further support the targeting processes. The information was labeled and marked in the photos, as well as described in text. Together this was compiled to a RECCEEXREP that was sent to the CAOC within two hours from landing. At CAOC 5 the intelligence personnel made further assessments based on the imagery, and sometimes would follow up with inquiries to the Swedish unit for further information on specific details.

From Skepticism to Appreciation

The arrival of the Swedish contingent at Sigonella, and its relatively good placement in the hangars, raised some eyebrows. It was at that stage unclear what the Swedes could and would do, why they were participating, and what types of missions they would fly.[37] The JAS 39 Gripen was unfamiliar to many, and cynical questions were raised as to whether the Swedish contribution would be of any substance, or if it was to be little more than a sales pitch for SAAB to get the jets "combat proven."[38] Sweden's initial political caveats did not help the skeptical reception. Nor did two of the early challenges discussed below—the incompatibility of jet fuel and the lack of access to the NATO Mission Secret Network (henceforth NATO Secrets). The prospects for a useful Swedish contribution seemed limited. However, the negative tune started changing only three weeks after the first deployment, as the fuel and communication challenges were being solved and as the Swedish contingent started producing high-quality reconnaissance images and reports.[39] This section analyzes what the Swedish contingent did and how it was received within the campaign as a whole. What did the Swedish contingent do to change the narrative from skeptical to highly favorable? The section emphasizes three factors without attempting to rank their relative importance—the quality and speed of intelligence reports, the reliability and flexibility of the Swedish contribution, and the likeability of the unit as a neighbor and cooperating partner.

As soon as the Swedish planes started flying, it became obvious that they were capable of making a substantial contribution to the operation. The quality of their reconnaissance photos was good, and the speed and quality of analysis were excellent. An absolutely central aspect in intelligence-gathering in general, and tactical recce mis-

---

[37] Interview with Lt. Col. Stefan Wilson, March 2012; Interview with officials at the Delegation of Sweden to NATO, May 2012.

[38] In 2011, marketing competition between the manufacturers of the Gripen, the Typhoon, and the Rafale was (and still is) intense as they vied for advantage in major fighter acquisition competitions in India, Brazil, Switzerland, and several other countries.

[39] Interview with Lt. Col. Stefan Wilson, March 7 and 20, 2012.

sions in particular, is the duration from initial observation to the delivery of analyzed data and reports to the higher level of command. The longer the process takes, the less relevant the information is likely to be. At the same time, the quality and accuracy of analysis never can be compromised, which makes the process a bit of a balancing act. The time from landing to delivered reports in the Swedish case most often was two hours, and the quality of both photos and analysis was surprisingly good from the coalition's point of view.[40] In July and August, Sweden provided about one-third of tactical reconnaissance within the coalition. As NATO continued to ask for more, the Swedish Air Force nevertheless worryingly reached maximum capacity. While more jets and pilots were available in Sweden, a lack of additional capacity remained to analyze the reconnaissance photos, which limited the possible scale of the Swedish contribution in Libya.[41] It should, however, be noted that this was partly due to national priorities, as some interpreters were used nationally, and as a Swedish UAV with interpreters was to be sent to Afghanistan around the same time.[42]

In addition, not only was the Swedish contingent quite reliable in terms of following orders and solving mission tasks, it gained respect by displaying great flexibility both mentally and technically. The Swedish contingent's culture of mission command meant it took a lot of initiative and dared to comment on and adjust air tasking orders and flight schedules from higher command when it was believed it would improve operations.[43] For example, while photographing oil cisterns outside Tripoli, the Swedish analysts discovered a number of them had floating lids. If photographed at a particular angle, the shade could easily be analyzed to calculate the level of consumption and refilling of these cisterns. The Swedish commander requested to change the flight schedules to photograph these cisterns at the same time each day to allow for the best possible comparative analysis. Small instances such as these, which showed a capability of seeing new possibilities within existing orders as well as in finding relevant targets of intelligence, plus initiative in questioning the air tasking orders, were highly appreciated at higher levels of command. The Swedish unit not only fulfilled its tasks with precision, it also came back with some extra value added because of this initiative.[44]

Moreover, the technical systems that the Gripen was carrying allowed for greater flexibility in operations than most coalition partners. For example, the recce pod and the Gripen allowed for the possibility of taking off with preplanned and programmed recce targets like all other contingents, but also had the capability to receive new targets while on the mission. This meant that after initial task accomplishment, the Swed-

---

[40] Interview with Lt. Col. Stefan Wilson, March 7, 2012; Interview with US DoD official, June 2012.

[41] Mikael Holmström, "För få fototolkar begränsar insats", *Svenska Dagbladet*, August 15, 2011; interview with Col. Fredrik Bergman, Contingent Commanders FL02, April 4, 2012.

[42] Interview with Lt. Col. Tommy Petersson, July 17, 2012.

[43] Interview with Col. Fredrik Bergman, April 4, 2012.

[44] Interview with Lt. Col. Stefan Wilson, March 7, 2012.

ish jets could wait in standby position after air-to-air refueling either to execute time-sensitive follow-up missions or to cover recce tasks that other contingents had failed to complete. As these types of tasks often came at very short notice, having the opportunity to task them to jets already in the air over the Mediterranean Sea substantially increased the speed and efficiency of tactical recce during OUP.[45]

Another factor was that the Swedish contingent proved to be a pleasant cooperating partner and neighbor at Sigonella. While this may seem trivial in the midst of combat, this factor often makes some of the most important impressions on commanding officers and other contingents. The Swedish work ethic, and the carefulness that was taken in keeping the hangar clean, returning rental vehicles on time, and participating in social events and ceremonies, contributed to an improving narrative of the Swedish contribution, as well as excellent working relationships with the base commander and neighboring units on the base.[46] The same useful working relationship reportedly was the case with the smaller Swedish satellites that worked with the CAOC in Poggio Renatico and the OUP headquarters (CJTF) at Joint Force Command (JFC) in Naples.

An indicator of the increasing appreciation of the Swedish contribution was the refueling priority list. The Swedish contingent initially was almost at the bottom of this priority list, which naturally had those contingents conducting the bombing at the top, followed by Qatar and United Arab Emirates. Sweden belonged to a third-tier group, which meant that its contingent could not fly at maximum capacity. Between April 18 and April 20, just as the unit reached full operational capability, the Swedish contingent commander nevertheless visited JFC in Naples and presented the early work of the Swedish contingent. The message was that if the Swedes could be placed higher on the refueling priority list, they could deliver more of the same. This visit, along with the ever-improving reputation, quickly had an impact, and the Swedish contingent rose in the priority list.[47]

Swedish NATO Interoperability and Operational Integration

Another important reason for the relative success of the Swedish contribution to OUP was the unit's interoperability with NATO. Apart from the already mentioned initial challenges of access to classified computers and crypto keys—issues discussed further below—the Swedish unit was well integrated from the beginning. In fact, the compatibility of the Swedish contingent was exceptionally good, given that this was the first Swedish Air Force contribution with combat aircraft to a NATO operation, and the first international Swedish Air Force operation with fighters since operations in the Congo in the early 1960s. This section seeks to illustrate a long and successful pro-

---

[45] Interview with Col. Fredrik Bergman, April 4, 2012.

[46] Interview with Col. Fredrik Bergman, April 4, 2012.

[47] Interview with Lt. Col. Stefan Wilson, March 7, 2012.

cess toward integration and interoperability with NATO despite Sweden's avoidance of membership in the Alliance.

The process of increasing compatibility with NATO has taken place over many years. Sweden has cooperated with NATO in the framework of the Partnership for Peace (PfP) since 1994, and work to make the Swedish Air Force interoperable with NATO began as early as 1996. Since then, technical and methodological interoperability has steadily improved, and today the Swedish Air Force has procedures, call signs, and technology that make it interoperable with NATO units. Over the years, the Swedish Air Force also has participated in numerous international air exercises, such as Red Flag and Cold Response, and has trained Swedish pilots in NATO countries. Moreover, while this was the first Swedish fighter contribution to a NATO operation, the Swedish Air Force already had been involved in ISAF (the International Security Assistance Force in Afghanistan) with transport aircraft and helicopters. Operating within a NATO air campaign framework, therefore, was far from unfamiliar.[48] Moreover, the Swedish armed forces' experience of participating in the NATO-led operations in Kosovo and Afghanistan also provided the larger Swedish bureaucracy with invaluable lessons—from the tactical command level to the Swedish Government Offices, and not least the Delegation of Sweden to NATO in Brussels.

As noted above, large parts of the Swedish unit also were part of the EAW that was on standby as part of EU Nordic Battle Group 11. This meant that the unit was unusually prepared for international operations within an EU framework, making it easy to plug into NATO systems. In essence, experience from NATO exercises, having standby units for international operations, in combination with the extensive past efforts to make technology, methodology, and language interoperable with NATO, meant that compatibility (beyond NATO Secrets) really was not an issue during the operation in Libya. One of the first Swedish pilots who entered Libyan airspace said: "I had to pinch my arm to remember that this was for real and not an exercise"— something that highlighted that the integration process and preparations for NATO interoperability had been successful.[49] In an analysis of operations in Libya, Adrian Johnson and Saqeb Mueen also noted that "Sweden's longstanding collaboration with NATO as a Partner for Peace made cooperation relatively seamless, and may mean that Sweden will participate more readily in future operations."[50]

This is not to say that no serious challenges arose. One of the main challenges was to integrate the tactical data exchange network, Link 16, on the Gripens. While the political challenges took time to resolve, the technical challenges were quickly and successfully overcome in cooperation with the Danish contingent, also based at Sigonella. The Swedish Air Force team members and the Danish military later were awarded

---

[48] Interviews with Col. Fredrik Bergman, April 4, 2012, and Lt. Col. Stefan Wilson, March 7, 2012.

[49] Interview with Col. Hans Einerth, July 18, 2012.

[50] Johnson and Mueen, 2012, p. 32.

Aviation Week Laureate Awards in the category of IT/Electronics "for successfully and quickly integrating Link 16 on the Saab JAS-39 Gripen in support of NATO operations over Libya."[51]

In terms of operational integration from a Swedish perspective, the Delegation of Sweden to NATO has highlighted that the involvement of partnership countries exceeded expectations as soon as the operation was under way. The vast majority of meetings in Brussels were held in OUP-format—meaning that troop contributions, rather than Alliance membership, determined access. All information (open and classified) also was shared among all OUP partners from the beginning.[52] To further facilitate Swedish integration, one Swedish officer was based at SHAPE and three were based at JFC in Naples. At JFC, the Swedish officers were given complete insight into the operations, as long as the Swedish contribution could deliver useful missions and analysis of high quality. The liaison officer wrote almost daily reports to provide the Swedish unit with increased understanding of the thinking and priorities of the staff in Naples. The most important contribution from an operational perspective nevertheless came from the two liaison and six staff officers working at CAOC 5, where the air campaign was led. As highlighted above, apart from performing the regular staff duties, the Swedish officers also were heavily involved in the tasking process to the Swedish contingent—not least during the period of strict national caveats.[53] Both the Swedish NATO delegation in Brussels and the contingent commanders have highlighted the importance of having Swedish staff officers at the important command levels during OUP.[54]

While information sharing and operational integration of partnership countries were good in general, the immediate quality and importance of the Swedish contribution provided an extra level of insight and access. While the Swedes were providing the most sought-after recce operations, they also were given access to the meetings of the "inner circle" (UK, United States, France), and to deliberations of "two eyes" and "five eyes"—the Anglophone communities of either the UK and United States, or of those two countries plus Canada, Australia, and New Zealand.[55] On the opposite end of the scale, during the period of fuel challenges, nonaccess to NATO Secrets and extreme interpretations of Swedish national caveats kept the Swedish contingent out of the loop at all levels of command. Liaison officers were not allowed to attend meetings in the

---

[51] "Congratulations to the Aviation Week Laureate Award Winners," *Aviation Week & Space Technology* online, 2012.

[52] Interview with officials at the Delegation of Sweden to NATO, May 20, 2012.

[53] Interview with Lt. Col. Tommy Petersson, July 17, 2012.

[54] Interview with Lt. Col. Stefan Wilson, March 7, 2012.

[55] Interview with officials at the Delegation of Sweden to NATO in Brussels, May 20, 2012.

inner circle, and access to relevant documents and briefings was limited until the caveats were lifted.[56]

Challenges to the Swedish Contribution

While the overall assessment of Swedish operations in OUP generally was quite positive, the contingent also faced a number of more or less serious challenges that provide important lessons and recommendations—both from Swedish and NATO perspectives—for improvement in future operations. This section focuses on three challenges: getting access to NATO Secrets and Link 16; the challenge of finding compatible jet fuel for the Gripens; and the Swedish political mistakes and national caveats. The first two are challenges stemming largely from Sweden not being a NATO member, while the final one is an internal Swedish problem. It should be noted most of the challenges could be described as start-up problems that successfully were resolved after a number of weeks of operations. This does not, however, take away from the importance of learning lessons from them for future operations.

Access to NATO Secrets and Link 16: The Nonmember Conundrum

Upon deployment, it became clear the Swedish communication systems, despite years of efforts to make them interoperable, could not be fully integrated into the NATO C2 systems. Two separate challenges became apparent: Most importantly, Sweden as a partnership country did not have access to NATO Secrets at the onset of operations, and the process of obtaining a license initially proved difficult. In addition, despite having made the JAS 39C compatible with Link 16 shortly before the operations in Libya, a crypto key had to be obtained, and the bureaucratic process to do so proved almost insurmountable.

The first challenge meant the Swedish contingent did not have a tool for receiving orders or submitting RECCEEXREPs. While this was temporarily solved by receiving orders via the neighboring Danish contingent and by sending images and recce reports physically on disc to CAOC 5, it meant that full operational capability (FOC) was delayed one week. Although this certainly was not the first time Sweden or other nonmembers contributed to NATO operations—KFOR (Kosovo Force) and ISAF being the most obvious examples—this challenge was dealt with very slowly until after the Swedish arrival at Sigonella. At that stage, intense work to solve the issue was launched at all levels within the Swedish contingent, as well as among liaison officers in different commands, and last but not least, within the Delegation of Sweden to NATO.[57]

---

[56] Interview with officials at the Delegation of Sweden to NATO.

[57] Interviews with Lt. Col. Stefan Wilson, March 7 and March 20, 2012.

Gaining access to classified NATO information and communication networks, including the necessary license or crypto key, obviously is not an automatic process for nonmembers. It was therefore quickly identified that formal NATO approval was necessary for access to secure networks. Using Link 16 required a number of formal tasks from the Swedish side, as well as decisions from the NATO Military Committee (MC). NATO expects a coordinated expression of information exchange needs from the contributing country. Based on this request, the appropriate systems and networks for access are identified. When the operational need is confirmed, a request goes to the MC, where the international military staff prepares a recommendation for the MC's decision. After intense work by both Sweden and the United States, it nevertheless became clear that NATO was not going to proactively work Sweden into the security networks and provide the relevant approvals. A number of bureaucratic roadblocks stood in the way. First, the Joint Task Force of OUP needed to define an operational requirement for each nation. Second, several individual requests for each partner nation created a prolonged process for Sweden in particular; other nations were politically more important to deal with. Third, a number of different requirements from different command control authorities were involved.[58] Further complicating matters was NATO's having to deal simultaneously with the requests from Sweden and the politically even more important partners, UAE and Qatar. The Swedish ambassador to NATO has highlighted the many occasions when she was told, "If it was only Sweden, there would be no problem."[59]

Final approval from MC did not come until May 30, at which point the Swedish communication systems could finally be fully integrated with NATO C2 systems. The process involved two time periods of different challenges. The first period, from April 2 until April 28, involved trying to figure out exactly what NATO needed and where to process it. The second period, from April 28 to May 30, involved getting the requirements through the NATO and OUP bureaucracies.[60] Getting a license for access to NATO Secrets was nevertheless not the only problem. The United States provides a number of the Air Force's communication and information systems for interoperability with NATO. Due to the nature of the agreements between the two countries, taking these systems abroad requires formal U.S. authorization. Moreover, using crypto keys that other actors provide also requires authorization. Nevertheless, the Swedish Armed Forces and Delegation of Sweden to NATO in relation to U.S. European Command (USEUCOM), as well as through the contacts of the air force

---

[58] Matthew P. Hill, "Operation Unified Protector," EUCOM briefing, November 2, 2011.

[59] Interview with Veronika Wand-Danielsson, September 10, 2012.

[60] Hill, "Operation Unified Protector."

attaché at the Embassy of Sweden in Washington, were able to quickly deal with these issues prior to deployment.[61]

From a Swedish perspective, three lessons were identified while navigating the formal procedures of the NATO bureaucracy. First was the need to identify useful points of contact at all appropriate levels of command to quickly navigate the formal processes. Second was the need to be prepared to present the formal expression of need immediately when the chance presents itself. This means that Sweden also must have a clear picture of what is necessary and helpful, to have in operations, and a quick-standing procedure for preparing the formal requests. The final need was to quickly identify and establish good relations with a sponsor nation in NATO. To navigate these testing waters of the NATO bureaucracy, as well as to influence and speed up the processes, the support of a powerful "sponsor nation" within NATO is essential. In this case, the Swedish NATO delegation received support from the U.S. delegation to NATO and USEUCOM in Brussels, as well as from the Pentagon in Washington. This relationship continued throughout the operation with nearly daily contacts between the U.S. and Swedish delegations during OUP.[62]

The fact that it took 58 days to integrate the Swedish contingent fully with the operational C2 system can be interpreted in two ways. On the one hand, it can be seen as completely unacceptable that a substantial contributor to the operation had to face such bureaucratic resistance and delay. Clearly, the Alliance was not prepared for the inclusion of partnership countries and the full integration of their communication systems. At the same time, Sweden had not prepared itself for the eventuality of having to go through these motions. On the other hand, these challenges were in the end resolved, and the force-contributing partnership countries were integrated in the operations in an unprecedented manner.

Nonetheless, not providing early access to NATO Secrets for substantial troop contributors was a failure on NATO's part, and the Alliance has also been critical of its own handling of this case.[63] Clearly, the processes for including nonmembers on classified networks will be essential in future operations. One possibility is changing the NATO policies by reducing the bureaucracy of the formal processes. Another possibility is having standing agreements between close partners and NATO that would take effect when contributing troops to operations.

Lack of Compatible Fuel

The second challenge that the Swedish contingent faced upon deployment was the lack of compatible fuel for the JAS 39 Gripen. Sigonella is a naval air station, which means

---

[61] Interviews with officials at the Delegation of Sweden to NATO, and the Embassy of Sweden in Washington, D.C., April 15, 2012.

[62] Interview with officials at the Delegation of Sweden to NATO, April 15, 2012.

[63] Hill, "Operation Unified Protector."

the jet fuel normally provided (JP-5) has a slightly lower flashpoint for increased security on aircraft carriers. This also means the fuel has lower conductivity and viscosity, which makes it incompatible with the Gripen, which normally runs on JP-8 fuel. The problem with JP-5 for the Gripen is that it has lower electrical conductivity, and is more prone to build up static electricity. This problem was discovered when the Swedish maintenance crews tested the fuel during the predeployment phase. The sensitivity to static electricity is not due to the engine, but to the fuel system. Since the Gripen is a small and compact aircraft, the fuel lines have been constructed thinner, which is compensated for by a higher fuel pressure and flow—something that increases the sensitivity to static electricity.[64]

The problem was known, but underestimated, within the Swedish HQ a few days before the deployment to Sigonella Naval Air Station. It was assumed that commercial jet fuel (JET-A1) could be bought and transported from the nearby civilian Catania Airport. JET-A1 fuel is essentially the same as JP-8, but without some military additives. The solution to get fuel from Catania Airport nevertheless faced two challenges. First, no fuel trucks were available on Sicily at this time. Second, JET-A1 is similar to JP-8, but not identical. The Gripen can fly shorter periods on this fuel, but it requires additives for extended use, which improves lubrication and decreases the risk of oxidation. This, in turn, decreases inspection and maintenance intervals on the Gripen. The problem of finding compatible fuel forced all parties involved to display great flexibility and resourcefulness.[65] The Swedish contingent was forced to fill up the Swedish C-130 at other bases so the Gripens could later be refueled in the air. The permanent solution, in the end, involved a convoy of fuel trucks traveling from Sweden through Europe arranged during the Easter break. The Swedish fuel trucks not only provided the correct fuel and the all-important fuel transport capability from Catania Airport; they carried pumps and a system that could automatically provide the appropriate additives to the JET-A1 fuel. The convoy nevertheless required military escort and provided not only logistical challenges, but also diplomatic ones, as military transports abroad require formal authorizations from each state they transit.[66]

While the fuel situation limited the extent of early missions flown, in the end the issue was resolved to an acceptable extent by the time that access to NATO Secrets was accomplished. Thus, the Swedish contingent reported FOC to NATO on April 21. Given the challenges described above, as well as the fact that this was the first Swedish contribution of fighter jets to a NATO air campaign, arriving at FOC in Sicily only 20 days after the parliamentary decision to contribute Swedish jets should be seen as quite an accomplishment.

---

[64] Interviews with Lt. Col. Hans Einerth, July 18, 2012, and Lt. Col. Stefan Wilson, March 25, 2012.

[65] Interview with Major General Anders Silwer, then-commander of the Swedish Air Tactical Command, May 12, 2012.

[66] Interviews with Lt. Col. Stefan Wilson, March 7, 2012, and Maj. Gen. Anders Silwer, May 12, 2012.

The National Caveats and the Failures of Swedish Politics

That the Swedish contingent was not authorized to strike ground targets in Libya was hardly surprising, given that this was the first time in 48 years that Swedish fighter jets were unleashed internationally. There was plenty of political nervousness in Stockholm regarding the potential impact of Swedish bombs causing civilian casualties. Thus, while Sweden supported the campaign in full, the political risks involved in engaging grounds targets were left to others. The caveat was nevertheless well understood within the coalition, which meant it did not have any substantial negative consequences in terms of the credibility of the Swedish contribution.[67] Moreover, the most important Swedish contribution was initially perceived to be the political legitimacy that Swedish participation provided for the operation.[68] Beyond that ground-target caveat, however, a number of unnecessary and strategically foolish caveats and limitations were placed on the Swedish contingent that could have been avoided. Two decisions stand out in this regard: First, beyond the bombing caveat, the Swedish Parliament initially decided that the only section of UNSCR 1973 that the Swedish contingent could implement was the task of creating and upholding the no-fly zone (NFZ). Second, political horse-trading meant that three Gripens were withdrawn from the mission halfway through—sending an unfortunate signal to OUP commanders and NATO HQ at a sensitive point in time for the operation.

As highlighted previously in the volume, UNSCR 1973 included three main operational tasks: establishment of an NFZ, enforcement of the arms embargo, and protection of Libyan civilians. Limiting the Swedish contribution to the NFZ made little sense and created great difficulties at the tactical level. In terms of tactical air doctrine, the NFZ is an aim of tactical operations rather than a task, and it was entirely unclear which tasks the Swedish contingent had the mandate to perform to achieve that aim. Creating and upholding an NFZ involves attacking ground targets such as air defense systems and C2 centers. Yet the Swedish unit was not allowed to do this, and the first two weeks of the operation were spent trying to understand what were legally and politically acceptable activities within the given political mandate. That the commander of the Swedish Air Tactical Command, Major General Anders Silwer, as well as a legal counsel, supported the unit at Sigonella to make this interpretation is an indication of both the perceived difficulty and importance of this interpretation.[69]

Initially, a relatively liberal interpretation was made. However, a combination of factors described below led to a much stricter interpretation after two weeks of sorties.

---

[67] NATO Secretary General Anders Fogh Rasmussen stressed while visiting Sweden on the day of the Parliamentary decision that the Swedish caveats did not represent a problem for NATO, in "Bred majoritet för Libyeninsats," *Svenska Dagbladet*, April 1, 2011.

[68] Interview with U.S. Department of Defense official, May 2012; interview with Embassy of Sweden official, April 2012.

[69] Interview with Maj. Gen. Anders Silwer, May 2012.

It was then decided that the NFZ caveat meant the Swedish contingent essentially was only allowed to conduct DCA operations and TAR against the NFZ. The Swedish contingent could not gather intelligence regarding civilians in danger or breaches of the weapons embargo. Libyan air capabilities essentially were destroyed by the time of Swedish deployment, and although a few relevant targets of reconnaissance related to the no-fly zone still existed during the early weeks, these also quickly disappeared. The Swedish contribution became increasingly useless and the caveats unsustainable. Moreover, the caveats did not come without a cost, as NATO reacted by throwing out diplomats and Swedish liaison officers from restricted meetings at all levels of command, and most importantly at JFC in Naples.[70]

A Swedish parliamentary delegation visited the Swedish unit at Sigonella base in late May and reportedly was shocked to hear that despite Sweden justifying the mission in humanitarian terms in general, and the protection of civilians in particular, the Swedish jets could not conduct reconnaissance with the purpose of leading to more effective airstrikes against threats to civilians, or even to help save civilian lives by identifying unsuitable targets. Recce sorties essentially had to ignore blatant threats to civilians, and officially were not allowed to photograph or report them.[71] Following the parliamentary visit, the mandate was first informally reinterpreted within a few days, then completely rewritten in the June 26 parliamentary decision to extend the Swedish mission by 90 days. All caveats beyond the prohibition on attacking ground targets were lifted at that point.

Why was the mandate of the Swedish unit so limited in the first parliamentary decision and why was it interpreted the way it was—with the effect of severely limiting the capability to contribute to the operation during April and May? The paragraphs below seek to explain the caveats by describing the impact of the nature of civil-military relations in Sweden, as well as by looking at the specific political context in which the main decisions regarding the Swedish contribution were made.

As described above, the political process leading up to the parliamentary decision was quite quick. Interestingly, the week before the decision was made, a draft government bill was produced with no caveats at all. However, after deliberations between the government and the main opposition parties, an agreement was reached that the Swedish jets would not engage ground targets. That agreement was reached on the morning of March 29. The government offices had less than an hour to rewrite the bill that had to be presented to Parliament the same day to avoid unnecessary delays in Parliament's formal political procedures. During that hour, the unfortunate redrafting solution, possibly reflecting a decision in the political agreement, was to include the no-ground-attacks caveat by focusing Swedish operations solely on the NFZ. This has

---

[70] Interviews with Lt. Col. Stefan Wilson, February 23, 2012; with senior civil servant at the Swedish Foreign Ministry, April 2012; with the Swedish Representation to Brussels, May 2012.

[71] Interview with Col. Stefan Wilson, February 23, 2012.

been described as a decision of pure convenience—an easy way of operationalizing the bombing caveat—as it was not anticipated that it would have a large impact on operations in the field.[72] Foreign Minister Carl Bildt's blog post, written the same day, also provides some interesting clues:

> The well-informed are likely to recall that our efforts in the air campaign at that time [the Congo in the 1960s]—with the J29 Flying Barrel—focused on attacks against ground targets. These efforts also became important for the UN mission in its entirety. Now, our efforts will involve the maintenance of air surveillance and—I hope—different forms of reconnaissance and intelligence efforts. Especially the latter have very clearly been requested, and here too I think that political support is very broad.[73]

The blog post can be interpreted as containing a kernel of disappointment about that fact that, for political reasons, the Swedish contingent would not be able to engage ground targets. The foreign minister also made clear that it was the Swedish reconnaissance and intelligence capabilities that were requested by NATO. Bildt was correct in his interpretation that broad political support was evident for reconnaissance and intelligence gathering at this stage, as the main opposition party was clearly on board for the full range of reconnaissance tasks.[74] In fact, a political consensus existed regarding the appropriate nature of the Swedish contribution (involving the full range of reconnaissance and intelligence gathering) but the mandate was still limited to the NFZ as a matter of bureaucratic convenience. This indicates the political leadership understood neither the tactical and legal challenges that the wording of the mandate would entail for the Swedish contingent, nor the limited utility that the Swedish contingent would provide for the operations as a whole with the mandate it was given. This lack of understanding was due to an all-too-common failure of communications in the civil-military interface.

A recurrent theme in Swedish contributions to international operations is the gap between the political leadership and the armed forces. The Swedish constitution demands a peculiar separation of the government ministries from the agencies that implement policy.[75] While this theoretically ensures unpoliticized implementation of government directives, it has some serious negative consequences for political control and leadership of military operations. On the one hand, it means the military leadership is detached from the political process and has remarkably limited *Fingerspitzengefühl*, or intuitive instinct, in understanding and implementing political

---

[72] Interview with senior civil servant at the Swedish Foreign Ministry, April 2012.

[73] Carl Bildt, "Hem från London" [Home from London], online (author's translation), March 29, 2011.

[74] Interview with Urban Ahlin, Social Democratic Party, May 5, 2012.

[75] Swedish Government, "Så Styrs Statliga Myndigheter" [How State Authorities Are Run], online, updated January 19, 2012.

wishes. On the other hand, and perhaps even more seriously, it means the departments of Defense and Foreign Affairs' understanding of the military instrument, and the consequent capability to control and direct them, is equally limited.[76] Thus, political deliberations and decisions often are made with little understanding of the general utility of force or the more specific military capabilities available to implement political ambitions. While this problem clearly is not limited to the Swedish system, it has led to a number of recent strategic blunders related to Swedish contributions to international operations.[77]

The limited arena for civil-military interaction also means that very few individuals within the Swedish system are capable of engaging in strategic thinking.[78] The foundation of strategy is how to translate political aims into suitable operation to achieve those aims. This is inherently difficult, however, and requires a deep understanding of the military instrument, as well as of political processes and interests. The Swedish bureaucracy simply does not produce individuals with the required breadth and depth of understanding, and the institutional setup also limits the possibility and frequency of meetings between representatives from the military and political fields.[79]

While the Swedish Parliament's mandate was problematic, an even bigger problem was the interpretation of that mandate. Why was an interpretation made that rendered the Swedish contribution almost useless during a number of weeks in April and May?

Three factors contributed to this, the first being that the political climate changed. The political deliberation process before the Swedish decision to contribute to OUP was quick and emotive. However, many politicians did not understand what the air campaign over Libya would actually involve. As this became clear, enthusiasm declined. In mid-May, the operation also was increasingly seen as problematic. It did not quickly deliver the anticipated results as the civil war on the ground dragged on with civilians as targets. It also became increasingly clear some of the leading contributing countries to OUP sought to instigate regime change by targeting Qaddafi and members of his family from the air. Another contributing factor to the belated political skepticism was the Swedish armed forces' response to growing criticism of not making a substantial contribution in Libya beyond political flag-waving. On the air force blog and when testifying before Parliament, the armed forces made it clear that the contribution was substantial by showing reconnaissance images from the Swedish jets. These involved graphic evidence of destroyed targets that had the unintended effect of making the

---

[76] Robert Egnell and Claes Nilsson, "Svensk Civil-Militär Samverkan för Internationella Insatser: Från Löftesrika Koncept till Konkret Handling" [Swedish Civil-Military Cooperation in International Operations: From Concept to Action], *KKrVA Handlingar och tidskrift*, No 1, 2011.

[77] Egnell and Nilsson, "Svensk Civil-militär samverkan."

[78] Interview with senior military officer, May 15, 2012.

[79] Interview with senior military officer, May 15, 2012.

antimilitaristic members of the political opposition extremely nervous about the Gripens over Libya. Most importantly, however, the main opposition party (and the biggest party in Sweden), the Social Democrats, had elected a new party chairman the weekend before the Parliamentary decision to participate. That official reversed the party position during April by stating: "The mandate has a time limit. I find it hard to imagine an extension [beyond the initial 90 days]."[80] While not taken seriously at the time, it fueled the political nervousness about Sweden's contribution in Libya, and had an impact on the interpretations of the mandate.

Another factor was that the actual "order" regarding the limited interpretation of the mandate came from the Swedish Defence Ministry. The armed forces received a very clear instruction from the Undersecretary of State for defense that the "agreement with the opposition is extremely important," and that no transgressions could be allowed.[81]

Finally, the armed forces, and especially the air force, were pleased that the long-standing political ban on fighter jets in international operations finally had been lifted with the decision to contribute in Libya. Therefore, they exercised great caution in the interpretation of the mandate in order to make sure that the political leadership would not have to regret the decision.[82]

These three factors meant the NFZ caveat that initially was a mere bureaucratic convenience hardened into a very real and harsh interpretation of the mandate. The Swedish contingent was hindered from playing the role it could have until the mandate was changed in June 2011. The initial mandate was unnecessary and based on misunderstandings. It was then followed by an unfortunate interpretation that did not reflect the intentions of the policymakers—all due to political infighting and poor communication within the civil-military interface.

The political bickering continued during the debate regarding the extension of the Swedish contribution. The chairman of the Social Democrats had, by that time, invested much prestige in the position that the mandate of the Swedish jets should not be extended. Instead of the jets, to save face he suggested a naval contribution and a boarding force. The political compromise that resulted from the negotiations involved withdrawing three Gripens while offering a boarding force. The boarding force, while it was on the list of requested assets in the initial Combined Joint Statement of Requirement, was unwanted at this stage of the operation—especially when it was being offered without a ship. This was well known within the Swedish administration, but in a complete bureaucratic circus, Sweden still was obligated to offer a force

---

[80] Håkan Juholt cited in "Oenighet om Svensk Libyen-Insats" [Disagreement About the Swedish Operation in Libya], *Svenska Dagbladet*, April 29, 2012.

[81] Interview with Maj. Gen. Anders Silwer, May 14, 2012.

[82] Interview with the Delegation of Sweden to NATO in Brussels, May 14, 2012.

no one wanted, and NATO was forced to politely decline the kind offer, just to allow Swedish politicians to save face.[83]

Conclusions and Recommendations

Given that it was the first foreign deployment of Swedish combat aircraft in nearly 50 years, the operation can, from a Swedish perspective, be described as nothing short of a major success—in political and diplomatic terms, as well as, for the military, an acknowledgment of well-functioning training and technical systems. The operations in Libya also provided a useful opportunity to develop and refine these systems. While the list of positive lessons could certainly be made longer than the one below, it is nevertheless more useful for the purpose of this chapter to focus on those aspects that were more problematic and that can be improved for future operations. Opportunities for improvement exist not only within the Swedish armed forces, but in the relationship between NATO and Sweden as a partnership country.

First, in relation to NATO, a number of positive lessons can be gleaned from the operations in Libya. Swedish soldiers and officers, as well as their technical systems, displayed not only great competence in international comparison but also an advantageous compatibility and interoperability with NATO forces. The Swedish military displayed it has useful air capabilities that, if allowed, have the potential to be quickly integrated into NATO structures. It can, therefore, be counted on in the future to provide not only political legitimacy, but substantial operational capabilities and effects. Other positive aspects include the increased openness toward troop-contributing partnership countries. From a Swedish perspective, this was highly appreciated, and the hope is it will serve as a new benchmark for future NATO operations. Finally, the invitation of liaison officers and staff at all relevant levels of command was not only highly appreciated, but considered essential for the operational integration and effectiveness of the partnership country contributions.

On the negative side, the nonmember conundrum of not having access to information, planning, and negotiations before the formal commitment of forces is a challenge that makes the predeployment planning difficult for partnership countries. The formal process for the inclusion of partners in operations clearly is too cumbersome for cases such as this, and a need exists for a new framework with greater flexibility and shorter time frames. Moreover, access to NATO mission secret networks proved highly problematic for partnership countries at the onset of operations. The Alliance's procedures were truly cumbersome to navigate to complete requests for such access, and the Alliance also proved to be overly bureaucratic when dealing with the Swedish request. This meant that full operational capability was delayed, as was the full C2

---

[83] Interview with the Delegation of Sweden to NATO.

integration of the Swedish jets. Given that coalition operations involving contributors beyond the NATO members is the norm rather than the exception in the contemporary context, policies and procedures to fully integrate troop contributors must further be improved to maximize operational efficacy. Several ways are available to improve the processes displayed in Libya. The most radical one would be to create standing agreements between common contributors and NATO that take effect as soon as a formal commitment is made. A less radical way of improving the procedures within the existing framework is to train more realistically by going through these formal processes in international exercises. This would provide the necessary knowledge of the formal processes among partners, as well as the necessary experience within NATO to deal with the requests. Whether NATO reforms its policies for including partner countries or not, the partners must always have a very good understanding of the formal processes required for access to NATO secrets, as well as standard operating procedures for these processes. This is particularly important in air campaigns that often require faster processes than traditional stability operations involving ground forces.

Looking at the Swedish conduct of operations, another positive set of conclusions can be drawn. First and foremost, for the Swedish Air Force, the operation displayed that its systems work. The quality of images and analysis, as well as the competence and flexibility of the technical and human systems, meant that the initial international skepticism toward the Swedish contribution was transformed into great appreciation. Worryingly, however, the armed forces worked at maximum capacity for air reconnaissance during OUP. While many more missions can be flown and pictures taken, the limiting factor is the number of deployable photo interpreters within the Air Force. Nonetheless, at the political and military strategic levels, the quality of the Swedish contribution created plenty of bilateral goodwill for Sweden—particularly within NATO and in the United States. This is something to carefully nurture.

On the negative side, the political strategic level again made unnecessary mistakes that limited the potential positive impact of the Swedish contribution. This was partly based on misunderstandings due to a general problem with a defunct civil-military interface within the Swedish system that led to poor strategic thinking. It was partly based on more situation-specific political bickering, which was allowed to be too much of an influence on operational decisions. These are familiar problems from past operations, and it seems that serious reforms of the civil-military interface are necessary to overcome the deficiencies.

With Operation Atalanta in the Gulf of Aden, and Operation Unified Protector in Libya, Sweden has taken two important steps as a credible contributor to international peace operations by moving out of its comfort zone as it deployed naval and air capabilities. OUP in Libya clearly was a continuation of Swedish ambitions to play a substantial role in international crisis management, and it is unlikely it was the last time Sweden will operate under the NATO banner. There are, therefore, good reasons for Sweden and NATO to continue making the procedures for partnership contributions to NATO operations as efficient and frictionless as possible. While OUP was in many ways a substantial improvement in terms of information sharing and operational integration of partner countries compared to KFOR and ISAF, a number of issues still can be improved. Part of this involves learning from past operations and changing the policies of the organization. Other parts are best developed as lessons from realistic exercises that force the organization to go through all the formal motions of partnership contributions. If this seems too cumbersome to introduce in exercises, it is probably a good sign that the procedures and policies need to be changed before the next international contingency arises.

CHAPTER TWELVE

The Arab States' Experiences

Bruce R. Nardulli

Introduction

The Libyan revolution and toppling of the regime with assistance from the NATO-led coalition had many distinctive features. In the larger political context, one of the more prominent ones involved the direct participation of Arab states in helping to bring down the Qaddafi regime, punctuated by the direct military participation of the Arab states of Qatar, the United Arab Emirates, and Jordan. These developments stood out as another dramatic development in a region already rocked by drama since the Tunisia uprising and the cascading events of the Arab Awakening that followed. The State of Qatar, in particular, staked out a leading position against the Qaddafi regime from the onset of the uprising and the initial violent crackdown in early February 2011.

The history of Arab state involvement in the Libyan campaign can be reconstructed in many different ways. All of them have the benefit of imposing logic and order on what was a complex, emotional, sometimes chaotic and rapidly unfolding situation. This chapter attempts to capture some of the major political and military elements that shaped the intervention and operations of the Arab state participants. It also emphasizes the manner in which the two Gulf states of Qatar and the UAE, in particular, managed to engage in direct military operations well outside their traditional operating area.

On the political front, the decade-long involvement of Western military forces in Afghanistan and Iraq, and the unfolding of the Arab Awakening, provided the strategic backdrop that helped set the conditions for Arab military involvement. The Libyan uprising provided the need for mutual support (and mutual opportunity) for the NATO-contributing countries and for the Arab state participants. The United States, Britain, and France all recognized the importance of having Arab political support to legitimize any military operations against Qaddafi and his regime. Likewise, the Arab states understood that Western military power was needed to bring down the Qaddafi regime and avoid a potential massacre of civilians in Libya. Active Arab participation also would provide an opening for Arab leadership to positively shape developments in light of the Arab Awakening. NATO provided them the necessary military coalition support structure to allow their militaries to become directly involved in the effort, something not possible in the absence of the much larger NATO effort.

The challenge lay in bringing the two sets of agendas and partners together to practical effect. An important part of this story, then, is how Arab-state military power was marshaled and employed in a rapidly unfolding "out-of-area" coalition campaign. This was accomplished in large part because of previously established security cooperation relationships with major Western coalition partners. Therefore, a proper understanding of the role of Arab partners in the Libyan campaign requires assessing how specific political conditions and previous operational military cooperation combined in this conflict.

Arab state contributions to the campaign can be placed into two broad categories. The first comprised political, diplomatic, and economic support to the anti-Qaddafi opposition that coalesced around the National Transitional Council (NTC). These actions proved to be of great importance, especially as the campaign quickly shifted from one designed to protect Libyan civilians to the more ambitious objective of removing *and replacing* the Qaddafi regime. For the latter to be successful, a viable and regionally legitimate governing alternative had to exist to avoid a vacuum and ensuing civil war or chaos—and the dark prospect of outside powers being forced to introduce ground forces to stabilize such a situation. Arab state efforts to support the NTC as that viable alternative were instrumental in this regard.

Second was direct military intervention. Led by Qatar and the UAE, this most visibly consisted of contributing combat aircraft to the NATO-led air effort. Less visible, but far more significant in terms of military impact, were activities to directly arm and train rebel forces and assist in providing ground intelligence to NATO. The full impact of this direct support to the opposition ground forces must await a detailed history. Available information, however, suggests this role, in conjunction with NATO's persistent air attacks on government forces over time, allowed for a military synergy that helped bring about the toppling of the regime.

This chapter covers both categories, with emphasis on the military component. It begins with a brief overview of the regional strategic context in which Arab participation occurred, a necessary prelude to understanding how that participation came about. It concludes with observations and initial lessons drawn from the Arab state participation.

The Road to Arab State Intervention

A series of regional developments linked to the Arab Awakening helped propel Qatar and the UAE into prominent roles in Libya among the Arab states. At the time, Egypt was in the midst of its own upheavals, and aside from concerns over the safety of its nationals in Libya and spillovers along its border, was in no position to take on a leadership role in Libya. Saudi Arabia was focused on unrest in nearby Bahrain, a far more pressing security priority than Libya. Several other Arab states concentrated on their own internal situations as popular Arab unrest continued to unfold. These conditions helped set the stage for the assertive and forward-leaning roles of Qatar and the UAE.

The nature and constraints of the NATO-led military operation itself also served to enhance the weight of Arab partner military participation. Most notably, training the rebels, especially via Arab special forces on the ground in Libya, took on added importance precisely because NATO had so much concern that none of its ground forces be part of the military effort, codified in UNSCR 1973. This provision, as well as the repeated statements that Operation Unified Protector was to defend civilians and not to support the rebels, set major constraints on any use of ground forces. Even the air operations were carefully framed with this protective-only role, with U.S. and NATO leaders making it clear that supporting the Libyan opposition forces and the NTC was not part of the coalition's mandate.[1] These constraints were essential to keeping the coalition together and maintaining Arab support for the operation, but also provided an opening into which the Qataris, in particular, would quickly move.

While the region still was reverberating from the news of the resignation of Egyptian President Hosni Mubarak on February 11, the first outbreaks of protest in Libya occurred on February 16 in Benghazi and quickly spread elsewhere. Counter-demonstrations and violence directed against the protestors soon escalated, and within the first week more than 200 people were reported killed. As the situation deteriorated, on February 22 Qaddafi made a highly charged televised speech in which he defiantly vowed resistance against the protestors, referring to them as "greasy rats" in the pay of Libya's enemies, and declared he would die a martyr and never flee Libya. In the course of his rambling speech, he made reference to the role of hostile Arab media in inciting the violence and specifically to Qatar's role here:

> These Arabic TV channels are the biggest enemy, and they are on to you. They want you to destroy the oil, the freedom, public authority and Libya, because they are jealous of you. Our brothers in Qatar, is this the end of it? Is that the friendship we had between us? You go against us in everything? Instead of going with us, you stand against us . . . You may regret this when it is too late.[2]

Likewise, in an early response to continuing media coverage of the violence in Libya by Doha-based *Al Jazeera*, Libyan officials noted: "We used to respect our brothers in Qatar. But the brothers in Qatar directed *Al Jazeera* to incitement and to spread lies . . . Libya has a problem with the brothers in Qatar."[3] It was clear that hostility

---

[1]   As noted in *Operations in Libya*, House of Commons Defence Committee, Ninth Report of Session 2012–12, Vol. 1, HC 950, February 8, 2012, pp. 36 and 38.

[2]   "Muammar Gaddafi speech TRANSLATED (2011 Feb 22)," posted on YouTube.

[3]   Statement by Libyan secretary general on Libyan television, as covered by "The Lede" blog (assembled by *The New York Times*), February 23, 2013.

was escalating between the two leaderships and setting a course for even more direct confrontation.[4]

The following day, at a press conference in London with British Prime Minister David Cameron, Prime Minister of Qatar His Excellency Sheikh Hamad Bin Jassim Bin Jabor Al-Thani reiterated Qatar's position on events in Libya: "We do not have any quarrels with the government of Libya. All that we have said officially was an expression of discomfort at the use of excessive force. This is unacceptable as far as we are concerned." He went on to note, "As far as any Qatari moves are concerned we move within the framework of the Arab League" and that "We do not consider this as an intervention. On the contrary, we want Libya to be an integral and important part of the Arab world. All we hope is what we have been witnessing in Libya should be ended as soon as possible."[5] The public position of Qatar at this time, while sharply critical of the Libyan government's actions against the protestors, did not yet imply that the Qaddafi regime had to go.

The first collective diplomatic action by Arab states on Libya came in early March by way of the Cooperation Council for the Arab States of the Gulf (GCC). By this time, a much harder line materialized toward the regime's future. In a Ministerial Statement on March 7, the GCC emphasized the "illegitimacy of the current Libyan regime and the necessity of having contacts/communication with the National Transition Council." Furthermore, it went on to state that the

> Council of Ministers calls on the Arab League to take on the responsibility for taking the necessary measures to spare the blood and realize the aspirations of the brotherly Libyan people and to study ways to achieve that including calling on the UN Security Council to impose a no-fly zone over Libya for the protection of civilians.[6]

With this, the GCC came out in favor of a no-fly zone and requested larger Arab League backing for it.[7]

The Arab League, in turn, met on March 11 in Cairo. At the ministerial level in its extraordinary session on Libya, the League took a watershed position on the conflict:

---

[4] As it would turn out, over the coming months *Al Jazeera* maintained 24-hour coverage of the conflict in both Arabic and English highlighting the brutality of the regime and with a clear underlying message in support of the uprising. The result was to keep the conflict front and center, the coverage serving as a constant pressure point. And to give direct voice to the opposition, Qatar would also later provide the means for the NTC opposition to set up its own satellite media channel, Libya al-Ahrar, with a studio in Doha and with Qatar transmitting its signal.

[5] "Press conference with the Prime Minister of Qatar," Wednesday, February 23, 2011, online at *10*, the official site of the British Prime Minister's Office, February 23, 2011.

[6] Translation from Arabic, original text found on GCC parallels website.

[7] At the time, the position of Secretary-General of the GCC was held by a Qatari, His Excellency Abdul Rahman Bin Hamad Al-Attiyah.

Recalling its commitment to preserve Libyan territorial integrity, regional security, political independence and civil peace; to ensure the safety and security of Libyan citizens, the national unity and independence of the Libyan people and their sovereignty over their territory; and to reject all forms of foreign intervention in Libya; and emphasizing that failure to take the measures necessary to end this crisis will lead to foreign intervention in Libyan internal affairs,

The League decided:

1. To call upon the Security Council, in view of the deterioration in the situation in Libya, to shoulder its responsibilities and take the measures necessary to immediately impose a no-fly zone on Libyan military aircraft and establish safe havens in areas that are exposed to bombardment, as precautionary measures that will provide protection for the Libyan people and the various foreign nationals resident in Libya while respecting the sovereignty and territorial integrity of neighbouring States.

2. To cooperate and liaise with the Interim Transitional National Council of Libya, and provide the Libyan people with urgent and sustained support and the necessary protection from the serious violations and grave crimes to which they are being subjected by the Libyan authorities, as a result of which those authorities have forfeited all legitimacy.[8]

The League went on to reiterate the ongoing importance of humanitarian assistance to the Libyan people and to continue its coordination with the U.N., African Union, Organization of the Islamic Conference, and European Union on the situation in Libya. With endorsement of the no-fly zone, this was the first time in its history that the Arab League called for military action against a fellow member state.

Diplomatic efforts for military intervention now were moving at an accelerated pace on all fronts. On March 17, the United Nations Security Council adopted Resolution 1973 (UNSCR 1973). It called for establishing a no-fly zone over Libya, robust enforcement of the arms embargo called for in UNSCR 1970, and for member states "to take all necessary measures . . . to protect civilians and civilian populated areas under threat of attack in the Libyan Arab Jamahiriya, including Benghazi, while excluding a foreign occupation force of any form on any part of Libyan territory."[9] French President Nicolas Sarkozy hosted the Paris summer two days later, which the Arab states of Iraq, Jordan, Morocco, Qatar, and the UAE all attended. Qatar and the

---

[8]   Council of the League of Arab States, Resolution No. 7360, extraordinary session, Cairo, March 12, 2011.

[9]   United Nations Security Council, Resolution 1973 (2011), March 17, 2011.

UAE were represented by their foreign ministers, who reportedly pledged a commitment of aircraft to help enforce a no-fly zone.[10]

While this move toward military intervention was reaching a critical phase, the GCC states faced a different type of intervention closer to home. Since mid-February, the Kingdom of Bahrain had been rocked with escalating protests that also had an intersectarian dimension and the specter of Iranian involvement. At the GCC Foreign Ministers meeting in Manama on February 17, the ministers stressed their full support and solidarity with the kingdom and its leadership. Per the GCC-adopted principle of indivisible security, "The ministerial council confirmed that protecting security and stability is a collective responsibility by all GCC member states."[11] Clearly, the tenor of the statement and presumably the meeting proceedings reflected growing concern among the GCC leadership that events in Bahrain could get out of control and potentially spread more widely. As the situation continued to deteriorate over the next few weeks, on March 13 the Bahraini leadership requested GCC assistance. The following evening, the GCC Jazeera (Peninsula) Shield Forces (GCC-JSF) began arriving in Bahrain, led by Saudi forces coming across the King Fahd Causeway. The forces had the stated purpose of assisting Bahraini forces to protect vital installations and to defend Bahrain against any foreign intervention. Forces from the UAE later joined the lead Saudi element, with Kuwait contributing to offshore security operations. Qatar backed the GCC response and was reported to have sent security personnel and observers, with a small contingent of Qatari troops on standby in Saudi Arabia's Eastern Province if required. The total number of GCC-JSF personnel inside Bahrain reportedly reached about 5,000.[12] Domestic unrest was therefore being confronted in two sharply contrasting ways at near-opposite ends of the Arab World, illustrating the dominance of core state security objectives and not a generalized support for popular Arab uprisings.

Qatar, the UAE, and Jordan Join the Coalition

As the situation continued to worsen in Libya, the Qataris in particular were very forward leaning in offering not only political and economic support, but also military

---

[10] Tim Ripley, "Power Brokers—Qatar and the UAE Take Centre Stage," *Jane's Intelligence Review*, Vol. 24, No. 2, February 2012, pp. 22–25.

[11] "Statement on the 30th Extraordinary GCC Foreign Ministers Council Meeting," Manama, Bahrain, February 17, 2011, Kingdom of Bahrain Ministry of Foreign Affairs website.

[12] *Report of the Bahrain Independent Commission of Inquiry*, Final Revision of December 10, 2011, subsection 501, p. 134. For troop numbers and composition see subsection 1580, p. 386. UAE Foreign Minister Sheikh Abdullah bin Zayed al-Nahayan confirmed that in response to a request for assistance from Bahrain, the Emirates dispatched roughly 500 police officers to the kingdom. See "UAE says sent 500 police officers into Bahrain," *Reuters*, March 14, 2011. HM King Hamad issued a Royal Decree the following day (March 15) declaring a State of National Safety throughout Bahrain for three months.

support following UNSCR 1973. It was the Qataris who made the initial move in offering to provide aircraft and other forms of military support to the opposition as the military strikes enforcing the no-fly zone commenced on March 19 under Operation Odyssey Dawn. The speed and willingness to commit forces reportedly came as a bit of a surprise even to Western officials in the region. So while the Western powers deemed Arab participation essential, Qatar actually took the initiative in pushing for their military participation.

The long and close relationship between France's President Sarkozy and the Emir of Qatar appears to have played an important role in this critical decisionmaking. It is noteworthy that when Sarkozy first took office in 2007, the Emir was the first Arab leader invited to France. Over the following years, the two worked together on diplomatic matters that included mediating talks between the Sudanese government and Darfur rebels and helping to broker a ceasefire in Gaza in 2008. Sarkozy's four visits to Qatar, the most he made to any Arab state, reflected the closeness of ties.[13]

As noted elsewhere in this volume, Sarkozy played a leading role—if not the leading role—in advocating outside intervention to staunch the bloodshed in Libya. The Emir of Qatar and the French president shared the view that the Libyan situation presented the potential for a humanitarian disaster unleashed by an erratic and lethal regime. Sarkozy also made clear in his public statements that Arab support was essential to any Western-led intervention. In addition to political support, having an Arab partner willing to commit military forces would be a dramatic way to bolster the legitimacy of the intervention. Therefore it is quite plausible these two leaders together forged the political-military alliance that led to Qatar's military involvement, essentially born of a bilateral arrangement at the highest levels. As subsequent events would show, the Qatari and French air forces would work closely as a team throughout the campaign.

The three Arab partner states' military contributions to the conflict varied, but collectively ended up consisting of three elements: (1) fighter aircraft used to conduct combat air patrols as part of the no-fly zone along with limited air-to-surface strike operations, (2) transport flights responsible for humanitarian assistance and military support of the Libyan opposition, and (3) the use of special forces inside Libya to help train and organize the opposition, assist them in planning military operations, and provide ground-based intelligence to the larger campaign effort. In terms of political significance and the "optics" of the coalition, the commitment of Arab states' fighter aircraft carried the most weight. During the early days of the conflict and the formation of the coalition, the early commitment and deployment of combat aircraft to the coalition effort (six Mirages by Qatar, shortly followed by the UAE's provision of six F-16s and six Mirages) received considerable publicity from NATO spokespersons and other Western leaders.

---

[13] Crown Prince Sheikh Tamim was also hosted by the president in February 2010. See John Irish and Regan E. Doherty, "Libyan Conflict Brings French-Qatari Ties to the Fore," *Reuters*, April 13, 2011; French Embassy in Doha, "Political Relations Between France and Qatar," May 31, 2011; and "The Ties That Bind Doha and Paris," *The National*, September 18, 2009.

While Arab-partner aircraft represented only about five percent of all coalition airpower, this was far outweighed by the political import of the combat aircraft commitments.[14]

Jordan's commitment of six F-16s in early April was, by contrast, done with a very low profile. Based at Aviano, in northern Italy, official Jordanian references to these aircraft emphasized they were deployed to protect humanitarian assistance operations that the Royal Jordanian Air Force was conducting with transport aircraft and would not be involved in any direct combat role. Official statements repeatedly emphasized that Jordan would not take part in air strike operations or actual enforcement sorties for the no-fly zone.[15]

Transport aircraft and their operations were less prominent in the public domain, but in many ways they were an equally or even more significant air contribution. These provided a direct link to the Libyan opposition, and over time became the key "air bridge" to providing continuous humanitarian relief and material support to the rebels. All three Arab states' air forces participated in humanitarian assistance and relief operations in Libya. Transport aircraft also became the means to bring in special forces to train the opposition, the most significant and high-leverage military contribution made by the Arab states to the conflict.

While the Libyan conflict presented a uniquely demanding operation for the Arab partner states, both Qatar and the UAE previously had shown growing interest in developing "expeditionary" capabilities and experience over the last several years that served them well. This was, in part, reflected in recent acquisitions of major transport capabilities in their air fleets. While focused primarily on national and then Gulf security, both Qatar and the UAE developed some military capacity to conduct out-of-area expeditionary missions. Prior to Libya, the primary focus had been on humanitarian assistance and relief efforts. Qatar, for example, was involved in the U.N. Interim Force in Lebanon (UNIFIL) operations in Lebanon, and humanitarian assistance in Haiti and Chile, the latter two involving long-distance shipments of food, water, and medical supplies in 2010 using newly purchased U.S. C-17 Globemaster III transports.[16] The UAE has maintained a military presence in Afghanistan for more than eight years focusing on humanitarian assistance, providing security to local Afghans, and imple-

---

[14] Shashank Joshi, "The Complexity of Arab Support," in Johnson and Mueen, 2012, p. 66.

[15] For one example, see Hani Hazaimeh, "Jordan Not Participating in No-Fly Zone," *Jordan Times*, March 20, 2011. Also, see "Jordan Sends Jets to Support Libya No-Fly Zone," *Reuters*, April 6, 2011; "'The fighter planes were sent to a European base to protect our humanitarian corridor and provide logistical support for the no-fly zone,' Foreign Minister Nasser Judeh told Reuters. 'The mission does not have a combat role.'"

[16] "Boeing, Qatar Emiri Air Force Laud C-17 Fleet's Achievements," Boeing Co. news release, Doha, Qatar, March 15, 2010. While not out-of-area, Qatar's first significant military deployment and combat outside its borders took place during the 1991 Gulf War, in which its ground forces achieved notoriety for their participation in the Battle of Khafji.

menting social and economic development programs.[17] The UAE also participated in peacekeeping and humanitarian relief operations in Somalia and Bosnia-Kosovo. Both countries have sought to expand their transport capabilities to extend their reach and the mobility of their forces. Qatar's purchase of two C-17s served as the backbone for its expeditionary activities, to be joined by four Lockheed C-130J-30 Hercules transport aircraft in the pipeline. One of Qatar's C-17s was painted in the nonmilitary livery of the Qatar national airline to explicitly raise public awareness of Qatar's participation in operations around the world. For its part, the UAE had ordered six C-17s and 12 C-130Js, with the initial C-17s delivered during Operation Unified Protector.[18]

In addition to acquiring capabilities and experience in out-of-area operations, a key enabler for Arab state participation in OUP was the long history of security cooperation with major NATO state militaries (U.S., French, and British). This served to help ease the demanding challenges of deploying and sustaining combat forces far from home basing. For example, among the bilateral security relationships that would prove especially important for sustaining the Qatari Mirages during the Libyan campaign were those with France. Since January 2011, two French pilots had been assigned to Qatar's Mirage 2000 and Alpha Jet squadrons. Also, in November–December 2010, French Mirage 2000s participated in a combined exercise with the Qataris, *Al Koot 5*, which emphasized bilateral training in joint and combined operations.[19] Longstanding U.S. ties with the Qatar military and Emiri air force would play a key role in facilitating the deployment of aircraft. Likewise with the UAE, the U.S. Air Force 363rd Flying Training Group (FTG), located at Al Dhafra Air Base, worked closely with the UAE Air Force and Air Defence (AFAD) throughout the Libyan campaign. A partnership developed over several years, the 363rd provided an ongoing training bond with the AFAD based on well-established relationships. This permitted timely cooperation and support to the AFAD once the UAE decision to commit forces was made. Liaison officers (LNOs) provided critical links for the AFAD to many functions and organizations as it integrated into coalition operations.[20]

---

[17] The role and experiences of the UAE forces in Afghanistan are described in a 2011 documentary and accompanying book entitled *Mission: Winds of Goodness*. See Shehab A. Makahleh, "UAE troops spare no effort to bring peace to Afghanistan," *gulfnews.com*, August 24, 2011. The two-part documentary with English translation is posted at YouTube.

[18] Tim Ripley, "Power Brokers—Qatar and the UAE Take Centre Stage." On the C-17 national markings scheme and motivation see "Boeing Delivers Second C-17 to Qatar," *Aerospace Daily & Defense Report*, September 14, 2009, p. 13. The C-17 in Qatar Airways livery is actually part of the Qatar Amiri Flight, the government-operated VIP fleet intended for use by the Royal Family and government officials.

[19] "Des Mirage 2000 en exercise au Qatar," Ministère de la Défense, December 10, 2010.

[20] The 363rd FTG took up station at Al Dhafra in June 2007. It was inactivated in July 2011 and redesignated the AFCENT Air Warfare Center (AWC), responsible for continued support to the UAE AFAD and providing high-level partnership training. The AWC is modeled after its counterpart at Nellis Air Force Base. See Air Force Historical Research Agency, "363 Flying Training Group (ACC)," online Fact Sheet, posted November 29, 2010;

Both Qatar and the UAE also joined the Istanbul Cooperation Initiative (ICI) launched in June 2004, a NATO-sponsored effort to provide mechanisms for bilateral security cooperation between participating states in the Middle East and the Alliance in a wide variety of military and security areas.[21] In mid-February 2011, as the Libyan conflict was heating up, NATO Secretary General Anders Fogh Rasmussen was conducting his first bilateral visit to the State of Qatar in which NATO-ICI cooperation was a topic of discussion.[22] The "menu" of bilateral activities offered in the original 2004 initiative included "promoting military-to-military cooperation to contribute to interoperability through participation in selected military exercises and related education and training activities that could improve the ability of participating countries' forces to operate with those of the Alliance in contributing to NATO-led operations consistent with the U.N. Charter."[23] Therefore, as Qatar and the UAE moved toward becoming military partners of the NATO-led coalition in the more distant Mediterranean theater, these prior engagements provided a foundation for cooperation with the Alliance. That said, when it came to bringing the Arab fighter aircraft into the NATO air campaign, it was the bilateral national-to-national ties that would prove most effective, being far more customized and flexible in meeting Arab needs than the NATO alliance structure.

Air Combat Operations

The State of Qatar notified the United Nations Secretary General on March 19 that it would undertake measures as authorized under UNSCR 1973. In an interview that day with *Al Jazeera*, Qatar's Prime Minister Sheikh Hamad Bin Jassim Al-Thani explained that "Qatar will participate in military action because we believe there must be Arab states undertaking this action, because the situation there is intolerable," without specifying the nature of Qatar's military participation.[24] The first public announcement from the West on Qatar's military involvement also came on March 19, inter-

---

and Master Sgt. Chance Babin, "AFCENT Stands Up Air Warfare Center," 380th Air Expeditionary Wing Office of Public Affairs, August 11, 2011.

[21] The six GCC states were initially invited to be participants in the ICI. By mid-2005 Kuwait, Bahrain, Qatar, and the UAE had joined. Saudi Arabia and Oman have expressed interest, but at the time of this writing have not joined the ICI.

[22] NATO online newsroom, "Secretary General Stresses Need for Further Cooperation with Qatar," February 14–16, 2011. On March 7, the NATO Secretary General also gave a speech in Manama on the importance of NATO–Gulf state cooperation and the importance of the ICI. The speech identified several threats and challenges that lay ahead, Libya went unmentioned. See NATO, "Speech by NATO Secretary General Anders Fogh Rasmussen on his visit to the Kingdom of Bahrain, Ritz Carlton Hotel, Manama, Bahrain," March 7, 2010.

[23] "Istanbul Cooperation Initiative," NATO Instanbul Summit, June 28–29, 2004, NATO policy document.

[24] "Qatar to take part in military action over Libya," Reuters, March 20, 2011.

estingly from a French Defense Ministry spokesman. That announcement noted that French and Qatari military aircraft would fly together to enforce the no-fly zone. On March 25, Qatar further specified it would provide military aircraft, military transports, and helicopters to coalition operations.[25] In another indication of the close Franco-Qatari collaboration, Qatar adopted the same code name for the Libyan campaign designated by the French, Operation Harmattan (the name given to the hot dry winds in the western Sahara).

The Qatar Emiri Air Force (QEAF) is officially based at Al Udeid Air Base, but most operations take place from a designated section on the south side of the Doha International Airport. Its Mirage 2000 fighters and helicopters operate from that location. Additional desert strips outside the airport also are used for helicopter operations. The Mirages belonged to the No. 7 Air Superiority Squadron, No. 1 Fighter Wing. Qatar's helicopter fleet is part of the QEAF, designated No. 2 Rotary Wing. The QEAF has 12 Dassault Mirage 2000-5s in its inventory, consisting of nine single-seat fighters and three two-seat variants also used for training. Purchased from France in the late 1990s, the aircraft were configured primarily for air-to-air combat for airspace protection. The Mirages were equipped with French-manufactured MICA and Magic 2 air-to-air missiles for their support of the no-fly zone. The QEAF transport wing is located at Al Udeid Air Base, home to the two C-17 Globemaster III transports in the Qatari inventory at the time.[26]

QEAF Mirage 2000-5 configured with MICA and Magic missiles.
Courtesy of the U.S. Navy, photo by Paul Farley.

[25] United Nations Security Council, *Final Report of the Panel of Experts Established Pursuant to Security Council Resolution 1973 (2011) Concerning Libya*, March 20, 2012, p. 24. For French announcement on Qatari participation see "France: Qatar to join Libya operation within hours," *The Associated Press*, March 20, 2011.

[26] "Qatar—Air Force," *Jane's Sentinel Security Assessment*, October 2011.

As a national policy–level matter, the decision to send aircraft was made by the Higher Authority leadership of His Highness Sheikh Hamad Bin Khalifa Al-Thani, Emir and commander-in-chief of the armed forces, and His Highness Sheikh Tamim bin Hamad al Thani, deputy Emir, heir apparent and deputy commander-in-chief of the armed forces.[27] The senior uniformed leadership had to begin preparations to launch the first set of aircraft quickly, with only a few days between the decision to participate and getting the first Mirages and C-17s en route. The top uniformed military leadership consisted of His Excellency Major-General Hamad Bin Ali Al-Attiyah, the chief of staff of the Qatar Armed Forces; Major-General Ghanim Bin Shaheen Al-Ghanim, assistant chief of staff for operations and training; and Brigadier-General Mubarak Mohammed Al Kumait Al Khayarin, Chief, QEAF. Upon being alerted, the first task was to prepare a plan for deploying the force and ensuring the deployed aircraft were sustained for their mission at their forward-based location. This was the first out-of-area expeditionary operation for the Qatari Mirages, and not surprisingly presented several challenges. One of the first was flight planning and securing overflight approvals necessary for routing the aircraft to their final beddown location at Souda Bay, Crete. This required considerable negotiation and real-time adjustments with Arab states in the region, including Saudi Arabia, Egypt, and Iraq. In some cases, rerouting of aircraft was required to work around airspace and en-route refueling constraints.[28] The United States provided assistance to the QEAF in securing the necessary diplomatic (DIP) clearances and other logistics support needed to deploy the aircraft. Recognizing this was the first combat aircraft deployment at distance for the QEAF, the Qatari leadership was comfortable reaching out to the United States and other Western partners for support in the endeavor.

The QEAF began deploying air assets over the local weekend of March 18–19, launching two Mirages and two C-17s. The preferred routing for the Mirages was from Doha to Tobuk in western Saudi Arabia, then through Egyptian airspace to Crete. The initial pair of Mirages made it to Tobuk, but issues arose in securing passage through Egyptian airspace and rerouting was required. Iraqi airspace was made available after negotiations and the Mirages completed their routing via Incirlik Air Base in Turkey, arriving at Souda on March 22. Additional Mirages followed over the next several days and all arrived by March 27.[29] The C-17s were routed through Incirlik as well. Two AgustaWestland A139 utility and two Sea King helicopters (primarily used for search and

---

[27] His Highness Sheikh Tamim bin Hamand al Thani became Emir of Qatar in June 2013.

[28] The Mirages were not capable of being air-refueled and therefore required various stopovers en route to Crete.

[29] *Flightglobal.com*, "Dubai Air Show Special," Libyan Air Force, 2012. As an example of the challenges encountered, two Mirages had to make an unscheduled landing at Larnaca in Cyprus due to fuel shortages, and landed without prior submitted flight plans and clearance request to do so. See Elias Hazou, "Qatari Warplanes Refuel in Cyprus," *Cyprus Mail*, March 23, 2011. The arrival of four additional Qatari Mirages at Souda on March 26–27 is noted in "Libya: point de situation opération Harmattan no9," Ministère de la Défense, March 29, 2011 [in French].

rescue) later joined the Qatari fixed-wing continent at Souda. While the total number of platforms deployed was relatively small, the State of Qatar committed half of its air superiority fighters and its entire C-17 strategic transport fleet to the campaign, a larger proportion of its air force inventory than any other member of the coalition.

The positioning at Souda placed Qatari aircraft relatively close to their operating sector over eastern Libya, approximately 525 kilometers from Benghazi with less than an hour of transit time to arrive on station (Figure 12.1). This airspace also became a prime routing for Qatar's C-17s flying into eastern Libya, and positioned the QEAF to help provide protection to the transports against any Libyan air force attempts to engage them. More important, it co-located them with the *Armée de l'Air* (French Air Force). With the well-established ties to the French Air Force along with the mutual use of the Mirage 2000 platform, the *Armée de l'Air* became a natural bridge for facilitating QEAF participation. This close coordination was reflected publicly when the French announced Qatar's participation at a joint French-Qatari news conference.[30] Indeed, it appears a portion of the French Mirage 2000-5 force deployed to Souda specifically was sent to work with and support the QEAF, perhaps part of the original arrangement to facilitate Qatari participation in the no-fly zone.

Figure 12.1
QEAF Positioning for the Campaign

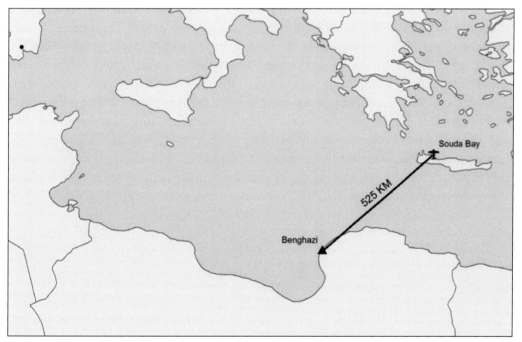

RAND *RR676-12.1*

---

[30] Irish and Doherty, "Libyan conflict brings French-Qatari ties to the fore."

The two air forces immediately set up a collaborative effort at Souda, effectively a joint Franco-Qatari detachment. French squadron commander Antoine Guillou, with two years of experience working with the Qatari military in Doha and now deployed forward to Souda, noted that a French and Qatari village was quickly set up which "involved installing the necessary logistics, communications systems and electronics required for the missions." Dual command centers were established in close proximity opposite each other, with about 300 personnel in place to support daily operations in addition to the pilots. The Qatari contingent was estimated at around 200. Speaking shortly after the arrival of the Qatari force, Guillou described the tactical profile: "Two French and two Qatari planes fly missions twice a day to patrol Libyan airspace." French and Qatari pilots were paired for the combat air patrols, with the first joint flights on March 25 consisting of a QEAF Mirage 2000-5 that flew alongside a French Mirage 2000-5 as part of a formation to enforce the no-fly zone in an eastern sector of airspace.[31] The Qatari Mirages were configured with air-to-air missiles to support the no-fly zone and not armed for conducting ground strikes.[32]

About 35 French engineers and mechanics were deployed to Souda, with five of these integrated into the Qatari team at the request of the QEAF; they provided expertise in maintenance of the Mirage 2000-5s. This French support would remain throughout the duration of the campaign.[33] The standard approach used throughout Harmattan involved joint patrols consisting of a two- or four-ship mix of Qatari and French Mirages flying combat air patrols over the northeastern sector of Libya, which was under rebel control and in relatively close proximity to Crete.[34] This proximity was important to maximize on-station time, as the QEAF Mirages lacked equipment for in-flight refueling. With a total deployment of six aircraft, two QEAF aircraft were regularly available for combat air patrols at any given time. The QEAF Mirages were placed on the NATO air tasking order on March 25 and flew air patrol missions paired with French Mirages. Despite the relatively small number of aircraft, accounts are that the QEAF sustained its sortie commitments throughout the duration of the campaign. For most of the operation, the QEAF continued to conduct patrols in the eastern sector of Libya airspace, although toward the end of the campaign it reportedly did execute some air-to-ground strikes as well.[35]

---

[31] USAFRICOM, "New Coalition Member Flies 1st Sortie Enforcing No-Fly Zone over Libya," Ramstein Air Base, Germany: Joint Task Force-Odyssey Dawn Public Affairs, March 25, 2011.

[32] "Years of Franco-Qatari Cooperation in Practice over Libya," *Agence France-Presse* (AFP), March 31, 2011. The French Mirages at Souda were configured to conduct both air-to-air and air-to-ground missions.

[33] "Libye cooperation franco-qatarienne pour le soutien technique," Ministere de la Defense, November 22, 2011.

[34] Jamey Keaten, "Tiny Qatar Flexes Muscles in No-Fly Libya Campaign," *Associated Press*, March 28, 2011.

[35] For example, according to former French Commander of Air Defense and Air Operations Lieutenant General Gilles Desclaux, toward the end of the air campaign the French were working with the Qataris to help them con-

At the higher command level, several Qatari officers also were embedded at NATO's Joint Forces Command Naples and the Allied Air Component Command Izmir to help coordinate planning and integration of QEAF assets with other allied forces.[36] The political importance of this early Qatari contribution was reflected in the official comments accompanying that participation. "We are very happy to have the Qatar Emiri air force become part of our coalition team," stated Major General Margaret Woodward, the Joint Force Air Component Commander for Operation Odyssey Dawn. "Having our first Arab nation join and start flying with us emphasizes that the world wants the innocent Libyan people protected from the atrocities perpetrated by pro-regime forces."[37]

The United Arab Emirates declared its intent to join the coalition on March 24.[38] It reported to the U.N. Secretary General on March 25 that it would provide military aircraft within the framework of the international coalition. The UAE Ministry of Foreign Affairs released a statement by His Highness Sheikh Abdulla bin Zayed Al Nahyan, the minister of foreign affairs: "In support of U.N. Resolution 1973, the UAE is fully engaged with humanitarian operations in Libya. As an extension of those humanitarian operations, the UAE air force has committed six F-16 and six Mirage aircraft to participate in the patrols that will enforce the No Fly Zone now established over Libya. UAE participation in the patrols will commence in the coming days."[39]

The UAE AFAD multirole fighter aircraft selected for deployment all were from Al Dhafra Air Base, the largest in the Emirates, and home at the time to both the Gulf Air Warfare Center (GAWC) and U.S. Air Force 363rd Flying Training Group (363rd FTG). The 363rd FTG (then from August onward, the Air Force Central Command (AFCENT) Air Warfare Center which replaced the 363rd) partnered closely with the AFAD to assist in Emirati participation throughout OUP.

The six "Desert Falcon" F-16E/Fs (Block 60) belonged to the 1st Shaheen Squadron at Al Dhafra. The Block 60 F-16 is equipped with some of the most advanced avionics available. Air-to-air weapons include the AIM-9 Sidewinder and AIM-120 AMRAAM.[40] Air-to-surface munitions included the AGM-65 Maverick. The six

---

duct some air-to-ground missions. "The Libyan Air Operation: A French Perspective," interview with Lt. General Desclaux, *Second Line of Defense* (SLD), October 22, 2011. General Jodice also noted that "Qatar and the UAE employed weapons from their aircraft for the first time" in OUP. Georg Mader, "Interview with Lieutenant General Ralph Jodice, Combined Forces Air Component Commander for Operation Unified Protector," *Jane's Defence Weekly*, April 25, 2012, p. 34.

[36] "NATO and Libya—Qatar's Contribution to Operation Unified Protector," interview with Lieutenant General Mubarak Al-Khayarin, Chief, Air Component Command, Qatar, May 5, 2011.

[37] USAFRICOM, "New Coalition Member Flies 1st Sortie Enforcing No-Fly Zone over Libya," Ramstein Air Base, Germany: Joint Task Force-Odyssey Dawn Public Affairs, March 25, 2011.

[38] USAFRICOM, "New Coalition Member Flies 1st Sortie Enforcing No-Fly Zone over Libya."

[39] "UAE to Send 12 Planes to Patrol Libya No-Fly Zone," *Dubai Chronicle*, March 25, 2011.

[40] The six aircraft consisted of five F-16E (single-seat) and one F-16F (two-seat) variants.

Mirage 2000-9s based at Al Dhafra were attached to the 71st and 76th Fighter Squadrons there. They were equipped with MICA and Magic air-to-air missiles. In addition to supporting the no-fly zone, later in the campaign both the F-16s and the Mirages would conduct air-to-surface strikes. The Mirages employed the Hakeem ("wise one"), a UAE-unique precision guided munition for striking surface targets, and the Black Shaheen cruise missile, a variant of the British Storm Shadow.

The UAE leadership gave the AFAD approximately 72 hours of warning that it would be deploying to support the air campaign. Within that short time frame, the AFAD was expected to be on the ramps at Al Dhafra and ready to begin moving forward to its beddown location at Decimomannu Air Base, on the Italian island of Sardinia. A series of preparatory actions quickly got under way. Training was stepped up and engagement intensified between the Emirati forces and the U.S. 363rd FTG. The Emiratis received briefing updates on Libyan military capabilities to include the status of the Libyan air force and surface-to-air missile threats. Communications plans and flows for integrating with coalition forces were reviewed, including what types of information would be available from assets such as AWACS aircraft. Mission planning procedures were covered. The Emiratis and 363rd personnel also worked closely together on the F-16 portion of the force package on all aspects of logistics, including munitions requirements, maintenance, parts inventories, support personnel, and working diplomatic clearances. This close cooperation during the predeployment phase all was aimed at facilitating the deployment itself and easing the transition to coalition combat operations once in theater. The U.S. teams for this were quite small (six to eight personnel) but provided substantial planning and support liaison on short notice. The well-established relations between these teams and the Emiratis made this possible.

Recent practice also facilitated coordination, as Emirati pilots and ground crews had just participated in the highly demanding Red Flag exercise at Nellis Air Force Base, Nevada, in January. As part of this deployment, for the first time the AFAD flew their F-16s from the UAE to the United States, a transatlantic flight of 9,000 miles. This provided hands-on experience with the demands of long-range deployment, and a dry run for the surge to Italian bases that would come less than two months later as part of OUP, the first out-of-area combat deployment for the fighters.[41]

Decimomannu Air Base is located in the south of the island of Sardinia, approximately 850 kilometers from Tripoli and 1,300 kilometers from Benghazi. The transit of the F-16s and Mirages from Al Dhafra to Decimomannu required multiple air refuelings from U.S. tanker aircraft. U.S. airlift assets also moved munitions, spare parts,

---

[41] Red Flag Nellis is the USAF's premier air combat training exercise and involves U.S. and allied air forces participation in air interdiction, air superiority, attack, SEAD, airlift, air refueling, air reconnaissance, and ground maintenance and logistics support. When the UAE AFAD participated in Red Flag for the first time in 2009, it flew F-16s that were based in nearby Tucson as part of the then-ongoing training program there. See Staff Sgt. Benjamin Wilson, "U.A.E. crosses Atlantic for Red Flag," Nellis Air Force Base, Nev.: Red Flag 11-2 Public Affairs, updated February 3, 2011.

A UAE Air Force F-16E Desert Falcon breaks away after refueling from a UK-based USAF KC-135R Stratotanker of the 100th Air Refueling Wing over the Mediterranean on July 19, 2011. Inbound to Libya, the fighter's armament comprises AIM-102C and AIM-9M air-to-air missiles, GBU-24 Paveway III laser-guided bombs, and an AN/AAQ-32 Internal FLIR Targeting System pod.
Courtesy of JetWashAviationPhotos.com, photo by Mike Green. Used with permission.

communications, and other support in coordination with the AFAD. At the time of the deployment, the AFAD had neither strategic airlift nor air tanker capabilities that were operational. (The UAE had purchased six Boeing C-17s; the first was delivered in May 2011, with three more delivered later in the year, so they were unavailable for the deployment.) [42]

The six F-16s arrived on March 27, followed by the six Mirages. The aircraft operated out of Decimomannu for the first month, conducting combat air patrols in support of the no-fly zone. On April 26 and April 27, the AFAD aircraft repositioned to Sigonella, Sicily, reportedly to reduce transit and response times and to save on fuel.[43] This repositioning significantly reduced the distance to Libya, with the straight flying distance between Sigonella to Tripoli reduced by some 300 kilometers to approximately 550 kilometers (Figure 12.2). The U.S. and Danish air forces had been operating F-16s from Sigonella since the beginning of the campaign. The French *Armée de l'Air* also had been operating Mirages from Sigonella.

---

[42] The AFAD also had on order three Airbus Military A330 Multi Role Tanker Transport (MRTT) aircraft, a modified version of the A330 commercial airliner, to provide an airborne refueling capability to the AFAD. The aircraft were delivered in 2013.

[43] "UAE Air Force on the Offensive in Libya," *Arabian Aerospace Online News Service*, posted August 24, 2011. During this transfer one of the F-16s overran the runway, resulting in a pilot ejection and temporary closing of the main runway.

AFAD pilots flew their own national sorties as directed by the air tasking order and were not paired with other coalition aircraft. The pilots received ground assistance from U.S. officers who received the air tasking order from the CAOC the night before and worked on the mission planning for the next day's sorties. At both Decimomannu and Sigonella, the F-16 and Mirage operations centers were co-located, and U.S. officers were able to assist in mission planning for both the F-16 and Mirage squadrons. This partnering on mission planning proved to be a key enabler for maintaining operational tempo and air tasking order commitments. During the course of the campaign, the AFAD reportedly conducted around 800 combat missions.[44]

The AFAD initially faced communications compatibility issues integrating into the NATO command network. Maj. Gen. Ibrahim Nasser Al Alawi, deputy commander of the AFAD, noted that "interoperability was a show-stopper in the beginning" and that AFAD initial missions were delayed due to unfamiliarity with NATO processes and regulations.[45] One of the early challenges the AFAD faced in its air patrol

Figure 12.2
UAE AFAD Positioning for the Campaign

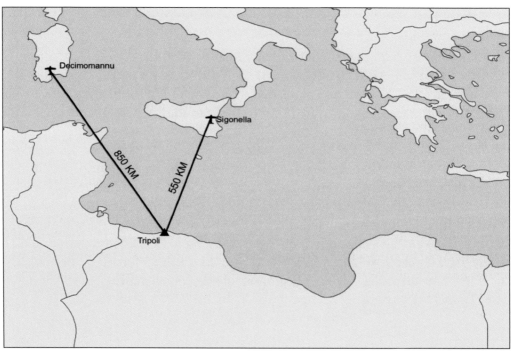

RAND RR676-12.2

---

[44] Robert Wall, "UAE Draws Lessons from Libya Ops," posted on "Ares Defense Technology Blog," hosted by *Aviation Week.com*, November 12, 2011.

[45] Robert Wall, "UAE Draws Lessons from Libya Ops."

role was that its pilots did not have access to NATO's encrypted communications. As a result, they could only communicate in the open, unsecured, and had to use code words in voice transmissions, which complicated operations. This also required UAE pilots to spend time translating coded NATO messages containing coordinates and other target information, a process that could take pilots 15 to 20 minutes.[46] Efforts to rectify these shortfalls were undertaken, but the approval process continued to face internal NATO hurdles and resistance, frustrating the AFAD partners. More broadly, and certainly not unique to the UAE experience, were limitations among national participants on sharing intelligence and targeting information, apparently due to a combination of established national and NATO procedures and classification protocols. [47] This was a problem even among NATO countries, but for non-NATO partner state participants it proved more challenging still. It became even more problematic as time-urgent and sensitive ISR was needed against mobile, fleeting targets as the campaign wore on. These limitations did constrain the types of ground-based targets the AFAD could engage.

While the AFAD initially focused on combat air patrols, by May and after the repositioning to Sigonella, it was anxious to undertake air-to-ground missions and began to do so. This represented the first time the AFAD conducted air-to-ground strikes in actual combat. These included cruise missile strikes employing the Black Shaheen system, named after the black shaheen falcon.[48] It is interesting to note that because the Black Shaheen (an export version of the Storm Shadow/SCALP-EG) has a range in excess of 300 kilometers, it was determined to be in conflict with the U.S. State Department's Missile Technology Control Regime (MTCR). As a result, the F-16s supplied to the UAE were barred from being configured to allow use of the weapon. Upgrades to the Mirage 2000-9s provided this capability and Mirages were used as the launch platform. Photographs at the time also showed the Mirage 2000s taking off from Sigonella armed with targeting pods and air-to-ground weapons that included the Al Hakeem PGM. The F-16s also conducted strike sorties using GBU-12 and GBU-32 laser-guided bombs. NATO sources reportedly confirmed the UAE AFAD had conducted more than 100 strike missions against preplanned or fixed targets such as ammunition dumps and vehicle parks.[49] No strikes were reported against mobile targets or AFAD participation in dynamic targeting, although aircraft were reportedly on station and available for such missions. The extremely strict rules of engagement to minimize collateral damage, and the associated training and tight C2 needed to exe-

---

[46] Based on comments of Maj Gen Ibrahim Naser Al-Alawi, Deputy Air Force Chief, in Stephen Trimble, "DUBAI: UAE Air Combat Debut Hit by Communications Issues," *Flight Daily News/Flightglobal*, November 12, 2011.

[47] Eric Schmitt, "NATO Sees Flaws in Air Campaign Against Qaddafi."

[48] Elizabeth Quintana, "The War from the Air," in Johnson and Mueen, 2012, p. 32.

[49] Tim Ripley, "Power Brokers—Qatar and the UAE Take Centre Stage."

cute complex strikes against dynamic targets, were limiting factors. Speculation also arose that the Italians imposed restrictions on such operations from Sigonella out of concerns over increased risk of collateral damage from striking dynamic targets.

One of the other challenges that the Emiratis (and some NATO state members as well) faced was in the specialty of weaponeering, the science of selecting specific types of weapons to achieve the intended effects against designated targets. This is a complex process involving many factors, and shortfalls in this skill-set can result in inefficient or ineffective use of weapons. Cases occurred in which the Emiratis released weapons that were not effective when hitting certain targets, on occasion glancing off them. Adjustments were made in the weaponeering process to rectify the problem. But this reflects a shortfall that partner members will want to further address, based on the Libyan experience.

As previously noted, given the absence of UAE strategic airlift assets at the onset of the Libyan campaign, the AFAD required considerable assistance to deploy its force. However, the AFAD demonstrated their rapid incorporation of strategic airlift assets with the return of the force to the UAE at the end of OUP. With their initial inventory of C-17s and trained air crews now in the force, in a little more than two weeks, the AFAD was able to pack up and move itself back home, including all of its associated cargo. This self-sufficient redeployment was a significant achievement for an air force that had just fought out-of-area for the first time and only had recently begun operating its C-17 fleet. This demonstrated ability to move the force with all of its support, now combined with AFAD air refuelers entering the inventory, shows an emerging organic capability to conduct out-of-area deployments with increasing self-sufficiency.

Arab Diplomatic and Political Pressure Continues

As Qatar and UAE direct military participation coalesced around their deployed combat air assets, events continued apace on the diplomatic front to further increase pressure on the Libyan regime. Qatar, the UAE, and Jordan were in the midst of these efforts. On March 29, the London Conference on Libya was held to discuss the way forward on the Libyan situation. On the issue of the future of Qaddafi and those around him, the chair's final statement was clear: "Participants agreed that Qadhafi and his regime have completely lost legitimacy" and that the "Libyan people must be free to determine their own future." While endorsing this position, Jordanian Foreign Minister Judeh reiterated: "Jordan rejects any invasion, occupation and the presence of foreign troops in Libya that violate Libya's sovereignty and calls for protecting the Libyan people, and ending bloodshed in line with the Arab League resolution."[50] As a

---

[50] "Judeh Takes Part in London Meeting on Libya," Petra News Agency, March 29, 2011.

way to coordinate support for the next steps on Libya from the international community, the conference established the Libya Contact Group.

Qatar hosted the first meeting of the Contact Group, which was held in Doha on April 13. It was co-chaired by the State of Qatar and the United Kingdom under the patronage of His Highness the Heir Apparent Sheikh Tamim Bin Hamad Al Thani. National representatives from 21 countries participated, as well as representatives from the United Nations, the Arab League, NATO, the European Union, the Organization of Islamic Conference, the GCC, and the African Union.[51] At that meeting, the Contact Group endorsed a proposal to establish a Temporary Financing Mechanism to support the immediate needs of the NTC as it sought to establish itself as a governing entity and gain access to foreign currency to finance food imports, among other things. A steering board was set up consisting of five members (three Libyan, one Qatari, one French). Qatar Central Bank was set up as trustee to supervise the account in the International Bank of Qatar.[52]

Economic support to the opposition included the financing needed to keep the opposition functioning, to provide basic services to Libyan civilians, and to support humanitarian assistance relief efforts. From the early period of the conflict, the NTC reached out to Qatar in particular and its offices for financial assistance in the wake of the freezing of Libyan assets. NTC leaders were frequent guests in Doha as they sought outside assistance. Qatari banking institutions soon became involved in facilitating the transfer of international funds during this critical phase. Doha also provided much-needed fuel to the opposition-held eastern part of the country and served as a conduit for marketing crude oil from the oil sectors under rebel control as a means for the NTC to generate revenue.[53] All of these efforts helped bolster the NTC as a viable alternative governing entity to the Qaddafi regime.

One of the more contentious topics at the April 13 Contact Group meeting was the issue of supplying arms to the rebel forces. The opening address of Qatar's Crown Prince Sheikh Tamim, and the early comments of the Qatari prime minister and Foreign Minister Sheikh Hamad bin Jassem bin Jabor al Thani, set the stage for this debate. His Highness Sheikh Tamim characterized the purpose of the meeting as being "to help the Libyan people defend themselves so they can decide their future." The foreign minister added that the Libyans had a right to defend themselves and that "our interpretation

---

[51] Foreign and Commonwealth Office, "Libya Contact Group: Chair's Statement," online at GOV.UK, April 13, 2011.

[52] By the end of 2011, the single largest direct contributor to the fund was Qatar ($100 million) followed by Kuwait ($50 million). Larger sums flowed into the Mechanism but these resulted from the unfreezing of Libyan funds. United Nations Security Council, *Final Report of the Panel of Experts Established Pursuant to Security Council Resolution 1973 (2011) Concerning Libya*, March 20, 2012, pp. 43–45.

[53] Mohammed Abbas, "Libya Rebels Reach to Qatar for Banking Lifeline," *Reuters*, May 19, 2011.

is that to defend yourself, you need certain equipment to do that."[54] The Emir, in an interview with CNN, maintained that UNSCR 1973 did permit military support to the opposition and "if they will ask for weapons, we are going to provide them."[55]

The Qatari leadership clearly advanced the case for direct military support to the rebels. In part, this was driven by the strong belief that Qaddafi would act on his threats to liquidate the opposition and would be able to do so without any internal restraints. Unlike Tunisia and Egypt, no military or other political institutions could act as brakes and alternative power centers as leverage against extremist leadership. Combined with Qaddafi's history of erratic behavior, and family and tribal control over all means of force, the prospect for a major bloodletting was deemed high. Absent direct military support beyond the air operations, the view was that the opposition faced not only the prospect of defeat, but with that, the likelihood of extremely large Libyan civilian casualties in its wake. At a more tactical level of concern, Qaddafi's forces were showing increasing signs of adapting to the threat of NATO air strikes, moving away from using easily identified and targetable military equipment such as tanks and armored personnel carriers, and toward civilian truck–mounted weapons ("technicals") that were more readily concealed among the general background traffic, including that of the opposition. Against the loosely armed and untrained opposition, even such weapons would exact a high price. So there was a growing sense of the urgency to provide additional means to counter Qaddafi's forces.

After the Libya Contact Group meeting, King Abdullah of Jordan visited Doha on April 19 for a Qatari-Jordanian summit to discuss regional developments. Regarding Libya, he stated:

> Our stance is in harmony with Qatar's stance aiming at protecting Libya's unity and we will continue exerting efforts to provide urgent humanitarian and medical aid for Libyan civilians . . . We are also trying, through cooperation with our brethren in Qatar, to set field hospitals in Libya, equipped with medical personnel and health professionals, thus enabling the Libyan people to receive adequate treatment and healthcare.[56]

On the humanitarian assistance front, Qatar established early cooperative arrangements with Malta to use it as a hub for providing aid to Libya. A small team of Qatari military officers worked closely with the Maltese to set up the means for ferrying to Libya food, water, and medical supplies, including ambulances. According to the Qatari military officer in charge of the operation, General Naser Al-Kabbi, 2,000 tons of food, two

---

[54] Charles McDermid, "Arming Libya's Rebels: A Debate in Doha," *Time*, April 14, 2011.

[55] Wolf Blitzer interview with the Emir of Qatar, Hamad bin Khalifa al-Thani, "The Situation Room with Wolf Blitzer," CNN, aired April 14, 2011.

[56] "Jordanian King Interviewed on Qatari-Jordanian Summit Talks, Libyan Crisis," *Al-Sharq Online*, April 19, 2011.

tons of medicine, and ambulances reached Libya by late September. Malta and Qatar also reached an agreement for treating injured Libyans and sick children at medical facilities in Malta. Transportation for this was provided at times by Qatar's C-17s serving as "air ambulances."[57] It is worth noting that the early destruction of Libya's IADS, and then combat air patrolling of the no-fly zone, provided important enablers for these air-transport-based humanitarian operations. While the threat of man-portable missiles and anti-aircraft guns remained, the absence of more sophisticated and lethal threats to transport aircraft provided much more operational flexibility.

Direct Support to Opposition Ground Forces

Aside from the policy constraints on supporting the Libyan opposition, in the early periods of the campaign the coalition forces had extremely limited information about individuals who were rising up against the regime and about the rebel forces more generally. As U.S. Secretary of Defense Robert Gates described in testimony to Congress in late March, "Other than a relative handful of leaders, we don't have much visibility into those who have risen against Qaddafi." He considered the term "opposition" a misnomer in that "it is very disparate, it is very scattered" and lacked any centralized command and organization. "At this point, we don't have a lot of visibility into those [elements]." So in addition to policy considerations, this limited information on the rebels, and the scattered nature of the uprising, presented practical operational impediments to any close working relationships. When asked specifically about U.S. plans to arm the opposition, Gates opined that other countries in the coalition were capable of providing such direct support: "And others have been taking a much more aggressive stance in that respect . . . My view would be if there is going to be that kind of assistance to the opposition, there are plenty of sources for it other than the United States." He later added that "I can see some individual countries, not the United States, at the invitation of the rebels, having somebody in there to do training and so on." U.S. Joint Chiefs of Staff Chairman Admiral Michael Mullen, in the same testimony, added that such training support "doesn't necessarily have to be a NATO country. It could be another country, an Arab country that's part of the coalition as well."[58] These were early signals of U.S. preferences that others take on the direct arming and training of the rebels. A related line of questioning involved a possible U.S. ground presence to assist in air strikes. Gates confirmed no U.S. military personnel were on the ground directing or coordinating air strikes. Admiral Mullen added, "We don't have any JTACs [Joint Terminal Attack Controllers] on the ground."[59]

---

[57] Anthony Manduca, "Qatar: Helping Libya from Malta," *The Times of Malta*, September 29, 2011.

[58] Testimony before U.S. House Armed Services Committee Hearing on Libya, March 31, 2011.

[59] Testimony before U.S. House Armed Services Committee Hearing on Libya, March 31, 2011.

The QEAF employed both of its C-17A Globemaster III transports during operations in Libya, one in standard military colors (left) and the other in the livery of Qatar Airways (right).
Courtesy of the U.S. Air Force, photo by Clayton Lenhardt (left); and of Wikipedia, photo by Ken Fielding (right), used in accordance with Creative Commons licensing provisions (CC BY-SA 3.0).

As for Arab states taking on such a role, Qatar reportedly began running C-17s from Souda to Benina airport outside Benghazi, the stronghold of the NTC, beginning early in the war. The flights reportedly were used to transport a mix of humanitarian assistance (to include evacuating those in need of medical treatment to facilities in Tunisia and Malta); military supplies and weapons to the NTC; and Qatari special-forces troops to provide training and other support to the opposition forces.[60] Both of Qatar's C-17s were utilized in this manner throughout the conflict. Given the shoulder-launched and other surface-to-air missile threats in the area, the C-17s were potential targets and often spent little on-ground time to reduce exposure. Maintenance and other support to the C-17s were provided via contractors at Souda and back in Qatar.[61]

As media reports emerged over the delivery of arms to the opposition forces, Qatari senior leadership—without confirming anything—made the point that the U.N. resolutions on Libya permitted "defensive weapons" to protect civilians against pro-government forces' attacks.[62] For its part, France in late June acknowledged publicly it had air-dropped weapons and other supplies to opposition forces in the western Nafusa Mountains outside Tripoli, defending its actions as consistent with UNSCR 1973 permitting "all necessary measures" to protect civilians.[63] The Qataris at times were relatively open about the assistance being provided, to include thinly veiled shipments of military supplies making their way to the rebels. In one *Al Jazeera* spot aired in June, a reporter showed material being loaded aboard a QEAF C-17 in Doha for the journey to Benghazi. In addition

---

[60] Tim Ripley, "Power Brokers—Qatar and the UAE Take Centre Stage."

[61] C-17 manufacturer Boeing provided operational support and depot-level maintenance to the Qataris as part of its Globemaster III Sustainment Partnership program. See "Boeing Delivers Qatar's 1st C-17 Globemaster III," Boeing news release, August 11, 2009.

[62] Ian Black, "Libyan Rebels Receiving Antitank Weapons from Qatar," *The Guardian*, April 14, 2011.

[63] Louis Charbonneau and Hamuda Hassan, "France Defends Arms Airlift to Libyan Rebels," *Reuters*, June 29, 2011.

to nonlethal supplies that members of the Qatari armed forces displayed, trucks were loaded containing wrapped cargo the reporter said upon close inspection were labeled as "munitions." A military police unit, with canines in tow, also was shown boarding the flight. The correspondent noted that the cargo flights were being run three to five times per week and had so far delivered over 200 tons of aid and evacuated around 150 injured people since the onset of hostilities. According to the reporter, authorities deemed as "classified" the cargo run observed in the *Al Jazeera* spot. The media clip concluded at a landing site in Benghazi, where members associated with the anti-government fighters drove off the trucks loaded with munitions.[64]

The UAE supported humanitarian operations initially from an airstrip it constructed in Libya, working closely with the NTC.[65] Jordan reportedly committed six transports to humanitarian assistance and cycled these routinely to Benghazi. These efforts included transporting Libyan civilians to Jordan for medical care.[66] Qatar and the UAE reportedly used small transport aircraft to shuttle personnel and weapons to the Nafusa Mountains. The UAE also reportedly seized a Libyan Ilyushin Il-76 airlifter at Dubai's airport that it turned over to the NTC and which was used to move supplies between the Gulf and Benghazi.[67]

The provision of arms and training to the rebel forces was a highly sensitive one, given the restrictive language of the U.N. resolutions and NATO member state resistance to exceeding that mandate. When it came to the Security Council resolutions and the associated missions of the no-fly zone, enforcing the arms embargo, and protection of civilians, Arab operations integrated into the NATO command and control structure for OUP and were under the same rules. According to testimony of Lt. Gen. Richard Barrons, Deputy Chief for Operations of the UK Defence Staff, "Any asset that was racked into Operation Unified Protector would be playing to exactly the same regulations" as NATO.[68] But "bilateral" arrangements existing outside the NATO command structure were matters for individual states to decide, and, by definition, were not bound by the same strictures. This provided the opening for military activities

---

[64] "Battle for Libya, Qatar Sending More Than Aid to Benghazi," *Al Jazeera* English, uploaded July 21, 2011. There were also reports of weapons transported from Tunisia along the Dehiba-Wazin border crossing. See Matt Robinson, "Qatari weapons reaching rebels in Libyan mountains," *Reuters*, May 31, 2011.

[65] Elizabeth Quintana, "The War from the Air," in Johnson and Mueen, 2012, p. 32.

[66] As the situation stabilized across Libya in the post-conflict period, Royal Jordanian flights also flew to Tripoli and Misrata. According to the head of Jordan's Private Hospitals Association, the kingdom treated over 55,000 Libyans in Jordanian hospitals in the months following the end of hostilities. See Kamal Taha, "Debt-Ridden Jordan Eager for Libya to Pay Bills," *The Daily Star* (Lebanon), June 18, 2012.

[67] Tim Ripley, "Power Brokers—Qatar and the UAE Take Centre Stage."

[68] Statement of Lieutenant-General Richard Barrons, Deputy Chief of the UK Defence Staff (Operations), Ministry of Defence, cited in *Operations in Libya*, House of Commons Defence Committee, Ninth Report of Session 2010–12, Vol. 1, HC 950, Oral evidence taken before the Defence Committee, Wednesday, October 26, 2011, Question 250.

not sanctioned by the U.N. resolutions or otherwise politically unacceptable to individual NATO members.[69] As noted in official testimony to the British House of Commons: "[T]here were representatives of Qatar and other Arab nations on the ground; they were there at the request of the NTC, sat alongside the NTC, and were able to provide advice, encouragement and guidance."[70] In addition to Arab state activities on the ground, this separate national chain of command also was the means for Western states to place personnel inside Libya, albeit in very small numbers.

It is likely that both the details and the importance of arms supplies to the opposition forces will remain controversial. Regarding the first, the U.N. final report on implementation of UNSCR 1973 raised concerns about both the UAE and Qatar making arms transfers in violation of the arms embargo, although details remained elusive. In its field trips to Benghazi, the U.N. team was "clearly informed that several countries, including Qatar, were supporting the opposition through deliveries of arms and ammunition." These same sources reported that between the beginning of the uprising and July 2011, "approximately 20 flights had delivered military material from Qatar to the revolutionaries in Libya, including French anti-tank weapon launchers (MILANs)." For its part, Qatar's official response to U.N. inquiries was that any weapons brought into Libya were to arm Qatari military personnel there to provide guidance to the rebels and to protect civilians and humanitarian aid convoys.[71] As to the importance of any such deliveries in determining the outcome, this judgment depends on a number of factors, including the particular battles being evaluated; the capacity of the opposition to effectively absorb the weapons; and the specialized nature of the weapons relative to the large quantities already available from local caches and weapons provided by defecting members of the Libyan National Army. What is clear is that this remains a sensitive political topic for many participants, revealing the tensions between the mandate of the U.N. resolution and other national activities undertaken outside of it.

---

[69] Much later in the conflict, in September, UNSCR 2009 (2011) was adopted making certain exceptions to the arms embargo originally imposed under UNSCR 1970. These exemptions related to material in support of establishing security under the new government as well as small arms for protection of UN personnel, media, and development assistance workers.

[70] Statement of Lieutenant-General Richard Barrons, Deputy Chief of the UK Defence Staff (Operations), Ministry of Defence, cited in *Operations in Libya*, House of Commons Defence Committee, Ninth Report of Session 2010–12, Vol. 1, HC 950, p. 40.

[71] United Nations Security Council, *Final Report of the Panel of Experts Established Pursuant to Security Council Resolution 1973 (2011) Concerning Libya*, March 20, 2012, pp. 24–25, and Annex V containing the official Qatari response to U.N. queries on arms shipments.

Stepping Up the Training and Air-Ground Integration

As the campaign wore on and air operations took their toll on the Libyan National Army's ground forces, the loyalist forces predictably adapted to complicate targeting from the air. As noted earlier, they blended into urban areas, shed their uniforms, and began using civilian trucks for movement and mounted weaponry that looked much like that of the rebel opposition. OUP Commander Lieutenant-General Charles Bouchard summarized the challenge: "[W]e found ourselves with both sides having the same equipment and both sides dressed in similar fashion. And in fact, a lot of the equipment would shift back and force within hours from one to the other."[72] Under such circumstances, having ground observers to help discriminate among forces took on even more importance, especially in the absence of regular coalition ground forces. Likewise, performing effective bomb damage assessments in the absence of ground forces' regular reporting proved problematic.[73]

Despite NATO's air campaign, by July the apparent stalemate increased the importance of improving the capabilities of opposition ground forces and air-ground synergies to turn the tide. This further elevated the need for close cooperation with the opposition ground forces. By this time, it was an open secret that Qatar had personnel on the ground in Benghazi training the opposition. Rebel forces openly remarked about the importance of Qatari training and advisors in improving their capabilities to fight, and how Qatar had been with them from the beginning.[74]

Operating in the range of 50 to 150 personnel on the ground at any one time, Qatar's special forces (SF) were used to train the opposition in a variety of small arms and tactics. Being fellow Arabs and sharing a common language greatly assisted the process. While it is difficult to get a detailed picture, the regular meetings in Doha with the NTC leadership likely facilitated the provision of weapons and training. The SF was not to play a direct combat role in fighting Libyan government forces. The objective was to ensure this was a Libyan uprising fought by the Libyan opposition. But the SF provided a great deal of the means for rebel forces to successfully engage pro-Qaddafi forces.[75] On-the-ground direct assistance reportedly was conducted via "embedded advisory teams" working directly with the main rebel brigades, especially toward the latter part of the campaign to surround and take Tripoli. These advisory teams also were reported to have "provided the main link between rebel ground units

---

[72] Elizabeth Quintana, "The War from the Air," in Johnson and Mueen, 2012, pp. 33–34.

[73] Joint and Coalition Operational Analysis, *Libya: Operation ODYSSEY DAWN (OOD)—Executive Summary*, Suffolk, Va.: JCOA, September 21, 2011.

[74] Portia Walker, "Qatari Military Advisers on the Ground, Helping Libyan Rebels Get into Shape," *The Washington Post*, May 12, 2011.

[75] For an early discussion of the role and contributions of SF from various nations, see Mueen and Turnbull, 2011, pp. 10–11.

and NATO's airpower."[76] The SF also reportedly helped to provide ground-based intelligence on Libyan government force movements and other military targets. This was used to supplement NATO targeting done by other means. And as Frederic Wehrey's chapter on the Libya experience shows, former regime military officers defecting to the opposition also played a substantial role in helping coordinate NTC ground operations with NATO's airpower, as did Western advisors.

The first official admission of Qatar's involvement in training the opposition forces came in late October. On the sidelines of a meeting with military supporters of the NTC, Qatari Chief of Staff of the Armed Forces Major-General Hamad bin Ali Al-Attiya remarked, "We were among them [the opposition forces] and the number of Qataris on the ground were hundreds in every region." He also noted that Qataris had had been "running the training and communication operations" and that "Qatar had supervised the rebels' plans because they are civilians and did not have enough military experience. We acted as the link between the rebels and NATO forces." A Qatari military staff officer also reported that a team of 60 Qataris assisted the opposition in setting up command centers in Benghazi, Zintan, and Tripoli.[77] Reports also surfaced that opposition forces were flown back to Qatar for training.

The final battle for Tripoli is detailed elsewhere in this volume. It is frequently cited as the culmination of the campaign as well as in the degree of coordination achieved between NATO air forces and opposition ground elements. Part of the explanation for this improved synergy is in the role that external parties on the ground were able to play. For example, the Tripoli brigade reportedly received several weeks of training in Benghazi from Qatari special forces before being relocated to the Nafusa Mountains for battles and then later conducted the assault on the capital. But it also appears that by August, the opposition was flush with defectors from the Libyan National Army and the police forces, providing indigenous sources of experience, training, and weapons. An established presence of Western advisors in Libya was on hand by that time to provide needed guidance and coordination. And despite the apparent coordination and speed of the uprising in Tripoli and the combined rebel force assault, participants have many differing accounts suggesting the absence of a master plan and a certain disorganized routing of the remaining demoralized Qaddafi forces at this stage, with citizens inside Tripoli playing a heavy role.[78]

---

[76] Tim Ripley, "Power Brokers—Qatar and the UAE Take Centre Stage."

[77] Sam Dagher, Charles Levinson, and Margaret Coker, "Tiny Kingdom's Huge Role in Libya Draws Concern," *Wall Street Journal*, October 17, 2011; Ian Black, "Qatar Admits Sending Hundreds of Troops to Support Libya Rebels," *The Guardian*, October 26, 2011; and "Qatari Forces to Remain in Libya After NATO Leaves," *The London Evening Post*, October 27, 2011.

[78] See, for example, the various descriptions in International Crisis Group, *Holding Libya Together: Security Challenges After Qadhafi*, Middle East/North Africa Report No. 115, December 14, 2011, pp. 1–5. For another narrative suggesting a long and well-planned operation, see Samia Nakhoul, "Special report: The secret plan to take

This military contribution was Qatar's most significant one, and is widely regarded as having been a major factor in helping the opposition to organize and ultimately defeat pro-regime forces along with coalition airpower. A more definitive conclusion on the impact of Qatari and other contributing Arab forces on the ground still must await a comprehensive evaluation that includes the role that western special operations and other teams in Libya played.[79]

Observations, Lessons, and Remaining Questions

Some observations, preliminary lessons, and remaining questions emerge from Arab state participation in the Libya campaign:

The Arab states' most important strategic contribution was in the political domain. Securing GCC, and then the League of Arab States', endorsements for military intervention against a fellow Arab state was a critical political enabler for military action against Libya. Qatar, in particular, took a leadership role in various Arab and international councils in advocating and mustering support for military intervention. In so doing, it helped secure legitimacy for the use of force, a significant accomplishment. Another key contribution lay in developing a political alternative to the Qaddafi regime. Qatari and UAE political, diplomatic, and financial support to the NTC was instrumental in providing breathing space for the NTC to form and survive, and to lend legitimacy to it as a governing alternative. These actions proved especially weighty as the campaign quickly shifted from one designed to immediately protect Libyan civilians to the more ambitious objective of removing and replacing the Qaddafi regime. For the latter to be successful, a viable and acceptable governing alternative had to exist. Qatar and the UAE played major roles in helping this to materialize.

Absent these efforts, any successful military involvement by the West would have been far more problematic. Likewise, the contribution of combat air forces by the Arab partner states was a highly valued demonstration of more than just rhetorical Arab commitment. The political and diplomatic import of this visible "show of force" carried far greater weight than the specific military contributions made by the combat aircraft themselves. Once committed, it also became politically essential that the Arab military partners succeed as part of the coalition.

How much did Arab state military activities on the ground contribute to air-ground synergies and the defeat of loyalist forces? This key issue is framed as a

---

Tripoli," *Reuters*, September 6, 2011. The plan was called "Operation Mermaid Dawn," Mermaid being a popular nickname for Tripoli.

[79] BBC News reported, for example, on the extensive role of UK special forces in Libya to help organize and train the NTC fighters (sometimes in conjunction with Qatari SF) as well as assisting in coordinating some NATO air strikes. See Mark Urban, "Inside story of the UK's secret mission to beat Gaddafi," *BBC News Magazine*, January 19, 2012.

question rather than a finding or lesson, reflecting the current limits of both information and analysis. A need exists to develop a more complete understanding of the roles played by Arab state ground forces to arrive at definitive conclusions. Doing so requires a deeper look at several areas.

One of the frequently cited military impediments in the Libyan campaign was the reduced effectiveness of air operations due to the absence of significant coalition ground forces and the resulting negative effects on air-ground combat synergies. A corollary to this is that the military campaign suffered from a lack of strong links between the opposition forces and the air campaign. As other chapters in this book also highlight, the absence of coalition ground forces placed a premium on finding alternative mechanisms for identifying loyalist forces and leadership targets. This became even more important as the conflict wore on and loyalist forces adopted tactics to frustrate air strikes, and concerns arose over possible stalemate on the ground.

Arab state partners on the ground provided a means for compensating, in many ways a unique one. Qatar's and the UAE's early decisions to support the NTC directly through military materiel deliveries and training helped to bolster the nascent capabilities of the patchwork opposition. As brotherly Arabs with preexisting ties to elements of the opposition leadership, shared language, and awareness of Islamic traditions, they were well-positioned to play this role in ways that were culturally and politically preferable to Western parties. And by acting as "national" entities for these activities falling outside the NATO-led structure, they had the latitude to take controversial actions others interpreted as beyond the mandate of the U.N. resolutions. By going in on the ground, they also demonstrated a willingness to accept the many risks of working in a dangerous and confused environment with an often-spotty opposition. Senior Western military leaders certainly observed that even though the NTC in effect served as the land element in the campaign, an "army" still was required for success, and that "this was delivered by our Arab partners, both from Libya and the Gulf."[80]

For the reasons discussed, this is a credible narrative. But in evaluating the specific impact of outside Arab forces on air-ground synergies—and by extension, the defeat of loyalist forces—four dimensions must be considered. First is the extent to which Arab state ground forces contributed to bolstering the opposition's combat capabilities. It is much easier to describe how the Arab states supported the opposition than it is to evaluate the practical effects of that support. To the degree these efforts helped buy time for airpower to take its toll, this represents an important synergy. Likewise, to the extent that airpower helped buy time for the opposition forces by attriting loyalist troops, it was important to take advantage of that time by providing training, equip-

---

[80] General Sir David Richards, "Annual Chief of the Defence Staff Lecture 2011," London: Royal United Services Institute, December 14, 2011.

ment, and other assistance to improve opposition military effectiveness.[81] Arguably, the Arab state presence provided that. But how much these efforts contributed to the overall outcome remains a matter of judgment as much as hard evidence.

The second dimension is the extent to which Arab state forces were able to provide ground-based intelligence to NATO that improved the waging of the air campaign. Information on potential targets, battle damage assessment, morale of loyalist forces and disposition of friendly opposition ones all could contribute to a more refined picture of the battlespace and more effective use of airpower. British Air Marshal Stuart Peach observed that conducting precision strikes in the absence of ground-based forward air controllers "pushed the boundaries" of the possible in utilizing technical solutions.[82] To what degree did Arab state activities on the ground help in providing intelligence to improve targeting? Was the information provided uniquely useful and unattainable by other means?

The third dimension is the extent to which the ground presence served as a liaison between the Libyan opposition and NATO member states, facilitating communication and coordination between ground and air force actions. Related to this, what role did Arab state forces play in facilitating linkages between the opposition and Western SF elements on the ground?

The fourth dimension is a negative evaluation. Were there circumstances in which the presence of Arab state forces on the ground *detracted* from synergies due to factors such as independent national actions and differing objectives? As with all coalitions, individual partners have individual motives, agendas, and desired outcomes. Balancing these in ways that contribute both to military and long-term political success requires careful consideration of the risks and trade-offs involved.[83] In the case of Libya, it certainly helped that the Qaddafi regime was widely detested and isolated including among the Arab states; presented a clear and present danger to Libya's civilian population; faced major defections; and that a viable opposition emerged as an alternative. This helped limit the prospects for core differences on the road to removing the regime. More complex and nuanced contingencies may not yield the same clarity of

---

[81] The clear imbalance in capabilities and effectivenss between the rebel and loyalist forces at the onset of hostilities, combined with the need for ground operations to ultimately defeat the loyalist forces, shows the importance of improving opposition force capabilities. Airpower bought critical time, but the real synergy lay in taking advantage of that time by improving opposition forces capacity to fight. For an excellent discussion of balance of technology (airpower) versus balance of skills (ground forces) as applied to Libya, see Erica D. Borghard and Costantino Pischedda, "Allies and Airpower in Libya," *Parameters*, Spring 2012, pp. 63–74.

[82] Chris Pocock, "Libya Defense: Boots on the Ground?" *AINonline*, November 13, 2011.

[83] Qatar, for example, came under criticism, including from some NTC leadership, that it was selectively arming and financially supporting specific partners with whom it had close relationships at the expense of the NTC. See Peter Beaumont, "Qatar Accused of Interfering in Libyan Affairs," *The Guardian*, October 4, 2011; and International Crisis Group, *Holding Libya Together: Security Challenges After Qadhafi*, Middle East/North Africa Report No. 115, December 14, 2011, pp. 21–25. Abdul Hakim Belhaj, head of the Tripoli Military Council, was one of those singled out in this regard.

purpose, producing sharper divisions over appropriate ends and means. In such cases, it is important to recognize that resulting frictions must be factored into any calculus of the benefits of synergy. The interplay of all these elements requires detailed examination before passing judgment on both the impact of Arab participation on the ground in Libya, and the applicability of the "Libya model" to future contingencies. At this stage, much is still unknown. Unsatisfying as it may be, the principal lesson is that in assessing the effectiveness of air-ground synergies, individual context is everything. Appreciating that individuality is a prerequisite for each conflict entered.

The Arab partners faced significant logistics and sustainment challenges in operating as expeditionary forces outside of their immediate region. A total force of about 20 combat aircraft and a small number of transports required considerable assistance from other coalition partners to make the commitment viable. The political benefits of this military involvement are clear, but so too are the real limitations on Arab state abilities to project combat power out-of-area. For example, operating in the Gulf region, the UAE AFAD presents a quite capable and substantial force with frontline capabilities. But projecting those capabilities outside the region on a significant scale is a very different proposition. To be clear, it was remarkable that the QEAF and AFAD were able to accomplish what they did. Even well-seasoned NATO forces operating much closer to home faced support and sustainment challenges in confronting the "logistics beast"—and as Christina Goulter observes in Chapter Six, there is a very important distinction between "deployed" and "expeditionary" operations. But this should not obscure what is involved in sustaining such partners and practical understanding of the military power they can generate at distance. In situations in which it is possible to build up combat power for many weeks or months before a conflict, the constraints would be lessened. In rapidly unfolding expeditionary operations, however, bringing in distant partners not configured or resourced for such operations will add to front-end demands. Future coalition planning and contingency resourcing must anticipate these potential additional demands. From the Arab perspective, efforts are under way to expand their airlift assets to help support future expeditionary operations. They must, however, look at the totality of their OUP experience in determining what is required of their forces to be full partners in future out-of-area combat operations. These are highly demanding undertakings for any military.

Bottlenecks resulted from communications incompatibility, as well as from classification-of-information considerations. These issues were flagged as concerns even among NATO members as the U.S.-managed Odyssey Dawn transitioned to become NATO's Operation Unified Protector.[84] The problem was magnified for "NATO-plus" partners, including the Arab states. This led to frustrations by Arab members, as these hurdles at times constrained their desire to participate fully in the

---

[84] Joint and Coalition Operational Analysis, *Libya: Operation ODYSSEY DAWN (OOD)—Executive Summary*, Suffolk, Va.: JCOA, September 21, 2011.

air campaign. It will be necessary to review how these bottlenecks can be reduced for future coalitions involving non-U.S./NATO forces under fast moving conditions. Major General Ibrahim Naser Al Alawi, deputy commander of the UAE air force, cited the need for better communications plans for integrating non-NATO partners, as well as increasing use of exchange officers and information sharing to ease future transitions.[85] Severe time compression in initiating operations, and in the transition from Operation Odyssey Dawn to Operation Unified Protector, presented an especially demanding environment.

Developing standardized procedures and templates for information sharing (to include classification protocols) with "NATO-plus" partners would ease some transition and integration issues. General Bouchard noted that "a lot of the information that we had was privileged national information from one side" that then had to be transferred to NATO channels. "So that transfer of intelligence and information became an issue as well. And it's probably another critical point we need to talk about, is exchange of information and the need to share, not the need to know." He went on to point out that because the operation involved four partners outside NATO—Sweden and three Arab states—"NATO Secret had to be declassified to Mission Secret," but in so doing, resulted in a level of information that limited its utility as actionable intelligence in a fast-moving target environment. "We had to create our own fusion cell, and that's probably the biggest point here for us was to establish a place where all of these various players would come in and actually share intelligence, turn it into actionable intel."[86] Partners recognize the need to improve sharing of information and intelligence if they are to fully participate. These might best be implemented through existing security-cooperation arrangements with select partners. Emphasis would be placed on the special challenges faced in out-of-area coalition operations, as opposed to established practices with partners for contingencies in their immediate region.

Previous security cooperation and engagement proved its value. The established relationships and shared equipment and procedures between the Arab state participants and Western militaries provided the means for rapid integration and support. Despite shortfalls, past experience and compatibilities did permit the Arab states to join the coalition quickly. The fact that Arab aircraft were actively participating in the no-fly zone less than ten days after passage of UNSCR 1973, and within a week of the start of the air campaign, is a noteworthy accomplishment. The importance of prior relationships and a long history of practical security and military-to-military cooperation, exercises, and leadership engagement proved a critical foundation for all parties. The traditional model of the last several decades has been of Western forces surging to the Middle East region in a crisis, utilizing the basing and other support infrastructures provided, and working with local partners as part of a coalition effort. OUP, in

---

[85] Robert Wall, "Fighter, UCAV Feature in UAE Air Force Plan," *Aviation Week*, November 12, 2011.

[86] Lt.-Gen. Charles Bouchard, "Coalition Building and the Future of NATO Operations: 2/14/2012—Transcript."

many ways, reversed these roles. Now it was Gulf state and Jordanian militaries that were deploying out-of-area to remote bases as part of a wider coalition campaign. The many challenges soon became manifest. But it was the well-established military relationships that made this role reversal possible. In several instances, it also was small training and liaison teams that paved the way for quick cooperation and responsiveness in engaging Arab partners, a bottom-up process in which field-grade officers were key links to successful operational compatibility. Trusted relations with their Arab counterparts allowed them "inside the tent." Such relations cannot be manufactured on short notice; entail long-term cooperative engagement of the sort reflected in the preexisting ties between U.S., French, and British forces and the Gulf militaries; and are likely best accomplished through small, seasoned in-country teams and not large bureaucracies. These "human enablers" will remain essential to working through the inevitable frictions of coalition operations.

Examine ways to best employ special forces of nontraditional partners to support air-ground integration. The Libya campaign often is characterized as an extension of the original "Afghanistan model" used to overthrow the Taliban. An added feature in the Libya case was the presence of third-party Arab state nationals as direct participants in the "unconventional warfare" mission of arming and training the indigenous opposition. Indeed, they represented the largest part of this effort among coalition participants. In these circumstances, it is important to examine what additional enablers would have helped to take full advantage of these ground-based elements to support the air effort and more importantly, the campaign outcome. Future coalition planning should include ways to most effectively integrate "nonstandard" partner special forces capabilities, such as those provided by Qatar and the UAE, into the larger campaign. This should include ways to directly support the SF elements consistent with coalition objectives.

A mechanism should be established for non-NATO partner involvement in after-action and lessons-learned processes. Western militaries and NATO have well-established, formal methods for analyzing past conflicts and deriving lessons to improve future performance.[87] Given the unique aspects and perspectives non-Western military partners bring, it is vitally important to capture their experiences and observations in a formal, systematic fashion. Such undertakings not only will help improve future performance, but will serve as another aspect to broaden mutual understanding leading to even more productive cooperation. These could be done bilaterally between individual militaries (e.g., QEAF and the *Armée de l'Air*), in a larger coalition/NATO setting, or through a combination of both. Emphasis should be on candid exchanges over what worked and what did not, differences in perspective, and the constraints each force worked under.

---

[87] In the case of NATO, see NATO, *The NATO Lessons Learned Handbook*, 2nd edition, Brussels: Joint Analysis and Lessons Learned Centre, September 2011.

CHAPTER THIRTEEN

Victory Through (Not By) Airpower

Karl P. Mueller

Introduction

Three years after the end of Operation Unified Protector, it is still too early to have a sense of finality when drawing conclusions about the campaign. Yet the process of trying to capture its lessons is best begun when events are still fresh in the memory of participants, which is very much what this volume has been about.[1]

Many of the preceding chapters discuss conclusions and implications regarding the intervention and the air campaign in Libya that have been identified either by the authors themselves or by the nations or air forces they examine, and this chapter will not seek to summarize them. Instead, it focuses on two main themes. The first is assessing what the air campaign in Libya did and did not accomplish, and why. The second is considering a number of overarching lessons to draw from the operation, focusing on two areas about which this case is particularly instructive: coalition operations, and the employment of airpower in situations like the Libyan intervention, where an air-centric campaign is conducted to cooperate with indigenous ground forces with few or no coalition "boots on the ground." We refer to this as a strategy of "aerial intervention," and the final sections of this chapter address the questions of how the United States and its allies can better prepare for future operations of this sort and whether one should regard the aerial intervention in Libya as an anomaly or as a potential model to emulate in future conflicts.

What Was Achieved?

No sensible observer would claim to know with certainty what the coming years hold for Libya so soon after the fall of the Qaddafi regime and the end of Operation Unified Protector. Consequently, it is impossible to predict without hedging whether the NATO-led coalition intervention in the Libyan civil war will appear in the fullness of

---

[1] This is also the motivation for a number of official "lessons learned" efforts among the armed forces and organizations that carried out the operation. Few of these have yet been officially released, and many are classified.

time to have been a grand strategic triumph for the states that undertook it, or a well-intentioned misstep that successfully achieved its immediate goals but resulted in a hollow victory. This volume's tale ends with the conclusion of the campaign to depose the regime, but the 2011 conflict is merely the first chapter in a much larger story, as the Libyan people struggle with the often-grim challenges of building a new state.[2]

Whether the intervention will appear worthwhile in the long run depends, of course, in large part on one's motives for intervening, about which there was not universal agreement. Reasons for supporting the intervention ranged from humanitarian altruism (protecting the Libyan populace from harm) to ideological principle (promoting democracy over tyranny or supporting the Arab Spring) to realist calculation (improving the strategic landscape of the region and establishing oneself as a friend of reform in the greater Middle East) to vengeance or justice (for Qaddafi's many crimes over more than four decades). Thus, some possible—and perhaps even probable—trajectories of Libyan politics in the coming years might make the coalition victory appear hollow to one observer without making much of a dent in its appeal for another.[3] Moreover, the effects of the war and of the demise of the Qaddafi regime already have been reverberating in other parts of North Africa, and there, too, the long-term consequences of the intervention are still emerging.

In any event, as the introductory chapter noted, the purpose of this study is to examine the conduct and results of the air campaign in Libya in more immediate terms, since this is central to understanding what such an aerial intervention might be expected to accomplish in other situations in the future. So that is where this final chapter begins.

Preventing Regime Victory

The first, and arguably the most important, accomplishment of the air campaign was enabling the Benghazi-centered Libyan opposition to survive Qaddafi's offensive against it in March 2011. Had the coalition not intervened when and how it did, there is every reason to think that regime forces would have succeeded in overrunning the rebel stronghold, potentially crushing the NTC and the uprising against Qaddafi more generally. Had this occurred, Libya presumably would have been counted, at least for the time being, as one of the first countries in the region where the flame of the Arab Spring flickered, but died.

Benghazi also might have become a name synonymous with "massacre," like Srebrenica in 1995. It is not certain the decisive defeat of the NTC that Qaddafi intended

---

[2] See Christopher S. Chivvis, Keith Crane, Peter Mandaville, and Jeffrey Martini, *Libya's Post-Qaddafi Transition: The Nation-Building Challenge*, Santa Monica, Calif.: RAND Corporation, RR-129-SRF, 2012.

[3] On the other hand, supporting the Libyan opposition never promised great economic rewards compared to the trade ties the West already enjoyed with the Qaddafi regime, and there was little reason to hope that even a very successful campaign would lead to much in the way of domestic political benefits for those who launched it (see John Mueller, "Will Obama's Libya 'Victory' Aid Re-Election Bid?" *The National Interest*, December 1, 2011.

would in fact have led to the slaughter of many thousands or tens of thousands, but leaders had every reason at the time to anticipate this, and in retrospect it still appears entirely plausible.[4]

That the initial airstrikes of the intervention turned back the regime's drive on Benghazi when it was in sight of its objective, and that the assault was never effectively renewed in the days that followed, was a diplomatic and military *tour de force* for the coalition. Few, even within the leading coalition governments' and militaries' own ranks, expected that effective action would actually be undertaken in time, yet against all the odds it was. The Arab League, the U.N. Security Council, and NATO all proved to be capable of unanticipated agility. Military planning was conducted with unprecedented speed. And the Libyan opposition movement—and the populace of Benghazi—survived.

Two key mechanisms were involved in airpower that enabled the rebels to survive in the early stages of the intervention. The first was physical: In the face of coalition airpower, regime forces could not mass for the substantial offensive operation that would have been required to overrun Benghazi. This echoes the pattern increasingly seen over the years in cases ranging from allied air interdiction in France in 1944–1945 to the 1972 Easter Offensive in Vietnam to the defeat of the January 1991 Iraqi drive toward Khafji in the Gulf War: Ground forces, especially mechanized and motorized ones, that expose themselves by massing and moving are vulnerable to air attack, provided the enemy enjoys reasonable air superiority when and where it is needed, and possesses sufficiently capable air-to-ground ISR and firepower to take advantage of the opportunity. Over the past two generations, the ability of modern airpower not merely to impede such movements, but actually to annihilate the ground forces in question has increased dramatically as PGMs, sensors, and battle management technologies and techniques have developed.[5] Libya was not the most daunting challenge for these abilities—the regime forces were modest in size and capability, and the terrain was favorable for air interdiction. However, the results the coalition achieved with a very small number of sorties—in fact, only a handful in the pivotal initial French attack on March 19—demonstrates the tactical, and in this case strategic, effect that a few capable aircraft in the right hands can have.

The second mechanism was psychological. As Frederic Wehrey vividly describes in Chapter Three, imposition of the no-fly zone and the beginning (and continuation) of coalition air strikes had a profound effect on the Libyan rebels beyond the protection those strikes provided from regime air and ground attacks. The commitment of coalition airpower signaled that the rebels were not alone, and gave the forces fighting

---

[4] See for example, Marc Lynch, "Why Obama Had to Act in Libya," posted to "Abu Aardvark Middle East Blog," hosted by *Foreign Policy*, March 29, 2011.

[5] David E. Johnson, *Learning Large Lessons: The Evolving Roles of Ground Power and Air Power in the Post–Cold War Era*, Santa Monica, Calif.: RAND Corporation, MG-405-1-AF, 2007.

against Qaddafi confidence that they could, and indeed likely would, prevail in the end. For forces and movements fighting against long odds, it is difficult to overstate the inspirational importance of such confidence.

Turning the Tide and Enabling Rebel Victory

The second great accomplishment of airpower in Libya, which overlapped with the first, was its role in turning the tide of the Libyan civil war, enabling the rebels not only to survive but to go successfully on the offensive to defeat Qaddafi's forces and ultimately to overthrow his regime—an outcome that appeared wildly far-fetched to most outside observers prior to the start of the air campaign. Indeed, it still seemed unlikely to many even after OUP was under way, when the Western media were peppered with prophecies that the NTC would not be able to achieve more than a stalemate until NATO sent its own ground forces to fight alongside them.

This was by no means an airpower-only story. NATO and partner airpower worked in concert with rebel forces on the ground to drive Qaddafi's forces back and finally break their resistance. This was a more gradual process than some initially had hoped for several reasons. One was that the air attacks were being carried out at a modest rate due to the limited numbers of available strike and tanker aircraft and above all due to constraints on the ISR capacity needed to generate satisfactory targets (see Figures 13.1 and 13.2). Strikes also were carried out with extreme care in the effort to avoid civilian casualties and fratricide against rebel forces, which was particularly

Figure 13.1
Operation Unified Protector Total Daily Sortie Rate

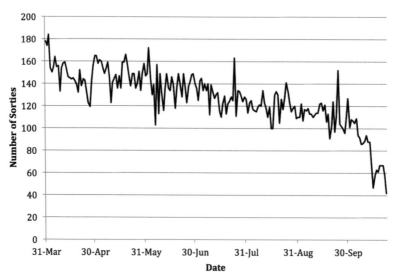

SOURCE: Data derived from NATO, "Operational Media Update: NATO and Libya," online, October 25, 2011.

RAND *RR676-13.1*

Figure 13.2
Operation Unified Protector Strike Daily Sortie Rate

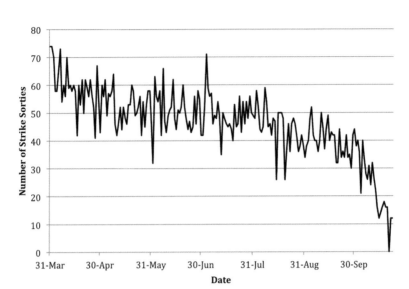

SOURCE: Data derived from NATO, "Operational Media Update: NATO and Libya,"
online, October 25, 2011.
NOTE: Not all strike sorties resulted in the dropping of munitions.
RAND *RR676-13.2*

challenging during combat in and around towns and cities—where so much of the
fighting in Libya took place.

Yet in spite of these and other constraints, coalition airpower was able to operate
effectively, paving the way for rebel victories, particularly by striking regime armored
vehicles, artillery, and other heavy weapons. The pace with which these targets were
struck was not as high as it might have been with a larger force more abundantly supplied with reconnaissance assets, tankers, and personnel skilled in the arcane arts of
air targeting, but it was fast enough to do the job. Faced with an enemy that sensibly
worked to make themselves hard to attack from the air, NATO aircraft still were able
to hit their targets with precision and discrimination. Even in the final battle of the
war, at Sirte in October, airpower played an essential role in reducing regime loyalist
forces' centers of resistance that the rebels were not able to overcome alone.

The tide also turned gradually because of the time needed to transform the
Libyan rebel forces into sufficiently capable units that could win against the regime
with NATO air support. This was a very different problem than the United States and
its allies faced working with the Northern Alliance in Afghanistan in 2001, where the
indigenous forces, for all of their shortcomings, at least were reasonably well-seasoned
combatants who had been holding their own against the enemy prior to Operation
Enduring Freedom. Training and assisting the Libyan rebels had to start from a far

more basic level; the full story of how this was accomplished, and even to some extent by whom, largely remains to be documented. But both Arab and NATO members of the coalition (particularly the former) played central roles in the process. Even here, airpower played an important but almost silent role, by airlifting essential supplies and equipment to the opposition forces.

Indeed, to describe the middle of the Libyan civil war as a "stalemate" is a bit of a misnomer, since that term implies neither side in a contest can gain the upper hand in spite of their best efforts. What looked like a frustrating stalemate in some Western capitals, and in the news media and the blogosphere, might be better described as a period of strategic preparation for the several months that it took to deploy advisors, to build the Libyan opposition into an effective fighting force, and to lay the groundwork for the offensive that would drive Qaddafi from Tripoli.

During this period of largely static front lines, one source of frustration was Qaddafi's refusal to buckle under the coercive pressure that airpower was applying. Many certainly hoped he might cave in and negotiate an acceptable settlement to the conflict, flee the country, or both. That this did not happen should not have been surprising, however, for neither the rebels nor the Western powers were interested in leaving him in power, and, especially under the threat of International Criminal Court prosecution, he did not have anywhere attractive to go. For its part, NATO was not putting a great deal of effort into coercing Qaddafi, wary of attacks that strayed too far afield from the civilian protection mission, but there is little reason to think that a more punitive approach to the air campaign would have been more effective in this respect.[6]

Where coercion did come more significantly into play was in encouraging members, supporters, and soldiers of the regime to defect or abandon the fight. This happened in considerable numbers as the conflict progressed, and airpower can claim some of the credit, particularly for demotivating the regime's troops in the field. Even some leading figures might have turned their coats in part because of fear for their immediate survival. But former regime loyalists made numerous defections in safe locations such as foreign embassies, so it seems sensible to attribute the decisions of cronies who abandoned Qaddafi more to the expectation that he would lose in the end (thanks to growing NTC ground power and highly visible coalition airpower), or to conscience and principle, than to fear of immediate risk to life and limb. For Qaddafi's cannon fodder as well, particularly his mercenary forces, the best incentive to run was the developing impression that they were fighting for a hopeless cause, and a doomed employer.

---

[6] On the use of airpower for coercion, see Robert A. Pape, *Bombing to Win: Air Power and Coercion in War*, Ithaca, N.Y.: Cornell University Press, 1996; Karl P. Mueller, "The Essence of Coercive Air Power: A Primer for Military Strategists," *Royal Air Force Air Power Review*, Vol. 4, No. 3, Autumn 2001, pp. 45–56.

Saving Lives

The central mission of Operations Odyssey Dawn and Unified Protector, based on UNSCR 1973 (which the coalition's leaders had authored), was the protection of Libyan civilians from the regime, so it is worth considering whether this was achieved. The answer involves a certain amount of hypothetical reasoning, and involves several aspects, but is fairly straightforward in the end.

Clearly at the tactical level, airpower protected many civilians in a very direct way. Coalition aircraft attacked and destroyed regime forces that were shooting at them or their towns or were preparing to do so. Air strikes also helped rebel forces to survive, and they in turn provided protection against harm from the regime's army. Here the assessment question is not whether civilians were protected, but whether they were protected well enough—that is, whether the coalition devoted enough capabilities to the effort to live up to its mandate as well as it intended.

At the strategic level, at least some room for debate exists regarding the net body count. The aerial intervention prevented an early regime victory, paving the way for a longer civil war, and civil wars tend to be extremely bloody. In this case, an NTC official estimated in September 2011 that deaths in the war to that point had amounted to some 30,000, roughly half of them loyalist troops, the other 15,000 comprising rebel fighters and civilians.[7] Assuming this count is roughly correct (the actual number might well be lower),[8] it is possible that fewer rebels and civilians ultimately would have died at Qaddafi's hands in the absence of foreign intervention. But these figures are not clearly higher than the numbers of casualties that Western leaders feared might occur if regime forces overran Benghazi and other cities in eastern Libya. Moreover, whatever the numbers killed in the civil war actually were, it is safe to conclude that they would have been considerably higher, particularly among rebel forces and the civilian populace, if the coalition intervention had been less energetic and therefore the war had dragged on for longer.

Not surprisingly, the aspect of the civilian-protection mission that drew the greatest attention during the war among the news media and national leaderships in the intervening states was the imperative to avoid causing civilian casualties through air strikes either hitting the wrong targets or causing collateral damage when hitting the right ones. As this volume describes, target planners and aircrews devoted enormous effort to avoiding civilian casualties, and were apparently quite successful. Postwar reports by Amnesty International and Human Rights Watch, which take NATO sternly to task for its apparent lack of interest in investigating civilian casualty estimates or sharing information about them, identify some 75 civilians killed in eight airstrikes, although this is presumably somewhat lower than the total number given

---

[7] "At Least 30,000 Killed, 50,000 Wounded in Libyan Conflict," *The Tripoli Post*, September 8, 2011.

[8] Rod Nordland, "Libya Counts More Martyrs Than Bodies," *New York Times*, September 16, 2011, p. A1.

difficulties in documenting some cases.[9] To the extent these estimates can be taken at face value, they suggest a civilian casualty rate on the order of one per 100 munitions delivered, which in turn is roughly on the order of half the rate for Operation Allied Force in 1999.[10]

Intervention at Low Cost

In addition to the positive goals that it achieved, the Libyan intervention accomplished a set of negative goals of great importance to Western leaders. First, no coalition personnel were killed, or even seriously wounded, carrying out operations over (or in) Libya; only one aircraft was lost, an F-15E whose crew was recovered. Second, in contrast to Stephen Biddle's March 25, 2011 warning that "warfare rarely allows big payoffs from small investments,"[11] the aerial intervention in Libya was in fact just such a case of a very small investment of resources paying off for the coalition. The war is estimated to have cost the coalition several billion dollars,[12] with the cost to the United States amounting to somewhat more than $1 billion (of which more than $250 million is the replacement costs for the TLAMs fired during Operation Odyssey Dawn).[13] Needless to say, the cost of the Libya intervention was microscopically small compared to the more than 6,000 military deaths U.S. forces have suffered in Iraq and Afghanistan (more than 7,500 coalition deaths) and the more than $1 trillion the United States has spent in those conflicts. However, this does not mean that the financial costs of the Libyan intervention were entirely trivial for the participating nations, particularly those that had to fund their operations by using funds that had been budgeted for procurement, maintenance, and other accounts.

Other costs the intervention did not incur include those that might have been associated with the ground war that the coalition ruled out of consideration in early March, and those that would have followed from an obligation to take on the burden

---

[9] NATO has identified one incident as being due to a technical failure in a laser-guided bomb causing the weapon to land far from its target. Details about the other cases have not been released. See Amnesty International, *Libya: The Forgotten Victims of NATO Strikes,* March 19, 2012; Human Rights Watch, *Unacknowledged Deaths: Civilian Casualties in NATO's Air Campaign in Libya,* May 14, 2012; C. J. Chivers and Eric Schmitt, "In Strikes on Libya by NATO, an Unspoken Civilian Toll," *The New York Times,* December 17, 2011.

[10] While the Libyan regime had strong incentives to exaggerate and fabricate apparent civilian casualties from air attacks, it also is worth noting that during the conflict the rebels and their sympathizers had similarly powerful motives to minimize and conceal civilian casualties that might discourage the energetic use of airpower against their enemies.

[11] Stephen Biddle, "The Libya Dilemma: The Limits of Air Power," *The Washington Post,* March 25, 2011.

[12] Some estimates run considerably higher as a result of not taking into account the peacetime costs that would have been associated with maintaining and operating the forces used in the intervention even if the operation had not occurred.

[13] Kevin Baron, "For the U.S., War Against Qaddafi Cost Relatively Little: $1.1 Billion," *The Atlantic* online, October 21, 2011; Z. Byron Wolf, "Cost of Libya Intervention $600 Million for First Week, Pentagon Says," *ABCNews* blog, March 28, 2011.

of reconstruction in Libya after the war. It seems likely the latter would have been considerably harder to avoid in the wake of a substantial intervention by coalition ground forces, although this cannot be stated with certainty.

This discussion of costs does raise the perhaps counterintuitive question of whether the Libyan intervention could have been carried out even more cheaply and still have succeeded. Given that virtually all of the forces deployed were quite actively used (with the arguable exception of fighter forces deployed by countries that did not commit them to operations over Libya), spending less on the operation essentially would have meant doing less—flying fewer missions, attacking fewer targets, or using less expensive ordnance. The second would have reduced the coalition's contribution to the eventual victory over the regime, presumably making the war longer and more costly for the rebels. Economizing on ordnance presumably either would have increased the difficulties associated with attacking regime targets while minimizing civilian casualties (for example, by substituting less expensive munitions for Brimstone missiles or other latest-generation PGMs), or would have increased risk to aircrews (by reducing the use of expensive cruise missiles in favor of more non-standoff weapons). As it turned out, the latter might have been a very reasonable choice, since Libya's actual air defense capabilities appear to have been overestimated by planners who had limited information about their status and therefore made conservative assumptions about the threats these weapons and their operators might pose to coalition forces. In retrospect, using large numbers of TLAMs to target Libyan air force and so-called integrated air defense system targets in the opening phase of the operation probably provided less "value for money" than most of the rest of the operation.[14]

A Libyan Victory

The coalition's aerial intervention achieved one more thing that is worth recognizing, yet often tends to be overlooked: It made possible not merely a victory against Qaddafi, but a *Libyan* victory. Supporting the rebel forces from the air while limiting assistance on the ground to an extremely small scale and keeping it inconspicuous meant that it was Libyans—Qaddafi's victims—who liberated Tripoli and later caught the dictator as he fled before them, not a foreign army.

Deploying allied ground forces to Libya to lead the offensive against Qaddafi certainly could have accelerated the victory. This was never the coalition's intention, and even if leaders' determination to avoid becoming entangled in a ground war had waned during the "stalemate," it would have been extremely difficult either to violate the prohibition on invasion and occupation that they had included in UNSCR 1973, or to pass a new resolution reversing that provision. But even setting this reality aside,

---

[14] The coalition may also have devoted more effort to DCA and perhaps SEAD escort and patrols than was strictly necessary given the anemic nature of the Libyan fighter and radar-guided SAM threats, but this too appears more obvious in hindsight than it did to planners at the time.

any approach that undermined the Libyans' sense of ownership of the victory against the regime would have produced a result that was substantially, perhaps profoundly, different in political terms, and that would almost certainly have been less desirable in terms of Libya's postwar politics.

What Have We Learned—Or Been Reminded Of?

After any war, there is a tendency to look for lessons to draw from the experience. For the victor, it is particularly important to examine what went wrong, or at least less well than it might have, and not focus exclusively on self-congratulations for achieving the positive overall outcome. This is all the more true when the enemy is weak or incompetent, which Qaddafi's forces certainly were compared to NATO, though they initially were far more powerful than those of the rebel movement.

It is certainly possible to look at the air campaign in Libya and identify such lessons amid the campaign's overall success. Yet it is worth noting that most of these do not represent major revelations so much as confirmation of things that other cases already had suggested. Indeed, the more one knew about airpower, particularly about recent developments in airpower, the less surprising the course and outcome of the Libyan air campaign and broader war. The Gulf War, Bosnia, Kosovo, and the opening phase of Operation Enduring Freedom all provided signposts on the road to Libya.

Airpower Ascendant but Not Abundant

As we noted at the outset of this volume, two aspects of the Libyan air campaign are particularly striking: the relationship between airpower and the Libyan rebel forces waging the civil war, and the deeply multinational character of the operation. This section focuses on lessons relating to airpower capabilities, while the next one deals with the coalition dimension.

Airpower as an Extension of Politics

One of the unsurprising yet noteworthy features of the Libyan air campaign was the extent to which the employment of airpower was intertwined with political considerations at multiple levels. This was most pivotal with respect to international diplomacy, where the cascading endorsements of imposing a no-fly zone by the GCC, then the Arab League, then the U.N. Security Council greatly affected, in turn, the decisions of some of the coalition members to participate in the operation. Diplomats and other actors not conspicuous to the general public subtly shaped the course of diplomatic events, and as is often the case one or a few relatively small countries—notably Qatar in this case—played a role far out of proportion to their nominal place on the international security chessboard. A variety of domestic political factors also were powerfully at work, either shaping choices about intervention (as described earlier in many of the national chapters) or affecting how the military effort could be sustained in the case of the hyper-partisan political conflict in the United States.

For airmen, Libya represents yet another case in which we are reminded of the importance of imparting knowledge about military strategy and operations to civilian leaders who often know little about the practice of warfare in general, and less about airpower in particular. In this instance, we see such information being an issue in multiple countries' deliberations about the challenges, utility, and implications of establishing a no-fly zone over Libya, for example, and then dysfunctionally affecting the caveats affecting Sweden's military participation in OUP. Addressing this problem by better educating leaders and populations about airpower always is easier to prescribe than to carry out, but that difficulty makes it no less important to try.

The Dynamic Limits of Airpower

Several trends in the ongoing evolution of airpower made themselves conspicuous in the coalition's aerial intervention on Libya.

One widely remarked upon—at least in conflicts such as this one—is the great and ever-growing importance of ISR, especially intelligence analysis and synthesis, but also tactical reconnaissance, staring surveillance, and other sensor capabilities. The pace of air strikes in Libya was affected by the availability of several different "enablers" and a limited number of strike aircraft, for that matter. But the availability of ISR, and especially of developed targets, was usually the most significant factor. Unfortunately, this is a problem not easily—or at least quickly—solved, since the solution depends not only on increased investment in a time of tight budgets, but on long-term development of human capital and career fields in which it can thrive.

A second pattern, and again one we have seen before, is the tendency for the evolving capabilities of airpower to outpace what many people expect it to be able to accomplish. In air campaigns through the past two decades, U.S. and allied airpower consistently has surprised observers, and even leaders, by accomplishing things that conventional wisdom said were unrealistic to expect. Airpower physically and psychologically ravaged the Iraqi army in 1991. It coerced Slobodan Milosevic into capitulating to NATO in 1999. It brought about a regime change in Afghanistan in 2001 that planners had expected would not be accomplished until multiple brigades of U.S. ground forces were introduced to the country during the next year. And in Libya, it reversed the course of the civil war and brought victory to the rebels. In short, the "limits of airpower" tend to recede over time, making it perilous to declare that airpower will not be able to do X simply because X was beyond its abilities in a war a decade ago. However, four very important caveats should be attached to this generalization.

First, none of these airpower successes was achieved by airpower alone. In each case, ground forces, or the threat of future combined arms operations, played an important, and usually game-changing, role in determining the outcome—something that wise airmen will recognize readily, no matter how often others suggest that they are intellectual descendants of Douhet who care for nothing but airpower.

Second, many airmen are among the serial underestimators of the potential of airpower. It was striking that when U.S. military leaders were discussing intervention in Libya, no great wave of enthusiasm emerged for such an operation among airmen who saw an opportunity to show the world what airpower could do, as one might have expected after years of often being bureaucratically overshadowed by the ground forces at the center of the counterinsurgencies in southwest Asia. Some of this doubtless was due to reluctance to further stretch an already extended force. But at the same time, Libya was about as good an opportunity for achievement at limited cost as an airman could reasonably hope to see.

Third, this discussion of recent airpower successes has an undeniable whiff of the panegyric about it, but should not be taken as a suggestion that airpower is omnipotent. Recognizing what airpower cannot do—and communicating this effectively to national leaders—remains at least as important as being able to envision what it can do, as the Israeli armed forces demonstrated in Lebanon in 2006.[15]

Finally, the Libyan rebels whose naïveté about airpower Frederic Wehrey describes in Chapter Three—imagining it has a near-magical ability to do anything—sometimes have their counterparts in the corridors of national power, where leaders can have wildly unrealistic expectations about the *deus ex machina* potential of airpower to solve difficult policy problems, or at least be quite impatient while waiting for success. The 2006 Israeli case certainly reflects this, but so did the U.S. leaders who imagined that Milosevic would surrender after two or three days of bombing in 1999. So long as this tendency exists, the problem of judiciously communicating what airpower has to offer as a strategic tool becomes significantly more challenging.

Quantity Still Has a Quality All Its Own

Operation Unified Protector was executed on a shoestring. Throughout the campaign, General Jodice requested additional forces, though he knew they would not be forthcoming.[16] The limited numbers of sorties that the coalition usefully could generate constrained what airpower could do in the conflict, sometimes to the frustration of rebel forces, especially in western Libya. That victory nevertheless came in the end is

---

[15] David E. Johnson, *Hard Fighting: Israel in Lebanon and Gaza*, Santa Monica, Calif.: RAND Corporation, MG1085-A/AF, 2011.

[16] Ralph J. Jodice II, remarks on Operation Unified Protector at the Atlantic Council, Washington, D.C., June 4, 2012.

important, but it should not obscure the basic dynamic of small numbers of aircraft seeking to extend their influence over a large country.

Several of the chapters above describe the plight of air forces stretched to the limit of their abilities to sustain deployments of aircraft. As Robert Owen notes, this was not a problem only for small coalition members with small defense budgets; the USAF also faced capacity limits. On the one hand, this is hardly surprising since Libya was not the only war under way—it was the combination of multiple contingencies, not just the relatively small deployment for OUP, that was stressing the U.S. and several of the European air forces. Yet the problem of preserving and maintaining sufficient force structure to meet plausible demands looms large for virtually every air force today. Libya provides both a cautionary lesson about the perils of overextension, and a warning about the potential opportunity costs of underinvesting in either combat air forces or the enablers needed for them to operate to their full capabilities—or indeed to operate at all, especially far from home.

Protecting Civilians

The Libyan aerial intervention was unusual in having a rationale that revolved around a mandate to protect civilians (though this was not unprecedented—protecting Kosovar civilians was central to the mission of Operation Allied Force, for example). Given this, and the wave of emphasis on the "responsibility to protect" doctrine in discussions preceding the intervention, one might expect that Operations Odyssey Dawn and Unified Protector would look quite different from air campaigns with dissimilar strategic objectives.

Perhaps surprisingly to some observers, this was not the case. It certainly was true that avoiding civilian casualties was a central focus of the campaign, and that this was strongly associated with an imperative to avoid causing collateral damage or striking targets that were not positively identified as enemies. However, this was not strikingly different from how airpower was employed in Operation Enduring Freedom in 2001, where as one member of the OEF CAOC later put it, "we *could not* have been more careful" in the effort to avoid damaging civilian targets.

That case is particularly instructive, since in the wake of the 9/11 terrorist attacks, many people expected that when the United States struck back at al Qaeda's base of operations in Afghanistan, it would do so with little restraint, and it seems very unlikely that the American people would have objected to such an approach. Yet OEF planners and battle managers exercised extremely high levels of care in selecting and approving attacks against targets when collateral damage concerns arose. Such restraint may have been less unexpected in the Balkans in the air campaigns of the 1990s, but even there, it is worth noting that NATO strategists, planners, and aircrews had strongly internalized civilian-protection norms even before receiving strategic direction from civilian leaders.

In the end, perhaps the most notable thing about the civilian-protection mission at the operational level (as opposed to the political/strategic level, where it was extremely significant in states' decisionmaking about participating in the operation) is how little it changed how the coalition waged war in Libya compared to other conflicts.

Alliances and Partnerships

The United States is no stranger to waging wars in coalitions and alliances—its first experience as a coalition member was the American Revolution itself, and every sizable war it has fought since 1917 has involved formal allies or coalition partners. But some coalitions are more equal than others.

The Gathering of Eagles

When interviewing U.S. Air Force leaders for this study regarding the lessons that they took away from OOD and OUP, it was striking how consistently and often intensely they expressed a high degree of regard for the performance of the other air forces that actively participated in the campaign, particularly those of the smallest NATO members. Of course, one expects leaders to say gracious things about allies and partners, but it is apparent in this case that expectations clearly were exceeded, whether in terms of willingness to take on difficult tasks, capability to do so expertly, or both.

Some of this had to do with a number of coalition members leaning forward assertively into the Libyan intervention because of its apparently worthy cause or for other reasons. But also at work was a fairly broad trend that saw a substantial number of smaller air forces, in both Europe and the Middle East, acquire capabilities during the past decade or so that markedly—even dramatically—increased their capabilities to perform effectively in the ISR- and precision-intensive Libyan intervention, and in some ways significantly narrowed the traditional gap between leading and secondary NATO members.

For Alliance and national strategists, this development stands in contrast to generally shrinking force sizes, at least in Europe. At the same time that many states are shedding force structure from their air forces, limiting their ability to deploy more than small numbers of aircraft for expeditionary operations, advanced munitions, targeting pods, and other capabilities are multiplying the potential effect of those aircraft. Consequently, future coalitions may tend to feature smaller national contributions than in the past, yet derive greater capabilities from those force elements—provided their air forces do not contract beyond the vanishing point at which providing any forces at all for out-of-area operations becomes impractical.

The Enabler Gap

It has become commonplace to look at the Libyan air campaign, note the shortfalls in available capacity for air refueling, SEAD, ISR collection and analysis, and other "enabling" functions that the United States predominantly contributed to the campaign, and conclude that the non-U.S. members of the Alliance need to invest more in these capabilities lest they remain dependent upon the United States to be able to project airpower. The conclusion may be correct, but it is important to approach it carefully rather than jump to it. Explaining why starts with recalling NATO's Balkan interventions in the 1990s.

In Operation Deliberate Force, many of the participating air forces discovered little or no capability to deliver PGMs, leaving the United States to undertake a disproportionate share of the precision attack task. As Christian Anrig describes in Chapter Ten, this experience was, quite properly, one of the factors that spurred smaller NATO air forces to invest in acquiring precision strike capabilities—if they did not do so, they would have multirole fighters whose ground attack capabilities would be of little use in a world that was tending more and more to demand the very discriminate use of air strikes, making the ability to deliver unguided bombs less and less relevant.

The situation with ISR and tankers in Libya was different. The Alliance did find these capabilities to be in relatively short supply, so investing in more capacity in these areas appears to be sensible. But that is not quite the same thing as saying that the European members need to increase their capabilities because they could not have conducted the Libyan air campaign alone. NATO is not, and never has been, designed to fight wars without the United States participating—in fact, the whole point of the Alliance originally was to tie U.S. and European defense together, making each indispensible to the other. In short, it is not necessarily a problem if European NATO members can't fight alone, as this is actually the traditional norm.[17]

Having noted that a European capability shortfall is not the same thing as a shortfall in NATO capabilities, at least two reasons remain why it is a sound idea that non-U.S. NATO members should invest more heavily in tankers, ISR, SEAD, strategists, and CAOC planners and battle managers. First, the Alliance is short of these capabilities relative to the capacity of its fighter forces, particularly if it is going to be carrying out expeditionary operations, and it is unlikely that the United States will jump at the opportunity to greatly increase its investment in these enablers in lieu of its allies doing so. Second, there is arguably significant value for the United States as well as for other NATO nations in Alliance (or European Union) members being able to conduct an operation like OUP on their own. It would be optimistic to imagine, in a world where wars are fought by coalitions of the willing, that the United States will

---

[17] This was exemplified in the Cold War by the U.S. argument that independent British and French nuclear forces were unnecessary, since the United States could and did provide a nuclear umbrella for its allies.

always be one of the willing when it should be—Washington has not been consistently infallible in its past choices about when to go to war.

Is it realistic to imagine that a coalition of European states could successfully conduct an operation like OOD or OUP with little or no serious assistance from the United States, short of building armed forces as capable as U.S. ones? It is likely this would depend on how the operation was carried out—the Libyan intervention looked as it did in part because the United States was participating. Having fewer tankers would call for some combination of flying fewer sorties and shifting bases forward to reduce sortie lengths. More limited SEAD capabilities might call for a less catastrophic demolition of enemy air defenses at the outset of an operation, and perhaps for accepting greater risks of losses. It is clear that the other members of the 2011 coalition could not have conducted OUP, let alone OOD, without the United States playing a major role. However, this is not the same thing as saying that they could not have conducted some sort of aerial intervention in Libya largely on their own, albeit a smaller, less elegant, less discriminating, and probably considerably costlier one.[18] It presumably would have been less effective as well, though whether it might still have been effective enough to enable the rebels eventually to win a longer and more difficult war against Qaddafi's regime is less certain.

NATO and Coalition Air Warfare

In the Libyan intervention, NATO operated in a nontraditional way, as an armature for the construction and operation of a coalition of willing participants that was both narrower and broader than the Alliance. As Christopher Chivvis notes in Chapter Two, the fact that NATO was able to adapt to a situation in which some of its major members chose to sit on the sidelines of the operation arguably is a hopeful sign of flexibility in an organization not widely associated with that quality. Every reason exists to think this will not be the last time the Alliance has occasion to take such an approach to dealing with a crisis.

If that is so, it behooves the Alliance to invest in developing provisions to enhance its ability to operate in this mode, anticipating that at least some operations in the future will be "pick-up games" in which the roster of players may be hard to predict, and may include some relatively unfamiliar faces. Building and maintaining partnerships with armed forces outside of the Alliance clearly is useful preparation for including them in Alliance-led operations, as proved to be the case in OUP with all four of the non-NATO members of the coalition. In addition to cultivating technical and tactical interoperability, building relationships and familiarity at the operational and strategic levels is invaluable, particularly in an environment in which one anticipates

---

[18] This counterfactual speculation sets aside the all-important question of whether many states would have been willing to participate in a coalition that did not include the United States as an active member—it seems certain that some of those that flew in OUP would not.

smaller air forces punching above their weight. As several of the chapters in this volume have emphasized, preparations for sharing classified intelligence, and for integrating communications and datalinks, are becoming increasingly central to the process of operating with partners, and can be stubbornly difficult to resolve on the fly once a crisis or operation is under way.

Conversely, it is also important to prepare to deal with the unanticipated absence of significant allies. This is a consideration that appears to argue in favor of investing in pooled resources, a measure usually associated mainly with the need to acquire expensive capabilities that smaller nations cannot afford on their own—if an ally decides to opt out of an operation, such arrangements can provide insurance against losing access to key capabilities, provided that operating the shared asset does not depend indispensably on the presence of the wayward ally's personnel.

Investing in serious partnerships—and for that matter, making hedging preparations against allied absenteeism—is not without cost. Even when dealing with inexpensive forms of collaboration rather than major exercises, it can consume substantial resources in terms of the time and attention of key personnel. Moreover, the investment has an air of speculation about it, since any given partner may or may not step up to participate in a particular contingency, and in general more partners are likely to sit out than join in. However, the value of being ready to integrate partners from outside the Alliance increases by the day as European-member defense budgets and armed forces contract and the military capabilities of states such as Qatar and the UAE catch up with their Western counterparts.

Is Libya a Model for the Future?

In Libya, the coalition achieved a conspicuous strategic success at remarkably limited cost—in contrast to some other recent operations in which it is fair to say that the United States and its partners have achieved remarkably limited strategic successes at conspicuous cost. It is natural to respond by turning to the Libyan intervention in hopes of finding a template on which to model future operations. Skeptics respond that Libya is an outlier case, and leaders should not imagine that it points the way to a future of inexpensive, low-risk military interventions. Of course, every war is unique; the question here is whether Libya's uniqueness makes it irrelevant.

In many ways, intervening in Libya was a best-case scenario for NATO. Libya has a small population[19] largely concentrated along an accessible coastline close to well-established NATO bases, which made it relatively easy to deploy and operate forces and kept air refueling demands manageable. Libya's topography also was largely favorable

---

[19] In spite of its southern geographical expanse, Libya's population of some 6.5 million is smaller than every member of the OUP coalition except Qatar, Norway, Denmark, and (barely) Jordan.

for the application of airpower. Qaddafi's regime was a weak opponent with limited military capabilities (though these were still far greater than those of the Libyan opposition).

The most challenging aspects of the intervention were situational, and many of these were resolved diplomatically prior to March 19 through the actions of the GCC, the Arab League, and the U.N. Security Council. What could not be resolved was the extent to which the military capabilities of the United States and a number of the other coalition members were already stretched near or actually to the limit by deployments in Afghanistan and elsewhere, which did much to offset the coalition members' structural advantages in size and resources compared to Libya.

However, the most important feature of the Libyan case from the point of view of the aerial intervention strategy option was the presence of a Libyan opposition movement whose capabilities were minimal, but which, in other ways, was a promising local partner for the coalition. It is difficult to overstate the importance of this. When comparing Libya to other places where one might think about intervening, the presence or absence of an indigenous political movement that is committed to its cause, palatable as a cobelligerent, capable of inspiring international sympathy, and with at least the potential to become effective on the battlefield with enough outside assistance is arguably a far more important prerequisite for intervention than features such as weak air defenses or proximity to one's bases. Such physical obstacles may be overcome with the right tools, and Libya demonstrates that airpower can do much to compensate for a local partner's physical weakness,[20] in fact more than many observers imagined when analyzing the "Afghan model" previously. But if no suitable political actor exists on whose behalf one can usefully intervene, it is extremely unlikely that one can be fabricated to effectively fill the vacuum.

One final, related observation about the potential value of aerial intervention is worth emphasizing, especially in light of the internal conflict that has developed in Libya since 2012. The intervening power or coalition is likely to have much more control over the fate of the regime it is fighting against than over what will succeed it. (In this sense, it resembles the dynamic of decapitation attacks against enemy leadership.) This is part of the aerial intervention bargain: Staying physically remote from local political struggles reduces costs and risks, but standoff distance also limits opportunities for influence.

Is Libya, then, a potential strategic model for the future? It was a relatively easy target for an aerial intervention, and repeating the exercise somewhere else almost certainly would be harder in military terms and because building the sort of broad international front against another enemy will be harder as a result of the Libyan precedent.

---

[20] This is also a lesson of OEF, though as noted earlier, the Northern Alliance was at a considerably smaller disadvantage with respect to the Taliban military capabilities than was the NTC with respect to Qaddafi's regime. Regarding the military dimension of the earlier case, see Richard B. Andres, Craig Wills, and Thomas E. Griffith Jr., "Winning with Allies: The Strategic Vaue of the Afghan Model," *International Security*, Vol. 30, No. 3, Winter 2005/06, pp. 124–160.

Whether or not Russia and China were genuinely surprised that UNSCR 1973 paved the way for regime change in Libya, gaining their acquiescence to a similar resolution against another country is likely to be an insurmountable hill to climb for the near future—in which case the next question will be whether countries such as Sweden and Norway, which placed great store in 2011 on the presence of a U.N. endorsement for the intervention, always will see this as a prerequisite for action. Yet while any "next Libya" is very likely to be a more difficult challenge, there is no *a priori* reason to think that suitable opportunities for such strategies will not emerge again in the future. Should that happen, NATO and its principal members would be well served by having prepared for the possibility.

Preparing for Future Aerial Interventions
Many of the capabilities called for by aerial intervention strategies are relevant to a far broader range of strategic approaches, but it is possible to identify some general rules of thumb in preparing for future operations of this type. Some of these derive from the likelihood that aerial interventions will be particularly attractive in situations where the intervening state or coalition has relatively modest stakes in the conflict, hence the appeal of an option to intervene at low cost and with limited risk.

- Aerial interventions may be even more likely than other sorts of operations to be carried out by coalitions, as multiple states each make limited contributions of forces in keeping with their limited interests.
- As in many other types of air operations, ISR, and especially intelligence, is a key bottleneck for generating and applying airpower. However, this pattern may be particularly pronounced in aerial interventions, where there is likely to be a particularly high priority on positively identifying combatant forces and avoiding collateral and other civilian damage.
- The convergence of coalition operations and the primacy of intelligence multiplies the importance of making provisions for sharing classified or restricted data among allies and coalition partners.
- Minimizing friendly losses always is likely to be a priority in aerial interventions, but is not likely always to be as easy as it was in Libya.
- Munitions with limited kinetic effects, such as Brimstone, demonstrated their worth in Libya, and are a natural priority area for future investment given their utility in a variety of conflict types in populated areas.
- Military-to-military contacts with the Libyan armed forces before the revolution proved to be valuable during the intervention, and Libya is unlikely to be the only place where that will turn out to be true.
- Cooperation with indigenous forces is all-important in cases such as Libya, and should be first among many areas of further investigation into improving strategies and techniques for aerial interventions.

The Age of Airpower

In the decade or so since the United States became mired in its counterinsurgency campaigns in Iraq and Afghanistan, some of the popular luster that airpower acquired from the campaigns of the 1990s apparently has worn off, and the suggestion is offered from time to time that airpower is of relatively minor importance in a world where wars are fought by irregular forces intermingled with civilian populations rather than mechanized armies like those of the Soviet Union during the Cold War or Iraq in 1991. Books such as Martin van Creveld's *The Age of Airpower* insist airpower has little to contribute to waging "wars among the people" and that the prevalence of such conflicts since the end of the Cold War has left modern airpower something of a relic of the past.[21]

In fact, airpower has played a major role in many modern counterinsurgencies, though often in ways that look fairly different from its roles in conventional warfare.[22] But perhaps there is no more crystalline example than the coalition air campaign in Libya to show not only that airpower can play a central role in a war among the people, but that its capabilities for doing so have developed remarkably during the past several decades. As often has been the case over the years, those who assume, either consciously or not, that airpower's capabilities of a generation earlier closely resemble its current potential are very likely to be surprised by actual events.

Using a modest amount of airpower and at relatively little cost, France, Britain, the United States, and their allies and partners reversed the course of the Libyan civil war, enabling the popular uprising against Muammar Qaddafi to survive and ultimately to triumph. It is certainly important not to overstate the significance of this military achievement, given the enemy's weaknesses and the favorable political and physical circumstances under which the war was fought, and the often-disheartening internal politics of Libya since the removal of the Qaddafi regime. Yet it is equally vital that we not forget about the campaign or write off what it did as a foregone conclusion or a historical fluke. It is surely true that no other war will be exactly like Libya, but every reason exists to expect that there will be crises and conflicts in coming years that we will be better prepared to deal with wisely if we understand and remember what happened in the aerial intervention in Libya in 2011.

---

[21] Martin van Creveld, *The Age of Airpower,* New York: Public Affairs, 2011. For critiques and corrections, see Karl P. Mueller, "Sky King," *The American Interest*, Vol. 7, No. 3, January/February 2012, pp. 104–108, and "Airpower: Two Centennial Appraisals," *Strategic Studies Quarterly*, Vol. 5, No. 4, Winter 2011, pp. 123–132.

[22] James S. Corum and Wray R. Johnson, *Airpower in Small Wars*, Lawrence, Kan.: University of Kansas Press, 2003; Alan J. Vick et al., *Air Power in the New Counterinsurgency Era: The Strategic Importance of USAF Advisory and Assistance Missions*, Santa Monica, Calif.: RAND Corporation, MG-509-AF, 2006; Robert C. Owen and Karl P. Mueller, *Airlift Capabilities for Future U.S. Counterinsurgency Operations*, Santa Monica, Calif.: RAND Corporation, MG-565-AF, 2007.

Timeline of Events in Libya

Compiler's Note

Every effort has been made to ensure this timeline of events in 2011 is as accurate as possible. When necessary, sources were verified against other timelines or newspaper articles; however, only the primary source for the item has been cited in the endnotes. Some events, especially the capture of cities, may cover several days. For ease of understanding, a single day, normally the most commonly referenced, was chosen. Timeline entries without sources were derived from the chapters contained in the report; please see the relevant chapter for citation.

Date	Military Events	Political Events
February 15–16		Anti-regime protests erupt in Benghazi.
February 17		A national "Day of Rage" is held throughout Libya.
February 20	Opposition forces secure control of Benghazi.	
February 21	Two Libyan air force (LARAF) pilots defect to Malta.[1] LARAF pilots at Banina Air Base (Benghazi) defect to the rebels.	Libyan Interior Minister Abdul Fattah Younis al Abidi, defects from the Qaddafi regime, joining the opposition.[2,3]
February 22	Portuguese and Dutch C-130s deploy to Sigonella to conduct Non-Combatant Evacuations (NEO).	Qaddafi, in a televised address, vows to remain in power and die as a "martyr" if necessary.[4,5] The Arab League suspends Libyan membership.[6]
February 23	Misrata falls to opposition forces.[7]	French President Nicolas Sarkozy calls for sanctions against Libya.[8]
February 24	UK begins NEO of its nationals.[9]	
February 25	U.S. citizens evacuated from Libya as the ferry *Maria Delores* departs from Tripoli.	U.S. Department of State suspends embassy operations in Libya.[10]
February 26	Ajdabiyah falls to opposition forces.[11] Canada's NEO, code-named Operation Mobile, begins.	United Nations Security Council adopts Resolution 1970 (UNSCR 1970), authorizing an arms embargo against Libya.[12] Canada suspends its diplomatic mission in Libya, withdrawing its staff from its embassy.

Date	Military Events	Political Events
February 27	A Dutch Lynx helicopter undertaking NEO operations near Sirte crashes and regime forces capture its crew.[13]	Former Qaddafi minister Mustafa Jalil is named interim prime minister for the Libyan National Transitional Council (NTC).[14]
March 2		Prime Minister David Cameron, during House of Commons Question Time, declares, "I think we should, and we are, looking at plans for a no-fly zone."[15]
March 3	The United States stands up Operation Odyssey Dawn.	President Barack Obama issues a statement: "Colonel Qaddafi needs to step down from power and leave."[16]
March 5	Pilots loyal to the Libyan opposition begin flying sorties against Regime forces near Ras Lanuf and Ajdabiya.	The NTC declares itself the legitimate government of Libya.[17]
March 6		A British delegation's effort to meet with Libyan opposition forces is aborted after it encounters difficulty. Members of the SAS and SIS leave Libya aboard a ship conducting NEO, HMS *Cumberland*.[18]
March 7	Fighting begins for control of the strategic city of Ras Lanuf.[19] Air strikes are launched by LARAF.[20]	The Gulf Cooperation Council (GCC) declares its support for a no-fly zone over Libya.
March 8	NATO AWACS aircraft from Operation Active Endeavor begin round-the-clock surveillance of Libya.[21]	Prime Minister Cameron and President Obama meet to discuss military options for intervention in Libya.[22] The Organization of the Islamic Conference (OIC) expresses support for a no-fly zone over Libya.
March 9	USS *Kearsarge* Amphibious Ready Group reported in the Mediterranean.[23]	
March 10	Libyan warplanes bomb Brega.[24]	France becomes the first country to extend official recognition to the NTC as the government of Libya.[25] NATO defense ministers meet in Brussels, deciding to send ships to monitor the Libyan situation.[26]
March 11	Captured Dutch helicopter crew freed.	President Nicolas Sarkozy issues a statement urging air strikes against Regime forces in the event of civilian casualties.[27]
A massive tsunami strikes Japan, causing widespread destruction.		
March 12		The Arab League asks the UN Security Council to authorize a no-fly zone over Libya, for the purpose of protecting civilians.[28]
March 13	Regime forces retake Brega.[29]	
March 16	Regime forces retake Ajdabiyah, pushing opposition forces back to Benghazi.[30]	
March 17		UNSCR 1973 authorizes a three-fold mission of protection of civilians, an arms embargo, and a no-fly zone.[31]

Date	Military Events	Political Events
March 18	Regime forces advance near the outskirts of the opposition-held city of Benghazi. Italian Air Force (ITAF) assets begin deploying to Trapani in anticipation of operations over Libya. Italian aircraft carrier *Giuseppe Garibaldi* (C551) departs Taranto. Qatar Emiri Air Force (QEAF) aircraft begin deploying to Souda Bay.	The Belgian government unanimously approves a military contribution to operations over Libya. Canada announces it will send assets to support the implementation of UNSCR 1973.
March 19	French fighters strike regime forces approaching Benghazi, marking the opening of Operation Harmattan. Military Operations for Operation Odyssey Dawn begin. British forces begin Operation Ellamy. Royal Danish Air Force (RDAF) aircraft depart Skrydstrup Air Base en route to Sigonella. Spanish Air Force assets deploy to Decimomannu. Seven Royal Canadian Air Force (RCAF) CF-188s arrive in-theater.	French President Sarkozy convenes a meeting of Arab and allied leaders, which OKs deployment of aircraft to establish a no-fly zone and assist opposition forces around Benghazi.
March 20	Ten British Typhoons deploy to Gioia del Colle, Italy. French aircraft carrier *Charles de Gaulle* departs Toulon to participate in the ongoing Operation Harmattan.[32] RDAF F-16s begin operations over Libya. ITAF aircraft begin operations over Libya. U.S. B-2 bombers strike targets in Sirte.	
March 21	A USAF F-15E Strike Eagle suffers an equipment malfunction, forcing the two-man crew to eject over Libya.[33] One crewman is picked up by coalition forces, the other by Libyan civilians.[34] Royal Norwegian Air Force (RNoAF) assets deploy to Souda Bay. Belgian Air Force F-16s begin combat air patrol (CAP) operations over Libya. RCAF aircraft begin operations over Libya.	
March 22	Admiral Locklear states in a briefing, "The no-fly zone is in place, no-fly zone is effective."[35] Both crewmembers of the downed F-15E are reported safe and in U.S. custody.[36] Non-U.S. coalition aircraft flew 35% of total sorties for the day.[37] QEAF assets arrive in Souda Bay.	
March 23	The no-fly zone over Libya expands to cover all Libyan coastline. Rear Admiral Hueber states in a briefing, "We have degraded the Libyan strategic surface-to-air missile systems to a negligible threat."[38] NATO begins maritime operations aimed at enforcing UNSCR 1973's arms embargo.[39]	Norway adopts a decree authorizing participation in Operation Odyssey Dawn, and enforcement of UNSCR 1973. The Netherlands green-lights participation in military operations over Libya.

Date	Military Events	Political Events
March 24	RNoAF F-16s begin operations over Libya. Royal Netherlands Air Force (RNLAF) aircraft deploy to Sardinia.	NATO agrees to take over control of the air operations enforcing the no-fly zone. The UAE announces it will deploy forces in support of operations over Libya.
March 25	NATO takes over enforcement of Libyan no-fly zone. QEAF and French Air Force fighters begin joint flights over Libya. Italian aircraft carrier *Giuseppe Garibaldi* (C551) transferred to NATO command to support the ongoing naval embargo.	
March 26	USAF A-10s and AC-130 gunships begin operating over Libya.[40] Opposition forces wrest the city of Ajdabiyah back from regime fighters.[41]	
March 27	Opposition forces retake Bin Jawad, Ras Lanuf, and Brega.[42] United Arab Emirates Air Force (UAEAF) assets deploy to Decimomannu.	NATO Secretary General Anders Fogh Rasmussen announces expansion of the NATO mission to include enforcing all of UNSCR 1973.[43]
March 28	RNLAF aircraft begin operations over Libya.	President Obama declares: "Going forward, the lead in enforcing the no-fly zone and protecting civilians on the ground will transition to our allies and partners, and I am fully confident that our coalition will keep the pressure on Qaddafi's remaining forces. In that effort, the United States will play a supporting role . . . "[44]
March 29		NATO and partner countries announce the formation of the "Libyan Contact Group" to promote coordination of international discussion regarding multiple aspects of Libyan situation.[45]
March 31	NATO, under Operation Unified Protector, takes over full operational control of the civilian protection mission in Libya.[46] Opposition forces withdraw from the town of Brega toward Ajdabiya.[47]	Libyan Foreign Minister Moussa Koussa defects to Great Britain.[48]
April 1–2	Swedish Air Force deploys eight JAS 39C Gripens to Sigonella.	The Swedish government agrees to participate in Operation Unified Protector.
April 4	The United States begins transitioning to a support role in OUP.[49]	
April 5	Regime forces push opposition fighters away from Brega.[50]	
April 6		Qaddafi issues a letter to President Obama, requesting that he put an end to the NATO intervention in Libya.[51]
April 7	NATO aircraft accidentally bomb opposition fighters, killing between five and 13 near Ajdabiya.[52] Swedish Air Force fighters begin operations over Libya.	The U.S. government responds to Qaddafi's letter, reiterating Washington's demands that Qaddafi abdicate power and live in exile.[53]
April 9	Regime forces assault Ajdabiya.[54]	

Date	Military Events	Political Events
April 11		Negotiators from the African Union attempt to broker a cease-fire between regime and opposition forces.[55]
April 13		First meeting of the Contact Group on Libya: A group of international ministers meet in Doha with Libyan opposition in a show of solidarity.[56]
April 14		NATO and allied foreign ministers meet in Berlin, commit to "using all necessary resources and operational flexibility" in support of the U.N. Mandate.[57]
April 15	Reports in the media indicate that NATO may be running short on PGMs.	
April 19	Britain announces it will send military advisors to assist the Libyan opposition.[58]	
April 20	Italy and France announce commitment of military advisors to support Libyan opposition.[59]	
April 21	United States approves use of UAVs for strikes over Libya.[60]	
April 23	Regime forces abandon the siege of Misrata.[61]	
April 26	UAEAF assets redeploy to Sigonella.	
April 27	NATO aircraft involved in "friendly fire" bombing of opposition forces near Misrata, killing twelve.[62] *Bataan* ARG assumes command of Task Force 62, replacing *Kearsarge* ARG.[63]	
April 30	Qaddafi's youngest son, Seif al-Arab Muammar el-Qaddafi, and other members of the Qaddafi family are killed in an airstrike.[64]	
May 5		The second meeting of the Libyan Contact Group is held in Rome.[65]
May 18	France begins deployment of attack helicopters to Libya aboard *Tonnerre*.	
May 19		NATO Secretary General Rasmussen declares regime military power to be "significantly degraded."[66] President Obama declares that Qaddafi must leave Libya in order for the transition to democracy to continue.[67]
May 20		President Obama fails to get congressional support for ongoing military operations in Libya, allowing the War Powers Resolution to lapse.[68]
May 22		European Union foreign policy official visits Benghazi.[69]
May 27	Britain begins deployment of Apache helicopter gunships to Libya aboard HMS *Ocean*.[70]	

Date	Military Events	Political Events
May 30	Approval is granted for Swedish Air Force systems to be fully integrated with NATO C2 systems.	
June 1		NATO extends its mission in Libya for 90 days.[71]
June 3		Congress issues a rebuke to President Obama over failure to obtain congressional approval for military action in Libya per the War Powers Resolution.[72]
June 4	British attack helicopters launch first strikes.[73]	
June 7		President Obama states during a joint news conference with German Chancellor Angela Merkel: "[We] have been clear—Qaddafi must step down and hand power to the Libyan people, and the pressure will only continue to increase until he does."[74]
June 8		NATO defense ministers convene in Brussels, upholding previous decisions of April 14, and encourage international institutions to begin planning for post-conflict Libya.[75]
June 9		In his concluding remarks at the NATO Defense Ministers' meeting, Secretary General Rasmussen reiterates his call for member nations, including those not actively contributing, to increase their support for the effort in Libya.[76] The third Libya Contact Group summit is held in Abu Dhabi.[77]
June 10	Norway announces it will reduce RNoAF participation in Operation Unified Protector from six aircraft to four by June 24 and withdraw from the operation by August 1.[78]	
June 21	A "drone helicopter" used by NATO goes down over Libya.[79]	
June 24		A resolution extending U.S. authority to conduct operations over Libya fails in the House of Representatives.[80]
June 26		The Swedish Parliament passes a resolution authorizing a continuation of the Swedish mission for another 90 days, and expanding its mandate.
July 7	Italy declares it will replace the *Garibaldi* with a smaller vessel, and will reduce its participation in Operation Unified Protector.[81]	
July 14		NATO Secretary General Rasmussen again calls on all Alliance members to increase their commitment to OUP.[82]

Date	Military Events	Political Events
July 15	Britain agrees to send an additional four Tornados to support the ongoing Operation Unified Protector.[83]	The fourth Libya Contact Group summit is held in Istanbul, Turkey.[84] The United States recognizes the NTC as the legitimate government of Libya.[85]
July 19	Opposition fighters encircle the strategic city of Brega.[86]	
July 21	NATO requests UAV and ISR assets from the United States.[87]	
July 26	Italian aircraft carrier *Garibaldi* is withdrawn from NATO operations over Libya.	
July 28		Opposition General Abdul Fattah Younes is killed in Benghazi.[88]
August 1	RNoAF aircraft depart Souda Bay.	
August 8	NATO bombs strike several homes in the village of Majer under disputed circumstances, killing 34 people.[89,90]	
August 10	French aircraft carrier *Charles de Gaulle* is withdrawn from OUP, returning to Toulon.[91]	
August 14	Opposition fighters seize the strategic city of Zawiyah, outside Tripoli.[92]	
August 18	British warplanes sink a Libyan ship.[93] French *Harfang* UAV deploys to Sigonella.[94]	
August 21	Opposition fighters enter Tripoli.[95]	
August 22		President Obama, in a written statement, declares, "Tripoli is slipping from the grasp of a tyrant. The Qadhafi regime is showing signs of collapse."[96]
August 23	Opposition fighters storm Qaddafi's compound.[97]	
October 20	Qaddafi killed in Sirte.	
October 31	Operation Unified Protector concludes.[98]	

[1] John Hooper and Ian Black, "Libya: Defections: Pilots Were 'Told to Bomb Protesters,'" *The Guardian*, Final Edition, February 22, 2011.

[2] CNN Wire Staff, "Interior Minister Resigns Rather Than Carry Out Gadhafi Orders," *CNN*, February 22, 2011.

[3] Helen Kennedy, "Die Here a Martyr!' Khadafy Not Leaving as Libya Shakes," *The Daily News*, February 23, 2011, p. 7.

[4] "Defiant Gaddafi Vows to Die as Martyr, Fight Revolt," Thomson Reuters, February 22, 2011.

[5] Brian Ferguson, "Defiant Gaddafi: I'll Die a Martyr," *The Scotsman*, 1st Edition, February 23, 2011.

[6] Molly Hennessy-Fiske, "Libya: Arab League Suspends Libyan Membership," blog entry, Los Angeles Times, February 22, 2011.

[7] Oren Kessler and the Associated Press, "Gaddafi Keeps Grip on Capital as Revolt Spreads Across Libya," *The Jerusalem Post*, February 24, 2011.

[8] "Libya; France Calls for Sanctions Against Libya," *Africa News*, February 23, 2011.

[9] Deborah Haynes and Laura Pitel, "Britain's First Plane Touches Down Long After Others Have Fled Tripoli," *The Times* (London), February 24, 2011.

[10] Patrick Kennedy and Janet Sanderson, "Briefing on Suspension of U.S. Embassy Operations in Libya [TRANSCRIPT]," Washington, D.C.: United States Department of State, February 25, 2011.

[11] The International Institute for Strategic Studies Armed Conflict Database, "Libya Uprising—Timeline."

[12] United Nations Security Council, UNSCR 1970, New York: The United Nations, February 26, 2011.

[13] "Three Dutch Marines Captured During Rescue in Libya," BBC, March 3, 2011.

[14] International Institute for Strategic Studies, "Libya Uprising—Timeline."

[15] David Cameron answers questions from members of Parliament, British House of Commons, March 2, 2011.

[16] Howard LaFranchi, "Obama to Pentagon: Give Me a List of Options to Protect Libyans," The Christian Science Monitor, March 3, 2011.

[17] "TIMELINE—Libya's Uprising Against Muammar Gaddafi," Thomson Reuters, August 22 2011.

[18] International Institute for Strategic Studies: "Libya Uprising—Timeline."

[19] International Institute for Strategic Studies: "Libya Uprising—Timeline."

[20] International Institute for Strategic Studies: "Libya Uprising—Timeline."

[21] NATO, "NATO and Libya—Operation Unified Protector," online.

[22] International Institute for Strategic Studies: "Libya Uprising—Timeline."

[23] Stratfor, "U.S. Naval Update Map: March 9, 2011," Austin, Texas: Stratfor, March 9, 2011.

[24] "TIMELINE—Libya's uprising against Muammar Gaddafi."

[25] "TIMELINE—Libya's uprising against Muammar Gaddafi."

[26] NATO, "NATO and Libya—Precursor to Operation Unified Protector," online, undated.

[27] International Institute for Strategic Studies: "Libya Uprising—Timeline."

[28] Reuters, "TIMELINE—Libya's uprising against Muammar Gaddafi."

[29] International Institute for Strategic Studies: "Libya Uprising—Timeline."

[30] International Institute for Strategic Studies: "Libya Uprising—Timeline."

[31] United Nations Security Council, Resolution 1973, New York: The United Nations, March 17, 2011.

[32] Tom Whithington, "France to Deploy More Rafales Over Libya to Cover Charles de Gaulle Exit," Jane's Defence Weekly, August 4, 2011.

[33] Rear Admiral Gerard Hueber, DOD News Briefing—Transcript Department of Defense, March 23, 2011.

[34] "Transcript: DoD News Briefing with Adm. Locklear via Teleconference from USS Mount Whitney," Story Number: NNS110322-22, March 22, 2011.

[35] "Transcript: DoD News Briefing with Adm. Locklear via Teleconference from USS Mount Whitney."

[36] "Transcript: DoD News Briefing with Adm. Locklear via Teleconference from USS Mount Whitney."

[37] "Transcript: DoD News Briefing with Adm. Locklear via Teleconference from USS Mount Whitney."

[38] Rear Admiral Gerard Hueber, DOD News Briefing, March 23, 2011.

[39] NATO, "NATO and Libya—Operation Unified Protector," online, undated.

[40] Jeremiah Gertler, "Operation Odyssey Dawn (Libya): Background and Issues for Congress," Congressional Research Service report R41725, Washington, D.C., March 30, 2011, p. 8.

[41] International Institute for Strategic Studies: "Libya Uprising—Timeline."

[42] International Institute for Strategic Studies: "Libya Uprising—Timeline."

[43] "Statement by NATO Secretary General Anders Fogh Rasmussen on Libya," North Atlantic Treaty Organization website, March 27, 2011.

[44] White House Press Office, "Remarks by the President in Address to the Nation on Libya," March 28, 2011.

[45] Reuters, "TIMELINE—Libya's Uprising Against Muammar Gaddafi."

[46] Oana Lungescu, Adm. Giampaolo Di Paola, and Lt.-Gen. Charles Bouchard, "Press Briefing," Brussels: North Atlantic Treaty Organization, March 31, 2011.

[47] "Events in Libya: A Chronology," *The New York Times*, August 29, 2011.

[48] "Events in Libya: A Chronology."

[49] "Events in Libya: A Chronology."

[50] "Events in Libya: A Chronology."

[51] International Institute for Strategic Studies: "Libya Uprising—Timeline."

[52] "Libyan Rebels Near Ajdabiya 'Killed in Nato Air Strike,'" *BBC,* April 7, 2011.

[53] International Institute for Strategic Studies: "Libya Uprising—Timeline"

[54] "Events in Libya: A Chronology."

[55] "Events in Libya: A Chronology."

[56] "Events in Libya: A Chronology."

[57] NATO, "NATO and Libya—Operation Unified Protector," online, undated.

[58] "Britain to Send Military Advisers to Libyan Rebels," *USA Today*, April 19, 2011.

[59] Alan Cowelland Ravi Somaiya, "France and Italy Will Also Send Advisers to Libya Rebels," *New York Times*, April 20, 2011.

[60] Greg Jaffe, Edward Cody, and William Branigin, "McCain Visits Benghazi; Libyan Rebels Welcome Armed Drone Aircraft," *The Washington Post*, April 21, 2011.

[61] "Events in Libya: A Chronology."

[62] "Events in Libya: A Chronology."

[63] *Kearsarge* and *Bataan* ARG Public Affairs, "*Kearsarge* and *Bataan* Amphibious Ready Groups Complete Turnover," United States Navy, April 28, 2011. Story Number: NNS110428-05.

[64] "Events in Libya: A Chronology."

[65] Foreign & Commonwealth Office, "Libya Contact Group Meeting in Rome Concludes," London, May 5, 2011.

[66] Anders Fogh Rasmussen, "Joint Press Point Secretary General and the President of Slovakia," Spoken Remarks, North Atlantic Treaty Organization (NATO), Brussels, Belgium [in Bratislava, Slovakia] May 19, 2011.

[67] International Institute for Strategic Studies: "Libya Uprising—Timeline."

[68] David A. Fahrenthold, "Obama Misses Deadline for Congressional Approval of Libya Operations," *The Washington Post*, May 20, 2011.

[69] "Events in Libya: A Chronology."

[70] "Libya: UK Apache Helicopters Used in Nato Attacks," *BBC*, June 4, 2011.

[71] "Libya: UK Apache Helicopters Used in Nato Attacks."

[72] David A. Fahrenthold, "House Rebukes Obama on Libya Mission, But Does Not Demand Withdrawal," *The Washington Post*, June 3, 2011; "Events in Libya: A Chronology."

[73] "Libya: UK Apache Helicopters Used in Nato Attacks."

[74] White House Press Office,"Remarks by President Obama and Chancellor Merkel in a Joint Press Conference," June 7, 2011.

[75] NATO, "NATO and Libya—Operation Unified Protector," online, undated.

[76] "Concluding Press Conference by NATO Secretary General Anders Fogh Rasmussen After the Meetings of NATO Defence Ministers," Press Conference Transcript, North Atlantic Treaty Organization, June 9, 2011.

[77] Libyan Contact Group, "Co-Chairs' Statement," third meeting of the International Contact Group on Libya, Abu Dhabi, June 9, 2011.

[78] "Norge Flyver Hjem Fra Libyen 1. august," *Jyllands-Posten*, June 10, 2011.

[79] "Press Briefing on Libya by NATO Spokesperson Oana Lungescu and Mike Bracken, Spokesperson for the Operation Unified Protector," North Atlantic Treaty Organization (NATO) website, June 21, 2011.

[80] International Institute for Strategic Studies: "Libya Uprising—Timeline."

[81] International Institute for Strategic Studies: "Libya Uprising—Timeline."

[82] International Institute for Strategic Studies: "Libya Uprising—Timeline."

[83] Gerrard Cowan, "UK Boosts Libya Tornado Force," *Jane's Defence Weekly*, July 15, 2011.

[84] Libya Contact Group, "Fourth Meeting of the Libya Contact Group Chair's Statement, 15 July 2011, Istanbul."

[85] William Wan and William Booth, "United States Recognizes Libyan Rebels as Legitimate Government," *The Washington Post*, July 15, 2011; Reuters, "TIMELINE—Libya's Uprising Against Muammar Gaddafi."

[86] International Institute for Strategic Studies: "Libya Uprising—Timeline."

[87] International Institute for Strategic Studies: "Libya Uprising—Timeline."

[88] William Booth, "Abdul Fattah Younis, Libyan Rebel Military Commander, Is Killed," *The Washington Post*, July 28, 2011.

[89] International Commission of Inquiry on Libya, "Report of the International Commission of Inquiry on Libya—Advance Unedited Version," New York: Human Rights Council, United Nations, A/HRC/19/68, March 2, 2012, p. 164.

[90] Amnesty International, "Libya: The Forgotten Victims of NATO Strikes," London: Amnesty International Publications, March 2012, p. 11.

[91] "France: Aircraft Carrier to Return for Maintenance," Austin, Texas, August 4, 2011.

[92] "TIMELINE—Libya's Uprising Against Muammar Gaddafi," Reuters.

[93] Damien McElroy, "Libya: RAF Airstrikes Sink Boat Filled with Gaddafi Troops After Refinery Battle," *The Telegraph*, August 18, 2011.

[94] Martin Streetly, "France Deploys Harfang UAV over Libya," *International Defence Review*, August 31, 2011.

[95] "Events in Libya: A Chronology."

[96] White House Press Office, "Statement of President Barack Obama on Libya," August 22, 2011.

[97] "Events in Libya: A Chronology."

[98] "Last Air Mission of Unified Protector Concluded," NATO website, October 31, 2011.

Air Order of Battle

Table B.1 lists aircraft assigned to the 2011 Libyan air campaign, excluding rotary-wing aircraft other than attack helicopters and transport aircraft operating from their home bases. Many of them participated in only part of the campaign; in particular, a considerable number of the aircraft employed in the early Odyssey Dawn air strikes did not fly in Operation Unified Protector. For a graphic depiction of base locations, see Figure 2.4 in Chapter Two. Table B.2 lists the distances from main operating bases to Tripoli.

Table B.1
Aircraft Assigned to Operations Odyssey Dawn and/or Unified Protector

Country	Assets	Base
Belgium		
	6 F-16AM Fighting Falcon	Araxos, GRC
	2 CC-130/130T Hercules	"
Canada		
	2 CP-140 Aurora	Sigonella, ITA
	2 CC-150T Polaris	Trapani, ITA
	2 CC-130/130T Hercules	"
	7 CF-18 Hornet	"
Denmark		
	6 F-16AM Fighting Falcon	Sigonella, ITA
France		
	2 E-2C Hawkeye	*Charles de Gaulle*
	8 Rafale M	"
	6 Super Étendard	"
	4 Tigre HAP	*Tonnerre/Mistral*
	20 Gazelle	"
	2 Atlantique 2	Sigonella, ITA
	5 Rafale B/C	"
	1 Harfang UAV	"
	8 Mirage 2000D	Souda Bay, GRC
	6 Mirage 2000N	"

Table B.1—Cont.

Country	Assets	Base
France, cont.		
	2 Mirage F1CT	Souda Bay, GRC
	2 Mirage F1CR	Solenzara, FRA
	8 Rafale B/C	"
	3 Mirage 2000-5	Dijon, FRA
	1 E-3F AWACS	Avord, FRA
	1 C-160G	Metz-Frescaty, FRA
	6 C-135FR	Istres-Le Tubé, FRA
Greece		
	1 EMB-145H Erieye	Souda Bay, GRC
Italy		
	4 AV-8B+ Harrier	*Giuseppe Garibaldi*
	1 KC-130J	Trapani, ITA
	4 F-16ADF Fighting Falcon	"
	5 Tornado IDS	"
	7 Tornado ECR	"
	8 Typhoon	"
	4 AMX Ghibli	"
	1 KC-767A	Pratica di Mare, ITA
Jordan		
	6 F-16AM Fighting Falcon	Aviano, ITA
NATO		
	3 E-3A Sentry	Trapani, ITA
Netherlands		
	1 KDC-10	Cagliari-Elmas Int'l, ITA
	6 F-16AM Fighting Falcon	Decimomannu, ITA
Norway		
	6 F-16AM Fighting Falcon	Souda Bay, GRC
Qatar		
	6 Mirage 2000-5EDA	Souda Bay, GRC
Spain		
	1 B-707	Decimomannu, ITA
	1 CN-235	"
	4 EF-18A Hornet	"
Sweden		
	1 Tp 84 (C-103H)	Sigonella, ITA
	8 JAS 39C Gripen	"
Turkey		
	2 KC-135R	Sigonella, ITA
	6 F-16C Fighting Falcon	"

Table B.1—Cont.

Country	Assets	Base
UAE		
	5 F-16E/F Desert Falcon	Decimomannu, ITA
	6 Mirage 2000-9DAD	(later to Sigonella)
United Kingdom		
	5 Apache AH.1	HMS *Ocean*
	2 E-3D Sentry AEW.1	Trapani, ITA
	2 VC10	"
	16 Tornado GR.4	Gioia del Colle, ITA
	8 Typhoon F.2	"
	1 E-3D Sentry AEW.1	Akrotiri, CYP
	1 Nimrod R.1	"
	2 Sentinel R.1	"
	1 VC10	"
	Tristar K.1/KC.1	Brize Norton, UK
	4 Tornado GR.4	Marham, UK
United States		
	6 AV-8B Harrier	USS *Kearsarge* (March 9)
	6 AV-8B Harrier	USS *Bataan* (April 27)
	12 F-16C Fighting Falcon	Aviano, ITA
	10 F-15E Strike Eagle	"
	6 F-16CJ Fighting Falcon	"
	6 A-10 Thunderbolt II	"
	5 EA-18G Growler	"
	4 EA-6B Prowler	"
	2 AC-130 Spectre	"
	1 EP-3E ARIES II	Sigonella, ITA
	1 P-3C Orion	"
	3 RQ-4 Global Hawk UAV	"
	8–10 MQ-1 Predator UAV	"
	1 EC-130H Compass Call	Souda Bay, GRC
	1 EC-130J Commando Solo	"
	2 RC-135 Rivet Joint	"
	10 F-15E Strike Eagle	RAF Lakenheath, UK
	15 KC-135 Stratotanker	Morón, ESP / Istres, FRA
	4 KC-10 Extender	"
	1 E-8C JSTARS	Rota, ESP
	2 E-3B/C Sentry	"
	3 B-2 Spirit	Whiteman AFB, USA
	2 B-1B Lancer	Ellsworth AFB, USA

Table B.2
Ranges from Main Operating Bases to Tripoli

Base	Distance to Tripoli (nmi)	Principal Users
Sigonella, Sicily, ITA	300	DEN, SWE, FRA, USA, CAN, TUR, UAE
Trapani, Sicily, ITA	300	ITA, CAN, GBR, NATO
Decimomannu, Sardinia, ITA	450	NED, UAE, ESP
Gioia del Colle, ITA	500	GBR
Araxos, GRC	500	BEL
Souda Bay, Crete, GRC	550	FRA, NOR, QAT, USA
Pratica di Mare, ITA	550	ITA
Solenzara, Corsica, FRA	600	FRA
Istres-Le Tubé, FRA	750	FRA, USA
Aviano, ITA	800	USA, JOR
Dijon, FRA	950	FRA
Morón, ESP	950	USA
Avord, FRA	1,000	FRA
Metz-Frascaty, FRA	1,000	FRA
Rota, ESP	1,000	USA
St. Dizier, FRA	1,000	FRA
Akrotiri, CYP	1,000	GBR, USA
RAF Lakenheath, UK	1,300	USA
RAF Marham, UK	1,300	GBR
Whiteman AFB, MO, USA	4,900	USA
Ellsworth AFB, SD, USA	5,000	USA

NOTE: Distances rounded to nearest 50 nautical miles and assume no overflight restrictions.

About the Authors

Gregory Alegi is a journalist and historian with over 25 years of experience in the aerospace field. Currently the editor-in-chief of the Italian defense daily www.dedalonews.it, he was previously the managing editor of the Italian airline pilot association's journal *Pegaso*. He has published 45 books and 60 essays, and is working on the first full-length biography of seminal airpower theorist Giulio Douhet. He teaches aerospace history at the Italian Air Force Academy, aviation management at Rome's LUISS Business School, and U.S. history at LUISS University.

Christian F. Anrig is deputy director of doctrine research and education, Swiss Air Force. From 2007 to 2009, he was a lecturer in air power studies in the Defence Studies Department of King's College London. The author of *The Quest for Relevant Air Power* (Air University Press, 2011), he has also published various articles and book chapters covering topics from European military transformation to modern air power and its ramifications for European nations. Dr. Anrig is a reviewer for *Air & Space Power Journal*, and he serves on the advisory panel of the RAF Centre for Air Power Studies. Various European air forces have invited him as a speaker to conferences and seminars.

Christopher S. Chivvis is a senior political scientist at the RAND Corporation and adjunct professor of European Studies at the Johns Hopkins, Paul H. Nitze School of Advanced International Studies (SAIS). A national security expert who specializes in Europe and North Africa, Chivvis is the author of *Toppling Qaddafi: Libya and the Limits of Liberal Intervention* (Cambridge University Press, 2013). He has worked on NATO-Russia issues in the Office of the Secretary of Defense for Policy and has held research positions at the French Institute for International Relations (IFRI) in Paris and at the German Institute for International and Security Affairs (SWP) in Berlin, in addition to teaching graduate courses at Johns Hopkins University, New York University, and Sciences Po in Paris. His articles have appeared in numerous journals including *Current History, International Affairs*, the *Journal of Contemporary History, Foreign Policy*, the *National Interest, Survival*, and the *Washington Quarterly*. His first book was *The Monetary Conservative*, an intellectual biography of the French thinker Jacques Rueff.

Robert Egnell is currently a visiting professor and director of teaching in the Security Studies Program at Georgetown University. He also holds a position as associate professor of war studies at the Swedish National Defence College. His previous positions include being a senior researcher at the Swedish Defence Reseach Agency and an assistant lecturer at the University of Dar es Salaam, Tanzania. His research concerns the conduct and effectiveness of peace operations, state-building, and civil-military relations. He is the author of numerous articles and of *Complex Peace Operations and Civil-Military Relations: Winning the Peace* (Routledge, 2009), co-author with David Ucko of *Counterinsurgency in Crisis: Britain and the Challenges of Modern Warfare* (Columbia University Press, 2013), and co-editor with Peter Haldén of *New Agendas in Statebuilding: Hybridity, Contingency and History* (Routledge, 2013).

Christina Goulter is a senior lecturer in the Defence Studies Department at King's College London, and teaches at the UK Defence Academy. From 1994 to 1997, she was visiting associate professor of strategy at the U.S. Naval War College. She serves on the advisory boards of the Royal Aeronautical Society, the RAF Centre for Air Power Studies, and the USAF Research Institute's *Strategic Studies Quarterly*. Her publications include *A Forgotten Offensive: Royal Air Force Coastal Command's Anti-Shipping Campaign, 1940–45*, and other publications on current aerospace subjects, intelligence, and counterinsurgency warfare. Her latest book deals with British Intervention in Greece, 1944–1945.

Camille Grand is director of the Fondation pour la Recherche Stratégique in Paris. He previously served as deputy director for disarmament and multilateral affairs in the Directorate for Strategic, Security and Disarmament Affairs of the French Ministry of Foreign Affairs and as the deputy diplomatic advisor to the French Minister of Defence. Grand also teaches graduate courses in international and security affairs at Sciences Po Paris and at the École Nationale d'Administration. Among past teaching positions, he was an associate professor in security studies at the École Spéciale Militaire (Saint Cyr-Coëtquidan). His publications include several books and monographs and numerous papers in European and American journals on current strategic affairs primarily focused on nuclear policy, nonproliferation, and disarmament.

Deborah C. Kidwell is a U.S. Air Force historian who has been assigned to the Historical Studies Office at the Pentagon and the Flight Test Center at Edwards Air Force Base in California, and is now the command historian for the Air Force Office of Special Investigations at Quantico, Va. She has taught at the U.S. Army Command and General Staff College in Ft. Leavenworth, Kan., where she was an associate professor of military history, staff group advisor, and Master's Thesis Committee chair. Dr. Kidwell has completed a study of Army contractors on the battlefield, published by the Combat Studies Institute at Ft. Leavenworth, and served as a guest lecturer for the Baltic Defense College (NATO) in Tartu, Estonia.

Richard Oliver Mayne is the director of air history and heritage for the Royal Canadian Air Force and has authored, co-authored, or co-edited a number of books, chapters for edited volumes, and articles on various aspects of Canadian military history and defense issues. Prior to working as a historian for the RCAF, Dr. Mayne was employed as a defense analyst with the Chief of Force Development and as a historian with the Directorate of History and Heritage at National Defence Headquarters in Ottawa. His work at the former location focused on the future security and defense environment, while the latter position involved research and writing as a member of the teams responsible for Volumes 2 and 3 of the official history of the Royal Canadian Navy. Dr. Mayne also served for 17 years as a reserve officer in the Canadian Forces.

Karl P. Mueller is a senior political scientist at the RAND Corporation and associate director of the RAND Arroyo Center's Strategy, Doctrine, and Resources Program. Dr. Mueller is also an adjunct professor at Johns Hopkins University and at Georgetown University's Walsh School of Foreign Service. His research focuses on military and national security strategy, particularly coercion, deterrence, and airpower, but has also extended to a wide variety of other subjects including defense planning, nuclear proliferation, economic sanctions, counterterrorism strategy, and space weapons. Among his RAND publications are *Striking First: Preemptive and Preventive Attack in U.S. National Security Policy* (2006); *Dangerous Thresholds: Managing Escalation in the 21st Century* (2008), and *Denying Flight: Strategic Options for Employing No-Fly Zones* (2013). Before joining RAND in 2001, Dr. Mueller taught at the University of Michigan and at the U.S. Air Force's School of Advanced Air and Space Studies (SAASS).

Bruce Nardulli is a senior political scientist with more than 25 years of experience at the RAND Corporation. Beginning in 2007 he spent over four years first as a senior researcher and then as director of the RAND-Qatar Policy Institute (RQPI) in Doha, Qatar. Prior to his RQPI assignment, Dr. Nardulli led defense and security projects for the RAND Arroyo Center, RAND Project AIR FORCE, and the RAND National Security Research Division, as well as a major study for the Qatar Armed Forces on alternative security strategies and force structures for the QAF; his RAND publications include *Disjointed War: Military Operations in Kosovo, 1999.* He has also been a visiting professor at the U.S. Naval War College, where he taught courses on defense planning and management.

Robert C. Owen is a professor in the Department of Aeronautical Science at Embry-Riddle Aeronautical University, Daytona Beach. He joined the Embry-Riddle faculty in 2002, following a 28-year career with the United States Air Force that included a mix of operational, staff, and advanced education assignments. Dr. Owen was rated as an Air Force command pilot, holds a civilian commercial license, and has logged over 4,000 hours as a pilot. He served on the HQ Air Force Staff and the HQ Staff of the Air Mobility Command, while his academic assignments included tours as an assistant professor of history at the U.S. Air Force Academy and as dean of the USAF's School of Advanced Airpower Studies, the service's graduate school for strategic planners. He has published numerous articles on air power history, strategy, and force structuring; his books include the *Chronology* volume of the *Gulf War Air Power Survey* (1995), *Deliberate Force: A Case Study in Effective Air Campaigning* (2000), and *Air Mobility: A Brief History of the American Experience* (2013).

Frederic Wehrey is a senior associate in the Middle East Program at the Carnegie Endowment for International Peace. His research focuses on political reform and security issues in the Arab Gulf states, Libya, and U.S. policy in the Middle East more broadly. Prior to joining Carnegie in 2012, he was a senior policy analyst at the RAND Corporation for seven years, where he was the lead author of monographs on Iran's Revolutionary Guards, Saudi-Iranian relations, and the impact of the Iraq War on the Middle East. Wehrey is also a lieutenant colonel in the U.S. Air Force Reserve and has completed tours in Iraq, Turkey, Uganda, and Libya prior to the 2011 revolution.

Bibliography

"22nd MEU to Return This Week," *The Daily News*, Jacksonville, N.C., February 2, 2012.

Abbas, Mohammed, "Libya Rebels Reach to Qatar for Banking Lifeline," *Reuters*, May 19, 2011. As of July 18, 2014:
http://www.reuters.com/article/2011/05/19/us-libya-qatar-idUSTRE74I5ZT20110519

Ackerman, Bruce, "Obama's Unconstitutional War," *Foreign Policy*, March 24, 2011. As of July 18, 2014:
http://www.foreignpolicy.com/articles/2011/03/24/obama_s_unconstitutional_war?

Adly, Farid, *La rivoluzione libica*, Milan: Il Saggiatore, 2012.

Aeronautica Militare, "The Italian Air Force in Operations Odyssey Dawn and Unified Protector," undated. As of July 18, 2014:
http://www.aeronautica.difesa.it/News/Documents/pdf/Cerimonia%20chiusura%20Unified%20Protector_151211/Brochure%20Libya%20EN.pdf

———, "Libya (2011): 'Odyssey Dawn' and 'Unified Protector' Operations," undated. As of July 18, 2014:
http://www.aeronautica.difesa.it/Operazioni/Internazionali/Pagine/Libia%282011%29_eng.aspx

Agresti, Francesco Saverio, "Potere aereo e strategia nell'era della 'Guerra al Terrore' . . . e oltre," *Rivista Aeronautica*, April 2011, p. 11.

Air Force Historical Research Agency, "Air Force Targeting Center (ACC)," online fact sheet, posted January 15, 2010. As of July 18, 2014:
http://www.afhra.af.mil/factsheets/factsheet.asp?id=16203

———, "363 Flying Training Group (ACC)," online fact sheet, posted November 29, 2010. As of July 18, 2014:
http://www.afhra.af.mil/factsheets/factsheet.asp?id=17565

Air Force Space Command, "Space Command TacSat 3 burns up in atmosphere," Peterson Air Force Base, Col.: AFSPC Public Affairs, posted May 5, 2012. As of July 18, 2014:
http://www.vandenberg.af.mil/news/story.asp?id=123300451

Air Mobility Command Office of Public Affairs, "'Calico' Wing Serves as Representation of Total Force Team Supporting Worldwide Operations," April 15, 2011. As of July 18, 2014:
http://www.amc.af.mil/news/story.asp?id=123251896

Alegi, Gregory, "Nei cieli della Libia. Colonialismo e i primi impieghi bellici dell'aeroplano," in R. H. Rainero and P. Alberini, eds., *Le forze armate e la nazione Italiana (1861–1914)*, Rome: CISM, 2003, pp. 247–263.

————, "A.M.: L'organismo è allo stremo. Ora è urgente ripristinare le funzioni vitali," Dedalonews. it, April 28, 2006. As of July 18, 2014:
http://www.dedalonews.it/it/index.php/04/2006/
am-lorganismo-e-allo-stremo-ora-e-urgente-ripristinare-le-funzioni-vitali/

————, "L'influenza della storia sul potere aereo," *Rivista Aeronautica*, No. 5, 2009, pp. 168–175.

————, "I tagli al bilancio metteranno l'aeronautica a terra nel 2010? Gli Scenari preoccupanti emersi dal seminario CESMA," *Dedalonews.it*, March 29, 2009. As of July 18, 2014:
http://www.dedalonews.it/it/index.php/03/2009/i-tagli-al-bilancio-metteranno-laeronautica-a-terra-nel-2010-gli-scenari-preoccupanti-emersi-dal-seminario-cesma/

————, "Libia verso ingresso in finmeccanica?" *Dedalonews.it*, July 5, 2009. As of July 18, 2014:
http://www.dedalonews.it/it/index.php/07/2009/libia-verso-ingresso-in-finmeccanica/

————, "Abrate subentra a camporini al vertice della difesa. In Afghanistan un soldato viene ucciso e uno ferito," Dedalonews.it, January 18, 2011. As of July 18, 2014:
http://www.dedalonews.it/it/index.php/01/2011/abrate-subentra-a-camporini-al-vertice-della-difesa-intanto-in-afghanistan-un-soldato-viene-ucciso-e-uno-ferito/

————, "Finmeccanica: La Libia detiene il 2%," *Dedalonews.it*, January 22, 2011. As of July 18, 2014:
http://www.dedalonews.it/it/index.php/01/2011/finmeccanica-la-libia-detiene-il-2/

————, "Gen. Tricarico: In Libia centrale il potere aereo. Le polemiche su trapani danneggiano le aspirazioni di altri aeroporti," *Dedalonenews.it*, May 4, 2011. As of July 18, 2014:
http://www.dedalonews.it/it/index.php/04/2011/gen-tricarico-in-libia-centrale-il-potere-aereo-le-polemiche-su-trapani-danneggiano-le-aspirazioni-di-altri-aeroporti/

————, "KC-767 ufficialmente in servizio con l'aeronautica militare," *Dedalonews.it*, May 17, 2011. As of July 18, 2014:
http://www.dedalonews.it/it/index.php/05/2011/
kc-767-ufficialmente-in-servizio-con-laeronautica-militare/

————, "Libia: C-130 italiano lancia volantini su Tripoli," *Dedalonews.it*, May 17, 2011. As of July 18, 2014:
http://www.dedalonews.it/it/index.php/05/2011/libia-c-130-italiano-lancia-volantini-su-tripoli/

————, "La Russa a Parigi: 'Nessun Taglio sugli investimenti della Difesa, manutenzione in sofferenza,'" *Dedalonews.it*, June 20, 2011. As of July 18, 2014:
http://www.dedalonews.it/it/index.php/06/2011/
la-russa-a-parigi-nessun-taglio-sugli-investimenti-della-difesa-manutenzione-in-sofferenza/

————, *La grande storia dell'aeronautica militare*, Milan: Fabbri, 2012, p. 698.

————, "Finmeccanica: Contratti con Israele per 850 mln di dollari, compresi i 30 M-346," *Dedalonews.it*, July 19, 2012. As of July 18, 2014:
http://www.dedalonews.it/it/index.php/07/2012/
finmeccanica-contratti-con-israele-per-850-mln-di-dollari-compresi-i-30-m-346/

————, "I Predator italiani debuttano nei cieli della Libia," *Dedalonews.it*, August 12, 2011. As of July 18, 2014:
http://www.dedalonews.it/it/index.php/08/2011/i-predator-italiani-debuttano-nei-cieli-della-libia/

Amato, Rosario, "Muti dirige Nabucco per i 150 anni dell'Unità Leo Nucci: 'Un inno alla Patria e alla libertà,'" *la Repubblica ROMA.it*, March 10, 2011. As of July 18, 2014:
http://roma.repubblica.it/cronaca/2011/03/10/news/nabucco_per_i_150_anni_dell_unit-13421243/

Amnesty International, *Libya: The Forgotten Victims of NATO Strikes*, March 19, 2012. As of July 18, 2014:
http://www.unhcr.org/refworld/docid/4f68451e2.html

Anderson, Lisa, "Demystifying the Arab Spring: Parsing the Differences Between Tunisia, Egypt, and Libya," *Foreign Affairs*, May/June 2011, pp. 2–7.

Andres, Richard B., Craig Wills, and Thomas Griffith Jr., "Winning with Allies: The Strategic Value of the Afghan Model," *International Security,* Vol. 30, No. 3, Winter 2005/06, pp. 124–160.

Anrig, Christian F., "Allied Air Power over Libya: A Preliminary Assessment," *Air and Space Power Journal*, Vol. XXV, No. 4, Winter 2011, pp. 89–109.

———, *The Quest for Relevant Air Power: Continental European Responses to the Air Power Challenges of the Post–Cold War Era*, Maxwell Air Force Base, Ala.: Air University Press, 2011.

Apps, Peter, and William Maclean, "Factbox: Libya's Military: What Does Gaddafi Have Left?" *Reuters*, March 1, 2011. As of July 18, 2014:
http://www.reuters.com/article/2011/03/01/us-libya-military-idUSTRE72027E20110301

Arpino, Gen. S. A. Mario, "L'Aeronautica Militare alle soglie del terzo millennio. Uno sguardo al future," lecture at the Centro Alti Studi Difesa, Rome, June 19, 1998.

———, "L'Italia Nelle Operazioni in Libia," *AffarInternazionali*, December 6, 2011. As of July 18, 2014:
http://www.affarinternazionali.it/articolo.asp?ID=1925

"Artikel 100: Handhaving of Bevordering Internationale Rechtsorde" [Article 100: Maintain or Advance International Legal Order], *Nederlandse Grondwet [Netherlands Constitution]*, 2008. As of July 18, 2014:
http://www.denederlandsegrondwet.nl/9353000/1/j9vvihlf299q0sr/vgrndcq2d9zm

Aruffo, Alessandro, *Qaddafi. Storia di una dittatura rivoluzionaria*, Urbino: Catelvecchi, 2011

"At Least 30,000 Killed, 50,000 Wounded in Libyan Conflict," *The Tripoli Post*, September 8, 2011. As of July 18, 2014:
http://www.tripolipost.com/articledetail.asp?c=1&i=6862&archive=1

Atha, Stuart, "Libyan Operations: A Defence Perspective," transcript, The Annual Defence Lecture 2011, London: Chatham House, September 28, 2011.

Auestad, Gunn Evy, "Held Tett om Norsk Role i Drapet på Gaddafi-Son" [Stays Silent on the Norwegian Role in the Killing of Gaddafi's Son], NRK [Norwegian Broadcasting Corporation], May 1, 2011. As of July 18, 2014:
http://www.nrk.no/nyheter/verden/1.7614348

Axe, David, "Two Bombers, 24 Hours, 100 Libyan Targets Destroyed," *Wired Danger Room*, July 13, 2011. As of July 18, 2014:
http://www.wired.com/2011/07/two-bombers-24-hours-100-libyan-targets-destroyed-ready/

Axworthy, Lloyd, and Allan Rock, "World Leaders Must Call R2P What It Is," *Ottawa Citizen*, March 2, 2011. As of July 18, 2014:
http://www2.canada.com/ottawacitizen/story.html?id=5d060bc4-fa80-4274-b639-edc1a71faf8f&p=2

"B-2 Bombers from Missouri Hit Libyan Targets," NPR Morning Edition, March 21, 2011, As of July 18, 2014:
http://www.npr.org/2011/03/21/134726240/No-Fly-Zone-Enforcer

Baastiens, Pieter, "Going Dutch," *Air Forces Monthly*, No. 287, February 2012, pp. 76–84.

Babin, Chance (Master Sgt., USAF) "AFCENT Stands Up Air Warfare Center," 380th Air Expeditionary Wing Office of Public Affairs, August 11, 2011. As of July 18, 2014 (no longer working):
http://www.380aew.afcent.af.mil/news/story.asp?id=123267671

Baldwin, Major Paul D., "That's a Wrap for 603rd AOC in 2011," USAFE–AFAFRICA: 3rd Air Force Public Affairs, January 3, 2012. As of July 18, 2014:
http://www.usafe.af.mil/news/story.asp?id=123284919

Baron, Kevin, "For the U.S., War Against Qaddafi Cost Relatively Little: $1.1 Billion," *The Atlantic* online, October 21, 2011. As of July 18, 2014:
http://www.theatlantic.com/international/archive/2011/10/
for-the-us-war-against-qaddafi-cost-relatively-little-11-billion/247133/

Batacchi, Pietro, "Il Futuro della Royal Navy," *Rivista Marittima*, October 2011.

"Battle for Libya: Key Moments," *Aljazeera.com*, August 23, 2011. As of July 18, 2014:
http://www.aljazeera.com/indepth/spotlight/libya/2011/08/20118219127303432.html

Baughn, Tom, "U.S. Marine Corps Operations During Libya Crisis," unpublished manuscript, February 3, 2012.

Beaumont, Peter, "Qatar Accused of Interfering in Libyan Affairs," *The Guardian*, October 4, 2011.

Beaumont, Peter, and Chris Stephen, "Gaddafi's Last Words as He Begged for Mercy: 'What Did I Do to You?'" *The Guardian*, October 22, 2011. As of July 18, 2014:
http://www.guardian.co.uk/world/2011/oct/23/gaddafi-last-words-begged-mercy

"Belgium Swears in New Government Headed by Elio di Rupo," *BBC News Europe*, online, December 6, 2011. As of July 18, 2014:
http://www.bbc.co.uk/news/world-europe-16042750

Benigh, Love, and Örjan Magnusson, "Nato Har Frågat Sverige om Jas-Plan till Libyen" [NATO Has Asked Sweden for JAS Aircraft to Libya], *SVT.SE*, March 28, 2011. As of July 18, 2014:
http://www.svt.se/nyheter/varlden/nato-har-fragat-sverige-om-jas-plan-till-libyen-1

Bensahel, Nora, Olga Oliker, Keith Crane, Richard R. Brennan Jr., Heather S. Gregg, Thomas Sullivan, and Andrew Rathmell, *After Saddam: Prewar Planning and the Occupation of Iraq*, Santa Monica, Calif.: RAND Corporation, MG-642-A, 2008. As of July 18, 2014:
http://www.rand.org/pubs/monographs/MG642.html

Bertoli, Lt. Col. Marco, "Appunti di Viaggio," *Rivista Aeronautica*, February 2011, pp. 26–29.

"Betreft Besluit Verlenging Nederlandse Inzet NAVO Mandaat Operatie Unified Protector" [Relating to the Decision of Extending the Netherlands Mission Within the Framework of NATO Operation Unified Protector], letter by the Minister of Foreign Affairs Dr. U. Rosenthal to the Chairman of the House of Representatives, The Hague: September 22, 2011.

"Betreft Kennisgevingsbrief Over Uitvoering Veiligheidsraad Resolutie 1973 Inzake Libië" [Letter of Information Relating to the Implementation of Security Council Resolution 1973 Concerning Libya] by the Minister of Foreign Affairs Dr. U. Rosenthal and the Minister of Defense J.S.J. Hillen to the Chairman of the Senate, The Hague: March 18, 2011.

"Betreft Nederlandse Bijdrage aan Uitvoering VN Veiligheidsraad Resolutie 1973 Inzake Libië" [Letter of Information Relating to a Netherlands Contribution to the Implementation of Security Council Resolution 1973 Concerning Libya], by the Minister of Foreign Affairs, Dr. U. Rosenthal, and the Minister of Defense, J.S.J. Hillen, to the Chairman of the Senate, The Hague: March 22, 2011.

"Betreft Uw Verzoek Inzake Nederlandse Bijdrage aan Uitvoering VN Veiligheidsraad Resolutie 1973—Libië" [Relating to Your Request for a Netherlands Contribution to the Implementation of Security Council Resolution 1973—Libya], letter by the Minister of Foreign Affairs, Dr. U. Rosenthal, and the Minister of Defense, J.S.J. Hillen, to the Chairman of the House of Representatives, The Hague: March 31, 2011.

"Betreft Verlenging van de Nederlandse Bijdrage aan Operatie Unified Protector—Libië" [Relating to the Extension of the Netherlands Contribution to Operation Unified Protector Concerning Libya], letter by the Minister of Foreign Affairs Dr. U. Rosenthal and the Minister of Defense J.S.J. Hillen to the Chairman of the House of Representatives and the Chairman of the Senate, The Hague: June 10, 2011.

Biagini, Antonello, ed., *C'era una Volta la Libia: 1911–2011. Storia e Cronaca,* Torino: Miraggi, 2011

Biddle, Stephen, "The Libya Dilemma: The Limits of Air Power," *Washington Post*, March 25, 2011.

Bildt, Carl, "Hem från London" [Home from London], online (author's translation), March 29, 2011. As of July 18, 2014:
http://carlbildt.wordpress.com/2011/03/29/8446/

Biscop, Sven, "Belgian Defence Policy: The Fight Goes On," December 2011. As of July 18, 2014:
http://www.egmontinstitute.be/publication_article/belgian-defence-policy-the-fight-goes-on/

Black, Dean, "Lieutenant General Charles Bouchard, Three Tenets of Allied Air Power Operations," *Air Force Magazine*, Vol. 35, No. 4, 2012.

Black, Ian, "Libyan Rebels Receiving Anti-Tank Weapons from Qatar," *The Guardian*, April 14, 2011a. As of July 18, 2014:
http://www.guardian.co.uk/world/2011/apr/14/libya-rebels-weapons-qatar

———, "Qatar Admits Sending Hundreds of Troops to Support Libya Rebels," *The Guardian*, October 26, 2011b. As of July 18, 2014:
http://www.guardian.co.uk/world/2011/oct/26/qatar-troops-libya-rebels-support

Black, Ian, and Owen Bowcott, "Libya Protests: Massacres Reported as Gaddafi Imposes News Blackout," *The Guardian*, online, February 18, 2011. As of July 18, 2014:
http://www.guardian.co.uk/world/2011/feb/18/libya-protests-massacres-reported

Black, Ian, and Ewen MacAskill, "US Threatens NATO Boycott over Belgian War Crimes Law," *The Guardian*, June 13, 2003. As of July 18, 2014:
http://www.guardian.co.uk/world/2003/jun/13/nato.warcrimes

Black, Ian, and Chris Stephen, "Libya: Gaddafi Son Spotted in Bani Walid as Heavy Fighting Continues," *The Guardian*, September 19, 2011. As of July 18, 2014:
http://www.guardian.co.uk/world/2011/sep/19/gaddafi-son-spotted-bani-walid

Blackwell, Tom, "Canada May Take on Large Share of Libya Mission," *The National Post*, March 21, 2011. As of July 18, 2014:
http://www.cdfai.org/PDF/Canada%20may%20take%20on%20large%20share%20of%20Libya%20mission.pdf

———, "Canada Contributed a Disproportionate Amount to Libya Air Strikes: Sources," *The National Post*, August 25, 2011. As of July 18, 2014:
http://news.nationalpost.com/2011/08/25/canada-contributed-a-disproportionate-amount-to-libya-air-strikes-sources/

Blanchard, Christopher M., *Libya: Unrest and U.S. Policy*, Washington, D.C.: Congressional Research Service, July 6, 2011. As of July 18, 2014
http://fpc.state.gov/documents/organization/169000.pdf

Blondin, Major General Yvan, Commander 1, Canadian Air Division, "Assisting Canadians—Making History!" *Prairie Flyer II*, Spring 2011.

Boeing, "767 Airplane Characteristics for Airport Planning," September 2005. As of July 18, 2014 (no longer working):
http://www.boeing.com/commercial/airports/767.htm

———, "Boeing Delivers Qatar's 1st C-17 Globemaster III," Boeing news release, August 11, 2009. As of July 18, 2014:
http://boeing.mediaroom.com/index.php?s=43&item=787

———, "Boeing, Qatar Emiri Air Force Laud C-17 Fleet's Achievements," Boeing news release, Doha, Qatar, March 15, 2010. As of July 18, 2014:
http://boeing.mediaroom.com/index.php?s=43&item=1117

"Boeing Delivers Second C-17 to Qatar," *Aerospace Daily & Defense Report*, September 14, 2009, p. 13.

Bolme Kühn, Kristina, and Johan Mast, "Dags att ta Ansvar" [Time to Take Responsibility], *Medecins San Frontieres*, May 19, 2011.

Bombeau, Bernard, "Afghanistan et Libye, l'arme Aérienne au Coeur des Combats," *Air & Cosmos*, No. 2270, June 17, 2011.

Booth, William, "Abdul Fattah Younis, Libyan Rebel Military Commander, Is Killed," *Washington Post*, July 28, 2011. As of July 18, 2014:
http://www.washingtonpost.com/world/middle-east/abdul-fattah-younis-libyan-rebel-military-commander-is-killed/2011/07/28/gIQASWDyfI_story.html

Booth, William, and William Wam, "United States Recognizes Libyan Rebels as Legitimate Government," *Washington Post*, July 15, 2011. As of July 18, 2014:
http://www.washingtonpost.com/world/middle-east/western-arab-leaders-meet-in-turkey-on-libyas-future/2011/07/15/gIQAZLbjFI_story.html

Borghard, Erica D., and Costantino Pischedda, "Allies and Airpower in Libya," *Parameters*, Spring 2012, pp. 63–74.

Bouchard, Charles (Lieutenant-General, Royal Canadian Air Force), "Coalition Building and the Future of NATO Operations: 2/14/2012—Transcript," remarks presented at Atlantic Council of the United States, Washington, D.C., February 14, 2012. As of July 18, 2014:
http://www.atlanticcouncil.org/news/transcripts/coalition-building-and-the-future-of-nato-operations-2-14-2012-transcript

Boyd, Henry, "Operation Unified Protector—Allied Assets Deployed to Libya," *IISS Voices*, undated. As of July 18, 2014:
http://archive.today/cKiH

Boyes, Roger, "Hesitant Obama Made Up His Mind Thanks to European Resolve," *The Times*, March 18, 2011, p. 7.

Branigin, William, Cody Edward, and Greg Jaffe, "McCain Visits Benghazi; Libyan Rebels Welcome Armed Drone Aircraft," *Washington Post*, April 21, 2011. As of July 18, 2014:
http://www.washingtonpost.com/world/obama-authorizes-predator-drone-strikes-in-libya/2011/04/21/AFWELQKE_story.html

"Bred Majoritet för Libyeninsats" [Broad Majority for Libyan Operation], *Svenska Dagbladet*, April 1, 2011. As of July 18, 2014:
http://www.svd.se/nyheter/inrikes/bred-majoritet-for-libyeninsats_6057571.svd

Brewster, Murray, "More Canadians Flee Libya as Dutch Commandos Captured," *Toronto Star*, March 3, 2011. As of July 18, 2014:
http://www.thestar.com/news/canada/article/948547--more-canadians-flee-libya-as-dutch-commandos-captured

"Britain to Send Military Advisers to Libyan Rebels," *USA Today*, April 19th, 2011. As of July 18, 2014:
http://www.usatoday.com/news/world/2011-04-19-libya-nato.htm

Butler, W., "Operation Odyssey Dawn/Operation Unified Protector," USAFE History Office list, March 27, 2012.

Byman, Daniel L., and Matthew C. Waxman, "Kosovo and the Great Air Power Debate," *International Security*, Vol. 24, No. 4, Spring 2000, pp. 5–38.

Calabrese, Antonio, and Luca Ricci, "Winter Hide 2011," *Rivista Aeronautica*, February 2011.

Calabresi, Massimo, "Susan Rice: A Voice for Intervention," *Time*, March 24, 2011. As of July 19, 2014:
http://www.time.com/time/magazine/article/0,9171,2061224,00.html

"Cameron: UK Working on 'No-Fly Zone' Plan for Libya," *Bbc.co.uk*, February 28, 2011. As of July 19, 2014:
http://www.bbc.co.uk/news/uk-politics-12598674

Cameron, Alastair, "The Channel Axis: France, the UK and NATO," in Adrian Johnson and Saqeb Mueen, eds., *Short War, Long Shadow: The Political and Military Legacies of the 2011 Libya Campaign*, London: Royal United Services Institute (RUSI), Whitehall Report 112, 2012, pp. 15–24. As of July 19, 2014:
http://www.rusi.org/downloads/assets/WHR_1-12.pdf

Cameron, David, "Answers to Questions from Members of Parliament, British House of Commons," March 2, 2011. As of July 19, 2014:
http://www.parliamentlive.tv/Main/Player.aspx?meetingId=7731&st=12:01:14

Campbell, Clark, and Steven Chase, "Canada Girds for Substantial Military Role in North Africa," *Globe and Mail*, March 1, 2011. As of July 19, 2014:
http://m.theglobeandmail.com/news/politics/canada-girds-for-substantial-military-role-in-north-africa/article568963/?service=mobile

"Canada Joins Propaganda War Aimed at Gadhafi Forces," *CTVNews.ca*, July 29, 2011. As of July 19, 2014:
http://www.ctvnews.ca/canada-joins-propaganda-war-aimed-at-gadhafi-forces-1.677289

"Canada's Actions Speak Volumes: Role in Libya Gives Heft to United Nations' Words," *www2.canada.com*, March 24, 2011. As of July 19, 2014:
http://www2.canada.com/calgaryherald/news/theeditorialpage/story.html?id=be9287aa-894a-4e91-b0ac-4897792ccc84

"Canadian Jets Destroy Libyan Arms Depot," *Ottawa Citizen*, March 24, 2011. As of July 19, 2014:
http://www2.canada.com/ottawacitizen/news/story.html?id=c150ebbe-deca-4873-852e-1e8bdabf703d

"Canadian Pilots Abort Bombing over Risk to Civilians," *CTVnews.ca*, March 22, 2011. As of July 19, 2014:
http://www.ctvnews.ca/canadian-pilots-abort-bombing-over-risk-to-civilians-1.621929

"Canadian Pilots Cautious of Collateral Damage in Libya," *theglobalmail.com*, April 4, 2011. As of July 19, 2014:
http://www.theglobeandmail.com/news/world/
canadian-pilots-cautious-of-collateral-damage-in-libya/article575169/

"Canadian to Lead NATO's Libya Mission," *cbc.ca*, March 25, 2011. As of July 19, 2014:
http://www.cbc.ca/news/world/story/2011/03/25/libya-nato-mission.html

Capasso, Matteo, "La Crisi in Libia," in N. Pedde, K. Mezran, and V. Cassar, eds., *Panorama 2012*, Rome: GAN, 2011, pp. 75–82.

Carden, Michael J., "Mullen Says No-Fly Zone 'Effectively in Place,'" *American Forces Press Service*, March 20, 2011. As of July 19, 2014:
http://www.defense.gov/news/newsarticle.aspx?id=63231

Central Intelligence Agency, "Country Comparison: Military Expenditures," *The World Factbook*, online. As of July 19, 2014:
https://www.cia.gov/library/publications/the-world-factbook/rankorder/2034rank.html

———, *The World Factbook*, online. As of July 19, 2014:
https://www.cia.gov/library/publications/the-world-factbook/

Charbonneau, Louis, and Hamuda Hassan, "France Defends Arms Airlift to Libyan Rebels," *Reuters*, June 29, 2011. As of July 19, 2014:
http://www.reuters.com/article/2011/06/29/us-libya-idUSTRE7270JP20110629

Charter, David, and Tom Coghlan, "Dutch Confirm Afghan Troop Pullout Sparking Fears of Domino Effect," *The Times*, February 22, 2010. As of July 19, 2014:
http://www.khilafah.com/index.php/news-watch/
south-asia/8859-dutch-confirm-afghan-troop-pullout-sparking-fears-of-domino-effect

Chenard, Terrance, "Everyday HMCS Vancouver's Sea King Gets the Job Done," helis.com, October 19, 2011. As of January 28, 2015:
http://www.helis.com/database/news/ch124_lybia/

Chivers, C. J., "Taking Airport, Rebels in Libya Loosen Noose," *New York Times*, May 11, 2011, p. A.1.

Chivers, C. J., and Eric Schmitt, "In Strikes on Libya by NATO, an Unspoken Civilian Toll," *New York Times*, December 17, 2011.

Chivvis, Christopher S., *Toppling Qaddafi: Libya and the Limits of Liberal Intervention*, Cambridge: Cambridge University Press, 2014.

Chivvis, Christopher S., Keith Crane, Peter Mandaville, and Jeffrey Martini, *Libya's Post-Qaddafi Transition: The Nation-Building Challenge*, Santa Monica, Calif.: RAND Corporation, RR-129-SRF, 2012. As of July 19, 2014:
http://www.rand.org/pubs/research_reports/RR129.html

Clark, Campbell, and Steven Chase, "Canada Girds for Substantial Military Role in North Africa," *Globe and Mail*, March 1, 2011.

Clarke, Michael, "The Road to War," in Saqeb Mueen and Grant Turnbull, eds., *Accidental Heroes: Britain, France, and the Libya Operation*, an Interim RUSI Campaign Report, London: Royal United Services Institute, September 2011. As of July 19, 2014:
http://www.rusi.org/downloads/assets/RUSIInterimLibyaReport.pdf

————, "The Making of Britain's Libya Strategy," in Adrian Johnson and Saqeb Mueen, eds., *Short War, Long Shadow: The Political and Military Legacies of the 2011 Libya Campaign*, London: Royal United Services Institute (RUSI), Whitehall Report 1–12, 2012, pp. 7–13. As of July 19, 2014: http://www.rusi.org/downloads/assets/WHR_1-12.pdf

Clinton, Hillary Rodham, "Holding the Qadhafi Government Accountable," press statement, Washington, D.C.: U.S. Department of State, February 26, 2011. As of July 19, 2014: http://allafrica.com/stories/201102281558.html

Cloud, David S., "Region in Turmoil: U.S. Cutting Its Craft from Libya Sorties," *Los Angeles Times*, April 1, 2011.

Coates, Sam, "A Lonely War for Cameron . . . But Now He Knows His Comrades in Arms," *The Times*, September 10, 2011.

Cody, Edward, "France, Britain Want NATO to Fight Harder Against Qaddafi's Forces," *Washington Post*, April 12, 2011.

Cohen, Eliot, and Thomas A. Keaney, eds., *Gulf War Air Power Survey, Volume 5—A Statistical Compendium and Chronology*, Washington, D.C.: Government Printing Office, 1993.

Cohen, Tobi, "Canadian Jets Destroy Libyan Arms Depot," *Ottawa Citizen*, March 24, 2011.

"Col. Gaddafi Killed: Condoleezza Rice Recounts His 'Eerie Obsession' with Her," *telegraph.co.uk*, October 21, 2011. As of July 19, 2014: http://www.telegraph.co.uk/news/worldnews/africaandindianocean/libya/8840259/Col-Gaddafi-killed-Condoleezza-Rice-recounts-his-eerie-obsession-with-her.html

"Comunicazioni del Governo su Recenti Sviluppi della Situazione in Libia," *Camera.it*, April 27, 2012. As of July 19, 2014: http://documenti.camera.it/_dati/leg16/lavori/stencomm/0304c0304/audiz2/2011/0427/pdf001.pdf

"Congratulations to the Aviation Week Laureate Award Winners," *Aviation Week Events*, 2012. As of July 19, 2014: http://events.aviationweek.com/archive/2012/lau/index.htm

Consulate General of the United States, "U.S. Citizens Evacuated Libya," February 25, 2012. As of July 19, 2014: http://istanbul.usconsulate.gov/libya_evacuation3.html

Coolsaet, Rik, "Atlantic Loyalty, European Autonomy. Belgium and the Atlantic Alliance 1949–2009," *Egmont Paper*, No. 28, March 2009.

Cooper, Helene, and Steven Lee Meyers, "Obama Takes Hard Line with Libya After Shift by Clinton," *New York Times*, March 18, 2011. As of July 19, 2014: http://www.nytimes.com/2011/03/19/world/africa/19policy.html?_r=1

————, "Shift by Clinton Helped Persuade President to Take a Harder Line," *New York Times*, March 19, 2011. As of July 19, 2014: http://www.nytimes.com/2011/03/19/world/africa/19policy.html?pagewanted=all&_r=0

Cornacchini, Lt. Col. Alessandro, editorial, *Rivista Aeronautica*, No. 5, 2011, p. 2.

Corum, James S., and Wray R. Johnson, *Airpower in Small Wars*, Lawrence, Kan.: University of Kansas Press, 2003.

Cosci, Lt. Col. Stefano, "A Poggio Renatico, Centro di Comando e Controllo di 'UP'," *Rivista Aeronautica*, March 2011, p. 47.

————, "Sigonella: Missione support," *Rivista Aeronautica*, May 2011, p. 20.

———, "Missione conclusa," *Rivista Aeronautica*, June 2011. As of July 19, 2014: http://www.aeronautica.difesa.it/News/Documents/pdf/Cerimonia%20chiusura%20Unified%20 Protector_151211/Brochure%20Libya%20EN.pdf

Cosentino, Cfr. Michele C. V., "La Saga dell'aviazione Navale Britannica," *Rivista Marittima*, October 2011.

"Cost of Libya Operations," *Mod.uk*, December 8, 2011. As of July 19, 2014: http://www.mod.uk/DefenceInternet/DefenceNews/DefencePolicyAndBusiness/ CostOfLibyaOperations.htm

Cowan, Gerrard, "UK Boosts Libya Tornado Force," *Jane's Defence Weekly*, July 2011.

Cowell, Alan, and Ravi Somaiya, "France and Italy Will Also Send Advisers to Libya Rebels," *NYtimes.com*, April 20, 2011. As of July 19, 2014: http://www.nytimes.com/2011/04/21/world/africa/21libya.html?pagewanted=all

Cresti, Federico, and Massimiliano Cricco, *Qaddafi. I Volti del Potere*, Rome:, Carocci, 2011

———, *Storia della Libia Contemporanea: dal Dominio Ottomano alla Morte di Qaddafi,* Rome: Carocci, 2012

Cutler, David, "Timeline: Libya's Uprising Against Muammar Gaddafi," *Thomson Reuters*, August 22, 2011. As of July 19, 2014: http://www.reuters.com/article/2011/08/22/us-libya-events-idUSTRE77K2QH20110822

Daalder, Ivo, "Libya—A NATO Success Story," prepared remarks to the Atlantic Council of the United States, November 7, 2011. As of July 19, 2014: http://nato.usmission.gov/sp110711.html

Daalder, Ivo, and James G. Stavridis, "NATO's Victory in Libya," *Foreign Affairs*, Vol. 91, Issue 2, March/April 2012, pp. 2–7.

Dagher, Sam, Charles Levinson, and Margaret Coker, "Tiny Kingdom's Huge Role in Libya Draws Concern," *Wall Street Journal*, October 17, 2011. As of July 19, 2014: http://online.wsj.com/article/SB10001424052970204002304576627000922764650.html

Dahl, Ann-Sofie, "Sweden and NATO: More Than a Partner? Reflections Post-Libya," NATO Defence College Paper, June 2012.

Dallaire, Roméo, *Shake Hands with the Devil: The Failure of Humanity in Rwanda*, Toronto: Random House Canada, 2003.

Dalton, Sir Stephen, Gen. Jean-Paul Paloméros, and Gen. Norton Schwartz, "Libyan Air Ops Showcase French, UK, U.S. Partnership," *Jane's Defence Weekly*, March 21, 2012, p. 19.

"Danmark Bliver i Libyen Trods Norsk Exit" [Denmark Stays in Libya Despite Norway's Exit], *Avisen.dk*, June 10, 2011.

Danish Defence Agreement 2005–2009, preliminary translation, Copenhagen: Danish Ministry of Defence, June 2004.

Danish Defence Agreement 2010–2014, Copenhagen: Danish Ministry of Defence, June 24, 2009.

"Danish Fighter Jets Deployed to Libya," Copenhagen: Danish Ministry of Defence, news release, March 21, 2011. As of July 19, 2014: http://www.fmn.dk/eng/news/Pages/DanishfighterjetsdeployedtoLibya.aspx

Davidson, Amy, "Eighty-Nine Questions: What Did Libya Do for the CIA?" *New Yorker Online*, September 3, 2011. As of July 19, 2014: http://www.newyorker.com/online/blogs/closeread/2011/09/eighty-nine-questions-what-did-libya-do-for-the-cia.html

De Crem, Pieter, "Note d'Orientation Politique" [Note of Political Orientation], Brussels: Ministry of Defence, June 2008, pp. 13, 15.

"De Crem Geeft Beelden Bombardementen Vrij" [De Crem Releases Bombing Images for Publication], *De Standard*, March 30, 2011. As of July 19, 2014: http://www.standaard.be/artikel/detail.aspx?artikelid=DMF20110330_177

La Défense [Defence (Belgium)], "Aperçu Hebdomadaire des Opérations Extérieures" [Weekly Report on Deployed Operations], March 17, 2011–March 23, 2011.

———, March 24, 2011–March 30, 2011.

———, May 12, 2011–May 18, 2011.

———, October 6, 2011–October 12, 2011, p. 2.

———, October 27, 2011–November 2, 2011, p. 2.

La Défense [Defence (Belgium)], "Libye: Six F16 et un navire," March 25, 2011.

———, "Vols de Nuit pour Nos F-16 en Libye" [Night Flights by Our F-16s over Libya], May 19, 2011.

———, "Khadafi et son régime neutralisés," October 20, 2011. As of July 19, 2014: http://www.pieterdecrem.be/index.php?id=36&tx_ttnews[tt_news]=1810&cHash=a134328ac039083a86bcb488c3c29e33&L=1

"Defiant Gaddafi Vows to Die as Martyr, Fight Revolt," *Thomson Reuters*, February 22, 2011. As of July 19, 2014: http://www.reuters.com/article/2011/02/22/us-libya-protests-idUSTRE71G0A620110222

Department of Defense Instruction (DoDI) 3020.47, *DoD Participation in the National Exercise Program (NEP)*, January 29, 2009. As of July 19, 2014: http://www.dtic.mil/whs/directives/corres/pdf/302047p.pdf

"Des helicopters français participent aux frappes," *France2.fr*, June 4, 2011. As of July 19, 2014: http://french.irib.ir/info/iran-actualite/item/117730-libye-des-helicopteres-francais-ont-participe-aux-frappes-etat-major

Deschamps, Lieutenant General André, "An Update on the Royal Canadian Air Force," transcript, Senate Committee on National Security and Defence, February 27, 2012.

Desens, Colonel Mark, "Forward Deployed Marines," excerpts from 26th Marine Expeditionary Unit Post Deployment Brief, December 6, 2011.

Det Kongelige Forsvarsdepartement [The Royal Ministry of Defence (Norway)] *Et Forsvar for Vår Tid, Prop. 73 S (2011–2012): Proposisjon til Stortinget (Forslag til Stortingsvedtak)* [A Defense for Our Time: Proposition to Parliament (Proposal for a Parliamentary Decision)], Oslo: Ministry of Defence, March 23, 2012.

DeYoung, Karen, and Scott Wilson, "Coalition Nears Agreement on Transition for Operations in Libya," *Washington Post*, March 23, 2011, p. A09.

Di Marco, Col. Roberto, "'Odyssey Dawn' e 'Unified Protector': L'impiego del Potere Aerospaziale e delle capacità operative dell'Aeronautica Militare," *Rivista Aeronautica*, March 2011.

Dionne, Major Bernard, "1st Canadian Division HQ Personnel Return from Op Mobile," *The Maple Leaf*, June 22, 2011. As of July 19, 2014: publications.gc.ca/collections/collection_2011/dn-nd/D12-7-14-22.pdf

DoD—*See* United States Department of Defense.

"La dottrina dell'Aeronautica Militare," supplement to *Rivista Aeronautica*, No. 1, 1998.

Douhet, Giulio, "Riepilogando" (1929), reprinted in *Il dominio dell'aria e altri scritti*, Luciano Bozzo ed., Rome: Stato Maggiore Aeronautica/Ufficio Storico, 2002.

Dreger, Paul, "JSF Partnership Takes Shape: A Review of the JSF Participation by Australia, Canada, Denmark, Israel, Italy, the Netherlands, Norway, Singapore, Turkey and the UK," *Military Technology*, 27, No. 4, April 2003, p. 29.

Dunridge, Neil, "ELLAMY Enabler," *Air Forces Monthly*, January 2012, pp. 42–46.

Durante, Serafino, Luca Ricci, and Emanuele Salvati, "Nel 'Cuore' della Missione Italiana," *Rivista Aeronautica*, March 2011, pp. 20–21.

——, ". . . l'impegno continua . . . ," *Rivista Aeronautica,* May 2011.

Egnell, Robert, "Är vi Beredda På Att ta Ansvar för Libyens Framtid?" [Are We Ready to Take Responsibility for the Future of Sweden?], *Dagens Nyheter*, March 3, 2011. As of July 19, 2014: http://www.dn.se/debatt/ar-vi-beredda-pa-att-ta-ansvar-for-libyens-framtid

Egnell, Robert, and Claes Nilsson, "Svensk Civil-Militär Samverkan för Internationella Insatser: Från Löftesrika Koncept till Konkret Handling" [Swedish Civil-Military Cooperation in International Operations: From Concept to Action], KKrVA Handlingar Och Tidskrift, No 1, 2011.

Eide, Minister of Defense Espen Barth, "Innledning: Luftforsvarets Luftmaktseminar: Internasjonal Krisehåndtering under Og Etter Libya" [Introduction: Air Force Air Power Seminar: International Crisis Management During and After Libya], January 31, 2012. As of July 19, 2014: http://www.regjeringen.no/nb/dep/fd/aktuelt/taler_artikler/ministeren/taler-og-artikler-av-forsvarsminister-es/2012/internasjonal-krisehandtering-under-og-e.html?id=671003

End of Tour Report—Task Force Libeccio, November 7, 2010, 1630-1 (Comd TF LIB).

"The EU Battlegroup Concept and the Nordic Battlegroup," *Government Offices of Sweden*, January 8, 2008. As of July 19, 2014: http://www.sweden.gov.se/sb/d/9133/a/82276

"Events in Libya: A Chronology," *New York Times*, August 29, 2011. As of July 19, 2014: http://www.nytimes.com/2011/08/29/timestopics/libyatimeline.html?pagewanted=all

Ewing, Philip, "DoD Denies Reports Navy Shot Down Libyan Scuds," *DoD.BUZZ*, August 31, 2011. As of July 19, 2014: http://www.dodbuzz.com/2011/08/31/dod-denies-reports-navy-shot-down-libyan-scuds/

"Executive Order 13566, Executive Order Blocking Property and Prohibiting Certain Transactions Related to Libya," Washington, D.C.: The White House, February 25, 2011. As of July 19, 2014: http://www.whitehouse.gov/the-press-office/2011/02/25/executive-order-libya

"Factbox: Pentagon Says U.S. Stepped Up Pace of Libya Air Strikes," *Reuters*, August 22, 2011. As of July 19, 2014: http://www.reuters.com/article/2011/08/23/us-libya-usa-strikes-idUSTRE77L76C20110823

Fahim, Kareem, "Libya Rebels Threaten a Supply Line to the Capital," *New York Times*, August 15, 2011, p. A8.

————, "Refugees Flee Libya Oil City as Qaddafi's Forces Dig In," *New York Times*, August 18, 2011, p. A4.

————, "Libyan Rebels Gain Control of Key Oil Refinery as Qaddafi Forces Flee," *New York Times*, August 19, 2011, p. A6.

Fahim, Kareen, and David D. Kirkpatrick, "Qaddafi's Grip on the Capital Tightens as Revolt Grows," *New York Times*, February 23, 2011, p. A.1.

Fahrenthold, David A.,"Obama Misses Deadline for Congressional Approval of Libya Operations," *Washington Post*, May 20, 2011. As of July 19, 2014:
http://www.washingtonpost.com/politics/obama-likely-to-miss-deadline-for-congressional-approval-of-libya-operations/2011/05/19/AFFLKn7G_story.html

————, "House Rebukes Obama on Libya Mission, But Does Not Demand Withdrawal," *Washington Post*, June 3, 2011. As of July 19, 2014:
http://www.washingtonpost.com/politics/house-rebukes-obama-on-libya-mission-but-does-not-demand-withdrawal/2011/06/03/AGdrK8HH_story.html

Faremo, Minister of Defence Grete, "Fullmakt til Deltakelse Med Norske Militære Bidrag i Operasjoner til Gjennomføring av FNs Sikkerhetsrådsresolusjon 1973 (2011)" [Authorization for the Participation of a Norwegian Military Contribution in Operations for the Implementation of UN Security Council Resolution 1973 (2011)], *Kongelig Resolusjon [Royal Decree]*, March 23, 2011. As of July 19, 2014:
http://www.regjeringen.no/upload/FD/Temadokumenter/Libya-deltakelse_kgl-res-23-3-2011.pdf

Ferguson, Brian, "Defiant Gaddafi: I'll Die a Martyr," *The Scotsman*, 1st ed., February 23, 2011.

Flightglobal.com, "Dubai Air Show Special," Libyan Air Force, 2012.

FN-Förbundet, "Inställningen till FN Och Internationella Frågor Bland Gymnasieungdomar i Sverige" [Attitudes Toward the U.N. and International Questions Among High School Students in Sweden], undated. As of July 19, 2014:
http://www.fn.se/PageFiles/18620/Rapport%20ungdomar%20och%20FN.pdf

Fontaine, Scott, "B-1B Crew Recalls Epic Mission to Libya," *Air Force Times*, April 2, 2011. As of July 19, 2014:
http://www.airforcetimes.com/article/20110402/
NEWS/104020301/B-1B-crew-recalls-epic-mission-Libya

————, "Libya Causing Cuts in Training, Other Programs," *Air Force Times*, June 17, 2011. As ofJuly 19, 2014:
http://www.airforcetimes.com/news/2011/06/airforce-libya-causing-cuts-in-training-061711w/

Foreign Affairs, Trade and Development Office of Canada, "Statement by Minister Cannon on Situation in Libya," No. 72, February 19, 2011. As of March 13, 2013:
http://www.international.gc.ca/media/aff/news-communiques/2011/72.aspx

————, "Statement by Minister Cannon on Situation of Civil Unrest in Libya," No. 73, February 21, 2011. As of July 19, 2014:
http://www.international.gc.ca/media/aff/news-communiques/2011/073.aspx

————, "Ministerial Statement on Libya," No. 76, February 22, 2011. As of July 19, 2014:
http://www.international.gc.ca/media/aff/news-communiques/2011/076.aspx

————, "Statement by Minister Cannon on Current Situation in Libya," No. 85, February 26, 2011. As of July 19, 2014:
http://www.international.gc.ca/media/aff/news-communiques/2011/085.aspx

————, "Statement by Minister Cannon on Situation in Libya," No. 86, February 26, 2011.

Foreign Commonwealth Office, "Libya Contact Group: Chair's Statement," online at GOV.UK, April 13, 2011. As of July 19, 2014:
http://www.fco.gov.uk/en/news/latest-news/?id=583592582&view=News#

Forsvaret [Defence (Norway)], "Sluttrapport Libya" [Final Report on Libya Operations], December 2, 2011. As of July 19, 2014 (no longer working):
http://forsvaret.no/operasjoner/rapporter/sluttrapporter/Sider/Sluttrapport-Libya.aspx

Forsvarsdepartementet [Ministry of Defence (Norway)], "Norge Med i Nato-Ledet Våpenembargo" [Norway Participates in NATO-Led Arms Embargo], *Nyheter* [news], March 24, 2011.

———, "Kommandooverføring til Nato" [Transfer of Command to NATO], *Nyheter* [news], March 30, 2011. As of July 19, 2014:
http://www.regjeringen.no/nb/dep/fd/aktuelt/nyheter/2011/kommandooverforing-til-nato.html?id=637010

———, "Forsvarsministerens Redegjørelse for Stortinget 9. Mai" [Defence Minister's Statement to Parliament on May 9], *Artikkel [Article]*, May 9, 2011. As of July 19, 2014:
http://www.regjeringen.no/nb/dep/fd/aktuelt/taler_artikler/ministeren/taler-og-artikler-av-forsvarsminister-gr/2011/forsvarsministerens-redegjorelse-for-sto.html?id=642484

———, "Viderefører Kampflybidraget til 1. August" [Continuing the Fighter Jet Contribution Til August 1], *Pressemelding* [press release], June 10, 2011. As of July 19, 2014:
http://www.regjeringen.no/nb/dep/fd/pressesenter/pressemeldinger/2011/fortsetter-med-fire-kampfly-i-libya-oper.html?id=647279

———, "Libya-Operasjonen: Billigere enn Forventet" [Libya Operations: Cheaper Than Expected], *Nyheter* [news], January 23, 2012. As of July 19, 2014:
http://www.regjeringen.no/nb/dep/fd/aktuelt/nyheter/2012/libya-operasjonen-billigere-enn-forvente.html?id=670331

Freedman, Lawrence, "Can the EU Develop an Effective Military Doctrine?" in Steven Everts, Lawrence Freedman, Charles Grant, François Heisbourg, Daniel Keohane and Michael O'Hanlon, *A European Way of War*, London: Centre for European Reform, 2004. As of July 19, 2014:
http://www.cer.org.uk/sites/default/files/publications/attachments/pdf/2011/p548_way_ofwar-4464.pdf

"French Confirm Arms Drops to Libyan Rebels," *Agence France-Presse*, June 29, 2011. As of July 19, 2014:
http://www.defensenews.com/article/20110629/DEFSECT04/106290306/French-Confirm-Arms-Drops-Libyan-Rebels

French Embassy in Doha, "Political Relations Between France and Qatar," May 31, 2011.

"French Fighter Jets Fly over Country," *Radio France Internationale (Paris)*, March 19, 2011.

"French Jets Attack Gaddafi Targets," *Aljazeera.com*, March 19, 2011. As of July 19, 2014:
http://www.aljazeera.com/news/europe/2011/03/2011319132058782326.html

Frigerio, Silvano, "Targeting Lessons from Libyan Air Operations and the Impact on Future Requirements," presentation at the International Fighter Conference, London, November 9, 2011.

Furlanis, Ermanno, "Aviano, Oh-Ahio," *Limes*, No. 4, 1999, pp. 107–124.

Gabelic, Alexander, and Linda Nordin Thorslund, "Nu Måste Omvärlden Ingripa" [Now You Need the Outside World to Intervene], *SvD OPINION*, March 15, 2012. As of July 19, 2014:
http://www.svd.se/opinion/brannpunkt/nu-maste-omvarlden-ingripa_6925557.svd

"Gaddafi Vows Long War," *Bbc.co.uk*, March 21, 2011. As of July 19, 2014:
http://www.bbc.co.uk/news/world-africa-12798568

"Gadhafi's Guns Silenced," *Reuters, Postmedia News*, March 24, 2011. As of July 19, 2014:
http://www2.canada.com/saskatoonstarphoenix/news/world/story.
html?id=12509b23-2cf5-44bb-8193-48ded93f44bd

Gaiani, Gianandrea, "Ma quanto mi costi," *Volare*, June 2011, pp. 8–13.

———, "Uno sguardo alle lezioni apprese (e non) nel conflitto libico," *Rivista Marittima*, October 2011, p. 18.

El Gamal, Rania, and Tim Gaynor, "Gaddafi Killed as Libya's Revolt Claims Hometown," *Reuters*, October 20, 2011. As of July 19, 2014:
http://www.reuters.com/article/2011/10/20/ozatp-libya-idAFJOE79J09O20111020

Garamone, Jim, "Leaders Describe Path to Peace in Libya," *American Forces Press Service*, April 15, 2011. As of July 19, 2014:
http://www.defense.gov/news/newsarticle.aspx?id=63580

———, "Panetta, Dempsey Discuss Risks, Threats of the Future," January 26, 2012. As of July 19, 2014:
http://www.army.mil/article/72614/Panetta__Dempsey_Discuss_Risks__Threats_of_the_Future/

———, "Strategy Drove Budget Decisions, Dempsey Says," *American Forces Press Service*, March 29, 2012. As of July 19, 2014:
http://www.defense.gov/News/NewsArticle.aspx?ID=67759

Gardner, Dan, "Why No One's Talking About Libya on the Campaign Trail," *Ottawa Citizen*, April 1, 2011. As of July 19, 2014:
http://www2.canada.com/ottawacitizen/columnists/story.
html?id=8fdff196-211c-4c1a-b89c-eb1cba371e50

Gelie, Philippe, "La France a parachuté des armes aux rebelles Libyens," *Le Figaro*, June 28, 2011. As of July 19, 2014:
http://www.lefigaro.fr/international/2011/06/28/01003-20110628ARTFIG00704-la-france-a-parachute-des-armes-aux-rebelles-libyens.php

Gentile, Tony, "Canada's Role? Opportunity to Lead Regime Change," *The London Free Press*, March 26, 2011.

German Marshall Fund, *Trans-Atlantic Trends 2011: Topline Data July 2011*, Brussels, 2011. As of July 19, 2014:
http://www.gmfus.org/publications_/TT/TTS2011Toplines.pdf

Gertler, Jeremiah, *Operation Odyssey Dawn (Libya): Background and Issues for Congress*, Washington, D.C.: Congressional Research Service, CRS R41725, March 28, 2011. As of July 19, 2014:
http://www.unhcr.org/refworld/publisher,USCRS,,LBY,4d99b5e12,0.html

Goldstone, Jack, "Understanding the Revolutions of 2011: Weakness and Resilience in Middle Eastern Autocracies," *Foreign Affairs*, May/June 2011, pp. 8–16.

Governo Italiano, Presidenza del Consiglio dei Ministri, Consiglio dei Ministri n. 131 (press release), March 18, 2011. As of July 19, 2014:
http://www.governo.it/Governo/ConsiglioMinistri/dettaglio.asp?d=62854

Graff, Peter, "Gaddafi Defiant as NATO Intensifies Tripoli Strikes," *Reuters.com*, June 7, 2011. As of July 19, 2014:
http://www.reuters.com/article/2011/06/07/us-libya-idUSTRE7270JP20110607

Gravemaker, Anno, "Dutch Air Force Hit by Spending Cuts," *Flight International*, April 11, 2011. As of July 19, 2014:
http://www.flightglobal.com/news/articles/dutch-air-force-hit-by-spending-cuts-355397/

Greenleaf, Jason R., "The Air War in Libya," *Air & Space Power Journal*, Vol. 27, No. 2 (2013), pp. 28–54.

Gros, Philippe, "De Odyssey Dawn à Unified Protector: Bilan transitoire, perspectives et premiers enseignements de l'engagement en Libye," Paris: Fondation pour la Recherche Stratégique, Note No. 04/11, April 2011. As of July 19, 2014:
http://www.frstrategie.org/barreFRS/publications/notes/2011/201104.pdf

Harding, Russell, "NATO Determined to Protect the People of Libya," text of speech delivered at press conference in Naples, April 6, 2011. As of July 19, 2014:
http://www.jfcnaples.nato.int/page16750104.aspx

Harding, Thomas, "Libya: SAS Leads Hunt for Gaddafi," *The Daily Telegraph*, August 24, 2011. As of July 19, 2014:
http://www.telegraph.co.uk/news/worldnews/africaandindianocean/libya/8721291/Libya-SAS-leads-hunt-for-Gaddafi.html

Hastings, Michael, "Inside Obama's War Room," *Rolling Stone*, October 13, 2011. As of July 19, 2014:
http://www.rollingstone.com/politics/news/inside-obamas-war-room-20111013

Haynes, Deborah, "Denmark's Tøp Guns Trump RAF in Libya," *The Times*, September 29, 2011, p. 13.

Haynes, Deborah, and Laura Pitel, "Britain's First Plane Touches Down Long After Others Have Fled Tripoli; Oilmen Stranded in the Libyan Desert Are the Big Problem Now," *The Times (London)*, February 24, 2011.

Hazaimeh, Hani, "Jordan Not Participating in No-Fly Zone," *Jordan Times*, March 20, 2011. As of July 19, 2014 (no longer working):
http://www.zawya.com/story/ZAWYA20110320043852/

Hazou, Elias, "Qatari Warplanes Refuel in Cyprus," *Cyprus Mail*, March 23, 2011. As of July 19, 2014 (no longer working):
http://www.parikia.co.uk/daily-news/cyprus-news/cyprus-news-in-english/14299-qatari-warplanes-refuel-in-cyprus.html

Headquarters United States Air Forces in Europe and 3 AF Lessons Learned (HQ USAFE/A9AL & 3 AF/A9O), *Operation ODYSSEY DAWN: Lessons Learned from a USAFE Perspective*, Ramstein Air Base, Germany: HQ USAFE, December 8, 2011, not available to the general public.

Headquarters United States Air Forces in Europe/Office of History, *The United States Air Forces in Europe in Operation Odyssey Dawn*, Ramstein Air Base, Germany: HQ USAFE/HO, February 28, 2012, not available to the general public.

Heertum, Serge Van, and Marc Arys, *F-16 Fighting Falcon: 30 Years in Action with the Belgian Air Force*, Brussels: Belgian Defence Composair IPR, 2009.

Hehs, Eric, "FWIT 2010," *Code One*, August 20, 2010. As of July 19, 2014:
http://www.codeonemagazine.com/article.html?item_id=51

Heilbrunn, Jacob, "Samantha and Her Subjects," *The National Interest*, April 19, 2011. As of July 19, 2014:
http://nationalinterest.org/article/samantha-her-subjects-5161

Heinbecker, Paul, *Getting Back in the Game: A Foreign Policy Playbook for Canada*, Toronto: Dundurn Press, 2011.

"Des Helicopters Français Participent aux Frappes," *France2.fr*, June 4, 2011. As of July 19, 2014: http://french.irib.ir/info/iran-actualite/item/117730-libye-des-helicopteres-francais-ont-participe-aux-frappes-etat-major

Hennessy-Fiske, Molly, "Libya: Arab League Suspends Libyan Membership," *Los Angeles Times*, February 22, 2011. As of July 19, 2014: http://latimesblogs.latimes.com/babylonbeyond/2011/02/libya-arab-lcaguc-suspends libyan-membership.html

Her Majesty's Government, *A Strong Britain in an Age of Uncertainty: The National Security Strategy*, London: The Stationery Office, CM7953, October 2010. As of July 19, 2014: https://www.gov.uk/government/publications/the-national-security-strategy-a-strong-britain-in-an-age-of-uncertainty

Higgs, Major Andra, "Maintainers 'Dance' Ensured NATO Success for OUP," 313th AEW Air Expeditionary Group, January 3, 2012. As of July 19, 2014: http://www.amc.af.mil/news/story.asp?id=123284979

Hill, Matthew P., "Operation Unified Protector," EUCOM briefing, November 2, 2011.

Hoedeman, Jan, and Theo Koelé, "Nederlands Helikopterfiasco in Libië: Wie Is de Schuldige?" [Dutch Helicopter Fiasco in Libya: Who Is Guilty?], *De Volkskrant*, March 21, 2011. As of July 19, 2014: http://www.volkskrant.nl/vk/nl/5444/VK-Dossier-De-opstand-in-Libie/article/detail/1862744/2011/03/21/Nederlands-helikopterfiasco-in-Libie-wie-is-de-schuldige.dhtml

Hoedeman, Jan, and Raoul du Pré, "Hillen Mixt een Fatale Cocktail" [Hillen Mixes a Fatal Cocktail], *De Volkskrant*, March 26, 2011. As of July 19, 2014: http://www.volkskrant.nl/vk/nl/5444/VK-Dossier-De-opstand-in-Libie/article/detail/1865376/2011/03/26/Hillen-mixt-een-fatale-cocktail.dhtml

Holcomb, Larry, Gregory K. James, and Chad T. Manske, "Joint Task Force Odyssey Dawn: A Model for Joint Experience, Training, and Education," *Joint Force Quarterly*, January 2012. As of July 19, 2014: http://www.cfr.org/libya/joint-task-force-odyssey-dawn-model-joint-experience-training-education/p27105

Hooper, John, and Ian Black, "Libya: Defections: Pilots Were 'Told to Bomb Protesters,'" *The Guardian*, February 21, 2011. As of July 19, 2014: http://www.guardian.co.uk/world/2011/feb/21/libya-pilots-flee-to-malta

Hosmer, Stephen T., *The Conflict over Kosovo: Why Milosevic Decided to Settle When He Did*, Santa Monica, Calif.: RAND Corporation, MR-1351-AF, 2001. As of July 19, 2014: http://www.rand.org/pubs/monograph_reports/MR1351.html

House of Commons Defence Committee, *The Strategic Defence and Security Review and the National Security Strategy: Government Response to the Committee's Sixth Report of Session 2010–12, Ninth Special Report of Session 2010–12*, London: The Stationery Office Limited, HC 1639, November 10, 2011. As of July 19, 2014: http://www.publications.parliament.uk/pa/cm201012/cmselect/cmdfence/1639/1639.pdf

House of Commons, Public Administration Select Committee, *Who Does UK National Strategy? First Report of Session 2010–11*, London: The Stationery Office, HC435, October 2010. As of July 19, 2014: http://www.publications.parliament.uk/pa/cm201011/cmselect/cmpubadm/435/435.pdf

Howorth, Jolyon, and Anand Menon, eds., *The European Union and National Defence Policy*, London: Routledge, 1997.

HQ USAFE—*See* Headquarters United States Air Forces in Europe.

Human Rights Watch, *Unacknowledged Deaths: Civilian Casualties in NATO's Air Campaign in Libya*, May 14, 2012. As of July 19, 2014:
http://www.unhcr.org/refworld/docid/4fb2472c2.html

"I Backspegeln—Hur Flygvapnets Libyeninsats 2011 Startade" [Looking Back—How the Air Campaign in Libya 2011 Started], *Flygvapenbloggen*, March 26, 2012. As of July 19, 2014:
http://blogg.forsvarsmakten.se/flygvapenbloggen/2012/03/26/i-backspegeln-%E2%80%93-hur-flygvapnets-libyeninsats-2011-startade/

"Immigrazione, accordo Italia-Libia," *Corriere della Sera.it*, December 29, 2007. As of July 19, 2014:
http://www.corriere.it/politica/07_dicembre_29/accordo_italia_libia_974aac78-b60a-11dc-ac5d-0003ba99c667.shtml

"Interior Minister Resigns Rather Than Carry Out Gadhafi Orders," *CNN.com*, February 22, 2011. As of July 19, 2014:
http://www.cnn.com/2011/WORLD/africa/02/22/libya.protests/index.html?hpt=T1&iref=BN1

International Commission of Inquiry on Libya, *Report of the International Commission of Inquiry on Libya—Advance Unedited Version*, New York: United Nations Human Rights Council, A/HRC/19/68, March 2, 2012, p. 208. As of July 19, 2014:
http://www.ohchr.org/Documents/HRBodies/HRCouncil/RegularSession/Session19/A.HRC.19.68.pdf

International Crisis Group, *Holding Libya Together: Security Challenges After Qadhafi*, Middle East/North Africa Report No. 115, December 14, 2011. As of July 19, 2014:
http://www.crisisgroup.org/~/media/Files/Middle%20East%20North%20Africa/North%20Africa/115%20Holding%20Libya%20Together%20--%20Security%20Challenges%20after%20Qadhafi.pdf

International Institute for Strategic Studies, "Libya Uprising—Timeline," online, undated. As of July 4, 2012:
http://acd.iiss.org/armedconflict/MainPages/dsp_ConflictTimeline.asp?ConflictID=224&YearID=1302&DisplayYear=2011

———, *The Military Balance 2011*, London: Routledge, March 2011.

Irish, John, and Regan E. Doherty, "Libyan Conflict Brings French-Qatari Ties to the Fore," *Reuters* online, April 13, 2011. As of July 19, 2014:
http://www.reuters.com/article/2011/04/13/france-qatar-idUSLDE73A0KW20110413

Italian Air Force, *Potere Aereo-Spaziale—Fondamenti* (SMA 9), June 2011.

Italian Embassy of Washington, D.C., "Media Availability with Secretary Panetta and Minister La Russa," undated. As of July 20, 2014:
http://www.ambwashingtondc.esteri.it/NR/rdonlyres/1246BB45-9EB7-464B-826B-557422D6E5D4/9202/LaRussaPanetta2.pdf

Jaffe, Greg, and Mary Beth Sheridan, "Coalition Agrees to Put NATO in Charge of No-Fly Zone in Libya," *Washington Post,* March 24, 2011. As of July 19, 2014:
http://www.washingtonpost.com/world/coalition-agrees-to-put-nato-in-charge-of-no-fly-zone-in-libya/2011/03/24/ABlZNLSB_story.html

Jakobsen, Peter Viggo, and Karsten Jakob Møller, "Good News: Libya and the Danish Way of War," in Nanna Hvidt and Hans Mouritzen, eds., *Danish Foreign Policy Yearbook 2012*, Copenhagen: Danish Institute for International Studies, 2012, pp. 106–130. As of July 19, 2014:
http://www.isn.ethz.ch/Digital-Library/Articles/Detail/?ots591=0c54e3b3-1e9c-be1e-2c24-a6a8c7060233&lng=en&v33=110617&id=144325

James, Gregory K., Larry Holcomb, and Chad T. Manske, "Joint Task Force Odyssey Dawn: A Model for Joint Experience, Training, and Education," *Joint Force Quarterly*, Issue 64, January 2012. As of July 19, 2014 (no longer working):
http://www.ndu.edu/press/lib/pdf/jfq-64/JFQ-64_24-29_James-Hokcomb-Manske.pdf

Jennings, Gareth, "Royal Air Force Downplays Carrier Aviation," *Jane's Defence Weekly*, Issue 48, No. 30, July 27, 2011, p. 12.

Johnson, Adrian, and Saqeb Mueen, eds., *Short War, Long Shadow: The Political and Military Legacies of the 2011 Libya Campaign*, London: Royal United Services Institute (RUSI), Whitehall Report 1–12, 2012. As of July 19, 2014:
http://www.rusi.org/downloads/assets/WHR_1-12.pdf

Johnson, David E., *Learning Large Lessons: The Evolving Roles of Ground Power and Air Power in the Post–Cold War Era*, Santa Monica, Calif.: RAND Corporation, MG-405-1-AF, 2007. As of July 19, 2014:
http://www.rand.org/pubs/monographs/MG405-1.html

———, *Hard Fighting: Israel in Lebanon and Gaza*, Santa Monica, Calif.: RAND Corporation, MG-1085-A/AF, 2011. As of July 19, 2014:
http://www.rand.org/pubs/monographs/MG1085.html.html

Joint and Coalition Operational Analysis, Libya: *Operation ODYSSEY DAWN (OOD)—Executive Summary*, Suffolk, Va.: JCOA, September 21, 2011.

Joint Chiefs of Staff, *Doctrine for the Armed Forces of the United States*, May 2, 2007, Incorporating Change 1, March 20, 2009. As of July 19, 2014:
http://www.dtic.mil/doctrine/new_pubs/jp1.pdf

———, 1-02, *Department of Defense Dictionary of Military and Associated Terms*, November 8, 2010, as amended through February 15, 2013. As of July 19, 2014:
http://www.dtic.mil/doctrine/dod_dictionary/

———, 3-03, *Joint Interdiction*, October 14, 2011. As of July 19, 2014:
http://www.dtic.mil/doctrine/new_pubs/jp3_03.pdf

———, 3-60, *Joint Targeting*, April 2007.

Jolly, David, "Britain Sends Supplies to Libyan Rebels," *New York Times*, June 30, 2011.

Jones, Barbara, and Ian Mcilgorm, "The Battle of Benghazi: City Seemed Lost to Gaddafi Forces but was Retaken by Rebels," *The Daily Mail Online*, March 20, 2011. As of July 19, 2014:
http://www.dailymail.co.uk/news/article-1368030/Libya-Benghazi-lost-Gaddafis-forces-retaken-rebels.html

Joshi, Shashank, "The Complexity of Arab Support," in Adrian Johnson and Saqeb Mueen, eds., *Short War, Long Shadow: The Political and Military Legacies of the 2011 Libya Campaign*, London: Royal United Services Institute (RUSI), Whitehall Report 1–12, 2012, pp. 63–69. As of July 19, 2014:
http://www.rusi.org/downloads/assets/WHR_1-12.pdf

"Judeh Takes Part in London Meeting on Libya," *Petra News Agency*, March 29, 2011. As of July 19, 2014 (by subscription only):
http://www.petra.gov.jo/Public_News/Nws_NewsDetails.aspx?lang=2&site_id=2&NewsID=26969&Type=P

Juholt, Håkan, "Oenighet om Svensk Libyen-Insats" [Disagreement About the Swedish Operation in Libya], *Svenska Dagbladet*, April 29, 2012. As of July 19, 2014:
http://www.svd.se/nyheter/inrikes/oenighet-om-svensk-libyen-insats_6125889.svd

Keaney, Thomas A., and Eliot A. Cohen, *Revolution in Warfare? Air Power in the Persian Gulf*, Annapolis: Naval Institute Press, 1995. As of July 19, 2014:
http://www.afhso.af.mil/shared/media/document/AFD-100927-061.pdf

Keaten, Jamey, "Tiny Qatar Flexes Muscles in No-Fly Libya Campaign," *Associated Press*, March 28, 2011.

Kennedy, Helen, "'Die Here a Martyr!' Khaday Not Leaving as Libya Shakes," *The Daily News*, February 23, 2011, p. 7.

Kenny, Colonel Eric, "Op Mobile/Task Force Libeccio Lessons Learned Symposium," Winnipeg, Manitoba, June 6, 2012.

Kessler, Oren, and the Associated Press, "Gaddafi Keeps Grip on Capital as Revolt Spreads Across Libya. Death Toll Estimates Continue to Climb as Eastern Region Slips Toward Rebel Control. US, EU Threaten Scantions," *Jerusalem Post*, February 24, 2011.

"Khadafi et Son Régime Neutralises," *La Défense [Defence (Belgium)]*, October 20, 2011.

Kingdom of Bahrain, Ministry of Foreign Affairs website, "Statement on the 30th Extraordinary GCC Foreign Ministers Council Meeting," Manama, Bahrain, February 17, 2011. As of July 19, 2014:
http://www.mofa.gov.bh/Default.aspx?tabid=7824&language=en-US&ItemId=732

Kington, Tom, "Small Bombs Loom Big as Libya War Grinds On," *Defense News*, June 27, 2011, pp. 1, 4.

Kirkpatrick, David D., "Gun Battle Disrupts Rebel Base in Libya," *New York Times*, August 1, 2011, p. A4.

———, "Qaddafi Defiant After Rebel Takeover," *New York Times*, August 23, 2011. As of July 19, 2014:
http://www.nytimes.com/2011/08/24/world/africa/24libya.html?_r=1

———, "Libya Democracy Clashes with Fervor for Jihad," *New York Times*, June 23, 2012, p. A1.

———, "Western Libya Earns a Taste of Freedom as Rebels Loosen Qaddafi's Grip," *New York Times*, June 26, 2012, p. A12.

Koring, Paul, "Canada's Hercs Star in Dangerous Ballet of Mid-Air Refuelling," *Globe and Mail*, June 14, 2011. As of July 19, 2014:
http://www.theglobeandmail.com/news/world/canadas-hercs-star-in-dangerous-ballet-of-mid-air-refuelling/article4192542/

Kreisher, Otto, "Strike Eagle Rescue," *Air Force Magazine*, March 2013, Vol. 96, No. 3. As of July 19, 2014 (by subscription only):
http://www.airforcemag.com/MagazineArchive/Pages/2013/March%202013/0313eagle.aspx

La Franchi, Howard, "Obama to Pentagon: Give Me a List of Options to Protect Libyans; President Obama Says He Has Asked the Pentagon and Other Agencies to Come Up with Ways That the US Could Help Protect Libyans in Case the 'Situation Deteriorates Rapidly,'" *Christian Science Monitor*, March 3, 2011.

Labott, Elise, "U.S. Mulling Military Options in Libya," CNN.com, March 2, 2011. As of July 19, 2014:
http://articles.cnn.com/2011-03-02/us/libya.military.options_1_gadhafi-government-arab-league-libyan-people?_s=PM:US

Lambeth, Benjamin S., *NATO's Air War for Kosovo: A Strategic and Operational Assessment*, Santa Monica, Calif.: RAND Corporation, MR-1365-AF, 2001. As of July 19, 2014:
http://www.rand.org/pubs/monograph_reports/MR1365.html

———, *Air Power Against Terror: America's Conduct of Operation Enduring Freedom*, Santa Monica, Calif.: RAND Corporation, MG-166-1-CENTAF, 2006. As of July 19, 2014:
http://www.rand.org/pubs/monographs/MG166-1.html

Larrabee, F. Stephen, Stuart E. Johnson, John Gordon IV, Peter A. Wilson, Caroline Baxter, Deborah Lai, and Calin Trenkov-Wermuth, *NATO and the Challenges of Austerity*, Santa Monica, Calif.: RAND Corporation, MG-1196-OSD, 2012. As of July 19, 2014:
http://www.rand.org/pubs/monographs/MG1196.html.html

Lee, Jesse, "The President on Libya: 'The Violence Must Stop; Muammar Gaddafi Has Lost the Legitimacy to Lead and He Must Leave,'" The White House blog, March 3, 2011. As of July 19, 2014:
http://www.whitehouse.gov/blog/2011/03/03/
president-libya-violence-must-stop-muammar-gaddafi-has-lost-legitimacy-lead-and-he-m

———, "The President on Libya: 'Our Goal Is Focused, Our Cause Is Just, and Our Coalition Is Strong," The White House blog, March 18, 2011. As of July 19, 2014:
http://www.whitehouse.gov/blog/2011/03/18/
president-libya-our-goal-focused-our-cause-just-and-our-coalition-strong

———, "The President on Libya: 'We Have Already Saved Lives,'" The White House blog, March 22, 2011. As of July 19, 2014:
http://www.whitehouse.gov/blog/2011/03/22/president-libya-we-have-already-saved-lives

Lehnberg, Anne-Li, "Vänstern Oenig om Libyenattacken" [The Left Cannot Agree on Attacking Libya], *Flamman Inrikes*, March 23, 2011. As of July 19, 2014:
http://www.flamman.se/vanstern-oenig-om-libyenattacken

Leiby, Richard, and Muhammad Mansour, "Arab League Asks U.N. for No-Fly Zone over Libya," *Washington Post*, March 12, 2011.

Levite, Jean-David, in Jean-Christophe Notin, *La Vérité sur Notre Guerre en Libye*, Paris: Fayard, October 10, 2012.

Lévy, Bernard-Henri, "Quando Sarkozy mi Disse 'Usa Assenti, Italia Senza Testa,'" *Corriere della Sera*, November 9, 2011.

Lewis, William, "Libya: Dream vs. Reality," *Mediterranean Quarterly*, Vol. 22, No. 3, Summer 2011, pp. 42–52.

"Libya: Canada to Send Fighter Jets for No-Fly Zone," *Bbc.co.uk*, March 18, 2011. As of July19, 2014:
http://www.bbc.co.uk/news/world-us-canada-12781682

"Libya: France Calls for Sanctions Against Libya," *Allafrica.com*, February 23, 2011. As of July 19, 2014:
http://allafrica.com/stories/201102230637.html

"Libya: France Recognizes Rebels as Government," *BBC News*, March 10, 2011. As of July 19, 2014:
http://www.bbc.co.uk/news/world-africa-12699183

"Libya: French Plane Fires on Military Vehicle," *BBC News*, March 19, 2011. As of July 19, 2014:
http://www.bbc.co.uk/news/world-africa-12795971

"Libya: Gaddafi Troops 'Force Rebels Out of Brega,'" *BBC News*, March 13, 2011. As of July 19, 2014:
http://www.bbc.co.uk/news/world-africa-12726032

"Libya: UK Apache Attack Helicopters Launch First Strikes," *The Telegraph*, June 4, 2011. As of July 19, 2014:
http://www.telegraph.co.uk/news/worldnews/africaandindianocean/libya/8556202/Libya-UK-Apache-attack-helicopters-launch-first-strikes.html

"Libya: UK Apache Helicopters Used in NATO Attacks," *BBC News*, June 4, 2011. As of July 19, 2014:
http://www.bbc.co.uk/news/uk-13651736

"Libya-Canada Diplomatic Relationship Halted," *CBC.ca*, February 26, 2011. As of July 19, 2014:
http://www.cbc.ca/news/world/story/2011/02/26/libya.html

"Libya Conflict: Rebels Battle Gaddafi Troops in Zawiya," *BBC News*, August 14, 2011. As of July 19, 2014:
http://www.bbc.co.uk/news/world-africa-14524132

"Libya Jails Russia, Ukraine, Belarus 'Mercenaries,'" *Agence France Press*, June 4, 2012. As of July 19, 2014:
http://www.portalangop.co.ao/angola/en_us/noticias/africa/2012/5/23/Libya-jails-Russia-Ukraine-Belarus-mercenaries,62cab560-66e1-4530-b985-5d951a732047.html

"Libya Rebels say Gaddafi Forces in Retreat," *Reuters.com*, July 18, 2011. As of July 19, 2014:
http://af.reuters.com/article/libyaNews/idAFLDE76H0MR20110718

"The Libyan Air Operation: A French Perspective," interview with Lt. General Desclaux, *Second Line of Defense (SLD)*, October 22, 2011. As of July 19, 2014:
http://www.sldinfo.com/the-libyan-air-operation-a-french-perspective/

Libyan Interim Transnational National Council, "Founding Statement of the Interim Transitional National Council (TNC)," March 5, 2011. As of July 19, 2014:
http://www.lcil.cam.ac.uk/sites/default/files/LCIL/documents/arabspring/libya/Libya_12_Founding_Statement_TNC.pdf

"Libyan Rebels Claim Victory in Battle for Brega," *BBC News*, July 18, 2011. As of July 19, 2014:
http://www.bbc.co.uk/news/world-africa-14180293

"Libyan Rebels Near Ajdabiya Killed in NATO Air Strike," *BBC News*, April 7, 2011. As of July 19, 2014:
http://www.bbc.co.uk/news/world-africa-12997181

"Libyan Rebels Retreat to Brega," *CBC.ca*, March 30, 2011. As of July 19, 2014:
http://www.cbc.ca/news/world/story/2011/03/30/libya-battle-wednesday.html

"Libye: Kadhafi prend le risque d'encourager une guerre civile," *LeMonde.fr*, February 22, 2011. As of July 19, 2014:
http://www.lemonde.fr/afrique/article/2011/02/22/libye-kadhafi-prend-le-risque-d-encourager-une-guerre-civile_1483828_3212.html

"Live Blog—Libya Feb 22," *Aljazeera.com*, February 22, 2011. As of July 19, 2014:
http://blogs.aljazeera.net/africa/2011/02/22/live-blog-libya-feb-22

"The Look Ahead: March 21–25, Election: Can PM Cast Off the Grime, Regain Moment," *Globe and Mail*, March 21, 2011.

Lungescu, Oana, NATO Spokesperson, and Brigadier General Mark van Uhm, Chief of Allied Operations, Allied Command Operations (SHAPE), "Press Briefing on Libya," April 19, 2011. As of July 19, 2014:
http://www.nato.int/cps/en/SID-57117436-C65ACBA0/natolive/news_72824.htm

Lynch, Marc, "Why Obama Had to Act in Libya," posted to "Abu Aardvark Middle East Blog," hosted by *Foreign Policy*, March 29, 2011. As of July 19, 2014:
http://lynch.foreignpolicy.com/posts/2011/03/29/the_case_against_the_libya_intervention

Mackey, Robert, "Feb. 23: Updates on the Uprising in Libya," blog entry ("The Lede"), *New York Times*, February 23, 2011. As of July 20, 2014:
http://thelede.blogs.nytimes.com/2011/02/23/latest-updates-on-the-uprising-in-libya/

MacKinnon, Douglas, "Canada, the Forgotten Ally," *Baltimore Sun*, May 29, 2012.

Mader, Georg, "Interview with Lieutenant General Ralph Jodice, Combined Forces Air Component Commander for Operation 'Unified Protector,'" *Jane's Defence Weekly*, April 25, 2012, p. 34.

Makahleh, Shehab, "UAE troops spare no effort to bring peace to Afghanistan," gulfnews.com, August 24, 2011. As of July 20, 2014:
http://gulfnews.com/news/gulf/uae/general/
uae-troops-spare-no-effort-to-bring-peace-to-afghanistan-1.856240

Manca, Vincenzo Ruggero, *Italia-Libia Stranamore*, Rome: Koiné, 2011

Manduca, Anthony, "Qatar: Helping Libya from Malta," *Times of Malta*, September 29, 2011. As of July 20, 2014:
http://www.timesofmalta.com/articles/view/20110929/business-news/
Qatar-Helping-Libya-from-Malta.386931

Mann, Shannon, "Dog in the Fight: 916th Airmen Support No Fly Zone over Libya," 916th Air Refueling Wing Public Affairs, April 4, 2011. As of July 20, 2014:
http://www.916arw.afrc.af.mil/news/story.asp?id=123249734

Marani, Gen. s.a. Giuseppe, interview with Lt. Col. Alessandro Cornacchini, *Rivista Aeronautica*, No. 3, 2011, p. 59.

Marroni, Carlo, "Italia-Libia, trattato sospeso," *IlSole24ore.com*, February 27, 2011. As of July 20, 2014:
http://www.ilsole24ore.com/art/notizie/2011-02-27/italialibia-trattato-sospeso-081205.
shtml?uuid=Aa0r50BD

Marucci, Arcangelo, "Il post-Gheddafi tra estremismo fondamentalista e minaccia terroristica," *Informazioni della Difesa*, January 2012, pp. 14-21.

Mazetti, Mark, and Eric Schmitt, "CIA Agents in Libya Aid Airstrikes and Meet Rebels," *New York Times*, March 30, 2011, p. A1. As of July 20, 2014:
http://www.nytimes.com/2011/03/31/world/africa/31intel.html

McConnell, Mitch, "Military Action in Libya," *Congressional Record*, 112 (2), Senate, March 28, 2011, p. S1880.

McCullough, Amy, "The Libya Mission," *Air Force Magazine*, Vol. 94, No. 8 (August 2011).

McDermid, Charles, "Arming Libya's Rebels: A Debate in Doha," *Time*, April 14, 2011. As of July 20, 2014:
http://www.time.com/time/world/article/0,8599,2065124,00.html

McElroy, Damien, "Libya: RAF Airstrikes Sink Boat Filled with Gaddafi Troops After Refinery Battle," *The Telegraph*, August 18, 2011. As of July 20, 2014: http://www.telegraph.co.uk/news/worldnews/africaandindianocean/libya/8709510/Libya-RAF-airstrikes-sink-boat-filled-with-Gaddafi-troops-after-refinery-battle.html

McGreal, Chris, Ian Black, Toby Helm, and Kim Willsher, "Allied Strikes Sweep Libya as West Intervenes in Conflict," *Guardian.co.uk*, March 19, 2011. As of July 20, 2014: http://www.theguardian.com/world/2011/mar/19/libya-air-strikes-gaddafi-france

McLean, Mark (Major, USAF), "Talking Paper on Operation Odyssey Dawn MAF Support (UNCLASS)," 18 AF staff paper, May 12, 2011.

Meyer, Carl, "Extent of Canadian Involvement in Libya Flying Under the Radar," *Embassy Magazine*, June 8, 2011. As of July 20, 2014: http://www.embassymag.ca/page/view/libya-04-06-2011

Mezran, Karim, "Come l'Italia ha Perso la Libia," *Limes*, February 2011.

———, "Piccolo Glossarietto delle Bufale Belliche," *La Guerra di Libia, Special Issue of Limes*, April 2011, pp. 70–71.

Mezran, Karim, and Arturo Varvelli, *Libia. Fine o Rinascita di una Rivoluzione?* Rome: Donzelli, 2012.

Michael, Maggie, and Paul Schemm, "'Fresh Air Strike' on Rebel-Held Libyan Town Brega," *Associated Press*, March 3, 2011.

Ministère de la Défense, "Des Mirage 2000 en exercise au Qatar," December 10, 2010. As of July 20, 2014: http://www.defense.gouv.fr/air/breves-migration/des-mirage-2000-en-exercice-au-qatar/(language)/fre-FR#SearchText=Al%20Koot#xtcr=5

———, "Libya: Point de situation Opération Harmattan no9," March 29, 2011 [in French]. As of July 20, 2014: http://www.defense.gouv.fr/actualites/operations/libye-point-de-situation-operation-harmattan-n-9

———, "Libye cooperation franco-qatarienne pour le soutien technique," November 22, 2011. As of July 20, 2014: http://www.defense.gouv.fr/actualites/international/libye-cooperation-franco-qatarienne-pour-le-soutien-technique

"Minister MacKay Salutes Evacuation Operations in Malta," *National Defence and the Canadian Forces*, March 12, 2011. As of July 20, 2014: http://www.forces.gc.ca/en/news/article.page?doc=minister-mackay-salutes-evacuation-operations-in-malta/hnps1vep

"Misión cumplida en Libia," *Revista Española de Defensa*, November 2011, pp. 6–11.

"Missile libico sfiora nave italiana cade in mare: Nessun ferito né danni," *Corriere Della Sera.it*, August 3, 2011. As of July 20, 2014: http://www.corriere.it/cronache/11_agosto_03/missile-libico-contro-nave-italiana_b1ef5c92-bdc5-11e0-99fd-c37f66002d24.shtml

"Missiles Rain on Gadhafi," *Edmonton Journal*, March 21, 2011.

Ministry of Defence—*See* United Kingdom Ministry of Defence.

Morelli, M., "Mille anime, un solo spirito," in Gregory Alegi and Alessandro Cornacchini, eds., *Al Lupo! Al Lupo! Il 4° Stormo Caccia da Gorizia a Grosseto, 1931–2011*, Rome: Aviator Edizioni/Rivista Aeronautica, 2011.

Morse, Eric, "The West Takes a Stand," *Ottawa Citizen*, March 18, 2011. As of July 20, 2014:
http://www2.canada.com/ottawacitizen/news/archives/story.
html?id=09f02730-da3c-4705-88d0-ed5d7573d671

Mostyn, Trevor, "Obituary: Gen Abdel Fatah Younis: Military Leader and Gaddafi's Trusted Aide Until He Defected to Libyan Rebel Forces," *The Guardian*, August 1, 2011, p. 32.

de la Motte, Eddy, "Gripen: When logic is part of the equation," briefing, July 11, 2012.

"Muammar Gaddafi Speech Translated (2011 Feb 22)," posted on YouTube. As of July 20, 2014:
http://www.youtube.com/watch?v=69wBG6ULNzQ

Mueen, Saqeb, and Grant Turnbull, eds., *Accidental Heroes: Britain, France, and the Libya Operation*, an Interim RUSI Campaign Report, London: Royal United Services Institute, September 2011.

Mueller, John, "Will Obama's Libya 'Victory' Aid Re-Election Bid?" *The National Interest*, December 1, 2011. As of July 20, 2014:
http://nationalinterest.org/blog/the-skeptics/
will-obama%E2%80%99s-libya-%E2%80%9Cvictory%E2%80%9D-aid-re-election-bid-6207

Mueller, Karl P., "The Essence of Coercive Air Power: A Primer for Military Strategists," *Royal Air Force Air Power Review*, Vol. 4, No. 3, Autumn 2001, pp. 45–56. As of July 20, 2014:
http://www.airpower.au.af.mil/airchronicles/cc/mueller.html

———, "Airpower: Two Centennial Appraisals," *Strategic Studies Quarterly*, Vol. 5, No. 4, Winter 2011, pp. 123–132.

———, "Sky King," *The American Interest*, Vol. 7, No. 3, January/February 2012, pp. 104–108.

———, *Denying Flight: Strategic Options for Employing No-Fly Zones*, Santa Monica, Calif.: RAND Corporation, RR-423-AF, 2013. As of January 28, 2015:
http://www.rand.org/pubs/research_reports/RR423.html

Nakhoul, Samia, "Special Report: The Secret Plan to Take Tripoli," *Reuters*, September 6, 2011. As of July 20, 2014:
http://www.reuters.com/article/2011/09/06/us-libya-endgame-idUSTRE7853C520110906

National Defence and the Canadian Forces, "Operation MOBILE: National Defence and Canadian Forces Response to the Situation in Libya," online, undated.

"National Post Editorial Board: A Better, Prouder Canadian Foreign Policy," *The National Post*, January 1, 2012. As of July 20, 2014:
http://fullcomment.nationalpost.com/2012/01/01/
national-post-editorial-board-a-better-prouder-canadian-foreign-policy

National Public Radio (NPR) staff, "NATO Allies Question Their Role in Libya" NPR, April 16, 2011. As of July 20, 2014:
http://www.npr.org/2011/04/16/135464254/nato-allies-question-their-role-in-libya

NATO—*See* North Atlantic Treaty Organization.

NATO Allied Maritime Command Naples, "Commander Allied Maritime Command," online, undated.

NATO Allied Maritime Command Naples website, "OUP Maritime Operations: Mission Accomplished," online, November 1, 2011.

"NATO and Libya—Qatar's Contribution to Operation Unified Protector," interview with Lieutenant General Mubarak Al-Khayarin, Chief of air component command, Qatar, May 5, 2011. As of July 20, 2014:
http://www.youtube.com/watch?v=A9Re_Pwdu10

NATO Media Operations Centre, "Operation UNIFIED PROTECTOR Final Mission Stats," November 2, 2011. As of July 20, 2014:
http://www.nato.int/nato_static/assets/pdf/
pdf_2011_11/20111108_111107-factsheet_up_factsfigures_en.pdf

"Nella Tana dei Predator, Operativi in Afghanistan e Pronti per la Libia," *Dedalonews*, June 29, 2011.

News conference transcript with Peter Mackay and Assistant Chief of the Air Staff Major General Tom Larson, Ottawa, March 21, 2011.

Nigro, Vincenzo, "La Russa 'buca' la riunione Nato e la spagna ci soffia la base radar," *La Republica*, June 19, 2011. As of July 27, 2012:
cca.analisidifesa.it/it/magazine_8034243544/numero119/
article_4566615020270005307161250487122_2683573816_0.jsp

Nordland, Rod, "Libya Counts More Martyrs Than Bodies," *New York Times*, September 16, 2011, p. A1. As of July 20, 2014:
http://www.nytimes.com/2011/09/17/world/africa/skirmishes-flare-around-qaddafi-strongholds.html?_r=1

———, "At Qaddafi Loyalists' Last Redoubts, A Struggle of Advances and Retreats," *New York Times*, September 18, 2011, p. A6.

"Norge Flyver Hjem fra Libyen 1. August" Jyllands-Posten, June 10, 2011. As of July 20, 2014:
http://jyllands-posten.dk/international/europa/ECE4540614/norge-flyver-hjem-fra-libyen-1-august/

North Atlantic Treaty Organization, "Operation Unified Protector Map," undated. As of July 20, 2014:
http://www.nato.int/nato_static/assets/pdf/pdf_2011_07/20110708_110708-map_OUP_Libya.pdf

———, "Political Military Framework for Partner Involvement in NATO-Led Operations," undated. As of July 20, 2014:
http://www.nato.int/nato_static/assets/pdf/pdf_2011_04/20110415_110415-PMF.pdf

———, "Istanbul Cooperation Initiative," NATO Instanbul Summit, June 28–29, 2004, NATO Policy document. As of July 20, 2014:
http://www.nato.int/docu/comm/2004/06-istanbul/docu-cooperation.htm

———, "Speech by NATO Secretary General Anders Fogh Rasmussen on His Visit to the Kingdom of Bahrain, Ritz Carlton Hotel, Manama, Bahrain," March 7, 2010. As of July 20, 2014:
http://www.nato.int/cps/en/natolive/opinions_62052.htm

———, "Secretary General Stresses Need for Further Cooperation with Qatar," February 14–16, 2011. As of July 20, 2014:
http://www.nato.int/cps/en/SID-D6804FBA-895188DF/natolive/news_70685.htm

———, "NATO Defence Ministers Will Discuss Situation in Libya and Longer-Term Prospects in Middle East," March 7, 2011. As of July 20, 2014:
http://www.nato.int/cps/en/natolive/news_71277.htm

———, "NATO Ready to Support International Efforts on Libya," March 11, 2011. As of July 20, 2014:
http://www.nato.int/cps/en/natolive/news_71446.htm

———, "Statement by the NATO Secretary General on Libya Arms Embargo," March 22, 2011. As of July 20, 2014:
http://www.nato.int/cps/en/natolive/news_71689.htm

————, *The NATO Lessons Learned Handbook*, 2nd edition, Brussels: Joint Analysis and Lessons Learned Centre, September 2011. As of July 20, 2014:
http://www.jallc.nato.int/newsmedia/publications.asp

————, "Evolution of the Frontlines in Libya—March–Sept. 2011," online maps, September 22, 2011. As of July 20, 2014:
http://www.nato.int/cps/en/natolive/photos_78403.htm

————, "Operational Media Update: NATO and Libya," online, October 25, 2011. As of July 20, 2014:
http://www.nato.int/cps/en/natolive/news_71994.htm

————, "'We Answered the Call'—The End of Operation Unified Protector," October 31, 2011. As of July 20, 2014:
http://www.nato.int/cps/en/natolive/news_80435.htm

————, "NATO and Libya: Operation Unified Protector—February–October 2011," online, last updated March 27, 2012. As of July 20, 2014:
http://www.nato.int/cps/en/natolive/71679.htm

————, "NATO and Libya," online, last updated March 28, 2012. As of July 20, 2014:
http://www.nato.int/cps/en/natolive/topics_71652.htm

————, "Strategic Airlift Capability (SAC): A Key Capability for the Alliance," online, last updated August 7, 2012. As of July 20, 2014
http://www.nato.int/cps/en/natolive/topics_50105.htm

Northrop Grumman, "Global Hawk—Global ISR Operations! 'March Madness,'" June 2011.

Norwegian Ministry of Defence, *Capable Force: Strategic Concept for the Norwegian Armed Forces*, Oslo: Ministry of Defence, November 2009.

Notin, Jean-Christophe, *La vérité sur notre guerre en Libye*, Paris: Fayard, 2011.

Norton-Taylor, Richard, and Chris Stephen, "Libya: SAS Veterans Helping NATO Identify Al-Qadhafi Targets in Misurata," *The Guardian*, May 31, 2011.

Nougayrède, Natalie, "Recit: Comment la France a-t-elle décidé d'intervenir en Libye?" *Le Monde*, April 19, 2011.

————, "La guerre de Nicolas Sarkozy," *Le Monde*, August 24, 2011.

————, "La guerre de Libye et la tentation du 'storytelling' Français, *Le Monde*, September 14, 2011.

OASD (PA)—*See* Office of the Assistant Secretary of Defense (Public Affairs).

"Obama Continues to Caution for Libya No-Fly Zone," *Ottawa Citizen*, March 12, 2011.

O'Dwyer, Gerard, "Libya Operations Threaten Nordic Budgets," *Defense News*, June 20, 2011, pp. 1, 8.

Office of the Assistant Secretary of Defense (Public Affairs), "DOD News Briefing with Secretary Gates and Adm. Mullen from the Pentagon," Washington, D.C.: U.S. Department of Defense, March 1, 2011. As of July 20, 2014:
http://www.defense.gov/transcripts/transcript.aspx?transcriptid=4777

————, "DOD News Briefing with Vice Adm. Gortney from the Pentagon on Libya Operation Odyssey Dawn," Washington, D.C.: U.S. Department of Defense, March 19, 2011. As of July 20, 2014:
http://www.defense.gov/transcripts/transcript.aspx?transcriptid=4786

————, "Media Availability with Secretary Gates enroute to Russia, from Andrews Air Force Base," Washington, D.C.: U.S. Department of Defense, March 20, 2011. As of July 20, 2014: http://www.defense.gov/transcripts/transcript.aspx?transcriptid=4788

————, "DOD News Briefing with Vice Adm. Gortney from the Pentagon on Libya Operation Odyssey Dawn," Washington, D.C.: U.S. Department of Defense, March 20, 2011. As of July 20, 2014: http://www.defense.gov/transcripts/transcript.aspx?transcriptid=4787

————, "DOD News Briefing with Adm. Locklear via Telephone from *USS Mount Whitney*," Washington, D.C.: U.S. Department of Defense, March 22, 2011. As of July 20, 2014: http://www.defense.gov/transcripts/transcript.aspx?transcriptid=4793

————, "DOD News Briefing with Rear Adm. Hueber via Telephone from *USS Mount Whitney*," Washington, D.C.: U.S. Department of Defense, March 23, 2011. As of July 20, 2014: http://www.defense.gov/transcripts/transcript.aspx?transcriptid=4794

————, "DOD News Briefing with Vice Adm. Gortney from the Pentagon on Libya Operation Odyssey Dawn," Washington, D.C.: U.S. Department of Defense, March 25, 2011. As of July 20, 2014: http://www.defense.gov/transcripts/transcript.aspx?transcriptid=4799

————, "ABC's 'This Week' interview with Secretary Gates and Secretary Clinton on Libya," Washington, D.C.: U.S. Department of Defense, March 27, 2011. As of July 20, 2014: http://www.defense.gov/transcripts/transcript.aspx?transcriptid=4800

————, "DOD News Briefing with Vice Adm. Gortney from the Pentagon on Libya Operation Odyssey Dawn," Washington, D.C.: U.S. Department of Defense, March 28, 2012. As of July 20, 2014: http://www.defense.gov/transcripts/transcript.aspx?transcriptid=4803

————, "DOD News Briefing with Secretary Gates and Gen. Cartwright from the Pentagon," Washington, D.C.: U.S. Department of Defense, April 21, 2011. As of July 20, 2014: http://www.defense.gov/transcripts/transcript.aspx?transcriptid=4815

Office of the Prime Minister of Canada, "Statement by the Prime Minister of Canada on the Current Situation in Libya," February 25, 2011. As of July 20, 2014: http://pm.gc.ca/eng/media.asp?id=3990

————, "Statement by the Prime Minister of Canada on Implementing Sanctions Against Libya," February 27, 2011. As of July 20, 2014: http://www.pm.gc.ca/eng/media.asp?id=3997

————, "Statement by the Prime Minister of Canada on the Current Situation in Libya," March 18, 2011. As of July 20, 2014: http://pm.gc.ca/eng/media.asp?id=4048

————, "Statement by the Prime Minister of Canada at an Emergency Meeting on Libya," March 19, 2011.

Office of the U.S. Joint Chiefs of Staff, "Comments by Secretary Robert Gates, Secretary of Defense and General James Cartwright, Vice Chairman of the Joint Chiefs of Staff," Washington, D.C. Thursday, April 21, 2011.

Office of U.S. Sen. John McCain, "Floor Statement by Senator McCain Introducing the Senate Resolution Calling for a No-Fly Zone in Libya," Washington, D.C.: U.S. Senate, March 14, 2011. As of July 19, 2014: http://www.mccain.senate.gov/public/index.cfm/ floor-statements?ID=b63b7b6f-a466-ba23-dea8-7bc024f54655

Office of U.S. Sen. Richard Lugar, "Lugar Says Costly, Ill-Defined War in Libya Looms," Washington, D.C.: United States Senate Committee on Foreign Relations, press release, April 6, 2011. As of July 19, 2014:
http://www.foreign.senate.gov/press/ranking/release/?id=c200ed42-710c-490b-a438-cdd4ee367871

O'Neil, Peter, "Canada Punching Above Its Weight in Military Alliance, Gates Tells Officials," *Winnipeg Free Press*, June 11, 2011. As of July 20, 2014:
http://www.winnipegfreepress.com/canada/CNS-GATES-CANADA-ALL.html

"On ne s'improvise pas diplomate," *Le Monde*, February 23, 2011, p. 7.

"Operation Ignition," *Crew Brief*, Vol. 9, No.1, pp. 8–9.

"L'opposition Libyenne Demande l'aide de l'Europe," *LeMonde.fr*, March 10, 2011. As of July 20, 2014:
http://www.lemonde.fr/afrique/article/2011/03/10/direct-bataille-diplomatique-entre-kadhafi-et-l-opposition_1490863_3212.html

"Ora Costringiamo Bengasi a Rispettare i Tripolitani," *Limes*, March 2011.

Österdahl, Inger, and Ylva L. Hartmann, "Omvärlden Bär ett Stort Ansvar" [The Outside World Has a Great Responsibility], *SvD OPINION*, March 2, 2012. As of July 20, 2014:
http://www.svd.se/opinion/brannpunkt/omvarlden-bar-ett-stort-ansvar_6893931.svd

Overhaus, Marco, "NATO's Operation in Libya: Not a Model for Military Intervention," Stiftung Wissenschaft und Politik [German Institute for International and Security Affairs], *SWP Comments,* No. 36, November 2011. As of July 20, 2014:
http://www.swp-berlin.org/fileadmin/contents/products/comments/2011C36_ovs_ks.pdf

Owen, Robert C., ed., *Deliberate Force: A Case Study in Effective Air Campaigning*, Maxwell Air Force Base, Ala.: Air University Press, 2000.

———, "Structuring Global Air Forces for Counterinsurgency Operations," *Silver Dart Canadian Aerospace Studies*, Vol. IV, Center for Defense and Security Studies, University of Manitoba, 2008.

Owen, Robert C., and Karl P. Mueller, *Airlift Capabilities for Future U.S. Counterinsurgency Operations*, Santa Monica, Calif.: RAND Corporation, MG-565-AF, 2007. As of July 20, 2014
http://www.rand.org/pubs/monographs/MG565.html

Pape, Robert A., *Bombing to Win: Air Power and Coercion in War*, Ithaca, N.Y.: Cornell University Press, 1996.

Parker, Geoffrey, ed., *The Cambridge Illustrated History of Warfare*, Cambridge, UK: Cambridge University Press, 1995.

"Parliament Honours UK Troops for Libya Operations," *Mod.uk*, April 25, 2012. As of July 20, 2014:
http://www.mod.uk/DefenceInternet/DefenceNews/HistoryAndHonour/ParliamentHonoursUkTroopsForLibyaOperations.htm

Parma, Gen. Vincenzo, "Il Ruolo del Comando Forze Mobilità e Supporto," *Rivista Aeronautica*, March 2011, pp. 37–38.

Parrish, Karen, "Locklear Nominated as Next Pacom Commander," *American Forces Press Service*, December 30, 2011. As of July 20, 2014:
http://www.defense.gov/news/newsarticle.aspx?id=66636

Peacock, Lindsay, and Eleanor Keymer, eds., *Jane's World Air Forces*, Issue 30, 2010.

Pelletier, Colonel Alain, "Task Force Libeccio—TF Lessons Learned on C2 and Intel Supt Commander TFL," Brief to 1 Cdn Air Div.

Petersson, Magnus, and Håkon Lunde Saxi, "Shifted Roles: Explaining Danish and Norwegian Alliance Strategy 1949–2009," *The Journal of Strategic Studies,* iFirst article, 2012. As of July 20, 2014:
http://dx.doi.org/10.1080/01402390.2011.608934

Phelps, Daniel, "NATO Called—Shaw Responded: Part 1 of 4," Shaw Air Force Base, S.C.: 20th Fighter Wing Public Affairs, online, February 3, 2012. As of July 20, 2014:
http://www.shaw.af.mil/news/story.asp?id=123288682

Pidd, Helen, "Nato Commander of Libya Mission Pleads for Specialised Fighter Jets," *The Guardian*, April 14, 2011. As of July 20, 2014:
http://www.guardian.co.uk/world/2011/apr/14/nato-commander-libya-fighter-jets

Pigott, Peter, "Answering the Call," *Frontline Defence*, Issue 6, 2011, p. 30.

Pocok, Chris, "Libya Defense: Boots on the Ground?" *AINonline*, November 13, 2011. As of July 20, 2014:
http://www.ainonline.com/aviation-news/dubai-air-show/2011-11-11/libya-defense-boots-ground

De Ponti, Gen. Giacomo, "Il coordinamento civile-militare nella gestione dello spazio aereo," *Rivista Aeronautica*, March 2011, pp. 40.

Posen, Barry R., "The War for Kosovo: Serbia's Political-Military Strategy," *International Security*, Vol. 24, No. 4, Spring 2000, pp. 39–84.

Potter, Mitch, "NATO Pushes Gadhafi Forces," therecord.com, March 24, 2011. As of July 20, 2014
http://www.therecord.com/news/world/article/506192--nato-pushes-gadhafi-forces

Presidenza del Consiglio dei Ministri/Sistema di informazione per la sicurezza della Repubblica, *Relazione sulla politica dell'informazione per la sicurezza 2010.*

"Press Conference with the Prime Minister of Qatar," online at 10, the official website of the British Prime Minister's Office, February 23, 2011. As of July 20, 2014:
http://www.number10.gov.uk/news/press-conference-with-the-prime-minister-of-qatar/

Prince, Rosa, and Richard Spencer, "Libya: Col Gaddafi 'Must Go Now,' Says PM amid Mounting Pressure on Dictator," *The Telegraph*, February 27, 2011. As of July 20, 2014:
http://www.telegraph.co.uk/news/worldnews/africaandindianocean/libya/8351119/Libya-Col-Gaddafi-must-go-now-says-PM-amid-mounting-pressure-on-dictator.html

"Public Wary of Military Intervention in Libya," Pew Research Center for the People and the Press, March 14, 2011. As of July 20, 2014:
http://www.people-press.org/2011/03/14/public-wary-of-military-intervention-in-libya/

Pugliese, David, "Development of Expeditionary Unit a Priority for RCAF," *Ottawa Citizen*, May 24, 2012. As of July 20, 2014:
http://rpdefense.over-blog.com/article-development-of-expeditionary-unit-a-priority-for-rcaf-105780809.html

Pusztai, Oberst Wolfgang, "Die militärstrategischen Lehren aus der Intervention in Libyen," in Johann Pucher and Johann Frank, eds., *Strategie und Sicherheit*, Vienna-Köln-Weimar, Böhlau, 2012.

"Qatar—Air Force," *Jane's Sentinel Security Assessment*, October 2011.

"Qatari Forces to Remain in Libya after NATO Leaves," *The London Evening Post*, October 27, 2011. As of July 20, 2014:
http://www.thelondoneveningpost.com/africa/qatari-forces-to-remain-in-libya-after-nato-leaves/

"Qatar to Take Part in Military Action over Libya," *Reuters Africa*, March 20, 2011. As of July 20, 2014:
http://af.reuters.com/article/topNews/idAFJOE72J00S20110320

Quartararo, Joe, Sr., Michael Rovenolt, and Randy White, "Libya's Operation Odyssey Dawn," *Prism,* Vol. 3, No. 2, March 2012, pp.141–156.

Quintana, Elizabeth, "The RAF and Expeditionary Operations," *RUSI Defence Systems,* Summer 2011, pp. 53–54.

———, "The War from the Air," in Adrian Johnson and Saqeb Mueen, eds., *Short War, Long Shadow: The Political and Military Legacies of the 2011 Libya Campaign,* London: Royal United Services Institute (RUSI), Whitehall Report 1–12, 2012, pp. 31–40. As of July 20, 2014: http://www.rusi.org/downloads/assets/WHR_1-12.pdf

Rachman, Gideon, "The Libyan War and the Gallant Belgians," *Financial Times,* October 28, 2011. As of July 20, 2014: http://blogs.ft.com/the-world/2011/10/the-libyan-war-and-the-gallant-belgians/

Radia, Kirit, "US Evacuates Embassy in Libya," *ABC Nnews.com,* February 25, 2011. As of July 20, 2014: http://abcnews.go.com/blogs/politics/2011/02/us-evacuates-embassy-in-libya/

Rampino, Antonella, "La Libia: Clandestini in Arrivo," *La Stampa,* May 13, 2012.

Redazione, "Nella tana dei Predator, operativi in Afghanistan e pronti per la Libia," *Dedalonews.it,* June 29, 2011. As of July 20, 2014: http://www.dedalonews.it/it/index.php/06/2011/nella-tana-dei-predator-operativi-in-afghanistan-e-pronti-per-la-libia/

Reguly, Eric, "Canadian Pilots Cautious of Collateral Damage in Libya," *Globe and Mail,* April 4, 2011. As of July 20, 2014: http://www.theglobeandmail.com/news/world/canadian-pilots-cautious-of-collateral-damage-in-libya/article575169/

Reguzzoni, Marco, "Speriamo finisca presto: la pace non è una parola priva di valore," *La Padania,* March 25, 2011.

"Relazione sulla politica dell'informazione per la sicurezza," *Presidenza del Consiglio dei Ministri/ Sistema di informazione per la sicurezza della Repubblica,* 2010, p. 53.

Report of the Bahrain Independent Commission of Inquiry, Final Revision of December 10, 2011, subsection 501, p. 134.

"Révoltes Arabes: Répression brutale en Libye, à Bahreïn et au Yémen," *Le Monde,* February 20, 2011.

Reychler, Luc, "The Passive Constrained: Belgian Security Policy in the 1980s," in Gregory Flynn, ed., *NATO's Northern Allies: The National Security Policies of Belgium, Denmark, the Netherlands, and Norway,* Totowa, N.J.: Rowman & Allanheld, 1985, pp. 1–56.

Ribezzo, Maria Elena, "Libia. Maggioranza compatta a Montecitorio," *La Padania,* March 25, 2011.

Richards, General Sir David, "Annual Chief of the Defence Staff Lecture 2011," Whitehall, London: Royal United Services Institute, December 14, 2011. As of July 20, 2014: http://www.rusi.org/events/past/ref:E4EA01B5272990/

Ripley, Tim, "US and Canadian Orions Direct UK Naval Gunfire off Libya," *Jane's Defence Weekly,* October 6, 2011. As of July 20, 2014: http://www.auroranewspaper.com/pdf/2011/3242news.pdf

———, "Power Brokers—Qatar and the UAE Take Centre Stage," *Jane's Intelligence Review,* Vol. 24, No. 2, February 2012, pp. 22–25.

Risen, James, "A Military and Intelligence Clash over Spy Satellites," *New York Times*, April 19, 2012. As of July 20, 2014:
http://www.nytimes.com/2012/04/20/us/politics/spy-satellite-clash-for-military-and-intelligence-officials.html?pagewanted=all

Riste, Olav, *Norway's Foreign Relations: A History*, Oslo: Universitetsforlaget, 2001.

Robinson, Matt, "Qatari weapons reaching rebels in Libyan mountains," *Reuters*, May 31, 2011. As of July 20, 2014:
http://www.reuters.com/article/2011/05/31/us-libya-weapons-idUSTRE74U3C520110531

———, "Libyan Rebel Advance Checked by NATO Strike Leaflets," *Reuters*, June 14, 2011.

Ronzitti, Natalino, "Il futuro dei trattati tra Italia e Libia," *AffarInternazionali*, February 2, 2012. As of July 20, 2014:
http://www.affarinternazionali.it/articolo.asp?ID=1961

Rose, Gideon, "Tell Me How This One Ends," *Washington Post*, March 27, 2011, p. B1.

Royal Air Force, "Libyan Air Force Neutered," March 24, 2011. As of July 20, 2014:
http://www.raf.mod.uk/news/archive.cfm?storyid=060DA2DC-5056-A318-A81DF37FD59CEDBA

Salvati, Cfr. Emanuele, "Gulfstream 550 Eitam. Il Piccolo CAEW," *Rivista Aeronautica*, February 2011, pp. 82–85.

Sanger, David E., and Thom Shanker, "Gates Warns of Risks of a No-Flight Zone," *New York Times*, March 3, 2011, p. A.12.

Scharper, Stephen Bede, "Libyan Intervention: A Just War or Just a War," *Toronto Star*, March 28, 2011. As of July 20, 2014:
http://www.thestar.com/opinion/editorialopinion/article/962164--libyan-intervention-a-just-war-or-just-a-war

Schemm, Paul, "Battle at Army Base Broke Gadhafi Hold in Benghazi," *Washington Post* (Associated Press story), February 25, 2011. As of July 20, 2014:
http://www.washingtonpost.com/wp-dyn/content/article/2011/02/25/AR2011022505021.html

Schmitt, Eric, "NATO Sees Flaws in Air Campaign Against Gaddafi," *New York Times*, April 14, 2012, p. A1. As of July 20, 2014:
http://www.nytimes.com/2012/04/15/world/africa/nato-sees-flaws-in-air-campaign-against-qaddafi.html?pagewanted=all&_r=0

Schwab, Orrin, *A Clash of Cultures: Civil-Military Relations During the Vietnam War*, Praeger, 2006.

Schwartz, Norton, "Air Force Contributions to Our Military and Our Nation," prepared remarks delivered at the World Affairs Council, Wilmington, Del., undated.

Sensini, Paolo, *Libia 2011,* Milan: Jaca Book, 2011.

Sewall, Sarah, Dwight Raymond, Sally Chin, et al., *MARO—Mass Atrocity Response Operations: A Military Planning Handbook*, Cambridge, Mass.: The President and Fellows of Harvard College, 2010. As of July 20, 2014:
http://www.hks.harvard.edu/cchrp/maro/pdf/MARO_Handbook_4.30.pdf

Shadid, Anthony, "Clashes in Libya Worsen as Army Crushes Dissent," *New York Times*, February 18, 2011, p. A.1.

Shanker, Thom, "U.S. Weighs Options, by Air and Sea," *New York Times*, March 7, 2011.

Sheridan, Mary Beth, and Greg Jaffee, "Coalition Agrees to Put NATO in Charge of No-Fly Zone in Libya," *Washington Post*, March 24, 2011.

Siccama, Jan G., "The Netherlands Depillarized: Security Policy in a New Domestic Context," in Gregory Flynn, ed., *NATO's Northern Allies: The National Security Policies of Belgium, Denmark, the Netherlands, and Norway*, Totowa, N.J.: Rowman & Allanheld, 1985, pp. 113–170.

Sloggett, Dave, *The RAF's Air War in Libya: New Conflicts in the Era of Austerity*, Barnsley: Pen and Sword, 2013.

Statsministerens Kontor [Prime Minister's Office], "Norge med i operasjoner i Libya" [Norway participates in operations in Libya], *Pressemelding* [press release], March 23, 2011. As of July 20, 2014:
http://www.regjeringen.no/nb/dep/smk/pressesenter/pressemeldinger/2011/norge-med-i-operasjoner-i-libya.html?id=636399

Stephen, Chris, "Libya Rebels Advance into NATO Bombing Path," *Guardian.co.uk*, June 14, 2011. As of July 20, 2014:
http://www.guardian.co.uk/world/2011/jun/14/misrata-rebels-nato-bomb-libya

Stokes, Tim (Capt., RCAF), "CC-177 assists in moving civilians out of Libya," Royal Canadian Air Force: 429 Transport Squadron, March 1, 2011.

Stolberg, Sheryl Gay, "Still Crusading, but Now on the Inside," *New York Times*, March 30, 2011, p. A10.

Strelieff, Jill (Captain), "17 Mission Support Flight Rolls into Mobile," Royal Canadian Air Force, October 27, 2011.

Stroobants, Jean-Pierre, "L'Alliance atlantique étale ses divisions à Bruxelles sur la gestion de la crise libyenne," *Le Monde*, March 23, 2011.

———, "Libye: batailles diplomatiques en coulisses," *Le Monde*, March 24, 2011, p. 1.

Swedish Government, "Svenskt Deltagande i Den Internationella Militära Insatsen i Libyen," [Swedish Participation in the International Military Operation in Libya], Prop. 2010/11:111, March 29, 2011. As of July 20, 2014:
http://www.regeringen.se/sb/d/14427/a/164975

———, "Så Styrs Statliga Myndigheter" [How State Authorities Are Run], online, updated January 19, 2012. As of July 20, 2014:
http://www.regeringen.se/sb/d/2462

Taha, Kamal, "Debt-Ridden Jordan Eager for Libya to Pay Bills," *The Daily Star* (Lebanon), June 18, 2012. As of July 20, 2014:
http://www.dailystar.com.lb/News/Middle-East/2012/Jun-18/177190-debt-ridden-jordan-eager-for-libya-to-pay-bills.ashx#axzz24foLdSHq

Talmon, Stefan, "Recognition of the Libyan National Transitional Council," *Insights*, Vol. 15, No. 16, Amerian Society of International Law (ASIL), June 16, 2011. As of July 20, 2014:
http://www.asil.org/insights/volume/15/issue/16/recognition-libyan-national-transitional-council

Tanguy, Jean-Marc, *Guerre Aérienne en Libye: L'Armée de l'Air au Combat*, Paris: Histoire & Collections, 2012.

Tani, Andrea, "La crisi libica," *Rivista Marittima*, June 2011, p. 31.

———, "Valutazioni politico-militari della campagna libica," *Rivista Marittima*, October 2011.

"Three Dutch Marines Captured During Rescue in Libya," *BBC News*, March 3, 2011. As of July 20, 2014:
http://www.bbc.co.uk/news/world-europe-12633415

"The Ties That Bind Doha and Paris," *The National* (UAE), September 18, 2009. As of July 20, 2014: http://www.thenational.ae/news/world/middle-east/the-ties-that-bind-doha-and-paris

"TIMELINE—Libya's Uprising Against Muammar Gaddafi," *Thomson Reuters*, August 22, 2011. As of July 20, 2014: http://www.reuters.com/article/2011/08/22/us-libya-events-idUSTRE77K2QH20110822

Tirpak, John A., "Odyssey Dawn Units Identified," *Air Force Association Daily Report*, March 22, 2011.

———, "Bombers over Libya," *Air Force Magazine*, July 2011, pp. 36–39.

———, "Lessons from Libya," *Air Force Magazine*, December 2011, pp. 34–38.

Tomes, Robert R., *U.S. Defense Strategy from Vietnam to Operation Iraqi Freedom: Military Innovation and the New American Way of War, 1973–2003*, London: Routledge, 2007.

Tosi, Gen. Tiziano, "La Dimensione Aerospaziale della Risposta," *Rivista Aeronautica*, March 2011, p. 27.

Tran, Pierre, "Why Did France Move So Forcefully on Libya?" *Defense News,* March 28, 2011.

"La trasformazione," supplement to *Rivista Aeronautica*, undated (2007).

Traynor, Ian, "Turkey and France Clash over Libya Air Campaign," *The Guardian*, March 24, 2011.

Treaty Between the United Kingdom of Great Britain and Northern Ireland and the French Republic for Defence and Security Co-operation, London: The Stationery Office, November 2, 2010. As of July 20, 2014: http://www.official-documents.gov.uk/document/cm79/7976/7976.pdf

Trimble, Stephen, "DUBAI: UAE Air Combat Debut Hit by Communications Issues," November 12, 2011, *Flight Daily News/Flightglobal*. As of July 20, 2014: http://www.flightglobal.com/news/articles/dubai-uae-air-combat-debut-hit-by-communications-issues-364702/

"Typhoon Joins Tornado in Libya Ground Attack Operations," *Mod.uk*, April 13, 2011. As of July 20, 2014: http://www.mod.uk/defenceinternet/defencenews/militaryoperations/typhoonjoinstornadoinlibyagroundattackoperations.htm

"UAE Air Force on the Offensive in Libya," *Arabian Aerospace Online News Service*, August 24, 2011. As of July 20, 2014: http://arabianaerospace.aero/uae-air-force-on-the-offensive-in-libya.html

"UAE Says Sent 500 Police Officers into Bahrain," *Reuters*, March 14, 2011. As of July 20, 2014: http://www.reuters.com/article/2011/03/14/us-g8-bahrain-uae-idUSTRE72D6DE20110314

"UAE to Send 12 Planes to Patrol Libya No-Fly Zone," *Dubai Chronicle*, March 25, 2011. As of November 30, 2012:

"UK, France Detail Sorties Mounted, Ordnance Expended," *Jane's Defence Weekly*, November 2, 2011, p. 5.

"UK-France Declaration on Security and Defence," *10* (official site of the British Prime Minister's Office), February 17, 2012. As of July 20, 2014: http://www.number10.gov.uk/news/uk-france-declaration-security/

"UN OKs Action Against Ghadhafi," *Jobsanger*, March 18, 2011. As of July 20, 2014: http://jobsanger.blogspot.com/2011/03/un-oks-all-necessary-action-against.html

"Le Unità d'Assalto Anfibio e Gli Elicotteri d'Attacco in Libia," *Rivista Marittima*, November 2011.

United Kingdom House of Commons, Defence Committee, "UK Contribution to the Operation," parliament.uk, prepared February 8, 2012. As of July 20, 2014:
http://www.publications.parliament.uk/pa/cm201012/cmselect/cmdfence/950/95007.htm

United Kingdom Ministry of Defence, "Brimstone Missiles Destroy Armoured Vehicles in Libya," *gov.uk*, March 26, 2011. As of July 20, 2014:
https://www.gov.uk/government/news/brimstone-missiles-destroy-armoured-vehicles-in-libya

———, "RAF Strikes Further Targets in Libya," *gov.uk*, March 28, 2011. As of July 20, 2014:
https://www.gov.uk/government/news/raf-strikes-further-targets-in-libya

———, "UK Military Liaison Advisory Team to be Sent to Libya," *gov.uk*, April 19, 2011. As of July 20, 2014:
https://www.gov.uk/government/news/uk-military-liaison-advisory-team-to-be-sent-to-libya

———, "RAF Destroys Gaddafi's Rocket Launchers," *gov.uk*, May 9, 2011. As of July 20, 2014:
https://www.gov.uk/government/news/raf-destroys-gaddafi-rocket-launchers

———, "Libya: Operations Updates," May 12, 2011–October 18, 2011, online.

United Nations General Assembly, *2005 World Summit Outcome*, document A/60/L.1, 15 September 14, 2005, outcomes 138–139.

United Nations Security Council, *Final Report of the Panel of Experts Established Pursuant to Security Council Resolution 1973 (2011) Concerning Libya*, March 20, 2012.

United Nations Security Council Resolution 1970 (2011), February 26, 2011.

United Nations Security Council Resolution 1973 (2011), March 17, 2011. As of July 20, 2014:
http://www.un.org/ga/search/view_doc.asp?symbol=S/RES/1973(2011)

United States Africa Command, "New Coalition Member Flies 1st Sortie Enforcing No-Fly Zone over Libya," Ramstein Air Base, Germany: Joint Task Force–Odyssey Dawn Public Affairs, March 25, 2011. As of July 20, 2014:
http://www.usafe.af.mil/news/story.asp?id=123248692

United States Air Forces Central Command, "Intelligence, Surveillance and Reconnaissance Division (ISRD)," Fact Sheet, posted online September 7, 2009. As of July 20, 2014 (no longer working):
http://www.afcent.af.mil/library/factsheets/factsheet.asp?id=12156

United States Department of State, "Humanitarian Assistance for Libya," Fact Sheet, February 28, 2011. As of July 20, 2014:
http://www.state.gov/r/pa/prs/ps/2011/02/157425.htm

United States House of Representatives, H.Res. 292, June 3, 2011. As of July 20, 2014:
http://www.govtrack.us/congress/bills/112/hres292/text

United States Joint Forces Command Joint Warfighting Center, and Office of the Secretary of Defense Joint Battle Damage Assessment Joint Test and Evaluation, *Commander's Handbook for Joint Battle Damage Assessment*, June 1, 2004. As of July 20, 2014:
http://www.dtic.mil/doctrine/doctrine/jwfc/hbk_jbda.pdf

United States Navy, "Amphibious Command Ships—LCC," online Fact File, November 1, 2012. As of July 20, 2014:
http://www.navy.mil/navydata/fact_display.asp?cid=4200&tid=500&ct=4

Uptegraff, Brigadier General Roy, et al., "U.S. Air Force Contingency Operations," Unprepared Remarks before the 2011 Air & Space Conference & Technology Exposition, September 21, 2011.

Urban, Mark, "Inside Story of the UK's Secret Mission to Beat Gaddafi," *BBC News Magazine*, January 19, 2012. As of July 20, 2014:
http://www.bbc.co.uk/news/magazine-16573516

"US Changes Diplomatic Tune," *Vancouver Sun*, March 17, 2011.

"US Sends 'Time to Go' Message to Gaddafi," *Al Jazeera*, July 19, 2011. As of July 20, 2014:
http://www.aljazeera.com/news/africa/2011/07/2011718233615749270.html

USAFRICOM—See United States Africa Command.

Utrikesdepartementet, "Sveriges Säkerhetspolitik" [Swedish Security Policy], online, updated March 24, 2011. As of July 20, 2014:
http://www.regeringen.se/sb/d/10660

van Creveld, Martin, *The Age of Airpower*, New York: Public Affairs, 2011.

van Genugten, Saskia, "Libya After Gadhafi," *Survival*, Vol. 53, No. 3, June–July 2011, pp. 61–75.

van Staden, Alfred, "The Netherlands," in Jolyon Howorth and Anand Menon, eds., *The European Union and National Defence Policy*, London: Routledge, 1997, pp. 87–104.

Vick, Alan J., Adam Grissom, William Rosenau, Beth Grill, and Karl P. Mueller, *Air Power in the New Counterinsurgency Era: The Strategic Importance of USAF Advisory and Assistance Missions*, Santa Monica, Calif.: RAND Corporation, MG-509-AF, 2006. As of July 20, 2014:
http://www.rand.org/pubs/monographs/MG509.html

"Vols de Nuit pour nos F-16 en Libye" [Night Flights by Our F-16s over Libya], *La Défense [Defence (Belgium)]*, May 19, 2011.

Wagnsson, Charlotte, "A Security Community in the Making? Sweden and NATO Post-Libya," *European Security*, Vol. 20, No. 4, December 2011, p. 598.

Walker, Portia, "Qatari Military Advisers on the Ground, Helping Libyan Rebels Get into Shape," *Washington Post*, May 12, 2011.

Wall, Robert, "Fighter, UCAV Feature in UAE Air Force Plan," *Aviation Week*, November 12, 2011.

———, "UAE Draws Lessons from Libya Ops," posted on "Ares Defense Technology Blog," hosted by *Aviation Week.com*, November 12, 2011.

Watt, Nicholas, and Patrick Wintour, "Libya No-Fly Zone Call by France Fails to Get David Cameron's Backing," *Guardian.co.uk*, February 23, 2011. As of July 20, 2014:
http://www.guardian.co.uk/world/2011/feb/23/libya-nofly-zone-david-cameron

Wells, R. A. C., "One Swallow Maketh Not a Summer: What Success in Libya Means for NATO," *JAPCC Journal*, No. 15, Spring/Summer 2012, pp. 67–71.

Westerhoven, Leo van, "FWIT 2012, New F-16 Weapon Instructors in the Making," Dutch Defence Press, June 8, 2012. As of July 20, 2014:
http://www.dutchdefencepress.com/?p=8351

"Western Military Action over Libya," *The London Free Press*, March 23, 2011.

The White House, Office of the Press Secretary, "Remarks by the President on Libya," Washington, D.C., February 23, 2011. As of July 20, 2014:
http://www.whitehouse.gov/the-press-office/2011/02/23/remarks-president-libya

———, "Readout of the President's Call with Prime Minister Berlusconi of Italy," press release, Washington, D.C., April 25, 2011. As of July 20, 2014:
http://www.whitehouse.gov/the-press-office/2011/04/25/readout-presidents-call-prime-minister-berlusconi-italy

———, "Remarks by President Obama at High-Level Meeting on Libya," Washington, D.C., September 20, 2011. As of July 20, 2014:
http://www.whitehouse.gov/the-press-office/2011/09/20/
remarks-president-obama-high-level-meeting-libya

White Paper '94, Brussels: Ministry of Defence, 1994.

Willsher, Kim, "Sarkozy Opposes NATO Taking Control of Libya Operation," *Guardian.co.uk*, March 22, 2011. As of July 20, 2014:
http://www.guardian.co.uk/world/2011/mar/22/sarkozy-nato-libya-france

Wilson, Staff Sgt. Benjamin, "U.A.E. Crosses Atlantic for Red Flag," Nellis Air Force Base, Nev.: Red Flag 11-2 Public Affairs, updated February 3, 2011. As of July 20, 2014:
http://www.nellis.af.mil/news/story.asp?id=123240956

Wilson, Scott, and Karen DeYoung, "Coalition Nears Agreement on Transition for Operations in Libya," *Washington Post*, March 23, 2011.

Wintour, Patrick, and Ewen MacAskill, "Is Muammar Gaddafi a Target? PM and Military Split over War Aims," *The Guardian*, March 21, 2011. As of July 20, 2014:
http://www.guardian.co.uk/world/2011/mar/21/muammar-gaddafi-david-cameron-libya

Wintour, Patrick, and Nicholas Watt, "David Cameron's Libyan War: Why the PM Felt Gaddafi Had to Be Stopped," *The Guardian*, October 2, 2011. As of July 20, 2014:
http://www.guardian.co.uk/politics/2011/oct/02/david-cameron-libyan-war-analysis

Wolf, Z. Byron, "Cost of Libya Intervention $600 Million for First Week, Pentagon Says," *ABCNews* blog, March 28, 2011. As of July 20, 2014:
http://abcnews.go.com/blogs/politics/2011/03/cost-of-libya-intervention-600-million-for-first-week-pentagon-says/

Woods, Allan, "Gadhafi: All My People Love Me," *Toronto Star*, March 1, 2011. As of July 20, 2014:
http://www.thestar.com/news/canada/2011/03/01/gadhafi_all_my_people_love_me.html

Woodward, Maj Gen Margaret H., "Defending America's Vital National Interests in Africa," Prepared Remarks before the 2011 Air & Space Conference & Technology Exposition, September 21, 2011. As of July 20, 2014:
http://www.af.mil/AboutUs/Speeches/Display/tabid/268/Article/143846/defending-americas-vital-national-interests-in-africa.aspx

"World Cannot Stand Aside from Libya, Says Cameron," *BBC News*, March 8, 2011. As of July 20, 2014:
http://www.bbc.co.uk/news/uk-12680280

"Years of Franco-Qatari Cooperation in Practice over Libya," *Agence France-Presse (AFP)*, March 31, 2011.